Mediterranean Diet Cookbook for Beginners

1000+ Easy Delightful Recipes to Change Your Life One Meal After Another

By Sara Dean

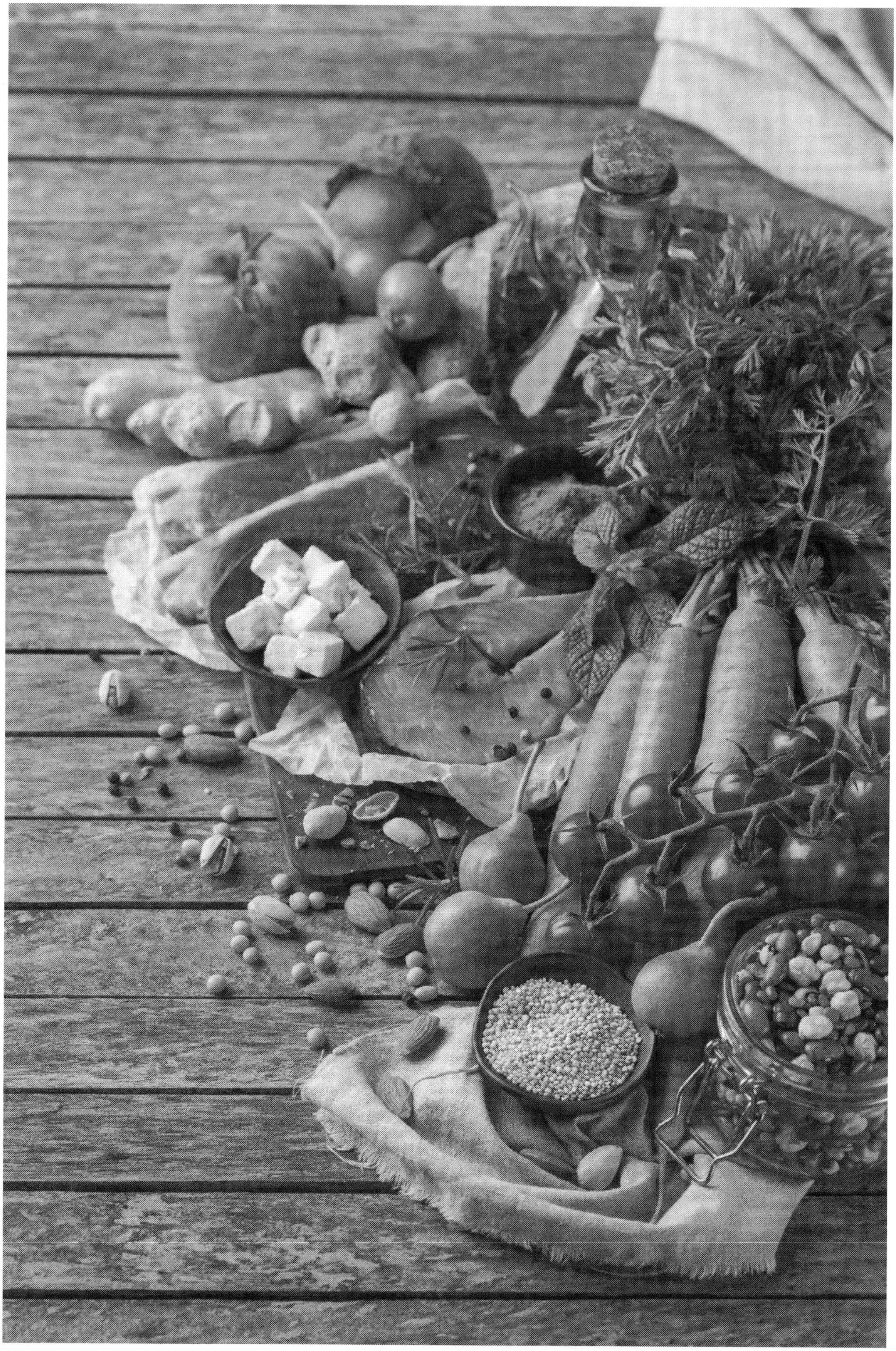

Table of Contents

Introduction 17

Chapter 1: Breakfast and Snack Recipes 18

- Mediterranean Omelet 19
- Hummus And Tomato Sandwich 19
- Sage Omelet 19
- Red Pepper and Artichoke Frittata 19
- Stuffed Figs 20
- Keto Egg Fast Snickerdoodle Crepes 20
- Quinoa and Potato Bowl 20
- Almond Cream Cheese Bake 21
- Slow-cooked Peppers Frittata 21
- Apricots with Yogurt, Honey, And Pistachios 21
- Mediterranean Garbanzo Chili 22
- Veggie Salad 22
- Fennel Bruschetta 22
- Cauliflower Hash Brown Breakfast Bowl 23
- Pumpkin Coconut Oatmeal 23
- Bacon, Vegetable And Parmesan Combo 23
- Mediterranean Crostini 24
- Heavenly Egg Bake with Blackberry 24
- Quick Cream ff Wheat 24
- Herbed Spinach Frittata 24
- Ham Spinach Ballet 25
- Banana Quinoa 25
- Cheesy Eggs Ramekins 25
- Mediterranean Frittata (Version 2) 25
- Cinnamon Apple And Lentils Porridge 26
- Creamy Oatmeal 26
- Stuffed Sweet Potato 26
- Couscous And Chickpeas Bowls 27
- Vegetarian Three Cheese Quiche Stuffed Peppers 27
- Sweet Bread With Dates 27
- Shrimp Toast 28
- Breakfast Beans (ful Mudammas) 28
- Seeds And Lentils Oats 28
- Couscous With Artichokes, Sun-dried Tomatoes And Feta 29
- Cinnamon Roll Oats 29
- Mediterranean Wrap 29
- Chicken Liver 30
- Avocado Spread 30
- Eggs with Zucchini Noodles 30
- Banana Oats 30
- Sun-dried Tomatoes Oatmeal 31
- Quinoa Muffins 31
- Watermelon "Pizza" 31
- Cheesy Yogurt 31
- Cauliflower Fritters 31
- Corn and Shrimp Salad 32
- Cottage Cheese and Berries Omelet 32
- Salmon Frittata 32
- Avocado and Olive Paste on Toasted Rye Bread .. 32
- Avocado and Chickpea Sandwiches 33
- Raisin Quinoa Breakfast 33
- Banana Cinnamon Fritters 33
- Veggie Casserole 33
- Ground Beef and Brussels Sprouts 33
- Italian Mini Meatballs 34
- Mushroom and Olives Steaks 34
- Salmon Kebabs 34
- Mediterranean Baked Salmon 34
- Feta Cheese Baked in Foil 34
- Avocado, Roasted Mushroom and Feta Spaghetti 35
- Tomato, Arugula and Feta Spaghetti 35
- Zucchini Fritters 35
- Cheesy Cauliflower Florets 35
- Wrapped Plums 36
- Tomato Cream Cheese Spread 36
- Italian Fries 36
- Tempeh Snack 36

Avocado Dip	37
Feta and Roasted Red Pepper Bruschetta	37
Meat-filled Phyllo (samboosek)	37
Tasty Black Bean Dip	38
Zucchini Cakes	38
Parsley Nachos	38
Plum Wraps	38
Parmesan Chips	39
Chicken Bites	39
Chicken Kale Wraps	39
Savory Pita Chips	39
Artichoke Skewers	40
Kidney Bean Spread	40
Mediterranean Polenta Cups Recipe	40
Tomato Triangles	41
Chili Mango And Watermelon Salsa	41
Tomato Olive Salsa	41
Lavash Chips	41
Homemade Salsa	41
Stuffed Zucchinis	42
Yogurt Dip	42
Popcorn-pine Nut Mix	42
Scallions Dip	43
Date Balls	43
Lavash Roll Ups	43
Chickpeas And Eggplant Bowls	43
Vinegar Beet Bites	43
Baked Sweet-potato Fries	44
Cucumber Rolls	44
Jalapeno Chickpea Hummus	44
Healthy Spinach Dip	45
Marinated Cheese	45
Za'atar Fries	45
Tuna Salad	45
Cheese Rolls	46
Olive, Pepperoni, And Mozzarella Bites	46
Eggplant Dip	46
Celery And Cucumber Snack	47
Oat Bites	47
Eggplant Bites	47
Creamy Pepper Spread	47
Creamy Eggplant Dip	48
Herbed Goat Cheese Dip	48
Italian Wheatberry Cakes	48
Healthy Kidney Bean Dip	48
Lentils Spread	49
Chickpeas Spread	49
Lime Yogurt Dip	49
Almond Bowls	49
Beet Spread	50
Calamari Mediterranean	50
Cheddar Dip	50
Olives And Cheese Stuffed Tomatoes	50
Feta Cheese Log With Sun-dried Tomatoes And Kalamata Olives	51
Lemon Salmon Rolls	51
Ginger And Cream Cheese Dip	51
Lemon Endive Bites	51
Perfect Italian Potatoes	52
Feta Artichoke Dip	52
Peach Skewers	52
Chickpeas Salsa	52
Hummus Appetizer Bites	52
Stuffed Avocado	53
Grilled Polenta Vegetables Bites	53
Grapefruit Salad	53
Hummus With Ground Lamb	54
Perfect Queso	54
Aromatic Artichokes	54
Parmesan Eggplant Bites	55
Quinoa Bars	55
Creamy Artichoke Dip	56
Olive Eggplant Spread	56
Cucumber Bites	56
Oregano Crackers	56
Tomato Salsa	57

Spicy Berry Dip 57
Mozzarella Chips 57
Salmon Rolls 57
Cream Cheese Rolls 57
Carrot Dip 58
Walnuts Yogurt Dip 58
Rosemary Cauliflower Dip 58
Light & Creamy Garlic Hummus 59
Mediterranean-style Nachos Recipe 59
Baked Goat Cheese Caprese Salad 59
Grilled Shrimp Kabobs 60
Red Pepper Tapenade 60
Collard Green Chicken Roll Ups 60
Cauliflower Spread 61
Coriander Falafel 61
Slow Cooked Cheesy Artichoke Dip 61
Marinated Chickpeas 62
Easy Tomato Dip 62
Zucchini Pizza Rolls 62
Creamy Spinach And Shallots Dip 62
French Baked Brie Recipe With Figs, Walnuts And Pistachios 63
Cucumber, Chicken And Mango Wrap 63
Greek Mountain Tea 63
Avocado And Spinach Breakfast Wrap 64
Paleo Almond Banana Pancakes 64
Italian Flat Bread Gluten Free 64
Spiced Breakfast Casserole 65
Italian Scrambled Eggs 65
Toasted Bagels 65
St Valentine's Mediterranean Pancakes 65
Sandwich With Hummus 66
Halibut Sandwiches Mediterranean Style 66
Quinoa Pizza Muffins 67
Pumpkin Pancakes 67
Breakfast Egg On Avocado 67
Breakfast Egg-artichoke Casserole 67
Garlic & Tomato Gluten Free Focaccia 68

Halibut Sandwiches Mediterranean Style 68
Rosemary-Walnut Loaf Bread 68
Italian Flat Bread Gluten Free 69

Chapter 2: Lunch & Dinner Recipes 70

Mediterranean Flank Steak 71
Spiced Grilled Flank Steak 71
Pan Roasted Chicken With Olives And Lemon 71
Creamy Salmon Soup 71
Grilled Salmon With Cucumber Dill Sauce 72
Grilled Basil-lemon Tofu Burgers 72
Creamy Green Pea Pasta 72
Meat Cakes 73
Herbed Roasted Cod 73
Mushroom Soup 73
Salmon Parmesan Gratin 73
Sweet And Sour Chicken Fillets 74
Salt Crusted Salmon 74
Sun-dried Tomato Pesto Penne 74
Herbed Marinated Sardines 74
Spicy Tomato Poached Eggs 75
Mediterranean Scones 75
Mixed Olives Braised Chicken 75
Coconut Chicken Meatballs 76
Grilled Turkey With White Bean Mash 76
Vegetable Turkey Casserole 76
Mediterranean Grilled Pork With Tomato Salsa 77
Beef And Macaroni Soup 77
Provencal Beef Stew 77
Greek Beef Meatballs 78
Sausage and Beans Soup 78
Jalapeno Grilled Salmon With Tomato Confit 78
Chicken And Rice Soup 79
Spicy Salsa Braised Beef Ribs 79
Pork and Prunes Stew 79
Low-carb And Paleo Mediterranean Zucchini Noodles 79
Pork And Rice Soup 80

Recipe	Page
Tomato Roasted Feta	80
Fettuccine With Spinach And Shrimp	81
Sage Pork And Beans Stew	81
Broccoli Pesto Spaghetti	81
Chorizo Stuffed Chicken Breasts	81
Grilled Mediterranean-style Chicken Kebabs	82
Sumac Salmon And Grapefruit	82
Bean Patties With And Salsa Avocado	82
Raisin Stuffed Lamb	83
Spinach Orzo Stew	83
Grapes, Cucumbers And Almonds Soup	83
Nutmeg Beef Soup	84
Parsnip Chickpea Veal Stew	84
Tuna And Couscous	84
Olive Oil Lemon Broiled Cod	85
Chicken And Spaghetti Soup	85
Mediterranean Flounder	85
Crunchy Baked Mussels	86
Mediterranean-style Tuna Wrap	86
Pear Braised Pork	86
Yogurt Baked Eggplants	86
Pancetta-wrapped Cod With Rosemary New Potatoes	87
Stuffed Peppers With Basil And Tomato Cream Sauce	87
Beef Stuffed Bell Peppers	88
Stuffed Eggplants	88
Mushroom Pilaf	88
Cream Cheese Artichoke Mix	89
Caramelized Shallot Steaks	89
Carrot And Potato Soup	89
Macedonian Greens And Cheese Pie	90
Chicken Stuffed Peppers	90
Turkey Fritters And Sauce	90
Garlic Clove Roasted Chicken	91
Chickpeas, Spinach And Arugula Bowl	91
Tuna Sandwiches	91
Cream Cheese Tart	92
Cherry Tomato Caper Chicken	92
Shrimp Pancakes	92
Herbed Chicken Stew	93
Spiced Seared Scallops With Lemon Relish	93
White Bean Soup	93
Coriander Pork And Chickpeas Stew	93
Crispy Pollock And Gazpacho	94
Falafel	94
Prosciutto Balls	95
Chicken Skillet	95
Salmon Bowls	95
Chicken And Parmesan Pasta Pudding	96
Pan-fried Ling With Olive And Tomato	96
Mediterranean-style Fish And White-bean Puree	96
Spiced Tortilla	97
Yogurt Marinated Pork Chops	97
White Beans And Orange Soup	97
Healthy Spinach Rice	98
Tasty Salsa Beans	98
Roasted Pepper Pasta	98
Tuna Pasta	99
Vegan Olive Pasta	99
Italian Chicken Pasta	99
Cucumber Lemon Rice	99
Bulgur Salad	100
Cheese Basil Tomato Rice	100
Delicious Chicken Pasta	100
Flavors Taco Rice Bowl	101
Sundried-Cheese Macaroni	101
Fried Balls with Tomato Sauce Rice	101
Delicious Pasta Primavera	102
Roasted Pepper and Feta Penne Pasta	102
Basil, Parmesan and Tomato Rice	102
Macaroni and Cheese	103
Flavors Herb Risotto	103
Pesto Chicken Pasta	103
Flavorful Mac & Cheese	103
Vegetable Herb Rice	104

Italian Two-Cheese Macaroni	104
Delicious Greek Chicken Pasta	104
Chicken Marinara Pasta	105
Fiber Packed Chicken Rice	105
Tasty Greek Rice	105
Mexican Taco Rice Bowl	105
Spinach Pesto Pasta	106
Tuna and Tomato Rotini Pasta	106
Olive Penne Pasta	106
Italian Mac & Cheese	107
Italian Chicken-Mozzarella Penne Pasta	107
Chicken Pasta with Vinaigrette Dressing	107
Creamy Chicken Pesto Pasta	107
Spinach and Mushroom Pesto	108
Chicken Fried Rice	108
Lemon Rice Pilaf	108
Bulgur, Mint and Parsley Salad	109
Perfect Herb Rice	109
Cod & Green Bean Dinner	109
Mediterranean Chicken Quinoa Bowl	109
Linguine with Shrimp	110
Sweet Yogurt Bulgur Bowl	110
Fried Halloumi & Avocados	110
Chicken Korma	110
Barley Risotto with Tomatoes	111
Chickpeas and Kale with Spicy Pomodoro Sauce	111
Mediterranean Chickpea Bowl	112
Curry Apple Couscous	112
Balsamic Roasted Carrots and Baby Onions	112
Chicken Souvlaki (Version 2)	113
Rosemary Roasted New Potatoes	113
Artichoke Feta Penne	113
Grilled Chicken And Rustic Mustard Cream	114
Balsamic Steak With Feta, Tomato, And Basil	114
Fried Chicken with Tzatziki Sauce	114
Spiced Lamb Patties	115
Chicken and Orzo Soup	115
Spanish Meatball Soup	115
Pesto, Avocado And Tomato Panini	115
Jew's Mallow Stew (mulukhiya)	116
Smoked Ham Split Pea Soup	116
Herbed Panini Fillet O'fish	117
Creamy Carrot Coriander Soup	117
Panini And Eggplant Caponata	117
Mixed Bean Minestrone	117
Creamy Panini	118
Tuna Melt Panini	118
Roasted Mushroom Creamy Soup	118
Eggplant Stew	119
Garlicky Roasted Sweet Potato Soup	119
Apple And Ham Flatbread Pizza	119
Red Beet Soup	120
Fig Relish Panini	120
Egg Muffin Sandwich	120
Buffalo Chicken Crust Pizza	121
Greek Bean Soup	121
Eggless Spinach & Bacon Quiche	121
Cauliflower Stew	122
Bbq Chicken Pizza	122
Fresh Bell Pepper Basil Pizza	122
Avocado And Turkey Mix Panini	123
Thin Crust Low Carb Pizza	123
Garlic-rosemary Dinner Rolls	123
Green Pea Stew (bazella)	124
Fig Relish Panini	124
Panini and Eggplant Caponata	124
Open Face Egg and Bacon Sandwich	124
Multi Grain & Gluten Free Dinner Rolls	125
Grilled Burgers with Mushrooms	125
Gorgonzola Sweet Potato Burgers	125

Chapter 3: Meat Recipes 127

Sage Tomato Beef	128
Square Meat Pies (sfeeha)	128
Lamb And Wine Sauce	128
Pork Meatloaf	128

Lamb And Rice	129
Italian Beef	129
Pork Chops And Peppercorns Mix	129
Pork And Tomato Meatloaf	129
Beef And Eggplant Moussaka	130
Hearty Meat And Potatoes	130
Ita Sandwiches	130
Easy Chicken With Capers Skillet	131
Lamb And Dill Apples	131
Tomatoes And Carrots Pork Mix	131
Cherry Stuffed Lamb	131
Rosemary Pork Chops	132
Cauliflower Tomato Beef	132
Pork And Sour Cream Mix	132
Honey Pork Strips	132
Orange Lamb And Potatoes	133
Pork Kebabs	133
Vegetable Lover's Chicken Soup	133
Lemony Lamb And Potatoes	133
Cumin Lamb Mix	134
Almond Lamb Chops	134
Pork And Figs Mix	134
Lamb Chops	134
Chicken Quinoa Pilaf	134
Greek Styled Lamb Chops	135
Bulgur And Chicken Skillet	135
Kibbeh With Yogurt	135
Mustard Chops With Apricot-basil Relish	136
Pork And Peas	136
Paprika And Feta Cheese On Chicken Skillet	137
Jalapeno Beef Chili	137
Kibbeh In A Pan	137
Saffron Beef	138
Cayenne Pork	138
Basil And Shrimp Quinoa	138
Ground Pork Salad	139
Beef And Dill Mushrooms	139
Beef Pitas	139
Lamb Burger On Arugula	140
Flavorful Beef Bourguignon	140
Kefta Burgers	140
Tasty Beef Stew	141
Beef Dish	141
Pork And Sage Couscous	141
Chicken Burgers With Brussel Sprouts Slaw	141
Beef And Potatoes With Tahini Sauce	142
Spicy Beef Chili Verde	142
Lime And Mustard Lamb	142
Steak with Olives and Mushrooms	143
Sausage & Bacon With Beans	143
Mediterranean Lamb Kebabs	143

Chapter 4: Poultry Recipes 144

Butter Chicken Thighs	145
Chicken And Olives Salsa	145
Slow Cooked Chicken And Capers Mix	145
Chili Chicken Mix	145
Ginger Duck Mix	146
Duck And Orange Warm Salad	146
Turmeric Baked Chicken Breast	146
Chicken Tacos	146
Chicken And Butter Sauce	147
Turkey And Cranberry Sauce	147
Coriander And Coconut Chicken	147
Chicken Pilaf	147
Chicken And Black Beans	148
Coconut Chicken	148
Ginger Chicken Drumsticks	148
Parmesan Chicken	149
Pomegranate Chicken	149
Chicken With Artichokes And Beans	149
Chicken Pie	149
Chicken And Semolina Meatballs	150
Lemon Chicken Mix	150
Turkey And Chickpeas	150
Cardamom Chicken And Apricot Sauce	150

- Chicken and Artichokes 151
- Buttery Chicken Spread 151
- Chicken And Spinach Cakes 151
- Cream Cheese Chicken 151
- Chicken And Lemongrass Sauce 152
- Spiced Chicken Meatballs 152
- Paprika Chicken Wings 152
- Chicken And Parsley Sauce 153
- Sage Turkey Mix 153
- Chipotle Turkey And Tomatoes 153
- Curry Chicken, Artichokes And Olives 153
- Roasted Chicken 154
- Curry Chicken Mix 154
- Creamy Chicken 154
- Chicken And Celery Quinoa Mix 155
- Chicken And Nutmeg Butter Sauce 155
- Turmeric Chicken And Eggplant Mix 155
- Honey Chicken 156
- Cheddar Chicken Mix 156
- Chicken And Veggie Saute 156
- Thyme Chicken And Potatoes 156
- Creamy Chicken And Mushrooms 157
- Basil Turkey And Zucchinis 157
- Herbed Almond Turkey 157
- Lime Chicken Thighs And Pomegranate Sauce .. 158
- Mediterranean Meatloaf 158
- Lemon Chicken 158
- Chicken And Mushroom Mix 158
- Chicken And Ginger Cucumbers Mix 159
- Dill Chicken Stew 159
- Chicken Stuffed Zucchini 159
- Creamy Coriander Chicken 159
- Chicken And Tomato Pan 160
- Smoked And Hot Turkey Mix 160
- Chicken With Artichokes 160
- Brown Rice, Chicken And Scallions 160
- Greek Chicken Bites 161
- Chicken Kebabs 161
- Chicken, Corn And Peppers 161
- Spicy Cumin Chicken 162
- Chives Chicken And Radishes 162
- Yogurt Chicken And Red Onion Mix 162
- Basil Chicken With Olives 162
- Chicken Skewers (shish Tawook) 163
- Oregano Chicken And Zucchini Pan 163
- Stuffed Chicken 163
- Chicken And Avocado Bowl 163
- Chicken And Grapes Salad 164
- Lime Turkey And Avocado Mix 164
- Coriander Chicken Drumsticks 164
- Turkey And Asparagus Mix 165
- Braised Chicken 165
- Pesto Chicken Mix 165
- Chicken And Salsa Enchiladas 165
- Paprika Chicken And Pineapple Mix 166
- Chicken And Apples Mix 166
- Oregano Turkey And Peppers 166
- Tomato Chicken And Lentils 166
- Chicken and Olives Tapenade 167
- Turkey, Leeks And Carrots 167
- Grilled Chicken On The Bone 167
- Saffron Chicken Thighs And Green Beans 167
- Sage And Nutmeg Chicken 168
- Herbed Chicken 168
- Duck And Blackberries 168
- Chicken And Onion Mix 168
- Cinnamon Duck Mix 169
- Lemony Turkey And Pine Nuts 169
- Spicy Mustard Chicken 169
- Walnut and Oregano Crusted Chicken 169
- Chicken and Mushrooms 170
- Blue Cheese and Mushroom Chicken 170
- Chicken and Onion Casserole 170
- Chicken And Mediterranean Tabbouleh 170
- Chicken Green Bean Soup 171
- Chicken Soup 171

Chapter 5: Fish and Seafood Recipes 172

- Cod And Mustard Sauce 173
- Garlic Scallops And Peas Mix 173
- Shrimp And Beans Salad 173
- Lemoney Prawns 173
- Pesto And Lemon Halibut 174
- Stuffed Branzino 174
- Tomato Olive Fish Fillets 174
- Steamed Mussels Thai Style 175
- Oregano Citrus Salmon 175
- Nutmeg Sea Bass 175
- Shrimp Kebabs 175
- Easy Broiled Lobster Tails 176
- Cajun Garlic Shrimp Noodle Bowl 176
- Red Peppers & Pineapple Topped Mahi-mahi 176
- Dill Halibut 177
- Kale, Beets And Cod Mix 177
- Shrimp Scampi 177
- Orange Rosemary Seared Salmon 177
- Salmon And Mango Mix 178
- Delicious Shrimp Alfredo 178
- Cod And Mushrooms Mix 178
- Baked Shrimp Mix 178
- Lemon And Dates Barramundi 179
- Cheesy Crab And Lime Spread 179
- Honey Lobster 179
- Fried Salmon 179
- Smoked Salmon And Veggies Mix 180
- Berries And Grilled Calamari 180
- Salmon And Zucchini Rolls 180
- Scallions And Salmon Tartar 181
- Flavors Cioppino 181
- Warm Caper Tapenade On Cod 181
- Spicy Tomato Crab Mix 181
- Salmon Bake 182
- Baked Trout And Fennel 182
- Salmon And Corn Salad 182
- Minty Sardines Salad 183
- Smoked Salmon And Watercress Salad 183
- Easy Salmon Stew 183
- Oregano Swordfish Mix 183
- Cheddar Tuna Bake 183
- Tarragon Trout And Beets 184
- Cod And Brussels Sprouts 184
- Salmon Tortillas 184
- Tasty Tuna Scaloppine 185
- Tuna And Tomato Salad 185
- Coriander Shrimps 185
- Leftover Salmon Salad Power Bowls 186
- Roasted Pollock Fillet With Bacon And Leeks ... 186
- Lemon Rainbow Trout 186
- Salmon With Pesto 186
- Baked Sea Bass 187
- Italian Tuna Pasta 187
- Mustard Cod 187
- Ginger Scallion Sauce Over Seared Ahi 187
- Creamy Scallops 188
- Fish And Rice (sayadieh) 188
- Creamy Bacon-fish Chowder 188
- Healthy Poached Trout 189
- Creamy Curry Salmon 189
- Cod And Cabbage 189
- Pecan Salmon Fillets 189
- Shrimp And Mushrooms Mix 190
- Leeks And Calamari Mix 190
- Cod With Lentils 190
- Honey Garlic Shrimp 190
- Pepper Salmon Skewers 191
- Marinated Tuna Steak 191
- Garlic and Shrimp Pasta 191
- Paprika Butter Shrimps 192
- Nicoise-inspired Salad with Sardines 192
- Mediterranean Avocado Salmon Salad 192
- Moroccan Fish 193

Broiled Chili Calamari 193
Salmon with Corn Pepper Salsa 193
Seafood Paella 194
Mediterranean Pearl Couscous 194
Potato and Tuna Salad 194
Tuna with Vegetable Mix 195
Tuna Bowl with Kale 195
Greek Baked Cod 196
Pistachio Sole Fish 196
Baked Tilapia 196
Mediterranean Salmon 197
A Great Mediterranean Snapper 197
Mediterranean Snapper 197
Heartthrob Mediterranean Tilapia 198
Spiced Swordfish 198
Anchovy Pasta Mania 198
Tuna Nutty Salad 198
Creamy Shrimp Soup 199
Spiced Salmon with Vegetable Quinoa 199
Baked Cod with Vegetables 200
Grilled Lemon Pesto Salmon 200
Dill Chutney Salmon 200
Steamed Trout with Lemon Herb Crust 201
Lemony Trout with Caramelized Shallots 201
Hazelnut Crusted Sea Bass 201
Swordfish Souvlaki 201
Stuffed Monkfish 202
Octopus with Figs and Peaches 202
Steamed Mussels with White Wine and Fennel 203
Skillet Braised Cod with Asparagus and Potatoes 203
Mediterranean Tuna Noodle Casserole 203
Acquapazza Snapper 204
Grilled Fish with Lemons 204
Seafood Corn Chowder 204
Creamy Bell Pepper Soup With Cod Fillets 205
Cod Potato Soup 205
White Wine Fish Soup 205

Chapter 6: Salads & Side Dishes 207

Balsamic Mushrooms 208
Greek Potato And Corn Salad 208
Mint Avocado Chilled Soup 208
Amazingly Fresh Carrot Salad 208
Feta And Almond Pasta 208
Italian-style Butter Beans 209
Leeks Salad 209
Broccoli And Mushroom Salad 209
Tomato Greek Salad 209
Saffron Zucchini Mix 210
Thai Salad With Cilantro Lime Dressing 210
Green Mediterranean Salad 210
Sautéed Zucchini And Mushrooms 210
Salad Greens With Pear And Persimmon 210
Easy Eggplant Salad 211
Wheatberry And Walnuts Salad 211
Lemony Butter Beans With Parsley 211
Spring Soup Recipe With Poached Egg 211
Eggplant Ragoût With Chickpeas, Tomatoes, And Peppers 212
Crispy Watermelon Salad 212
Red Wine Dressed Arugula Salad 212
Artichoke Farro Salad 213
Balsamic Tomato Mix 213
Gigantes Plaki 213
Squash And Tomatoes Mix 213
Chickpeas, Corn And Black Beans Salad 214
Eggplant And Bell Pepper Mix 214
Broccoli Salad With Caramelized Onions 214
Easy Butternut Squash Soup 214
Mediterranean Veggie Bowl 215
Grilled Veggie and Hummus Wrap 215
Spanish Green Beans 215
Roasted Cauliflower and Tomatoes 215
Rustic Cauliflower and Carrot Hash 216
Roasted Acorn Squash 216

Sweet Veggie-Stuffed Peppers	216
Garlicky Sautéed Zucchini with Mint	217
Stewed Okra	217
Moussaka	217
Vegetable-Stuffed Grape Leaves	217
Grilled Eggplant Rolls	218
Crispy Zucchini Fritters	218
Green Beans and Potatoes in Olive Oil	218
Cheesy Spinach Pies	218
Instant Pot Black Eyed Peas	219
Nutritious Vegan Cabbage	219
Instant Pot Horta and Potatoes	219
Instant Pot Artichokes with Mediterranean Aioli	219
Instant Pot Jackfruit Curry	220
Instant Pot Collard Greens with Tomatoes	220
Instant Pot Millet Pilaf	220
Barley & Mushroom Soup	220
Instant Pot Stuffed Sweet Potatoes	221
Instant Pot Couscous and Vegetable Medley	221
Chickpea Pasta Salad	221
Bean Lettuce Wraps	221
Easy Lentil & Rice Bowl	222
Chickpea Pita Patties	222
Mushrooms with Soy Sauce Glaze	222
California Grilled Vegetable Sandwich	223
Delicious Sweet Potato Casserole	223
Light and Fluffy Spinach Quiche	223
Spicy Bean Salsa	224
Hot Artichoke and Spinach Dip	224
Harvest Salad	224
Sweet Potato Casserole Dessert	225
Cranberry Sauce	225
Vegetarian Meatloaf	225
Eggs Over Kale Hash	225
Baba Ganoush	226
Leek And Potato Soup	226
Mast-o Khiar (Aka Persian Yogurt And Cucumbers)	227
Homemade Greek Yogurt	227
Curried Chicken, Chickpeas And Raita Salad	227
Bulgur Tomato Pilaf	228
Garbanzo And Kidney Bean Salad	228
Rice & Currant Salad Mediterranean Style	229
Orange, Dates And Asparagus On Quinoa Salad	229
Stuffed Tomatoes With Green Chili	230
Red Wine Risotto	230
Chicken Pasta Parmesan	231
Tasty Lasagna Rolls	231
Raisins, Nuts And Beef On Hashweh Rice	232
Yangchow Chinese Style Fried Rice	232
Cinnamon Quinoa Bars	233
Cucumber Olive Rice	233
Chicken And White Bean	234
Chorizo-kidney Beans Quinoa Pilaf	234
Belly-filling Cajun Rice & Chicken	235
Quinoa & Black Bean Stuffed Sweet Potatoes	235
Feta, Eggplant And Sausage Penne	236
Bell Peppers 'n Tomato-chickpea Rice	236
Lipsmacking Chicken Tetrazzini	236
Spaghetti In Lemon Avocado White Sauce	237
Simple Penne Anti-pasto	237
Kidney Beans And Beet Salad	238
Filling Macaroni Soup	238
Squash And Eggplant Casserole	238
Blue Cheese And Grains Salad	239
Creamy Artichoke Lasagna	240
Brown Rice Pilaf With Butternut Squash	240
Cranberry And Roasted Squash Delight	241
Mexican Quinoa Bake	241
Spanish Rice Casserole With Cheesy Beef	242
Kidney Bean And Parsley-lemon Salad	242
Italian White Bean Soup	243
Citrus Quinoa & Chickpea Salad	243
Chickpea Salad Moroccan Style	243

Garlicky Peas And Clams On Veggie Spiral	244
Leek, Bacon And Pea Risotto	244
Chickpea Fried Eggplant Salad	245
Turkey And Quinoa Stuffed Peppers	245
Brussels Sprouts 'n White Bean Medley	246
Pastitsio An Italian Dish	246
Rice And Chickpea Stew	247
Mediterranean Diet Pasta With Mussels	247
Sun-dried Tomatoes And Chickpeas	247
Puttanesca Style Bucatini	248
Garlic Avocado-pesto And Zucchini Pasta	248
Mushroom Chickpea Marsala	249
Creamy Alfredo Fettuccine	249
Chickpea-crouton Kale Caesar Salad	249
Lemon Asparagus Risotto	250
Seafood Paella With Couscous	250
Amazingly Good Parsley Tabbouleh	251
Greek Farro Salad	251
Exotic Chickpea Tagine	252
Zucchini And Brown Rice	252
Perfect Herb Rice	253
Baked Parmesan And Eggplant Pasta	253
Greek Couscous Salad And Herbed Lamb Chops	253
Fresh Herbs And Clams Linguine	254
Garbanzo And Lentil Soup	254
Pasta And Tuna Salad	255
Quinoa Buffalo Bites	255
Feta On Tomato-black Bean	255
Nutty And Fruity Amaranth Porridge	256
Black Beans And Quinoa	256
Veggie Pasta With Shrimp, Basil And Lemon	256
Kasha With Onions And Mushrooms	257
Chickpea Alfredo Sauce	257
Lime-cilantro Rice Chipotle Style	257
Lentils And Rice (mujaddara With Rice)	258
Gorgonzola And Chicken Pasta	258
Pasta Shells Stuffed With Feta	258
Kefta Styled Beef Patties With Cucumber Salad	259
Italian Mac & Cheese	259
Saffron Green Bean-quinoa Soup	260
Black Bean Hummus	260
White Bean And Tuna Salad	260
Beans And Spinach Mediterranean Salad	261
Grilled Veggie And Pasta With Marinara Sauce	261
Chicken And Sweet Potato Stir Fry	262
Shrimp Paella Made With Quinoa	262
Fasolakia – Potatoes & Green Beans In Olive Oil	263
Pesto Pasta And Shrimps	263
Seafood And Veggie Pasta	264
Cilantro-dijon Vinaigrette On Kidney Bean Salad	264
Tasty Mushroom Bolognese	265
Delicious Chicken Pasta	265
Garlicky Lemon-parsley Hummus	265
Black Eyed Peas Stew	266
Breakfast Salad From Grains And Fruits	266
Pasta Primavera Without Cream	267
Spicy Sweet Red Hummus	267
Veggies And Sun-dried Tomato Alfredo	267
Aioli Sauce	268
Italian Meatball Soup	268
Dill And Tomato Frittata	269
Eggs With Dill, Pepper, And Salmon	269
Kale And Red Pepper Frittata	269
Tahini Sauce	270
Mediterranean Wild Mushroom Pie	270
Simple And Easy Hummus	271
Grilled Mediterranean Vegetables	271
Greek Salad And Mediterranean Vinaigrette	271
Cream Of Asparagus Soup	272
Mediterranean-style Spread	272
Spicy Tortilla Soup	272
Muhammara Spread	273
Mixed Greens And Ricotta Frittata	273

Baked Mediterranean Halibut 274
Mediterranean Baba Ghanoush 274
Mushroom, Spinach And Turmeric Frittata 275
White Bean Kale Soup 275
Hearty Brown Lentil Soup 275
Cheesy Vegetable Soup 276
Tomato-bacon Quiche 276
Spicy Silan Aka Date Syrup 277
Fried Caprese Pistachio Bites 277
Dill, Havarti & Asparagus Frittata 278
Pistachio Oil Drizzled Robiola, And Pickled Fig Crostini 278
Mediterranean Lentil Sloppy Joes 279
Zucchini-Eggplant Gratin 279
Tuscan Bread Dipper 279
Sandwich with Spinach and Tuna Salad 280

Chapter 7: Dessert Recipes 281

Soothing Red Smoothie 282
Minty Orange Greek Yogurt 282
Yogurt Mousse With Sour Cherry Sauce 282
Fruit Salad With Orange Blossom Water 282
Vanilla Apple Pie 283
Spinach Pancake Cake 283
Blueberry Frozen Yogurt 283
Apple Pear Compote 284
Cream Cheese Cake 284
Nutmeg Lemon Pudding 284
Yogurt Panna Cotta With Fresh Berries 285
Flourless Chocolate Cake 285
Strawberry And Avocado Medley 285
Creamy Mint Strawberry Mix 285
Watermelon Ice Cream 286
Creamy Pie 286
Hazelnut Pudding 287
Mediterranean Cheesecakes 287
Melon Cucumber Smoothie 287
Mediterranean Style Fruit Medley 288
White Wine Grapefruit Poached Peaches 288

Cinnamon Stuffed Peaches 288
Eggless Farina Cake (namoura) 289
Banana And Berries Trifle 289
Mixed Berry Sorbet 289
Almonds And Oats Pudding 290
Chocolate Rice 290
Lemon And Semolina Cookies 290
Strawberry Sorbet 291
Halva (halawa) 291
Semolina Cake 291
Shredded Phyllo And Sweet Cheese Pie (knafe) . 292
Lemon Pear Compote 292
Banana Kale Smoothie 292
Cinnamon Pear Jam 293
Apple And Walnut Salad 293
Phyllo Custard Pockets (shaabiyat) 293
Chocolate Baklava 293
Apricot Rosemary Muffins 294
Blueberry Yogurt Mousse 295
Pistachio Cheesecake 295
Almond Citrus Muffins 295
Custard-filled Pancakes (atayef) 295
Mediterranean Bread Pudding (aish El Saraya) 296
Cinnamon Apple Rice Pudding 296
Pomegranate Granita With Lychee 297
Lime Grapes And Apples 297
Mediterranean Baked Apples 297
Poached Cherries 297
Watermelon Salad 298
Easy Fruit Compote 298
Minty Tart 298
Papaya Cream 299
Orange-sesame Almond Tuiles 299
Strawberry Ice Cream 300
Creamy Strawberries 300
Almond Rice Dessert 300
Greek Yogurt Pie 300
Five Berry Mint Orange Infusion 301

Cocoa Yogurt Mix	301
Frozen Strawberry Greek Yogurt	301
Almond Peaches Mix	301
Raisin Pecan Baked Apples	302
Walnuts Cake	302
Spiced Cookies	302
Scrumptious Cake With Cinnamon	303
Yogurt Cake	303
Chunky Apple Sauce	303
Olive Oil Cake	304
Grapes Stew	304
Lemon Cranberry Sauce	304
Delectable Mango Smoothie	305
Blackberries And Pomegranate Parfait	305
Yellow Cake With Jam Topping	305
Raspberry Tart	306
Coconut Risotto Pudding	306
Mango And Honey Cream	306
Raw Truffles	306
Baked Peaches	307
Greek Yogurt Muesli Parfaits	307
Lemon Cream	307
Sweet Tropical Medley Smoothie	307
Mediterranean Fruit Tart	307
Green Tea And Vanilla Cream	308
Semolina Pie	308
Vanilla Apple Compote	309
Cold Lemon Squares	309
Minty Coconut Cream	309
Cherry Cream	310
Warm Peach Compote	310
Honey Walnut Bars	310
Lime Vanilla Fudge	310
Pear Sauce	311
Honey Cream	311
Dragon Fruit, Pear, And Spinach Salad	311
Mediterranean Biscotti	312
Kataifi	312
Walnuts Kataifi	313
Cinnamon Tea	313
Tiny Orange Cardamom Cookies	313
Chocolate Ganache	314
Chocolate Covered Strawberries	314
Strawberry Angel Food Dessert	314
Key Lime Pie	315
Ice Cream Sandwich Dessert	315
Bananas Foster	315
Rhubarb Strawberry Crunch	315
Frosty Strawberry Dessert	316
Dessert Pie	316
Fruit Dip	316
Sugar-Coated Pecans	316
Jalapeño Popper Spread	317
Brown Sugar Smokies	317
Banana & Tortilla Snacks	317
Caramel Popcorn	317
Apple and Berries Ambrosia	318
Chocolate, Almond, and Cherry Clusters	318
Mascarpone and Fig Crostini	318
Chocolate and Avocado Mousse	319
Coconut Blueberries with Brown Rice	319
Glazed Pears with Hazelnuts	319
Lemony Blackberry Granita	319
Lemony Tea and Chia Pudding	320
Mint Banana Chocolate Sorbet	320
Yogurt Sundae	320
Raspberry Yogurt Basted Cantaloupe	320
Simple Apple Compote	321
Simple Peanut Butter and Chocolate Balls	321
Simple Spiced Sweet Pecans	321
Overnight Oats with Raspberries	321
Blackberry-Yogurt Green	322
Minty Watermelon Salad	322
Creamy Rice Pudding	322
Ricotta-Lemon Cheesecake	322
Strawberry Coconut Parfait	323

Moroccan Stuffed Dates	323
Almond Cookies	323
Spanish Nougat	324
Cinnamon Butter Cookies	324
Pumpkin Baked with Dry Fruit	324
Best French Meringues	324
Cinnamon Palmier	325
Baked Apples	325
Quick Peach Tarts	325
Bulgarian Rice Pudding	325
Caramel Cream	326
Yogurt-Strawberries Ice Pops	326
Fresh Strawberries in Mascarpone and Rose Water	326
Delicious French Éclairs	326
Blueberry Yogurt Dessert	327
Banana Yogurt with Walnuts	327

Copyright 2021 by Sara Dean - All rights reserved.

The following Book is reproduced below with the goal of providing information that is as accurate and reliable as possible. Regardless, purchasing this Book can be seen as consent to the fact that both the publisher and the author of this book are in no way experts on the topics discussed within and that any recommendations or suggestions that are made herein are for entertainment purposes only. Professionals should be consulted as needed prior to undertaking any of the action endorsed herein.

This declaration is deemed fair and valid by both the American Bar Association and the Committee of Publishers Association and is legally binding throughout the United States.

Furthermore, the transmission, duplication, or reproduction of any of the following work including specific information will be considered an illegal act irrespective of if it is done electronically or in print. This extends to creating a secondary or tertiary copy of the work or a recorded copy and is only allowed with the express written consent from the Publisher. All additional right reserved.

The information in the following pages is broadly considered a truthful and accurate account of facts and as such, any inattention, use, or misuse of the information in question by the reader will render any resulting actions solely under their purview. There are no scenarios in which the publisher or the original author of this work can be in any fashion deemed liable for any hardship or damages that may befall them after undertaking information described herein.

Additionally, the information in the following pages is intended only for informational purposes and should thus be thought of as universal. As befitting its nature, it is presented without assurance regarding its prolonged validity or interim quality. Trademarks that are mentioned are done without written consent and can in no way be considered an endorsement from the trademark holder.

Introduction

Mediterranean diet is based on the eating habits of the inhabitants of the regions along the Mediterranean Sea, mostly from Italy, Spain and Greece; it is considered more a life style then a diet, in fact it also promotes physical activity and proper liquid (mostly water) consumption.

Depending on fresh seasonal local foods there are no strict rules, because of the many cultural differences, but there are some common factors.

Mediterranean diet has become famous for its ability to reduce heart disease and obesity, thanks to the low consumption of unhealthy fats that increase blood glucose.

Mediterranean diet is mostly plant based, so it's rich of antioxidants; vegetables, fruits like apple and grapes, olive oil, whole grains, herbs, beans and nuts are consumed in large quantities.

Moderate amounts of poultry, eggs, dairy and seafood are also common aliments, accompanied by a little bit of red wine (some studies say that in small amount it helps to stay healthy).
Red meat and sweets like cookies and cakes are accepted but are more limited in quantity.

Foods to avoid:
refined grains, such as white bread and pasta
dough containing white flour refined oils (even canola oil and soybean oil)
foods with added sugars (like pastries, sodas, and candies)
processed meats processed or packaged foods

Chapter 1: Breakfast and Snack Recipes

Mediterranean Omelet

Servings: 1 Omelet | Cooking: 10 min

Ingredients
- 2 TB. extra-virgin olive oil
- 2 TB. yellow onion, finely chopped
- 1 small clove garlic, minced
- 1/2 tsp. salt
- 1 cup fresh spinach, chopped
- 1/2 medium tomato, diced
- 2 large eggs
- 2 TB. whole or 2 percent milk
- 4 kalamata olives, pitted and chopped
- 1/2 tsp. ground black pepper
- 3 TB. crumbled feta cheese
- 1 TB. fresh parsley, finely chopped

Directions
1. In a nonstick pan over medium heat, cook extra-virgin olive oil, yellow onion, and garlic for 3 minutes.
2. Add salt, spinach, and tomato, and cook for 4 minutes.
3. In a small bowl, whisk together eggs and whole milk.
4. Add kalamata olives and black pepper to the pan, and pour in eggs over sautéed vegetables.
5. Using a rubber spatula, slowly push down edges of eggs, letting raw egg form a new layer, and continue for about 2 minutes or until eggs are cooked.
6. Fold omelet in half, and slide onto a plate. Top with feta cheese and fresh parsley, and serve warm.

Hummus And Tomato Sandwich

Servings: 3 | Cooking: 2 min

Ingredients
- 6 whole grain bread slices
- 1 tomato
- 3 Cheddar cheese slices
- ½ teaspoon dried oregano
- 1 teaspoon green chili paste
- ½ red onion, sliced
- 1 teaspoon lemon juice
- 1 tablespoon hummus
- 3 lettuce leaves

Directions
1. Slice tomato into 6 slices.
2. In the shallow bowl mix up together dried oregano, green chili paste, lemon juice, and hummus.
3. Spread 3 bread slices with the chili paste mixture.
4. After this, place the sliced tomatoes on them.
5. Add sliced onion, Cheddar cheese, and lettuce leaves.
6. Cover the lettuce leaves with the remaining bread slices to get the sandwiches.
7. Preheat the grill to 365F.
8. Grill the sandwiches for 2 minutes.

Nutrition: calories 269; fat 12.1; fiber 5.1; carbs 29.6; protein 13.9

Sage Omelet

Servings: 8 | Cooking: 25 min

Ingredients
- 8 eggs, beaten
- 6 oz Goat cheese, crumbled
- ½ teaspoon salt
- 3 tablespoons sour cream
- 1 teaspoon butter
- ½ teaspoon canola oil
- ¼ teaspoon sage
- ¼ teaspoon dried oregano
- 1 teaspoon chives, chopped

Directions
1. Put butter in the skillet. Add canola oil and preheat the mixture until it is homogenous.
2. Meanwhile, in the mixing bowl combine together salt, sour cream, sage, dried oregano, and chives. Add eggs and stir the mixture carefully with the help of the spoon/fork.
3. Pour the egg mixture in the skillet with butter-oil liquid.
4. Sprinkle the omelet with goat cheese and close the lid.
5. Cook the breakfast for 20 minutes over the low heat. The cooked omelet should be solid.
6. Slice it into the servings and transfer in the plates.

Nutrition: calories 176; fat 13.7; fiber 0; carbs 0; protein 12.2

Red Pepper and Artichoke Frittata

Servings: 2 | Cooking: 15 min

Ingredients

- 4 large eggs
- 1 can (14-ounce) artichoke hearts, rinsed, coarsely chopped
- 1 medium red bell pepper, diced
- 1 teaspoon dried oregano
- 1/4 cup Parmesan cheese, freshly grated
- 1/4 teaspoon red pepper, crushed
- 1/4 teaspoon salt, or to taste
- 2 garlic cloves, minced
- 2 teaspoons extra-virgin olive oil, divided
- Freshly ground pepper, to taste

Directions

1. In a 10-inch non-stick skillet, heat 1 teaspoon of the olive oil over medium heat. Add the bell pepper; cook for about 2 minutes or until tender. Add the garlic and the red pepper; cook for about 30 seconds, stirring. Transfer the mixture to a plate and wipe the skillet clean.
2. In a medium mixing bowl, whisk the eggs. Stir in the artichokes, cheese, the bell pepper mixture, and season with salt and pepper.
3. Place an over rack 4 inches from the source of heat; preheat broiler.
4. Brush the skillet with the remaining 1 teaspoon olive oil and heat over medium heat. Pour the egg mixture into the skillet and tilt to evenly distribute. Reduce the heat to medium low; cook for about 3-4 minutes, lifting the edges to allow the uncooked egg to flow underneath, until the bottom of the frittata is light golden.
5. Transfer the pan into the broiler, cook for about 1 1/2-2 1/2 minutes, or until the top is set.
6. Slide into a platter; cut into wedges and serve.

Nutrition: 305 Cal, 18 g total fat (6 g sat. fat, 8 g mono), 432 mg chol., 734 mg sodium, 1639 mg pot., 18 g carb.,8 g fiber, 21 g protein.

Stuffed Figs

Servings: 2 | Cooking: 15 min

Ingredients

- 7 oz fresh figs
- 1 tablespoon cream cheese
- ½ teaspoon walnuts, chopped
- 4 bacon slices
- ¼ teaspoon paprika
- ¼ teaspoon salt
- ½ teaspoon canola oil
- ½ teaspoon honey

Directions

1. Make the crosswise cuts in every fig.
2. In the shallow bowl mix up together cream cheese, walnuts, paprika, and salt.
3. Fill the figs with cream cheese mixture and wrap in the bacon.
4. Secure the fruits with toothpicks and sprinkle with honey.
5. Line the baking tray with baking paper.
6. Place the prepared figs in the tray and sprinkle them with olive oil gently.
7. Bake the figs for 15 minutes at 350F.

Nutrition: Calories 299; fat 19.4; fiber 2.3; carbs 16.7; protein 15.2

Keto Egg Fast Snickerdoodle Crepes

Servings: 2 | Cooking: 15 min

Ingredients

- 5 oz cream cheese, softened
- 6 eggs
- 1 teaspoon cinnamon
- Butter, for frying
- 1 tablespoon Swerve
- 2 tablespoons granulated Swerve
- 8 tablespoons butter, softened
- 1 tablespoon cinnamon

Directions

1. For the crepes: Put all the ingredients together in a blender except the butter and process until smooth.
2. Heat butter on medium heat in a non-stick pan and pour some batter in the pan.
3. Cook for about 2 minutes, then flip and cook for 2 more minutes.
4. Repeat with the remaining mixture.
5. Mix Swerve, butter and cinnamon in a small bowl until combined.
6. Spread this mixture onto the centre of the crepe and serve rolled up.

Nutrition: Calories: 543 Carbs: 8g Fats: 51.6g Proteins: 15.7g Sodium: 455mg Sugar: 0.9g

Quinoa and Potato Bowl

Servings: 4 | Cooking: 20 min

Ingredients
- 1 sweet potato, peeled, chopped
- 1 tablespoon olive oil
- ½ teaspoon chili flakes
- ½ teaspoon salt
- 1 cup quinoa
- 2 cups of water
- 1 teaspoon butter
- 1 tablespoon fresh cilantro, chopped

Directions
1. Line the baking tray with parchment.
2. Arrange the chopped sweet potato in the tray and sprinkle it with chili flakes, salt, and olive oil.
3. Bake the sweet potato for 20 minutes at 355F.
4. Meanwhile, pour water in the saucepan.
5. Add quinoa and cook it over the medium heat for 7 minutes or until quinoa will absorb all liquid.
6. Add butter in the cooked quinoa and stir well.
7. Transfer it in the bowls, add baked sweet potato and chopped cilantro.

Nutrition: calories 221; fat 7.1; fiber 3.9; carbs 33.2; protein 6.6

Almond Cream Cheese Bake

Servings: 4 | Cooking: 2 Hours

Ingredients
- 1 cup cream cheese
- 4 tablespoons honey
- 1 oz almonds, chopped
- ½ teaspoon vanilla extract
- 3 eggs, beaten
- 1 tablespoon semolina

Directions
1. Put beaten eggs in the mixing bowl.
2. Add cream cheese, semolina, and vanilla extract.
3. Blend the mixture with the help of the hand mixer until it is fluffy.
4. After this, add chopped almonds and mix up the mass well.
5. Transfer the cream cheese mash in the non-sticky baking mold.
6. Flatten the surface of the cream cheese mash well.
7. Preheat the oven to 325F.
8. Cook the breakfast for 2 hours.
9. The meal is cooked when the surface of the mash is light brown.
10. Chill the cream cheese mash little and sprinkle with honey.

Nutrition: calories 352; fat 27.1; fiber 1; carbs 22.6; protein 10.4

Slow-cooked Peppers Frittata

Servings: 6 | Cooking: 3 Hours

Ingredients
- ½ cup almond milk
- 8 eggs, whisked
- Salt and black pepper to the taste
- 1 teaspoon oregano, dried
- 1 and ½ cups roasted peppers, chopped
- ½ cup red onion, chopped
- 4 cups baby arugula
- 1 cup goat cheese, crumbled
- Cooking: spray

Directions
1. In a bowl, combine the eggs with salt, pepper and the oregano and whisk.
2. Grease your slow cooker with the cooking spray, arrange the peppers and the remaining ingredients inside and pour the eggs mixture over them.
3. Put the lid on and cook on Low for 3 hours.
4. Divide the frittata between plates and serve.

Nutrition: calories 259; fat 20.2; fiber 1; carbs 4.4; protein 16.3

Apricots with Yogurt, Honey, And Pistachios

Servings: 1 | Cooking: 5 min

Ingredients
- 1 ripe apricot, halved, pitted
- 4 tablespoons Greek yogurt, plain
- 1 tablespoon roasted pistachios, unsalted, roughly chopped
- Honey (try wildflower or lavender)

Directions
1. Top each apricot with 2 tablespoons of Greek yogurt, drizzle with honey, and sprinkle with the chopped pistachios. Serve.

Nutrition: 143 Cal, 6 g total fat (2 g sat. fat), 7 mg chol., 27 mg sodium, 19 g carb., 1 g fiber, 6 g protein.

Mediterranean Garbanzo Chili

Servings: 6 | Cooking: 15 min

Ingredients
- 1 can (14 1/2 ounces) chicken broth, reduced-sodium
- 3 cans (15 ounces each) garbanzo beans or chickpeas, rinsed, drained
- 1 large (about 1 1/4 cups) sweet green pepper, cut into bite-size strips
- 1 pint grape tomatoes, halved
- 1/2 cup feta cheese, crumble, plus more for sprinkling
- 1/3 cup Kalamata olives, pitted, halved
- 1/4 teaspoon red pepper, crushed
- 2 large (about 2 cups) onions, sliced
- 2 tablespoons olive oil, extra-virgin
- 2 teaspoons dried basil, crushed
- 2 teaspoons lemon peel, finely shredded
- 5 garlic cloves, minced

Directions
1. Over medium-high heat, heat the olive oil in a Dutch oven. Add the garlic, onions, basil, and red pepper; cook for about 4-5 minutes, frequently stirring, until softened.
2. Add the sweet peppers; cook, stirring, for about 2 minutes.
3. Add the garbanzo beans; cook for about 2 minutes, occasionally stirring.
4. Add the broth and the olives; bring to a boil, reduce the heat to medium, and simmer uncovered for about 5 minutes, occasionally stirring.
5. Add the grape tomatoes in; cook, stirring, for about 2 minutes, or just until heated through and wilted. Remove the Dutch oven from the heat.
6. Add in the feta cheese and the lemon peel. Stir until the cheese is melted.
7. Divide the chili between 6 bowls. If desired, trop with additional crumbled feta cheese.

Nutrition: 385 Cal, 11 g total fat (3 g sat. fat, 2 g poly. Fat, 4 g mono), 11 mg chol., 812 mg sodium, 59 g carb.,12 g fiber,15 g sugar, 15 g protein.

Veggie Salad

Servings: 4 | Cooking: 0 min

Ingredients
- 2 tomatoes, cut into wedges
- 2 red bell peppers, chopped
- 1 cucumber, chopped
- 1 red onion, sliced
- ½ cup kalamata olives, pitted and sliced
- 2 ounces feta cheese, crumbled
- ¼ cup lime juice
- ½ cup olive oil
- 2 garlic cloves, minced
- 1 tablespoon oregano, chopped
- Salt and black pepper to the taste

Directions
1. In a large salad bowl, combine the tomatoes with the peppers and the rest of the ingredients except the cheese and toss.
2. Divide the salad into smaller bowls, sprinkle the cheese on top and serve for breakfast.

Nutrition: calories 327; fat 11.2; fiber 4.4; carbs 16.7; protein 6.4

Fennel Bruschetta

Servings: 20 | Cooking: 10 min

Ingredients
- 6 large-sized tomatoes, diced
- 2 garlic cloves, minced
- 1/4 cup olive oil, extra-virgin, for brushing
- 1/3 cup fresh basil, minced
- 1/2 large Bermuda onion, diced
- 1 loaf (20 ounces) French bread, sliced into 1/2-inch thick pieces
- 1 1/2 tablespoons fennel seed
- 1/3 cup olive oil, extra-virgin
- Salt and black pepper, to taste

Directions
1. In a mixing bowl, combine the tomatoes, fennel seeds, garlic, onion, basil, the 1/3 cup of olive oil, and season of salt and then pepper. Refrigerate for a minimum of 1 hour to allow the flavors to blend.
2. Preheat the oven to 350F or 175C.
3. Brush the sides of the slices of bread with a little of the1/4 cup olive oil. Place them into baking sheet, and toast for 3 minutes each side until golden brown.
4. To serve, scoop the chilled tomato toppings into each toasted bread slice, arrange them on a serving plate.

Nutrition: 146 Cal, 6.6 g total fat (1 g sat. fat), 0 mg chol., 188 mg sodium, 18.8 g carb., 1.6 g fiber, 4 g protein.

Cauliflower Hash Brown Breakfast Bowl

Servings: 2 | Cooking: 30 min

Ingredients
- 1 tablespoon lemon juice
- 1 egg
- 1 avocado
- 1 teaspoon garlic powder
- 2 tablespoons extra virgin olive oil
- 2 oz mushrooms, sliced
- ½ green onion, chopped
- ¼ cup salsa
- ¾ cup cauliflower rice
- ½ small handful baby spinach
- Salt and black pepper, to taste

Directions
1. Mash together avocado, lemon juice, garlic powder, salt and black pepper in a small bowl.
2. Whisk eggs, salt and black pepper in a bowl and keep aside.
3. Heat half of olive oil over medium heat in a skillet and add mushrooms.
4. Sauté for about 3 minutes and season with garlic powder, salt, and pepper.
5. Sauté for about 2 minutes and dish out in a bowl.
6. Add rest of the olive oil and add cauliflower, garlic powder, salt and pepper.
7. Sauté for about 5 minutes and dish out.
8. Return the mushrooms to the skillet and add green onions and baby spinach.
9. Sauté for about 30 seconds and add whisked eggs.
10. Sauté for about 1 minute and scoop on the sautéed cauliflower hash browns.
11. Top with salsa and mashed avocado and serve.

Nutrition: Calories: 400 Carbs: 15.8g Fats: 36.7g Proteins: 8g Sodium: 288mg Sugar: 4.2g

Pumpkin Coconut Oatmeal

Servings: 6 | Cooking: 13 min

Ingredients
- 2 cups oatmeal
- 1 cup of coconut milk
- 1 cup milk
- 1 teaspoon Pumpkin pie spices
- 2 tablespoons pumpkin puree
- 1 tablespoon Honey
- ½ teaspoon butter

Directions
1. Pour coconut milk and milk in the saucepan. Add butter and bring the liquid to boil.
2. Add oatmeal, stir well with the help of a spoon and close the lid.
3. Simmer the oatmeal for 7 minutes over the medium heat.
4. Meanwhile, mix up together honey, pumpkin pie spices, and pumpkin puree.
5. When the oatmeal is cooked, add pumpkin puree mixture and stir well.
6. Transfer the cooked breakfast in the serving plates.

Nutrition: calories 232; fat 12.5; fiber 3.8; carbs 26.2; protein 5.9

Bacon, Vegetable And Parmesan Combo

Servings: 2 | Cooking: 25 min

Ingredients
- 2 slices of bacon, thick-cut
- ½ tbsp mayonnaise
- ½ of medium green bell pepper, deseeded, chopped
- 1 scallion, chopped
- ¼ cup grated Parmesan cheese
- 1 tbsp olive oil

Directions
1. Switch on the oven, then set its temperature to 375°F and let it preheat.
2. Meanwhile, take a baking dish, grease it with oil, and add slices of bacon in it.
3. Spread mayonnaise on top of the bacon, then top with bell peppers and scallions, sprinkle with Parmesan cheese and bake for about 25 minutes until cooked thoroughly.
4. When done, take out the baking dish and serve immediately.
5. For meal prepping, wrap bacon in a plastic sheet and refrigerate for up to 2 days.
6. When ready to eat, reheat bacon in the microwave and then serve.

Nutrition: Calories 197, Total Fat 13.8g, Total Carbs 4.7g, Protein 14.3g, Sugar 1.9g, Sodium 662mg

Mediterranean Crostini

Servings: 4 | Cooking: 15 min

Ingredients

- 12 slices (1/3-inch thick) whole-wheat baguette, toasted
- Coarse salt and freshly ground pepper
- For the spread:
- 1 can chickpeas (15 1/2 ounces), drained, rinsed
- 1/4 cup olive oil, extra-virgin
- 1 tablespoon lemon juice, freshly squeezed
- 1 small clove garlic, minced
- 2 tablespoons olive oil, extra-virgin, divided
- 2 tablespoons celery, finely diced, plus celery leaves for garnish
- 8 large green olives, pitted, cut into 1/8-inch slivers

Directions

1. In a food processor, combine the spread ingredients and season with salt and pepper; set aside.
2. In a small mixing bowl, combine 1 tablespoon of olive oil and the remaining ingredients. Season with salt and pepper. Set aside.
3. Divide the spread between the toasted baguette slices, top with the relish. Drizzle the remaining1 tablespoon of olive oil over each and season with pepper. If desired, garnish with the celery leaves. Serve immediately.

Nutrition: 603 Cal, 3.7 g total fat (3.7 g sat. fat), 0 mg chol., 781 mg sodium, 483 mg pot, 79.2 g carb.,9.6 g fiber,6.8 g sugar, 19.1 g protein.

Heavenly Egg Bake with Blackberry

Servings: 4 | Cooking: 15 min

Ingredients

- Chopped rosemary
- 1 tsp lime zest
- ½ tsp salt
- ¼ tsp vanilla extract, unsweetened
- 1 tsp grated ginger
- 3 tbsp coconut flour
- 1 tbsp unsalted butter
- 5 organic eggs
- 1 tbsp olive oil
- ½ cup fresh blackberries
- Black pepper to taste

Directions

1. Switch on the oven, then set its temperature to 350°F and let it preheat.
2. Meanwhile, place all the ingredients in a blender, reserving the berries and pulse for 2 to 3 minutes until well blended and smooth.
3. Take four silicon muffin cups, grease them with oil, evenly distribute the blended batter in the cups, top with black pepper and bake for 15 minutes until cooked through and the top has golden brown.
4. When done, let blueberry egg bake cool in the muffin cups for 5 minutes, then take them out, cool them on a wire rack and then serve.
5. For meal prepping, wrap each egg bake with aluminum foil and freeze for up to 3 days.
6. When ready to eat, reheat blueberry egg bake in the microwave and then serve.

Nutrition: Calories 144, Total Fat 10g, Total Carbs 2g, Protein 8.5g

Quick Cream ff Wheat

Servings: 1 Cup | Cooking: 12 min

Ingredients

- 4 cups whole milk
- 1/2 cup farina
- 1/2 tsp. salt
- 3 TB. sugar
- 3 TB. butter
- 3 TB. pine nuts

Directions

1. In a large saucepan over medium heat, bring whole milk to a simmer, and cook for about 4 minutes. Do not allow milk to scorch.
2. Whisk in farina, salt, and sugar, and bring to a slight boil. Cook for 2 minutes, reduce heat to low, and cook for 3 more minutes. Stay close to the pan to ensure it doesn't boil over.
3. Pour mixture into 4 bowls, and let cool for 5 minutes.
4. Meanwhile, in a small pan over low heat, cook butter and pine nuts for about 3 minutes or until pine nuts are lightly toasted.
5. Evenly spoon butter and pine nuts over each bowl, and serve warm.

Herbed Spinach Frittata

Servings: 4 | Cooking: 20 min

Ingredients
- 5 eggs, beaten
- 1 cup fresh spinach
- 2 oz Parmesan, grated
- 1/3 cup cherry tomatoes
- ½ teaspoon dried oregano
- 1 teaspoon dried thyme
- 1 teaspoon olive oil

Directions
1. Chop the spinach into the tiny pieces and or use a blender.
2. Then combine together chopped spinach with eggs, dried oregano and thyme.
3. Add Parmesan and stir frittata mixture with the help of the fork.
4. Brush the springform pan with olive oil and pour the egg mixture inside.
5. Cut the cherry tomatoes into the halves and place them over the egg mixture.
6. Preheat the oven to 360F.
7. Bake the frittata for 20 minutes or until it is solid.
8. Chill the cooked breakfast till the room temperature and slice into the servings.

Nutrition: calories 140; fat 9.8; fiber 0.5; carbs 2.1; protein 11.9

Ham Spinach Ballet

Servings: 2 | Cooking: 40 min

Ingredients
- 4 teaspoons cream
- ¾ pound fresh baby spinach
- 7-ounce ham, sliced
- Salt and black pepper, to taste
- 1 tablespoon unsalted butter, melted

Directions
1. Preheat the oven to 360 degrees F. and grease 2 ramekins with butter.
2. Put butter and spinach in a skillet and cook for about 3 minutes.
3. Add cooked spinach in the ramekins and top with ham slices, cream, salt and black pepper.
4. Bake for about 25 minutes and dish out to serve hot.
5. For meal prepping, you can refrigerate this ham spinach ballet for about 3 days wrapped in a foil.

Nutrition: Calories: 188 Fat: 12.5g Carbohydrates: 4.9g Protein: 14.6g Sugar: 0.3g Sodium: 1098mg

Banana Quinoa

Servings: 4 | Cooking: 12 min

Ingredients
- 1 cup quinoa
- 2 cup milk
- 1 teaspoon vanilla extract
- 1 teaspoon honey
- 2 bananas, sliced
- ¼ teaspoon ground cinnamon

Directions
1. Pour milk in the saucepan and add quinoa.
2. Close the lid and cook it over the medium heat for 12 minutes or until quinoa will absorb all liquid.
3. Then chill the quinoa for 10-15 minutes and place in the serving mason jars.
4. Add honey, vanilla extract, and ground cinnamon.
5. Stir well.
6. Top quinoa with banana and stir it before serving.

Nutrition: Calories 279; fat 5.3; fiber 4.6; carbs 48.4; protein 10.7

Cheesy Eggs Ramekins

Servings: 2 | Cooking: 10 min

Ingredients
- 1 tablespoon chives, chopped
- 1 tablespoon dill, chopped
- A pinch of salt and black pepper
- 2 tablespoons cheddar cheese, grated
- 1 tomato, chopped
- 2 eggs, whisked
- Cooking: spray

Directions
1. In a bowl, mix the eggs with the tomato and the rest of the ingredients except the cooking spray and whisk well.
2. Grease 2 ramekins with the cooking spray, divide the mix into each ramekin, bake at 400 degrees F for 10 minutes and serve.

Nutrition: calories 104; fat 7.1; fiber 0.6; carbs 2.6; protein 7.9

Mediterranean Frittata (Version 2)

Servings: 6 | Cooking: 15 min

Ingredients
- 8 eggs
- 3 tablespoons olive oil, divided
- 2 tablespoons Parmesan cheese, finely shredded
- 1/8 teaspoon ground black pepper
- 1/4 cup low-fat milk
- 1/4 cup fresh basil, slivered
- 1/2 of a 7-ounce jar (about 1/2 cup) roasted red sweet peppers, drained, chopped
- 1/2 cup onion-and-garlic croutons, purchased, coarsely crushed
- 1/2 cup kalamata or ripe olives, sliced, pitted
- 1/2 cup (2 ounces) feta cheese, crumbled
- 1 teaspoon garlic, bottled minced
- 1 cup onion, chopped

Directions
1. Preheat broiler.
2. In a cast-iron skillet over medium heat, heat 2 tablespoons of the olive oil. Add the garlic and the onion; cook until the onions are just tender.
3. In a large bowl, combine the eggs and the milk; beat. Stir in the feta, sweet peppers, basil, olives, and black pepper. Pour the egg mixture into the skillet and cook. As the mixture sets, using a spatula, lift the egg mixture to allow the uncooked liquid to flow underneath. Continue cooking and lifting until the egg is almost set but the surface is still moist. Reduce the heat, if necessary, to prevent overcooking.
4. In a small-sized bowl, combine the parmesan, croutons, and the remaining 1 tablespoon of olive oil; sprinkle the mixture over the frittata.
5. Transfer the skillet under the broiler about 4-5 inches from the source of heat; broil for about 1-2 minutes, or until the top is set.

Nutrition: 242 Cal, 19 g total fat (6 g sat. fat), 297 mg chol., 339 mg sodium, 7g carb.,1 g fiber,12 g protein.

Cinnamon Apple And Lentils Porridge

Servings: 4 | Cooking: 10 min

Ingredients
- ½ cup walnuts, chopped
- 2 green apples, cored, peeled and cubed
- 3 tablespoons maple syrup
- 3 cups almond milk
- ½ cup red lentils
- ½ teaspoon cinnamon powder
- ½ cup cranberries, dried
- 1 teaspoon vanilla extract

Directions
1. Put the milk in a pot, heat it up over medium heat, add the walnuts, apples, maple syrup and the rest of the ingredients, toss, simmer for 10 minutes, divide into bowls and serve.

Nutrition: calories 150; fat 2; fiber 1; carbs 3; protein 5

Creamy Oatmeal

Servings: 2 | Cooking: 15 min

Ingredients
- 1 ½ cup oatmeal
- 1 tablespoon cocoa powder
- ½ cup heavy cream
- ¼ cup of water
- 1 teaspoon vanilla extract
- 1 tablespoon butter
- 2 tablespoons Splenda

Directions
1. Mix up together oatmeal with cocoa powder and Splenda.
2. Transfer the mixture in the saucepan.
3. Add vanilla extract, water, and heavy cream. Stir it gently with the help of the spatula.
4. Close the lid and cook it for 10-15 minutes over the medium-low heat.
5. Remove the cooked cocoa oatmeal from the heat and add butter. Stir it well.

Nutrition: calories 230; fat 10.6; fiber 3.5; carbs 28.1; protein 4.6

Stuffed Sweet Potato

Servings: 8 | Cooking: 40 min

Ingredients
- 8 sweet potatoes, pierced with a fork
- 14 ounces canned chickpeas, drained and rinsed
- 1 small red bell pepper, chopped
- 1 tablespoon lemon zest, grated
- 2 tablespoons lemon juice
- 3 tablespoons olive oil
- 1 teaspoon garlic, minced
- 1 tablespoon oregano, chopped
- 2 tablespoons parsley, chopped
- A pinch of salt and black pepper
- 1 avocado, peeled, pitted and mashed

- ¼ cup water
- ¼ cup tahini paste

Directions
1. Arrange the potatoes on a baking sheet lined with parchment paper, bake them at 400 degrees F for 40 minutes, cool them down and cut a slit down the middle in each.
2. In a bowl, combine the chickpeas with the bell pepper, lemon zest, half of the lemon juice, half of the oil, half of the garlic, oregano, half of the parsley, salt and pepper, toss and stuff the potatoes with this mix.
3. In another bowl, mix the avocado with the water, tahini, the rest of the lemon juice, oil, garlic and parsley, whisk well and spread over the potatoes.
4. Serve cold for breakfast.

Nutrition: calories 308; fat 2; fiber 8; carbs 38; protein 7

Couscous And Chickpeas Bowls

Servings: 4 | Cooking: 6 min

Ingredients
- ¾ cup whole wheat couscous
- 1 yellow onion, chopped
- 1 tablespoon olive oil
- 1 cup water
- 2 garlic cloves, minced
- 15 ounces canned chickpeas, drained and rinsed
- A pinch of salt and black pepper
- 15 ounces canned tomatoes, chopped
- 14 ounces canned artichokes, drained and chopped
- ½ cup Greek olives, pitted and chopped
- ½ teaspoon oregano, dried
- 1 tablespoon lemon juice

Directions
1. Put the water in a pot, bring to a boil over medium heat, add the couscous, stir, take off the heat, cover the pan, leave aside for 10 minutes and fluff with a fork.
2. Heat up a pan with the oil over medium-high heat, add the onion and sauté for 2 minutes.
3. Add the rest of the ingredients, toss and cook for 4 minutes more.
4. Add the couscous, toss, divide into bowls and serve for breakfast.

Nutrition: calories 340; fat 10; fiber 9; carbs 51; protein 11

Vegetarian Three Cheese Quiche Stuffed Peppers

Servings: 2 | Cooking: 50 min

Ingredients
- 2 large eggs
- ¼ cup mozzarella, shredded
- 1 medium bell peppers, sliced in half and seeds removed
- ¼ cup ricotta cheese
- ¼ cup grated Parmesan cheese
- ½ teaspoon garlic powder
- 1/8 cup baby spinach leaves
- ¼ teaspoon dried parsley
- 1 tablespoon Parmesan cheese, to garnish

Directions
1. Preheat oven to 375 degrees F.
2. Blend all the cheeses, eggs, garlic powder and parsley in a food processor and process until smooth.
3. Pour the cheese mixture into each sliced bell pepper and top with spinach leaves.
4. Stir with a fork, pushing them under the cheese mixture and cover with foil.
5. Bake for about 40 minutes and sprinkle with Parmesan cheese.
6. Broil for about 5 minutes and dish out to serve.

Nutrition: Calories: 157 Carbs: 7.3g Fats: 9g Proteins: 12.7g Sodium: 166mg Sugar: 3.7g

Sweet Bread With Dates

Servings: 1 Roll | Cooking: 30 min

Ingredients
- 2 3/4 cups all-purpose flour
- 1/4 cup dry milk
- 1/4 cup sugar
- 1 1/4 tsp. salt
- 1 TB. instant yeast
- 3 large eggs
- 1/3 cup plus 1 TB. water
- 10 TB. butter
- 12 medjool dates, pitted
- 1 TB. orange blossom water
- 1/2 tsp. cinnamon
- 1 large egg white

Directions

1. In a food processor fitted with a dough attachment or in a blender, knead all-purpose flour, dry milk, sugar, salt, instant yeast, eggs, 1/3 cup water, and 8 tablespoons butter for 15 minutes.
2. Transfer dough to a bowl lightly sprayed with olive oil spray, cover the bowl with plastic wrap, and let rise in the refrigerator for 24 hours.
3. In a food processor fitted with a chopping blade, blend medjool dates, orange blossom water, and cinnamon for 2 minutes or until smooth.
4. Grease a 12-cup muffin tin with remaining 2 tablespoons butter.
5. Form dough into 12 equal pieces. Spoon 1 tablespoon date mixture into center of each dough piece, tightly seal dough around date mixture, and place seal side down into the prepared muffin tin.
6. Set aside dough to rise for 1 hour.
7. Preheat the oven to 375°F.
8. In a small bowl, whisk together egg white and remaining 1 tablespoon water. Brush each roll with egg wash.
9. Bake for 30 minutes.
10. Remove rolls from the oven, and let rest for 20 minutes before serving.

Shrimp Toast

Servings: 4 | Cooking: 10 min

Ingredients

- 13 oz shrimps, peeled
- 1 tablespoon tomato sauce
- ½ teaspoon Splenda
- ¼ teaspoon garlic powder
- 1 teaspoon fresh parsley, chopped
- ½ teaspoon olive oil
- 1 teaspoon lemon juice
- 4 whole-grain bread slices
- 1 cup water, for cooking

Directions

1. Pour water in the saucepan and bring it to boil.
2. Add shrimps and boil them over the high heat for 5 minutes.
3. After this, drain shrimps and chill them to the room temperature.
4. Mix up together shrimps with Splenda, garlic powder, tomato sauce, and fresh parsley.
5. Add lemon juice and stir gently.
6. Preheat the oven to 360F.
7. Brush the bread slices with olive oil and bake for 3 minutes.
8. Then place the shrimp mixture on the bread. Bruschetta is cooked.

Nutrition: calories 199; fat 3.7; fiber 2.1; carbs 15.3; protein 24.1

Breakfast Beans (ful Mudammas)

Servings: 1 Cup | Cooking: 10 min

Ingredients

- 1 (15-oz.) can chickpeas, rinsed and drained
- 1 (15-oz.) can fava beans, rinsed and drained
- 1 cup water
- 1 TB. minced garlic
- 1 tsp. salt
- 1/2 cup fresh lemon juice
- 1/2 tsp. cayenne
- 1/2 cup fresh parsley, chopped
- 1 large tomato, diced
- 3 medium radishes, sliced
- 1/4 cup extra-virgin olive oil

Directions

1. In a 2-quart pot over medium-low heat, combine chickpeas, fava beans, and water. Simmer for 10 minutes.
2. Pour bean mixture into a large bowl, and add garlic, salt, and lemon juice. Stir and smash half of beans with the back of a wooden spoon.
3. Sprinkle cayenne over beans, and evenly distribute parsley, tomatoes, and radishes over top. Drizzle with extra-virgin olive oil, and serve warm or at room temperature.

Seeds And Lentils Oats

Servings: 4 | Cooking: 50 min

Ingredients

- ½ cup red lentils
- ¼ cup pumpkin seeds, toasted
- 2 teaspoons olive oil
- ¼ cup rolled oats
- ¼ cup coconut flesh, shredded
- 1 tablespoon honey
- 1 tablespoon orange zest, grated
- 1 cup Greek yogurt
- 1 cup blackberries

Directions
1. Spread the lentils on a baking sheet lined with parchment paper, introduce in the oven and roast at 370 degrees F for 30 minutes.
2. Add the rest of the ingredients except the yogurt and the berries, toss and bake at 370 degrees F for 20 minutes more.
3. Transfer this to a bowl, add the rest of the ingredients, toss, divide into smaller bowls and serve for breakfast.

Nutrition: calories 204; fat 7.1; fiber 10.4; carbs 27.6; protein 9.5

Couscous With Artichokes, Sun-dried Tomatoes And Feta

Servings: 6 | Cooking: 15 min

Ingredients
- 3 cups chicken breast, cooked, chopped
- 2 1/3 cups water, divided
- 2 jars (6-ounces each) marinated artichoke hearts, undrained
- 1/4 teaspoon black pepper, freshly ground
- 1/2 cup tomatoes, sun-dried
- 1/2 cup (2 ounces) feta cheese, crumbled
- 1 cup flat-leaf parsley, fresh, chopped
- 1 3/4 cups whole-wheat Israeli couscous, uncooked
- 1 can (14 1/2 ounces) vegetable broth

Directions
1. In a microwavable bowl, combine 2 cups of the water and the tomatoes. Microwave on HIGH for about 3 minutes or until the water boils. When water is boiling, remove from the microwave, cover, and let stand for about 3 minutes or until the tomatoes are soft; drain, chop, and set aside.
2. In a large saucepan, place the vegetable broth and the remaining 1/3 cup of water; bring to boil. Stir in the couscous, cover, reduce heat, and simmer for about 8 minutes or until tender.
3. Remove the pan from the heat; add the tomatoes and the remaining ingredients. Stir to combine.

Nutrition: 419 Cal, 14.1 g total fat (3.9 g sat. fat, 0.8 g poly. Fat, 1.4 g mono), 64 mg chol.,677 mg sodium, 42.5 g carb.,2.6 g fiber, 30.2 g protein.

Cinnamon Roll Oats

Servings: 4 | Cooking: 10 min

Ingredients
- ½ cup rolled oats
- 1 cup milk
- 1 teaspoon vanilla extract
- 1 teaspoon ground cinnamon
- 2 teaspoon honey
- 2 tablespoons Plain yogurt
- 1 teaspoon butter

Directions
1. Pour milk in the saucepan and bring it to boil.
2. Add rolled oats and stir well.
3. Close the lid and simmer the oats for 5 minutes over the medium heat. The cooked oats will absorb all milk.
4. Then add butter and stir the oats well.
5. In the separated bowl, whisk together Plain yogurt with honey, cinnamon, and vanilla extract.
6. Transfer the cooked oats in the serving bowls.
7. Top the oats with the yogurt mixture in the shape of the wheel.

Nutrition: Calories 243; fat 20.2; fiber 1; carbs 2.8; protein 13.3

Mediterranean Wrap

Servings: 4 | Cooking: 10 min

Ingredients
- 4 pieces (10-inch) spinach wraps (or whole wheat tortilla or sun-dried tomato wraps)
- 1 pound chicken tenders
- 1 cup cucumber, chopped
- 3 tablespoons extra-virgin olive oil
- 1 medium tomato, chopped
- 1/3 cup couscous, whole-wheat
- 2 teaspoons garlic, minced
- 1/4 teaspoon salt, divided
- 1/4 teaspoon freshly ground pepper
- 1/4 cup lemon juice
- 1/2 cup water
- 1/2 cup fresh mint, chopped
- 1 cup fresh parsley, chopped

Directions
1. In a small saucepan, pour the water and bring to a boil. Stir in the couscous, remove pan from heat, cover, and allow to stand for 5 minutes, then fluff using a fork; set aside.

2. Meanwhile, in a small mixing bowl, combine the mint, parsley, oil, lemon juice, garlic, 1/8 teaspoon of the salt, and the pepper.
3. In a medium mixing bowl, toss the chicken with the 1 tablespoon of the mint mixture and the remaining 1/8 teaspoon of salt.
4. Place the chicken mixture into a large non-stick skillet; cook for about 3-5 minutes each side, or until heated through. Remove from the skillet, allow to cool enough to handle, and cut into bite-sized pieces.
5. Stir the remaining mint mixture, the cucumber, and the tomato into the couscous.
6. Spread about 3/4 cup of the couscous mix onto each wrap and divide the chicken between the wraps, roll like a burrito, tucking the sides in to hold to secure the ingredients in. Cut in halves and serve.

Nutrition: 479 Cal, 17 g total fat (3 g sat. fat, 11 g mono), 67 mg chol., 653 mg sodium, 382 pot., 49 g carb.,5 g fiber, 15 g protein.

Chicken Liver

Servings: ¾ Cup | Cooking: 7 min

Ingredients
- 2 lb. chicken liver
- 3 TB. extra-virgin olive oil
- 3 TB. minced garlic
- 1 tsp. salt
- 1/2 tsp. ground black pepper
- 1 cup fresh cilantro, finely chopped
- 1/4 cup fresh lemon juice

Directions
1. Cut chicken livers in half, rinse well, and pat dry with paper towels.
2. Preheat a large skillet over medium heat. Add extra-virgin olive oil and garlic, and cook for 2 minutes.
3. Add chicken liver and salt, and cook, tossing gently, for 5 minutes. Remove the skillet from heat, and spoon liver onto a plate.
4. Add black pepper, cilantro, and lemon juice. Lightly toss, and serve warm.

Avocado Spread

Servings: 8 | Cooking: 0 min

Ingredients
- 2 avocados, peeled, pitted and roughly chopped
- 1 tablespoon sun-dried tomatoes, chopped
- 2 tablespoons lemon juice
- 3 tablespoons cherry tomatoes, chopped
- ¼ cup red onion, chopped
- 1 teaspoon oregano, dried
- 2 tablespoons parsley, chopped
- 4 kalamata olives, pitted and chopped
- A pinch of salt and black pepper

Directions
1. Put the avocados in a bowl and mash with a fork.
2. Add the rest of the ingredients, stir to combine and serve as a morning spread.

Nutrition: calories 110; fat 10; fiber 3.8; carbs 5.7; protein 1.2

Eggs with Zucchini Noodles

Preparation: 10 min | Cooking: 11 min | Servings: 2

Ingredients
- 2 tablespoons extra-virgin olive oil
- 3 zucchinis, cut with a spiralizer
- 4 eggs
- A pinch of red pepper flakes
- 1 tablespoon basil, chopped

Directions
1. In a bowl, combine the zucchini noodles with salt, pepper and the olive oil and toss well.
2. Grease a baking sheet using cooking spray and divide the zucchini noodles into 4 nests on it.
3. Whisk an egg on top of each nest, sprinkle salt, pepper and the pepper flakes on top then bake at 350 F for 11 min.
4. Divide the mix between plates, sprinkle the basil on top and serve.

Nutrition: 296 calories; 23g fat; 3.3g fiber;

Banana Oats

Preparation: 10 min | Cooking: 0 min | Servings: 2

Ingredients
- ½ cup cold brewed coffee
- 2 dates, pitted
- 2 tablespoons cocoa powder
- 1 cup rolled oats

- 1 and ½ tablespoons chia seeds

Directions
1. In a blender, combine the 1 banana with the ¾ almond milk and the rest of the ingredients, pulse, divide into bowls and serve for breakfast.

Nutrition: 451 calories; 25g fat; 9.9g fiber;

Sun-dried Tomatoes Oatmeal

Preparation: 10 min | Cooking: 25 min | Servings: 4

Ingredients
- 3 cups water
- 1 cup almond milk
- 1 tablespoon olive oil
- 1 cup steel-cut oats
- ¼ cup sun-dried tomatoes, chopped

Directions
1. In a pan, scourge water with the milk, bring to a boil over medium heat.
2. Meanwhile, pre-heat pan with the oil over medium-high heat, add the oats, cook them for about 2 min and transfer m to the pan with the milk.
3. Stir the oats, add the tomatoes and simmer over medium heat for 23 min.
4. Divide the mix into bowls, sprinkle the red pepper flakes on top and serve for breakfast.

Nutrition: 170 calories; 17.8g fat; 1.5g protein

Quinoa Muffins

Preparation: 10 min | Cooking: 30 min | Servings: 12

Ingredients
- 6 eggs, whisked
- 1 cup Swiss cheese, grated
- 1 small yellow onion, chopped
- 1 cup quinoa, white mushrooms
- ½ cup sun-dried tomatoes, chopped

Directions
1. In a bowl, combine the eggs with salt, pepper and the rest of the ingredients and whisk well.
2. Divide this into a silicone muffin pan, bake at 350 degrees F for 30 min and serve for breakfast.

Nutrition: 123 calories; 5.6g fat; 7.5g protein

Watermelon "Pizza"

Preparation: 10 min | Cooking: 0 min | Servings: 4

Ingredients
- 1 watermelon slice cut 1-inch thick and then from the center cut into 4 wedges resembling pizza slices
- 6 kalamata olives, pitted and sliced
- 1-ounce feta cheese, crumbled
- ½ tablespoon balsamic vinegar
- 1 teaspoon mint, chopped

Directions
1. Arrange the watermelon "pizza" on a plate, sprinkle the olives and the rest of the ingredients on each slice and serve right away for breakfast.

Nutrition: 90 calories; 3g fat; 2g protein

Cheesy Yogurt

Preparation: 4 hs and 5 min | Cooking: 0 min | Servings: 4

Ingredients
- 1 cup Greek yogurt
- 1 tablespoon honey
- ½ cup feta cheese, crumbled

Directions
1. In a blender, combine the yogurt with the honey and the cheese and pulse well.
2. Divide into bowls and freeze for 4 hs before serving for breakfast.

Nutrition: 161 calories; 10g fat; 6.6g protein

Cauliflower Fritters

Preparation: 10 min | Cooking: 50 min | Servings: 4

Ingredients
- 30 ounces canned chickpeas, drained and rinsed
- 2 and ½ tablespoons olive oil
- 1 small yellow onion, chopped
- 2 cups cauliflower florets chopped
- 2 tablespoons garlic, minced

Directions
1. Lay out half of the chickpeas on a baking sheet lined with parchment pepper, pour in 1

tablespoon oil, season well, toss and bake at 400 degrees F for 30 min.
2. Transfer the chickpeas to a food processor, pulse well and put the mix into a bowl.
3. Heat up a pan with the ½ tablespoon oil over medium-high heat, add the garlic and the onion and sauté for 3 min.
4. Add the cauliflower, cook for 6 min more, transfer this to a blender, add the rest of the chickpeas, pulse, pour over the crispy chickpeas mix from the bowl, stir and shape medium fritters out of this mix.
5. Heat up a pan with the rest of the oil over medium-high heat, add the fritters, cook them for 6 min on both side and serve for breakfast.

Nutrition: 333 calories; 12.6g fat; 13.6g protein

Corn and Shrimp Salad

Preparation: 10 min | Cooking: 10 min | Servings: 4

Ingredients
- 4 ears of sweet corn, husked
- 1 avocado, peeled, pitted and chopped
- ½ cup basil, chopped
- 1-pound shrimp, peeled and deveined
- 1 and ½ cups cherry tomatoes, halved

Directions
1. Put the corn in a pot, boil water and cover, over medium heat for 6 min, drain, cool down, cut corn from the cob and put it in a bowl.
2. Thread the shrimp onto skewers and brush with some of the oil.
3. Situate the skewers on the prepared grill, cook over medium heat for 2 min on each side, remove from skewers and add over the corn.
4. Place the rest of the ingredients to the bowl, toss, divide between plates and serve for breakfast.

Nutrition: 371 calories; 22g fat; 23g protein

Cottage Cheese and Berries Omelet

Preparation: 5 min | Cooking: 4 min | Servings: 1

Ingredients
- 1 egg, whisked
- 1 teaspoon cinnamon powder
- 1 tablespoon almond milk
- 3 ounces cottage cheese
- 4 ounces blueberries

Directions
1. Scourge egg with the rest of the ingredients except the oil and toss.
2. Preheat pan with the oil over medium heat, add the eggs mix, spread, cook for 4 min on both sides, then serve.

Nutrition: 190 calories; 8g fat; 2g protein

Salmon Frittata

Preparation: 5 min | Cooking: 27 min | Servings: 4

Ingredients
- 1-pound gold potatoes, roughly cubed
- 1 tablespoon olive oil
- 2 salmon fillets, skinless and boneless
- 8 eggs, whisked
- 1 teaspoon mint, chopped

Directions
1. Put the potatoes in a boiling water at medium heat, then cook for 12 min, drain and transfer to a bowl.
2. Spread the salmon on a baking sheet lined with parchment paper, grease with cooking spray, broil at medium-high heat for 10 min on both sides, cool down, flake and put in a separate bowl.
3. Warm up a pan with the oil over medium heat, add the potatoes, salmon, and the rest of the ingredients excluding the eggs and toss.
4. Add the eggs on top, put the lid on and cook over medium heat for 10 min.
5. Divide the salmon between plates and serve.

Nutrition: 289 calories; 11g fat; 4g protein

Avocado and Olive Paste on Toasted Rye Bread

Preparation: 5 min | Cooking: 0 minute | Servings: 4

Ingredients
- 1 avocado, halved, peeled and finely chopped
- 1 tbsp green onions, finely chopped
- 2 tbsp green olive paste
- 4 lettuce leaves
- 1 tbsp lemon juice

Directions
1. Crush avocados with a fork or potato masher until almost smooth. Add the onions, green olive

paste and lemon juice. Season with salt and pepper to taste. Stir to combine.
2. Toast 4 slices of rye bread until golden. Spoon 1/4 of the avocado mixture onto each slice of bread, top with a lettuce leaf and serve.

Nutrition: 291 calories; 13g fat; 3g protein

Avocado and Chickpea Sandwiches

Preparation: 4 min | Cooking: 0 minute | Servings: 4

Ingredients
- 1/2 cup canned chickpeas
- 1 small avocado
- 2 green onions, finely chopped
- 1 egg, hard boiled
- 1/2 tomato, cucumber

Directions
1. Mash the avocado and chickpeas with a fork or potato masher until smooth. Add in green onions and salt and combine well.
2. Spread this mixture on the four slices of bread. Top each piece with tomato, cucumber and egg, and serve.

Nutrition: 309 calories; 9g fat; 2g protein

Raisin Quinoa Breakfast

Preparation: 15 min | Cooking: 0 minute | Servings: 4

Ingredients
- 1 cup quinoa
- 2 cups milk
- 2 tbsp. walnuts, crushed
- 2 tbsp. raisins, cranberries
- 1 tbsp. chia seeds

Directions
1. Rinse quinoa with cold water and drain. Place milk and quinoa into a saucepan and bring to a boil. Add ½ tsp. of vanilla. Adjust heat to low and simmer for 16 min stirring from time to time.
2. Set aside to cool then serve in a bowl, topped with honey, chia seeds, raisins, cranberries and crushed walnuts.

Nutrition: 299 calories; 7g fat; 1g protein

Banana Cinnamon Fritters

Preparation: 15 min | Cooking: 6 min | Servings: 4

Ingredients
- 1 cup self-rising flour
- 1 egg, beaten
- 3/4 cup sparkling water
- 2 tsp ground cinnamon
- 2-3 bananas, cut diagonally into 4 pieces each

Directions
1. Sift flour and cinnamon into a bowl and make a well in the center. Add egg and enough sparkling water to mix to a smooth batter.
2. Heat sunflower oil in a saucepan, enough to cover the base by 1-2 inch, so when a little batter dropped into the oil sizzles and rises to the surface.
3. Dip banana pieces into the batter, and then fry for 2-3 min or until golden. Pull out using slotted spoon and strain on paper towels. Sprinkle with sugar and serve hot.

Nutrition: 209 calories; 10g fat; 2g protein

Veggie Casserole

Preparation: 25 min | Cooking: 45 min | Servings: 4

Ingredients
- 1 lb. okra, trimmed
- 3 tomatoes, cut into wedges
- 3 garlic cloves, chopped
- 1 cup fresh parsley leaves, finely cut

Directions
1. In a deep ovenproof baking dish, combine okra, sliced tomatoes, olive oil and garlic. Add in salt and black pepper to taste, and toss to combine.
2. Bake in a prepared oven at 350 F for 45 min. Garnish with parsley and serve.

Nutrition: 302 calories; 13g fat; 6g protein

Ground Beef and Brussels Sprouts

Preparation: 20 min | Cooking: 36 min | Servings: 4

Ingredients
- 6 oz. ground beef
- 2 garlic cloves, crushed
- ½ cup grated sweet potato

- 1 cup grated Brussels sprouts
- 1 egg, boiled

Directions
1. In a medium saucepan, cook olive oil over medium heat. Gently sauté the ½ onion and garlic until the onion is soft and translucent. Add in the beef and the sweet potato and cook until the meat is fully cooked.
2. Mix in the Brussels sprouts and cook for about 5 min more. Season well and serve topped with a boiled egg.

Nutrition: 314 calories; 15g fat; 6g protein

Italian Mini Meatballs

Preparation: 13 min | Cooking: 20 min | Servings: 6

Ingredients
- 1 lb. ground beef
- 1 onion, grated
- 1 egg, lightly whisked
- 1 tsp garlic powder
- 1 tsp dried basil, oregano, parsley

Directions
1. Combine ground beef, onion, egg, parsley, garlic powder, basil and oregano. Mix very well with hands. Roll tablespoonful of the meat mixture into balls.
2. Place meatballs on a lined baking tray. Bake 20 min or until brown. Transfer to a serving plate and serve.

Nutrition: 275 calories; 9g fat; 1g protein

Mushroom and Olives Steaks

Preparation: 20 min | Cooking: 9 min | Servings: 6

Ingredients
- 1 lb. boneless beef sirloin steak
- 1 large onion, sliced
- 5-6 white mushrooms
- 1/2 cup green olives, coarsely chopped
- 1 cup parsley leaves, finely cut

Directions
1. Cook olive oil in a heavy bottomed pan at medium-high heat. Cook the steaks until well browned on each side then keep aside.
2. Gently sauté the onion in the same pan, for 3 min. Cook the mushrooms and olives until the mushrooms are done.
3. Situate the steaks back to the skillet, and cook for 5-6 min. Stir in parsley and serve.

Nutrition: 281 calories; 14g fat; 3g protein

Salmon Kebabs

Preparation: 30 min | Cooking: 6 min | Servings: 5

Ingredients
- 2 shallots, ends trimmed, halved
- 2 zucchinis, cut in 2-inch cubes
- 1 cup cherry tomatoes
- 6 skinless salmon fillets, cut into 1-inch pieces
- 3 limes, cut into thin wedges

Directions
1. Preheat barbecue or char grill on medium-high. Thread fish cubes onto skewers, then zucchinis, shallots and tomatoes.
2. Repeat to make 12 kebabs. Bake the kebabs for about 3 min each side for medium cooked.
3. Situate to a plate, wrap with foil and set aside for 5 min to rest.

Nutrition: 268 calories; 9g fat; 3g protein

Mediterranean Baked Salmon

Preparation: 35 min | Cooking: 11 min | Servings: 5

Ingredients
- 2 (6 oz) boneless salmon fillets
- 1 onion, tomato
- 1 tbsp. capers
- 1 tsp dry oregano
- 3 tbsp. Parmesan cheese

Directions
1. Set oven to 350 F. Place the salmon fillets in a baking dish, sprinkle with oregano, top with onion and tomato slices, drizzle with olive oil, and sprinkle with capers and Parmesan cheese.
2. Wrap the dish with foil and bake for 30 min.

Nutrition: 291 calories; 14g fat; 2g protein

Feta Cheese Baked in Foil

Preparation: 15 min | Cooking: 16 min | Servings: 5

Ingredients
- 14 oz. feta cheese, cut in slices
- 4 oz. butter
- 1 tbsp. paprika
- 1 tsp dried oregano

Directions
1. Cut the cheese into four medium-thick slices and place on sheets of butter lined aluminum foil.
2. Place a little bit of butter on top each feta cheese piece, sprinkle with paprika and dried oregano and wrap. Situate on a tray and bake in a prepared to 350 F oven for 15 min.

Nutrition: 279 calories; 9g fat; 2g protein

Avocado, Roasted Mushroom and Feta Spaghetti

Preparation: 20 min | Cooking: 17 min | Servings: 5

Ingredients
- 12 oz. spaghetti
- 2 avocados, peeled and diced
- 10-15 white mushrooms, halved
- 1 cup feta, crumbled
- 2 tbsp. green olive paste

Directions
1. Wrap baking tray with baking paper and place mushrooms on it. Spray with olive oil and season with salt and black pepper to taste. Roast in a prepared to 375 F oven for 15 min.
2. Using big pot of boiling salted water, cook spaghetti following package's instructions. Drain and set aside.
3. In a blender, combine lemon juice, 2 garlic cloves, olive paste and avocados and blend until smooth.
4. Combine pasta, mushrooms and avocado sauce. Sprinkle with feta cheese and serve immediately.

Nutrition: 278 calories; 10g fat; 4g protein

Tomato, Arugula and Feta Spaghetti

Preparation: 20 min | Cooking: 3 min | Servings: 6

Ingredients
- 12 oz. spaghetti
- 2 cups grape tomatoes, halved
- 1 cup fresh basil leaves, roughly torn
- 1 cup baby arugula leaves
- 1 cup feta, crumbled

Directions
1. In a very big saucepan with salted boiling water, cook spaghetti according to package directions. Drain and keep aside.
2. Return saucepan to medium heat. Add olive oil, 2 garlic cloves and tomatoes. Season with pepper and cook, tossing, for 1-2 min or until tomatoes are hot. Add spaghetti, basil and feta. Toss lightly for 1 minute. Sprinkle with arugula and serve.

Nutrition: 278 calories; 15g fat; 3g protein

Zucchini Fritters

Preparation: 20 min | Cooking: 26 min | Servings: 6

Ingredients
- 5 zucchinis, grated
- 3 eggs
- 2 garlic cloves, crushed
- 5 spring onions, finely chopped
- 1 cup feta cheese, crumbled

Directions
1. Grate zucchinis and situate them in a colander. Sprinkle with salt and leave aside to drain. After 20 min, squeeze and place in a bowl. Add in all other ingredients except for 1 cup of flour and sunflower oil. Combine everything very well. Add in flour and stir to combine again.
2. Cook sunflower oil in a frying pan. Drop a few scoops of the zucchini batter and fry them on medium heat for 3-5 min, until golden brown. Serve with yogurt.

Nutrition: 293 calories; 13g fat; 6g protein

Cheesy Cauliflower Florets

Preparation: 25 min | Cooking: 16 min | Servings: 6

Ingredients
- 1 small cauliflower, cut into florets
- 1 tbsp. garlic powder
- 1 tsp paprika
- 4 tbsp. extra virgin olive oil
- 1/2 cup grated Parmesan cheese

Directions

1. Combine olive oil, paprika, salt, pepper and garlic powder. Throw in the cauliflower florets and position in a baking dish in single layer.
2. Bake in a prepared to 350 F oven for 20 min. Pull out from the oven, stir, and topped with Parmesan cheese. Bake for 5 min more.

Nutrition: 297 calories; 13g fat; 6g protein

Wrapped Plums

Servings: 8 | Cooking: 0 min

Ingredients

- 2 ounces prosciutto, cut into 16 pieces
- 4 plums, quartered
- 1 tablespoon chives, chopped
- A pinch of red pepper flakes, crushed

Directions

1. Wrap each plum quarter in a prosciutto slice, arrange them all on a platter, sprinkle the chives and pepper flakes all over and serve.

Nutrition: calories 30; fat 1; fiber 0; carbs 4; protein 2

Tomato Cream Cheese Spread

Servings: 6 | Cooking: 0 min

Ingredients

- 12 ounces cream cheese, soft
- 1 big tomato, cubed
- ¼ cup homemade mayonnaise
- 2 garlic clove, minced
- 2 tablespoons red onion, chopped
- 2 tablespoons lime juice
- Salt and black pepper to the taste

Directions

1. In your blender, mix the cream cheese with the tomato and the rest of the ingredients, pulse well, divide into small cups and serve cold.

Nutrition: calories 204; fat 6.7; fiber 1.4; carbs 7.3; protein 4.5

Italian Fries

Servings: 4 | Cooking: 40 min

Ingredients

- 1/3 cup baby red potatoes
- 1 tablespoon Italian seasoning
- 3 tablespoons canola oil
- 1 teaspoon turmeric
- ½ teaspoon of sea salt
- ½ teaspoon dried rosemary
- 1 tablespoon dried dill

Directions

1. Cut the red potatoes into the wedges and transfer in the big bowl.
2. After this, sprinkle the vegetables with Italian seasoning, canola oil, turmeric, sea salt, dried rosemary, and dried dill.
3. Shake the potato wedges carefully.
4. Line the baking tray with baking paper.
5. Place the potatoes wedges in the tray. Flatten it well to make one layer.
6. Preheat the oven to 375F.
7. Place the tray with potatoes in the oven and bake for 40 minutes. Stir the potatoes with the help of the spatula from time to time.
8. The potato fries are cooked when they have crunchy edges.

Nutrition: calories 122; fat 11.6; fiber 0.5; carbs 4.5; protein 0.6

Tempeh Snack

Servings: 6 | Cooking: 8 min

Ingredients

- 11 oz soy tempeh
- 1 teaspoon olive oil
- ½ teaspoon ground black pepper
- ¼ teaspoon garlic powder

Directions

1. Cut soy tempeh into the sticks.
2. Sprinkle every tempeh stick with ground black pepper, garlic powder, and olive oil.
3. Preheat the grill to 375F.
4. Place the tempeh sticks in the grill and cook them for 4 minutes from each side. The time of cooking depends on the tempeh sticks size.
5. The cooked tempeh sticks will have a light brown color.

Nutrition: calories 88; fat 2.5; fiber 3.6; carbs 10.2; protein 6.5

Avocado Dip

Servings: 8 | Cooking: 0 min

Ingredients
- ½ cup heavy cream
- 1 green chili pepper, chopped
- Salt and pepper to the taste
- 4 avocados, pitted, peeled and chopped
- 1 cup cilantro, chopped
- ¼ cup lime juice

Directions
1. In a blender, combine the cream with the avocados and the rest of the ingredients and pulse well.
2. Divide the mix into bowls and serve cold as a party dip.

Nutrition: calories 200; fat 14.5; fiber 3.8; carbs 8.1; protein 7.6

Feta and Roasted Red Pepper Bruschetta

Servings: 24 | Cooking: 15 min

Ingredients
- 6 Kalamata olives, pitted, chopped
- 2 tablespoons green onion, minced
- 1/4 cup Parmesan cheese, grated, divided
- 1/4 cup extra-virgin olive oil brushing, or as needed
- 1/4 cup cherry tomatoes, thinly sliced
- 1 teaspoon lemon juice
- 1 tablespoon extra-virgin olive oil
- 1 tablespoon basil pesto
- 1 red bell pepper, halved, seeded
- 1 piece (12 inch) whole-wheat baguette, cut into 1/2-inch thick slices
- 1 package (4 ounce) feta cheese with basil and sun-dried tomatoes, crumbled
- 1 clove garlic, minced

Directions
1. Preheat the oven broiler. Place the oven rack 6 inches from the source of heat.
2. Brush both sides of the baguette slices, with the 1/4 cup olive oil. Arrange the bread slices on a baking sheet; toast for about 1 minute each side, carefully watching to avoid burning. Remove the toasted slices, transferring into another baking sheet.
3. With the cut sides down, place the red peppers in a baking sheet; broil for about 8 to 10 minutes or until the skin is charred and blistered. Transfer the roasted peppers into a bowl; cover with plastic wrap. Let cool, remove the charred skin. Discard skin and chop the roasted peppers.
4. In a bowl, mix the roasted red peppers, cherry tomatoes, feta cheese, green onion, olives, pesto, 1 tablespoon olive oil, garlic, and lemon juice.
5. Top each bread with 1 tablespoon of the roasted pepper mix, sprinkle lightly with the Parmesan cheese.
6. Return the baking sheet with the topped bruschetta; broil for about 1-2 minutes or until the topping is lightly browned.

Nutrition: 73 cal., 4.8 g total fat (1.4 sat. fat), 5 mg chol., 138 mg sodium, 5.3 g total carbs., 0.4 g fiber, 0.6 g sugar, and 2.1 g protein.

Meat-filled Phyllo (samboosek)

Servings: 1 Phyllo Pie | Cooking: 10 min

Ingredients
- 1 lb. ground beef or lamb
- 1 medium yellow onion, finely chopped
- 1 TB. seven spices
- 1 tsp. salt
- 1 pkg. frozen phyllo dough (12 sheets)
- 2/3 cup butter, melted

Directions
1. In a medium skillet over medium heat, brown beef for 3 minutes, breaking up chunks with a wooden spoon.
2. Add yellow onion, seven spices, and salt, and cook for 5 to 7 minutes or until beef is browned and onions are translucent. Set aside, and let cool.
3. Place first sheet of phyllo on your work surface, brush with melted butter, lay second sheet of phyllo on top, and brush with melted butter. Cut sheets into 3-inch-wide strips.
4. Spoon 2 tablespoons meat filling at end of each strip, and fold end strip to cover meat and form a triangle. Fold pointed end up and over to the opposite end, and you should see a triangle forming. Continue to fold up and then over until you come to the end of strip.
5. Place phyllo pies on a baking sheet, seal side down, and brush tops with butter. Repeat with remaining phyllo and filling.
6. Bake for 10 minutes or until golden brown.

7. Remove from the oven and set aside for 5 minutes before serving warm or at room temperature.

Tasty Black Bean Dip

Servings: 6 | Cooking: 18 min

Ingredients
- 2 cups dry black beans, soaked overnight and drained
- 1 1/2 cups cheese, shredded
- 1 tsp dried oregano
- 1 1/2 tsp chili powder
- 2 cups tomatoes, chopped
- 2 tbsp olive oil
- 1 1/2 tbsp garlic, minced
- 1 medium onion, sliced
- 4 cups vegetable stock
- Pepper
- Salt

Directions
1. Add all ingredients except cheese into the instant pot.
2. Seal pot with lid and cook on high for 18 minutes.
3. Once done, allow to release pressure naturally. Remove lid. Drain excess water.
4. Add cheese and stir until cheese is melted.
5. Blend bean mixture using an immersion blender until smooth.
6. Serve and enjoy.

Nutrition: Calories 402 Fat 15.3 g Carbohydrates 46.6 g Sugar 4.4 g Protein 22.2 g Cholesterol 30 mg

Zucchini Cakes

Servings: 4 | Cooking: 10 min

Ingredients
- 1 zucchini, grated
- ¼ carrot, grated
- ¼ onion, minced
- 1 teaspoon minced garlic
- 3 tablespoons coconut flour
- 1 teaspoon Italian seasonings
- 1 egg, beaten
- 1 teaspoon coconut oil

Directions
1. In the mixing bowl combine together grated zucchini, carrot, minced onion, and garlic.
2. Add coconut flour, Italian seasoning, and egg.
3. Stir the mass until homogenous.
4. Heat up coconut oil in the skillet.
5. Place the small zucchini fritters in the hot oil. Make them with the help of the spoon.
6. Roast the zucchini fritters for 4 minutes from each side.

Nutrition: calories 65; fat 3.3; fiber 3; carbs 6.3; protein 3.3

Parsley Nachos

Servings: 3 | Cooking: 0 min

Ingredients
- 3 oz tortilla chips
- ¼ cup Greek yogurt
- 1 tablespoon fresh parsley, chopped
- ¼ teaspoon minced garlic
- 2 kalamata olives, chopped
- 1 teaspoon paprika
- ¼ teaspoon ground thyme

Directions
1. In the mixing bowl mix up together Greek yogurt, parsley, minced garlic, olives, paprika, and thyme.
2. Then add tortilla chips and mix up gently.
3. The snack should be served immediately.

Nutrition: calories 81; fat 1.6; fiber 2.2; carbs 14.1; protein 3.5

Plum Wraps

Servings: 4 | Cooking: 10 min

Ingredients
- 4 plums
- 4 prosciutto slices
- ¼ teaspoon olive oil

Directions
1. Preheat the oven to 375F.
2. Wrap every plum in prosciutto slice and secure with a toothpick (if needed).
3. Place the wrapped plums in the oven and bake for 10 minutes.

Nutrition: calories 62; fat 2.2; fiber 0.9; carbs 8; protein 4.3

Parmesan Chips

Servings: 4 | Cooking: 20 min

Ingredients
- 1 zucchini
- 2 oz Parmesan, grated
- ½ teaspoon paprika
- 1 teaspoon olive oil

Directions
1. Trim zucchini and slice it into the chips with the help of the vegetable slices.
2. Then mix up together Parmesan and paprika.
3. Sprinkle the zucchini chips with olive oil.
4. After this, dip every zucchini slice in the cheese mixture.
5. Place the zucchini chips in the lined baking tray and bake for 20 minutes at 375F.
6. Flip the zucchini sliced onto another side after 10 minutes of cooking.
7. Chill the cooked chips well.

Nutrition: calories 64; fat 4.3; fiber 0.6; carbs 2.3; protein 5.2

Chicken Bites

Servings: 6 | Cooking: 5 min

Ingredients
- ½ cup coconut flakes
- 8 oz chicken fillet
- ¼ cup Greek yogurt
- 1 teaspoon dried dill
- 1 teaspoon salt
- 1 teaspoon ground black pepper
- 1 tablespoon tomato sauce
- 1 teaspoon honey
- 4 tablespoons sunflower oil

Directions
1. Chop the chicken fillet on the small cubes (popcorn cubes)
2. Sprinkle them with dried dill, salt, and ground black pepper.
3. Then add Greek yogurt and stir carefully.
4. After this, pour sunflower oil in the skillet and heat it up.
5. Coat chicken cubes in the coconut flakes and roast in the hot oil for 3-4 minutes or until the popcorn cubes are golden brown.
6. Dry the popcorn chicken with the help of the paper towel.
7. Make the sweet sauce: whisk together honey and tomato sauce.
8. Serve the popcorn chicken hot or warm with sweet sauce.

Nutrition: calories 107; fat 5.2; fiber 0.8; carbs 2.8; protein 12.1

Chicken Kale Wraps

Servings: 4 | Cooking: 10 min

Ingredients
- 4 kale leaves
- 4 oz chicken fillet
- ½ apple
- 1 tablespoon butter
- ¼ teaspoon chili pepper
- ¾ teaspoon salt
- 1 tablespoon lemon juice
- ¾ teaspoon dried thyme

Directions
1. Chop the chicken fillet into the small cubes.
2. Then mix up together chicken with chili pepper and salt.
3. Heat up butter in the skillet.
4. Add chicken cubes. Roast them for 4 minutes.
5. Meanwhile, chop the apple into small cubes and add it in the chicken.
6. Mix up well.
7. Sprinkle the ingredients with lemon juice and dried thyme.
8. Cook them for 5 minutes over the medium-high heat.
9. Fill the kale leaves with the hot chicken mixture and wrap.

Nutrition: calories 106; fat 5.1; fiber 1.1; carbs 6.3; protein 9

Savory Pita Chips

Servings: 1 Cup | Cooking: 10 min

Ingredients
- 3 pitas
- 1/4 cup extra-virgin olive oil
- 1/4 cup zaatar

Directions
1. Preheat the oven to 450°F.
2. Cut pitas into 2-inch pieces, and place in a large bowl.
3. Drizzle pitas with extra-virgin olive oil, sprinkle with zaatar, and toss to coat.
4. Spread out pitas on a baking sheet, and bake for 8 to 10 minutes or until lightly browned and crunchy.
5. Let pita chips cool before removing from the baking sheet. Store in an airtight container for up to 1 month.

Artichoke Skewers

Servings: 4 | Cooking: 0 min

Ingredients
- 4 prosciutto slices
- 4 artichoke hearts, canned
- 4 kalamata olives
- 4 cherry tomatoes
- ¼ teaspoon cayenne pepper
- ¼ teaspoon sunflower oil

Directions
1. Skewer prosciutto slices, artichoke hearts, kalamata olives, and cherry tomatoes on the wooden skewers.
2. Sprinkle antipasto skewers with sunflower oil and cayenne pepper.

Nutrition: calories 152; fat 3.7; fiber 10.8; carbs 23.2; protein 11.1

Kidney Bean Spread

Servings: 4 | Cooking: 18 min

Ingredients
- 1 lb dry kidney beans, soaked overnight and drained
- 1 tsp garlic, minced
- 2 tbsp olive oil
- 1 tbsp fresh lemon juice
- 1 tbsp paprika
- 4 cups vegetable stock
- 1/2 cup onion, chopped
- Pepper
- Salt

Directions
1. Add beans and stock into the instant pot.
2. Seal pot with lid and cook on high for 18 minutes.
3. Once done, allow to release pressure naturally. Remove lid.
4. Drain beans well and reserve 1/2 cup stock.
5. Transfer beans, reserve stock, and remaining ingredients into the food processor and process until smooth.
6. Serve and enjoy.

Nutrition: Calories 461 Fat 8.6 g Carbohydrates 73 g Sugar 4 g Protein 26.4 g Cholesterol 0 mg

Mediterranean Polenta Cups Recipe

Servings: 24 | Cooking: 5 min

Ingredients
- 1 cup yellow cornmeal
- 1 garlic clove, minced
- 1/2 teaspoon fresh thyme, minced or 1/4 teaspoon dried thyme
- 1/2 teaspoon salt
- 1/4 cup feta cheese, crumbled
- 1/4 teaspoon pepper
- 2 tablespoons fresh basil, chopped
- 4 cups water
- 4 plum tomatoes, finely chopped

Directions
1. In a heavy, large saucepan, bring the water and the salt to a boil; reduce the heat to a gentle boil. Slowly whisk in the cornmeal; cook, stirring with a wooden spoon for about 15 to 20 minutes, or until the polenta is thick and pulls away cleanly from the sides of the pan. Remove from the heat; stir in the pepper and the thyme.
2. Grease miniature muffin cups with cooking spray. Spoon a heaping tablespoon of the polenta mixture into each muffin cups.
3. With the back of a spoon, make an indentation in the center of each; cover and chill until the mixture is set.
4. Meanwhile, combine the feta cheese, tomatoes, garlic, and basil in a small-sized bowl.
5. Unmold the chilled polenta cups; place them on an ungreased baking sheet. Tops each indentation with 1 heaping tablespoon of the feta mixture. Broil the cups 4 inches from the heat source for about 5 to 7 minutes, or until heated through.

Nutrition: 26 cal, 1 mg chol., 62 mg sodium, 5 g carbs., 1 g fiber, and 1 g protein.

Tomato Triangles

Servings: 6 | Cooking: 0 min

Ingredients
- 6 corn tortillas
- 1 tablespoon cream cheese
- 1 tablespoon ricotta cheese
- ½ teaspoon minced garlic
- 1 tablespoon fresh dill, chopped
- 2 tomatoes, sliced

Directions
1. Cut every tortilla into 2 triangles.
2. Then mix up together cream cheese, ricotta cheese, minced garlic, and dill.
3. Spread 6 triangles with cream cheese mixture.
4. Then place sliced tomato on them and cover with remaining tortilla triangles.

Nutrition: calories 71; fat 1.6; fiber 2.1; carbs 12.8; protein 2.3

Chili Mango And Watermelon Salsa

Servings: 12 | Cooking: 0 min

Ingredients
- 1 red tomato, chopped
- Salt and black pepper to the taste
- 1 cup watermelon, seedless, peeled and cubed
- 1 red onion, chopped
- 2 mangos, peeled and chopped
- 2 chili peppers, chopped
- ¼ cup cilantro, chopped
- 3 tablespoons lime juice
- Pita chips for serving

Directions
1. In a bowl, mix the tomato with the watermelon, the onion and the rest of the ingredients except the pita chips and toss well.
2. Divide the mix into small cups and serve with pita chips on the side.

Nutrition: calories 62; fat 4.7; fiber 1.3; carbs 3.9; protein 2.3

Tomato Olive Salsa

Servings: 4 | Cooking: 5 min

Ingredients
- 2 cups olives, pitted and chopped
- 1/4 cup fresh parsley, chopped
- 1/4 cup fresh basil, chopped
- 2 tbsp green onion, chopped
- 1 cup grape tomatoes, halved
- 1 tbsp olive oil
- 1 tbsp vinegar
- Pepper
- Salt

Directions
1. Add all ingredients into the inner pot of instant pot and stir well.
2. Seal pot with lid and cook on high for 5 minutes.
3. Once done, allow to release pressure naturally for 5 minutes then release remaining using quick release. Remove lid.
4. Stir well and serve.

Nutrition: Calories 119 Fat 10.8 g Carbohydrates 6.5 g Sugar 1.3 g Protein 1.2 g Cholesterol 0 mg

Lavash Chips

Servings: 4 | Cooking: 10 min

Ingredients
- 1 lavash sheet, whole grain
- 1 tablespoon canola oil
- 1 teaspoon paprika
- ½ teaspoon chili pepper
- ½ teaspoon salt

Directions
1. In the shallow bowl whisk together canola oil, paprika, chili pepper, and salt.
2. Then chop lavash sheet roughly (in the shape of chips).
3. Sprinkle lavash chips with oil mixture and arrange in the tray to get one thin layer.
4. Bake the lavash chips for 10 minutes at 365F. Flip them on another side from time to time to avoid burning.
5. Cool the cooked chips well.

Nutrition: calories 73; fat 4; fiber 0.7; carbs 8.4; protein 1.6

Homemade Salsa

Servings: 8 | Cooking: 5 min

Ingredients

- 12 oz grape tomatoes, halved
- 1/4 cup fresh cilantro, chopped
- 1 fresh lime juice
- 28 oz tomatoes, crushed
- 1 tbsp garlic, minced
- 1 green bell pepper, chopped
- 1 red bell pepper, chopped
- 2 onions, chopped
- 6 whole tomatoes
- Salt

Directions

1. Add whole tomatoes into the instant pot and gently smash the tomatoes.
2. Add remaining ingredients except cilantro, lime juice, and salt and stir well.
3. Seal pot with lid and cook on high for 5 minutes.
4. Once done, allow to release pressure naturally for 10 minutes then release remaining using quick release. Remove lid.
5. Add cilantro, lime juice, and salt and stir well.
6. Serve and enjoy.

Nutrition: Calories 146 Fat 1.2 g Carbohydrates 33.2 g Sugar 4 g Protein 6.9 g Cholesterol 0 mg

Stuffed Zucchinis

Servings: 6 | Cooking: 40 min

Ingredients

- 6 zucchinis, halved lengthwise and insides scooped out
- 2 garlic cloves, minced
- 2 tablespoons oregano, chopped
- Juice of 2 lemons
- Salt and black pepper to the taste
- 2 tablespoons olive oil
- 8 ounces feta cheese, crumbed

Directions

1. Arrange the zucchini halves on a baking sheet lined with parchment paper, divide the cheese and the rest of the ingredients in each zucchini half and bake at 450 degrees F for 40 minutes.
2. Arrange the stuffed zucchinis on a platter and serve as an appetizer.

Yogurt Dip

Servings: 6 | Cooking: 0 min

Ingredients

- 2 cups Greek yogurt
- 2 tablespoons pistachios, toasted and chopped
- A pinch of salt and white pepper
- 2 tablespoons mint, chopped
- 1 tablespoon kalamata olives, pitted and chopped
- ¼ cup za'atar spice
- ¼ cup pomegranate seeds
- 1/3 cup olive oil

Directions

1. In a bowl, combine the yogurt with the pistachios and the rest of the ingredients, whisk well, divide into small cups and serve with pita chips on the side.

Nutrition: calories 294; fat 18; fiber 1; carbs 21; protein 10

Popcorn-pine Nut Mix

Servings: 10 | Cooking: 10 min

Ingredients

- 1 tablespoon olive oil
- 1/2 cup pine nuts
- 1/2 teaspoon Italian seasoning
- 1/4 cup popcorn, white kernels, popped
- 1/4 teaspoon salt
- 2 tablespoons honey
- 1/2 lemon zest

Directions

1. Place the popped corn in a medium bowl.
2. In a dry pan or skillet over low heat, toast the pine nuts, stirring frequently for about 4 to 5 minutes, until fragrant and some begin to brown; remove from the heat.
3. Stir the oil in; add honey, the Italian seasoning, the lemon zest, and the salt. Stir to mix and pour over the popcorn; toss the ingredients to coat the popcorn kernels with the honey syrup.
4. It's alright if most of the nuts sink in the bowl bottom.
5. Let the mixture sit for about 2 minutes to allow the honey to cool and to get stickier.
6. Transfer the bowl contents into a Servings: bowl so the nuts are on the top. Gently stir and serve.

Nutrition: 80 cal, 6 g total fat (0.5 g sat. fat), 0 mg chol., 105 mg sodium, 60 mg pot., 5 total carbs., <1 g fiber, 4 g sugar, 2 g protein, 2% vitamin A, 8% vitamin C, 4% calcium, and 4% iron.

Scallions Dip

Servings: 8 | Cooking: 0 min

Ingredients
- 6 scallions, chopped
- 1 garlic clove, minced
- 3 tablespoons olive oil
- Salt and black pepper to the taste
- 1 tablespoon lemon juice
- 1 and ½ cups cream cheese, soft
- 2 ounces prosciutto, cooked and crumbled

Directions
1. In a bowl, mix the scallions with the garlic and the rest of the ingredients except the prosciutto and whisk well.
2. Divide into bowls, sprinkle the prosciutto on top and serve as a party dip.

Nutrition: calories 144; fat 7.7; fiber 1.4; carbs 6.3; protein 5.5

Date Balls

Servings: 3 | Cooking: 5 min

Ingredients
- 3 dates, pitted
- 3 pistachio nuts
- ½ teaspoon butter, softened, salted

Directions
1. Fill dates with butter and pistachio nuts.
2. Bake the prepared dates for 5 minutes at 395F.
3. Chill the cooked appetizer to the room temperature.

Nutrition: calories 42; fat 1.8; fiber 0.9; carbs 6.9; protein 0.7

Lavash Roll Ups

Servings: 2-4 | Cooking: 10 min

Ingredients
- 2 lavash wraps (whole-wheat)
- 1/4 cup roasted red peppers, sliced
- 1/4 cup black olives, sliced
- 1/2 cup hummus of choice
- 1/2 cup grape tomatoes, halved
- 1 Medium cucumber, sliced
- Fresh dill, for garnish

Directions
1. Lay out the lavash wraps on a clean surface. Evenly spread hummus over each piece.
2. Layer the cucumbers across the wraps, about 1/2-inch from each other, leaving about 2-icnh empty space at the bottom of the wrap for rolling purposes.
3. Place the roasted pepper slices around the cucumbers. Sprinkle with black olives and the tomatoes. Garnish with freshly chopped dill.
4. Tightly roll each wrap, using the hummus at the end to almost glue the wrap into a roll.
5. Slice each roll into 4 equal pieces. Secure each piece by sticking a toothpick through the center of each roll slice.
6. Lay each on a serving bowl or tray; garnish more with fresh dill.

Nutrition: 250 cal, 8 g total fat (0.5 g sat. fat), 0 mg chol., 440 mg sodium, 340 mg pot., 43 total carbs., 40 g fiber, 3 g sugar, 10 g protein, 15% vitamin A, 25% vitamin C, 6% calcium, and 8% iron.

Chickpeas And Eggplant Bowls

Servings: 4 | Cooking: 10 min

Ingredients
- 2 eggplants, cut in half lengthwise and cubed
- 1 red onion, chopped
- Juice of 1 lime
- 1 tablespoon olive oil
- 28 ounces canned chickpeas, drained and rinsed
- 1 bunch parsley, chopped
- A pinch of salt and black pepper
- 1 tablespoon balsamic vinegar

Directions
1. Spread the eggplant cubes on a baking sheet lined with parchment paper, drizzle half of the oil all over, season with salt and pepper and cook at 425 degrees F for 10 minutes.
2. Cool the eggplant down, add the rest of the ingredients, toss, divide between appetizer plates and serve.

Nutrition: calories 263; fat 12; fiber 9.3; carbs 15.4; protein 7.5

Vinegar Beet Bites

Servings: 4 | Cooking: 30 min

Ingredients
- 2 beets, sliced
- A pinch of sea salt and black pepper
- 1/3 cup balsamic vinegar
- 1 cup olive oil

Directions
1. Spread the beet slices on a baking sheet lined with parchment paper, add the rest of the ingredients, toss and bake at 350 degrees F for 30 minutes.
2. Serve the beet bites cold as a snack.

Nutrition: calories 199; fat 5.4; fiber 3.5; carbs 8.5; protein 3.5

Baked Sweet-potato Fries

Servings: 6 | Cooking: 25 min

Ingredients
- 1 1/2 teaspoons dried oregano
- 1 teaspoon dried thyme
- 1 teaspoon garlic powder
- 1/2 teaspoon salt
- 2 large sweet potatoes (about 2 pounds), skins on, scrubbed, cut into 1/2-inch thick 4-inch long sticks
- 3 large egg whites (a scant 1/2 cup)
- Vegetable oil, for the parchment
- For the Mediterranean spice:
- Oregano
- Thyme
- Garlic

Directions
1. Place all of the Mediterranean spice ingredients in a small food processor or a spice grinder; briefly grind or process to blend.
2. Place the oven racks in the middle and upper position; preheat the oven to 450F.
3. Line 2 baking sheets with parchment paper; rub the form with the oil.
4. Put the potatoes in a microwavable container, cover, and microwave for 2 minutes. Stir gently, body, and microwave for about 1-2 minutes more or until the pieces are pliable; let rest for about 5 minutes covered. Pour into a platter.
5. In a large-sized bowl, whisk the eggs until frothy. Add the spice mix and whisk again to blend.
6. Working in batches, toss the sweet potatoes in the seasoned egg whites letting the excess liquid drip back into the bowl. Arrange the coated potatoes in a single layer on the prepared baking sheets.
7. Bake for 10 minutes; flip the pieces over using a spatula. Rotate the baking sheets from back to front and one to the other; bake for about 15 minutes or until dark golden brown. Serve immediately.

Nutrition: 100 cal., 4 g total fat (0 g sat. fat), 0 mg chol., 60 mg sodium, 230 mg pot., 12 g total carbs., 2 g fiber, 2 g sugar, 3 g protein, 150% vitamin A, 2% vitamin C, 4% calcium, and 6% iron.

Cucumber Rolls

Servings: 6 | Cooking: 0 min

Ingredients
- 1 big cucumber, sliced lengthwise
- 1 tablespoon parsley, chopped
- 8 ounces canned tuna, drained and mashed
- Salt and black pepper to the taste
- 1 teaspoon lime juice

Directions
1. Arrange cucumber slices on a working surface, divide the rest of the ingredients, and roll.
2. Arrange all the rolls on a platter and serve as an appetizer.

Nutrition: calories 200; fat 6; fiber 3.4; carbs 7.6; protein 3.5

Jalapeno Chickpea Hummus

Servings: 4 | Cooking: 25 min

Ingredients
- 1 cup dry chickpeas, soaked overnight and drained
- 1 tsp ground cumin
- 1/4 cup jalapenos, diced
- 1/2 cup fresh cilantro
- 1 tbsp tahini
- 1/2 cup olive oil
- Pepper
- Salt

Directions
1. Add chickpeas into the instant pot and cover with vegetable stock.
2. Seal pot with lid and cook on high for 25 minutes.

3. Once done, allow to release pressure naturally. Remove lid.
4. Drain chickpeas well and transfer into the food processor along with remaining ingredients and process until smooth.
5. Serve and enjoy.

Nutrition: Calories 425 Fat 30.4 g Carbohydrates 31.8 g Sugar 5.6 g Protein 10.5 g Cholesterol 0 mg

Healthy Spinach Dip

Servings: 4 | Cooking: 8 min

Ingredients
- 14 oz spinach
- 2 tbsp fresh lime juice
- 1 tbsp garlic, minced
- 2 tbsp olive oil
- 2 tbsp coconut cream
- Pepper
- Salt

Directions
1. Add all ingredients except coconut cream into the instant pot and stir well.
2. Seal pot with lid and cook on low pressure for 8 minutes.
3. Once done, allow to release tension naturally for 5 minutes then release remaining using quick release. Remove lid.
4. Add coconut cream and stir well and blend spinach mixture using a blender until smooth.
5. Serve and enjoy.

Nutrition: Calories 109 Fat 9.2 g Carbohydrates 6.6 g Sugar 1.1 g Protein 3.2 g Cholesterol 0 mg

Marinated Cheese

Servings: 18 | Cooking: 10 min

Ingredients
- 8 ounces cream cheese
- 6 sprigs fresh thyme
- 3 sprigs fresh rosemary
- 2 garlic cloves, sliced
- 1/2 cup sun-dried tomato vinaigrette dressing
- 1 teaspoon black pepper
- 1 lemon peel, cut into thin strips

Directions
1. Cut the cream cheese into 36 cubes. Place on a serving tray.
2. Combine the remaining ingredients together.
3. Pour the dressing over the cheese; toss lightly.
4. Refrigerate for at least 1 hour to marinate.

Nutrition: 44 cal., 4.3 g total fat (2.4 sat. fat), 13.9 mg chol., 40.6 mg sodium, 0.7 g total carbs., 0 g fiber, 0.4 g sugar, and 0.8 g protein.

Za'atar Fries

Servings: 5 | Cooking: 35 min

Ingredients
- 1 teaspoon Za'atar spices
- 3 sweet potatoes
- 1 tablespoon dried dill
- 1 teaspoon salt
- 3 teaspoons sunflower oil
- ½ teaspoon paprika

Directions
1. Pour water in the crockpot. Peel the sweet potatoes and cut them into the fries.
2. Line the baking tray with parchment.
3. Place the layer of the sweet potato in the tray.
4. Sprinkle the vegetables with dried dill, salt, and paprika.
5. Then sprinkle sweet potatoes with Za'atar and mix up well with the help of the fingertips.
6. Sprinkle the sweet potato fries with sunflower oil.
7. Preheat the oven to 375F.
8. Bake the sweet potato fries for 35 minutes. Stir the fries every 10 minutes.

Nutrition: calories 28; fat 2.9; fiber 0.2; carbs 0.6; protein 0.2

Tuna Salad

Servings: 2-4 | Cooking: 10 min

Ingredients
- 1 can (5 ounce) albacore tuna, solid white
- 1 to 2 tablespoons mayo or Greek yogurt
- 1 whole-wheat crackers
- 1/4 cup chickpeas, rinsed, drained (or preferred white beans)
- 1/4 cup Kalamata olives, quartered
- 1/4 cup roughly chopped marinated artichoke hearts

Directions
1. Flake the tuna out of the can into medium-sized bowl.
2. Add the chickpeas, olives, and artichoke hearts; toss to combine.
3. Add mayo or Greek yogurt according to your taste; stir until well combined.
4. Spoon the salad mixture onto crackers; serve.

Nutrition: 130 cal., 5 g total fat (0.5 g sat. fat), 25 mg chol., 240 mg sodium, 240 mg pot., 8 g total carbs., 1 g fiber, <1 g sugar, 12 g protein, 2% vitamin A, 2% vitamin C, 4% calcium, and 6% iron.

Cheese Rolls

Servings: 1 Roll | Cooking: 5 min

Ingredients
- 1 cup ackawi cheese
- 1 cup shredded mozzarella cheese
- 2 TB. fresh parsley, finely chopped
- 1 large egg
- 1/2 tsp. ground black pepper
- 1 large egg yolk, beaten
- 2 TB. water
- 1 pkg. egg roll dough (20 count)
- 4 TB. extra-virgin olive oil

Directions
1. In a large bowl, combine ackawi cheese, mozzarella cheese, parsley, egg, and black pepper.
2. In a small bowl, whisk together egg yolk and water.
3. Lay out 1 egg roll, place 2 tablespoons cheese mixture at one corner of egg roll, and brush opposite corner with egg yolk mixture.
4. Fold over side of egg roll, with cheese, to the middle. Fold in left and right sides, and complete rolling egg roll, using egg-brushed side to seal. Set aside, fill side down, and repeat with remaining egg rolls and cheese mixture.
5. In a skillet over low heat, heat 2 tablespoons extra-virgin olive oil. Add up to 4 cheese rolls, seal side down, and cook for 1 or 2 minutes per side or until browned. Repeat with remaining 2 tablespoons extra-virgin olive oil and egg rolls.
6. Serve warm.

Olive, Pepperoni, And Mozzarella Bites

Servings: 2 | Cooking: 10 min

Ingredients
- 1 pound block Mozzarella cheese
- 1 package pepperoni
- 1 can whole medium black olives

Directions
1. Slice the block of mozzarella cheese into 1/2x1/2-inch cubes. Drain the olives from the liquid.
2. With a toothpick, skewer the olive, pushing it 1/3 way up the toothpick.
3. Fold a pepperoni into half or quarters and skewer after the olive.
4. Finally, skewer a mozzarella cheese, not pushing all the way through the cube, about only half way through. Repeat with the remaining olives, pepperoni, and mozzarella cubes.

Nutrition: 75 cal., 5.6 g total fat (2.5 g sat. fat), 14 mg chol., 221 mg sodium, 16 mg pot., 0.8 g total carbs., 0 g fiber, 0 g sugar, 5.6 g protein, 3% vitamin A, 0% vitamin C, 11% calcium, and 1% iron.

Eggplant Dip

Servings: 4 | Cooking: 40 min

Ingredients
- 1 eggplant, poked with a fork
- 2 tablespoons tahini paste
- 2 tablespoons lemon juice
- 2 garlic cloves, minced
- 1 tablespoon olive oil
- Salt and black pepper to the taste
- 1 tablespoon parsley, chopped

Directions
1. Put the eggplant in a roasting pan, bake at 400 degrees F for 40 minutes, cool down, peel and transfer to your food processor.
2. Add the rest of the ingredients except the parsley, pulse well, divide into small bowls and serve as an appetizer with the parsley sprinkled on top.

Nutrition: calories 121; fat 4.3; fiber 1; carbs 1.4; protein 4.3

Celery And Cucumber Snack

Servings: 4 | Cooking: 0 min

Ingredients
- 6 oz celery stalk, roughly chopped
- 2 cucumbers, roughly chopped
- 1 teaspoon mustard
- 1 teaspoon honey
- 2 teaspoons lemon juice
- 1 tablespoon fresh cilantro, chopped

Directions
1. Place celery stalk, cucumbers, and fresh cilantro in the big bowl.
2. In the shallow bowl combine together mustard, honey, and lemon juice.
3. Pour the liquid over the vegetables and shake them well.
4. Transfer the vegetables in the jars and close with the lid.
5. Store the vegetable snack jars up to 2 hours in the fridge.

Nutrition: calories 39; fat 0.5; fiber 1.6; carbs 8.5; protein 1.5

Oat Bites

Servings: 4 | Cooking: 10 min

Ingredients
- 1 teaspoon honey
- 4 dates, pitted
- 1 tablespoon rolled oats
- 1 tablespoon raisins, chopped
- ¼ teaspoon ground cinnamon
- 1 teaspoon chia seeds, dried

Directions
1. Mash the dates with the help of the fork until you get a mashed mixture.
2. Then add honey, rolled oats, raisins, ground cinnamon, and chia seeds.
3. Mix up the mixture with the help of the spoon until homogenous.
4. Make the small balls and refrigerate them for at least 10-15 minutes.

Nutrition: calories 52; fat 0.9; fiber 1.8; carbs 11.4; protein 0.9

Eggplant Bites

Servings: 8 | Cooking: 15 min

Ingredients
- 2 eggplants, cut into 20 slices
- 2 tablespoons olive oil
- ½ cup roasted peppers, chopped
- ½ cup kalamata olives, pitted and chopped
- 1 tablespoon lime juice
- 1 teaspoon red pepper flakes, crushed
- Salt and black pepper to the taste
- 2 tablespoons mint, chopped

Directions
1. In a bowl, mix the roasted peppers with the olives, half of the oil and the rest of the ingredients except the eggplant slices and stir well.
2. Brush eggplant slices with the rest of the olive oil on both sides, place them on the preheated grill over medium high heat, cook for 7 minutes on each side and transfer them to a platter.
3. Top each eggplant slice with roasted peppers mix and serve.

Nutrition: calories 214; fat 10.6; fiber 5.8; carbs 15.4; protein 5.4

Creamy Pepper Spread

Servings: 4 | Cooking: 15 min

Ingredients
- 1 lb red bell peppers, chopped and remove seeds
- 1 1/2 tbsp fresh basil
- 1 tbsp olive oil
- 1 tbsp fresh lime juice
- 1 tsp garlic, minced
- Pepper
- Salt

Directions
1. Add all ingredients into the inner pot of instant pot and stir well.
2. Seal pot with lid and cook on high for 15 minutes.
3. Once done, allow to release pressure naturally for 10 minutes then release remaining using quick release. Remove lid.
4. Transfer bell pepper mixture into the food processor and process until smooth.
5. Serve and enjoy.

Nutrition: Calories 41 Fat 3.6 g Carbohydrates 3.5 g Sugar 1.7 g Protein 0.4 g Cholesterol 0 mg

Creamy Eggplant Dip

Servings: 4 | Cooking: 20 min

Ingredients
- 1 eggplant
- 1/2 tsp paprika
- 1 tbsp olive oil
- 1 tbsp fresh lime juice
- 2 tbsp tahini
- 1 garlic clove
- 1 cup of water
- Pepper
- Salt

Directions
1. Add water and eggplant into the instant pot.
2. Seal pot with the lid and select manual and set timer for 20 minutes.
3. Once done, release pressure using quick release. Remove lid.
4. Drain eggplant and let it cool.
5. Once the eggplant is cool then remove eggplant skin and transfer eggplant flesh into the food processor.
6. Add remaining ingredients into the food processor and process until smooth.
7. Serve and enjoy.

Nutrition: Calories 108 Fat 7.8 g Carbohydrates 9.7 g Sugar 3.7 g Protein 2.5 g Cholesterol 0 mg

Herbed Goat Cheese Dip

Servings: 4 | Cooking: 0 min

Ingredients
- ¼ cup mixed parsley, chopped
- ¼ cup chives, chopped
- 8 ounces goat cheese, soft
- Salt and black pepper to the taste
- A drizzle of olive oil

Directions
1. In your food processor mix the goat cheese with the parsley and the rest of the ingredients and pulse well.
2. Divide into small bowls and serve as a party dip.

Nutrition: calories 245; fat 11.3; fiber 4.5; carbs 8.9; protein 11.2

Italian Wheatberry Cakes

Servings: 6 | Cooking: 15 min

Ingredients
- 1 cup wheatberry, cooked
- 2 eggs
- ¼ cup ground chicken
- 1 tablespoon wheat flour, whole grain
- 1 teaspoon Italian seasoning
- 1 tablespoon olive oil
- 1 teaspoon salt

Directions
1. In the mixing bowl mix up together wheatberry and ground chicken.
2. Crack eggs in the mixture.
3. Then add wheat flour, Italian seasoning, and salt.
4. Mix up the mass with the help of the spoon until homogenous.
5. Then make burgers and freeze them in the freezer for 20 minutes.
6. Heat up olive oil in the skillet.
7. Place frozen burgers in the hot oil and roast them for 4 minutes from each side over the high heat.
8. Then cook burgers for 10 minutes more over the medium heat. Flip them onto another side from time to time.

Nutrition: calories 97; fat 5.7; fiber 1.5; carbs 9.2; protein 5.2

Healthy Kidney Bean Dip

Servings: 6 | Cooking: 10 min

Ingredients
- 1 cup dry white kidney beans, soaked overnight and drained
- 1 tbsp fresh lemon juice
- 2 tbsp water
- 1/2 cup coconut yogurt
- 1 roasted garlic clove
- 1 tbsp olive oil
- 1/4 tsp cayenne
- 1 tsp dried parsley
- Pepper
- Salt

Directions
1. Add soaked beans and 1 3/4 cups of water into the instant pot.
2. Seal pot with lid and cook on high for 10 minutes.
3. Once done, allow to release pressure naturally. Remove lid.
4. Drain beans well and transfer them into the food processor.
5. Add remaining ingredients into the food processor and process until smooth.
6. Serve and enjoy.

Nutrition: Calories 136 Fat 3.2 g Carbohydrates 20 g Sugar 2.1 g Protein 7.7 g Cholesterol 0 mg

Lentils Spread

Servings: 12 | Cooking: 0 min

Ingredients
- 1 garlic clove, minced
- 12 ounces canned lentils, drained and rinsed
- 1 teaspoon oregano, dried
- ¼ teaspoon basil, dried
- 3 tablespoons olive oil
- 1 tablespoon balsamic vinegar
- Salt and black pepper to the taste

Directions
1. In a blender, combine the lentils with the garlic and the rest of the ingredients, pulse well, divide into bowls and serve as an appetizer.

Nutrition: calories 287; fat 9.5; fiber 3.5; carbs 15.3; protein 9.3

Chickpeas Spread

Servings: 7 | Cooking: 45 min

Ingredients
- 1 cup chickpeas, soaked
- 6 cups of water
- ½ cup lemon juice
- 3 tablespoon olive oil
- 1 teaspoon salt
- 1/3 teaspoon harissa

Directions
1. Combine together chickpeas and water and boil for 45 minutes or until chickpeas are tender.
2. Then transfer chickpeas in the food processor.
3. Add 1 cup of chickpeas water and lemon juice.
4. After this, add salt and harissa.
5. Blend the hummus until it is smooth and fluffy.
6. Add olive oil and pulse it for 10 seconds more.
7. Transfer the cooked hummus in the bowl and store it in the fridge up to 2 days.

Nutrition: calories 160; fat 7.9; fiber 5. carbs 17.8; protein 5.7

Lime Yogurt Dip

Servings: 4 | Cooking: 0 min

Ingredients
- 1 large cucumber, trimmed
- 3 oz Greek yogurt
- 1 teaspoon olive oil
- 3 tablespoons fresh dill, chopped
- 1 tablespoon lime juice
- ¾ teaspoon salt
- 1 garlic clove, minced

Directions
1. Grate the cucumber and squeeze the juice from it.
2. Then place the squeezed cucumber in the bowl.
3. Add Greek yogurt, olive oil, dill, lime juice, salt, and minced garlic.
4. Mix up the mixture until homogenous.
5. Store tzaziki in the fridge up to 2 days.

Nutrition: calories 44; fat 1.8; fiber 0.7; carbs 5.1; protein 3.2

Almond Bowls

Servings: 5 | Cooking: 15 min

Ingredients
- 1 cup almonds
- 3 tablespoons salt
- 2 cups of water

Directions
1. Bring water to boil.
2. After this, add 2 tablespoons of salt in water and stir it.
3. When salt is dissolved, add almonds and let them soak for at least 1 hour.
4. Meanwhile, line the tray with baking paper and preheat oven to 350F.
5. Dry the soaked almonds with a paper towel well and arrange them in one layer in the tray.
6. Sprinkle buts with remaining salt.

7. Bake the snack for 15 minutes. Mix it from time to time with the help of the spatula or spoon.

Nutrition: calories 110; fat 9.5; fiber 2.4; carbs 4.1; protein 4

Beet Spread

Servings: 4 | Cooking: 35 min

Ingredients
- 1 tablespoon pumpkin puree
- 1 beet, peeled
- 1 teaspoon tahini paste
- ½ teaspoon sesame seeds
- 1 teaspoon paprika
- 1 tablespoon olive oil
- ¼ cup water, boiled
- 1 tablespoon lime juice
- ½ teaspoon salt

Directions
1. Place beet in the oven and bake it at 375F for 35 minutes.
2. Then chop it roughly and put in the food processor.
3. Blend the beet until smooth.
4. After this, add tahini paste, pumpkin puree, paprika, olive oil, water, lime juice, and salt.
5. Blend the hummus until smooth and fluffy.
6. Then transfer the appetizer in the bowl and sprinkle with sesame seeds.

Nutrition: calories 99; fat 8.6; fiber 1.6; carbs 3.9; protein 2.1

Calamari Mediterranean

Servings: 2 | Cooking: 10 min

Ingredients
- 1 tablespoon Italian parsley
- 1 teaspoon ancho chili, chopped
- 1 teaspoon cumin
- 1 teaspoon red pepper flakes
- 1/2 cup white wine
- 2 cups calamari
- 2 medium plum tomatoes, diced
- 2 tablespoons capers
- 2 tablespoons garlic cloves, roasted
- 2 tablespoons olive oil
- 2 tablespoons unsalted butter
- 3 tablespoons lime juice
- Salt

Directions
1. Heat a sauté pan. Add the oil, garlic, and the calamari; sauté for 1 minute. Add the capers, red pepper flakes, cumin, ancho chili and the diced tomatoes; cook for 1 minute.
2. Add the wine and the lime juice; simmer for 4 minutes.
3. Stir in the butter, parsley, and the salt; continue cooking until the sauce is thick.
4. Serve with whole-wheat French bread.

Nutrition: 308.8 cal., 25.7 g total fat (9.3 sat. fat), 30.5 mg chol., 267.8 mg sodium, 10.2 g total carbs., 1.7 g fiber, 2.8 g sugar, and 1.9 g protein.

Cheddar Dip

Servings: 6 | Cooking: 10 min

Ingredients
- 1 cup Cheddar cheese
- ¼ cup cilantro, chopped
- 1 chili pepper, chopped
- 1 teaspoon garlic powder
- ¼ cup milk

Directions
1. Bring the milk to boil.
2. Then add Cheddar cheese in the milk and simmer the mixture for 2 minutes. Stir it constantly.
3. After this, add cilantro, chili pepper, and garlic powder. Mix up the mixture well. If it doesn't get a smooth texture, use the hand blender to blend the mass.
4. It is recommended to serve the dip when it gets the room temperature.

Nutrition: calories 83; fat 6.5; fiber 0.1; carbs 1.2; protein 5.1

Olives And Cheese Stuffed Tomatoes

Servings: 24 | Cooking: 0 min

Ingredients
- 24 cherry tomatoes, top cut off and insides scooped out
- 2 tablespoons olive oil
- ¼ teaspoon red pepper flakes
- ½ cup feta cheese, crumbled

- 2 tablespoons black olive paste
- ¼ cup mint, torn

Directions
1. In a bowl, mix the olives paste with the rest of the ingredients except the cherry tomatoes and whisk well.
2. Stuff the cherry tomatoes with this mix, arrange them all on a platter and serve as an appetizer.

Nutrition: calories 136; fat 8.6; fiber 4.8; carbs 5.6; protein 5.1

Feta Cheese Log With Sun-dried Tomatoes And Kalamata Olives

Servings: 2 | Cooking: 20 min

Ingredients
- 8 ounces feta cheese, crumbled
- 4 ounces cream cheese, softened
- 2 tablespoons extra-virgin olive oil
- 1/8-1/4 teaspoon cayenne pepper (depending on your taste)
- 1/4 cup chopped sun-dried tomato
- 1/4 cup chopped Kalamata olive
- 1/2 teaspoon dried Mediterranean oregano, crumbled
- 1 small garlic clove, minced
- 1/2 cup walnuts, toasted, chopped
- 1/4 cup fresh parsley, minced

Directions
1. With a mixer, combine the feta cheese, cream cheese, and the olive oil on medium speed until well combined. Add the remaining ingredients and mix well.
2. Shape the soft mixture into a 10-inch long log.
3. Combine the parsley and the walnuts; roll the log over the mixture, pressing slightly to stick the parsley and the walnuts on the sides of the log.
4. Wrap the log with plastic wrap; refrigerate for at least 5 hours to let the flavors blend.
5. Remove the plastic wrap, lay the log on a parsley-lined serving platter. Serve with whole-wheat crackers and toasted whole-wheat slices of baguette.

Nutrition: 1154 cal., 106.3 g total fat (43.9 sat. fat), 226.2 mg chol., 2395.3 mg sodium, 23 g total carbs., 5 g fiber, 13.5 g sugar, and 35.2 g protein.

Lemon Salmon Rolls

Servings: 6 | Cooking: 0 min

Ingredients
- 6 wonton wrappers
- 7 oz salmon, grilled
- 6 lettuce leaves
- 1 carrot, peeled
- 1 cucumber, trimmed
- 1 tablespoon lemon juice
- 1 teaspoon olive oil
- ¼ teaspoon dried oregano

Directions
1. Cut the carrot and cucumber onto the wedges.
2. Then chop the grilled salmon.
3. Arrange the salmon, carrot and cucumber wedges, and lettuce leaves on 6 wonton wraps.
4. In the shallow bowl whisk together dried oregano, olive oil, and lemon juice.
5. Sprinkle the roll mixture with oil dressing and wrap.

Nutrition: calories 90; fat 3.4; fiber 0.7; carbs 7.7; protein 7.7

Ginger And Cream Cheese Dip

Servings: 6 | Cooking: 0 min

Ingredients
- ½ cup ginger, grated
- 2 bunches cilantro, chopped
- 3 tablespoons balsamic vinegar
- ½ cup olive oil
- 1 and ½ cups cream cheese, soft

Directions
1. In your blender, mix the ginger with the rest of the ingredients and pulse well.
2. Divide into small bowls and serve as a party dip.

Nutrition: calories 213; fat 4.9; fiber 4.1; carbs 8.8; protein 17.8

Lemon Endive Bites

Servings: 10 | Cooking: 0 min

Ingredients
- 6 oz endive
- 2 pears, chopped

- 4 oz Blue cheese, crumbled
- 1 teaspoon olive oil
- 1 teaspoon lemon juice
- ¾ teaspoon ground cinnamon

Directions
1. Separate endive into the spears (10 spears).
2. In the bowl combine together chopped pears, olive oil, lemon juice, ground cinnamon, and Blue cheese.
3. Fill the endive spears with cheese mixture.

Nutrition: calories 72; fat 3.8; fiber 1.9; carbs 7.4; protein 2.8

Perfect Italian Potatoes

Servings: 6 | Cooking: 7 min

Ingredients
- 2 lbs baby potatoes, clean and cut in half
- 3/4 cup vegetable broth
- 6 oz Italian dry dressing mix

Directions
1. Add all ingredients into the inner pot of instant pot and stir well.
2. Seal pot with lid and cook on high for 7 minutes.
3. Once done, allow to release pressure naturally for 3 minutes then release remaining using quick release. Remove lid.
4. Stir well and serve.

Nutrition: Calories 149 Fat 0.3 g Carbohydrates 41.6 g Sugar 11.4 g Protein 4.5 g Cholesterol 0 mg

Feta Artichoke Dip

Servings: 8 | Cooking: 30 min

Ingredients
- 8 ounces artichoke hearts, drained and quartered
- ¾ cup basil, chopped
- ¾ cup green olives, pitted and chopped
- 1 cup parmesan cheese, grated
- 5 ounces feta cheese, crumbled

Directions
1. In your food processor, mix the artichokes with the basil and the rest of the ingredients, pulse well, and transfer to a baking dish.
2. Introduce in the oven, bake at 375 degrees F for 30 minutes and serve as a party dip.

Nutrition: calories 186; fat 12.4; fiber 0.9; carbs 2.6; protein 1.5

Peach Skewers

Servings: 2 | Cooking: 0 min

Ingredients
- 1 peach
- 4 Mozzarella balls, cherry size
- ½ teaspoon pistachio, chopped
- 1 teaspoon honey

Directions
1. Cut the peach on 4 cubes.
2. Then skewer peach cubes and Mozzarella balls on the skewers.
3. Sprinkle them with honey and chopped pistachio.

Nutrition: calories 202; fat 14.3; fiber 1.2; carbs 10; protein 10.8

Chickpeas Salsa

Servings: 6 | Cooking: 0 min

Ingredients
- 4 spring onions, chopped
- 1 cup baby spinach
- 15 ounces canned chickpeas, drained and rinsed
- Salt and black pepper to the taste
- 2 tablespoons olive oil
- 2 tablespoons lemon juice
- 1 tablespoon cilantro, chopped

Directions
1. In a bowl, mix the chickpeas with the spinach, spring onions and the rest of the ingredients, toss, divide into small cups and serve as a snack.

Nutrition: calories 224; fat 5.1; fiber 1; carbs 9.9; protein 15.1

Hummus Appetizer Bites

Servings: 1 Bite | Cooking: 10 min

Ingredients
- 11/4 cups all-purpose flour
- 1/2 tsp. salt
- 5 TB. cold butter
- 2 TB. vegetable shortening

- 1/4 cup ice water
- 1 batch Traditional Hummus (recipe in Chapter 11)
- 1 tsp. paprika
- 12 kalamata olives
- 12 fresh parsley leaves

Directions
1. In a food processor fitted with a chopping blade, pulse 1 cup all-purpose flour and salt 5 times.
2. Add cold butter and vegetable shortening, and pulse for 1 minute or until mixture resembles coarse meal.
3. Continue to pulse while adding water for about 1 minute. Test dough; if it holds together when you pinch it, it doesn't require any additional moisture. If it does not come together, add another 3 tablespoons water.
4. Remove dough from the food processor, place in a plastic bag, form into a flat disc, and refrigerate for 30 minutes.
5. Preheat the oven to 425°F.
6. Remove dough from the plastic bag, and dust both sides with flour. Sprinkle your counter with flour.
7. Using a rolling pin, roll out dough to 1/4 inch thickness. Using a 2-inch circle cookie cutter, cut out 12 circles of dough. Gently mold dough circles into a mini muffin tin, and using a fork, gently poke dough.
8. Bake for 10 minutes. Remove from the oven, and set aside to cool.
9. Spoon about 1 tablespoon Traditional Hummus on top of each cooled piecrust, sprinkle with paprika, and top with 1 kalamata olive and 1 parsley leaf each. Serve immediately or refrigerate.

Stuffed Avocado

Servings: 2 | Cooking: 0 min

Ingredients
- 1 avocado, halved and pitted
- 10 ounces canned tuna, drained
- 2 tablespoons sun-dried tomatoes, chopped
- 1 and ½ tablespoon basil pesto
- 2 tablespoons black olives, pitted and chopped
- Salt and black pepper to the taste
- 2 teaspoons pine nuts, toasted and chopped
- 1 tablespoon basil, chopped

Directions
1. In a bowl, combine the tuna with the sun-dried tomatoes and the rest of the ingredients except the avocado and stir.
2. Stuff the avocado halves with the tuna mix and serve as an appetizer.

Nutrition: calories 233; fat 9; fiber 3.5; carbs 11.4; protein 5.6

Grilled Polenta Vegetables Bites

Servings: 6-8 | Cooking: 15 min

Ingredients
- 1 1/2 to 2 tablespoons olive oil
- 1 green bell pepper, chopped
- 1 tomato sliced
- 1 tube (18-ounce) Polenta, pre-cooked
- 1/2 teaspoon garlic powder
- 1/2 yellow onion, chopped into big chunks
- 2 jalapenos, sliced, de-seeded
- 2-3 slices Swiss cheese or your cheese of choice
- 5-6 pieces baby Bella mushrooms
- Optional: Chopped parsley and black olives
- Salt and pepper, to taste

Directions
1. Preheat the grill.
2. Meanwhile, slice the polenta into 1/4-1/2 slices. Brush both sides with the olive oil and set aside.
3. Place the chopped vegetables into a mixing bowl, add the garlic, remaining oil, and season with salt and pepper to taste; toss lightly.
4. Grill the polenta and the vegetables for about 15 to 20 minutes, turning at least once, until lightly browned.
5. Remove from the grill and assemble the sandwiches with cheese, vegetables, and tomato slice. Top with the olives and parsley, if desired. Secure with toothpicks.

Nutrition: 150 cal., 11 g total fat (3.5 sat. fat), 10 mg chol., 410 mg sodium, 360 mg pot., 16 g total carbs., 2 g fiber, 2 g sugar, 6 g protein, 15% vitamin A, 45% vitamin C, 10% calcium, and 6% iron.

Grapefruit Salad

Servings: 6 | Cooking: 0 min

Ingredients
- 2 cups arugula

- 1 tablespoon honey
- 1 teaspoon mustard
- 1 teaspoon lemon juice
- ½ teaspoon olive oil
- 1 grapefruit, peeled
- ¾ cup walnuts, chopped

Directions
1. Chop arugula roughly and place in the bowl.
2. Add chopped walnuts.
3. Then chop grapefruit and add it in the bowl too.
4. Shake the salad well.
5. After this, make salad dressing: whisk together mustard, honey, lemon juice, and olive oil.
6. Pour the dressing over salad.

Nutrition: calories 122; fat 9.8; fiber 1.5; carbs 6.6; protein 4.2

Hummus With Ground Lamb

Servings: 8 | Cooking: 15 min

Ingredients
- 10 ounces hummus
- 12 ounces lamb meat, ground
- ½ cup pomegranate seeds
- ¼ cup parsley, chopped
- 1 tablespoon olive oil
- Pita chips for serving

Directions
1. Heat up a pan with the oil over medium-high heat, add the meat, and brown for 15 minutes stirring often.
2. Spread the hummus on a platter, spread the ground lamb all over, also spread the pomegranate seeds and the parsley and sere with pita chips as a snack.

Nutrition: calories 133; fat 9.7; fiber 1.7; carbs 6.4; protein 5.4

Perfect Queso

Servings: 16 | Cooking: 15 min

Ingredients
- 1 lb ground beef
- 32 oz Velveeta cheese, cut into cubes
- 10 oz can tomatoes, diced
- 1 1/2 tbsp taco seasoning
- 1 tsp chili powder
- 1 onion, diced
- Pepper
- Salt

Directions
1. Set instant pot on sauté mode.
2. Add meat, onion, taco seasoning, chili powder, pepper, and salt into the pot and cook until meat is no longer pink.
3. Add tomatoes and stir well. Top with cheese and do not stir.
4. Seal pot with lid and cook on high for 4 minutes.
5. Once done, release pressure using quick release. Remove lid.
6. Stir everything well and serve.

Nutrition: Calories 257 Fat 15.9 g Carbohydrates 10.2 g Sugar 4.9 g Protein 21 g Cholesterol 71 mg

Aromatic Artichokes

Servings: 1 Artichoke | Cooking: 45 min

Ingredients
- 4 artichokes
- 6 cups water
- 2 cloves garlic
- 1 bay leaf
- 2 tsp. minced garlic
- 1/3 cup fresh lemon juice
- 1/4 cup extra-virgin olive oil
- 1/2 tsp. salt
- 1/2 tsp. ground black pepper

Directions
1. Using a pair of kitchen scissors, cut off the tips of artichoke leaves. With a sharp knife, cut 1 inch off top of artichokes. Pull off small leaves along base and stem, leaving only a 1-inch stem. Rinse artichokes in cold water.
2. In a steamer or large saucepan over medium-high heat, bring water, garlic cloves, and bay leaf to a simmer. Add steaming basket, place artichokes inside, cover, and steam for 40 minutes.
3. In a small bowl, whisk together minced garlic, lemon juice, extra-virgin olive oil, salt, and black pepper.
4. Transfer artichokes from the steamer to a serving dish, and spoon dressing over artichokes, being sure to get it between leaves.
5. Serve warm or cold.

Rosemary Olive Bread
Servings: 1 Pita | Cooking: 20 min

Ingredients

- 1 1/2 TB. active dry yeast
- 1 1/2 cups warm water
- 1 tsp. sugar
- 1 tsp. salt
- 1/4 cup plus 3 TB. extra-virgin olive oil
- 3 TB. fresh rosemary, roughly chopped
- 10 kalamata olives, pitted and roughly chopped
- 1 tsp. ground black pepper
- 3 cups all-purpose flour

Directions

1. In a large bowl, combine yeast, warm water, and sugar, and set aside for 5 minutes.
2. Add salt, 1/4 cup extra-virgin olive oil, rosemary, kalamata olives, black pepper, and 1 cup all-purpose flour, and stir to combine. Add another 1 cup all-purpose flour, and begin to knead dough. Add remaining 1 cup all-purpose flour, and knead for about 3 minutes or until dough comes together in a ball. If you're using an electric stand mixer, use the dough attachment to knead dough.
3. Remove dough from the bowl, and grease the bowl with 1 tablespoon extra-virgin olive oil. Return dough to the bowl, and turn over to coat dough in oil. Cover the bowl with plastic wrap and a thick towel, and set aside to rise for 2 hours.
4. Uncover the bowl, and gently pull dough together into a ball. Divide dough into 10 equal-size pieces, lightly dust with flour and cover with plastic wrap or a moist towel.
5. Flour your rolling pin and work surface. Roll out each dough ball to 1/4 inch thick, and place on a baking sheet. Let rolled-out dough sit for 10 minutes before cooking.
6. Preheat an iron or cast-iron skillet over medium-low heat, and brush lightly with extra-virgin olive oil. Add 1 rolled-out dough to the skillet, and cook for 2 or 3 minutes or until lightly browned. Flip over and cook for 2 more minutes. Transfer to a plate, and cover with a slightly damp towel. Brush the skillet with more extra-virgin olive oil before cooking next piece.
7. Store in an airtight container, and serve with a good extra-virgin olive oil and olives.

Parmesan Eggplant Bites

Servings: 8 | Cooking: 30 min

Ingredients

- 2 eggs, beaten
- 3 oz Parmesan, grated
- 1 tablespoon coconut flakes
- ½ teaspoon ground paprika
- 1 teaspoon salt
- 2 eggplants, trimmed

Directions

1. Slice the eggplants into the thin circles. Use the vegetable slicer for this step.
2. After this, sprinkle the vegetables with salt and mix up. Leave them for 5-10 minutes.
3. Then drain eggplant juice and sprinkle them with ground paprika.
4. Mix up together coconut flakes and Parmesan.
5. Dip every eggplant circle in the egg and then coat in Parmesan mixture.
6. Line the baking tray with parchment and place eggplants on it.
7. Bake the vegetables for 30 minutes at 360F. Flip the eggplants into another side after 12 minutes of cooking.

Nutrition: calories 87; fat 3.9; fiber 5; carbs 8.7; protein 6.2

Quinoa Bars

Servings: 15 | Cooking: 25 min

Ingredients

- 1 cup rolled oats
- 6 oz quinoa
- 7 oz almonds, chopped
- 5 tablespoons maple syrup
- 3 tablespoons peanut butter
- 1 teaspoon ground cinnamon
- 1 tablespoon coconut flakes

Directions

1. In the bog bowl mix up together rolled oats, quinoa, almonds, and coconut flakes.
2. Then add peanut butter and maple syrup.
3. Stir the mixture carefully with the help of the spoon.
4. Line the baking tray with parchment.
5. Transfer the quinoa mixture in the tray and flatten it well.
6. Bake granola for 25 minutes at 355F.
7. Chill the cooked granola well and crack on the servings.

Nutrition: calories 177; fat 9.4; fiber 3.3; carbs 19.1; protein 5.9

Creamy Artichoke Dip

Servings: 8 | Cooking: 5 min

Ingredients
- 28 oz can artichoke hearts, drain and quartered
- 1 1/2 cups parmesan cheese, shredded
- 1 cup sour cream
- 1 cup mayonnaise
- 3.5 oz can green chilies
- 1 cup of water
- Pepper
- Salt

Directions
1. Add artichokes, water, and green chilis into the instant pot.
2. Seal pot with the lid and select manual and set timer for 1 minute.
3. Once done, release pressure using quick release. Remove lid. Drain excess water.
4. Set instant pot on sauté mode. Add remaining ingredients and stir well and cook until cheese is melted.
5. Serve and enjoy.

Nutrition: Calories 262 Fat 7.6 g Carbohydrates 14.4 g Sugar 2.8 g Protein 8.4 g Cholesterol 32 mg

Olive Eggplant Spread

Servings: 12 | Cooking: 8 min

Ingredients
- 1 3/4 lbs eggplant, chopped
- 1/2 tbsp dried oregano
- 1/4 cup olives, pitted and chopped
- 1 tbsp tahini
- 1/4 cup fresh lime juice
- 1/2 cup water
- 2 garlic cloves
- 1/4 cup olive oil
- Salt

Directions
1. Add oil into the inner pot of instant pot and set the pot on sauté mode.
2. Add eggplant and cook for 3-5 minutes. Turn off sauté mode.
3. Add water and salt and stir well.
4. Seal pot with lid and cook on high for 3 minutes.
5. Once done, release pressure using quick release. Remove lid.
6. Drain eggplant well and transfer into the food processor.
7. Add remaining ingredients into the food processor and process until smooth.
8. Serve and enjoy.

Nutrition: Calories 65 Fat 5.3 g Carbohydrates 4.7 g Sugar 2 g Protein 0.9 g Cholesterol 0 mg

Cucumber Bites

Servings: 12 | Cooking: 0 min

Ingredients
- 1 English cucumber, sliced into 32 rounds
- 10 ounces hummus
- 16 cherry tomatoes, halved
- 1 tablespoon parsley, chopped
- 1 ounce feta cheese, crumbled

Directions
1. Spread the hummus on each cucumber round, divide the tomato halves on each, sprinkle the cheese and parsley on to and serve as an appetizer.

Nutrition: calories 162; fat 3.4; fiber 2; carbs 6.4; protein 2.4

Oregano Crackers

Servings: 8 | Cooking: 15 min

Ingredients
- ½ cup wheat flour, whole grain
- ¼ cup Feta cheese, crumbled
- ¾ cup of water
- 1 teaspoon dried oregano
- 1 teaspoon salt
- ½ teaspoon sesame seeds

Directions
1. Mix up together water and flour.
2. Add dried oregano, salt, and Feta cheese.
3. Knead the non-sticky dough.
4. After this, roll up the dough into the thick sheet and cut the sheet on the crackers.
5. Line the baking tray with baking paper.
6. Arrange the uncooked crackers in the tray and bake for 14 minutes at 365F.

7. After this, flip the crackers on another side and cook for 1 minute more.
8. Chill the cooked crackers well.

Nutrition: calories 38; fat 1.1; fiber 0.3; carbs 5.6; protein 1.4

Tomato Salsa

Servings: 6 | Cooking: 0 min

Ingredients
- 1 garlic clove, minced
- 4 tablespoons olive oil
- 5 tomatoes, cubed
- 1 tablespoon balsamic vinegar
- ¼ cup basil, chopped
- 1 tablespoon parsley, chopped
- 1 tablespoon chives, chopped
- Salt and black pepper to the taste
- Pita chips for serving

Directions
1. In a bowl, mix the tomatoes with the garlic and the rest of the ingredients except the pita chips, stir, divide into small cups and serve with the pita chips on the side.

Nutrition: calories 160; fat 13.7; fiber 5.5; carbs 10.1; protein 2.2

Spicy Berry Dip

Servings: 4 | Cooking: 15 min

Ingredients
- 10 oz cranberries
- 1/4 cup fresh orange juice
- 3/4 tsp paprika
- 1/2 tsp chili powder
- 1 tsp lemon zest
- 1 tbsp lemon juice

Directions
1. Add all ingredients into the inner pot of instant pot and stir well.
2. Seal pot with lid and cook on high for 15 minutes.
3. Once done, allow to release pressure naturally for 5 minutes then release remaining using quick release. Remove lid.
4. Blend cranberry mixture using a blender until getting the desired consistency.
5. Serve and enjoy.

Nutrition: Calories 49 Fat 0.2 g Carbohydrates 8.6 g Sugar 4.1 g Protein 0.3 g Cholesterol 0 mg

Mozzarella Chips

Servings: 8 | Cooking: 10 min

Ingredients
- 4 phyllo dough sheets
- 4 oz Mozzarella, shredded
- 1 tablespoon olive oil

Directions
1. Place 2 phyllo sheets in the pan and brush it with sprinkle it with Mozzarella.
2. Then cover the cheese with 2 remaining phyllo sheets.
3. Brush the top of Phyllo with olive oil and cut on 8 squares.
4. Bake the chips for 10 minutes at 365F or until they are light brown.

Nutrition: calories 130; fat 5; fiber 0.5; carbs 15.5; protein 6.5

Salmon Rolls

Servings: 12 | Cooking: 0 min

Ingredients
- 1 big long cucumber, thinly sliced lengthwise
- 2 teaspoons lime juice
- 4 ounces cream cheese, soft
- 1 teaspoon lemon zest, grated
- Salt and black pepper to the taste
- 2 teaspoons dill, chopped
- 4 ounces smoked salmon, cut into strips

Directions
1. Arrange cucumber slices on a working surface and top each with a salmon strip.
2. In a bowl, mix the rest of the ingredients, stir and spread over the salmon.
3. Roll the salmon and cucumber strips, arrange them on a platter and serve as an appetizer.

Nutrition: calories 245; fat 15.5; fiber 4.8; carbs 16.8; protein 17.3

Cream Cheese Rolls

Servings: 2 | Cooking: 0 min

Ingredients
- 1 lavash sheet
- 1 tablespoon cream cheese
- 1 bell pepper
- 2 ham slices
- 1 tomato, sliced
- 3 lettuce leaves

Directions
1. Spread lavash with cream cheese from one side.
2. Then cut bell pepper on the wedges and arrange it over the cream cheese.
3. Add sliced ham, tomato, and lettuce.
4. Roll the lavash.
5. Cut it on 2 servings and secure every lavash roll with a toothpick.

Nutrition: calories 169; fat 5.1; fiber 2.6; carbs 23.1; protein 8.9

Carrot Dip

Servings: 10 | Cooking: 12 min

Ingredients
- 1 piece (2 inches) fresh ginger root, peeled, thinly sliced
- 1 1/2 teaspoons ground coriander
- 1 pound carrots, peeled, thinly sliced
- 1/3 cup apricot preserves
- 1/8 teaspoon cayenne pepper
- 2 tablespoons fresh lemon juice
- 3 cloves garlic, thinly sliced
- 3/4 teaspoon salt, divided
- 4 teaspoons toasted sesame oil
- 2 cups water

Directions
1. Place the carrots, ginger, garlic, and 1/4 teaspoon salt in a large-sized saucepan. Add the water, cover, and bring to a boil. When boiling, reduce the heat, simmer covered for about 10-12 minutes, or until the carrots are drained. Drain.
2. Transfer the carrots to a food processor. Add the remaining 1/2 teaspoon salt and the rest of the ingredients; process until the mixture is smooth.

Nutrition: 65 cal., 2.1 g total fat (0.3 sat. fat), 0 mg chol., 210 mg sodium, 12.1 g total carbs., 1.5 g fiber, 6.9 g sugar, and 0.6 g protein.

Walnuts Yogurt Dip

Servings: 8 | Cooking: 0 min

Ingredients
- 3 garlic cloves, minced
- 2 cups Greek yogurt
- ¼ cup dill, chopped
- 1 tablespoon chives, chopped
- ¼ cup walnuts, chopped
- Salt and black pepper to the taste

Directions
1. In a bowl, mix the garlic with the yogurt and the rest of the ingredients, whisk well, divide into small cups and serve as a party dip.

Nutrition: calories 200; fat 6.5; fiber 4.6; carbs 15.5; protein 8.4

Rosemary Cauliflower Dip

Servings: 4 | Cooking: 15 min

Ingredients
- 1 lb cauliflower florets
- 1 tbsp fresh parsley, chopped
- 1/2 cup heavy cream
- 1/2 cup vegetable stock
- 1 tbsp garlic, minced
- 1 tbsp rosemary, chopped
- 1 tbsp olive oil
- 1 onion, chopped
- Pepper
- Salt

Directions
1. Add oil into the inner pot of instant pot and set the pot on sauté mode.
2. Add onion and sauté for 5 minutes.
3. Add remaining ingredients except for parsley and heavy cream and stir well.
4. Seal pot with lid and cook on high for 10 minutes.
5. Once done, allow to release pressure naturally for 10 minutes then release remaining using quick release. Remove lid.
6. Add cream and stir well. Blend cauliflower mixture using immersion blender until smooth.
7. Garnish with parsley and serve.

Nutrition: Calories 128 Fat 9.4 g Carbohydrates 10.4 g Sugar 4 g Protein 3.1 g Cholesterol 21 mg

Light & Creamy Garlic Hummus

Servings: 12 | Cooking: 40 min

Ingredients
- 1 1/2 cups dry chickpeas, rinsed
- 2 1/2 tbsp fresh lemon juice
- 1 tbsp garlic, minced
- 1/2 cup tahini
- 6 cups of water
- Pepper
- Salt

Directions
1. Add water and chickpeas into the instant pot.
2. Seal pot with a lid and select manual and set timer for 40 minutes.
3. Once done, allow to release pressure naturally. Remove lid.
4. Drain chickpeas well and reserved 1/2 cup chickpeas liquid.
5. Transfer chickpeas, reserved liquid, lemon juice, garlic, tahini, pepper, and salt into the food processor and process until smooth.
6. Serve and enjoy.

Nutrition: Calories 152 Fat 6.9 g Carbohydrates 17.6 g Sugar 2.8 g Protein 6.6 g Cholesterol 0 mg

Mediterranean-style Nachos Recipe

Servings: 12 | Cooking: 15 min

Ingredients
- 6 pieces whole-wheat pita breads
- Cooking: spray
- 1/2 teaspoon ground cumin
- 1/2 teaspoon ground coriander
- 1/2 teaspoon paprika
- 1/2 teaspoon pepper
- 1/2 teaspoons salt
- 1/2 cup hot water
- 1/2 teaspoon beef stock concentrate
- 1 pound ground lamb or beef
- 2 garlic cloves, minced
- 1 teaspoon cornstarch
- 2 medium cucumbers, peeled, seeded, grated
- 2 cups Greek yogurt, plain
- 2 tablespoons lemon juice
- 1/4 teaspoon grated lemon peel
- 1 teaspoon salt, divided
- 1/4 teaspoon pepper
- 1/2 cup pitted Greek olives, sliced
- 4 green onions, thinly sliced
- 1/2 cup crumbled feta cheese
- 2 cups torn romaine lettuce
- 2 medium tomatoes, seeded and chopped

Directions
1. In a colander set over a bowl, toss the cucumbers with 1/2 teaspoon of the salt; let stand for 30 minutes, then squeeze and pat dry. Set aside.
2. In a small-sized bowl, combine the coriander, cumin, 1/2 teaspoon pepper, paprika, and 1/2 teaspoon salt; set aside.
3. Cut each pita bread into 8 wedges. Arrange them in a single layer on ungreased baking sheets. Sprits both sides of the wedges with cooking spray. Sprinkle with 3/4 teaspoon of the seasoning mix. Broil 3-4 inches from the heat source for about 3-4 minutes per side, or until golden brown. Transfer to wire racks, let cool.
4. Whisk hot water and beef stock cube in a 1-cup liquid measuring cup until blended. In a large-sized skillet, cook the lamb, seasoning with the remaining seasoning mix, over medium heat until the meat is no longer pink. Add the garlic; cook for 1 minute. Drain.
5. Stir in the cornstarch into the broth; mix until smooth. Gradually stir into the skillet; bring to a boil and cook, stirring, for 2 minutes or until thick.
6. In a small-sized bowl, combine the cucumbers, yogurt, lemon peel, lemon juice, and the remaining salt and 1/4 teaspoon pepper.
7. Arrange the pita wedges on a serving platter. Layer with the lettuce, lamb mixture, tomatoes, onions, olives, and cheese; serve immediately with the cucumber sauce.

Nutrition: 232 cal, 6.7 g total fat (2.9 g sat. fat), 42 mg chol., 630 mg sodium, 412 mg pot., 24 total carbs., 3.3 g fiber, 4.1 g sugar, 20.2 g protein, 8% vitamin A, 12% vitamin C, 11% calcium, and 15% iron.

Baked Goat Cheese Caprese Salad

Servings: 4 | Cooking: 15 min

Ingredients
- 1 (log 4 ounce) fresh goat cheese, halved
- 1 pinch cayenne pepper, or to taste
- 16 cherry tomatoes, diagonally cut into halves
- 2 tablespoons olive oil, divided
- 3 tablespoons basil chiffonade (thinly sliced fresh basil leaves), divided
- Freshly ground black pepper, to taste

Directions
1. Preheat the oven to 400F or 200C.
2. Drizzle about 1 1/2 teaspoons olive oil into the bottom of 2 pieces 6-ounch ramekin. Sprinkle about 1 tablespoon of basil per ramekin.
3. Place 1 goat half over each ramekin; surround with cherry tomato halves.
4. Sprinkle with the black pepper and the cayenne. Spread the remaining basil on top of each.
5. Place the ramekins on a baking sheet. Drizzle each serve with the remaining olive oil; bake for about 15 minutes or until bubbling. Serve warm.

Nutrition: 178 cal., 15.5 g total fat (6.8 sat. fat), 22 mg chol., 152 mg sodium, 4.1 g total carbs., 0.9 g fiber, 0.7 g sugar, and 6.8 g protein.

Grilled Shrimp Kabobs

Servings: 4 | Cooking: 4 min

Ingredients
- 1 1/2 cups whole-wheat dry breadcrumbs
- 1 clove garlic, finely minced or pressed
- 1 teaspoon dried basil leaves
- 1/4 cup olive oil
- 2 pounds shrimp, peeled, deveined, leaving the tails on
- 2 tablespoons vegetable oil
- 2 teaspoons dried parsley flakes
- Salt and pepper
- 16 skewers, soaked for at least 20 minutes in water or until ready to use if using wooden

Directions
1. Rinse the shrimps and dry.
2. Put the vegetable and the olive oil in a re-sealable plastic bag; add the shrimp and toss to coat with the oil mixture.
3. Add the breadcrumbs, parsley, garlic, basil, salt, and pepper; toss to coat with the dry mix.
4. Seal the bag, refrigerate for 1 hour. Thread the shrimps on the skewers.
5. Grill on preheated grill for about 2 minutes each side or until golden, making sure not to overcook.

Nutrition: 502.7 cal., 24.8 g total fat (3.5 sat. fat), 285.8 mg chol., 1581.8 mg sodium, 31.7 g total carbs., 2 g fiber, 2.5 g sugar, and 36.4 g protein.

Red Pepper Tapenade

Servings: 4 | Cooking: 0 min

Ingredients
- 7 ounces roasted red peppers, chopped
- ½ cup parmesan, grated
- 1/3 cup parsley, chopped
- 14 ounces canned artichokes, drained and chopped
- 3 tablespoons olive oil
- ¼ cup capers, drained
- 1 and ½ tablespoons lemon juice
- 2 garlic cloves, minced

Directions
1. In your blender, combine the red peppers with the parmesan and the rest of the ingredients and pulse well.
2. Divide into cups and serve as a snack.

Nutrition: calories 200; fat 5.6; fiber 4.5; carbs 12.4; protein 4.6

Collard Green Chicken Roll Ups

Servings: 4 | Cooking: 20 min

Ingredients
- 4 large collard greens
- 1/2 teaspoon hot sauce
- 1/2 cup black olives, diced
- 1 tablespoon fresh cilantro, de-stemmed and chopped
- 1 small seedless cucumber cut into long match sticks
- 1 pound of Foster Farms Simply Raised chicken
- 1 large avocado
- Juice of 1/2 lime
- Salt and pepper, to taste

Directions
1. Place a large-sized grill pan over medium heat. Season both sides of the chicken with the salt and pepper. Place on the grill, cook until the meat is no longer pink and opaque all the way through. Remove from the heat.
2. Meanwhile, fill the bottom of a large skillet with few inches of water; bring to a boil over high heat. Ready a large-sized bowl filled with iced cubes and cold water near the stove.
3. Slice off the stems and the tough backbones from the collard greens using a paring knife.

4. Add one leaf at a time into the boiling water, blanching for about 30 to 45 seconds until they are pliable but not soft to fall apart when rolled. Remove from the boiling water and immediately add to the iced water, letting the water cool. Once cool, place the leaf on a paper towel or dish towel; dry well. Repeat the process with the remaining leaves.
5. Place the avocado in a bowl, add the cilantro, lime, hot sauce, and season with salt and pepper to taste; mash together to combine.
6. Place a leaf on a clean, flat surface. Spread a dollop of the avocado mixture at the larger part of the collard greens. Top the avocado mixture with the chicken, cucumber, and olives.
7. Fold the top end of the collard over the filling; roll the leaf, tucking in the sides as you roll the bottom. Cut the rolls into halves; serve.

Nutrition: 250 cal., 13 g total fat (2.5 g sat. fat), 75 mg chol., 450 mg sodium, 670 mg pot., 12 g total carbs., 6 g fiber, 2 g sugar, 25 g protein, 4% vitamin A, 20% vitamin C, 6% calcium, and 15% iron.

Cauliflower Spread

Servings: 4 | Cooking: 15 min

Ingredients
- 1 cup cauliflower
- 1 teaspoon tahini paste
- 3 tablespoons lemon juice
- ½ teaspoon minced garlic
- 1 teaspoon dried oregano
- ¼ teaspoon cayenne pepper
- ½ teaspoon salt
- ¼ teaspoon dried thyme
- 1 cup of water

Directions
1. Pour water in the pan and add cauliflower.
2. Boil cauliflower for 15 minutes.
3. Then drain ½ part of liquid from cauliflower.
4. Transfer remaining liquid and cauliflower in the food processor.
5. Add tahini paste, lemon juice, minced garlic, dried oregano, cayenne pepper, salt, and dried thyme.
6. Blend the mixture until you get a smooth and fluffy mixture.
7. Store the cooked hummus in the fridge up to 3 days.

Nutrition: calories 19; fat 0.9; fiber 1; carbs 2.3; protein 0.9

Coriander Falafel

Servings: 8 | Cooking: 10 min

Ingredients
- 1 cup canned garbanzo beans, drained and rinsed
- 1 bunch parsley leaves
- 1 yellow onion, chopped
- 5 garlic cloves, minced
- 1 teaspoon coriander, ground
- A pinch of salt and black pepper
- ¼ teaspoon cayenne pepper
- ¼ teaspoon baking soda
- ¼ teaspoon cumin powder
- 1 teaspoon lemon juice
- 3 tablespoons tapioca flour
- Olive oil for frying

Directions
1. In your food processor, combine the beans with the parsley, onion and the rest the ingredients except the oil and the flour and pulse well.
2. Transfer the mix to a bowl, add the flour, stir well, shape 16 balls out of this mix and flatten them a bit.
3. Heat up a pan with some oil over medium-high heat, add the falafels, cook them for 5 minutes on each side, transfer to paper towels, drain excess grease, arrange them on a platter and serve as an appetizer.

Nutrition: calories 112; fat 6.2; fiber 2; carbs 12.3; protein 3.1

Slow Cooked Cheesy Artichoke Dip

Servings: 6 | Cooking: 60 min

Ingredients
- 10 oz can artichoke hearts, drained and chopped
- 4 cups spinach, chopped
- 8 oz cream cheese
- 3 tbsp sour cream
- 1/4 cup mayonnaise
- 3/4 cup mozzarella cheese, shredded
- 1/4 cup parmesan cheese, grated
- 3 garlic cloves, minced
- 1/2 tsp dried parsley
- Pepper

- Salt

Directions
1. Add all ingredients into the inner pot of instant pot and stir well.
2. Seal the pot with the lid and select slow cook mode and set the timer for 60 minutes. Stir once while cooking.
3. Serve and enjoy.

Nutrition: Calories 226 Fat 19.3 g Carbohydrates 7.5 g Sugar 1.2 g Protein 6.8 g Cholesterol 51 mg

Marinated Chickpeas

Servings: 4 | Cooking: 10 min

Ingredients
- 1 can (15 ounce) chickpeas (or garbanzo beans), drained, rinsed
- 1 tablespoon fresh oregano, chopped
- 1 tablespoon lemon juice
- 1 tablespoon lemon zest
- 1 teaspoon fresh parsley, chopped
- 1/4 teaspoon minced garlic
- 3 tablespoons olive oil
- Sea salt, to taste

Directions
1. Place the chickpeas in a bowl. Add the rest of the ingredients; toss to mix well. Marinate the chickpeas for 8 hours or overnight in the refrigerator.

Nutrition: 176 cal., 11 g total fat (1.5 sat. fat), 0 mg chol., 290 mg sodium, 16.6 g total carbs., 3.3 g fiber, 0.2 g sugar, and 3.6 g protein.

Easy Tomato Dip

Servings: 4 | Cooking: 13 min

Ingredients
- 2 cups tomato puree
- 1/2 tsp ground cumin
- 1 tsp garlic, minced
- 1/4 cup vinegar
- 1 onion, chopped
- 1 tbsp olive oil
- Pepper
- Salt

Directions
1. Add oil into the inner pot of instant pot and set the pot on sauté mode.
2. Add onion and sauté for 3 minutes.
3. Add remaining ingredients and stir well.
4. Seal pot with lid and cook on high for 10 minutes.
5. Once done, allow to release pressure naturally for 10 minutes then release remaining using quick release. Remove lid.
6. Blend tomato mixture using an immersion blender until smooth.
7. Serve and enjoy.

Nutrition: Calories 94 Fat 3.9 g Carbohydrates 14.3 g Sugar 7.3 g Protein 2.5 g Cholesterol 0 mg

Zucchini Pizza Rolls

Servings: 8 | Cooking: 15 min

Ingredients
- 4 large zucchini, sliced lengthwise into 1/4-inch thick slices
- 1/2 cup sun-dried tomatoes, chopped
- 1/2 cup black olives, chopped
- 1 tablespoon olive oil
- 1 cup pizza sauce
- Freshly ground black pepper
- Red pepper flakes (optional)
- Sea salt

Directions
1. Preheat a grill or a broiler.
2. Brush each slice of zucchini lightly with the olive oil and season with salt and pepper; grill or broil for about 2 minutes each side, or until softened. Let cool slightly.
3. On 1/2 side of the zucchini slices, spread a thin layer of pizza sauce. Sprinkle the olives, sun-dried tomato, and if using, red pepper flakes over the sauce. Starting on the end with the pizza sauce, roll each slice. If necessary, secure with toothpicks.

Nutrition: 20 cal., 1 g total fat (0 g sat. fat), 0 mg chol., 85 mg sodium, 140 mg pot., 2 g total carbs., <1 g fiber, 1 g sugar, <1 g protein, 10% vitamin A, 10% vitamin C, 2% calcium, and 2% iron.

Creamy Spinach And Shallots Dip

Servings: 4 | Cooking: 0 min

Ingredients
- 1 pound spinach, roughly chopped
- 2 shallots, chopped
- 2 tablespoons mint, chopped
- ¾ cup cream cheese, soft
- Salt and black pepper to the taste

Directions
1. In a blender, combine the spinach with the shallots and the rest of the ingredients, and pulse well.
2. Divide into small bowls and serve as a party dip.

Nutrition: calories 204; fat 11.5; fiber 3.1; carbs 4.2; protein 5.9

French Baked Brie Recipe With Figs, Walnuts And Pistachios

Servings: 6 To 8 | Cooking: 10 min

Ingredients
- 13 ounces French brie
- 4 tablespoons fig jam or preserves, divided
- 1/3 cup walnut hearts, roughly chopped
- 1/3 cup pistachios, shelled and roughly chopped
- 1/3 cup dried mission figs, sliced

Directions
1. Preheat the oven to 375F.
2. Place the fig preserves or jam in a microwavable dish; microwave for 30 seconds or until soft.
3. In a small-sized bowl, combine the nuts and the dried figs. Add in 1/2 of the softened fig preserve; mix well until well combined.
4. Place the brie into a small-sized ovenproof dish or a cast-iron skillet. With a knife, coat the brie with remaining 1/2 of the softened fig preserve/jam.
5. Top the brie with the nut and fig mixture.
6. Place the dish or the skillet in the oven and bake for 10 minutes at 375F or until the brie starts to ooze, but not melt.
7. Serve warm with your favorite crackers.

Nutrition: 330 cal.,22.8 g total fat (11.1 g sat. fat), 61 mg chol., 410 mg sodium, 250 mg pot., 18.1 g total carbs., 2 g fiber, 12.3 g sugar, 15.5 g protein, 7% vitamin A, 2% vitamin C, 14% calcium, and 5% iron

Cucumber, Chicken And Mango Wrap

Servings: 1 | Cooking: 20 min

Ingredients
- ½ of a medium cucumber cut lengthwise
- ½ of ripe mango
- 1 tbsp salad dressing of choice
- 1 whole wheat tortilla wrap
- 1-inch thick slice of chicken breast around 6-inch in length
- 2 tbsp oil for frying
- 2 tbsp whole wheat flour
- 2 to 4 lettuce leaves
- Salt and pepper to taste

Directions
1. Slice a chicken breast into 1-inch strips and just cook a total of 6-inch strips. That would be like two strips of chicken. Store remaining chicken for future use.
2. Season chicken with pepper and salt. Dredge in whole wheat flour.
3. On medium fire, place a small and nonstick fry pan and heat oil. Once oil is hot, add chicken strips and fry until golden brown around 5 minutes per side.
4. While chicken is cooking, place tortilla wraps in oven and cook for 3 to 5 minutes. Then remove from oven and place on a plate.
5. Slice cucumber lengthwise, use only ½ of it and store remaining cucumber. Peel cucumber cut into quarter and remove pith. Place the two slices of cucumber on the tortilla wrap, 1-inch away from the edge.
6. Slice mango and store the other half with seed. Peel the mango without seed, slice into strips and place on top of the cucumber on the tortilla wrap.
7. Once chicken is cooked, place chicken beside the cucumber in a line.
8. Add cucumber leaf, drizzle with salad dressing of choice.
9. Roll the tortilla wrap, serve and enjoy.

Nutrition: Calories: 434; Fat: 10g; Protein: 21g; Carbohydrates: 65g

Greek Mountain Tea

Servings: 1 | Cooking: 5 min

Ingredients
- Greek Mountain Tea
- 1 Cup Water
- Honey or sugar, optional

Directions
1. Get about 1 to 2 Greek Mountain Tea leaves and break them into thirds.

2. Fill a pot or a briki with water. Turn the flame or heat on to medium-high. Put the tealeaves into the pot or briki; bring the water to a boil. When boiling, remove the pot or briki from the heat, and let the tea steep for 7 minutes.
3. After steeping, pour the tea into a cup over a strainer to catch the tealeaves.
4. If desired, sweeten with honey and sugar. Enjoy!

Nutrition: 3 cal., 0 g total fat (0 g sat. fat), 0 mg chol., 8 mg sodium, 19 mg pot., 0.9 g total carbs., 0 g fiber, 0.7 g sugar, 0 g protein, 0% vitamin A, 0% vitamin C, 1% calcium, and 0% iron.

Avocado And Spinach Breakfast Wrap

Servings: 4 | Cooking: 10 min

Ingredients
- ¼ tsp pepper
- ½ tsp salt
- 1 5-oz box or bag of baby spinach, chopped
- 1 avocado, sliced
- 4 egg whites
- 4 eggs
- 4 oz shredded pepper jack cheese
- 4 thin, whole wheat pita bread, 8-inch
- Hot sauce, optional
- Nonstick cooking spray

Directions
1. On medium high fire, place a nonstick skillet greased with cooking spray.
2. Once hot, sauté spinach for 2 minutes or until wilted.
3. Meanwhile, in a small bowl whisk egg whites and eggs. Season with pepper and salt, whisk again. Pour into skillet and scramble. Cook for 3 to 4 minutes or to desired doneness.
4. Evenly divide egg into 4 equal portions and place in middle of pita bread and add 2 to 4 slices of avocadoes beside the egg and roll tortilla like a burrito.
5. Serve and enjoy with a side of hot sauce.

Nutrition: Calories: 532; Carbs: 42.7g; Protein: 28.2g; Fat: 27.6g

Paleo Almond Banana Pancakes

Servings: 3 | Cooking: 10 min

Ingredients
- ¼ cup almond flour
- ½ teaspoon ground cinnamon
- 3 eggs
- 1 banana, mashed
- 1 tablespoon almond butter
- 1 teaspoon vanilla extract
- 1 teaspoon olive oil
- Sliced banana to serve

Directions
1. Whisk the eggs in a mixing bowl until they become fluffy.
2. In another bowl mash the banana using a fork and add to the egg mixture.
3. Add the vanilla, almond butter, cinnamon and almond flour.
4. Mix into a smooth batter.
5. Heat the olive oil in a skillet.
6. Add one spoonful of the batter and fry them from both sides.
7. Keep doing these steps until you are done with all the batter.
8. Add some sliced banana on top before serving.

Nutrition: Calories per serving: 306; Protein: 14.4g; Carbs: 3.6g; Fat: 26.0g

Italian Flat Bread Gluten Free

Servings: 8 | Cooking: 30 min

Ingredients
- 1 tbsp apple cider
- 2 tbsp water
- ½ cup yogurt
- 2 tbsp butter
- 2 tbsp sugar
- 2 eggs
- 1 tsp xanthan gum
- ½ tsp salt
- 1 tsp baking soda
- 1 ½ tsp baking powder
- ½ cup potato starch, not potato flour
- ½ cup tapioca flour
- ¼ cup brown rice flour
- 1/3 cup sorghum flour

Directions
1. With parchment paper, line an 8 x 8-inch baking pan and grease parchment paper. Preheat oven to 375°F.
2. Mix xanthan gum, salt, baking soda, baking powder, all flours, and starch in a large bowl.
3. Whisk well sugar and eggs in a medium bowl until creamed. Add vinegar, water, yogurt, and butter. Whisk thoroughly.

4. Pour in egg mixture into bowl of flours and mix well.
5. Transfer sticky dough into prepared pan and bake in the oven for 25 to 30 minutes.
6. If tops of bread start to brown a lot, cover top with foil and continue baking until done.
7. Remove from oven and pan right away and let it cool.
8. Best served when warm.

Nutrition: Calories: 166; Carbs: 27.8g; Protein: 3.4g; Fat: 4.8g

Spiced Breakfast Casserole

Servings: 6 | Cooking: 35 min

Ingredients
- 1 tablespoon nutritional yeast
- ¼ cup water
- 6 large eggs
- 1 teaspoon coriander
- 1 teaspoon cumin
- 8 kale leaves, stems removed and torn into small pieces
- 2 sausages, cooked and chopped
- 1 large sweet potato, peeled and chopped

Directions
1. Preheat the oven to 375°F.
2. Grease an 8" x 8" baking pan with olive oil and set aside.
3. Place sweet potatoes in a microwavable bowl and add ¼ cup water. Cook the chopped sweet potatoes in the microwave for three to five minutes. Drain the excess water then set aside.
4. Fry in a skillet heated over medium flame the sausage and cook until brown. Mix in the kale and cook until wilted.
5. Add the coriander, cumin and cooked sweet potatoes.
6. In another bowl, mix together the eggs, water and nutritional yeast. Add the vegetable and meat mixture into the bowl and mix completely.
7. Place the mixture in the baking dish and make sure that the mixture is evenly distributed within the pan.
8. Bake for 20 minutes or until the eggs are done.
9. Slice into squares.

Nutrition: Calories per serving: 137; Protein: 10.1g; Carbs: 10.0g; Fat: 6.6g

Italian Scrambled Eggs

Servings: 1 | Cooking: 7 min

Ingredients
- 1 teaspoon balsamic vinegar
- 2 large eggs
- ¼ teaspoon rosemary, minced
- ½ cup cherry tomatoes
- 1 ½ cup kale, chopped
- ½ teaspoon olive oil

Directions
1. Melt the olive oil in a skillet over medium high heat.
2. Sauté the kale and add rosemary and salt to taste. Add three tablespoons of water to prevent the kale from burning at the bottom of the pan. Cook for three to four minutes.
3. Add the tomatoes and stir.
4. Push the vegetables on one side of the skillet and add the eggs. Season with salt and pepper to taste.
5. Scramble the eggs then fold in the tomatoes and kales.

Nutrition: Calories per serving: 230; Protein: 16.4g; Carbs: 15.0g; Fat: 12.4g

Toasted Bagels

Servings: 6 | Cooking: 10 min

Ingredients
- 6 teaspoons butter
- 3 bagels, halved

Directions
1. Preheat the Airfryer to 375 degrees F and arrange the bagels into an Airfryer basket.
2. Cook for about 3 minutes and remove the bagels from Airfryer.
3. Spread butter evenly over bagels and cook for about 3 more minutes.

Nutrition: Calories: 169 Carbs: 26.5g Fats: 4.7g Proteins: 5.3g Sodium: 262mg Sugar: 2.7g

St Valentine's Mediterranean Pancakes

Servings: 2 | Cooking: 20 min

Ingredients
- 4 eggs, preferably organic

- 2 pieces banana, peeled and then cut into small pieces
- 1/2 teaspoon extra-virgin olive oil (for the pancake pan)
- 1 tablespoon milled flax seeds, preferably organic
- 1 tablespoon bee pollen, milled, preferably organic

Directions
1. Crack the eggs into a mixing bowl. Add in the banana, flax seeds, and bee pollen. With a hand mixer, blend the ingredients until smooth batter inn texture.
2. Put a few drops of the olive oil in a nonstick pancake pan over medium flame or heat. Pour some batter into the pan; cook for about 2 minutes, undisturbed until the bottom of the pancake is golden and can be lifted easily from the pan. With a silicon spatula, lift and flip the pancake; cook for about 30seconds more and transfer into a plate.
3. Repeat the process with the remaining batter, oiling the pan with every new batter.
4. Serve the pancake as you cook or serve them all together topped with vanilla, strawberry, pine nuts jam.

Nutrition: 272 cal.,11.6 g total fat (3 g sat. fat), 327 mg chol., 125 mg sodium, 633 mg pot., 32.7 g total carbs., 4.5 g fiber, 17.3 g sugar, 13.3 g protein, 10% vitamin A, 20% vitamin C, 6% calcium, and 12% iron

Sandwich With Hummus

Servings: 4 | Cooking: 0 min

Ingredients
- 4 cups alfalfa sprouts
- 1 cup cucumber sliced 1/8 inch thick
- 4 red onion sliced ¼-inch thick
- 8 tomatoes sliced ¼-inch thick
- 2 cups shredded Bibb lettuce
- 12 slices 1-oz whole wheat bread
- 1 can 15.5-oz chickpeas, drained
- 2 garlic cloves, peeled
- ¼ tsp salt
- ½ tsp ground cumin
- 1 tbsp tahini
- 1 tbsp lemon juice
- 2 tbsp water
- 3 tbsp plain fat free yogurt

Directions
1. In a food processor, blend chickpeas, garlic, salt, cumin, tahini, lemon juice, water and yogurt until smooth to create hummus.
2. On 1 slice of bread, spread 2 tbsp hummus, top with 1 onion slice, 2 tomato slices, ½ cup lettuce, another bread slice, 1 cup sprouts, ¼ cup cucumber and cover with another bread slice. Repeat procedure for the rest of the ingredients.

Nutrition: Calories: 407; Carbs: 67.7g; Protein: 18.8 g; Fat: 6.8g

Halibut Sandwiches Mediterranean Style

Servings: 4 | Cooking: 23 min

Ingredients
- 2 packed cups arugula or 2 oz.
- Grated zest of 1 large lemon
- 1 tbsp capers, drained and mashed
- 2 tbsp fresh flat leaf parsley, chopped
- ¼ cup fresh basil, chopped
- ¼ cup sun dried tomatoes, chopped
- ¼ cup reduced fat mayonnaise
- 1 garlic clove, halved
- 1 pc of 14 oz of ciabatta loaf bread with ends trimmed and split in half, horizontally
- 2 tbsp plus 1 tsp olive oil, divided
- Kosher salt and freshly ground pepper
- 2 pcs or 6 oz halibut fillets, skinned
- Cooking: spray

Directions
1. Heat oven to 450oF.
2. With cooking spray, coat a baking dish. Season halibut with a pinch of pepper and salt plus rub with a tsp of oil and place on baking dish. Then put in oven and bake until cooked or for ten to fifteen minutes. Remove from oven and let cool.
3. Get a slice of bread and coat with olive oil the sliced portions. Put in oven and cook until golden, around six to eight minutes. Remove from heat and rub garlic on the bread.
4. Combine the following in a medium bowl: lemon zest, capers, parsley, basil, sun dried tomatoes and mayonnaise. Then add the halibut, mashing with fork until flaked. Spread the mixture on one side of bread, add arugula and cover with the other bread half and serve.

Nutrition: Calories: 125; Carbs: 8.0g; Protein: 3.9g; Fat: 9.2g

Quinoa Pizza Muffins

Servings: 4 | Cooking: 30 min

Ingredients
- 1 cup uncooked quinoa
- 2 large eggs
- ½ medium onion, diced
- 1 cup diced bell pepper
- 1 cup shredded mozzarella cheese
- 1 tbsp dried basil
- 1 tbsp dried oregano
- 2 tsp garlic powder
- 1/8 tsp salt
- 1 tsp crushed red peppers
- ½ cup roasted red pepper, chopped*
- Pizza Sauce, about 1-2 cups

Directions
1. Preheat oven to 350oF.
2. Cook quinoa according to directions.
3. Combine all ingredients (except sauce) into bowl. Mix all ingredients well.
4. Scoop quinoa pizza mixture into muffin tin evenly. Makes 12 muffins.
5. Bake for 30 minutes until muffins turn golden in color and the edges are getting crispy.
6. Top with 1 or 2 tbsp pizza sauce and enjoy!

Nutrition: Calories: 303; Carbs: 41.3g; Protein: 21.0g; Fat: 6.1g

Pumpkin Pancakes

Servings: 8 | Cooking: 20 min

Ingredients
- 2 squares puff pastry
- 6 tablespoons pumpkin filling
- 2 small eggs, beaten
- ¼ teaspoon cinnamon

Directions
1. Preheat the Airfryer to 360 degrees F and roll out a square of puff pastry.
2. Layer it with pumpkin pie filling, leaving about ¼-inch space around the edges.
3. Cut it up into equal sized square pieces and cover the gaps with beaten egg.
4. Arrange the squares into a baking dish and cook for about 12 minutes.
5. Sprinkle some cinnamon and serve.

Nutrition: Calories: 51 Carbs: 5g Fats: 2.5g Proteins: 2.4g Sodium: 48mg Sugar: 0.5g

Breakfast Egg On Avocado

Servings: 6 | Cooking: 15 min

Ingredients
- 1 tsp garlic powder
- 1/2 tsp sea salt
- 1/4 cup Parmesan cheese (grated or shredded)
- 1/4 tsp black pepper
- 3 medium avocados (cut in half, pitted, skin on)
- 6 medium eggs

Directions
1. Prepare muffin tins and preheat the oven to 350oF.
2. To ensure that the egg would fit inside the cavity of the avocado, lightly scrape off 1/3 of the meat.
3. Place avocado on muffin tin to ensure that it faces with the top up.
4. Evenly season each avocado with pepper, salt, and garlic powder.
5. Add one egg on each avocado cavity and garnish tops with cheese.
6. Pop in the oven and bake until the egg white is set, about 15 minutes.
7. Serve and enjoy.

Nutrition: Calories per serving: 252; Protein: 14.0g; Carbs: 4.0g; Fat: 20.0g

Breakfast Egg-artichoke Casserole

Servings: 8 | Cooking: 35 min

Ingredients
- 16 large eggs
- 14 ounce can artichoke hearts, drained
- 10-ounce box frozen chopped spinach, thawed and drained well
- 1 cup shredded white cheddar
- 1 garlic clove, minced
- 1 teaspoon salt
- 1/2 cup parmesan cheese
- 1/2 cup ricotta cheese
- 1/2 teaspoon dried thyme
- 1/2 teaspoon crushed red pepper
- 1/4 cup milk
- 1/4 cup shaved onion

Directions
1. Lightly grease a 9x13-inch baking dish with cooking spray and preheat the oven to 350oF.
2. In a large mixing bowl, add eggs and milk. Mix thoroughly.

3. With a paper towel, squeeze out the excess moisture from the spinach leaves and add to the bowl of eggs.
4. Into small pieces, break the artichoke hearts and separate the leaves. Add to the bowl of eggs.
5. Except for the ricotta cheese, add remaining ingredients in the bowl of eggs and mix thoroughly.
6. Pour egg mixture into the prepared dish.
7. Evenly add dollops of ricotta cheese on top of the eggs and then pop in the oven.
8. Bake until eggs are set and doesn't jiggle when shook, about 35 minutes.
9. Remove from the oven and evenly divide into suggested servings. Enjoy.

Nutrition: Calories per serving: 302; Protein: 22.6g; Carbs: 10.8g; Fat: 18.7g

Garlic & Tomato Gluten Free Focaccia

Preparation: 6 min | Cooking: 19 min | Servings: 8

Ingredients
- 1 egg
- ½ tsp lemon juice
- 1 tbsp. honey
- 4 tbsp. olive oil
- A pinch of sugar
- 1 ¼ cup warm water
- 1 tbsp. active dry yeast
- 2 tsp rosemary, chopped
- 2 tsp thyme, chopped
- 2 tsp basil, chopped
- 2 cloves garlic, minced
- 1 ¼ tsp sea salt
- 2 tsp xanthan gum
- ½ cup millet flour
- 1 cup potato starch, not flour
- 1 cup sorghum flour
- Gluten free cornmeal for dusting

Directions
1. For 5 min, turn on the oven and then turn it off, while keeping oven door closed. Dissolve warm water and pinch of sugar. Add yeast and swirl gently. Leave for 7 min.
2. In a large mixing bowl, whisk well herbs, garlic, salt, xanthan gum, starch, and flours. Once yeast is done proofing, pour into bowl of flours. Whisk in egg, lemon juice, honey, and olive oil.
3. Mix thoroughly and place in a well-greased square pan, dusted with cornmeal. Top with fresh garlic, more herbs, and sliced tomatoes. Place in the warmed oven and let it rise for half an h.
4. Turn on oven to 375F and after preheating time it for 20 min. Focaccia is done once tops are lightly browned. Remove from oven and pan immediately and let it cool. Best served when warm.

Nutrition: Calories: 251; Protein: 5.4g; Fat: 9.0g

Halibut Sandwiches Mediterranean Style

Preparation: 9 min | Cooking: 23 min | Servings: 4

Ingredients
- 2 packed cups arugula
- 2 oz. Grated zest of 1 large lemon
- 1 tbsp. capers, drained and mashed
- 2 tbsp. fresh flat leaf parsley, chopped
- ¼ cup fresh basil, chopped
- ¼ cup sun dried tomatoes, chopped
- ¼ cup reduced fat; mayonnaise
- 1 garlic clove, halved
- 1 pc of 14 oz. of ciabatta loaf bread with ends trimmed and split in half, horizontally
- 2 tbsp. plus 1 tsp olive oil, divided
- Kosher salt and freshly ground pepper
- 2 pcs or 6 oz. halibut fillets, skinned
- Cooking spray

Directions
1. Heat oven to 450oF. With cooking spray, coat a baking dish. Season halibut with a pinch of pepper and salt plus rub with a tsp of oil and place on baking dish. Then put in oven and bake until cooked or for ten to fifteen min.
2. Remove from oven and let cool. Get a slice of bread and coat with olive oil the sliced portions. Put in oven and cook until golden, around six to eight min. Remove from heat and rub garlic on the bread.
3. Combine the following in a medium bowl: lemon zest, capers, parsley, basil, sun dried tomatoes and mayonnaise. Then add the halibut, mashing with fork until flaked. Brush the mix on one side of bread, add arugula and cover with the other bread half and serve.

Nutrition: Calories: 125; Protein: 3.9g; Fat: 9.2g

Rosemary-Walnut Loaf Bread

Preparation: 9 min | Cooking: 47 min | Servings: 8

Ingredients
- ½ cup chopped walnuts
- 4 tbsp. fresh, chopped rosemary
- 1 1/3 cups lukewarm carbonated water
- 1 tbsp. honey
- ½ cup extra virgin olive oil
- 1 tsp apple cider vinegar
- 3 eggs
- 5 tsp instant dry yeast granules
- 1 tsp salt
- 1 tbsp. xanthan gum
- ¼ cup buttermilk powder
- 1 cup white rice flour
- 1 cup tapioca starch
- 1 cup arrowroot starch
- 1 ¼ cups all-purpose Bob's Red Mill gluten-free flour mix

Directions
1. In a large mixing bowl, whisk well eggs. Add 1 cup warm water, honey, olive oil, and vinegar. While beating continuously, stir in the rest of the ingredients except for rosemary and walnuts. Continue beating. Dough should be shaggy and thick.
2. Then add rosemary and walnuts continue kneading until evenly distributed. Cover bowl of dough with a clean towel, place in a warm spot, and let it rise for 30 min. Fifteen min into rising time, preheat oven to 400F.
3. Generously grease with olive oil a 2-quart Dutch oven and preheat inside oven without the lid. Once dough is done rising, remove pot from oven, and place dough inside. With a wet spatula, spread top of dough evenly in pot.
4. Brush tops of bread with 2 tbsp. of olive oil, cover Dutch oven and bake for 35 to 45 min. Once bread is done, remove from oven. And gently remove bread from pot. Allow bread to cool at least ten min before slicing. Serve and enjoy.

Nutrition: Calories: 424; Protein: 7.0g; Fat: 19.0g

Italian Flat Bread Gluten Free

Preparation: 6 min | Cooking: 31 min | Servings: 8

Ingredients
- 1 tbsp. apple cider
- 2 tbsp. water
- ½ cup yogurt
- 2 tbsp. butter
- 2 tbsp. sugar
- 2 eggs
- 1 tsp xanthan gum
- ½ tsp salt
- 1 tsp baking soda
- 1 ½ tsp baking powder
- ½ cup potato starch, not potato flour
- ½ cup tapioca flour
- ¼ cup brown rice flour
- 1/3 cup sorghum flour

Directions
1. With parchment paper, line an 8 x 8-inch baking pan and grease parchment paper. Preheat oven to 375F. Mix xanthan gum, salt, baking soda, baking powder, all flours, and starch in a large bowl.
2. Whisk well sugar and eggs in a medium bowl until creamed. Add vinegar, water, yogurt, and butter. Whisk thoroughly. Pour in egg mixture into bowl of flours and mix well. Transfer sticky dough into prepared pan and bake in the oven for 25 to 30 min.
3. If tops of bread start to brown a lot, cover top with foil and continue baking until done. Remove from oven and pan right away and let it cool. Best served when warm.

Nutrition: Calories: 166; Protein: 3.4g; Fat: 4.8g

Chapter 2: Lunch & Dinner Recipes

Mediterranean Flank Steak

Servings: 4 | Cooking: 40 min

Ingredients
- 4 flank steaks
- 1 lemon, juiced
- 1 orange, juiced
- 4 garlic cloves, chopped
- 1 teaspoon Dijon mustard
- 1 teaspoon chopped thyme
- 1 teaspoon dried sage
- 2 tablespoons olive oil
- Salt and pepper to taste

Directions
1. Combine the flank steaks and the rest of the ingredients in a zip lock bag.
2. Refrigerate for 30 minutes.
3. Heat a grill pan over medium flame and place the steaks on the grill.
4. Cook on each side for 6-7 minutes.
5. Serve the steaks warm and fresh.

Nutrition: Calories:234 Fat:13.4g Protein:21.6g Carbohydrates:6.7g

Spiced Grilled Flank Steak

Servings: 4 | Cooking: 40 min

Ingredients
- 4 flank steaks
- 1 teaspoon chili powder
- 1 teaspoon ground coriander
- 1 teaspoon ground cumin
- 1 teaspoon mustard powder
- Salt and pepper to taste

Directions
1. Season the steaks with salt and pepper then sprinkle with chili, coriander, cumin and mustard powder.
2. Allow to rest for 20 minutes then heat a grill pan over medium flame and place the steaks on the grill.
3. Cook on each side for 5-7 minutes and serve the steaks warm and fresh.

Nutrition: Calories:202 Fat:8.8g Protein:28.2g Carbohydrates:0.9g

Pan Roasted Chicken With Olives And Lemon

Servings: 4 | Cooking: 50 min

Ingredients
- 4 chicken legs
- Salt and pepper to taste
- 3 tablespoons olive oil
- 1 lemon, juiced
- 1 orange, juiced
- 1 jalapeno, sliced
- 2 garlic cloves, chopped
- ½ cup green olives, sliced
- ¼ cup black olives, pitted and sliced
- 1 thyme sprig
- 1 rosemary sprig

Directions
1. Season the chicken with salt and pepper.
2. Heat the oil in a skillet and add the chicken.
3. Cook on each side for 5 minutes until golden brown then add the rest of the ingredients and continue cooking on medium heat for 15 minutes.
4. Serve the chicken and the sauce warm.

Nutrition: Calories:319 Fat:18.9g Protein:29.7g Carbohydrates:8.0g

Creamy Salmon Soup

Servings: 6 | Cooking: 15 min

Ingredients
- 2 tablespoon olive oil
- 1 red onion, chopped
- Salt and white pepper to the taste
- 3 gold potatoes, peeled and cubed
- 2 carrots, chopped
- 4 cups fish stock
- 4 ounces salmon fillets, boneless and cubed
- ½ cup heavy cream
- 1 tablespoon dill, chopped

Directions
1. Heat up a pan with the oil over medium heat, add the onion, and sauté for 5 minutes.
2. Add the rest of the ingredients expect the cream, salmon and the dill, bring to a simmer and cook for 5-6 minutes more.
3. Add the salmon, cream and the dill, simmer for 5 minutes more, divide into bowls and serve.

Nutrition: calories 214; fat 16.3; fiber 1.5; carbs 6.4; protein 11.8

Grilled Salmon With Cucumber Dill Sauce

Servings: 4 | Cooking: 40 min

Ingredients
- 4 salmon fillets
- 1 teaspoon smoked paprika
- 1 teaspoon dried sage
- Salt and pepper to taste
- 4 cucumbers, sliced
- 2 tablespoons chopped dill
- ½ cup Greek yogurt
- 1 tablespoon lemon juice
- 1 tablespoon olive oil

Directions
1. Season the salmon with salt, pepper, paprika and sage.
2. Heat a grill pan over medium flame and place the salmon on the grill.
3. Cook on each side for 4 minutes.
4. For the sauce, mix the cucumbers, dill, yogurt, lemon juice and oil in a bowl. Add salt and pepper and mix well.
5. Serve the salmon with the cucumber sauce.

Nutrition: Calories:224 Fat:10.3g Protein:26.3g Carbohydrates:8.9g

Grilled Basil-lemon Tofu Burgers

Servings: 6 | Cooking: 6 min

Ingredients
- 6 slices (1/4-inch thick each) tomato
- 6 pieces (1 1/2-ounce) whole-wheat hamburger buns
- 1 pound tofu, firm or extra-firm, drained
- 1 cup watercress, trimmed
- Cooking: spray
- 1/3 cup fresh basil, finely chopped
- 2 tablespoons Dijon mustard
- 2 tablespoons honey
- 1/4 cup freshly squeezed lemon juice
- 2 teaspoons grated lemon rind
- 1 tablespoon olive oil, extra-virgin,
- 1/2 teaspoon salt
- 1/4 teaspoon black pepper (freshly ground)
- 3 garlic cloves, minced
- 1 garlic cloves, minced
- 1/3 cup Kalamata olives, finely, chopped pitted
- 3 tablespoons sour cream, reduced-fat
- 3 tablespoons light mayonnaise

Directions
1. Combine the marinade ingredients in a small-sized bowl. In a crosswise direction, cut the tofu into 6 slices. Pat each piece dry using paper towels. Place them in a jelly roll pan and brush both sides of the slices with the marinade mixture; reserve any leftover marinade. Marinate for 1 hour.
2. Preheat the grill and coated the grill rack with cooking spray. Place the tofu slices; grill for about 3 minutes per side, brushing the tofu with the reserved marinade mixture.
3. In a small-sized bowl, combine the garlic-olive mayonnaise ingredients. Spread about 1 1/2 tablespoons of the mixture over the bottom half of the hamburger buns. Top each with 1 slice tofu, 1 slice tomato, about 2 tablespoons of watercress, and top with the top buns.

Nutrition: 276 Cal, 11.3 g total fat (1.9 g sat. fat, 5.7 g mono fat, 2.2 g poly fat), 10.5 g protein, 34.5 g carb., 1.5 g fiber, 5 mg chol., 2.4 mg iron, 743 mg sodium, and 101 mg calcium.

Creamy Green Pea Pasta

Servings: 4 | Cooking: 25 min

Ingredients
- 8 oz. whole wheat spaghetti
- 1 cup green peas
- 1 avocado, peeled and cubed
- 2 tablespoons olive oil
- 2 garlic cloves, chopped
- 2 mint leaves
- 1 tablespoon lemon juice
- ¼ cup heavy cream
- 2 tablespoons vegetable stock
- Salt and pepper to taste

Directions
1. Pour a few cups of water in a deep pot and bring to a boil with a pinch of salt.
2. Add the spaghetti and cook for 8 minutes then drain well.
3. For the sauce, combine the remaining ingredients in a blender and pulse until smooth.

4. Mix the cooked the spaghetti with the sauce and serve the pasta fresh.

Nutrition: Calories:294 Fat:20.1g Protein:6.4g Carbohydrates:25.9g

Meat Cakes

Servings: 4 | Cooking: 10 min

Ingredients
- 1 cup broccoli, shredded
- ½ cup ground pork
- 2 eggs, beaten
- 1 teaspoon salt
- 1 tablespoon Italian seasonings
- 1 teaspoon olive oil
- 3 tablespoons wheat flour, whole grain
- 1 tablespoon dried dill

Directions
1. In the mixing bowl combine together shredded broccoli and ground pork,
2. Add salt, Italian seasoning, flour, and dried dill.
3. Mix up the mixture until homogenous.
4. Then add eggs and stir until smooth.
5. Heat up olive oil in the skillet.
6. With the help of the spoon make latkes and place them in the hot oil.
7. Roast the latkes for 4 minutes from each side over the medium heat.
8. The cooked latkes should have a light brown crust.
9. Dry the latkes with the paper towels if needed.

Nutrition: calories 143; fat 6; fiber 0.9; carbs 7; protein 15.1

Herbed Roasted Cod

Servings: 4 | Cooking: 45 min

Ingredients
- 4 cod fillets
- 4 parsley sprigs
- 2 cilantro sprigs
- 2 basil sprigs
- 1 lemon, sliced
- Salt and pepper to taste
- 2 tablespoons olive oil

Directions
1. Season the cod with salt and pepper.
2. Place the parsley, cilantro, basil and lemon slices at the bottom of a deep dish baking pan.
3. Place the cod over the herbs and cook in the preheated oven at 350F for 15 minutes.
4. Serve the cod warm and fresh with your favorite side dish.

Nutrition: Calories:192 Fat:8.1g Protein:28.6g Carbohydrates:0.1g

Mushroom Soup

Servings: 2 | Cooking: 20 min

Ingredients
- 1 cup cremini mushrooms, chopped
- 1 cup Cheddar cheese, shredded
- 2 cups of water
- ½ teaspoon salt
- 1 teaspoon dried thyme
- ½ teaspoon dried oregano
- 1 tablespoon fresh parsley, chopped
- 1 tablespoon olive oil
- 1 bell pepper, chopped

Directions
1. Pour olive oil in the pan.
2. Add mushrooms and bell pepper. Roast the vegetables for 5 minutes over the medium heat.
3. Then sprinkle them with salt, thyme, and dried oregano.
4. Add parsley and water. Stir the soup well.
5. Cook the soup for 10 minutes.
6. After this, blend the soup until it is smooth and simmer it for 5 minutes more.
7. Add cheese and stir until cheese is melted.
8. Ladle the cooked soup into the bowls. It is recommended to serve soup hot.

Nutrition: calories 320; fat 26; fiber 1.4; carbs 7.4; protein 15.7

Salmon Parmesan Gratin

Servings: 4 | Cooking: 45 min

Ingredients
- 4 salmon fillets, cubed
- 2 garlic cloves, chopped
- 1 fennel bulb, sliced
- ½ teaspoon ground coriander
- ½ teaspoon Dijon mustard
- ½ cup vegetable stock
- 1 cup heavy cream

- 2 eggs
- Salt and pepper to taste
- 1 cup grated Parmesan cheese

Directions
1. Combine the salmon, garlic, fennel, coriander and mustard in a small deep dish baking pan.
2. Mix the eggs with cream and stock and pour the mixture over the fish.
3. Top with Parmesan cheese and bake in the preheated oven at 350F for 25 minutes.
4. Serve the gratin right away.

Nutrition: Calories:414 Fat:25.9g Protein:41.0g Carbohydrates:6.1g

Sweet And Sour Chicken Fillets

Servings: 4 | Cooking: 40 min

Ingredients
- 4 chicken fillets
- 3 tablespoons olive oil
- 1 red pepper, sliced
- 1 lemon, juiced
- 1 tablespoon honey
- Salt and pepper to taste
- Chopped parsley for serving

Directions
1. Season the chicken with salt and pepper.
2. Heat the oil in a skillet and add the chicken.
3. Cook on each side for 10 minutes.
4. Add the red pepper, lemon juice and honey and cook just for 1 additional minute.
5. Serve the chicken and the sauce warm and fresh.

Nutrition: Calories:309 Fat:18.0g Protein:29.4g Carbohydrates:7.5g

Salt Crusted Salmon

Servings: 6 | Cooking: 40 min

Ingredients
- 1 whole salmon (3 pounds)
- 3 cups salt
- ½ cup chopped parsley
- 3 tablespoons olive oil

Directions
1. Spread a very thin layer of salt in a baking tray.
2. Place the salmon over the salt and top with parsley. Drizzle with oil then top with the rest of the salt.
3. Cook in the preheated oven at 350F for 30 minutes.
4. Serve the salmon warm.

Nutrition: Calories:362 Fat:21.0g Protein:44.1g Carbohydrates:0.3g

Sun-dried Tomato Pesto Penne

Servings: 4 | Cooking: 20 min

Ingredients
- 8 oz. penne
- ½ cup sun-dried tomatoes, drained well
- 2 tablespoons olive oil
- 4 garlic cloves, minced
- 2 tablespoons lemon juice
- 2 tablespoons pine nuts
- 2 tablespoons grated Parmesan cheese
- 1 pinch chili flakes

Directions
1. Cook the penne in a large pot of salty water for 8 minutes or as long as it says on the package, just until al dente.
2. Drain the penne well.
3. For the pesto, combine the remaining ingredients in a blender and pulse until well mixed and smooth.
4. Mix the pesto with the penne and serve right away.

Nutrition: Calories:308 Fat:14.4g Protein:11.9g Carbohydrates:34.1g

Herbed Marinated Sardines

Servings: 4 | Cooking: 50 min

Ingredients
- 8 sardines
- ½ cup chopped parsley
- 2 tablespoons chopped cilantro
- 2 tablespoons pesto sauce
- 2 tablespoons olive oil
- 2 garlic cloves
- Salt and pepper to taste
- 2 tablespoons lemon juice

Directions
1. Combine the herbs, pesto, oil, garlic, salt and pepper in a blender and pulse until smooth.
2. Spread the herb mixture over the sardines and season with salt and pepper.
3. Place the sardines in the fridge for 30 minutes.
4. Heat a grill pan over medium flame and place the sardines on the grill.
5. Cook on each side for 5-7 minutes.
6. Serve the sardines warm and fresh with your favorite side dish.

Nutrition: Calories:201 Fat:15.9g Protein:13.0g Carbohydrates:1.7g

Spicy Tomato Poached Eggs

Servings: 4 | Cooking: 30 min

Ingredients
- 2 tablespoons olive oil
- 2 shallots, chopped
- 2 garlic cloves, chopped
- 2 red bell peppers, cored and sliced
- 2 yellow bell peppers, cored and sliced
- 2 tomatoes, peeled and diced
- 1 cup vegetable stock
- 1 jalapeno, chopped
- Salt and pepper to taste
- 4 eggs

Directions
1. Heat the oil in a saucepan and stir in the shallots, garlic, bell peppers and jalapeno. Cook for 5 minutes.
2. Add the tomatoes, stock, thyme and bay leaf, as well as salt and pepper to taste.
3. Cook for 10 minutes on low heat.
4. Crack open the eggs and drop them in the hot sauce.
5. Cook on low heat for 5 additional minutes.
6. Serve the eggs and the sauce fresh and warm.

Nutrition: Calories:179 Fat:11.9g Protein:7.6g Carbohydrates:11.7g

Mediterranean Scones

Servings: 8 | Cooking: 15-20 min

Ingredients
- 1 egg, beaten, to glaze
- 1 tablespoon baking powder
- 1 tablespoon olive oil
- 1/4 tsp salt
- 10 black olives, pitted, halved
- 100 g feta cheese, cubed
- 300 ml full-fat milk
- 350 g self-rising whole-wheat flour
- 50 g butter, cut in pieces
- 8 halves Italian sundried tomatoes, coarsely chopped

Directions
1. Preheat the oven to 220C, gas to 7, or fan to 200C.
2. Grease a large-sized baking sheet with butter.
3. In a large mixing bowl, mix the flour, the baking powder, and the salt. Rub in the oil and the butter, until the flour mix resembles fine crumbs. Add the cheese, tomatoes, and the olives.
4. Create a well in the center of the flour mix, pour the milk, and with a knife, mix using cutting movements, until the flour mixture is a stickyish, soft dough. Make sure that you do not over mix the dough.
5. Flour the work surface and your hands well; shape the dough into 3 to 4-cm think round. Cut into 8 wedges; place the wedges well apart in the prepared baking sheet. Brush the wedges with the beaten egg; bake for about 15-20 minutes, until the dough has risen, golden, and springy.
6. Transfer into a wire rack; cover with a clean tea towel to keep them soft.
7. Serve warm and buttered.
8. Store in airtight container for up to 2 to 3 days.

Nutrition: 293 Cal, 14 g total fat (7 g sat. fat), 36 g carb.,0 g sugar, 2 g fiber, 8 g protein, and 2 g sodium.

Mixed Olives Braised Chicken

Servings: 4 | Cooking: 1 Hour

Ingredients
- 4 chicken breasts
- 2 shallots, sliced
- 4 garlic cloves, chopped
- 2 red bell peppers, cored and sliced
- ½ cup black olives
- ½ cup green olives
- ½ cup kalamata olives
- 2 tablespoons olive oil
- ¼ cup white wine
- ½ cup vegetable stock
- Salt and pepper to taste

- 1 bay leaf
- 1 thyme sprig

Directions
1. Combine the shallots, garlic, bell peppers, olives, oil, wine and stock in a deep dish baking pan.
2. Season with salt and pepper and place the chicken in the pan over the olives.
3. Cook in the preheated oven at 350F for 45 minutes.
4. Serve the chicken warm and fresh.

Nutrition: Calories:280 Fat:16.3g Protein:22.9g Carbohydrates:7.9g

Coconut Chicken Meatballs

Servings: 4 | Cooking: 10 min

Ingredients
- 2 cups ground chicken
- 1 teaspoon minced garlic
- 1 teaspoon dried dill
- 1/3 carrot, grated
- 1 egg, beaten
- 1 tablespoon olive oil
- ¼ cup coconut flakes
- ½ teaspoon salt

Directions
1. In the mixing bowl mix up together ground chicken, minced garlic, dried dill, carrot, egg, and salt.
2. Stir the chicken mixture with the help of the fingertips until homogenous.
3. Then make medium balls from the mixture.
4. Coat every chicken ball in coconut flakes.
5. Heat up olive oil in the skillet.
6. Add chicken balls and cook them for 3 minutes from each side. The cooked chicken balls will have a golden brown color.

Nutrition: calories 200; fat 11.5; fiber 0.6; carbs 1.7; protein 21.9

Grilled Turkey With White Bean Mash

Servings: 4 | Cooking: 45 min

Ingredients
- 4 turkey breast fillets
- 1 teaspoon chili powder
- 1 teaspoon dried parsley
- Salt and pepper to taste
- 2 cans white beans, drained
- 4 garlic cloves, minced
- 2 tablespoons lemon juice
- 3 tablespoons olive oil
- 2 sweet onions, sliced
- 2 tablespoons tomato paste

Directions
1. Season the turkey with salt, pepper and dried parsley.
2. Heat a grill pan over medium flame and place the turkey on the grill. Cook on each side for 7 minutes.
3. For the mash, combine the beans, garlic, lemon juice, salt and pepper in a blender and pulse until well mixed and smooth.
4. Heat the oil in a skillet and add the onions. Cook for 10 minutes until caramelized. Add the tomato paste and cook for 2 more minutes.
5. Serve the grilled turkey with bean mash and caramelized onions.

Nutrition: Calories:337 Fat:8.2g Protein:21.1g Carbohydrates:47.2g

Vegetable Turkey Casserole

Servings: 8 | Cooking: 1 ¼ Hours

Ingredients
- 3 tablespoons olive oil
- 2 pounds turkey breasts, cubed
- 1 sweet onion, chopped
- 3 carrots, sliced
- 2 celery stalks, sliced
- 2 garlic cloves, chopped
- ½ teaspoon cumin powder
- ½ teaspoon dried thyme
- 2 cans diced tomatoes
- 1 cup chicken stock
- 1 bay leaf
- Salt and pepper to taste

Directions
1. Heat the oil in a deep heavy pot and stir in the turkey.
2. Cook for 5 minutes until golden on all sides then add the onion, carrot, celery and garlic. Cook for 5 more minutes then add the rest of the ingredients.
3. Season with salt and pepper and cook in the preheated oven at 350F for 40 minutes.

4. Serve the casserole warm and fresh.

Nutrition: Calories:186 Fat:7.3g Protein:20.1g Carbohydrates:9.9g

Mediterranean Grilled Pork With Tomato Salsa

Servings: 4 | Cooking: 1 Hour

Ingredients
- 4 pork chops
- 1 teaspoon dried oregano
- 1 teaspoon dried basil
- 1 teaspoon dried marjoram
- Salt and pepper to taste
- 4 tomatoes, peeled and diced
- 1 jalapeno, chopped
- 1 shallot, chopped
- 2 garlic cloves, minced
- 1 green onion, chopped
- 2 tablespoons chopped parsley
- 1 tablespoon lemon juice

Directions
1. Season with salt and pepper, oregano, basil and marjoram.
2. Heat a grill pan over medium flame and place the pork chops on the grill.
3. Cook on each side for 5-6 minutes.
4. For the salsa, mix the tomatoes, jalapeno, shallot, garlic, onion and parsley. Add salt and pepper to taste. Add the lemon juice as well.
5. Serve the pork chops with salsa.

Nutrition: Calories:286 Fat:20.3g Protein:19.4g Carbohydrates:6.3g

Beef And Macaroni Soup

Servings: 6 | Cooking: 30 min

Ingredients
- ½ cup elbow macaroni
- 1 teaspoon coconut oil
- 1/3 teaspoon minced garlic
- 2 oz yellow onion, diced
- 1 ½ cup ground beef
- ½ teaspoon dried oregano
- ½ teaspoon dried thyme
- 1 teaspoon salt
- 1 teaspoon chili flakes
- 3 oz Mozzarella, shredded
- 1 teaspoon dried basil
- 5 cups beef broth
- 1 tablespoon cream cheese
- 1 cup water, for cooking macaroni

Directions
1. Pour water in the pan and bring it to boil.
2. Add elbow macaroni and cook them according to the manufacturer directions.
3. Then drain water from the cooked elbow macaroni.
4. Put coconut oil in the big pot and melt it.
5. Add minced garlic, yellow onion, ground beef, dried oregano, dried thyme, salt, chili flakes, and dried basil.
6. Cook the ingredients for 10 minutes over the medium-low heat. Stir the mixture from time to time.
7. Add beef broth and cream cheese. Stir the soup until it is homogenous.
8. Cook the soup for 10 minutes.
9. Then add cooked elbow macaroni and stir well.
10. Bring the soup to boil and remove from the heat.
11. Ladle the cooked soup in the serving bowls and garnish with Mozzarella.

Nutrition: calories 180; fat 9.2; fiber 0.5; carbs 7.6; protein 15.7

Provencal Beef Stew

Servings: 8 | Cooking: 1 ½ Hours

Ingredients
- 3 tablespoons olive oil
- 2 pounds beef roast, cubed
- 2 sweet onions, chopped
- 4 garlic cloves, chopped
- 2 carrots, diced
- 2 celery stalks, diced
- 1 can diced tomatoes
- 2 tomatoes, peeled and diced
- 1 cup vegetable stock
- 1 jalapeno, chopped
- 1 bay leaf
- 1 thyme sprig
- Salt and pepper to taste

Directions
1. Heat the oil in a skillet and stir in the beef. Cook for 10 minutes on all sides.

2. Add the onions and garlic and cook for 5 more minutes.
3. Stir in the remaining ingredients and season with salt and pepper.
4. Place a lid on and cook on low heat for 1 hour.
5. Serve the stew warm and fresh.

Nutrition: Calories:284 Fat:12.5g Protein:35.4g Carbohydrates:6.5g

Greek Beef Meatballs

Servings: 8 | Cooking: 1 Hour

Ingredients
- 2 pounds ground beef
- 6 garlic cloves, minced
- 1 teaspoon dried mint
- 1 teaspoon dried oregano
- 1 shallot, finely chopped
- 1 carrot, grated
- 1 egg
- 1 tablespoon tomato paste
- 3 tablespoons chopped parsley
- Salt and pepper to taste

Directions
1. Combine all the ingredients in a bowl and mix well.
2. Season with salt and pepper then form small meatballs and place them in a baking tray lined with baking paper.
3. Bake in the preheated oven at 350F for 25 minutes.
4. Serve the meatballs warm and fresh.

Nutrition: Calories:229 Fat:7.7g Protein:35.5g Carbohydrates:2.4g

Sausage and Beans Soup

Servings: 4 | Cooking: 20 min

Ingredients
- 1 pound Italian pork sausage, sliced
- ¼ cup olive oil
- 1 carrot, chopped
- 1 yellow onion, chopped
- 1 celery stalk, chopped
- 2 garlic cloves, minced
- ½ pound kale, chopped
- 4 cups chicken stock
- 28 ounces canned cannellini beans, drained and rinsed
- 1 bay leaf
- 1 teaspoon rosemary, dried
- Salt and black pepper to the taste
- ½ cup parmesan, grated

Directions
1. Heat up a pot with the oil over medium heat, add the sausage and brown for 5 minutes.
2. Add the onion, carrots, garlic and celery and sauté for 3 minutes more.
3. Add the rest of the ingredients except the parmesan, bring to a simmer and cook over medium heat for 30 minutes.
4. Discard the bay leaf, ladle the soup into bowls, sprinkle the parmesan on top and serve.

Nutrition: calories 564; fat 26.5; fiber 15.4; carbs 37.4; protein 26.6

Jalapeno Grilled Salmon With Tomato Confit

Servings: 4 | Cooking: 30 min

Ingredients
- 4 salmon fillets
- 1 jalapeno
- 4 garlic cloves
- 2 tablespoons tomato paste
- 2 tablespoons olive oil
- Salt and pepper to taste
- 2 cups cherry tomatoes, halved
- 1 shallot, chopped
- 1 tablespoon olive oil

Directions
1. Combine the jalapeno, garlic, tomato paste and oil in a mortar. Mix well until a smooth paste is formed.
2. Spread the spicy paste over the salmon and season it with salt and pepper.
3. Heat a grill pan over medium flame then place the fish on the grill.
4. Cook on each side for 5-6 minutes.
5. For the confit, heat 1 tablespoon of oil in a skillet. Add the shallot and cook for 1 minute then stir in the cherry tomatoes, salt and pepper. Cook for 2 minutes on high heat.
6. Serve the grilled salmon with the tomatoes.

Nutrition: Calories:237 Fat:14.5g Protein:24.0g Carbohydrates:4.4g

Chicken And Rice Soup

Servings: 4 | Cooking: 35 min

Ingredients

- 6 cups chicken stock
- 1 and ½ cups chicken meat, cooked and shredded
- 1 bay leaf
- 1 yellow onion, chopped
- 2 tablespoons olive oil
- 1/3 cup white rice
- 1 egg, whisked
- Juice of ½ lemon
- 1 cup asparagus, trimmed and halved
- 1 cup carrots, chopped
- ½ cup dill, chopped
- Salt and black pepper to the taste

Directions

1. Heat up a pot with the oil over medium heat, add the onions and sauté for 5 minutes.
2. Add the stock, dill, the rice and the bay leaf, stir, bring to a boil over medium heat and cook for 10 minutes.
3. Add the rest of the ingredients except the egg and the lemon juice, stir and cook for 15 minutes more.
4. Add the egg whisked with the lemon juice gradually, whisk the soup, cook for 2 minutes more, divide into bowls an serve.

Nutrition: calories 263; fat 18.5; fiber 4.5; carbs 19.8; protein 14.5

Spicy Salsa Braised Beef Ribs

Servings: 12 | Cooking: 4 Hours

Ingredients

- 6 pounds beef ribs
- 4 tomatoes, diced
- 2 jalapenos, chopped
- 2 shallots, chopped
- 1 cup chopped parsley
- ½ cup chopped cilantro
- 3 tablespoons olive oil
- 2 tablespoons balsamic vinegar
- 1 teaspoon Worcestershire sauce
- Salt and pepper to taste

Directions

1. Combine the tomatoes, jalapenos, shallots, parsley, cilantro, oil, vinegar, sauce, salt and pepper in a deep dish baking pan.
2. Place the ribs in the pan and cover with aluminum foil.
3. Cook in the preheated oven at 300F for 3 1/3 hours.
4. Serve the ribs warm.

Nutrition: Calories:464 Fat:17.8g Protein:69.4g Carbohydrates:2.5g

Pork and Prunes Stew

Servings: 8 | Cooking: 1 ¼ Hours

Ingredients

- 2 pounds pork tenderloin, cubed
- 2 tablespoons olive oil
- 1 sweet onions, chopped
- 4 garlic cloves, chopped
- 2 carrots, diced
- 2 celery stalks, chopped
- 2 tomatoes, peeled and diced
- 1 cup vegetable stock
- ½ cup white wine
- 1 pound prunes, pitted
- 1 bay leaf
- 1 thyme sprig
- 1 teaspoon mustard seeds
- 1 teaspoon coriander seeds
- Salt and pepper to taste

Directions

1. Combine all the ingredients in a deep dish baking pan.
2. Add salt and pepper to taste and cook in the preheated oven at 350F for 1 hour, adding more liquid as it cooks if needed.
3. Serve the stew warm and fresh.

Nutrition: Calories:363 Fat:7.9g Protein:31.7g Carbohydrates:41.4g

Low-carb And Paleo Mediterranean Zucchini Noodles

Servings: 4 | Cooking: 10 min

Ingredients

- 4 medium (about 8 inches long) zucchini

- 3-4 garlic cloves, peeled
- 1 tablespoon olive oil (or slightly more if you have a lot of noodles)
- 2 tablespoons olive oil
- 1/4 cup red onion, finely chopped
- 1 tablespoon garlic, finely minced, plus
- 1/2 teaspoon dried oregano
- 1/2 teaspoon Italian herb blend
- Red pepper flakes, to taste (1/2 teaspoon, less or more)
- 1/4 cup parsley, chopped
- 2 cups cherry tomatoes, cut into halves
- 1/2 cup Kalamata olives, drained, cut in half (or regular black olives)
- 1/4 cup capers, drained, chopped

Directions
1. Except for the zucchini, prepare and ready the rest of the ingredients.
2. Wash the zucchini well and pat dry with paper towel. Spiralize the noodles using a spiralizer. With a kitchen shear, cut through the pile of zoodles (zucchini noodles) a few times to shorten them.
3. For the sauce:
4. In a medium-frying pan, heat the 2 tablespoons olive oil over medium-high heat. Add the red onions; cook for 2 minutes. Add the minced garlic and the dried herbs, cook for 1 minute. Add the tomatoes; cook for 2 minutes. Add the capers, olives, and red pepper flakes; cook for about 1-2 minutes. Turn the heat off; stir the parsley in to mix.
5. For the zoodles:
6. In a large-sized-sized nonstick wok or pan, heat the remaining 1 tablespoon olive oil. When hot, add the whole garlic cloves, cook for about 30 seconds, or just until fragrant, discard the garlic. Add the zoodles; cook for 2 to 3 minutes on high heat, stirring a couple of times, just until the zoodles are beginning to soften and hot.
7. Divide the zoodles between 4 bowls. Top each serve with a generous scoop of the sauce. Best when freshly made and served. However, if there are any leftovers, you can keep them in the fridge and reheat gently in a pan.

Nutrition: 190 cal., 13 g total fat (1.5 g sat fat), 0 mg chol., 420 mg sodium, 8400 mg potassium, 16 g carb., 5 g fiber, 9 g sugar, and 4 g protein.

Pork And Rice Soup

Servings: 4 | Cooking: 7 Hours

Ingredients
- 2 pounds pork stew meat, cubed
- A pinch of salt and black pepper
- 6 cups water
- 1 leek, sliced
- 2 bay leaves
- 1 carrot, sliced
- 3 tablespoons olive oil
- 1 cup white rice
- 2 cups yellow onion, chopped
- ½ cup lemon juice
- 1 tablespoon cilantro, chopped

Directions
1. In your slow cooker, combine the pork with the water and the rest of the ingredients except the cilantro, put the lid on and cook on Low for 7 hours.
2. Stir the soup, ladle into bowls, sprinkle the cilantro on top and serve.

Nutrition: calories 300; fat 15; fiber 7.6; carbs 17.4; protein 22.4

Tomato Roasted Feta

Servings: 4 | Cooking: 45 min

Ingredients
- 8 oz. feta cheese
- 2 tomatoes, peeled and diced
- 2 garlic cloves, chopped
- 1 cup tomato juice
- 1 thyme sprig
- 1 oregano sprig

Directions
1. Mix the tomatoes, garlic, tomato juice, thyme and oregano in a small deep dish baking pan.
2. Place the feta in the pan as well and cover with aluminum foil.
3. Cook in the preheated oven at 350F for 10 minutes.
4. Serve the feta and the sauce fresh.

Nutrition: Calories:173 Fat:12.2g Protein:9.2g Carbohydrates:7.8g

Fettuccine With Spinach And Shrimp

Servings: 4-6 | Cooking: 10 min

Ingredients
- 8 ounces whole-wheat fettuccine pasta, uncooked
- 3 garlic cloves, peeled, chopped
- 2 teaspoons dried basil, crushed
- 12 ounces medium raw shrimp, peeled, deveined
- 1/4 teaspoon crushed red pepper flakes
- 1/2 cup crumbled feta cheese
- 1 teaspoon salt
- 1 package (10 ounce) frozen spinach, thawed
- 1 cup sour cream

Directions
1. In a large-sized mixing bowl, combine sour cream, the feta, basil, garlic, salt, and red pepper.
2. According to the package instructions, cook the fettucine. After the first 8 minutes of cooking, add the spinach and the shrimp to the boiling water with pasta; boil for 2 minutes more and then drain thoroughly.
3. Add the hot pasta, spinach, and shrimp mixture into the bowl with the sour cream mix; lightly toss and serve immediately.

Nutrition: 417.9 Cal, 18 g total fat (9.8 g sat. fat), 197.6 mg chol., 1395.6 mg sodium, 39.7 g carb., 2.5 g fiber, 3.3 g sugar, and 25.2 g protein.

Sage Pork And Beans Stew

Servings: 4 | Cooking: 4 Hours And 10 min

Ingredients
- 2 pounds pork stew meat, cubed
- 2 tablespoons olive oil
- 1 sweet onion, chopped
- 1 red bell pepper, chopped
- 3 garlic cloves, minced
- 2 teaspoons sage, dried
- 4 ounces canned white beans, drained
- 1 cup beef stock
- 2 zucchinis, chopped
- 2 tablespoons tomato paste
- 1 tablespoon cilantro, chopped

Directions
1. Heat up a pan with the oil over medium-high heat, add the meat, brown for 10 minutes and transfer to your slow cooker.
2. Add the rest of the ingredients except the cilantro, put the lid on and cook on High for 4 hours.
3. Divide the stew into bowls, sprinkle the cilantro on top and serve.

Nutrition: calories 423; fat 15.4; fiber 9.6; carbs 27.4; protein 43

Broccoli Pesto Spaghetti

Servings: 4 | Cooking: 35 min

Ingredients
- 8 oz. spaghetti
- 1 pound broccoli, cut into florets
- 2 tablespoons olive oil
- 4 garlic cloves, chopped
- 4 basil leaves
- 2 tablespoons blanched almonds
- 1 lemon, juiced
- Salt and pepper to taste

Directions
1. For the pesto, combine the broccoli, oil, garlic, basil, lemon juice and almonds in a blender and pulse until well mixed and smooth.
2. Cook the spaghetti in a large pot of salty water for 8 minutes or until al dente. Drain well.
3. Mix the warm spaghetti with the broccoli pesto and serve right away.

Nutrition: Calories:284 Fat:10.2g Protein:10.4g Carbohydrates:40.2g

Chorizo Stuffed Chicken Breasts

Servings: 4 | Cooking: 1 ¼ Hours

Ingredients
- 4 chicken breasts
- 2 chorizo links, diced
- 4 oz. mozzarella, shredded
- 3 tablespoons olive oil
- 1 shallot, chopped
- 2 garlic cloves, minced
- 1 can diced tomatoes
- ½ cup dry white wine
- ½ cup vegetable stock
- Salt and pepper to taste

Directions
1. Mix the chorizo and mozzarella in a bowl.

2. Cut a small pocket into each chicken breast and stuff it with the chorizo.
3. Season the chicken with salt and pepper.
4. Heat the oil in a skillet and add the chicken.
5. Cook on each side for 5 minutes or until golden brown.
6. Add the shallot, garlic and tomatoes, as well as wine, stock, salt and pepper.
7. Cook on low heat for 40 minutes.
8. Serve the chicken and the sauce warm.

Nutrition: Calories:435 Fat:30.8g Protein:30.2g Carbohydrates:4.2g

Grilled Mediterranean-style Chicken Kebabs

Servings: 10 | Cooking: 10-15 min

Ingredients
- 3 chicken filets, diced in 1-inch cubes
- 2 green bell peppers
- 2 red bell peppers
- 1 red onion
- 2 teaspoon black pepper (freshly ground), divided
- 2 teaspoon paprika, divided
- 2 teaspoon thyme, divided
- 2/3 cup extra virgin olive oil, divided
- 4 teaspoon oregano, divided
- 4 teaspoon of salt, divided
- 6 cloves of garlic (minced), divided
- Juice of 1 lemon, divided

Directions
1. Mix 1/2 amount of all the marinade ingredients in a small bowl, place the chicken in a Ziploc bag and add the marinade. Refrigerate for at least 30 minutes to marinate
2. Mix the remaining 1/2 amount of the marinade ingredients in the same bowl. Pour in the Ziploc bag and add the vegetables. Refrigerate for at least 30 minutes to marinate.
3. When marinated, thread the chicken, the peppers, and the onions into skewers, about 5 to 6 pieces chicken with a combination of onion and peppers between each chicken cubes.
4. Heat an indoor or outdoor grill pan over medium high heat. Lightly oil the grates. Grill the chicken for about 5 minutes per side, or until the center of the cubes are no longer pink.
5. Serve with favorite Mediterranean side dish, salad, or baked potato slices or fries.

Nutrition: 150 cal., 15 g total fat (2 g sat fat), 0 mg chol., 950 mg sodium, 150 mg potassium, 6 g carb., 2 g fiber, 2 g sugar, and <1 g protein.

Sumac Salmon And Grapefruit

Servings: 4 | Cooking: 5 min

Ingredients
- 1 cup parsley leaves, flat-leaf
- 1 teaspoon ground cumin
- 1/4 cup (60ml) olive oil, plus more to brush
- 2 oranges, peeled, segmented
- 2 pink grapefruits, peeled, segmented
- 2 tablespoons sumac
- 4 pieces (180 g each) salmon fillets, skinless, pin-boned
- Juice of 1/2 lemon, and wedges to serve

Directions
1. In a mixing bowl, combine the sumac and the cumin.
2. Brush the fillets with the olive oil; season with the sumac mixture.
3. In a large frying pan, heat 1 tablespoon olive oil over medium heat. Add the fish fillets; cook for about 2 minutes per side, or until charred on the outside and almost cooked through, but still pink in the middle. Transfer to a plate and loosely cover with foil.
4. Meanwhile, whisk the remaining 2 tablespoons of olive oil and lemon juice; season. Add the fruits and the parsley, toss to coat.
5. Serve the fish fillets with the salad and wedges of lemon.

Nutrition: 567.9 Cal, 34 g total fat (7 g sat. fat), 16 g carb., 7 g fiber, 47 g protein, and 95.39 mg sodium.

Bean Patties With And Salsa Avocado

Servings: 4 | Cooking: 10 min
Ingredients
- 60 g mixed salad leaves, washed, dried
- 5 pieces 13-cm round pocket bread (whole wheat pita bread)
- 1/4 cup chopped fresh coriander
- 1 small red onion, finely chopped
- 1 egg white
- 1 container (170 g) chunky tomato salsa dip
- 1 can (750 g) red kidney beans, rinsed, drained
- 1 avocado, halved, seed removed, peeled, sliced lengthways

- 1 1/2 tablespoons olive oil

Directions
1. Tear 1 round of pita into pieces; place in the bowl of the food processor and process until breadcrumb-like in texture. Transfer into a medium-sized bowl; set aside.
2. Reserve 185 g (or 1 cup) of the beans; place the remaining beans into the bowl of a food processor. In short bursts, process until roughly mashed.
3. Transfer into a bowl. Add the coriander, onion, reserved beans, egg white, and the pita crumbs; stir well until combined. With damp hands, divide the mixture into 4 portions, and shape into 8-cm thick and 8-cm wide diameter.
4. In a large nonstick frying pan, heat the oil over medium heat. Add the patties; cook for 4 minutes per side or until golden brown and the patties are heated through.
5. Meanwhile, preheat grill to medium-high. Grill the remaining pita under the preheated grill for about 1 to 2 minutes per side or until toasted.
6. Place the toasted pita into serving plates, top with the mixed salad, the slices of avocado, the bean patties, and the salsa; serve immediately.

Nutrition: 549 cal., 22 g fat (4 g sat fat), 62 g carb., 8 g sugar, 18 g protein, and 964.9 mg sodium.

Raisin Stuffed Lamb

Servings: 10 | Cooking: 2 ½ Hours

Ingredients
- 4 pounds lamb shoulder
- 1 teaspoon garlic powder
- 1 teaspoon onion powder
- 1 teaspoon chili powder
- Salt and pepper to taste
- 1 cup golden raisins
- 2 red apples, cored and diced
- 1 teaspoon mustard powder
- 1 teaspoon cumin powder
- 2 tablespoons pine nuts
- 1 cup dry white wine

Directions
1. Season the lamb with garlic powder, onion powder, chili, salt and pepper.
2. Cut a pocket into the lamb.
3. Mix the raisins, red apples, mustard, cumin and pine nuts and stuff the mixture into the lamb.
4. Place the lamb in a deep dish baking pan and cover with aluminum foil.
5. Cook in the preheated oven at 330F for 2 hours.
6. Serve the lamb warm and fresh.

Nutrition: Calories:436 Fat:14.8g Protein:52.0g Carbohydrates:18.1g

Spinach Orzo Stew

Servings: 8 | Cooking: 1 Hour

Ingredients
- 3 tablespoons olive oil
- 1 sweet onion, chopped
- 2 garlic cloves, minced
- 1 celery stalk, diced
- 2 carrots, diced
- 1 cup orzo, rinsed
- 2 cups vegetable stock
- Salt and pepper to taste
- 4 cups baby spinach
- 1 tablespoon lemon juice

Directions
1. Heat the oil in a skillet and stir in the onion, garlic, celery and carrots. Cook for 2 minutes until softened then add the orzo.
2. Cook for another 5 minutes then pour in the stock.
3. Add the salt and pepper and cook on low heat for 20 minutes.
4. Add the spinach and lemon juice and cook for another 5 minutes.
5. Serve the stew warm and fresh.

Nutrition: Calories:143 Fat:5.8g Protein:3.5g Carbohydrates:19.8g

Grapes, Cucumbers And Almonds Soup

Servings: 4 | Cooking: 0 min

Ingredients
- ¼ cup almonds, chopped and toasted
- 3 cucumbers, peeled and chopped
- 3 garlic cloves, minced
- ½ cup warm water
- 6 scallions, sliced
- ¼ cup white wine vinegar
- 3 tablespoons olive oil

- Salt and white pepper to the taste
- 1 teaspoon lemon juice
- ½ cup green grapes, halved

Directions
1. In your blender, combine the almonds with the cucumbers and the rest of the ingredients except the grapes and lemon juice, pulse well and divide into bowls.
2. Top each serving with the lemon juice and grapes and serve cold.

Nutrition: calories 200; fat 5.4; fiber 2.4; carbs 7.6; protein 3.3

Nutmeg Beef Soup

Servings: 8 | Cooking: 30 min

Ingredients
- 1 yellow onion, chopped
- 1 tablespoon olive oil
- 1 garlic clove, minced
- 1 pound beef meat, ground
- 1 pound eggplant, chopped
- ¾ cup carrots, chopped
- Salt and black pepper to the taste
- 30 ounces canned tomatoes, drained and chopped
- 1 quart beef stock
- ½ teaspoon nutmeg, ground
- 2 teaspoons parsley, chopped

Directions
1. Heat up a pot with the oil over medium heat, add the meat, onion and the garlic and brown for 5 minutes.
2. Add the rest of the ingredients except the parsley, bring to a boil and cook over medium heat for 25 minutes.
3. Add the parsley, divide the soup into bowls and serve.

Nutrition: calories 232; fat 5.4; fiber 7.6; carbs 20.1; protein 6.5

Parsnip Chickpea Veal Stew

Servings: 10 | Cooking: 2 Hours

Ingredients
- 2 pounds veal meat, cubed
- 3 tablespoons olive oil
- 2 shallots, chopped
- 4 garlic cloves, chopped
- 2 red bell peppers, cored and sliced
- 2 yellow bell peppers, cored and sliced
- 4 parsnips, peeled and sliced
- 2 carrots, sliced
- 1 can diced tomatoes
- 1 ½ cups beef stock
- 1 bay leaf
- 1 rosemary sprig
- 1 oregano sprig
- 1 can chickpeas, drained
- Salt and pepper to taste

Directions
1. Heat the oil in a heavy saucepan and stir in the veal. Cook for 5 minutes until slightly browned.
2. Add the shallots, garlic, bell peppers, parsnips and carrots.
3. Cook for another 5 minutes then stir in the rest of the ingredients.
4. Season with salt and pepper and cook for 1 ½ hours on low heat.
5. Serve the stew warm and fresh.

Nutrition: Calories:332 Fat:12.7g Protein:27.8g Carbohydrates:26.9g

Tuna And Couscous

Servings: 4 | Cooking: 0 min

Ingredients
- 1 cup chicken stock
- 1 and ¼ cups couscous
- A pinch of salt and black pepper
- 10 ounces canned tuna, drained and flaked
- 1 pint cherry tomatoes, halved
- ½ cup pepperoncini, sliced
- 1/3 cup parsley, chopped
- 1 tablespoon olive oil
- ¼ cup capers, drained
- Juice of ½ lemon

Directions
1. Put the stock in a pan, bring to a boil over medium-high heat, add the couscous, stir, take off the heat, cover, leave aside for 10 minutes, fluff with a fork and transfer to a bowl.
2. Add the tuna and the rest of the ingredients, toss and serve for lunch right away.

Nutrition: calories 253; fat 11.5; fiber 3.4; carbs 16.5; protein 23.2

Olive Oil Lemon Broiled Cod

Servings: 4 | Cooking: 35 min

Ingredients
- 4 cod fillets
- 1 teaspoon dried marjoram
- 4 tablespoons olive oil
- 1 lemon, juiced
- 1 thyme sprig
- Salt and pepper to taste

Directions
1. Season the cod with salt, pepper and marjoram.
2. Heat the oil in a large skillet and place the cod in the hot oil.
3. Fry on medium heat on both sides until golden brown then add the lemon juice.
4. Place the thyme sprig on top and cover with a lid.
5. Cook for 5 more minutes then remove from heat.
6. Serve the cod and sauce fresh.

Nutrition: Calories:304 Fat:15.5g Protein:40.0g Carbohydrates:0.1g

Chicken And Spaghetti Soup

Servings: 5 | Cooking: 35 min

Ingredients
- 4 chicken drumsticks, skinless
- 3 oz whole grain spaghetti
- 3 cups chicken stock
- 1 teaspoon salt
- ½ teaspoon dried oregano
- 1 tablespoon chives, chopped
- 1 onion, chopped
- 1 tablespoon canola oil
- ½ teaspoon cilantro, chopped
- 2 potatoes, chopped

Directions
1. Pour chicken stock in the pan. Add chicken drumsticks and simmer them for 20 minutes.
2. Meanwhile, roast together onion with canola oil.
3. When the onion is light brown, add the potato and roast the vegetables for 3-4 minutes more. Stir them from time to time.
4. Then add the roasted vegetables in the pan with drumsticks.
5. Sprinkle soup with chives, salt, and cilantro.
6. When the potato is half-cooked, add spaghetti, stir well, and cook soup for 10 minutes.
7. Ladle the cooked soup in the bowls.

Nutrition: calories 287; fat 6.6; fiber 6.8; carbs 39.4; protein 17.6

Mediterranean Flounder

Servings: 4 | Cooking: 30 min

Ingredients
- 6 leaves fresh basil, chopped
- 5 roma tomatoes, chopped or 1 (15 ounce) can chopped tomatoes
- 4 tablespoons capers
- 3 tablespoons parmesan cheese
- 24 Kalamata olives, pitted, chopped
- 2 tablespoons olive oil
- 2 garlic cloves, chopped
- ¼ cup white wine
- ½ onion, chopped
- 1 teaspoon lemon juice, freshly squeezed
- 1 pound flounder (or sole, halibut, mahi-mahi or tilapia fillet
- 1 pinch Italian seasoning

Directions
1. Preheat the oven to 425F.
2. Bring water to a boil and place a bowl of ice water near the oven. Plunge the tomatoes into the boiling water, immediately remove them and plunge into the ice water; peel the skins. Alternatively, you can chop them with the skins on or you can use canned if you prefer.
3. In a medium-sized skillet, heat the olive oil over medium flame or heat. Add the onion; sauté until tender. Add the garlic and the Italian seasoning, stirring to combine. Add the tomatoes; cook until tender. Mix in the wine, capers, olives, 1/2 of the basil, and lemon juice. Alternatively, you can use a couple teaspoons of dried basil. However, fresh is preferred.
4. Reduce the heat, add the parmesan cheese; cook until the mixture is bubbly and hot. If you want a thicker sauce, cook for about 15 minutes or up to thick.
5. Place the fish in a shallow baking dish, pour the sauce over the fish, and bake for about 15 to 20 minutes until it easily flakes with a fork. Take note, the mah-mahi will not easily flake even when it is done.

Nutrition: 221.9 Cal, 13.1 g total fat (2.5 g sat. fat), 54.4 mg chol., 848.1 mg sodium, 7.5 g carb., 2.3 g fiber, 2.9 g sugar, and 16.9 g protein.

Crunchy Baked Mussels

Servings: 4 | Cooking: 45 min

Ingredients

- 2 pounds mussels
- ½ cup breadcrumbs
- 1 teaspoon lemon zest
- 4 garlic cloves, minced
- 2 tablespoons chopped parsley
- ½ teaspoon chili flakes
- 2 tablespoons butter, melted

Directions

1. Mix the breadcrumbs, lemon zest, garlic, parsley, chili and butter in a bowl.
2. Wash the mussels well and place them in a steamer.
3. Cook for a few minutes until they all open up.
4. Carefully remove them from the steamer and place the opened up ones in a baking tray.
5. Top each mussel with the breadcrumb mixture and cook in the preheated oven at 400F for 5 minutes.
6. Serve right away.

Nutrition: Calories:305 Fat:11.6g Protein:29.1g Carbohydrates:19.3g

Mediterranean-style Tuna Wrap

Servings: 4 | Cooking: 13 min

Ingredients

- 1/2 teaspoon lemon zest
- 1/4 cup fresh parsley, chopped
- 1/4 cup Kalamata olives, chopped
- 1/4 cup red onion, finely diced
- 2 cans (6-ounce each) chunk light tuna in water, drained well
- 2 large tomatoes, sliced
- 2 tablespoons lemon juice, freshly squeezed
- 3 tablespoons olive oil
- 4 whole-grain (about 2 ounces each) wrap breads
- 6 cups (about 3 ounces) mixed greens, pre-washed
- Freshly ground black pepper
- Salt

Directions

1. In a medium mixing bowl, combine the tuna, parsley, onion, and olives.
2. In a small mixing bowl, whisk the olive oil, lemon juice, lemon zest, salt, and pepper. Pour about 2/3 of the dressing over the tuna mixture; toss to incorporate.
3. In another bowl, combine the greens and the remaining 1/3 dressing; toss to coat.
4. Into each piece of wrap bread, top tuna salad, then with 1 1/2 cup greens, and a few slices of tomatoes. Roll the wrap; serve.

Nutrition: 379 Cal, 16.5 g total fat (2 g sat. fat), 29 g carb., 4 g sugar, 5 g fiber, 26 g protein, and 701 mg sodium.

Pear Braised Pork

Servings: 10 | Cooking: 2 ¼ Hours

Ingredients

- 3 pounds pork shoulder
- 4 pears, peeled and sliced
- 2 shallots, sliced
- 4 garlic cloves, minced
- 1 bay leaf
- 1 thyme sprig
- ½ cup apple cider
- Salt and pepper to taste

Directions

1. Season the pork with salt and pepper.
2. Combine the pears, shallots, garlic, bay leaf, thyme and apple cider in a deep dish baking pan.
3. Place the pork over the pears then cover the pan with aluminum foil.
4. Cook in the preheated oven at 330F for 2 hours.
5. Serve the pork and the sauce fresh.

Nutrition: Calories:455 Fat:29.3g Protein:32.1g Carbohydrates:14.9g

Yogurt Baked Eggplants

Servings: 4 | Cooking: 45 min

Ingredients

- 2 eggplants
- 4 garlic cloves, minced
- 1 teaspoon dried basil

- 2 tablespoons lemon juice
- Salt and pepper to taste
- 1 cup Greek yogurt
- 2 tablespoons chopped parsley

Directions
1. Cut the eggplants in half and score the halves with a sharp knives.
2. Season the eggplants with salt and pepper, as well as the basil then drizzle with lemon juice and place the eggplant halves on a baking tray.
3. Spread the garlic over the eggplants and bake in the preheated oven at 350F for 20 minutes.
4. When done, place the eggplants on serving plates and top with yogurt and parsley.
5. Serve the eggplants right away.

Nutrition: Calories:113 Fat:1.6g Protein:8.1g Carbohydrates:19.4g

Pancetta-wrapped Cod With Rosemary New Potatoes

Servings: 6 | Cooking: 1 ¼ Hours

Ingredients
- 6 cod fillets
- 6 pancetta slices
- 1 pound new potatoes, rinsed
- ½ green beans, trimmed and halved
- 3 tablespoons olive oil
- 2 tablespoons lemon juice
- 2 rosemary sprigs
- Salt and pepper to taste

Directions
1. Season the fish with salt and pepper and wrap it in pancetta.
2. Combine the new potatoes, beans, oil, lemon juice and rosemary in a deep dish baking pan. Season with salt and pepper.
3. Place the cod over the vegetables and cover the pan with aluminum foil.
4. Cook in the preheated oven at 350F for 40 minutes.
5. Serve the fish and the veggies warm and fresh.

Nutrition: Calories: 291 Fat: 8.6g Protein: 39.5g Carbohydrates: 12.5g

Stuffed Peppers With Basil And Tomato Cream Sauce

Servings: 4 | Cooking: 50 min

Ingredients
- 1 1/2 cups cooked brown rice
- 1 can (29 ounces) tomato sauce
- 1 pound ground chicken breast (or turkey)
- 1/2 onion, chopped
- 1/3 cup fresh basil, chopped, reserving a few for garnish
- 1/3 cup heavy cream
- 1 tablespoon olive oil
- 3 garlic cloves, minced
- 3/4 cup parmesan cheese, divided
- 4 red, orange, green, or yellow peppers
- Salt and pepper

Directions
1. Preheat the oven to 400F. Slice the top of the peppers off, remove the seeds and the seeds; set aside. Save the pepper tops.
2. Over medium flame or heat, put the oil in a skillet. Add the onion; sauté for 5 minutes, or until soft. Add the garlic; cook for 1 minute.
3. Season the ground chicken with the salt and the pepper; cook for about 10 to 12 minutes, stirring occasionally, until brown.
4. While the chicken is cooking, mix the tomato sauce, the heavy cream, and the remaining garlic in another skillet; heat over low heat. Stir in the basil.
5. Stir the cooked brown rice into the skillet of chicken. Add 1/2 cup of the parmesan cheese, about 1/2 cup of the tomato-cream mixture; toss to coat. Turn the heat off.
6. Divide the chicken mixture between 4 peppers, filling them to the top. Place the stuffed peppers in a baking dish that will allow them to stand; spoon a bit of the tomato-cream sauce over the top of the stuffed peppers. Pour the remaining sauce in the bottom of the dish; place the pepper tops back into the stuffed peppers. Bake for about 20 minutes, cover the dish with foil, and bake for 30 minutes more.
7. Serve with more parmesan and with basil garnishing, and mashed potato on the side.

Nutrition: 660 cal., 33 g total fat (13 g sat fat), 145 mg chol., 1420 mg sodium, 1660 mg potassium, 58 g carb., 11 g fiber, 24 g sugar, and 34 g protein.

Beef Stuffed Bell Peppers

Servings: 6 | Cooking: 1 Hour

Ingredients
- 6 red bell peppers
- 1 pound ground beef
- 2 sweet onions, chopped
- 1 garlic cloves, minced
- 1 carrot, grated
- 1 celery stalk, finely chopped
- 1 tablespoon pesto sauce
- 2 tablespoons tomato paste
- ½ cup white rice
- Salt and pepper to taste
- 1 cup tomato juice
- 1 ½ cups beef stock
- 1 thyme sprig

Directions
1. Place the thyme sprig at the bottom of a pot.
2. Mix the beef, onions, garlic, carrot, celery, pesto sauce and tomato paste, as well as rice, salt and pepper in a bowl.
3. Cut the top of each bell pepper and remove the vines.
4. Stuff the bell peppers with the beef mixture and place them in the pot.
5. Pour in the tomato juice and stock and cover with a lid.
6. Cook on low heat for 45 minutes.
7. Serve the bell peppers warm and fresh.

Nutrition: Calories:280 Fat:6.5g Protein:27.2g Carbohydrates:27.1g

Stuffed Eggplants

Servings: 4 | Cooking: 35 min

Ingredients
- 2 eggplants, halved lengthwise and 2/3 of the flesh scooped out
- 3 tablespoons olive oil
- 1 red onion, chopped
- 2 garlic cloves, minced
- 1 pint white mushrooms, sliced
- 2 cups kale, torn
- 2 cups quinoa, cooked
- 1 tablespoon thyme, chopped
- Zest and juice of 1 lemon
- Salt and black pepper to the taste
- ½ cup Greek yogurt
- 3 tablespoons parsley, chopped

Directions
1. Rub the inside of each eggplant half with half of the oil and arrange them on a baking sheet lined with parchment paper.
2. Heat up a pan with the rest of the oil over medium heat, add the onion and the garlic and sauté for 5 minutes.
3. Add the mushrooms and cook for 5 minutes more.
4. Add the kale, salt, pepper, thyme, lemon zest and juice, stir, cook for 5 minutes more and take off the heat.
5. Stuff the eggplant halves with the mushroom mix, introduce them in the oven and bake 400 degrees F for 20 minutes.
6. Divide the eggplants between plates, sprinkle the parsley and the yogurt on top and serve for lunch.

Nutrition: calories 512; fat 16.4; fiber 17.5; carbs 78; protein 17.2

Mushroom Pilaf

Servings: 4 | Cooking: 50 min

Ingredients
- 2 tablespoons olive oil
- 1 shallot, chopped
- 2 garlic cloves, minced
- 1 pound button mushrooms
- 1 cup brown rice
- 2 cups chicken stock
- 1 bay leaf
- 1 thyme sprig
- Salt and pepper to taste

Directions
1. Heat the oil in a skillet and stir in the shallot and garlic. Cook for 2 minutes until softened and fragrant.
2. Add the mushrooms and rice and cook for 5 minutes.
3. Add the stock, bay leaf and thyme, as well as salt and pepper and continue cooking for 20 more minutes on low heat.
4. Serve the pilaf warm and fresh.

Nutrition: Calories:265 Fat:8.9g Protein:7.6g Carbohydrates:41.2g

Cream Cheese Artichoke Mix

Servings: 6 | Cooking: 45 min

Ingredients
- 4 sheets matzo
- ½ cup artichoke hearts, canned
- 1 cup cream cheese
- 1 cup spinach, chopped
- ½ teaspoon salt
- 1 teaspoon ground black pepper
- 3 tablespoons fresh dill, chopped
- 3 eggs, beaten
- 1 teaspoon canola oil
- ½ cup cottage cheese

Directions
1. In the bowl combine together cream cheese, spinach, salt, ground black pepper, dill, and cottage cheese.
2. Pour canola oil in the skillet, add artichoke hearts and roast them for 2-3 minutes over the medium heat. Stir them from time to time.
3. Then add roasted artichoke hearts in the cheese mixture.
4. Add eggs and stir until homogenous.
5. Place one sheet of matzo in the casserole mold.
6. Then spread it with cheese mixture generously.
7. Cover the cheese layer with the second sheet of matzo.
8. Repeat the steps till you use all ingredients.
9. Then preheat oven to 360F.
10. Bake matzo mina for 40 minutes.
11. Cut the cooked meal into the servings.

Nutrition: calories 272; fat 17.3; fiber 4.3; carbs 20.2; protein 11.8

Caramelized Shallot Steaks

Servings: 6 | Cooking: 45 min

Ingredients
- 6 flank steaks
- Salt and pepper to taste
- 1 teaspoon dried oregano
- 1 teaspoon dried basil
- 6 shallots, sliced
- 4 tablespoons olive oil
- ¼ cup dry white wine

Directions
1. Season the steaks with salt, pepper, oregano and basil.
2. Heat a grill pan over medium flame and place the steaks on the grill.
3. Cook on each side for 6-7 minutes.
4. Heat the oil in a skillet and stir in the shallots. Cook for 15 minutes, stirring often, until the shallots are caramelized.
5. Add the wine and cook for another 5 minutes.
6. Serve the steaks with shallots.

Nutrition: Calories:258 Fat:16.3g Protein:23.5g Carbohydrates:2.1g

Carrot And Potato Soup

Servings: 6 | Cooking: 35 min

Ingredients
- 5 cups beef broth
- 4 carrots, peeled
- 1 teaspoon dried thyme
- ½ teaspoon ground cumin
- 1 teaspoon salt
- 1 ½ cup potatoes, chopped
- 1 tablespoon olive oil
- ½ teaspoon ground black pepper
- 1 tablespoon lemon juice
- 1/3 cup fresh parsley, chopped
- 1 chili pepper, chopped
- 1 tablespoon tomato paste
- 1 tablespoon sour cream

Directions
1. Line the baking tray with baking paper.
2. Put sweet potatoes and carrot on the tray and sprinkle with olive oil and salt.
3. Bake the vegetables for 25 minutes at 365F.
4. Meanwhile, pour the beef broth in the pan and bring it to boil.
5. Add dried thyme, ground cumin, chopped chili pepper, and tomato paste.
6. When the vegetables are cooked, add them in the pan.
7. Boil the vegetables until they are soft.
8. Then blend the mixture with the help of the blender until smooth.
9. Simmer it for 2 minutes and add lemon juice. Stir well.
10. Then add sour cream and chopped parsley. Stir well.
11. Simmer the soup for 3 minutes more.

Nutrition: calories 123; fat 4.1; fiber 2.9; carbs 16.4; protein 5.3

Macedonian Greens And Cheese Pie

Servings: 6 | Cooking: 50 min

Ingredients
- 1 bunch chicory
- 1 bunch rocket or arugula
- 1 bunch mint
- 1 bunch dill
- 10 sheets whole-wheat filo pastry
- 150 g halloumi, finely diced
- 150 g ricotta
- 200 g baby spinach
- 250 g Greek feta, crumbled
- 4 eggs
- 50 g dried whole-wheat breadcrumbs
- 6 green onions, trimmed
- Olive oil, to brush

Directions
1. Trim the rocket stalks and the chicory. Finely chop the green onions and the dill (include the dill stems). Strip the mint leaves.
2. Pour water into a large-sized pan; bring to boil. Ready a bowl with iced water beside the stove. Add the chicory into the boiling water; blanch for 3 minutes and using a slotted spoon, transfer to the bowl with iced water. Repeat the process with the spinach and the rocket, blanching each for 1 minute; drain well.
3. A handful at a time, tightly wring the greens to squeeze out the excess liquid, then pat dry with paper towel. Finely chop the blanched greens. Combine them with the eggs, herbs, feta, 30 g of the breadcrumbs, ricotta, and 3/4 of the halloumi; season.
4. Preheat the oven to 180C.
5. Grease a 5-cm deep 25cmx pie tin.
6. Brush a filo sheet with the olive oil, place it in the pie tin, extending the edge of the filo outside the edge of the tin. Brush the remaining sheets of filo and add them to the pie tin, arranging them like wheel spokes.
7. Sprinkle the remaining breadcrumbs over the base of the layered filo sheets. Top with the filling mixture. Loosely fold the filo sheets over to cover the filling, brush with oil, sprinkle with water, and scatter the halloumi over.
8. Bake for 45 minutes. After 45 minutes, cover, and bake for additional 15 minutes, or until heated through.

Nutrition: 374.8 Cal, 20 g total fat (12 g sat. fat), 22 g carb., 2 g fiber, 3 g sugar, 25g protein, and 1506.7 mg sodium.

Chicken Stuffed Peppers

Servings: 6 | Cooking: 0 min

Ingredients
- 1 cup Greek yogurt
- 2 tablespoons mustard
- Salt and black pepper to the taste
- 1 pound rotisserie chicken meat, cubed
- 4 celery stalks, chopped
- 2 tablespoons balsamic vinegar
- 1 bunch scallions, sliced
- ¼ cup parsley, chopped
- 1 cucumber, sliced
- 3 red bell peppers, halved and deseeded
- 1 pint cherry tomatoes, quartered

Directions
1. In a bowl, mix the chicken with the celery and the rest of the ingredients except the bell peppers and toss well.
2. Stuff the peppers halves with the chicken mix and serve for lunch.

Nutrition: calories 266; fat 12.2; fiber 4.5; carbs 15.7; protein 3.7

Turkey Fritters And Sauce

Servings: 4 | Cooking: 30 min

Ingredients
- 2 garlic cloves, minced
- 1 egg
- 1 red onion, chopped
- 1 tablespoon olive oil
- ¼ teaspoon red pepper flakes
- 1 pound turkey meat, ground
- ½ teaspoon oregano, dried
- Cooking: spray

For the sauce:
- 1 cup Greek yogurt
- 1 cucumber, chopped
- 1 tablespoon olive oil
- ¼ teaspoon garlic powder

- 2 tablespoons lemon juice
- ¼ cup parsley, chopped

Directions
1. Heat up a pan with 1 tablespoon oil over medium heat, add the onion and the garlic, sauté for 5 minutes, cool down and transfer to a bowl.
2. Add the meat, turkey, oregano and pepper flakes, stir and shape medium fritters out of this mix.
3. Heat up another pan greased with cooking spray over medium-high heat, add the turkey fritters and brown for 5 minutes on each side.
4. Introduce the pan in the oven and bake the fritters at 375 degrees F for 15 minutes more.
5. Meanwhile, in a bowl, mix the yogurt with the cucumber, oil, garlic powder, lemon juice and parsley and whisk really well.
6. Divide the fritters between plates, spread the sauce all over and serve for lunch.

Nutrition: calories 364; fat 16.8; fiber 5.5; carbs 26.8; protein 23.4

Garlic Clove Roasted Chicken

Servings: 8 | Cooking: 1 ½ Hours

Ingredients
- 8 chicken legs
- 40 garlic cloves, crushed
- 1 shallot, sliced
- ½ cup white wine
- 1 bay leaf
- 1 thyme sprig
- Salt and pepper to taste

Directions
1. Season the chicken with salt and pepper.
2. Combine it with the rest of the ingredients in a deep dish baking pan.
3. Cover the pan with aluminum foil and cook in the preheated oven at 350F for 1 hour.
4. Serve the chicken warm and fresh.

Nutrition: Calories:225 Fat:7.5g Protein:29.9g Carbohydrates:5.6g

Chickpeas, Spinach And Arugula Bowl

Servings: 5 | Cooking: 25 min

Ingredients
- 1 cup chickpeas, canned, drained
- ½ teaspoon butter
- ½ teaspoon salt
- ½ teaspoon ground paprika
- ¾ teaspoon onion powder
- 6 oz quinoa, dried
- 12 oz chicken stock
- 2 tomatoes, chopped
- 1 cucumber, chopped
- ½ cup fresh spinach, chopped
- ½ cup arugula, chopped
- ½ cup lettuce chopped
- 1 tablespoon olive oil
- 4 teaspoons hummus

Directions
1. Place chickpeas in the skillet. Add butter and salt.
2. Roast the chickpeas for 5 minutes over the high heat. Stir them from time to time.
3. After this, place quinoa and chicken stock in the pan.
4. Cook the quinoa for 15 minutes over the medium heat.
5. Then make the salad: mix up together tomatoes, cucumber, spinach, arugula, lettuce, and olive oil. Shake the salad gently.
6. Arrange roasted chickpeas in every serving bowl.
7. Add salad and hummus.
8. Then add quinoa. Buddha bowl is cooked.

Nutrition: calories 330; fat 8.4; fiber 10.9; carbs 51.6; protein 14.1

Tuna Sandwiches

Servings: 4 | Cooking: 10 min

Ingredients
- 1/3 cup sun-dried tomato packed in oil, drained
- 1/4 cup red bell pepper, finely chopped (optional)
- 1/4 cup red onions or 1/4 cup sweet Spanish onion, finely chopped
- 1/4 cup ripe green olives or 1/4 cup ripe olives, sliced
- 1/4 teaspoon black pepper, fresh ground
- 2 cans (6 ounce) tuna in water, drained, flaked
- 2 teaspoons capers (more to taste)
- 4 romaine lettuce or curly green lettuce leaves
- 4 teaspoons balsamic vinegar
- 4 teaspoons roasted red pepper
- 8 slices whole-grain bread (or 8 slices whole-wheat pita bread)
- Olive oil

Optional:
- 3 tablespoons mayonnaise (or low-fat mayonnaise)

Directions
1. Toast the bread, if desired.
2. In a small mixing bowl, mix the vinegar and the olive oil. Brush the oil mixture over 1 side of each bread slices or on the inside of the pita pockets.
3. Except for the lettuce, combine the remaining of the ingredients in a mixing bowl.
4. Place 1 lettuce leaf on the oiled side of 4 bread slices.
5. Top the leaves with the tuna mix; top with the remaining bread slices with the oiled side in.
6. If using pita, place 1 lettuce leave inside each pita slices, then fill with the tuna mixture; serve immediately.

Nutrition: 338.1 Cal, 11.7 g total fat (2.1 g sat. fat), 28.5 g carb., 4.7 g sugar, 5.5 g fiber, 29.4 g protein, and 801.9 mg sodium.

Cream Cheese Tart

Servings: 6 | Cooking: 20 min

Ingredients
- 1 cup wheat flour, whole grain
- ½ teaspoon salt
- 1/3 cup butter, softened
- 1 cup Mozzarella, shredded
- 3 tablespoons chives, chopped
- 1 tablespoon cream cheese
- ½ teaspoon ground paprika
- 4 eggs, beaten
- 1 teaspoon dried oregano

Directions
1. In the mixer bowl combine together flour and salt. Add butter and blend the mixture until you get non-sticky dough or knead it with the help of the fingertips.
2. Roll up the dough and arrange it in the round tart mold.
3. Flatten it gently and bake for 10 minutes at 365F.
4. Meanwhile, mix up together eggs with Mozzarella cheese, cream cheese, and chives.
5. Remove the tart crust from the oven and chill for 5-10 minutes.
6. Then place the cheese mixture in the tart crust and flatten it well with the help of a spatula.
7. Bake the tart for 10 minutes.
8. Use the kitchen torch to make the grilled tart surface.
9. Chill the cooked tart well and only after this slice it onto the servings.

Nutrition: calories 229; fat 14.8; fiber 0.8; carbs 16.7; protein 7.5

Cherry Tomato Caper Chicken

Servings: 4 | Cooking: 1 Hour

Ingredients
- 4 chicken breasts
- 3 tablespoons olive oil
- 4 garlic cloves, chopped
- 2 cups cherry tomatoes, halved
- 1 teaspoon capers, chopped
- ½ cup black olives, pitted and sliced
- 1 thyme sprig

Directions
1. Heat the oil in a skillet and add the chicken. Cook on high heat for 5 minutes on each side.
2. Add the rest of the ingredients and season with salt and pepper.
3. Cook in the preheated oven at 350F for 35 minutes.
4. Serve the chicken and the sauce warm and fresh.

Nutrition: Calories:320 Fat:19.9g Protein:30.1g Carbohydrates:5.6g

Shrimp Pancakes

Servings: 4 | Cooking: 10 min

Ingredients
- 4 eggs, beaten
- 4 teaspoons sour cream
- 1 cup shrimps, peeled, boiled
- 1 teaspoon butter
- 1 teaspoon olive oil
- 1/3 cup Mozzarella, shredded
- ½ teaspoon salt
- 1 teaspoon dried oregano

Directions
1. In the mixing bowl, combine together sour cream, eggs, salt, and dried oregano.
2. Place butter and olive oil in the crepe skillet and heat the ingredients up.
3. Separate the egg liquid into 4 parts.

4. Ladle the first part of the egg liquid in the skillet and flatten it in the shape of crepe.
5. Sprinkle the egg crepe with ¼ part of shrimps and a small amount of Mozzarella.
6. Roast the crepe for 2 minutes from one side and then flip it onto another.
7. Cook the crepe for 30 seconds more.
8. Repeat the same steps with all remaining ingredients.

Nutrition: calories 148; fat 8.5; fiber 0.2; carbs 1.5; protein 16.1

Herbed Chicken Stew

Servings: 6 | Cooking: 1 Hour

Ingredients
- 3 tablespoons olive oil
- 6 chicken legs
- 2 shallots, chopped
- 4 garlic cloves, minced
- 2 tablespoons pesto sauce
- ½ cup chopped cilantro
- ½ cup chopped parsley
- 2 tablespoons lemon juice
- 4 tablespoons vegetable stock
- Salt and pepper to taste

Directions
1. Heat the oil in a skillet and place the chicken in the hot oil.
2. Cook on each side until golden brown then add the shallots, garlic and pesto sauce.
3. Cook for 2 more minutes then add the rest of the ingredients.
4. Season with salt and pepper and continue cooking on low heat, covered with a lid, for 30 minutes.
5. Serve the stew warm and fresh.

Nutrition: Calories:357 Fat:19.6g Protein:41.4g Carbohydrates:2.0g

Spiced Seared Scallops With Lemon Relish

Servings: 4 | Cooking: 45 min

Ingredients
- 2 pounds scallops, cleaned
- ½ teaspoon cumin powder
- ¼ teaspoon ground ginger
- ½ teaspoon ground coriander
- ½ teaspoon smoked paprika
- ½ teaspoon salt
- 3 tablespoons olive oil

Directions
1. Pat the scallops dry with a paper towel.
2. Sprinkle them with spices and salt.
3. Heat the oil in a skillet and place half of the scallops in the hot oil. Cook for 1-2 minutes per side, just until the scallops look golden brown on the sides.
4. Remove the scallops and place the remaining ones in the hot oil.
5. Serve the scallops warm and fresh with your favorite side dish.

Nutrition: Calories:292 Fat:12.3g Protein:38.2g Carbohydrates:5.7g

White Bean Soup

Servings: 6 | Cooking: 8 Hours

Ingredients
- 1 cup celery, chopped
- 1 cup carrots, chopped
- 1 yellow onion, chopped
- 6 cups veggie stock
- 4 garlic cloves, minced
- 2 cup navy beans, dried
- ½ teaspoon basil, dried
- ½ teaspoon sage, dried
- 1 teaspoon thyme, dried
- A pinch of salt and black pepper

Directions
1. In your slow cooker, combine the beans with the stock and the rest of the ingredients, put the lid on and cook on Low for 8 hours.
2. Divide the soup into bowls and serve right away.

Nutrition: calories 264; fat 17.5; fiber 4.5; carbs 23.7; protein 11.5

Coriander Pork And Chickpeas Stew

Servings: 4 | Cooking: 8 Hours

Ingredients
- ½ cup beef stock
- 1 tablespoon ginger, grated
- 1 teaspoon coriander, ground
- 2 teaspoons cumin, ground

- Salt and black pepper to the taste
- 2 and ½ pounds pork stew meat, cubed
- 28 ounces canned tomatoes, drained and chopped
- 1 red onion, chopped
- 4 garlic cloves, minced
- ½ cup apricots, cut into quarters
- 15 ounces canned chickpeas, drained
- 1 tablespoon cilantro, chopped

Directions
1. In your slow cooker, combine the meat with the stock, ginger and the rest of the ingredients except the cilantro and the chickpeas, put the lid on and cook on Low for 7 hours and 40 minutes.
2. Add the cilantro and the chickpeas, cook the stew on Low for 20 minutes more, divide into bowls and serve.

Nutrition: calories 283; fat 11.9; fiber 4.5; carbs 28.8; protein 25.4

Crispy Pollock And Gazpacho

Servings: 4 | Cooking: 15 min

Ingredients
- 85 g whole-wheat bread, torn into chunks
- 4 tablespoons olive oil
- 4 pieces Pollock fillets, skinless
- 4 large tomatoes, cut into chunks
- 3/4 cucumber, cut into chunks
- 2 tablespoons sherry vinegar
- 2 garlic cloves, crushed
- 1/2 red onion, thinly sliced
- 1 yellow pepper, deseeded, cut into chunks

Directions
1. Preheat the oven to 200C, gas to 6, or fan to 180C.
2. Over a baking tray, scatter the chunks of bread. Toss with 1 tablespoon of the olive oil and bake for about 10 minutes, or until golden and crispy.
3. Meanwhile, mix the cucumber, tomatoes, onion, pepper, crushed garlic, sherry vinegar, and 2 tablespoons of the olive oil; season well.
4. Heat a non-stick large frying pan. Add the remaining 1 tablespoon of the olive oil and heat. When the oil is hot, add the fish; cook for about 4 minutes or until golden. Flip the fillet; cook for additional 1 to 2 minutes or until the fish cooked through.
5. In a mixing bowl, quickly toss the salad and the croutons; divide among 4 plates and then serve with the fish.

Nutrition: 296 Cal, 13 g total fat (2 g sat. fat), 19 g carb., 9 g sugar, 3 g fiber, 27 g protein, and 0.67 g sodium.

Falafel

Servings: 2 | Cooking: 40 min

Ingredients
- 1 pound (about 2 cups) dry chickpeas or garbanzo beans (use dry, DO NOT use canned)
- 1 1/2 tablespoons flour
- 1 3/4 teaspoons salt
- 1 small onion, roughly chopped
- 1 teaspoon ground coriander
- 1/4 cup fresh parsley, chopped
- 1/4 teaspoon black pepper
- 1/4 teaspoon cayenne pepper
- 2 teaspoons cumin
- 3-5 cloves garlic, roasted, if desired
- Pinch ground cardamom
- Canola, grapeseed, peanut oil, or oil with high smoking point, for frying

Directions
1. Pour the chickpeas into a large-sized bowl, cover with about 3-inch cold water, and soak overnight. The chickpeas will double to about 4-5 cups after soaking.
2. Drain and then rinse well, pour into a food processor. Except for the oil for frying, add the remaining of the ingredients into the processor; pulse until the texture resembles a coarse meal. Periodically scrape the sides of the processor, pushing the mixture down the sides, process until the mixture resembles a texture that is between couscous and paste, making sure not to over process or they will turn into hummus.
3. Transfer into a bowl. With a fork, stir the mixture, removing any large chickpeas that remained unprocessed. Cover the bowl with a plastic wrap; refrigerate for about 1 to 2 hours.
4. Fill a skillet with 1 1/2-inch worth of oil. Slowly heat the oil over medium flame or heat.
5. Meanwhile, scoop out 2 tablespoons worth of the falafel mixture; with wet hands form it into round ball or slider-shaped. You can make them smaller or larger if you want. They may stick together loosely, but when they start to fry, they will bind

nicely. If the balls won't hold, add flour by the 1 tablespoon-worth until they hold. If they still don't hold, add 1-2 eggs.
6. Test the hotness of your oil with 1 piece falafel in the center of the pan. If the oil is at the right temperature the falafel will brown 5-6 minutes total or 2-3 minutes each side. If it browns faster, the oil is too hot. Slightly cool the oil down and then test again. When you reach the right temperature, cook the falafel in 5-6 pieces batches until both sides are golden brown. With a slotted spoon, remove from the skillet, and drain on paper towels.
7. Serve fresh and hot with hummus and then topped with tahini sauce.

Nutrition: 60 cal., 1.5 g total fat (0 g sat fat), 0 mg chol., 135 mg sodium, 140 mg potassium, 10 g carb., 3 g fiber, 2 g sugar, and 3 g protein.

Prosciutto Balls

Servings: 4 | Cooking: 10 min

Ingredients
- 8 Mozzarella balls, cherry size
- 4 oz bacon, sliced
- ¼ teaspoon ground black pepper
- ¾ teaspoon dried rosemary
- 1 teaspoon butter

Directions
1. Sprinkle the sliced bacon with ground black pepper and dried rosemary.
2. Wrap every Mozzarella ball in the sliced bacon and secure them with toothpicks.
3. Melt butter.
4. Brush wrapped Mozzarella balls with butter.
5. Line the tray with the baking paper and arrange Mozzarella balls in it.
6. Bake the meal for 10 minutes at 365F.

Nutrition: calories 323; fat 26.8; fiber 0.1; carbs 0.6; protein 20.6

Chicken Skillet

Servings: 6 | Cooking: 35 min

Ingredients
- 6 chicken thighs, bone-in and skin-on
- Juice of 2 lemons
- 1 teaspoon oregano, dried
- 1 red onion, chopped
- Salt and black pepper to the taste
- 1 teaspoon garlic powder
- 2 garlic cloves, minced
- 2 tablespoons olive oil
- 2 and ½ cups chicken stock
- 1 cup white rice
- 1 tablespoon oregano, chopped
- 1 cup green olives, pitted and sliced
- 1/3 cup parsley, chopped
- ½ cup feta cheese, crumbled

Directions
1. Heat up a pan with the oil over medium heat, add the chicken thighs skin side down, cook for 4 minutes on each side and transfer to a plate.
2. Add the garlic and the onion to the pan, stir and sauté for 5 minutes.
3. Add the rice, salt, pepper, the stock, oregano, and lemon juice, stir, cook for 1-2 minutes more and take off the heat.
4. Add the chicken to the pan, introduce the pan in the oven and bake at 375 degrees F for 25 minutes.
5. Add the cheese, olives and the parsley, divide the whole mix between plates and serve for lunch.

Nutrition: calories 435; fat 18.5; fiber 13.6; carbs 27.8; protein 25.6

Salmon Bowls

Servings: 4 | Cooking: 40 min

Ingredients
- 2 cups farro
- Juice of 2 lemons
- 1/3 cup olive oil+ 2 tablespoons
- Salt and black pepper
- 1 cucumber, chopped
- ¼ cup balsamic vinegar
- 1 garlic cloves, minced
- ¼ cup parsley, chopped
- ¼ cup mint, chopped
- 2 tablespoons mustard
- 4 salmon fillets, boneless

Directions
1. Put water in a large pot, bring to a boil over medium-high heat, add salt and the farro, stir, simmer for 30 minutes, drain, transfer to a bowl, add the lemon juice, mustard, garlic, salt, pepper and 1/3 cup oil, toss and leave aside for now.

2. In another bowl, mash the cucumber with a fork, add the vinegar, salt, pepper, the parsley, dill and mint and whisk well.
3. Heat up a pan with the rest of the oil over medium heat, add the salmon fillets skin side down, cook for 5 minutes on each side, cool them down and break into pieces.
4. Add over the farro, add the cucumber dressing, toss and serve for lunch.

Nutrition: calories 281; fat 12.7; fiber 1.7; carbs 5.8; protein 36.5

Chicken And Parmesan Pasta Pudding

Servings: 10 | Cooking: 1 ¼ Hours

Ingredients
- 3 chicken breasts, cubed
- 2 tablespoons olive oil
- 1 teaspoon dried oregano
- 1 teaspoon dried basil
- 8 oz. penne
- 1 cup green peas
- 1 cup frozen sweet corn
- 1 celery stalk, sliced
- 2 carrots, diced
- 1 cup heavy cream
- 6 oz. mozzarella, crumbled

Directions
1. Heat the oil in a skillet and add the chicken. Cook for a few minutes on all sides then add the oregano and basil. Cook for another 2 minutes then transfer in a deep dish baking pan.
2. Cook the penne in a large pot of salty water until al dente, not more than 8 minutes. Drain and place in the baking pan as well.
3. Stir in the peas, corn, celery and carrots and season with salt and pepper.
4. Drizzle in the cream and top with mozzarella cheese.
5. Bake in the preheated oven at 350F for 30 minutes.
6. Serve the pudding warm and fresh.

Nutrition: Calories:266 Fat:13.2g Protein:17.7g Carbohydrates:19.8g

Pan-fried Ling With Olive And Tomato

Servings: 4 | Cooking: 10 min

Ingredients
- 800 g baby washed potatoes, steamed
- 4 pink ling fillets, skinless
- 350 g tomato medley, sliced or halved
- 3/4 cup Mediterranean mixed pitted olives, coarsely chopped
- 2 truss tomatoes, cut into thin wedges
- 2 tablespoons Wattle Valley Chunky Basil with Cashew and Parmesan Dip
- 2 tablespoons olive oil spread or butter, divided (I Can't Believe It's Not Butter! ®)
- 1/4 cup olive oil
- 1/3 cup basil leaves
- 1 tablespoon lemon juice
- 1 tablespoon flat-leaf parsley, chopped

Directions
1. Brush both sides of the fillets with 1 tablespoon of the olive oil. Over medium-high heat, heat a nonstick frying skillet or pan. Add the fish, cook per side for about 2 to 3 minutes or until just cooked through.
2. In a bowl, combine the olives, tomatoes, and basil. In another small bowl, combine the lemon juice, the dip, and the remaining olive oil.
3. In another bowl, toss the potatoes with the spread and the basil. Drizzle the dip and lemon dressing over r the cooked fish; serve with the potatoes and the mixed olive-tomato.

Nutrition: 543 cal., 30 g fat (9.5 g sat fat), 31.20 g carb., 7 g sugar, 6.3 g fiber, 33.30 g protein, and 623 mg sodium.

Mediterranean-style Fish And White-bean Puree

Servings: 4 | Cooking: 5 min

Ingredients
- 4 pieces (about 120 g each) white fish fillets (red snapper or ocean perch)
- 15 ml olive oils
- 1 1/2 tablespoons almond flour
- Salt and pepper, to season
- 1/2 cup Kalamata olives, chopped
- 1 tablespoons fresh oregano, chopped
- 2 tomatoes, vine-ripened, peeled, seeded, finely chopped
- 1 small fennel bulb, finely chopped, reserve fronds
- 30 ml olive oil

- 1 tablespoon balsamic vinegar
- 1 garlic clove
- Salt and pepper, to season
- 2 cans (400 g each) cannellini beans, drained, and rinsed
- 1/2 cup ground almonds
- 1 tablespoon lemon juice
- 1 garlic clove
- 125 ml olive oil
- 1 tablespoons fresh oregano, chopped

Directions

For the puree:
1. Except for the olive oil and the oregano, process the rest of the ingredients in a food processor to combine. With the motor continuously running, add the olive oil in a steady, slow stream. Transfer into a bowl, stir the oregano, and cover with plastic wrap; set aside.

For the olive-tomato mix:
2. In a bowl, place the olives, fennel, oregano, tomatoes, and garlic. Chop the fennel fronds roughly; add into the olive mixture. Add the vinegar and the olive oil; season with the salt and the pepper and set aside.

For the fish:
3. Season the flour with the salt and the pepper; toss the fish in the coat.
4. In a frying pan, heat the olive oil over medium heat. Add the fish, cook for about 1 to 2 minutes per side or until cooked through.
5. Place a spoonful of the bean puree into each serving plate. Place the fish on top of the puree. Divide the salsa between the plates; serve.

Nutrition: 745 cal., 53 g fat (8 g sat fat), 33 g carb., 5 g sugar, 33 g protein, 65 mg chol., and 705.72 mg sodium.

Spiced Tortilla

Servings: 4 | Cooking: 20 min

Ingredients

- 8 eggs, beaten
- 500 g cooked potato, sliced
- 300 g cherry tomato
- 2 teaspoon curry spice (we used cumin, coriander, and turmeric)
- 1 tablespoon sunflower oil
- 1 red chili, deseeded, shredded
- 1 onion, sliced
- 1 bunch coriander, finely chopped stalks, roughly chopped leaves

Directions

1. Preheat the broiler.
2. In a large oven-safe frying pan, heat the oil. When the oil is hot, add the onion and 1/2 of the red chili; cook for about 5 minutes or until softened.
3. Add the spices, cook for 1 minute. Add the tomatoes, the potatoes, and the coriander stalks. Stir to mix and distribute. Pour the eggs over the veggies; cook for about 8 to 10 minutes, or until almost set.
4. Transfer the pan into the broiler; broil for about 1 to 2 minutes until the top is set.
5. Scatter the coriander leaves and the remaining 1/2 chili over the top.
6. Slice the tortilla into wedges; serve with green Mediterranean salad.

Nutrition: 327 Cal, 17 g total fat (4 g sat. fat), 27 g carb., 5 g sugar, 3 g fiber, 19 g protein, and 0.69 g sodium.

Yogurt Marinated Pork Chops

Servings: 6 | Cooking: 2 Hours

Ingredients

- 6 pork chops
- 1 cup plain yogurt
- 1 mandarin, sliced
- 2 garlic cloves, chopped
- 1 red pepper, chopped
- Salt and pepper to taste

Directions

1. Season the pork with salt and pepper and mix it with the remaining ingredients in a zip lock bag.
2. Marinate for 1 ½ hours in the fridge.
3. Heat a grill pan over medium flame and cook the pork chops on each side until browned.
4. Serve the pork chops fresh and warm.

Nutrition: Calories:293 Fat:20.4g Protein:20.6g Carbohydrates:4.4g

White Beans And Orange Soup

Servings: 4 | Cooking: 37 min

Ingredients

- 1 yellow onion, chopped
- 5 celery sticks, chopped
- 4 carrots, chopped

- 1 cup olive oil
- ½ teaspoon oregano, dried
- 1 bay leaf
- 3 orange slices, peeled
- 30 ounces canned white beans, drained
- 2 tablespoons tomato paste
- 2 cups water
- 6 cups chicken stock

Directions
1. Heat up a pot with the oil over medium heat, add the onion, celery, carrots, the bay leaf and the oregano, stir and sauté for 5 minutes.
2. Add the orange slices and cook for 2 minutes more.
3. Add the rest of the ingredients, stir, bring to a simmer and cook over medium heat for 30 minutes.
4. Ladle the soup into bowls and serve.

Nutrition: calories 273; fat 16.3; fiber 8.4; carbs 15.6; protein 7.4

Healthy Spinach Rice

Preparation: 10 min | Cooking: 16 min | Servings: 4

Ingredients
- 1/2 cups rice
- 1 tbsp. fresh lemon juice
- 1/2 cups vegetable stock
- 12 oz. spinach, chopped
- 1/2 cup onion, chopped
- 2 tbsp. olive oil
- 1 tsp garlic, minced Pepper
- Salt

Directions
1. Add oil into the inner pot of instant pot and set the pot on sauté mode.
2. Sauté onion and garlic for 5 min.
3. Stir in remaining ingredients except spinach and stir well.
4. Seal pot with lid and cook on high for 8 min.
5. When done, release the pressure naturally for 6 min then release remaining using quick release. Remove lid.
6. Add spinach and stir well and cook on sauté mode for 3 min.
7. Serve and enjoy.

Nutrition: Calories 347, Fat 8g, Protein 8g

Tasty Salsa Beans

Preparation: 10 min | Cooking: 40 min | Servings: 6

Ingredients
- 20 oz. package ham pinto beans, rinsed
- 1 jalapeno pepper, diced
- 1 onion, diced
- 5 cups vegetable broth
- 1/4 cup parsley, chopped
- 1/2 cup salsa
- 1/2 tsp garlic, chopped Pepper
- Salt

Directions
1. Incorporate all ingredients into the inner pot of instant pot and stir well.
2. Seal pot with lid and cook on high for 40 min.
3. Once done, allow to release pressure naturally. Remove lid.
4. Stir well and serve.

Nutrition: Calories 147, Fat 2.3g, Protein 12.5g

Roasted Pepper Pasta

Preparation: 10 min | Cooking: 13 min | Servings: 6

Ingredients
- 1 lb. whole wheat penne pasta
- 1 tbsp. Italian seasoning
- 4 cups vegetable broth
- 1 tbsp. garlic, minced
- 1/2 onion, chopped
- 14 oz. jar roasted red peppers
- 1 cup feta cheese, crumbled
- 1 tbsp. olive oil
- Pepper Salt

Directions
1. Add roasted pepper into the blender and blend until smooth.
2. Add oil into the inner pot of instant pot and set the pot on sauté mode.
3. Add garlic and onion and sauté for 2-3 min.
4. Add blended roasted pepper and sauté for 2 min.
5. Add remaining ingredients except feta cheese and stir well.
6. Seal pot with lid and cook on high for 8 min.
7. When done, release the pressure naturally for 7 min then release remaining using quick release. Remove lid.
8. Top with feta cheese and serve.

Nutrition: Calories 459, Fat 10.6g, Protein 21.3g

Tuna Pasta

Preparation: 10 min | Cooking: 8 min | Servings: 6

Ingredients
- 10 oz. can tuna, drained
- 15 oz. whole wheat rotini pasta
- 4 oz. mozzarella cheese, cubed
- 1/2 cup parmesan cheese, grated
- 1 tsp dried basil
- 14 oz. can tomato, diced
- 4 cups vegetable broth
- 1 tbsp. garlic, minced
- 8 oz. mushrooms, sliced
- 2 zucchinis, sliced
- 1 onion, chopped
- 2 tbsp. olive oil Pepper
- Salt

Directions
1. Add oil into the inner pot of instant pot and set the pot on sauté mode.
2. Add mushrooms, zucchini, and onion and sauté until onion is softened.
3. Add garlic and sauté for a minute.
4. Add pasta, basil, tuna, tomatoes, and broth and stir well.
5. Seal pot with lid and cook on high for 4 min.
6. When done, release the pressure naturally for 6 min then release remaining using quick release. Remove lid.
7. Add remaining ingredients and stir well and serve.

Nutrition: Calories 346, Fat 11.9g, Protein 6.3g

Vegan Olive Pasta

Preparation: 10 min | Cooking: 5 min | Servings: 4

Ingredients
- 4 cups whole grain penne pasta
- 1/2 cup olives, sliced
- 1 tbsp. capers
- 1/4 tsp red pepper flakes
- 3 cups of water
- 4 cups pasta sauce, homemade
- 1 tbsp. garlic, minced
- Pepper Salt

Directions
1. Incorporate all ingredients into the inner pot of instant pot and stir well.
2. Seal pot with lid and cook on high for 5 min.
3. Once done, release pressure using quick release. Remove lid.
4. Stir and serve.

Nutrition: Calories 441, Fat 10.1g, Protein 11.8g

Italian Chicken Pasta

Preparation: 10 min | Cooking: 9 min | Servings: 8

Ingredients
- 1 lb. chicken breast, skinless, boneless, and cut into chunks
- 1/2 cup cream cheese
- 1 cup mozzarella cheese, shredded
- 1 1/2 tsp Italian seasoning
- 1 tsp garlic, minced
- 1 cup mushrooms, diced
- 1/2 onion, diced
- 2 tomatoes, diced
- 2 cups of water
- 16 oz. whole wheat penne pasta
- Pepper
- Salt

Directions
1. Add all ingredients except cheeses into the inner pot of instant pot and stir well.
2. Seal pot with lid and cook on high for 9 min.
3. When done, release the pressure naturally for 6 min then release remaining using quick release. Remove lid.
4. Add cheeses and stir well and serve.

Nutrition: Calories 328, Fat 8.5g, Protein 23.7g

Cucumber Lemon Rice

Preparation: 10 min | Cooking: 10 min | Servings: 8

Ingredients
- 2 cups rice, rinsed
- 1/2 cup olives, pitted
- 1 cup cucumber, chopped
- 1 tbsp. red wine vinegar
- 1 tsp. lemon zest, grated
- 1 tbsp. fresh lemon juice
- 2 tbsp. olive oil

- 2 cups vegetable broth
- 1/2 tsp dried oregano
- 1 red bell pepper, chopped
- 1/2 cup onion, chopped
- 1 tbsp. olive oil
- Pepper
- Salt

Directions
1. Add oil into the inner pot of instant pot and set the pot on sauté mode.
2. Add onion and sauté for 3 min.
3. Add bell pepper and oregano and sauté for 1 minute.
4. Add rice and broth and stir well.
5. Seal pot with lid and cook on high for 6 min.
6. When done, release the pressure naturally for 11 min then release remaining using quick release. Remove lid.
7. Add remaining ingredients and stir everything well to mix.
8. Serve immediately and enjoy it.

Nutrition: Calories 229, Fat 5.1g, Protein 4.9g

Bulgur Salad

Preparation: 10 min | Cooking: 1 minute | Servings: 2

Ingredients
- 1/2 cup bulgur wheat
- 1/4 cup fresh parsley, chopped
- 1 tbsp. fresh mint, chopped
- 1/3 cup feta cheese, crumbled
- 2 tbsp. fresh lemon juice
- 1 tbsp. olives, chopped
- 1/4 cup olive oil
- 1/2 cup tomatoes, chopped
- 1/3 cup cucumber, chopped
- 1/2 cup water
- Salt

Directions
1. Add the bulgur wheat, water, and salt into the instant pot.
2. Seal pot with lid and cook on high for 1 minute.
3. Once done, release pressure using quick release. Remove lid.
4. Transfer bulgur wheat to the mixing bowl. Stir the remaining ingredients well.
5. Serve and enjoy.

Nutrition: Calories 430, Fat 32.2g, Protein 8.9g

Cheese Basil Tomato Rice

Preparation: 10 min | Cooking: 26 min | Servings: 8

Ingredients
- 1 1/2 cups brown rice
- 1 cup parmesan cheese, grated
- 1/4 cup fresh basil, chopped
- 2 cups grape tomatoes, halved
- 8 oz. can tomato sauce
- 1 3/4 cup vegetable broth
- 1 tbsp. garlic, minced
- 1/2 cup onion, diced
- 1 tbsp. olive oil Pepper
- Salt

Directions
1. Add oil into the inner pot of instant pot and set the pot on sauté mode.
2. Add garlic and onion and sauté for 4 min.
3. Add rice, tomato sauce, broth, pepper, and salt and stir well.
4. Seal pot with lid and cook on high for 22 min.
5. When done, release the pressure naturally for 11 min then release remaining using quick release. Remove lid.
6. Add remaining ingredients and stir well.
7. Serve and enjoy.

Nutrition: Calories 208, Fat 5.6g, Protein 8.3g

Delicious Chicken Pasta

Preparation: 10 min | Cooking: 17 min | Servings: 4

Ingredients
- 3 chicken breasts, skinless, boneless, cut into pieces
- 9 ounces whole-grain pasta
- ½ cup of olives, sliced
- ½ cup of sun-dried tomatoes
- 1 tablespoon of roasted red peppers, chopped
- 14-ounces can tomato, diced
- 2 cups of marinara sauce
- 1 cup of chicken broth
- Pepper
- Salt

Directions
1. Add all ingredients except whole-grain pasta into the Instant Pot and stir well.
2. Close and cook over high heat for 12 min.

3. Once done, allow to release pressure naturally. Remove lid.
4. Add pasta and stir well. Seal the pot again and select manual and set timer for 5 min.
5. Allow to release pressure naturally for about 5 min, then release remaining using quick release. Remove lid.
6. Stir well and serve.

Nutrition: Calories: 615 ; Fat: 15.4g ; Protein: 48g

Flavors Taco Rice Bowl

Preparation: 10 min | Cooking: 14 min | Servings: 8

Ingredients
- 1-pound ground beef
- 8 ounces cheddar cheese, shredded
- 14-ounces can of red beans
- 2 ounces taco seasoning
- 16 ounces salsa
- 2 cups of water
- 2 cups of brown rice
- Pepper
- Salt

Directions
1. Set the Instant Pot on sauté mode.
2. Add meat to the pot and sauté until brown.
3. Add water, beans, rice, taco seasoning, pepper, and salt and stir well.
4. Top with salsa. Seal the pot with the lid and cook over high heat for 14 min.
5. Once done, release pressure using quick release. Remove lid.
6. Stir in cheddar cheese until melted.
7. Serve and enjoy.

Nutrition: Calories: 464 ; Fat: 15.3g ; Protein: 32.2g

Sundried-Cheese Macaroni

Preparation: 10 min | Cooking: 10 min | Servings: 6

Ingredients
- 16 ounces whole-grain elbow pasta
- 4 cups of water
- 1 cup of tomatoes, diced
- 1 teaspoon of garlic, chopped
- 2 tablespoons of olive oil
- ¼ cup of green onions, chopped
- ½ cup of Parmesan cheese, grated
- ½ cup of mozzarella cheese, grated
- 1 cup of cheddar cheese, grated
- ¼ cup of passata
- 1 cup of unsweetened almond milk
- 1 cup of marinated artichoke, diced
- ½ cup of sun-dried tomatoes, sliced
- ½ cup of olives, sliced
- 1 teaspoon of salt

Directions
1. Add pasta, water, tomatoes, garlic, oil, and salt into the Instant Pot and stir well.
2. Seal the pot with the lid and cook over high heat for 4 min.
3. When done, release the pressure naturally for about 5 min, then release remaining using quick release. Remove lid.
4. Set pot on sauté mode. Add green onion, Parmesan cheese, mozzarella cheese, cheddar cheese, passata, almond milk, artichoke, sun-dried tomatoes, and olive. Mix well.
5. Stir well and cook until cheese is melted.
6. Serve and enjoy.

Nutrition: Calories: 519 ; Fat: 17. g ; Protein: 25g

Fried Balls with Tomato Sauce Rice

Preparation: 15 min | Cooking: 20 min | Servings: 4

Ingredients
- 1 cup bread crumbs
- 2 cups cooked risotto (see tip)
- 2 large eggs, divided
- ¼ cup freshly grated Parmesan cheese
- 8 fresh baby mozzarella balls, or 1 (4-inch) log fresh mozzarella, cut into 8 pieces
- 2 tablespoons water
- 1 cup corn oil
- 1 cup Basic Tomato Basil Sauce, or store-bought

Directions
1. Prep the bread crumbs then set aside.
2. Incorporate the risotto, 1 egg, and the Parmesan cheese until well combined.
3. Dampen your hands with some water to prevent sticking and divide the risotto mixture into 8 pieces. Situate them on a clean work surface and flatten each piece.
4. Situate 1 mozzarella ball on each flattened rice disk. Seal the rice around the mozzarella to form a ball. Repeat until finish.
5. Scourge remaining egg and the water.
6. Soak each prepared risotto ball into the egg wash and roll it in the bread crumbs. Set aside.

7. Using big sauté pan or skillet over high heat, heat the corn oil for about 3 min.
8. Mildly lower the risotto balls into the hot oil and fry for 7 min.
9. Using a saucepan over medium heat, heat the tomato sauce for 5 min, then serve the warm sauce alongside the rice balls.

Nutrition: Calories: 255; Fat: 15g; Protein: 11g

Delicious Pasta Primavera

Preparation: 10 min | Cooking: 4 min | Servings: 4

Ingredients
- 8 ounces whole-wheat penne pasta
- 1 tablespoon of fresh lemon juice
- 2 tablespoons of fresh parsley, chopped
- ¼ cup of almonds slivered
- ¼ cup of Parmesan cheese, grated
- 14-ounce can tomato, diced
- ½ cup of prunes
- ½ cup of zucchini, chopped
- ½ cup of asparagus, and then cut into 1-inch pieces
- ½ up carrots, chopped
- ½ cup of broccoli, chopped
- 1 ¾ cups of vegetable stock
- Pepper
- Salt

Directions
1. Add stock, pars, tomatoes, prunes, zucchini, asparagus, carrots, and broccoli into the Instant Pot and stir well.
2. Seal the pot with the lid and cook over high heat for 4 min.
3. Once done, release pressure using quick release. Remove lid.
4. Add the remaining ingredients and stir well and serve.

Nutrition: Calories: 303 ; Fat: 2.6g ; Protein: 12.8g

Roasted Pepper and Feta Penne Pasta

Preparation: 10 min | Cooking: 13 min | Servings: 6

Ingredients
- 1-pound whole-wheat penne pasta
- 1 tablespoon of Italian seasoning
- 4 cups of vegetable broth
- 1 tablespoon of garlic, minced
- ½ onion, chopped
- 14-ounce jar roasted red peppers
- 1 cup of feta cheese, crumbled
- 1 tablespoon of olive oil
- Pepper
- Salt

Directions
1. Add roasted pepper into the blender and blend until smooth.
2. Add oil to the inner pot of the instant pot and set the pot on sauté mode.
3. Add garlic and onion and sauté for 2–3 min.
4. Add blended roasted pepper and sauté for 2 min.
5. Add the remaining ingredients except for feta cheese and stir well.
6. Seal the pot with the lid and cook over high heat for 8 min.
7. When done, release the pressure naturally for 5 min, then release remaining using quick release. Remove lid.
8. Top with feta cheese and serve.

Nutrition: Calories: 459 ; Fat: 10.6g ; Protein: 21.3g

Basil, Parmesan and Tomato Rice

Preparation: 10 min | Cooking: 26 min | Servings: 8

Ingredients
- 1 ½ cup of brown rice
- 1 cup of Parmesan cheese, grated
- ¼ cup of fresh basil, chopped
- 2 cups of grape tomatoes, halved
- 8-ounce can tomato sauce
- 1 ¾ cup of vegetable broth
- 1 tablespoon of garlic, minced
- ½ cup of onion, diced
- 1 tablespoon of olive oil
- Pepper
- Salt

Directions
1. Pour oil to the pot of Instant Pot and set the pot on sauté mode.
2. Add garlic and onion and sauté for 4 min.
3. Add rice, tomato sauce, broth, pepper, and salt and stir well.
4. Seal the pot with the lid and cook over high heat for 22 min.
5. When done, release the pressure naturally for 11 min, then release remaining using quick release. Remove lid.
6. Add the remaining ingredients and stir well.

7. Serve and enjoy.

Nutrition: Calories: 208 ; Fat: 5.6g ; Protein: 8.3g

Macaroni and Cheese

Preparation: 10 min | Cooking: 4 min | Servings: 8

Ingredients
- 1-pound whole-grain pasta
- ½ cup of Parmesan cheese, grated
- 4 cups of cheddar cheese, shredded
- 1 cup of milk
- ¼ teaspoon of garlic powder
- ½ teaspoon of ground mustard
- 2 tablespoons of olive oil
- 4 cups of water
- Pepper
- Salt

Directions
1. Add pasta, garlic powder, mustard, oil, water, pepper, and salt into the Instant Pot.
2. Seal the pot with the lid and cook on high for 4 min.
3. Once done, release pressure using quick release. Remove lid.
4. Add the remaining ingredients and stir well and serve.

Nutrition: Calories: 509 ; Fat: 25.7g ; Protein: 27.3g

Flavors Herb Risotto

Preparation: 10 min | Cooking: 15 min | Servings: 4

Ingredients
- 2 cups of rice
- 2 tbsp. parmesan cheese, grated
- oz. heavy cream
- 1 tbsp. fresh oregano, chopped
- 1 tbsp. fresh basil, chopped
- 1/2 tbsp. sage, chopped
- 1 onion, chopped
- 2 tbsp. olive oil
- 1 tsp garlic, minced
- 4 cups vegetable stock
- Pepper
- Salt

Directions
1. Add oil into the inner pot of instant pot and set the pot on sauté mode.
2. Add garlic and onion and sauté for 2-3 min.
3. Add remaining ingredients except for parmesan cheese and heavy cream and stir well.
4. Seal pot with lid and cook on high for 12 min.
5. When done, release the pressure naturally for 11 min then release remaining using quick release. Remove lid.
6. Stir in cream and cheese and serve.

Nutrition: Calories 514Fat 17.6gProtein 8.8g

Pesto Chicken Pasta

Preparation: 10 min | Cooking: 10 min | Servings: 6

Ingredients
- 1 lb. chicken breast, skinless, boneless, and diced
- 3 tbsp. olive oil
- 1/2 cup parmesan cheese, shredded
- 1 tsp Italian seasoning
- 1/4 cup heavy cream
- 16 oz. whole wheat pasta
- 6 oz. basil pesto
- 3 1/2 cups water Pepper
- Salt

Directions
1. Season chicken with Italian seasoning, pepper, and salt.
2. Add oil into the inner pot of instant pot and set the pot on sauté mode.
3. Add chicken to the pot and sauté until brown.
4. Add remaining ingredients except for parmesan cheese, heavy cream, and pesto and stir well.
5. Seal pot with lid and cook on high for 5 min.
6. Once done, release pressure using quick release. Remove lid.
7. Stir in parmesan cheese, heavy cream, and pesto and serve.

Nutrition: Calories 475, Fat 14g, Protein 28.7g

Flavorful Mac & Cheese

Preparation: 10 min | Cooking: 10 min | Servings: 6

Ingredients
- 16 oz. whole-grain elbow pasta
- 4 cups of water
- cup can tomato, diced

- 1 tsp garlic, chopped
- Tbsp. olive oil
- 1/4 cup green onions, chopped
- 1/2 cup parmesan cheese, grated
- 1/2 cup mozzarella cheese, grated
- 1 cup cheddar cheese, grated
- 1/4 cup passata
- 1 cup unsweetened almond milk
- 1 cup marinated artichoke, diced
- 1/2 cup sun-dried tomatoes, sliced
- 1/2 cup olives, sliced
- tsp salt

Directions
1. Add pasta, water, tomatoes, garlic, oil, and salt into the instant pot and stir well.
2. Seal pot with lid and cook on high for 4 min.
3. When done, release the pressure naturally for 6 min then release remaining using quick release. Remove lid.
4. Set pot on sauté mode. Add green onion, parmesan cheese, mozzarella cheese, cheddar cheese, passata, almond milk, artichoke, sun-dried tomatoes, and olive. Mix well.
5. Stir well and cook until cheese is melted.
6. Serve and enjoy.

Nutrition: Calories 519, Fat 17.1g, Protein 25g

Vegetable Herb Rice

Preparation: 10 min | Cooking: 27 min | Servings: 6

Ingredients
- 1 1/2 cups brown rice, rinsed and drained
- 1/2 cup fresh parsley, chopped
- 1 3/4 cup water
- 1/4 tsp dried oregano
- 1/2 celery, chopped
- 1/2 cup bell pepper, chopped
- 1 tbsp. garlic, minced
- 1 cup onion, chopped
- 1 1/2 tbsp. olive oil Pepper
- Salt

Directions
1. Add oil into the inner pot of instant pot and set the pot on sauté mode.
2. Add celery, bell pepper, garlic, and onion and sauté for 5 min.
3. Add remaining ingredients and stir well.
4. Seal pot with lid and cook on high for 22 min.
5. Once done, allow to release pressure naturally. Remove lid.
6. Serve and enjoy.

Nutrition: Calories 217, Fat 4.9g, Protein 4.1g

Italian Two-Cheese Macaroni

Preparation: 10 min | Cooking: 6 min | Servings: 4

Ingredients
- 1 lb. whole grain pasta
- 2 tsp Italian seasoning
- 1 1/2 tsp garlic powder
- 1 1/2 tsp onion powder
- 1 cup sour cream
- 4 cups of water
- 4 oz. parmesan cheese, shredded
- 12 oz. ricotta cheese
- Pepper Salt

Directions
1. Add all ingredients except ricotta cheese into the inner pot of instant pot and stir well.
2. Seal pot with lid and cook on high for 6 min.
3. When done, release the pressure naturally for 6 min then release remaining using quick release. Remove lid.
4. Add ricotta cheese and stir well and serve.

Nutrition: Calories 388, Fat 25.8g, Protein 22.8g

Delicious Greek Chicken Pasta

Preparation: 10 min | Cooking: 10 min | Servings: 6

Ingredients
- 2 chicken breasts, skinless, boneless, and cut into chunks
- 1/2 cup olives, sliced
- 2 cups vegetable stock
- 12 oz. Greek vinaigrette dressing
- 1 lb. whole grain pasta
- Pepper
- Salt

Directions
1. Incorporate all ingredients into the inner pot of instant pot and stir well.
2. Seal pot with lid and cook on high for 10 min.
3. Once done, release pressure using quick release. Remove lid.
4. Stir well and serve.

Nutrition: Calories 325, Fat 25.8g, Protein 15.6g

Chicken Marinara Pasta

Preparation: 10 min | Cooking: 17 min | Servings: 4

Ingredients
- 3 chicken breasts, skinless, boneless, cut into pieces
- 9 oz. whole-grain pasta
- 1/2 cup olives, sliced
- 1/2 cup sun-dried tomatoes
- 1 tbsp. roasted red peppers, chopped
- 14 oz. can tomato, diced
- 2 cups marinara sauce
- 1 cup chicken broth Pepper
- Salt

Directions
1. Add all ingredients except whole-grain pasta into the instant pot and stir well.
2. Seal pot with lid and cook on high for 12 min.
3. Once done, allow to release pressure naturally. Remove lid.
4. Add pasta and stir well. Seal pot again and select manual and set timer for 5 min.
5. When done, release the pressure naturally for 6 min then release remaining using quick release. Remove lid.
6. Stir well and serve.

Nutrition: Calories 615, Fat 15.4g, Protein 48g

Fiber Packed Chicken Rice

Preparation: 10 min | Cooking: 16 min | Servings: 6

Ingredients
- 3 lb. chicken breast, skinless, boneless, and cut into chunks
- oz. can cannellini beans
- 4 cups chicken broth
- 2 cups wild rice
- 1 tbsp. Italian seasoning
- 1 small onion, chopped
- 1 tbsp. garlic, chopped
- 1 tbsp. olive oil
- Pepper Salt

Directions
1. Add oil into the inner pot of instant pot and set the pot on sauté mode.
2. Add garlic and onion and sauté for 2 min.
3. Add chicken and cook for 2 min.
4. Add remaining ingredients and stir well.
5. Seal pot with lid and cook on high for 12 min.
6. Once done, release pressure using quick release. Remove lid.
7. Stir well and serve.

Nutrition: Calories 399, Fat 6.4g, Protein 31.6g

Tasty Greek Rice

Preparation: 10 min | Cooking: 10 min | Servings: 6

Ingredients
- 1 3/4 cup brown rice, rinsed and drained
- 3/4 cup roasted red peppers, chopped
- 1 cup olives, chopped
- 1 tsp dried oregano
- 1 tsp Greek seasoning
- 3/4 cup vegetable broth
- 2 tbsp. olive oil
- Salt

Directions
1. Add oil into the inner pot of instant pot and set the pot on sauté mode.
2. Add rice and cook for 5 min.
3. Add remaining ingredients except for red peppers and olives and stir well.
4. Seal pot with lid and cook on high for 5 min.
5. When done, release the pressure naturally for 11 min then release remaining using quick release. Remove lid.
6. Add red peppers and olives and stir well.
7. Serve and enjoy.

Nutrition: Calories 285, Fat 9.1g, Protein 6g

Mexican Taco Rice Bowl

Preparation: 10 min | Cooking: 14 min | Servings: 8

Ingredients
- 1 lb. ground beef
- 8 oz. cheddar cheese, shredded
- 14 oz. can red beans
- 2 oz. taco seasoning
- 16 oz. salsa
- 2 cups of water
- 2 cups brown rice Pepper
- Salt

Directions
1. Set instant pot on sauté mode.

2. Add meat to the pot and sauté until brown.
3. Add water, beans, rice, taco seasoning, pepper, and salt and stir well.
4. Top with salsa. Seal pot with lid and cook on high for 14 min.
5. Once done, release pressure using quick release. Remove lid.
6. Mix in cheddar cheese until melted.
7. Serve and enjoy.

Nutrition: Calories 464, Fat 15.3g, Protein 32.2g

Spinach Pesto Pasta

Preparation: 10 min | Cooking: 10 min | Servings: 4

Ingredients

- 8 oz. whole-grain pasta
- 1/3 cup mozzarella cheese, grated
- 1/2 cup pesto
- 5 oz. fresh spinach
- 1 3/4 cup water
- 8 oz. mushrooms, chopped
- 1 tbsp. olive oil
- Pepper
- Salt

Directions

1. Add oil into the inner pot of instant pot and set the pot on sauté mode.
2. Add mushrooms and sauté for 5 min.
3. Add water and pasta and stir well.
4. Seal pot with lid and cook on high for 5 min.
5. Once done, release pressure using quick release. Remove lid.
6. Stir in remaining ingredients and serve.

Nutrition: Calories 213, Fat 17.3g, Protein 7.4g

Tuna and Tomato Rotini Pasta

Preparation: 10 min | Cooking: 8 min | Servings: 6

Ingredients

- 10-ounce can tuna, drained
- 15-ounce whole-wheat rotini pasta
- 4-ounce mozzarella cheese, cubed
- ½ cup of Parmesan cheese, grated
- 1 teaspoon of dried basil
- 14-ounce can tomato, diced
- 4 cups of vegetable broth
- 1 tablespoon of garlic, minced
- 8-ounce mushrooms, sliced
- 2 zucchinis, sliced
- 1 onion, chopped
- 2 tablespoons of olive oil
- Pepper
- Salt

Directions

1. Pour oil to the pot of Instant Pot and set the pot on sauté mode.
2. Add mushrooms, zucchini, and onion and sauté until onion is softened.
3. Add garlic and sauté for 1 minute.
4. Add pasta, basil, tuna, tomatoes, and broth and stir well.
5. Seal the pot with the lid and cook over high heat for 4 min.
6. When done, release the pressure naturally for 5 min, then release remaining using quick release. Remove lid.
7. Add the remaining ingredients and stir well and serve.

Nutrition: Calories: 346 ; Fat: 11.9g ; Protein: 6.3g

Olive Penne Pasta

Preparation: 10 min | Cooking: 5 min | Servings: 4

Ingredients

- 4 cups of whole grain penne pasta
- ½ cup of olives, sliced
- 1 tablespoon of capers
- ¼ teaspoon of red pepper flakes
- 3 cups of water
- 4 cups of pasta sauce, homemade
- 1 tablespoon of garlic, minced
- Pepper
- Salt

Directions

1. Incorporate all of the ingredients into the pot of Instant Pot and stir well.
2. Seal the pot with the lid and cook over high heat for 5 min.
3. Once done, release pressure using quick release. Remove lid.
4. Stir and serve.

Nutrition: Calories: 441; Fat: 10.1g ; Protein: 11.8g

Italian Mac & Cheese

Preparation: 10 min | Cooking: 6 min | Servings: 4

Ingredients
- 1-pound whole-grain pasta
- 2 teaspoons of Italian seasoning
- 1 ½ teaspoon of garlic powder
- 1 ½ teaspoon of onion powder
- 1 cup of sour cream
- 4 cups of water
- 4 ounces Parmesan cheese, shredded
- 12 ounces ricotta cheese
- Pepper
- Salt

Directions
1. Add all ingredients except ricotta cheese into the inner pot of Instant Pot and stir well.
2. Seal the pot with the lid and cook over high heat for 6 min.
3. When done, release the pressure naturally for 5 min, then release remaining using quick release. Remove lid.
4. Add ricotta cheese and stir well and serve.

Nutrition: Calories: 388 ; Fat: 25.8g; Protein: 22.8g

Italian Chicken-Mozzarella Penne Pasta

Preparation: 10 min | Cooking: 9 min | Servings: 8

Ingredients
- 1-pound chicken breast, skinless, boneless, and cut into chunks
- ½ cup of cream cheese
- 1 cup of mozzarella cheese, shredded
- 1 ½ teaspoon of Italian seasoning
- 1 teaspoon of garlic, minced
- 1 cup of mushrooms, diced
- ½ onion, diced
- 2 tomatoes, diced
- 2 cups of water
- 16 ounces whole-wheat penne pasta
- Pepper
- Salt

Directions
1. Add all ingredients except cheeses into the inner pot of Instant Pot and stir well.
2. Seal the pot with the lid and cook over high heat for 9 min.
3. When done, release the pressure naturally for 5 min, then release remaining using quick release. Remove lid.
4. Add cheeses and stir well and serve.

Nutrition: Calories: 328 ; Fat: 8.5g ; Protein: 23.7g

Chicken Pasta with Vinaigrette Dressing

Preparation: 10 min | Cooking: 10 min | Servings: 6

Ingredients
- 2 chicken breasts, skinless, boneless, and cut into chunks
- ½ cup of olives, sliced
- 2 cups of vegetable stock
- 12 ounces Greek vinaigrette dressing
- 1-pound whole-grain pasta
- Pepper
- Salt

Directions
1. Incorporate all of the ingredients in the inner pot of Instant Pot and stir well.
2. Seal the pot with the lid and cook over high heat for 10 min.
3. Once done, release pressure using quick release. Remove lid.
4. Stir well and serve.

Nutrition: Calories: 325 ; Fat: 25.8g ; Protein: 15.6g

Creamy Chicken Pesto Pasta

Preparation: 10 min | Cooking: 10 min | Servings: 6

Ingredients
- 1-ounce chicken breast, skinless, boneless, and diced
- 3 tablespoon of olive oil
- ½ cup of Parmesan cheese, shredded
- 1 teaspoon of Italian seasoning
- ¼ cup of heavy cream
- 16 ounces whole-wheat pasta
- 6 ounces basil pesto
- 3 ½ cups of water
- Pepper
- Salt

Directions

1. Season chicken with Italian seasoning, pepper, and salt.
2. Pour oil to the pot of Instant Pot and set the pot on sauté mode.
3. Add chicken to the pot and sauté until brown.
4. Add the remaining ingredients except for Parmesan cheese, heavy cream, and pesto, and stir well.
5. Seal the pot with the lid and cook over high heat for 5 min.
6. Once done, release pressure using quick release. Remove lid.
7. Stir in Parmesan cheese, heavy cream, and pesto and serve.

Nutrition: Calories: 475 ; Fat: 14.7g ; Protein: 28.7g

Spinach and Mushroom Pesto

Preparation: 10 min | Cooking: 10 min | Servings: 4

Ingredients

- 8 ounces whole-grain pasta
- 1/3 cup of mozzarella cheese, grated
- ½ cup of pesto
- 5-ounce fresh spinach
- 1 ¾ cup of water
- 8 ounces mushrooms, chopped
- 1 tablespoon of olive oil
- Pepper
- Salt

Directions

1. Pour oil to the pot of Instant Pot and set the pot on sauté mode.
2. Add mushrooms and sauté for 5 min.
3. Add water and pasta and stir well.
4. Seal the pot with the lid and cook over high heat for 5 min.
5. Once done, release pressure using quick release. Remove lid.
6. Stir in the remaining ingredients and serve.

Nutrition: Calories: 213 ; Fat: 17.3g ; Protein: 7.4g

Chicken Fried Rice

Preparation: 10 min | Cooking: 16 min | Servings: 6

Ingredients

- 1-pound chicken breast, skinless, boneless, and cut into chunks
- 14.5-ounce can cannellini beans
- 4 cups of chicken broth
- 2 cups of wild rice
- 1 tablespoon of Italian seasoning
- 1 small onion, chopped
- 1 tablespoon of garlic, chopped
- 1 tablespoon of olive oil
- Pepper
- Salt

Directions

1. Pour oil to the pot of Instant Pot and set the pot on sauté mode.
2. Add garlic and onion and sauté for 2 min.
3. Add chicken and cook for 2 min.
4. Add the remaining ingredients and stir well.
5. Seal the pot with the lid and cook over high heat for 12 min.
6. Once done, release pressure using quick release. Remove lid.
7. Stir well and serve.

Nutrition: Calories: 399 ; Fat: 6.4g ; Protein: 31.6g

Lemon Rice Pilaf

Preparation: 10 min | Cooking: 10 min | Servings: 6

Ingredients

- 1 ¾ cup of brown rice
- ¾ cup of roasted red peppers, chopped
- 1 cup of olives, chopped
- 1 teaspoon of dried oregano
- 1 teaspoon of Greek seasoning
- 1 ¾ cup of vegetable broth
- 2 tablespoons of olive oil
- Salt

Directions

1. Pour oil to the pot of Instant Pot and set the pot on sauté mode.
2. Add rice and cook for 5 min.
3. Add the remaining ingredients except for red peppers and olives and stir well.
4. Seal the pot with the lid and cook over high heat for 5 min.
5. When done, allow to release pressure for 10 min, then release remaining using quick release. Remove lid.
6. Add red peppers and olives and stir well.
7. Serve and enjoy.

Nutrition: Calories: 285 ; Fat: 9.1g ; Protein: 6g

Bulgur, Mint and Parsley Salad

Preparation: 10 min | Cooking: 1 minute | Servings: 2

Ingredients
- ½ cup of bulgur wheat
- ¼ cup of fresh parsley, chopped
- 1 tablespoon of fresh mint, chopped
- 1/3 cup of feta cheese, crumbled
- 2 tablespoons of fresh lemon juice
- 2 tablespoons of olives, chopped
- ¼ cup of olive oil
- ½ cup of tomatoes, chopped
- 1/3 cup of cucumber, chopped
- ½ cup of water
- Salt

Directions
1. Add the bulgur wheat, water, and salt into the instant pot.
2. Seal the pot with the lid and cook over high heat for 1 minute.
3. Once done, release pressure using quick release. Remove lid.
4. Transfer bulgur wheat to the mixing bowl. Mix the remaining ingredients.
5. Serve.

Nutrition: Calories: 430 ; Fat: 32.2g ; Protein: 8.9g

Perfect Herb Rice

Preparation: 10 min | Cooking: 4 min | Servings: 4

Ingredients
- 1 cup of brown rice, rinsed
- 1 tablespoon of olive oil
- 1 ½ cups of water
- ½ cup of fresh mixed herbs, chopped
- 1 teaspoon of salt

Directions
1. First, add all ingredients into the inner pot of Instant Pot and stir well.
2. Seal the pot with the lid and cook over high heat for 4 min.
3. When done, release the pressure naturally for 11 min, then release remaining using quick release. Remove lid.
4. Stir well and serve.

Nutrition: Calories: 264 ; Fat: 9.9g ; Protein: 7.3g

Cod & Green Bean Dinner

Preparation: 10 min | Cooking: 10 min | Serves: 2

Ingredients
- 1 Tbsp. Olive Oil
- ½ Tbsp. Balsamic Vinegar
- 2 Cod Fillets
- 4 oz. Each
- 1 ½ Cups Green Beans
- ½ Pint Cherry Grapes

Directions
1. Heat oven to 390° F, and get out two rimmed baking sheets. Coat them with nonstick cooking spray.
2. Whisk vinegar and oil together in the bowl before setting it to the side.
3. Place two pieces of fish on each baking sheet.
4. Get out a bowl and combine tomatoes and beans.
5. Pour the oil and vinegar over it, and toss to coat.
6. Pour half of the green bean mixture over the fish on one baking sheet and the remaining fish and green beans on the other.
7. Turn the fish over, and coat it with the oil mixture.
8. Bake for five to eight min.

Nutrition: Calories: 440 ; Protein: 14g ; Fat: 22g

Mediterranean Chicken Quinoa Bowl

Preparation: 10 min | Cooking: 15 min | Servings: 8

Ingredients
- ½ cup almonds, slivered
- 1/8 teaspoon black pepper
- 2 tablespoons extra-virgin olive oil, divided
- 1/8 teaspoon crushed red pepper
- 1 tablespoon fresh parsley, finely chopped
- 1 cup cooked quinoa
- 1/8 cup feta cheese, crumbled
- ½ teaspoon salt
- 1 small garlic clove, crushed
- ½ pound boneless, skinless chicken breasts, trimmed
- ½ (7-ounce) jar roasted red peppers, rinsed
- ½ teaspoon paprika
- 1/8 cup pitted Kalamata olives, chopped
- ½ cup cucumber, diced
- ¼ teaspoon ground cumin
- 1/8 cup red onions, finely chopped

Directions
1. Preheat the oven on broiler setting and lightly grease a baking sheet.
2. Sprinkle the chicken with salt and black pepper.
3. Transfer it on the baking sheet and broil for about 15 min.
4. Let the chicken cool for about 5 min and transfer to a cutting board.
5. Shred the chicken and keep aside.
6. Put almonds, paprika, black pepper, garlic, half of olive oil, red pepper and cumin in a blender.
7. Blend until smooth and dish out in a bowl.
8. Toss quinoa, red onions, 2 tablespoons oil, quinoa and olives in a bowl.
9. Divide the quinoa mixture in the serving bowls and top with cucumber, red pepper sauce and chicken.
10. Garnish with feta cheese and parsley to immediately serve.

Nutrition: Calories 741 Fat 33.7g Protein 48.4g

Linguine with Shrimp

Preparation: 10 min | Cooking: 15 min | Servings: 4

Ingredients
- 3 tablespoons extra virgin olive oil
- 12 ounces linguine
- 1 tablespoon garlic, minced
- 30 large shrimp, peeled and deveined
- A pinch of red pepper flakes, crushed
- 1 cup green olives, pitted and chopped
- 3 tablespoons lemon juice
- 1 teaspoon lemon zest, grated
- ¼ cup parsley, chopped

Directions
1. Put some water in a large saucepan, add water, bring to a boil over medium high heat, add linguine, cook according to instructions, take off heat, drain and put in a bowl and reserve ½ cup cooking liquid.
2. Heat a pan with 2 tablespoons oil over medium high heat, add shrimp, stir and cook for 3 min.
3. Add pepper flakes and garlic, stir and cook 10 seconds more.
4. Add remaining oil, lemon zest and juice and stir well.
5. Add pasta and olives, reserved cooking liquid and parsley, stir, cook for 2 min more, take off heat, divide between plates and serve.

Nutrition: Calories 500, Fat 20g, Protein 34g

Sweet Yogurt Bulgur Bowl

Preparation: 10 min | Cooking: 0 min | Servings: 4

Ingredients
- 1 cup grapes, halved
- ½ cup bulgur, cooked
- ¼ cup celery stalk, chopped
- 2 oz. walnuts, chopped
- ¼ cup plain yogurt
- ½ teaspoon ground cinnamon

Directions
1. Mix grapes with bulgur, celery stalk, and walnut. Then add plain yogurt and ground cinnamon. Stir the mixture with the help of the spoon and transfer in the serving bowls.

Fried Halloumi & Avocados

Preparation: 5 min | Cooking: 5 min | Servings: 2

Ingredients
- 10oz halloumi cheese
- 2 tbsp. butter
- 2 avocados
- 0.5 cup sour cream
- 0.25 cucumber
- 2 tbsp. olive oil
- 2 tbsp. pistachio nuts
- Salt
- Pepper

Directions
1. Chop the cheese into slices and put to a frying pan, with the butter for cooking
2. Cook for 5 min on each side
3. Place the cheese onto a plate
4. Slice up the cucumber and arrange on the plate
5. Remove the skin and seed from the avocado and cut into slices
6. Garnish cheese on top of the avocado, drizzle with olive oil and season

Nutrition: Fat: 100g ; Protein: 36g Calories: 1112

Chicken Korma

Preparation: 5 min | Cooking: 10 min | Servings: 4

Ingredients
- 1 sliced red onion
- 4oz yogurt (Greek yogurt works best)
- 4 tbsp. ghee
- 3 cloves
- 1 bay leaf
- 1-star anise
- 1 cinnamon stick
- 3 cardamom pods
- 8 black peppercorns
- 15oz chicken thighs, skinless
- 1 tsp garlic paste
- 0.5 tsp turmeric
- 1 tsp red chili powder
- 1 tsp coriander seeds, ground
- 0.5 tsp garam masala
- 1 tsp cumin, ground
- Salt

Directions
1. Take a large saucepan and melt the ghee
2. Once melted, add the onions and cook until they turn golden
3. Take the onions out and mix in a bowl with the yogurt, blending if necessary
4. Warm up the ghee once more and add the bay leaf, cloves, star anise, cardamom pods, black peppercorns, and the cinnamon stick
5. Cook for half a minute
6. Add the chicken and season with salt
7. Add the garlic paste and cook for two min, stirring often
8. Add the coriander, garam masala, turmeric, red chili powder, and cumin, combine well and cook for two more minute
9. Add the onion and yogurt mixture and combine everything once more
10. Add a little water and combine
11. Close then cook for 15 min
12. Serve whilst still warm

Nutrition: Fat: 48g ; Protein: 27g Calories: 568

Barley Risotto with Tomatoes

Preparation: 20 min | Cooking: 45 min | Servings: 4

Ingredients
- 2 tablespoons extra-virgin olive oil
- 2 celery stalks, diced
- ½ cup shallots, diced
- 4 garlic cloves, minced
- 3 cups no-salt-added vegetable stock
- 1 (14.5-ounce) can no-salt-added diced tomatoes
- 1 (14.5-ounce) can no-salt-added crushed tomatoes
- 1 cup pearl barley
- Zest of 1 lemon
- 1 teaspoon kosher salt
- ½ teaspoon smoked paprika
- ¼ teaspoon red pepper flakes
- ¼ teaspoon freshly ground black pepper
- 4 thyme sprigs
- 1 dried bay leaf
- 2 cups baby spinach
- ½ cup crumbled feta cheese
- 1 tablespoon fresh oregano, chopped
- 1 tablespoon fennel seeds, toasted (optional)

Directions
1. Cook the olive oil in a big saucepan over medium heat. Add the celery and shallots and sauté, about 4 to 5 min. Add the garlic and sauté 30 seconds. Add the vegetable stock, diced tomatoes, crushed tomatoes, barley, lemon zest, salt, paprika, red pepper flakes, black pepper, thyme, and the bay leaf, and mix well. Bring to a boil, then lower to low, and simmer. Cook, stirring occasionally, for 40 min.
2. Remove the bay leaf and thyme sprigs. Stir in the spinach. In a small bowl, combine the feta, oregano, and fennel seeds. Serve the barley risotto in bowls topped with the feta mixture.

Nutrition: 375 Calories: 12g fat; 11g Protein:

Chickpeas and Kale with Spicy Pomodoro Sauce

Preparation: 10 min | Cooking: 35 min | Servings: 4

Ingredients
- 2 tablespoons extra-virgin olive oil
- 4 garlic cloves, sliced
- 1 teaspoon red pepper flakes
- 1 (28-ounce) can no-salt-added crushed tomatoes
- 1 teaspoon kosher salt
- ½ teaspoon honey
- 1 bunch kale, stemmed and chopped
- 2 (15-ounce) cans low-sodium chickpeas, drained and rinsed
- ¼ cup fresh basil, chopped
- ¼ cup grated pecorino Romano cheese

Directions

1. Cook the olive oil in a big skillet or sauté pan over medium heat. Stir in garlic and red pepper flakes and sauté until the garlic is a light golden brown, about 2 min. Add the tomatoes, salt, and honey and mix well. Adjust the heat to low and simmer for 21 min.
2. Add the kale and mix in well. Cook about 5 min. Add the chickpeas and simmer about 5 min. Remove from heat and stir in the basil. Serve topped with pecorino cheese.

Nutrition: 420 Calories: 13g fat; 20g Protein:

Mediterranean Chickpea Bowl

Preparation: 12 min | Cooking: 13 min | Servings: 2

Ingredients

- ½ tbs. of cumin seeds
- 1 large julienned carrot
- A ¼ cup of tomatoes (chopped)
- 1 medium julienned zucchini
- A ¼ cup of lemon juice
- 2 sliced green chilies
- ¼ cup of olive oil
- A ½ cup of chopped parsley leaves
- 1 minced clove of garlic
- ¼ tbs. salt
- ¼ tbs. cayenne pepper powder
- A ¼ cup of radish (sliced)
- 3 tbs. walnuts (chopped)
- 1/3 feta cheese (crumbled)
- 1 big can of chickpeas
- Proportionate salad greens

Directions

1. Another ingredient that you will see on the Mediterranean Diet list is chickpeas. The Mediterranean Chickpea Bowl is a popular snack that can be enjoyed at all times. You can use fresh or canned chickpeas as per preference.
2. For the salad, you will have to make a special dressing that will make the dish tasty. You need to roast the cumin seeds on a dry pan. Make sure the heat is at medium.
3. When the seeds begin releasing the aroma, put the seeds in a different mixing bowl.
4. In this bowl, add the olive oil, garlic, lemon juice, and tomatoes. Also, add the cayenne pepper and salt, and mix well to blend in all the ingredients.
5. Take a big bowl and add the chickpeas into it. Then put in the sliced and chopped veggies, and parsley leaves.
6. Adding walnut pieces will add an extra crunch to the Mediterranean chickpea salad.
7. Put in the seasoning you just prepared and then, mix all the ingredients well.

Nutrition: ; Protein: 12g ; Fat: 38g, Calories: 492

Curry Apple Couscous

Preparation: 20 min | Cooking: 5 min | Servings: 4

Ingredients

- 2 teaspoons olive oil
- 2 leeks, white parts only, sliced
- 1 apple, diced
- 2 tablespoons curry powder
- 2 cups couscous, cooked & whole wheat
- 1/2 cup pecans, chopped

Directions

1. Heat your oil in a skillet using medium heat. Add the leeks, and cook until tender, which will take five min. Add in your apple, and cook until soft.
2. Add in your curry powder and couscous, and stir well. Remove from heat, and mix in your nuts before serving immediately.

Nutrition: 330 calories; 30g protein, 12g fat;

Balsamic Roasted Carrots and Baby Onions

Preparation: 50 min | Cooking: 26 min | Servings: 4

Ingredients

- 2 bunches baby carrots, scrubbed, ends trimmed
- 10 small onions, peeled, halved
- 4 tbsp. 100% pure maple syrup (unprocessed)
- tsp thyme
- 1 tbsp. extra virgin olive oil

Directions

1. Preheat oven to 350F. Line a baking tray with baking paper.
2. Place the carrots, onion, thyme and oil in a large bowl and toss until well coated. Spread carrots and onion, in a single layer, on the baking tray. Roast for 25 min or until tender.
3. Sprinkle over the maple syrup and vinegar and toss to coat. Roast for 25-30 min more or until

vegetables are tender and caramelized. Season well and serve.

Nutrition: 401 calories; 49g fat; 20g protein

Chicken Souvlaki (Version 2)

Servings: 4-6 | Cooking: 12-15 min

Ingredients
- 4-6 chicken breasts, boneless, skinless

For the marinade:
- 1 tablespoon dried oregano (use Greek or Turkish oregano)
- 1 tablespoon garlic, finely minced (or garlic puree from a jar)
- 1 tablespoon red wine vinegar
- 1 teaspoon dried thyme
- 1/2 cup lemon juice, freshly squeezed
- 1/2 cup olive oil

Directions
1. If there are any visible fat on the chicken, trim them off. Cut each breasts into 5-6 pieces 1-inch thick crosswise strips. Put them in a Ziploc bag or a container with tight lid.
2. Whisk the marinade ingredients together until combined. Pour into the bag or container with the chicken, seal, and shake the bag or the container to coat the chicken. Marinade for 6 to 8 hours or more in the refrigerator.
3. When marinated, remove the chicken from the fridge, let thaw to room temperature, and drain; discard the marinade. Thread the chicken strips into skewers, about 6 pieces on each skewer, the meat folded over to it would not spin around on the skewers.
4. Mist the grill with olive oil. Preheat the charcoal or gas grill to medium high.
5. Grill the skewers for about 12-15 minutes, turning once as soon as you see grill marks. Souvlaki is done when the chicken is slightly browned and firm, but not hard to the touch.

Nutrition: 360 cal., 26 g total fat (4.5 g sat fat), 90 mg chol., 170 mg sodium, 570 mg potassium, 3 g carb., 0 g fiber, <1 g sugar, and 30 g protein.

Rosemary Roasted New Potatoes

Servings: 6 | Cooking: 1 Hour

Ingredients
- 2 pounds new potatoes, washed
- 3 tablespoons olive oil
- 2 rosemary sprigs
- 4 garlic cloves, crushed
- Salt and pepper to taste

Directions
1. Place the new potatoes in a large pot and cover them with water. Cook for 15 minutes then drain well.
2. Heat the oil in a skillet and add the rosemary and garlic.
3. Stir in the potatoes and continue cooking on medium flame for 20 minutes or until evenly golden brown.
4. Serve the potatoes warm.

Nutrition: Calories:168 Fat:7.2g Protein:2.7g Carbohydrates:24.6g

Artichoke Feta Penne

Servings: 4 | Cooking: 40 min

Ingredients
- 8 oz. penne pasta
- 2 tablespoons olive oil
- 1 shallot, chopped
- 4 garlic cloves, chopped
- 1 jar artichoke hearts, drained and chopped
- 1 cup diced tomatoes
- ¼ cup white wine
- ½ cup vegetable stock
- Salt and pepper to taste
- 4 oz. feta cheese, crumbled

Directions
1. Heat the oil in a skillet and stir in the shallot and garlic. Cook for 2 minutes until softened.
2. Add the artichoke hearts, tomatoes, wine and stock, as well as salt and pepper to taste.
3. Cook on low heat for 15 minutes.
4. In the meantime, cook the penne in a large pot of water until al dente, not more than 8 minutes.
5. Drain the pasta well and mix it with the artichoke sauce.
6. Serve the penne with crumbled feta cheese.

Nutrition: Calories:325 Fat:14.4g Protein:11.1g Carbohydrates:35.8g

Grilled Chicken And Rustic Mustard Cream

Servings: 4 | Cooking: 12 min

Ingredients

- 1 tablespoon plus 1 teaspoon whole-grain Dijon mustard, divided
- 1 tablespoon water
- 1 teaspoon fresh rosemary, chopped
- 1/4 teaspoon black pepper
- 1/4 teaspoon of salt
- 1 tablespoon olive oil
- 3 tablespoons light mayonnaise
- 4 pieces (6-ounces each) chicken breast halves, skinless, boneless
- Rosemary sprigs (optional)
- Cooking: spray

Directions

1. Preheat the grill.
2. In a small-sized bowl, combine the olive oil, 1-teaspoon of mustard; brush evenly over each chicken breast.
3. Coat the grill rack with the cooking spray, place and chicken, and grill for 6 minutes per side or until cooked.
4. While the chicken is grilling, combine the mayonnaise, the 1 tablespoon of mustard, and the water in a bowl.
5. Serve the grilled chicken with the mustard cream. If desired garnish with some rosemary sprigs.

Nutrition: 262 Cal, 10 g total fat (1 g sat. fat, 4 g mono fat, 3 g poly fat), 39.6 g protein, 1.7 g carb., 0.2 g fiber, 102 mg chol., 1.4 mg iron, 448 mg sodium, and 25 mg calcium.

Balsamic Steak With Feta, Tomato, And Basil

Servings: 4 | Cooking: 23 min

Ingredients

- 1 tablespoon balsamic vinegar
- 1/4 cup basil leaves
- 175 g Greek fetta, crumbled
- 2 tablespoons olive oil
- 2 teaspoons baby capers
- 4 sirloin steaks, trimmed
- 4 whole garlic cloves, skin on
- 6 roma tomatoes, halved
- Olive oil spray
- Salt and cracked black pepper

Directions

1. Preheat the oven to 200C.
2. Line a baking tray with baking paper. Place the tomatoes and then scatter with the capers, crumbled feta, and the garlic cloves. Drizzle with 1 tablespoon of the olive oil and season with salt and pepper; cook for about 15 minutes or until the tomatoes are soft. Remove from the oven, set aside.
3. In a large non-metallic bowl, toss the steak with the remaining 1 tablespoon of olive oil, vinegar, salt and pepper; cover and refrigerate for 5 minutes.
4. Preheat the grill pan to high heat; grill the steaks for about 4 minutes per side or until cooked to your preference.
5. Serve with the prepared tomato mixture and sprinkle with basil.

Nutrition: 520.3 Cal, 30 g total fat (12 g sat. fat), 3 g carb., 2 g fiber, 2 g sugar, 59 g protein, and 622.82 mg sodium.

Fried Chicken with Tzatziki Sauce

Servings: 4 | Cooking: 45 min

Ingredients

- 4 chicken breasts, cubed
- 4 tablespoons olive oil
- 1 teaspoon dried basil
- 1 teaspoon dried oregano
- ½ teaspoon chili flakes
- Salt and pepper to taste
- 1 cup Greek yogurt
- 1 cucumber, grated
- 4 garlic cloves, minced
- 1 teaspoon lemon juice
- 1 teaspoon chopped mint
- 2 tablespoons chopped parsley

Directions

1. Season the chicken with salt, pepper, basil, oregano and chili.
2. Heat the oil in a skillet and add the chicken. Cook on each side for 5 minutes on high heat just until golden brown.
3. Cover the chicken with a lid and continue cooking for 15-20 more minutes.
4. For the sauce, mix the yogurt, cucumber, garlic, lemon juice, mint and parsley, as well as salt and pepper.

5. Serve the chicken and the sauce fresh.

Nutrition: Calories:366 Fat:22.6g Protein:34.8g Carbohydrates:6.2g

Spiced Lamb Patties

Servings: 8 | Cooking: 1 Hour

Ingredients
- 2 pounds ground lamb
- 4 garlic cloves, minced
- 1 shallot, finely chopped
- 1 teaspoon ground coriander
- 1 teaspoon ground cumin
- ½ teaspoon chili powder
- 1 teaspoon dried mint
- 2 tablespoons pine nuts, crushed
- Salt and pepper to taste
- 2 tablespoons chopped parsley
- 1 tablespoon chopped cilantro

Directions
1. Mix the lamb meat and the remaining ingredients in a bowl.
2. Add salt and pepper and mix well.
3. Form small patties and place them on a chopping board.
4. Heat a grill pan over medium flame and cook on each side for 4-5 minutes or until browned and the juices run out clean.
5. Serve the patties warm.

Nutrition: Calories:231 Fat:9.9g Protein:32.4g Carbohydrates:1.3g

Chicken and Orzo Soup

Servings: 4 | Cooking: 11 min

Ingredients
- ½ cup carrot, chopped
- 1 yellow onion, chopped
- 12 cups chicken stock
- 2 cups kale, chopped
- 3 cups chicken meat, cooked and shredded
- 1 cup orzo
- ¼ cup lemon juice
- 1 tablespoon olive oil

Directions
1. Heat up a pot with the oil over medium heat, add the onion and sauté for 3 minutes.
2. Add the carrots and the rest of the ingredients, stir, bring to a simmer and cook for 8 minutes more.
3. Ladle into bowls and serve hot.

Nutrition: calories 300; fat 12.2; fiber 5.4; carbs 16.5; protein 12.2

Spanish Meatball Soup

Servings: 8 | Cooking: 1 Hour

Ingredients
- 2 tablespoons olive oil
- 1 onion, chopped
- 2 garlic cloves, chopped
- 2 red bell peppers, cored and diced
- 2 carrots, diced
- 1 celery stalk, diced
- 2 cups vegetable stock
- 6 cups water
- 1 pound ground veal
- 1 egg
- 2 tablespoons chopped parsley
- 1 can crushed tomatoes
- Salt and pepper to taste

Directions
1. Heat the oil in a soup pot and stir in the onion, garlic, bell peppers, carrots, celery, stock and water. Season with salt and pepper and bring to a boil.
2. In the meantime, mix the veal, egg and parsley in a bowl. Form small meatballs and place them in the boiling liquid.
3. Add the tomatoes and adjust the taste with salt and pepper.
4. Cook on low heat for 20 minutes.
5. Serve the soup war and fresh.

Nutrition: Calories:166 Fat:8.5g Protein:15.6g Carbohydrates:6.5g

Pesto, Avocado And Tomato Panini

Servings: 4 | Cooking: 10 min

Ingredients
- 2 tbsp extra virgin olive oil
- 8 oz fresh buffalo mozzarella cheese

- 2 vine-ripened tomatoes cut into ¼ inch thick slices
- 2 avocados, peeled, pitted, quartered and cut into thin strips
- 1 ciabatta loaf
- Pepper and salt
- ½ lemon
- 1/3 cup extra virgin olive oil
- 1/3 cup parmesan cheese
- 1/3 cup pine nuts, toasted
- 1 ½ bunches fresh basil leaves
- 2 garlic cloves, peeled

Directions
1. To make the pesto, puree garlic in a food processor and transfer to a mortar and pestle and add in basil and smash into a coarse paste like consistency. Mix in the pine nuts and continue crushing. Once paste like, add the parmesan cheese and mix. Pour in olive oil and blend thoroughly while adding lemon juice. Season with pepper and salt. Put aside.
2. Prepare Panini by slicing ciabatta loaf in three horizontal pieces. To prepare Panini, over bottom loaf slice layer the following: avocado, tomato, pepper, salt and mozzarella cheese. Then top with the middle ciabatta slice and repeat layering process again and cover with the topmost ciabatta bread slice.
3. Grill in a Panini press until cheese is melted and bred is crisped and ridged.

Nutrition: Calories: 577; Carbs: 15.5g; Protein: 24.2g; Fat: 49.3g

Jew's Mallow Stew (mulukhiya)

Servings: 1 Cup | Cooking: 2 Hours

Ingredients
- 2 whole chicken thighs, including drumstick
- 1 (2-in.) cinnamon stick
- 2 bay leaves
- 8 cups water
- 2 tsp. salt
- 1/2 cup extra-virgin olive oil
- 6 cups rehydrated Jew's mallow leaves, drained
- 1 large yellow onion, chopped
- 6 TB. minced garlic
- 1 cup fresh cilantro, finely chopped
- 1/2 tsp. cayenne
- 1/2 cup fresh lemon juice

Directions
1. In a large pot over medium heat, combine chicken thighs, cinnamon stick, bay leaves, water, and 1 teaspoon salt. Cook for 30 minutes. Skim off any foam that comes to the top.
2. Meanwhile, in another large pot over medium heat, heat 1/4 cup extra-virgin olive oil. Add Jew's mallow leaves, and cook, tossing leaves, for 10 minutes. Remove leaves, and set aside.
3. Reduce heat to medium-low. Add remaining 1/4 cup extra-virgin olive oil, yellow onion, and 3 tablespoons garlic, and cook for 5 minutes.
4. Return Jew's mallow leaves to onions. Add 8 cups chicken broth strained to the first pot to onions and Jew's mallow leaves in the second pot. Add remaining 1 teaspoon salt, and cook for 1 hour.
5. Meanwhile, separate chicken meat from bones. Discard bones and remaining contents of first pot.
6. After leaves have been cooking for 1 hour, add chicken, cilantro, cayenne, and remaining 3 tablespoons garlic, and cook for 20 more minutes.
7. Add lemon juice, and cook for 10 more minutes.
8. Serve with brown rice.

Smoked Ham Split Pea Soup

Servings: 8 | Cooking: 1 Hour

Ingredients
- 2 tablespoons olive oil
- 4 oz. smoked ham, diced
- 1 sweet onion, chopped
- 1 jalapeno pepper, chopped
- 2 red bell peppers, cored and diced
- 2 garlic cloves, chopped
- 2 carrots, diced
- 1 parsnip, diced
- 2 tomatoes, peeled and diced
- 2 cups vegetable stock
- 6 cups water
- ½ cup split peas
- Salt and pepper to taste
- 1 lemon, juiced
- Crème fraiche for serving

Directions
1. Heat the oil in a soup pot and stir in the ham. Cook for 5 minutes then add the rest of the ingredients.
2. Season with salt and pepper and cook on low heat for 30 minutes.
3. Serve the soup warm, topped with crème fraiche.

Nutrition: Calories:139 Fat:5.1g Protein:6.7g Carbohydrates:18.0g

Herbed Panini Fillet O'fish

Servings: 4 | Cooking: 25 min

Ingredients
- 4 slices thick sourdough bread
- 4 slices mozzarella cheese
- 1 portabella mushroom, sliced
- 1 small onion, sliced
- 6 tbsp oil
- 4 garlic and herb fish fillets

Directions
1. Prepare your fillets by adding salt, pepper and herbs (rosemary, thyme, parsley whatever you like). Then dredged in flour before deep frying in very hot oil. Once nicely browned, remove from oil and set aside.
2. On medium high fire, sauté for five minutes the onions and mushroom in a skillet with 2 tbsp oil.
3. Prepare sourdough breads by layering the following over it: cheese, fish fillet, onion mixture and cheese again before covering with another bread slice.
4. Grill in your Panini press until cheese is melted and bread is crisped and ridged.

Nutrition: Calories: 422; Carbs: 13.2g; Protein: 51.2g; Fat: 17.2g

Creamy Carrot Coriander Soup

Servings: 8 | Cooking: 50 min

Ingredients
- 2 tablespoons olive oil
- 2 shallots, chopped
- 2 garlic cloves, chopped
- 6 carrots, sliced
- 1 teaspoon coriander seeds
- 1 red pepper, sliced
- 2 cups vegetable stock
- 2 cups water
- Salt and pepper to taste
- ½ cup heavy cream

Directions
1. Heat the oil in a soup pot and stir in the shallots, garlic and carrots, as well as coriander seeds.
2. Cook for 5 minutes, then stir in the red pepper, stock, water, salt and pepper.
3. Cook for another 10-15 minutes on low heat then remove from heat. Add the cream and puree the soup with an immersion blender.
4. Serve the soup warm and fresh.

Nutrition: Calories:84 Fat:6.3g Protein:0.9g Carbohydrates:6.5g

Panini And Eggplant Caponata

Servings: 4 | Cooking: 10 min

Ingredients
- ¼ cup packed fresh basil leaves
- ¼ of a 7oz can of eggplant caponata
- 4 oz thinly sliced mozzarella
- 1 tbsp olive oil
- 1 ciabatta roll 6-7-inch length, horizontally split

Directions
1. Spread oil evenly on the sliced part of the ciabatta and layer on the following: cheese, caponata, basil leaves and cheese again before covering with another slice of ciabatta.
2. Then grill sandwich in a Panini press until cheese melts and bread gets crisped and ridged.

Nutrition: Calories: 295; Carbs: 44.4g; Protein: 16.4g; Fat: 7.3g

Mixed Bean Minestrone

Servings: 10 | Cooking: 1 Hour

Ingredients
- 2 tablespoons olive oil
- 2 chicken sausages, sliced
- 2 shallots, chopped
- 1 green bell pepper, cored and diced
- 1 garlic clove, chopped
- 2 celery stalks, sliced
- 2 carrots, diced
- 1 can red beans, drained
- 1 can white beans, drained
- 4 cups chicken stock
- 4 cups water
- 1 cup diced tomatoes
- 1 tablespoon tomato paste
- Salt and pepper to taste
- ½ cup short pasta

- 2 tablespoons lemon juice

Directions
1. Heat the oil in a soup pot and stir in the sausages. Cook for 5 minutes then add the vegetables.
2. Cook for 10 minutes then add the liquids and season with salt and pepper.
3. Cook on low heat for 25 minutes.
4. The soup is best served warm or chilled.

Nutrition: Calories:174 Fat:3.5g Protein:9.7g Carbohydrates:27.3g

Creamy Panini

Servings: 4 | Cooking: 16 min

Ingredients
- 1 jar of 7 oz roasted red peppers, drained and sliced
- 4 slices provolone cheese
- 1 small zucchini, thinly sliced
- 8 slices rustic whole grain bread
- 2 tbsp finely chopped oil-cured black olives
- ¼ cup chopped fresh basil leaves
- ½ cup Mayonnaise dressing with olive oil, divided

Directions
1. In a small bowl, mix together olives, basil and mayonnaise dressing.
2. Spread the dressing evenly on 4 slices of whole grain bread.
3. Then top it with zucchini, bacon, peppers and provolone before covering with another slice of bread.
4. Spread the remaining mayonnaise mixture around the bread and cook over medium heat on a nonstick skillet for two minutes on each side or until bread is golden brown on both sides and cheese is melted.

Nutrition: Calories: 350; Carbs: 24.2g; Protein: 14.4g; Fat: 21.8g

Tuna Melt Panini

Servings: 4 | Cooking: 10 min

Ingredients
- 2 tbsp softened unsalted butter
- 16 pcs of 1/8-inch kosher dill pickle
- 8 pcs of ¼ inch thick cheddar or Swiss cheese
- Mayonnaise and Dijon mustard
- 4 ciabatta rolls, split
- Pepper and salt
- ½ tsp crushed red pepper
- 1 tbsp minced basil
- 1 tbsp balsamic vinegar
- ¼ cup extra virgin olive oil
- ¼ cup finely diced red onion
- 2 cans of 6oz albacore tuna

Directions
1. Combine thoroughly the following in a bowl: salt pepper, crushed red pepper, basil, vinegar, olive oil, onion and tuna.
2. Smear with mayonnaise and mustard the cut sides of the bread rolls then layer on: cheese, tuna salad and pickles. Cover with the remaining slice of roll.
3. Grill in a Panini press ensuring that cheese is melted and bread is crisped and ridged.

Nutrition: Calories: 539; Carbs: 27.7g; Protein: 21.6g; Fat: 38.5g

Roasted Mushroom Creamy Soup

Servings: 8 | Cooking: 55 min

Ingredients
- 3 tablespoons olive oil
- 4 garlic cloves, chopped
- 2 shallots, chopped
- ½ teaspoon chili powder
- ½ teaspoon cumin powder
- 1 ½ pounds mushrooms, halved
- 2 cups vegetable stock
- ½ cup heavy cream
- Salt and pepper to taste

Directions
1. Combine the oil, garlic, shallots, chili powder, cumin and mushrooms in a baking tray.
2. Cook in the preheated oven at 350F for 20 minutes.
3. Transfer the mushrooms in a soup pot and stir in the stock, as well as salt and pepper.
4. Cook for 10 more minutes then add the cream and puree the soup with an immersion blender.
5. Serve the soup warm.

Nutrition: Calories:96 Fat:8.4g Protein:3.1g Carbohydrates:4.3g

Eggplant Stew

Servings: 1 Cup | Cooking: 35 min

Ingredients
- 3 TB. extra-virgin olive oil
- 1 medium white onion, chopped
- 2 large carrots, sliced diagonally
- 4 medium Italian eggplant, trimmed and diced
- 2 large potatoes, peeled and diced
- 1 large tomato, diced
- 1 (16-oz.) can tomato sauce
- 1 tsp. garlic powder
- 1 tsp. paprika
- 1 1/2 tsp. salt
- 1 cup fresh cilantro, chopped

Directions
1. In a 3-quart pot over medium heat, heat extra-virgin olive oil. Add white onion and carrots, and cook for 5 minutes.
2. Add Italian eggplant and potatoes, and cook for 7 minutes.
3. Add tomato, and cook for 3 minutes.
4. Add tomato sauce, garlic powder, paprika, and salt, and simmer, stirring occasionally, for 15 minutes.
5. Stir in cilantro, and cook for 5 more minutes.
6. Serve with brown rice.

Garlicky Roasted Sweet Potato Soup

Servings: 8 | Cooking: 1 Hour

Ingredients
- 3 tablespoons olive oil
- 4 sweet potatoes, peeled and cubed
- 1 teaspoon dried oregano
- 1 tablespoon balsamic vinegar
- 6 garlic cloves
- 3 cups vegetable stock
- 1 cup water
- Salt and pepper to taste
- 1 thyme sprig

Directions
1. Combine the potatoes, oil, oregano, vinegar and garlic in a baking tray.
2. Season with salt and pepper and cook in the preheated oven at 350F for 25 minutes.
3. Transfer the ingredients in a soup pot and add the remaining ingredients.
4. Adjust the taste with salt and pepper.
5. Cook on low heat for 10 minutes.
6. When done, puree the soup with an immersion blender.
7. Serve the soup warm.

Nutrition: Calories:140 Fat:5.4g Protein:1.5g Carbohydrates:22.1g

Apple And Ham Flatbread Pizza

Servings: 8 | Cooking: 15 min

Ingredients
- ¾ cup almond flour
- ½ teaspoon sea salt
- 2 cups mozzarella cheese, shredded
- 2 tablespoons cream cheese
- 1/8 teaspoon dried thyme
- ½ small red onion, cut into thin slices
- 4 ounces low carbohydrate ham, cut into chunks
- Salt and black pepper, to taste
- 1 cup Mexican blend cheese, grated
- ¼ medium apple, sliced
- 1/8 teaspoon dried thyme

Directions
1. Preheat the oven to 425 degrees F and grease a 12-inch pizza pan.
2. Boil water and steam cream cheese, mozzarella cheese, almond flour, thyme, and salt.
3. When the cheese melts enough, knead for a few minutes to thoroughly mix dough.
4. Make a ball out of the dough and arrange in the pizza pan.
5. Poke holes all over the dough with a fork and transfer in the oven.
6. Bake for about 8 minutes until golden brown and reset the oven setting to 350 degrees F.
7. Sprinkle ¼ cup of the Mexican blend cheese over the flatbread and top with onions, apples, and ham.
8. Cover with the remaining ¾ cup of the Mexican blend cheese and sprinkle with the thyme, salt, and black pepper.
9. Bake for about 7 minutes until cheese is melted and crust is golden brown.
10. Remove the flatbread from the oven and allow to cool before cutting.
11. Slice into desired pieces and serve.

Nutrition: Calories: 179 Carbs: 5.3g Fats: 13.6g Proteins: 10.4g Sodium: 539mg Sugar: 2.1g

Red Beet Soup

Servings: 8 | Cooking: 1 Hour

Ingredients
- 2 tablespoons olive oil
- 2 leeks, sliced
- 1 celery stalk, sliced
- 2 carrots, diced
- 1 parsnip, diced
- 3 red beets, peeled and diced
- 4 cups vegetable stock
- 1 cup diced tomatoes
- 2 cups shredded cabbage
- 2 cups water
- 1 bay leaf
- 1 thyme sprig
- 1 rosemary sprig
- Salt and pepper to taste

Directions
1. Heat the oil in a soup pot and stir in the leeks, celery, carrots, parsnip and beets, as well as cabbage.
2. Cook for 5 minutes then add the rest of the ingredients and season with salt and pepper.
3. Cook for 20-25 minutes.
4. Serve the soup warm or chilled.

Nutrition: Calories:91 Fat:3.8g Protein:1.9g Carbohydrates:13.9g

Fig Relish Panini

Servings: 4 | Cooking: 40 min

Ingredients
- Grated parmesan cheese, for garnish
- Olive oil
- Fig relish (recipe follows)
- Arugula
- Basil leaves
- Toma cheese, grated or sliced
- Sweet butter
- 4 ciabatta slices
- 1 tsp dry mustard
- Pinch of salt
- 1 tsp mustard seed
- ½ cup apple cider vinegar
- ½ cup sugar
- ½ lb. Mission figs, stemmed and peeled

Directions
1. Create fig relish by mincing the figs. Then put in all ingredients, except for the dry mustard, in a small pot and simmer for 30 minutes until it becomes jam like. Season with dry mustard according to taste and let cool before refrigerating.
2. Spread sweet butter on two slices of ciabatta rolls and layer on the following: cheese, basil leaves, arugula and fig relish then cover with the remaining bread slice.
3. Grill in a Panini press until cheese is melted and bread is crisped and ridged.

Nutrition: Calories: 264; Carbs: 55.1g; Protein: 6.0g; Fat: 4.2g

Egg Muffin Sandwich

Servings: 2 | Cooking: 10 min

Ingredients
- 1 large egg, free-range or organic
- 1/4 cup almond flour (25 g / 0.9 oz)
- 1/4 cup flax meal (38 g / 1.3 oz)
- 1/4 cup grated cheddar cheese (28 g / 1 oz)
- 1/4 tsp baking soda
- 2 tbsp heavy whipping cream or coconut milk
- 2 tbsp water
- pinch salt
- 1 tbsp butter or 2 tbsp cream cheese for spreading
- 1 tbsp ghee
- 1 tsp Dijon mustard
- 2 large eggs, free-range or organic
- 2 slices cheddar cheese or other hard type cheese (56 g / 2 oz)
- Optional: 1 cup greens (lettuce, kale, chard, spinach, watercress, etc.)
- salt and pepper to taste

Directions
1. Make the Muffin: In a small mixing bowl, mix well almond flour, flax meal, baking soda, and salt. Stir in water, cream, and eggs. Mix thoroughly.
2. Fold in cheese and evenly divide in two single-serve ramekins.
3. Pop in the microwave and cook for 75 seconds.
4. Make the filing: on medium the fire, place a small nonstick pan, heat ghee and cook the eggs to the desired doneness. Season with pepper and salt.

5. To make the muffin sandwiches, slice the muffins in half. Spread cream cheese on one side and mustard on the other side.
6. Add egg and greens. Top with the other half of sliced muffin.
7. Serve and enjoy.

Nutrition: Calories per serving: 639; Protein: 26.5g; Carbs: 10.4g; Fat: 54.6g

Buffalo Chicken Crust Pizza

Servings: 6 | Cooking: 25 min

Ingredients
- 1 cup whole milk mozzarella, shredded
- 1 teaspoon dried oregano
- 2 tablespoons butter
- 1 pound chicken thighs, boneless and skinless
- 1 large egg
- ¼ teaspoon black pepper
- ¼ teaspoon salt
- 1 stalk celery
- 3 tablespoons Franks Red Hot Original
- 1 stalk green onion
- 1 tablespoon sour cream
- 1 ounce bleu cheese, crumbled

Directions
1. Preheat the oven to 400 degrees F and grease a baking dish.
2. Process chicken thighs in a food processor until smooth.
3. Transfer to a large bowl and add egg, ½ cup of shredded mozzarella, oregano, black pepper, and salt to form a dough.
4. Spread the chicken dough in the baking dish and transfer in the oven
5. Bake for about 25 minutes and keep aside.
6. Meanwhile, heat butter and add celery, and cook for about 4 minutes.
7. Mix Franks Red Hot Original with the sour cream in a small bowl.
8. Spread the sauce mixture over the crust, layer with the cooked celery and remaining ½ cup of mozzarella and the bleu cheese.
9. Bake for another 10 minutes, until the cheese is melted

Nutrition: Calories: 172 Carbs: 1g Fats: 12.9g Proteins: 13.8g Sodium: 172mg Sugar: 0.2g

Greek Bean Soup

Servings: 8 | Cooking: 1 Hour

Ingredients
- 3 tablespoons olive oil
- 2 sweet onions, chopped
- 2 garlic cloves, chopped
- 2 celery stalks, sliced
- 2 carrots, diced
- 1 cup diced tomatoes
- 1 can red beans, drained
- ½ teaspoon dried mint
- ½ teaspoon dried oregano
- ½ teaspoon dried basil
- 2 cups vegetable stock
- 4 cups water
- Salt and pepper to taste

Directions
1. Heat the oil in a soup pot and stir in the onions. Cook for 5 minutes then add the garlic and cook for 1 more minute.
2. Add the rest of the ingredients and season with salt and pepper.
3. Cook for 20 minutes.
4. The soup is best served warm.

Nutrition: Calories:147 Fat:5.6g Protein:6.0g Carbohydrates:19.7g

Eggless Spinach & Bacon Quiche

Servings: 8 | Cooking: 20 min

Ingredients
- 1 cup fresh spinach, chopped
- 4 slices of bacon, cooked and chopped
- ½ cup mozzarella cheese, shredded
- 4 tablespoons milk
- 4 dashes Tabasco sauce
- 1 cup Parmesan cheese, shredded
- Salt and freshly ground black pepper, to taste

Directions
1. Preheat the Airfryer to 325 degrees F and grease a baking dish.
2. Put all the ingredients in a bowl and mix well.
3. Transfer the mixture into prepared baking dish and cook for about 8 minutes.
4. Dish out and serve.

Nutrition: Calories: 72 Carbs: 0.9g Fats: 5.2g Proteins: 5.5g Sodium: 271mg Sugar: 0.4g

Cauliflower Stew

Servings: 2 Cups | Cooking: 25 min

Ingredients

- 1/2 lb. ground beef
- 2 tsp. salt
- 1 tsp. black pepper
- 1 (16-oz.) can plain tomato sauce
- 1 (16-oz.) can crushed tomatoes
- 2 cups water
- 1 TB. fresh thyme
- 1 tsp. garlic powder
- 1/2 tsp. onion powder
- 4 cups cauliflower florets
- 2 large potatoes
- 2 large carrots, finely diced
- 1 (16-oz.) can chickpeas, rinsed and drained

Directions

1. In a small bowl, combine beef, 1/2 teaspoon salt, and 1/2 teaspoon black pepper. Form mixture into 20 to 30 mini meatballs about 1 teaspoon each.
2. In a large, 3-quart pot over medium heat, add meatballs. Cover and cook for 5 minutes.
3. Add tomato sauce, crushed tomatoes, water, thyme, garlic powder, onion powder, remaining 1 1/2 teaspoons salt, and remaining 1/2 teaspoon black pepper, and simmer for 5 minutes.
4. Stir in cauliflower, potatoes, carrots, and chickpeas, and simmer for 20 minutes.
5. Serve with brown rice.

Bbq Chicken Pizza

Servings: 4 | Cooking: 30 min

Ingredients

Dairy Free Pizza Crust:
- 6 tablespoons Parmesan cheese
- 6 large eggs
- 3 tablespoons psyllium husk powder
- Salt and black pepper, to taste
- 1½ teaspoons Italian seasoning

Toppings:
- 6 oz. rotisserie chicken, shredded
- 4 oz. cheddar cheese
- 1 tablespoon mayonnaise
- 4 tablespoons tomato sauce
- 4 tablespoons BBQ sauce

Directions

1. Preheat the oven to 400 degrees F and grease a baking dish.
2. Place all Pizza Crust ingredients in an immersion blender and blend until smooth.
3. Spread dough mixture onto the baking dish and transfer in the oven.
4. Bake for about 10 minutes and top with favorite toppings.
5. Bake for about 3 minutes and dish out.

Nutrition: Calories: 356 Carbs: 2.9g Fats: 24.5g Proteins: 24.5g Sodium: 396mg Sugar: 0.6g

Fresh Bell Pepper Basil Pizza

Servings: 3 | Cooking: 25 min

Ingredients

Pizza Base:
- ½ cup almond flour
- 2 tablespoons cream cheese
- 1 teaspoon Italian seasoning
- ½ teaspoon black pepper
- 6 ounces mozzarella cheese
- 2 tablespoons psyllium husk
- 2 tablespoons fresh Parmesan cheese
- 1 large egg
- ½ teaspoon salt

Toppings:
- 4 ounces cheddar cheese, shredded
- ¼ cup Marinara sauce
- 2/3 medium bell pepper
- 1 medium vine tomato
- 3 tablespoons basil, fresh chopped

Directions

1. Preheat the oven to 400 degrees F and grease a baking dish.
2. Microwave mozzarella cheese for about 30 seconds and top with the remaining pizza crust.
3. Add the remaining pizza ingredients to the cheese and mix together.
4. Flatten the dough and transfer in the oven.
5. Bake for about 10 minutes and remove pizza from the oven.
6. Top the pizza with the toppings and bake for another 10 minutes.
7. Remove pizza from the oven and allow to cool.

Nutrition: Calories: 411 Carbs: 6.4g Fats: 31.3g Proteins: 22.2g Sodium: 152mg Sugar: 2.8g

Avocado And Turkey Mix Panini

Servings: 2 | Cooking: 8 min

Ingredients
- 2 red peppers, roasted and sliced into strips
- ¼ lb. thinly sliced mesquite smoked turkey breast
- 1 cup whole fresh spinach leaves, divided
- 2 slices provolone cheese
- 1 tbsp olive oil, divided
- 2 ciabatta rolls
- ¼ cup mayonnaise
- ½ ripe avocado

Directions
1. In a bowl, mash thoroughly together mayonnaise and avocado. Then preheat Panini press.
2. Slice the bread rolls in half and spread olive oil on the insides of the bread. Then fill it with filling, layering them as you go: provolone, turkey breast, roasted red pepper, spinach leaves and spread avocado mixture and cover with the other bread slice.
3. Place sandwich in the Panini press and grill for 5 to 8 minutes until cheese has melted and bread is crisped and ridged.

Nutrition: Calories: 546; Carbs: 31.9g; Protein: 27.8g; Fat: 34.8g

Thin Crust Low Carb Pizza

Servings: 6 | Cooking: 25 min

Ingredients
- 2 tablespoons tomato sauce
- 1/8 teaspoon black pepper
- 1/8 teaspoon chili flakes
- 1 piece low-carb pita bread
- 2 ounces low-moisture mozzarella cheese
- 1/8 teaspoon garlic powder
- Bacon, roasted red peppers, spinach, olives, pesto, artichokes, salami, pepperoni, roast beef, prosciutto, avocado, ham, chili paste, Sriracha

Directions
1. Preheat the oven to 450 degrees F and grease a baking dish.
2. Mix together tomato sauce, black pepper, chili flakes, and garlic powder in a bowl and keep aside.
3. Place the low-carb pita bread in the oven and bake for about 2 minutes.
4. Remove from oven and spread the tomato sauce on it.
5. Add mozzarella cheese and top with your favorite toppings.
6. Bake again for 3 minutes and dish out.

Nutrition: Calories: 254 Carbs: 12.9g Fats: 16g Proteins: 19.3g Sodium: 255mg Sugar: 2.8g

Garlic-rosemary Dinner Rolls

Servings: 8 | Cooking: 20 min

Ingredients
- 2 garlic cloves, minced
- 1 tsp dried crushed rosemary
- ½ tsp apple cider vinegar
- 2 tbsp olive oil
- 2 eggs
- 1 ¼ tsp salt
- 1 ¾ tsp xanthan gum
- ½ cup tapioca starch
- ¾ cup brown rice flour
- 1 cup sorghum flour
- 2 tsp dry active yeast
- 1 tbsp honey
- ¾ cup hot water

Directions
1. Mix well water and honey in a small bowl and add yeast. Leave it for exactly 7 minutes.
2. In a large bowl, mix the following with a paddle mixer: garlic, rosemary, salt, xanthan gum, sorghum flour, tapioca starch, and brown rice flour.
3. In a medium bowl, whisk well vinegar, olive oil, and eggs.
4. Into bowl of dry ingredients pour in vinegar and yeast mixture and mix well.
5. Grease a 12-muffin tin with cooking spray. Transfer dough evenly into 12 muffin tins and leave it 20 minutes to rise.
6. Then preheat oven to 375oF and bake dinner rolls until tops are golden brown, around 17 to 19 minutes.
7. Remove dinner rolls from oven and muffin tins immediately and let it cool.
8. Best served when warm.

Nutrition: Calories: 200; Carbs: 34.3g; Protein: 4.2g; Fat: 5.4g

Green Pea Stew (bazella)

Servings: 1 Cup | Cooking: 43 min

Ingredients
- 1/2 lb. ground beef
- 3 TB. extra-virgin olive oil
- 1 large yellow onion, finely chopped
- 2 TB. garlic, minced
- 2 cups fresh or frozen green peas
- 2 large carrots, diced (1 cup)
- 1 (16-oz.) can plain tomato sauce
- 2 cups water
- 1 1/2 tsp. salt
- 1 tsp. ground black pepper
- 1/2 cup fresh Italian parsley, finely chopped

Directions
1. In a 3-quart pot over medium heat, brown beef for 5 minutes, breaking up chunks with a wooden spoon.
2. Add extra-virgin olive oil, yellow onion, and garlic, and cook for 5 minutes.
3. Add peas and carrots, and cook for 3 minutes.
4. Add tomato sauce, water, salt, and black pepper, and simmer for 25 minutes.
5. Stir in Italian parsley, and simmer for 5 more minutes.
6. Serve warm with brown rice.

Fig Relish Panini

Preparation: 9 min | Cooking: 40 min | Servings: 4

Ingredients
- Grated parmesan cheese, for garnish
- Olive oil
- Fig relish (recipe follows)
- Arugula
- Basil leaves
- Toma cheese, grated or sliced
- Sweet butter
- 4 ciabatta slices

For Fig Relish:
- 1 tsp dry mustard
- Pinch of salt
- 1 tsp mustard seed
- 1/2 cup apple cider vinegar
- 1/2 cup sugar
- 1/2 lb. Mission figs, stemmed and peeled

Directions
1. Create fig relish by mincing the figs. Then put in all ingredients, except for the dry mustard, in a small pot and simmer for 30 min until it becomes jam like.
2. Season with dry mustard according to taste and let cool before refrigerating. Spread sweet butter on two slices of ciabatta rolls and layer on the following: cheese, basil leaves, arugula and fig relish then cover with the remaining bread slice.
3. Grill in a Panini press until toasted.

Nutrition: Calories: 264; Protein: 6.0g; Fat: 4.2g

Panini and Eggplant Caponata

Preparation: 9 min | Cooking: 10 min | Servings: 4

Ingredients
- 1/4 cup packed fresh basil leaves
- 1/4 of a 7oz can of eggplant Caponata
- 4 oz. thinly sliced mozzarella
- 1 tbsp. olive oil
- 1 ciabatta roll
- 6-7-inch length horizontally split

Directions
1. Spread oil evenly on the sliced part of the ciabatta and layer on the following: cheese, Caponata, basil leaves and cheese again before covering with another slice of ciabatta.
2. Then grill sandwich in a Panini press until cheese melts and bread gets crisped and ridged.

Nutrition: Calories: 295; Protein: 16.4g; Fat: 7.3g

Open Face Egg and Bacon Sandwich

Preparation: 9 min | Cooking: 19 min | Servings: 1

Ingredients
- 1/4 oz. reduced fat; cheddar, shredded
- 1/2 small jalapeno, thinly sliced
- 1/2 whole grain English muffin, split
- 1 large organic egg
- 1 thick slice of tomato
- 1-piece turkey bacon
- 2 thin slices red onion
- 4-5 sprigs fresh cilantro
- Cooking spray

- Pepper to taste

Directions

1. On medium fire, place a skillet, cook bacon until crisp tender and set aside. In same skillet, drain oils, and place ½ of English muffin and heat for at least a minute per side. Transfer muffin to a serving plate.
2. Grease the same skillet with cooking spray and fry egg to desired doneness. Once cooked, place egg on top of muffin. Add cilantro, tomato, onion, jalapeno and bacon on top of egg. Serve and enjoy.

Nutrition: Calories: 245; Protein: 11.8g; Fat: 11g

Multi Grain & Gluten Free Dinner Rolls

Preparation: 7 min | Cooking: 19 min | Servings: 8

Ingredients
- ½ tsp apple cider vinegar
- 3 tbsp. olive oil
- 2 eggs
- 1 tsp baking powder
- 1 tsp salt
- 2 tsp xanthan gum
- ½ cup tapioca starch
- ¼ cup brown teff flour
- ¼ cup flax meal
- ¼ cup amaranth flour
- ¼ cup sorghum flour
- ¾ cup brown rice flour

Directions
1. Mix well water and honey in a small bowl and add yeast. Leave it for exactly 10 min. Incorporate the following with a paddle mixer: baking powder, salt, xanthan gum, flax meal, sorghum flour, teff flour, tapioca starch, amaranth flour, and brown rice flour.
2. In a medium bowl, whisk well vinegar, olive oil, and eggs. Into bowl of dry ingredients pour in vinegar and yeast mixture and mix well. Grease a 12-muffin tin with cooking spray. Transfer dough evenly into 12 muffin tins and leave it for an h to rise.
3. Then preheat oven to 375F and bake dinner rolls until tops are golden brown, around 20 min. Remove dinner rolls from oven and muffin tins immediately and let it cool. Best served when warm.

Nutrition: Calories: 207; Protein: 4.6g; Fat: 8.3g

Grilled Burgers with Mushrooms

Preparation: 7 min | Cooking: 10 min | Servings: 4

Ingredients
- 2 Bibb lettuce, halved
- 4 slices red onion
- 4 slices tomato
- 4 whole wheat buns, toasted
- 2 tbsp. olive oil
- ¼ tsp cayenne pepper, optional
- 1 garlic clove, minced
- 1 tbsp. sugar
- ½ cup water
- 1/3 cup balsamic vinegar
- 4 large Portobello mushroom caps, around 5-inches in diameter

Directions
1. Remove stems from mushrooms and clean with a damp cloth. Transfer into a baking dish with gill-side up. In a bowl, mix thoroughly olive oil, cayenne pepper, garlic, sugar, water and vinegar.
2. Pour over mushrooms and marinate mushrooms in the ref for at least an h. Once the one h is nearly up, preheat grill to medium high fire and grease grill grate. Grill mushrooms for five min per side or until tender. Baste mushrooms with marinade so it doesn't dry up.
3. To assemble, place ½ of bread bun on a plate, top with a slice of onion, mushroom, tomato and one lettuce leaf. Cover with the other top half of the bun. Repeat process with remaining ingredients, serve and enjoy.

Nutrition: Calories: 244.1; Protein: 8.1g; Fat: 9.3g

Gorgonzola Sweet Potato Burgers

Preparation: 9 min | Cooking: 16 min | Servings: 4

Ingredients
- 1 large sweet potato (about 8 ounces)
- 2 tablespoons extra-virgin olive oil, divided
- 1 cup chopped onion (about ½ medium onion)
- 1 cup old-fashioned rolled oats
- 1 large egg
- 1 tablespoon balsamic vinegar
- 1 tablespoon dried oregano

- 1 garlic clove
- ¼ teaspoon kosher or sea salt
- ½ cup crumbled blue cheese
- Salad greens or 4 whole-wheat rolls, for serving (optional)

Directions
1. Poke the sweet potato all over and microwave on high for 4 to 5 min, until tender in the center. Cool slightly, and then slice in half.
2. While the sweet potato is cooking, in a large skillet over medium-high heat, heat 1 tablespoon of oil. Cook the onion for 5 min.
3. Using a spoon, carefully scoop the sweet potato flesh out of the skin and put the flesh in a food processor. Add the onion, oats, egg, vinegar, oregano, garlic, and salt. Process until smooth. Add the cheese and pulse four times to barely combine. With your hands, form the mixture into four (½-cup-size) burgers. Place the burgers on a plate, and press to flatten each to about ¾-inch thick.
4. Wipe the skillet using a paper towel, then heat the remaining 1 tablespoon of oil at medium-high heat for 2 min. Add the burgers to the hot oil, then turn the heat down to medium. Cook the burgers for 5 min, flip with a spatula, then cook an additional 5 min. Enjoy as is or serve on salad greens or whole-wheat rolls.

Nutrition: Calories: 223; Fat: 13g; Protein: 7g

Chapter 3: Meat Recipes

Sage Tomato Beef

Servings: 4 | Cooking: 40 min

Ingredients
- 2 lbs beef stew meat, cubed
- 1/4 cup tomato paste
- 1 tsp garlic, minced
- 2 cups chicken stock
- 1 onion, chopped
- 2 tbsp olive oil
- 1 tbsp sage, chopped
- Pepper
- Salt

Directions
1. Add oil into the instant pot and set the pot on sauté mode.
2. Add garlic and onion and sauté for 5 minutes.
3. Add meat and sauté for 5 minutes.
4. Add remaining ingredients and stir well.
5. Seal pot with lid and cook on high for 30 minutes.
6. Once done, allow to release pressure naturally. Remove lid.
7. Serve and enjoy.

Nutrition: Calories 515 Fat 21.5 g Carbohydrates 7 g Sugar 3.6 g Protein 70 g Cholesterol 203 mg

Square Meat Pies (sfeeha)

Servings: 1 Meat Pie | Cooking: 20 min

Ingredients
- 1 large yellow onion
- 2 large tomatoes
- 1 lb. ground beef
- 11/4 tsp. salt
- 1/2 tsp. ground black pepper
- 1 tsp. seven spices
- 1 batch Multipurpose Dough

Directions
1. Preheat the oven to 425°F.
2. In a food processor fitted with a chopping blade, pulse yellow onion and tomatoes for 30 seconds.
3. Transfer tomato-onion mixture to a large bowl. Add beef, salt, black pepper, and seven spices, and mix well.
4. Form Multipurpose Dough into 18 balls, and roll out to 4-inch circles. Spoon 2 tablespoons meat mixture onto center of each dough circle. Pinch together the two opposite sides of dough up to meat mixture, and pinch the opposite two sides together, forming a square. Place meat pies on a baking sheet, and bake for 20 minutes.
5. Serve warm or at room temperature.

Lamb And Wine Sauce

Servings: 4 | Cooking: 2 Hours And 40 min

Ingredients
- 2 tablespoons olive oil
- 2 pounds leg of lamb, trimmed and sliced
- 3 garlic cloves, chopped
- 2 yellow onions, chopped
- 3 cups veggie stock
- 2 cups dry red wine
- 2 tablespoons tomato paste
- 4 tablespoons avocado oil
- 1 teaspoon thyme, chopped
- Salt and black pepper to the taste

Directions
1. Heat up a pan with the oil over medium-high heat, add the meat, brown for 5 minutes on each side and transfer to a roasting pan.
2. Heat up the pan again over medium heat, add the avocado oil, add the onions and garlic and sauté for 5 minutes.
3. Add the remaining ingredients, stir, bring to a simmer and cook for 10 minutes.
4. Pour the sauce over the meat, introduce the pan in the oven and bake at 370 degrees F for 2 hours and 20 minutes.
5. Divide everything between plates and serve.

Nutrition: calories 273; fat 21; fiber 11.1; carbs 16.2; protein 18.3

Pork Meatloaf

Servings: 6 | Cooking: 1 Hour And 20 min

Ingredients
- 1 red onion, chopped
- Cooking: spray
- 2 garlic cloves, minced
- 2 pounds pork stew, ground
- 1 cup almond milk
- ¼ cup feta cheese, crumbled
- 2 eggs, whisked
- 1/3 cup kalamata olives, pitted and chopped
- 4 tablespoons oregano, chopped
- Salt and black pepper to the taste

Directions
1. In a bowl, mix the meat with the onion, garlic and the other ingredients except the cooking spray, stir well, shape your meatloaf and put it in a loaf pan greased with cooking spray.
2. Bake the meatloaf at 370 degrees F for 1 hour and 20 minutes.
3. Serve the meatloaf warm.

Nutrition: calories 350; fat 23; fiber 1; carbs 17; protein 24

Lamb And Rice

Servings: 4 | Cooking: 1 Hour And 10 min

Ingredients
- 1 tablespoon lime juice
- 1 yellow onion, chopped
- 1 pound lamb, cubed
- 1 ounce avocado oil
- 2 garlic cloves, minced
- Salt and black pepper to the taste
- 2 cups veggie stock
- 1 cup brown rice
- A handful parsley, chopped

Directions
1. Heat up a pan with the avocado oil over medium-high heat, add the onion, stir and sauté for 5 minutes.
2. Add the meat and brown for 5 minutes more.
3. Add the rest of the ingredients except the parsley, bring to a simmer and cook over medium heat for 1 hour.
4. Add the parsley, toss, divide everything between plates and serve.

Nutrition: calories 302; fat 13.2; fiber 10.7; carbs 15.7; protein 14.3

Italian Beef

Servings: 4 | Cooking: 35 min

Ingredients
- 1 lb ground beef
- 1 tbsp olive oil
- 1/2 cup mozzarella cheese, shredded
- 1/2 cup tomato puree
- 1 tsp basil
- 1 tsp oregano
- 1/2 onion, chopped
- 1 carrot, chopped
- 14 oz can tomatoes, diced
- Pepper
- Salt

Directions
1. Add oil into the instant pot and set the pot on sauté mode.
2. Add onion and sauté for 2 minutes.
3. Add meat and sauté until browned.
4. Add remaining ingredients except for cheese and stir well.
5. Seal pot with lid and cook on high for 35 minutes.
6. Once done, release pressure using quick release. Remove lid.
7. Add cheese and stir well and cook on sauté mode until cheese is melted.
8. Serve and enjoy.

Nutrition: Calories 297 Fat 11.3 g Carbohydrates 11.1 g Sugar 6.2 g Protein 37.1 g Cholesterol 103 mg

Pork Chops And Peppercorns Mix

Servings: 4 | Cooking: 20 min

Ingredients
- 1 cup red onion, sliced
- 1 tablespoon black peppercorns, crushed
- ¼ cup veggie stock
- 5 garlic cloves, minced
- A pinch of salt and black pepper
- 2 tablespoons olive oil
- 4 pork chops

Directions
1. Heat up a pan with the oil over medium-high heat, add the pork chops and brown for 4 minutes on each side.
2. Add the onion and the garlic and cook for 2 minutes more.
3. Add the rest of the ingredients, cook everything for 10 minutes, tossing the mix from time to time, divide between plates and serve.

Nutrition: calories 232; fat 9.2; fiber 5.6; carbs 13.3; protein 24.2

Pork And Tomato Meatloaf

Servings: 8 | Cooking: 55 min

Ingredients
- 2 cups ground pork
- 1 egg, beaten
- ¼ cup crushed tomatoes
- 1 teaspoon salt

- 1 teaspoon ground black pepper
- 1 oz Swiss cheese, grated
- 1 teaspoon minced garlic
- 1/3 onion, diced
- ¼ cup black olives, chopped
- 1 jalapeno pepper, chopped
- 1 teaspoon dried basil
- Cooking: spray

Directions
1. Spray the loaf mold with cooking spray.
2. Then combine together ground pork, egg, crushed tomatoes, salt, ground black pepper. Grated Swiss cheese, minced garlic, onion, olives, jalapeno pepper, and dried basil.
3. Stir the mass until it is homogenous and transfer it in the prepared loaf mold.
4. Flatten the surface of meatloaf well and cover with foil.
5. Bake the meatloaf for 40 minutes at 375F.
6. Then discard the foil and bake the meal for 15 minutes more.
7. Chill the cooked meatloaf to the room temperature and then remove it from the loaf mold.
8. Slice it on the servings.

Nutrition: calories 265; fat 18.3; fiber 0.6; carbs 1.9; protein 22.1

Beef And Eggplant Moussaka

Servings: 3 | Cooking: 50 min

Ingredients
- 1 small eggplant, sliced
- 1 teaspoon olive oil
- ½ cup cream
- 1 egg, beaten
- 1 tablespoon wheat flour, whole grain
- 1 teaspoon cornstarch
- 3 oz Romano cheese, grated
- ½ cup ground beef
- ¼ teaspoon minced garlic
- 1 tablespoon Italian parsley, chopped
- 3 tablespoons tomato sauce
- ¾ teaspoon ground nutmeg

Directions
1. Sprinkle the eggplants with olive oil and ground nutmeg and arrange in the casserole mold in one layer.
2. After this, place the ground beef in the skillet.
3. Add minced garlic, Italian parsley, and ground nutmeg.
4. Then add tomato sauce and mix up the mixture well.
5. Roast it for 10 minutes over the medium heat.
6. Make the sauce: in the saucepan whisk together cream with egg.
7. Bring the liquid to boil (simmer it constantly) and add wheat flour, cornstarch, and cheese. Stir well.
8. Bring the liquid to boil and stir till cheese is melted. Remove the sauce from the heat.
9. Put the cooked ground beef over the eggplants and flatten well.
10. Then pour the cream sauce over the ground beef.
11. Cover the meal with foil and secure the edges.
12. Bake moussaka for 30 minutes at 365F.

Nutrition: calories 271; fat 16.1; fiber 5.9; carbs 15.4; protein 17.6

Hearty Meat And Potatoes

Servings: 2 Cups | Cooking: 30 min

Ingredients
- 1 lb. ground beef or lamb
- 1/4 cup extra-virgin olive oil
- 1 large yellow onion, chopped
- 5 large potatoes, peeled and cubed
- 1 1/2 tsp. salt
- 1 TB. seven spices
- 1/2 tsp. ground black pepper

Directions
1. In a large, 3-quart pot over medium heat, brown beef for 5 minutes, breaking up chunks with a wooden spoon.
2. Add extra-virgin olive oil and yellow onion, and cook for 5 minutes.
3. Toss in potatoes, salt, seven spices, and black pepper. Cover and cook for 10 minutes. Toss gently, and cook for 10 more minutes.
4. Serve warm with a side of Greek yogurt.

Ita Sandwiches

Servings: 1 Pita Sandwich | Cooking: 20 min

Ingredients
- 1 lb. ground beef
- 1 tsp. salt
- 1/2 tsp. ground black pepper
- 1 tsp. seven spices
- 4 (6- or 7-in.) pitas

Directions
1. Preheat the oven to 400°F.
2. In a medium bowl, combine beef, salt, black pepper, and seven spices.
3. Lay out pitas on the counter, and divide beef mixture evenly among them, and spread beef to edge of pitas.
4. Place pitas on a baking sheet, and bake for 20 minutes.
5. Serve warm with Greek yogurt.

Easy Chicken With Capers Skillet

Servings: 4 | Cooking: 35 min

Ingredients
- 4 boneless skinless chicken breast halves (6 ounces each)
- 1/4 teaspoon salt
- 1/4 teaspoon pepper
- 3 tablespoons olive oil
- 1-pint grape tomatoes
- 16 pitted Greek or ripe olives, sliced
- 3 tablespoons capers, drained

Directions
1. Place a cast iron skillet on medium high fire and heat for 5 minutes.
2. Meanwhile, season chicken with pepper and salt.
3. Add oil to pan and heat for another minute. Add chicken and increase fire to high. Brown sides for 4 minutes per side.
4. Lower fire to medium and add capers and tomatoes.
5. Bake uncovered in a 475oF preheated oven for 12 minutes.
6. Remove from oven and let it sit for 5 minutes before serving.

Nutrition: Calories: 336; Carbs: 6.0g; Protein: 36.0g; Fats: 18.0g

Lamb And Dill Apples

Servings: 4 | Cooking: 25 min

Ingredients
- 3 green apples, cored, peeled and cubed
- Juice of 1 lemon
- 1 pound lamb stew meat, cubed
- 1 small bunch dill, chopped
- 3 ounces heavy cream
- 2 tablespoon olive oil
- Salt and black pepper to the taste

Directions
1. Heat up a pan with the oil over medium-high heat, add the lamb and brown for 5 minutes.
2. Add the rest of the ingredients, bring to a simmer and cook over medium heat for 20 minutes.
3. Divide the mix between plates and serve.

Nutrition: calories 328; fat 16.7; fiber 10.5; carbs 21.6; protein 14.7

Tomatoes And Carrots Pork Mix

Servings: 4 | Cooking: 7 Hours

Ingredients
- 2 tablespoons olive oil
- ½ cup chicken stock
- 1 tablespoon ginger, grated
- Salt and black pepper to the taste
- 2 and ½ pounds pork stew meat, roughly cubed
- 2 cups tomatoes, chopped
- 4 ounces carrots, chopped
- 1 tablespoon cilantro, chopped

Directions
1. In your slow cooker, combine the oil with the stock, ginger and the rest of the ingredients, put the lid on and cook on Low for 7 hours.
2. Divide the mix between plates and serve.

Nutrition: calories 303; fat 15; fiber 8.6; carbs 14.9; protein 10.8

Cherry Stuffed Lamb

Servings: 2 | Cooking: 40 min

Ingredients
- 9 oz lamb loin
- 1 oz pistachio, chopped
- 1 teaspoon cherries, pitted
- ½ teaspoon olive oil
- ¼ teaspoon dried thyme
- 1 teaspoon dried rosemary
- 1 garlic clove, minced
- ¼ teaspoon liquid honey

Directions
1. Rub the lamb loin with dried thyme and rosemary.
2. Then make a lengthwise cut in the meat.
3. Mix up together pistachios, minced garlic, and cherries.
4. Fill the meat with this mixture and secure the cut with the toothpick.
5. Then brush the lamb loin with liquid honey and olive oil.

6. Wrap the meat in the foil and bake at 365F for 40 minutes.
7. When the meat is cooked, remove it from the foil.
8. Let the meat chill for 10 minutes and then slice it.

Nutrition: calories 353; fat 20.4; fiber 1.8; carbs 6; protein 36.9

Rosemary Pork Chops

Servings: 4 | Cooking: 35 min

Ingredients
- 4 pork loin chops, boneless
- Salt and black pepper to the taste
- 4 garlic cloves, minced
- 1 tablespoon rosemary, chopped
- 1 tablespoon olive oil

Directions
1. In a roasting pan, combine the pork chops with the rest of the ingredients, toss, and bake at 425 degrees F for 10 minutes.
2. Reduce the heat to 350 degrees F and cook the chops for 25 minutes more.
3. Divide the chops between plates and serve with a side salad.

Nutrition: calories 161; fat 5; fiber 1; carbs 1; protein 25

Cauliflower Tomato Beef

Servings: 2 | Cooking: 25 min

Ingredients
- 1/2 lb beef stew meat, chopped
- 1 tsp paprika
- 1 tbsp balsamic vinegar
- 1 celery stalk, chopped
- 1/4 cup grape tomatoes, chopped
- 1 onion, chopped
- 1 tbsp olive oil
- 1/4 cup cauliflower, chopped
- Pepper
- Salt

Directions
1. Add oil into the instant pot and set the pot on sauté mode.
2. Add meat and sauté for 5 minutes.
3. Add remaining ingredients and stir well.
4. Seal pot with lid and cook on high for 20 minutes.
5. Once done, allow to release pressure naturally. Remove lid.
6. Stir and serve.

Nutrition: Calories 306 Fat 14.3 g Carbohydrates 7.6 g Sugar 3.5 g Protein 35.7 g Cholesterol 101 mg

Pork And Sour Cream Mix

Servings: 4 | Cooking: 40 min

Ingredients
- 1 and ½ pounds pork meat, boneless and cubed
- 1 red onion, chopped
- 1 tablespoon avocado oil
- 1 garlic clove, minced
- ½ cup chicken stock
- 2 tablespoons hot paprika
- Salt and black pepper to the taste
- 1 and ½ cups sour cream
- 1 tablespoon cilantro, chopped

Directions
1. Heat up a pot with the oil over medium heat, add the pork and brown for 5 minutes.
2. Add the onion and the garlic and cook for 5 minutes more.
3. Add the rest of the ingredients except the cilantro, bring to a simmer and cook over medium heat for 30 minutes.
4. Add the cilantro, toss, divide between plates and serve.

Nutrition: calories 300; fat 9.5; fiber 4.5; carbs 15.5; protein 22

Honey Pork Strips

Servings: 4 | Cooking: 8 min

Ingredients
- 10 oz pork chops
- 1 teaspoon liquid honey
- 1 teaspoon tomato sauce
- 1 teaspoon sunflower oil
- ½ teaspoon sage
- ½ teaspoon mustard

Directions
1. Cut the pork chops on the strips and place in the bowl.
2. Add liquid honey, tomato sauce, sunflower oil, sage, and mustard.
3. Mix up the meat well and leave for 15-20 minutes to marinate.
4. Meanwhile, preheat the grill to 385F.

5. Arrange the pork strips in the grill and roast them for 4 minutes from each side.
6. Sprinkle the meat with remaining honey liquid during to cooking to make the taste of meat juicier.

Nutrition: calories 245; fat 18.9; fiber 0.1; carbs 1.7; protein 16.1

Orange Lamb And Potatoes

Servings: 4 | Cooking: 7 Hours

Ingredients
- 1 pound small potatoes, peeled and cubed
- 2 cups stewed tomatoes, drained
- Zest and juice of 1 orange
- 4 garlic cloves, minced
- 3 and ½ pounds leg of lamb, boneless and cubed
- Salt and black pepper to the taste
- ½ cup basil, chopped

Directions
1. In your slow cooker, combine the lamb with the potatoes and the rest of the ingredients, toss, put the lid on and cook on Low for 7 hours.
2. Divide the mix between plates and serve hot.

Nutrition: calories 287; fat 9.5; fiber 7.3; carbs 14.8; protein 18.2

Pork Kebabs

Servings: 6 | Cooking: 14 min

Ingredients
- 1 yellow onion, chopped
- 1 pound pork meat, ground
- 3 tablespoons cilantro, chopped
- 1 tablespoon lime juice
- 1 garlic clove, minced
- 2 teaspoon oregano, dried
- Salt and black pepper to the taste
- A drizzle of olive oil

Directions
1. In a bowl, mix the pork with the other ingredients except the oil, stir well and shape medium kebabs out of this mix.
2. Divide the kebabs on skewers, and brush them with a drizzle of oil.
3. Place the kebabs on your preheated grill and cook over medium heat for 7 minutes on each side.
4. Divide the kebabs between plates and serve with a side salad.

Nutrition: calories 229; fat 14; fiber 8.3; carbs 15.5; protein 12.4

Vegetable Lover's Chicken Soup

Servings: 4 | Cooking: 20 min

Ingredients
- 1 ½ cups baby spinach
- 2 tbsp orzo (tiny pasta)
- ¼ cup dry white wine
- 1 14oz low sodium chicken broth
- 2 plum tomatoes, chopped
- 1/8 tsp salt
- ½ tsp Italian seasoning
- 1 large shallot, chopped
- 1 small zucchini, diced
- 8-oz chicken tenders
- 1 tbsp extra virgin olive oil

Directions
1. In a large saucepan, heat oil over medium heat and add the chicken. Stir occasionally for 8 minutes until browned. Transfer in a plate. Set aside.
2. In the same saucepan, add the zucchini, Italian seasoning, shallot and salt and stir often until the vegetables are softened, around 4 minutes.
3. Add the tomatoes, wine, broth and orzo and increase the heat to high to bring the mixture to boil. Reduce the heat and simmer.
4. Add the cooked chicken and stir in the spinach last.
5. Serve hot.

Nutrition: Calories: 207; Carbs: 14.8g; Protein: 12.2g; Fat: 11.4g

Lemony Lamb And Potatoes

Servings: 4 | Cooking: 2 Hours And 10 min

Ingredients
- 2 pound lamb meat, cubed
- 2 tablespoons olive oil
- 2 springs rosemary, chopped
- 2 tablespoons parsley, chopped
- 1 tablespoon lemon rind, grated
- 3 garlic cloves, minced
- 2 tablespoons lemon juice
- 2 pounds baby potatoes, scrubbed and halved
- 1 cup veggie stock

Directions

1. In a roasting pan, combine the meat with the oil and the rest of the ingredients, introduce in the oven and bake at 400 degrees F for 2 hours and 10 minutes.
2. Divide the mix between plates and serve.

Nutrition: calories 302; fat 15.2; fiber 10.6; carbs 23.3; protein 15.2

Cumin Lamb Mix

Servings: 2 | Cooking: 10 min

Ingredients

- 2 lamb chops (3.5 oz each)
- 1 tablespoon olive oil
- 1 teaspoon ground cumin
- ½ teaspoon salt

Directions

1. Rub the lamb chops with ground cumin and salt.
2. Then sprinkle them with olive oil.
3. Let the meat marinate for 10 minutes.
4. After this, preheat the skillet well.
5. Place the lamb chops in the skillet and roast them for 10 minutes. Flip the meat on another side from time to time to avoid burning.

Nutrition: calories 384; fat 33.2; fiber 0.1; carbs 0.5; protein 19.2

Almond Lamb Chops

Servings: 4 | Cooking: 20 min

Ingredients

- 1 teaspoon almond butter
- 2 teaspoons minced garlic
- 1 teaspoon butter, softened
- ½ teaspoon salt
- ½ teaspoon chili flakes
- ½ teaspoon ground paprika
- 12 oz lamb chop

Directions

1. Churn together minced garlic, butter, salt, chili flakes, and ground paprika.
2. Carefully rub every lamb chop with the garlic mixture.
3. Toss almond butter in the skillet and melt it.
4. Place the lamb chops in the melted almond butter and roast them for 20 minutes (for 10 minutes from each side) over the medium-low heat.

Nutrition: calories 194; fat 9.5; fiber 0.5; carbs 1.4; protein 24.9

Pork And Figs Mix

Servings: 4 | Cooking: 40 min

Ingredients

- 3 tablespoons avocado oil
- 1 and ½ pounds pork stew meat, roughly cubed
- Salt and black pepper to the taste
- 1 cup red onions, chopped
- 1 cup figs, dried and chopped
- 1 tablespoon ginger, grated
- 1 tablespoon garlic, minced
- 1 cup canned tomatoes, crushed
- 2 tablespoons parsley, chopped

Directions

1. Heat up a pot with the oil over medium-high heat, add the meat and brown for 5 minutes.
2. Add the onions and sauté for 5 minutes more.
3. Add the rest of the ingredients, bring to a simmer and cook over medium heat for 30 minutes more.
4. Divide the mix between plates and serve.

Nutrition: calories 309; fat 16; fiber 10.4; carbs 21.1; protein 34.2

Lamb Chops

Servings: 1 Chop | Cooking: 6 min

Ingredients

- 6 (3/4-in.-thick) lamb chops
- 2 TB. fresh rosemary, finely chopped
- 3 TB. minced garlic
- 1 tsp. salt
- 1 tsp. ground black pepper
- 3 TB. extra-virgin olive oil

Directions

1. In a large bowl, combine lamb chops, rosemary, garlic, salt, black pepper, and extra-virgin olive oil until chops are evenly coated. Let chops marinate at room temperature for at least 25 minutes.
2. Preheat a grill to medium heat.
3. Place chops on the grill, and cook for 3 minutes per side for medium well.
4. Serve warm.

Chicken Quinoa Pilaf

Servings: 1 Cup | Cooking: 35 min

Ingredients
- 2 (8-oz.) boneless, skinless chicken breasts, cut into 1/2-in. cubes
- 3 TB. extra-virgin olive oil
- 1 medium red onion, finely chopped
- 1 TB. minced garlic
- 1 (16-oz.) can diced tomatoes, with juice
- 2 cups water
- 2 tsp. salt
- 1 TB. dried oregano
- 1 TB. turmeric
- 1 tsp. paprika
- 1 tsp. ground black pepper
- 2 cups red or yellow quinoa
- 1/2 cup fresh parsley, chopped

Directions
1. In a large, 3-quart pot over medium heat, heat extra-virgin olive oil. Add chicken, and cook for 5 minutes.
2. Add red onion and garlic, stir, and cook for 5 minutes.
3. Add tomatoes with juice, water, salt, oregano, turmeric, paprika, and black pepper. Stir, and simmer for 5 minutes.
4. Add red quinoa, and stir. Cover, reduce heat to low, and cook for 20 minutes. Remove from heat.
5. Fluff with a fork, cover again, and let sit for 10 minutes.
6. Serve warm.

Greek Styled Lamb Chops

Servings: 4 | Cooking: 4 min

Ingredients
- ¼ tsp black pepper
- ½ tsp salt
- 1 tbsp bottled minced garlic
- 1 tbsp dried oregano
- 2 tbsp lemon juice
- 8 pcs of lamb loin chops, around 4 oz
- Cooking: spray

Directions
1. Preheat broiler.
2. In a big bowl or dish, combine the black pepper, salt, minced garlic, lemon juice and oregano. Then rub it equally on all sides of the lamb chops.
3. Then coat a broiler pan with the cooking spray before placing the lamb chops on the pan and broiling until desired doneness is reached or for four minutes.

Nutrition: Calories: 131.9; Carbs: 2.6g; Protein: 17.1g; Fat: 5.9g

Bulgur And Chicken Skillet

Servings: 4 | Cooking: 40 min

Ingredients
- 4 (6-oz.) skinless, boneless chicken breasts
- 1 tablespoon olive oil, divided
- 1 cup thinly sliced red onion
- 1 tablespoon thinly sliced garlic
- 1 cup unsalted chicken stock
- 1 tablespoon coarsely chopped fresh dill
- 1/2 teaspoon freshly ground black pepper, divided
- 1/2 cup uncooked bulgur
- 2 teaspoons chopped fresh or 1/2 tsp. dried oregano
- 4 cups chopped fresh kale (about 2 1/2 oz.)
- 1/2 cup thinly sliced bottled roasted red bell peppers
- 2 ounces feta cheese, crumbled (about 1/2 cup)
- 3/4 teaspoon kosher salt, divided

Directions
1. Place a cast iron skillet on medium high fire and heat for 5 minutes. Add oil and heat for 2 minutes.
2. Season chicken with pepper and salt to taste.
3. Brown chicken for 4 minutes per side and transfer to a plate.
4. In same skillet, sauté garlic and onion for 3 minutes. Stir in oregano and bulgur and toast for 2 minutes.
5. Stir in kale and bell pepper, cook for 2 minutes. Pour in stock and season well with pepper and salt.
6. Return chicken to skillet and turn off fire. Pop in a preheated 400oF oven and bake for 15 minutes.
7. Remove form oven, fluff bulgur and turn over chicken. Let it stand for 5 minutes.
8. Serve and enjoy with a sprinkle of feta cheese.

Nutrition: Calories: 369; Carbs: 21.0g; Protein: 45.0g; Fats: 11.3g

Kibbeh With Yogurt

Servings: 1 Kibbeh | Cooking: 50 min

Ingredients
- 1/2 cup bulgur wheat, grind #1
- 4 cups water

- 1 large yellow onion, chopped
- 2 fresh basil leaves
- 1 lb. lean ground chuck beef
- 2 tsp. salt
- 1 tsp. ground black pepper
- 1/2 tsp. ground allspice
- 1/2 tsp. ground coriander
- 1/2 tsp. ground cumin
- 1/2 tsp. ground nutmeg
- 1/2 tsp. ground cloves
- 1/2 tsp. ground cinnamon
- 1/2 tsp. dried sage
- 1/4 cup long-grain rice
- 1/2 lb. ground beef
- 3 TB. extra-virgin olive oil
- 1/2 cup pine nuts
- 1 tsp. seven spices
- 4 cups Greek yogurt
- 2 TB. minced garlic
- 1 tsp. dried mint

Directions
1. In a small bowl, soak bulgur wheat in 1 cup water for 30 minutes.
2. In a food processor fitted with a chopping blade, blend 1/2 of yellow onion and basil for 30 seconds. Add bulgur, and blend for 30 more seconds.
3. Add ground chuck, 1 1/2 teaspoons salt, black pepper, allspice, coriander, cumin, nutmeg, cloves, cinnamon, and sage, and blend for 1 minute.
4. Transfer mixture to a large bowl, and knead for 3 minutes.
5. In a large pot, combine long-grain rice and remaining 3 cups water, and cook for 30 minutes.
6. In a medium skillet over medium heat, brown beef for 5 minutes, breaking up chunks with a wooden spoon.
7. Add remaining 1/2 of yellow onion, extra-virgin olive oil, remaining 1/2 teaspoon salt, pine nuts, and seven spices, and cook for 7 minutes. Set aside to cool.
8. Whisk Greek yogurt into cooked rice, add garlic and mint, reduce heat to low, and cook for 5 minutes.
9. Form meat-bulgur mixture into 12 equal-size balls. Create a groove in center of each ball, fill with beef and onion mixture, and seal groove.
10. Carefully drop balls into yogurt sauce, and cook for 15 minutes. Serve warm.

Mustard Chops With Apricot-basil Relish

Servings: 4 | Cooking: 12 min

Ingredients
- ¼ cup basil, finely shredded
- ¼ cup olive oil
- ½ cup mustard
- ¾ lb. fresh apricots, stone removed, and fruit diced
- 1 shallot, diced small
- 1 tsp ground cardamom
- 3 tbsp raspberry vinegar
- 4 pork chops
- Pepper and salt

Directions
1. Make sure that pork chops are defrosted well. Season with pepper and salt. Slather both sides of each pork chop with mustard. Preheat grill to medium-high fire.
2. In a medium bowl, mix cardamom, olive oil, vinegar, basil, shallot, and apricots. Toss to combine and season with pepper and salt, mixing once again.
3. Grill chops for 5 to 6 minutes per side. As you flip, baste with mustard.
4. Serve pork chops with the Apricot-Basil relish and enjoy.

Nutrition: Calories: 486.5; Carbs: 7.3g; Protein: 42.1g; Fat: 32.1g

Pork And Peas

Servings: 4 | Cooking: 20 min

Ingredients
- 4 ounces snow peas
- 2 tablespoons avocado oil
- 1 pound pork loin, boneless and cubed
- ¾ cup beef stock
- ½ cup red onion, chopped
- Salt and white pepper to the taste

Directions
1. Heat up a pan with the oil over medium-high heat, add the pork and brown for 5 minutes.
2. Add the peas and the rest of the ingredients, toss, bring to a simmer and cook over medium heat for 15 minutes.
3. Divide the mix between plates and serve right away.

Nutrition: calories 332; fat 16.5; fiber 10.3; carbs 20.7; protein 26.5

Paprika And Feta Cheese On Chicken Skillet

Servings: 6 | Cooking: 35 min

Ingredients
- ¼ cup black olives, sliced in circles
- ½ teaspoon coriander
- ½ teaspoon paprika
- 1 ½ cups diced tomatoes with the juice
- 1 cup yellow onion, chopped
- 1 teaspoon onion powder
- 2 garlic cloves, peeled and minced
- 2 lb. free range organic boneless skinless chicken breasts
- 2 tablespoons feta cheese
- 2 tablespoons ghee or olive oil
- Crushed red pepper to taste
- Salt and black pepper to taste

Directions
1. Preheat oven to 400oF.
2. Place a cast-iron pan on medium high fire and heat for 5 minutes. Add oil and heat for 2 minutes more.
3. Meanwhile in a large dish, mix well pepper, salt, crushed red pepper, paprika, coriander, and onion powder. Add chicken and coat well in seasoning.
4. Add chicken to pan and brown sides for 4 minutes per side. Increase fire to high.
5. Stir in garlic and onions. Lower fire to medium and mix well.
6. Pop pan in oven and bake for 15 minutes.
7. Remove from oven, turnover chicken and let it stand for 5 minutes before serving.

Nutrition: Calories: 232; Carbs: 5.0g; Protein: 33.0g; Fats: 8.0g

Jalapeno Beef Chili

Servings: 8 | Cooking: 40 min

Ingredients
- 1 lb ground beef
- 1 tsp garlic powder
- 1 jalapeno pepper, chopped
- 1 tbsp ground cumin
- 1 tbsp chili powder
- 1 lb ground pork
- 4 tomatillos, chopped
- 1/2 onion, chopped
- 5 oz tomato paste
- Pepper
- Salt

Directions
1. Add oil into the instant pot and set the pot on sauté mode.
2. Add beef and pork and cook until brown.
3. Add remaining ingredients and stir well.
4. Seal pot with lid and cook on high for 35 minutes.
5. Once done, allow to release pressure naturally. Remove lid.
6. Stir well and serve.

Nutrition: Calories 217 Fat 6.1 g Carbohydrates 6.2 g Sugar 2.7 g Protein 33.4 g Cholesterol 92 mg

Kibbeh In A Pan

Servings: 1 Kibbeh | Cooking: 37 min

Ingredients
- 1/2 cup bulgur wheat, grind #1
- 1 cup water
- 1 large yellow onion, chopped
- 2 fresh basil leaves
- 1 lb. lean ground chuck beef
- 2 tsp. salt
- 1 tsp. ground black pepper
- 1/2 tsp. ground allspice
- 1/2 tsp. ground coriander
- 1/2 tsp. ground cumin
- 1/2 tsp. ground nutmeg
- 1/2 tsp. ground cloves
- 1/2 tsp. ground cinnamon
- 1/2 tsp. dried sage
- 1/2 lb. ground beef
- 4 TB. extra-virgin olive oil
- 1/2 cup pine nuts
- 1 tsp. seven spices

Directions
1. In a small bowl, soak bulgur wheat in water for 30 minutes.
2. In a food processor fitted with a chopping blade, blend 1/2 of yellow onion and basil for 30 seconds. Add bulgur, and blend for 30 more seconds.
3. Add ground chuck, 11/2 teaspoons salt, black pepper, allspice, coriander, cumin, nutmeg,

cloves, cinnamon, and sage, and blend for 1 minute.
4. Transfer mixture to a large bowl, and knead for 3 minutes.
5. In a medium skillet over medium heat, brown beef for 5 minutes, breaking up chunks with a wooden spoon.
6. Add remaining 1/2 of yellow onion, 2 tablespoons extra-virgin olive oil, remaining 1/2 teaspoon salt, pine nuts, and seven spices, and cook for 7 minutes.
7. Preheat the oven to 450°F. Grease an 8×8-inch baking dish with extra-virgin olive oil.
8. Divide kibbeh dough in half, spread a layer of dough on bottom of the prepared baking dish, add a layer of sautéed vegetables, and top with remaining kibbeh dough.
9. Paint top of kibbeh with remaining 2 tablespoons extra-virgin olive oil, and cut kibbeh into 12 equal-size pieces. Bake for 25 minutes.
10. Let kibbeh rest for 15 minutes before serving.

Saffron Beef

Servings: 2 | Cooking: 15 min

Ingredients
- ¾ teaspoon saffron
- ¾ teaspoon dried thyme
- ¾ teaspoon ground coriander
- ¼ teaspoon ground cinnamon
- 1 tablespoon butter
- 1/3 teaspoon salt
- 9 oz beef sirloin

Directions
1. Rub the beef sirloin with dried thyme, ground coriander, saffron, ground cinnamon, and salt.
2. Leave the meat for at least 10 minutes to soak all the spices.
3. Then preheat the grill to 395F.
4. Place the beef sirloin in the grill and cook it for 5 minutes.
5. Then spread the meat with butter carefully and cook for 10 minutes more. Flip it on another side from time to time.

Nutrition: calories 291; fat 13.8; fiber 0.3; carbs 0.6; protein 38.8

Cayenne Pork

Servings: 4 | Cooking: 50 min

Ingredients
- 8 oz beef sirloin
- 1 poblano pepper, grinded
- 1 teaspoon minced garlic
- ½ cup of water
- 1 tablespoon butter
- 1 teaspoon ground black pepper
- 1 teaspoon salt
- ½ teaspoon paprika
- 1 teaspoon cayenne pepper

Directions
1. Toss the butter in the saucepan and melt it.
2. Meanwhile rub the beef sirloin with minced garlic, salt, ground black pepper, paprika, and cayenne pepper.
3. Put the meat in the hot butter and roast for 5 minutes from each side over the medium heat.
4. After this, add water and poblano pepper.
5. Cook the meat for 50 minutes over the medium heat.
6. Then transfer the beef sirloin on the cutting board and shred it with the help of the fork.

Nutrition: calories 97; fat 5.5; fiber 0.5; carbs 3; protein 9.5

Basil And Shrimp Quinoa

Servings: 1 Cup | Cooking: 20 min

Ingredients
- 3 TB. extra-virgin olive oil
- 2 TB. minced garlic
- 1 cup fresh broccoli florets
- 3 stalks asparagus, chopped (1 cup)
- 4 cups chicken or vegetable broth
- 11/2 tsp. salt
- 1 tsp. ground black pepper
- 1 TB. lemon zest
- 2 cups red quinoa
- 1/2 cup fresh basil, chopped

Directions
1. 1/2 lb. medium raw shrimp (18 to 20), shells and veins removed
2. In a 2-quart pot over low heat, heat extra-virgin olive oil. Add garlic, and cook for 3 minutes.
3. Increase heat to medium, add broccoli and asparagus, and cook for 2 minutes.
4. Add chicken broth, salt, black pepper, and lemon zest, and bring to a boil. Stir in red quinoa, cover, and cook for 15 minutes.
5. Fold in basil and shrimp, cover, and cook for 10 minutes.

6. Remove from heat, fluff with a fork, cover, and set aside for 10 minutes. Serve warm.

Ground Pork Salad

Servings: 8 | Cooking: 15 min

Ingredients
- 1 cup ground pork
- ½ onion, diced
- 4 bacon slices
- 1 teaspoon sesame oil
- 1 teaspoon butter
- 1 cup lettuce, chopped
- 1 tablespoon lemon juice
- 4 eggs, boiled
- ½ teaspoon salt
- 1 teaspoon chili pepper
- ¼ teaspoon liquid honey

Directions
1. Make burgers: in the mixing bowl combine together ground pork, diced onion, salt, and chili pepper.
2. Make the medium size burgers.
3. Melt butter in the skillet and add prepared burgers.
4. Roast them for 5 minutes from each side over the medium heat.
5. When the burgers are cooked, chill them little.
6. Place the bacon in the skillet and roast it until golden brown. Then chill the bacon and chop it roughly.
7. In the salad bowl combine together chopped bacon, sesame oil, lettuce, lemon juice, and honey. Mix up salad well.
8. Peel the eggs and cut them on the halves.
9. Arrange the eggs and burgers over the salad. Don't mix salad anymore.

Nutrition: calories 213; fat 15.4; fiber 0.1; carbs 1.5; protein 16.5

Beef And Dill Mushrooms

Servings: 3 | Cooking: 35 min

Ingredients
- 1 cup cremini mushrooms, sliced
- 4 oz beef loin, sliced onto the wedges
- 1 tablespoon olive oil
- 1 teaspoon dried oregano
- ½ cup of water
- ¼ cup cream
- 1 teaspoon tomato paste
- 1 teaspoon ground black pepper
- 1 teaspoon salt
- 1 tablespoon fresh dill, chopped

Directions
1. In the saucepan combine together olive oil and cremini mushrooms.
2. Add dried oregano, ground black pepper, salt, and dill. Mix up well.
3. Cook the mushrooms for 2-3 minutes and add sliced beef loin.
4. Cook the ingredients for 5 minutes over the medium heat.
5. After this, add cream, water, tomato paste, and mix up the meal well.
6. Simmer the beef stroganoff for 25 minutes over the medium heat.

Nutrition: calories 196; fat 11.8; fiber 0.8; carbs 3.3; protein 20.1

Beef Pitas

Servings: 4 | Cooking: 15 min

Ingredients
- 1 ½ cup ground beef
- ½ red onion, diced
- 1 teaspoon minced garlic
- ¼ cup fresh spinach, chopped
- 1 teaspoon salt
- ½ teaspoon chili pepper
- 1 teaspoon dried oregano
- 1 teaspoon fresh mint, chopped
- 4 tablespoons Plain yogurt
- 1 cucumber, grated
- ½ teaspoon dill
- ½ teaspoon garlic powder
- 4 pitta bread

Directions
1. In the mixing bowl combine together ground beef, onion, minced garlic, spinach, salt, chili pepper, and dried oregano.
2. Make the medium size balls from the meat mixture.
3. Line the baking tray with baking paper and arrange the meatballs inside.
4. Bake the meatballs for 15 minutes at 375F. Flip them on another side after 10 minutes of cooking.
5. Meanwhile, make tzaziki: combine together fresh mint, yogurt, grated cucumber, dill, and garlic powder. Whisk the mixture for 1 minute.

6. When the meatballs are cooked, place the over pitta bread and top with tzaziki.

Nutrition: calorie 253; fat 7.1; fiber 4; carbs 30.1; protein 16.3

Lamb Burger On Arugula

Servings: 6 | Cooking: 6 min

Ingredients
- ½ oz fresh mint, divided
- 1 tbsp salt
- 2 lbs. ground lamb
- 2 tbsp shelled and salted Pistachio nuts
- 3 oz dried apricots, diced
- 3 oz Feta crumbled – you can omit if you do not eat dairy
- 4 cups arugula

Directions
1. In a bowl, with your hands blend feta, salt, ½ of fresh mint (diced), apricots and ground lamb.
2. Then form into balls or patties with an ice cream scooper. Press ball in between palm of hands to flatten to half an inch. Do the same for remaining patties.
3. In a nonstick thick pan on medium fire, place patties without oil and cook for 3 minutes per side or until lightly browned. Flip over once and cook the other side.
4. Meanwhile, arrange 1 cup of arugula per plate. Total of 4 plates.
5. Divide evenly and place cooked patties on top of arugula.
6. In a food processor, process until finely chopped the remaining mint leaves and nuts.
7. Sprinkle on top of patties, serve and enjoy.

Nutrition: Calories: 458.2; Carbs: 12.0g; Protein: 23.8g; Fat: 35.0g

Flavorful Beef Bourguignon

Servings: 4 | Cooking: 20 min

Ingredients
- 1 1/2 lbs beef chuck roast, cut into chunks
- 2/3 cup beef stock
- 2 tbsp fresh thyme
- 1 bay leaf
- 1 tsp garlic, minced
- 8 oz mushrooms, sliced
- 2 tbsp tomato paste
- 2/3 cup dry red wine
- 1 onion, sliced
- 4 carrots, cut into chunks
- 1 tbsp olive oil
- Pepper
- Salt

Directions
1. Add oil into the instant pot and set the pot on sauté mode.
2. Add meat and sauté until brown. Add onion and sauté until softened.
3. Add remaining ingredients and stir well.
4. Seal pot with lid and cook on high for 12 minutes.
5. Once done, allow to release pressure naturally. Remove lid.
6. Stir well and serve.

Nutrition: Calories 744 Fat 51.3 g Carbohydrates 14.5 g Sugar 6.5 g Protein 48.1 g Cholesterol 175 mg

Kefta Burgers

Servings: 1 Burger | Cooking: 10 min

Ingredients
- 1 lb. ground beef
- 1 cup fresh parsley, finely chopped
- 1 tsp. seven spices
- 1 1/2 tsp. salt
- 1 large yellow onion, finely sliced
- 1 TB. sumac
- 1/2 cup mayonnaise
- 3 TB. tahini paste
- 2 TB. balsamic vinegar
- 1/2 tsp. ground black pepper
- 4 (4-in.) pitas
- 1 medium tomato, sliced

Directions
1. In a large bowl, combine beef, 1/2 cup parsley, seven spices, 1 teaspoon salt. Form mixture into 4 patties.
2. In a medium bowl, combine remaining 1/2 cup parsley, yellow onion, and sumac.
3. In a small bowl, whisk together mayonnaise, tahini paste, remaining 1/2 teaspoon salt, balsamic vinegar, and black pepper.
4. Preheat a large skillet over medium-high heat. Place patties in the skillet, and cook for 5 minutes per side.
5. To assemble burgers, open each pita into a pocket, and spread both sides with tahini mayonnaise. Add 1 burger patty, some parsley mixture, and a few tomato slices, and serve.

Tasty Beef Stew

Servings: 4 | Cooking: 30 min

Ingredients
- 2 1/2 lbs beef roast, cut into chunks
- 1 cup beef broth
- 1/2 cup balsamic vinegar
- 1 tbsp honey
- 1/2 tsp red pepper flakes
- 1 tbsp garlic, minced
- Pepper
- Salt

Directions
1. Add all ingredients into the inner pot of instant pot and stir well.
2. Seal pot with lid and cook on high for 30 minutes.
3. Once done, allow to release pressure naturally. Remove lid.
4. Stir well and serve.

Nutrition: Calories 562 Fat 18.1 g Carbohydrates 5.7 g Sugar 4.6 g Protein 87.4 g Cholesterol 253 mg

Beef Dish

Servings: ¼ Pound | Cooking: 20 min

Ingredients
- 1 lb. skirt steak
- 2 TB. minced garlic
- 1/4 cup fresh lemon juice
- 2 TB. apple cider vinegar
- 3 TB. extra-virgin olive oil
- 1 tsp. salt
- 1/2 tsp. ground black pepper
- 1/4 tsp. ground cinnamon
- 1/4 tsp. ground cardamom
- 1 tsp. seven spices

Directions
1. Using a sharp knife, cut skirt steak into thin, 1/4-inch strips. Place strips in a large bowl.
2. Add garlic, lemon juice, apple cider vinegar, extra-virgin olive oil, salt, black pepper, cinnamon, cardamom, and seven spices, and mix well.
3. Place steak in the refrigerator and marinate for at least 20 minutes and up to 24 hours.
4. Preheat a large skillet over medium heat. Add meat and marinade, and cook for 20 minutes or until meat is tender and marinade has evaporated.
5. Serve warm with pita bread and tahini sauce.

Pork And Sage Couscous

Servings: 4 | Cooking: 7 Hours

Ingredients
- 2 pounds pork loin boneless and sliced
- ¾ cup veggie stock
- 2 tablespoons olive oil
- ½ tablespoon chili powder
- 2 teaspoon sage, dried
- ½ tablespoon garlic powder
- Salt and black pepper to the taste
- 2 cups couscous, cooked

Directions
1. In a slow cooker, combine the pork with the stock, the oil and the other ingredients except the couscous, put the lid on and cook on Low for 7 hours.
2. Divide the mix between plates, add the couscous on the side, sprinkle the sage on top and serve.

Nutrition: calories 272; fat 14.5; fiber 9.1; carbs 16.3; protein 14.3

Chicken Burgers With Brussel Sprouts Slaw

Servings: 4 | Cooking: 15 min

Ingredients
- ¼ cup apple, diced
- ¼ cup green onion, diced
- ½ avocado, cubed
- ½ pound Brussels sprouts, shredded
- 1 garlic clove, minced
- 1 tablespoon Dijon mustard
- 1/3 cup apple, sliced into strips
- 1/8 teaspoon red pepper flakes, optional
- 1-pound cooked ground chicken
- 3 slices bacon, cooked and diced
- Salt and pepper to taste

Directions
1. In a mixing bowl, combine together chicken, green onion, Dijon mustard, garlic, apple, bacon and pepper flakes. Season with salt and pepper to taste. Mix the ingredients then form 4 burger patties.
2. Heat a grill pan over medium-high flame and grill the burgers. Cook for five minutes on side. Set aside.
3. In another bowl, toss the Brussels sprouts and apples.

4. In a small pan, heat coconut oil and add the Brussels sprouts mixture until everything is slightly wilted. Season with salt and pepper to taste.
5. Serve burger patties with the Brussels sprouts slaw.

Nutrition: Calories: 325.1; Carbs: 11.5g; Protein: 32.2g; Fat: 16.7g

Beef And Potatoes With Tahini Sauce

Servings: 1/6 Casserole | Cooking: 35 min

Ingredients
- 1/2 large yellow onion
- 1 lb. ground beef
- 2 1/2 tsp. salt
- 1/2 tsp. ground black pepper
- 6 small red potatoes, washed
- 3 TB. extra-virgin olive oil
- 2 cups plain Greek yogurt
- 3/4 cup tahini paste
- 1 1/2 cups water
- 1/4 cup fresh lemon juice
- 1 TB. minced garlic
- 1/2 cup pine nuts

Directions
1. Preheat the oven to 425°F.
2. In a food processor fitted with a chopping blade, blend yellow onion for 30 seconds.
3. Transfer onion to a large bowl. Add beef, 1 teaspoon salt, black pepper, and mix well.
4. Spread beef mixture evenly in the bottom of a 9-inch casserole dish, and bake for 20 minutes.
5. Cut red potatoes into 1/4-inch-thick pieces, place in a bowl, and toss with 2 tablespoons extra-virgin olive oil and 1/2 teaspoon salt. Spread potatoes on a baking sheet, and bake for 20 minutes.
6. In a large bowl, combine Greek yogurt, tahini paste, water, lemon juice, garlic, and remaining 1 teaspoon salt.
7. Remove beef mixture and potatoes from the oven. Using a spatula, transfer potatoes to the casserole dish. Pour yogurt sauce over top, and bake for 15 more minutes.
8. In a small pan over low heat, heat remaining 1 tablespoon extra-virgin olive oil. Add pine nuts, and toast for 1 or 2 minutes.
9. Remove casserole dish from the oven, spoon pine nuts over top, and serve warm with brown rice.

Spicy Beef Chili Verde

Servings: 2 | Cooking: 23 min

Ingredients
- 1/2 lb beef stew meat, cut into cubes
- 1/4 tsp chili powder
- 1 tbsp olive oil
- 1 cup chicken broth
- 1 Serrano pepper, chopped
- 1 tsp garlic, minced
- 1 small onion, chopped
- 1/4 cup grape tomatoes, chopped
- 1/4 cup tomatillos, chopped
- Pepper
- Salt

Directions
1. Add oil into the instant pot and set the pot on sauté mode.
2. Add garlic and onion and sauté for 3 minutes.
3. Add remaining ingredients and stir well.
4. Seal pot with lid and cook on high for 20 minutes.
5. Once done, allow to release pressure naturally. Remove lid.
6. Stir well and serve.

Nutrition: Calories 317 Fat 15.1 g Carbohydrates 6.4 g Sugar 2.6 g Protein 37.8 g Cholesterol 101 mg

Lime And Mustard Lamb

Servings: 2 | Cooking: 25 min

Ingredients
- 8 oz lamb ribs, trimmed
- 1 tablespoon olive oil
- 1 tablespoon lime juice
- ½ teaspoon lime zest, grated
- ¼ teaspoon mustard
- ½ teaspoon salt

Directions
1. In the shallow bowl combine together olive oil, lime juice, lime zest, mustard, and salt.
2. Rub the lamb ribs with the lime mixture well and place in the skillet.
3. Roast the meat for 5 minutes from each side.
4. Then add remaining lime mixture and close the lid.
5. Cook the lamb ribs for 20 minutes over the medium heat. You can flip the ribs on another side during cooking.

Nutrition: calories 325; fat 22.2; fiber 0.1; carbs 0.2; protein 29.8

Steak with Olives and Mushrooms

Preparation: 20 min | Cooking: 9 min | Servings: 6

Ingredients
- lb. boneless beef sirloin steak
- 1 large onion, sliced
- 5-6 white button mushrooms
- 1/2 cup green olives, coarsely chopped
- 4 tbsp. extra virgin olive oil

Directions
1. Heat olive oil in a heavy bottomed skillet over medium-high heat. Brown the steaks on both sides then put aside.
2. Gently sauté the onion in the same skillet, for 2-3 min, stirring rarely. Sauté in the mushrooms and olives.
3. Return the steaks to the skillet, cover, cook for 5-6 min and serve.

Nutrition: 299 calories; 56g fat; 16g protein

Sausage & Bacon With Beans

Servings: 12 | Cooking: 30 min

Ingredients
- 12 medium sausages
- 12 bacon slices
- 8 eggs
- 2 cans baked beans
- 12 bread slices, toasted

Directions
1. Preheat the Airfryer at 325 degrees F and place sausages and bacon in a fryer basket.
2. Cook for about 10 minutes and place the baked beans in a ramekin.
3. Place eggs in another ramekin and the Airfryer to 395 degrees F.
4. Cook for about 10 more minutes and divide the sausage mixture, beans and eggs in serving plates.
5. Serve with bread slices.

Nutrition: Calories: 276 Carbs: 14.1g Fats: 17g Proteins: 16.3g Sodium: 817mg Sugar: 0.6g

Mediterranean Lamb Kebabs

Servings: 4 | Cooking: 40 min

Ingredients
- 1 pound ground lamb
- 2 tablespoons scallions, chopped
- 2 tablespoons extra-virgin olive oil
- 2 tablespoons of crème fraîche
- 12 large-sized shallots; peel, halved lengthwise, and then trim root ends but keep intact
- 1/3 cup of water
- 1/2 teaspoon black pepper, freshly ground
- 1 teaspoon freshly squeezed lemon juice
- 1 tablespoon parsley, flat-leaf, chopped
- 1 garlic clove, minced
- 1 1/4 teaspoons salt
- 1 1/2 teaspoons pomegranate molasses, divided
- Warm pita bread, for serving

Directions
1. Light an outdoor grill.
2. In medium-sized bowl, gently mix the ground lamb, garlic, crème fraîche, salt, and the pepper until combined. With moistened hands, roll lamb mixture to form 16 balls.
3. Into 8 pieces 10-inch or less metal skewers, alternate skewer 3 halves shallots and 2 pieces lamb balls. Brush kebabs with olive oil. Place on the grill and cook over medium high heat for about 3 minutes, turning once, until the outside of the lamb balls and the shallots are browned but are not cooked all the way through.
4. Transfer the semi-cooked kebabs into very large-sized deep skillet, about 12-14 inches. Add water, the lemon juice, and 1 teaspoon pomegranate molasses to the water; bring the water mixture to a boil. When boiling, cover and gently simmer for about 30 minutes over low flame or heat or until the meatballs are cooked through and the shallots are very tender.
5. Uncover the skillet; increase heat to high. Add remaining 1/2 teaspoon pomegranate molasses. Continue cooking for 5 minutes more, basting the shallots and the meatballs occasionally until they are glazed.
6. Transfer kebabs into a serving platter. Drizzle with the remaining sauce from the skillet. Garnish with parsley and scallions. Serve with warmed pita bread.

Nutrition: 379 cal.,16.9 g total fat (4.8 g sat. fat), 909 mg sodium, 105 mg chol., 665 mg pot., 21.3 g total carbs., 0.5 g fiber, 1.7 g sugar, 35.1 g protein, 17% vitamin A, 13% vitamin C, 7% calcium, and 23% iron

Chapter 4: Poultry Recipes

Butter Chicken Thighs

Servings: 4 | Cooking: 30 min

Ingredients
- 1 teaspoon fennel seeds
- 1 garlic clove, peeled
- 1 tablespoon butter
- 1 teaspoon coconut oil
- ¼ teaspoon thyme
- ½ teaspoon salt
- 1 oz fennel bulb, chopped
- 1 oz shallot, chopped
- 4 chicken thighs, skinless, boneless
- 1 teaspoon ground black pepper

Directions
1. Rub the chicken thighs with ground black pepper.
2. In the skillet mix up together butter and coconut oil.
3. Add fennel seeds, garlic clove, thyme, salt, and shallot.
4. Roast the mixture for 1 minute.
5. Then add fennel bulb and chicken thighs.
6. Roast the chicken thighs for 2 minutes from each side over the high heat.
7. Then transfer the skillet with chicken in the oven and cook the meal for 20 minutes at 360F.

Nutrition: calories 324; fat 14.9; fiber 0.6; carbs 2.6; protein 42.7

Chicken And Olives Salsa

Servings: 4 | Cooking: 25 min

Ingredients
- 2 tablespoon avocado oil
- 4 chicken breast halves, skinless and boneless
- Salt and black pepper to the taste
- 1 tablespoon sweet paprika
- 1 red onion, chopped
- 1 tablespoon balsamic vinegar
- 2 tablespoons parsley, chopped
- 1 avocado, peeled, pitted and cubed
- 2 tablespoons black olives, pitted and chopped

Directions
1. Heat up your grill over medium-high heat, add the chicken brushed with half of the oil and seasoned with paprika, salt and pepper, cook for 7 minutes on each side and divide between plates.
2. Meanwhile, in a bowl, mix the onion with the rest of the ingredients and the remaining oil, toss, add on top of the chicken and serve.

Nutrition: calories 289; fat 12.4; fiber 9.1; carbs 23.8; protein 14.3

Slow Cooked Chicken And Capers Mix

Servings: 4 | Cooking: 7 Hours

Ingredients
- 2 chicken breasts, skinless, boneless and halved
- 2 cups canned tomatoes, crushed
- 2 garlic cloves, minced
- 1 yellow onion, chopped
- 2 cups chicken stock
- 2 tablespoons capers, drained
- ¼ cup rosemary, chopped
- Salt and black pepper to the taste

Directions
1. In your slow cooker, combine the chicken with the tomatoes, capers and the rest of the ingredients, put the lid on and cook on Low for 7 hours.
2. Divide the mix between plates and serve.

Nutrition: calories 292; fat 9.4; fiber 11.8; carbs 25.1; protein 36.4

Chili Chicken Mix

Servings: 4 | Cooking: 18 min

Ingredients
- 2 pounds chicken thighs, skinless and boneless
- 2 tablespoons olive oil
- 2 cups yellow onion, chopped
- 1 teaspoon onion powder
- 1 teaspoon smoked paprika
- 1 teaspoon chili pepper
- ½ teaspoon coriander seeds, ground
- 2 teaspoons oregano, dried
- 2 teaspoon parsley flakes
- 30 ounces canned tomatoes, chopped
- ½ cup black olives, pitted and halved

Directions
1. Set the instant pot on Sauté mode, add the oil, heat it up, add the onion, onion powder and the rest of the ingredients except the tomatoes, olives and the chicken, stir and sauté for 10 minutes.
2. Add the chicken, tomatoes and the olives, put the lid on and cook on High for 8 minutes.
3. Release the pressure naturally 10 minutes, divide the mix into bowls and serve.

Nutrition: calories 153; fat 8; fiber 2; carbs 9; protein 12

Ginger Duck Mix

Servings: 4 | Cooking: 1 Hour And 50 min

Ingredients
- 4 duck legs, boneless
- 4 shallots, chopped
- 2 tablespoons olive oil
- 1 tablespoon ginger, grated
- 2 tablespoons rosemary, chopped
- 1 cup chicken stock
- 1 tablespoon chives, chopped

Directions
1. In a roasting pan, combine the duck legs with the shallots and the rest of the ingredients except the chives, toss, introduce in the oven at 250 degrees F and bake for 1 hour and 30 minutes.
2. Divide the mix between plates, sprinkle the chives on top and serve.

Nutrition: calories 299; fat 10.2; fiber 9.2; carbs 18.1; protein 17.3

Duck And Orange Warm Salad

Servings: 4 | Cooking: 25 min

Ingredients
- 2 tablespoons balsamic vinegar
- 2 oranges, peeled and cut into segments
- 1 teaspoon orange zest, grated
- 1 tablespoons orange juice
- 3 shallot, minced
- 2 tablespoons olive oil
- Salt and black pepper to the taste
- 2 duck breasts, boneless and skin scored
- 2 cups baby arugula
- 2 tablespoons chives, chopped

Directions
1. Heat up a pan with the oil over medium-high heat, add the duck breasts skin side down and brown for 5 minutes.
2. Flip the duck, add the shallot, and the other ingredients except the arugula, orange and the chives, and cook for 15 minutes more.
3. Transfer the duck breasts to a cutting board, cool down, cut into strips and put in a salad bowl.
4. Add the remaining ingredients, toss and serve warm.

Nutrition: calories 304; fat 15.4; fiber 12.6; carbs 25.1; protein 36.4

Turmeric Baked Chicken Breast

Servings: 2 | Cooking: 40 min

Ingredients
- 8 oz chicken breast, skinless, boneless
- 2 tablespoons capers
- 1 teaspoon olive oil
- ½ teaspoon paprika
- ½ teaspoon ground turmeric
- ½ teaspoon salt
- ½ teaspoon minced garlic

Directions
1. Make the lengthwise cut in the chicken breast.
2. Rub the chicken with olive oil, paprika, capers, ground turmeric, salt, and minced garlic.
3. Then fill the chicken cut with capers and secure it with the toothpicks.
4. Bake the chicken breast for 40 minutes at 350F.
5. Remove the toothpicks from the chicken breast and slice it.

Nutrition: calories 156; fat 5.4; fiber 0.6; carbs 1.3; protein 24.4

Chicken Tacos

Servings: 4 | Cooking: 20 min

Ingredients
- 2 bread tortillas
- 1 teaspoon butter
- 2 teaspoons olive oil
- 1 teaspoon Taco seasoning
- 6 oz chicken breast, skinless, boneless, sliced
- 1/3 cup Cheddar cheese, shredded
- 1 bell pepper, cut on the wedges

Directions
1. Pour 1 teaspoon of olive oil in the skillet and add chicken.
2. Sprinkle the meat with Taco seasoning and mix up well.
3. Roast chicken for 10 minutes over the medium heat. Stir it from time to time.
4. Then transfer the cooked chicken in the plate.
5. Add remaining olive oil in the skillet.
6. Then add bell pepper and roast it for 5 minutes. Stir it all the time.
7. Mix up together bell pepper with chicken.

8. Toss butter in the skillet and melt it.
9. Put 1 tortilla in the skillet.
10. Put Cheddar cheese on the tortilla and flatten it.
11. Then add chicken-pepper mixture and cover it with the second tortilla.
12. Roast the quesadilla for 2 minutes from each side.
13. Cut the cooked meal on the halves and transfer in the serving plates.

Nutrition: calories 194; fat 8.3; fiber 0.6; carbs 16.4; protein 13.2

Chicken And Butter Sauce

Servings: 5 | Cooking: 30 min

Ingredients
- 1-pound chicken fillet
- 1/3 cup butter, softened
- 1 tablespoon rosemary
- ½ teaspoon thyme
- 1 teaspoon salt
- ½ lemon

Directions
1. Churn together thyme, salt, and rosemary.
2. Chop the chicken fillet roughly and mix up with churned butter mixture.
3. Place the prepared chicken in the baking dish.
4. Squeeze the lemon over the chicken.
5. Chop the squeezed lemon and add in the baking dish.
6. Cover the chicken with foil and bake it for 20 minutes at 365F.
7. Then discard the foil and bake the chicken for 10 minutes more.

Nutrition: calories 285; fat 19.1; fiber 0.5; carbs 1; protein 26.5

Turkey And Cranberry Sauce

Servings: 4 | Cooking: 50 min

Ingredients
- 1 cup chicken stock
- 2 tablespoons avocado oil
- ½ cup cranberry sauce
- 1 big turkey breast, skinless, boneless and sliced
- 1 yellow onion, roughly chopped
- Salt and black pepper to the taste

Directions
1. Heat up a pan with the avocado oil over medium-high heat, add the onion and sauté for 5 minutes.
2. Add the turkey and brown for 5 minutes more.
3. Add the rest of the ingredients, toss, introduce in the oven at 350 degrees F and cook for 40 minutes

Nutrition: calories 382; fat 12.6; fiber 9.6; carbs 26.6; protein 17.6

Coriander And Coconut Chicken

Servings: 4 | Cooking: 30 min

Ingredients
- 2 pounds chicken thighs, skinless, boneless and cubed
- 2 tablespoons olive oil
- Salt and black pepper to the taste
- 3 tablespoons coconut flesh, shredded
- 1 and ½ teaspoons orange extract
- 1 tablespoon ginger, grated
- ¼ cup orange juice
- 2 tablespoons coriander, chopped
- 1 cup chicken stock
- ¼ teaspoon red pepper flakes

Directions
1. Heat up a pan with the oil over medium-high heat, add the chicken and brown for 4 minutes on each side.
2. Add salt, pepper and the rest of the ingredients, bring to a simmer and cook over medium heat for 20 minutes.
3. Divide the mix between plates and serve hot.

Nutrition: calories 297; fat 14.4; fiber 9.6; carbs 22; protein 25

Chicken Pilaf

Servings: 4 | Cooking: 30 min

Ingredients
- 4 tablespoons avocado oil
- 2 pounds chicken breasts, skinless, boneless and cubed
- ½ cup yellow onion, chopped
- 4 garlic cloves, minced
- 8 ounces brown rice
- 4 cups chicken stock
- ½ cup kalamata olives, pitted
- ½ cup tomatoes, cubed
- 6 ounces baby spinach
- ½ cup feta cheese, crumbled

- A pinch of salt and black pepper
- 1 tablespoon marjoram, chopped
- 1 tablespoon basil, chopped
- Juice of ½ lemon
- ¼ cup pine nuts, toasted

Directions
1. Heat up a pot with 1 tablespoon avocado oil over medium-high heat, add the chicken, some salt and pepper, brown for 5 minutes on each side and transfer to a bowl.
2. Heat up the pot again with the rest of the avocado oil over medium heat, add the onion and garlic and sauté for 3 minutes.
3. Add the rice, the rest of the ingredients except the pine nuts, also return the chicken, toss, bring to a simmer and cook over medium heat for 20 minutes.
4. Divide the mix between plates, top each serving with some pine nuts and serve.

Nutrition: calories 283; fat 12.5; fiber 8.2; carbs 21.5; protein 13.4

Chicken And Black Beans

Servings: 4 | Cooking: 20 min

Ingredients
- 12 oz chicken breast, skinless, boneless, chopped
- 1 tablespoon taco seasoning
- 1 tablespoon nut oil
- ½ teaspoon cayenne pepper
- ½ teaspoon salt
- ½ teaspoon garlic, chopped
- ½ red onion, sliced
- 1/3 cup black beans, canned, rinsed
- ½ cup Mozzarella, shredded

Directions
1. Rub the chopped chicken breast with taco seasoning, salt, and cayenne pepper.
2. Place the chicken in the skillet, add nut oil and roast it for 10 minutes over the medium heat. Mix up the chicken pieces from time to time to avoid burning.
3. After this, transfer the chicken in the plate.
4. Add sliced onion and garlic in the skillet. Roast the vegetables for 5 minutes. Stir them constantly. Then add black beans and stir well. Cook the ingredients for 2 minute more.
5. Add the chopped chicken and mix up well. Top the meal with Mozzarella cheese.
6. Close the lid and cook the meal for 3 minutes.

Nutrition: calories 209; fat 6.4; fiber 2.8; carbs 13.7, 22.7

Coconut Chicken

Servings: 4 | Cooking: 5 min

Ingredients
- 6 oz chicken fillet
- ¼ cup of sparkling water
- 1 egg
- 3 tablespoons coconut flakes
- 1 tablespoon coconut oil
- 1 teaspoon Greek Seasoning

Directions
1. Cut the chicken fillet on small pieces (nuggets).
2. Then crack the egg in the bowl and whisk it.
3. Mix up together egg and sparkling water.
4. Add Greek seasoning and stir gently.
5. Dip the chicken nuggets in the egg mixture and then coat in the coconut flakes.
6. Melt the coconut oil in the skillet and heat it up until it is shimmering.
7. Then add prepared chicken nuggets.
8. Roast them for 1 minute from each or until they are light brown.
9. Dry the cooked chicken nuggets with the help of the paper towel and transfer in the serving plates.

Nutrition: calories 141; fat 8.9; fiber 0.3; carbs 1; protein 13.9

Ginger Chicken Drumsticks

Servings: 4 | Cooking: 30 min

Ingredients
- 4 chicken drumsticks
- 1 apple, grated
- 1 tablespoon curry paste
- 4 tablespoons milk
- 1 teaspoon coconut oil
- 1 teaspoon chili flakes
- ½ teaspoon minced ginger

Directions
1. Mix up together grated apple, curry paste, milk, chili flakes, and minced garlic.
2. Put coconut oil in the skillet and melt it.
3. Add apple mixture and stir well.
4. Then add chicken drumsticks and mix up well.
5. Roast the chicken for 2 minutes from each side.
6. Then preheat oven to 360F.

7. Place the skillet with chicken drumsticks in the oven and bake for 25 minutes.

Nutrition: calories 150; fat 6.4; fiber 1.4; carbs 9.7; protein 13.5

Parmesan Chicken

Servings: 3 | Cooking: 30 min

Ingredients
- 1-pound chicken breast, skinless, boneless
- 2 oz Parmesan, grated
- 1 teaspoon dried oregano
- ½ teaspoon dried cilantro
- 1 tablespoon Panko bread crumbs
- 1 egg, beaten
- 1 teaspoon turmeric

Directions
1. Cut the chicken breast on 3 servings.
2. Then combine together Parmesan, oregano, cilantro, bread crumbs, and turmeric.
3. Dip the chicken servings in the beaten egg carefully.
4. Then coat every chicken piece in the cheese-bread crumbs mixture.
5. Line the baking tray with the baking paper.
6. Arrange the chicken pieces in the tray.
7. Bake the chicken for 30 minutes at 365F.

Nutrition: calories 267; fat 9.5; fiber 0.5; carbs 3.2; protein 40.4

Pomegranate Chicken

Servings: 6 | Cooking: 25 min

Ingredients
- 1-pound chicken breast, skinless, boneless
- 1 tablespoon za'atar
- ½ teaspoon salt
- 1 tablespoon pomegranate juice
- 1 tablespoon olive oil

Directions
1. Rub the chicken breast with za'atar seasoning, salt, olive oil, and pomegranate juice.
2. Marinate the chicken or 15 minutes and transfer in the skillet.
3. Roast the chicken for 15 minutes over the medium heat.
4. Then flip the chicken on another side and cook for 10 minutes more.
5. Slice the chicken and place in the serving plates.

Nutrition: calories 107; fat 4.2; fiber 0; carbs 0.2; protein 16.1

Chicken With Artichokes And Beans

Servings: 4 | Cooking: 40 min

Ingredients
- 2 tablespoons olive oil
- 2 chicken breasts, skinless, boneless and halved
- Zest of 1 lemon, grated
- 3 garlic cloves, crushed
- Juice of 1 lemon
- Salt and black pepper to the taste
- 1 tablespoon thyme, chopped
- 6 ounces canned artichokes hearts, drained
- 1 cup canned fava beans, drained and rinsed
- 1 cup chicken stock
- A pinch of cayenne pepper
- Salt and black pepper to the taste

Directions
1. Heat up a pan with the oil over medium-high heat, add chicken and brown for 5 minutes.
2. Add lemon juice, lemon zest, salt, pepper and the rest of the ingredients, bring to a simmer and cook over medium heat for 35 minutes.
3. Divide the mix between plates and serve right away.

Nutrition: calories 291; fat 14.9; fiber 10.5; carbs 23.8; protein 24.2

Chicken Pie

Servings: 6 | Cooking: 50 min

Ingredients
- ¼ cup green peas, frozen
- 1 carrot, chopped
- 1 cup ground chicken
- 5 oz puff pastry
- 1 tablespoon butter, melted
- ¼ cup cream
- 1 teaspoon ground black pepper
- 1 oz Parmesan, grated

Directions
1. Roll up the puff pastry and cut it on 2 parts.
2. Place one puff pastry part in the non-sticky springform pan and flatten.
3. Then mix up together green peas, chopped carrot, ground chicken, and ground black pepper.

4. Place the chicken mixture in the puff pastry.
5. Pour cream over mixture and sprinkle with Parmesan.
6. Cover the mixture with second puff pastry half and secure the edges of it with the help of the fork.
7. Brush the surface of the pie with melted butter and bake it for 50 minutes at 365F.

Nutrition: calories 223; fat 14.3; fiber 1; carbs 13.2; protein 10.5

Chicken And Semolina Meatballs

Servings: 8 | Cooking: 10 min

Ingredients
- 1/3 cup carrot, grated
- 1 onion, diced
- 2 cups ground chicken
- 1 tablespoon semolina
- 1 egg, beaten
- ½ teaspoon salt
- 1 teaspoon dried oregano
- 1 teaspoon dried cilantro
- 1 teaspoon chili flakes
- 1 tablespoon coconut oil

Directions
1. In the mixing bowl combine together grated carrot, diced onion, ground chicken, semolina, egg, salt, dried oregano, cilantro, and chili flakes.
2. With the help of scooper make the meatballs.
3. Heat up the coconut oil in the skillet.
4. When it starts to shimmer, put meatballs in it.
5. Cook the meatballs for 5 minutes from each side over the medium-low heat.

Nutrition: calories 102; fat 4.9; fiber 0.5; carbs 2.9; protein 11.2

Lemon Chicken Mix

Servings: 2 | Cooking: 10 min

Ingredients
- 8 oz chicken breast, skinless, boneless
- 1 teaspoon Cajun seasoning
- 1 teaspoon balsamic vinegar
- 1 teaspoon olive oil
- 1 teaspoon lemon juice

Directions
1. Cut the chicken breast on the halves and sprinkle with Cajun seasoning.
2. Then sprinkle the poultry with olive oil and lemon juice.
3. Then sprinkle the chicken breast with the balsamic vinegar.
4. Preheat the grill to 385F.
5. Grill the chicken breast halves for 5 minutes from each side.
6. Slice Cajun chicken and place in the serving plate.

Nutrition: calories 150; fat 5.2; fiber 0; carbs 0.1; protein 24.1

Turkey And Chickpeas

Servings: 4 | Cooking: 5 Hours

Ingredients
- 2 tablespoons avocado oil
- 1 big turkey breast, skinless, boneless and roughly cubed
- Salt and black pepper to the taste
- 1 red onion, chopped
- 15 ounces canned chickpeas, drained and rinsed
- 15 ounces canned tomatoes, chopped
- 1 cup kalamata olives, pitted and halved
- 2 tablespoons lime juice
- 1 teaspoon oregano, dried

Directions
1. Heat up a pan with the oil over medium-high heat, add the meat and the onion, brown for 5 minutes and transfer to a slow cooker.
2. Add the rest of the ingredients, put the lid on and cook on High for 5 hours.
3. Divide between plates and serve right away!

Nutrition: calories 352; fat 14.4; fiber 11.8; carbs 25.1; protein 26.4

Cardamom Chicken And Apricot Sauce

Servings: 4 | Cooking: 7 Hours

Ingredients
- Juice of ½ lemon
- Zest of ½ lemon, grated
- 2 teaspoons cardamom, ground
- Salt and black pepper to the taste
- 2 chicken breasts, skinless, boneless and halved
- 2 tablespoons olive oil
- 2 spring onions, chopped
- 2 tablespoons tomato paste

- 2 garlic cloves, minced
- 1 cup apricot juice
- ½ cup chicken stock
- ¼ cup cilantro, chopped

Directions
1. In your slow cooker, combine the chicken with the lemon juice, lemon zest and the other ingredients except the cilantro, toss, put the lid on and cook on Low for 7 hours.
2. Divide the mix between plates, sprinkle the cilantro on top and serve.

Nutrition: calories 323; fat 12; fiber 11; carbs 23.8; protein 16.4

Chicken and Artichokes

Servings: 4 | Cooking: 20 min

Ingredients
- 2 pounds chicken breast, skinless, boneless and sliced
- A pinch of salt and black pepper
- 4 tablespoons olive oil
- 8 ounces canned roasted artichoke hearts, drained
- 6 ounces sun-dried tomatoes, chopped
- 3 tablespoons capers, drained
- 2 tablespoons lemon juice

Directions
1. Heat up a pan with half of the oil over medium-high heat, add the artichokes and the other ingredients except the chicken, stir and sauté for 10 minutes.
2. Transfer the mix to a bowl, heat up the pan again with the rest of the oil over medium-high heat, add the meat and cook for 4 minutes on each side.
3. Return the veggie mix to the pan, toss, cook everything for 2-3 minutes more, divide between plates and serve.

Nutrition: calories 552; fat 28; fiber 6; carbs 33; protein 43

Buttery Chicken Spread

Servings: 6 | Cooking: 20 min

Ingredients
- 8 oz chicken liver
- 3 tablespoon butter
- 1 white onion, chopped
- 1 bay leaf
- 1 teaspoon salt
- ½ teaspoon ground black pepper
- ½ cup of water

Directions
1. Place the chicken liver in the saucepan.
2. Add onion, bay leaf, salt, ground black pepper, and water.
3. Mix up the mixture and close the lid.
4. Cook the liver mixture for 20 minutes over the medium heat.
5. Then transfer it in the blender and blend until smooth.
6. Add butter and mix up until it is melted.
7. Pour the pate mixture in the pate ramekin and refrigerate for 2 hours.

Nutrition: calories 122; fat 8.3; fiber 0.5; carbs 2.3; protein 9.5

Chicken And Spinach Cakes

Servings: 4 | Cooking: 15 min

Ingredients
- 8 oz ground chicken
- 1 cup fresh spinach, blended
- 1 teaspoon minced onion
- ½ teaspoon salt
- 1 red bell pepper, grinded
- 1 egg, beaten
- 1 teaspoon ground black pepper
- 4 tablespoons Panko breadcrumbs

Directions
1. In the mixing bowl mix up together ground chicken, blended spinach, minced garlic, salt, grinded bell pepper, egg, and ground black pepper.
2. When the chicken mixture is smooth, make 4 burgers from it and coat them in Panko breadcrumbs.
3. Place the burgers in the non-sticky baking dish or line the baking tray with baking paper.
4. Bake the burgers for 15 minutes at 365F.
5. Flip the chicken burgers on another side after 7 minutes of cooking.

Nutrition: calories 171; fat 5.7; fiber 1.7; carbs 10.5; protein 19.4

Cream Cheese Chicken

Servings: 2 | Cooking: 20 min

Ingredients
- 1 onion, chopped
- 1 sweet red pepper, roasted, chopped
- 1 cup spinach, chopped
- ½ cup cream
- 1 teaspoon cream cheese
- 1 tablespoon olive oil
- ½ teaspoon ground black pepper
- 8 oz chicken breast, skinless, boneless, sliced

Directions
1. Mix up together sliced chicken breast with ground black pepper and put in the saucepan.
2. Add olive oil and mix up.
3. Roast the chicken for 5 minutes over the medium-high heat. Stir it from time to time.
4. After this, add chopped sweet pepper, onion, and cream cheese.
5. Mix up well and bring to boil.
6. Add spinach and cream. Mix up well.
7. Close the lid and cook chicken Alfredo for 10 minutes more over the medium heat.

Nutrition: calories 279; fat 14; fiber 2.5; carbs 12.4; protein 26.4

Chicken And Lemongrass Sauce

Servings: 4 | Cooking: 20 min

Ingredients
- 1 tablespoon dried dill
- 1 teaspoon butter, melted
- ½ teaspoon lemongrass
- ½ teaspoon cayenne pepper
- 1 teaspoon tomato sauce
- 3 tablespoons sour cream
- 1 teaspoon salt
- 10 oz chicken fillet, cubed

Directions
1. Make the sauce: in the saucepan whisk together lemongrass, tomato sauce, sour cream, salt, and dried dill.
2. Bring the sauce to boil.
3. Meanwhile, pour melted butter in the skillet.
4. Add cubed chicken fillet and roast it for 5 minutes. Stir it from time to time.
5. Then place the chicken cubes in the hot sauce.
6. Close the lid and cook the meal for 10 minutes over the low heat.

Nutrition: calories 166; fat 8.2; fiber 0.2; carbs 1.1; protein 21

Spiced Chicken Meatballs

Servings: 4 | Cooking: 20 min

Ingredients
- 1 pound chicken meat, ground
- 1 tablespoon pine nuts, toasted and chopped
- 1 egg, whisked
- 2 teaspoons turmeric powder
- 2 garlic cloves, minced
- Salt and black pepper to the taste
- 1 and ¼ cups heavy cream
- 2 tablespoons olive oil
- ¼ cup parsley, chopped
- 1 tablespoon chives, chopped

Directions
1. In a bowl, combine the chicken with the pine nuts and the rest of the ingredients except the oil and the cream, stir well and shape medium meatballs out of this mix.
2. Heat up a pan with the oil over medium-high heat, add the meatballs and cook them for 4 minutes on each side.
3. Add the cream, toss gently, cook everything over medium heat for 10 minutes more, divide between plates and serve.

Nutrition: calories 283; fat 9.2; fiber 12.8; carbs 24.4; protein 34.5

Paprika Chicken Wings

Servings: 4 | Cooking: 8 min

Ingredients
- 4 chicken wings, boneless
- 1 tablespoon honey
- ½ teaspoon paprika
- ¼ teaspoon cayenne pepper
- ¾ teaspoon ground black pepper
- 1 tablespoon lemon juice
- ½ teaspoon sunflower oil

Directions
1. Make the honey marinade: whisk together honey, paprika, cayenne pepper, ground black pepper, lemon juice, and sunflower oil.
2. Then brush the chicken wings with marinade carefully.
3. Preheat the grill to 385F.
4. Place the chicken wings in the grill and cook them for 4 minutes from each side.

Nutrition: calories 26; fat 0.8; fiber 0.3; carbs 5.1; protein 0.3

Chicken And Parsley Sauce

Servings: 4 | Cooking: 25 min

Ingredients
- 1 cup ground chicken
- 2 oz Parmesan, grated
- 1 tablespoon olive oil
- 2 tablespoons fresh parsley, chopped
- 1 teaspoon chili pepper
- 1 teaspoon paprika
- ½ teaspoon dried oregano
- ¼ teaspoon garlic, minced
- ½ teaspoon dried thyme
- 1/3 cup crushed tomatoes

Directions
1. Heat up olive oil in the skillet.
2. Add ground chicken and sprinkle it with chili pepper, paprika, dried oregano, dried thyme, and parsley. Mix up well.
3. Cook the chicken for 5 minutes and add crushed tomatoes. Mix up well.
4. Close the lid and simmer the chicken mixture for 10 minutes over the low heat.
5. Then add grated Parmesan and mix up.
6. Cook chicken bolognese for 5 minutes more over the medium heat.

Nutrition: calories 154; fat 9.3; fiber 1.1; carbs 3; protein 15.4

Sage Turkey Mix

Servings: 4 | Cooking: 40 min

Ingredients
- 1 big turkey breast, skinless, boneless and roughly cubed
- Juice of 1 lemon
- 2 tablespoons avocado oil
- 1 red onion, chopped
- 2 tablespoons sage, chopped
- 1 garlic clove, minced
- 1 cup chicken stock

Directions
1. Heat up a pan with the avocado oil over medium-high heat, add the turkey and brown for 3 minutes on each side.
2. Add the rest of the ingredients, bring to a simmer and cook over medium heat for 35 minutes.
3. Divide the mix between plates and serve with a side dish.

Nutrition: calories 382; fat 12.6; fiber 9.6; carbs 16.6; protein 33.2

Chipotle Turkey And Tomatoes

Servings: 4 | Cooking: 1 Hour

Ingredients
- 2 pounds cherry tomatoes, halved
- 3 tablespoons olive oil
- 1 red onion, roughly chopped
- 1 big turkey breast, skinless, boneless and sliced
- 3 garlic cloves, chopped
- 3 red chili peppers, chopped
- 4 tablespoons chipotle paste
- Zest of ½ lemon, grated
- Juice of 1 lemon
- Salt and black pepper to the taste
- A handful coriander, chopped

Directions
1. Heat up a pan with the oil over medium-high heat, add the turkey slices, cook for 4 minutes on each side and transfer to a roasting pan.
2. Heat up the pan again over medium-high heat, add the onion, garlic and chili peppers and sauté for 2 minutes.
3. Add chipotle paste, sauté for 3 minutes more and pour over the turkey slices.
4. Toss the turkey slices with the chipotle mix, also add the rest of the ingredients except the coriander, introduce in the oven and bake at 400 degrees F for 45 minutes.
5. Divide everything between plates, sprinkle the coriander on top and serve.

Nutrition: calories 264; fat 13.2; fiber 8.7; carbs 23.9; protein 33.2

Curry Chicken, Artichokes And Olives

Servings: 6 | Cooking: 7 Hours

Ingredients
- 2 pounds chicken breasts, boneless, skinless and cubed
- 12 ounces canned artichoke hearts, drained
- 1 cup chicken stock
- 1 red onion, chopped
- 1 tablespoon white wine vinegar
- 1 cup kalamata olives, pitted and chopped

- 1 tablespoon curry powder
- 2 teaspoons basil, dried
- Salt and black pepper to the taste
- ¼ cup rosemary, chopped

Directions
1. In your slow cooker, combine the chicken with the artichokes, olives and the rest of the ingredients, put the lid on and cook on Low for 7 hours.
2. Divide the mix between plates and serve hot.

Nutrition: calories 275; fat 11.9; fiber 7.6; carbs 19.7; protein 18.7

Roasted Chicken

Servings: ¼ Chicken | Cooking: 1 Hour 15 min

Ingredients
- 1 (5-lb.) whole chicken
- 1 TB. extra-virgin olive oil
- 2 TB. minced garlic
- 1 tsp. salt
- 1 tsp. paprika
- 1 tsp. black pepper
- 1 tsp. ground coriander
- 1 tsp. seven spices
- 1/2 tsp. ground cinnamon
- 1/2 large lemon, cut in 1/2
- 1/2 large yellow onion, cut in 1/2
- 2 sprigs fresh rosemary
- 2 sprigs fresh thyme
- 2 sprigs fresh sage
- 2 large carrots, cut into 1-in. pieces
- 6 small red potatoes, washed and cut in 1/2
- 4 cloves garlic

Directions
1. Preheat the oven to 450°F. Wash chicken and pat dry with paper towels. Place chicken in a roasting pan, and drizzle and then rub chicken with extra-virgin olive oil.
2. In a small bowl, combine garlic, salt, paprika, black pepper, coriander, seven spices, and cinnamon. Sprinkle and then rub entire chicken with spice mixture to coat.
3. Place 1/4 lemon, 1/4 yellow onion, 1 sprig rosemary, 1 sprig thyme, and 1 sprig sage in chicken cavity.
4. Place remaining rosemary, thyme, sage, lemon, and onion around chicken in the roasting pan. Add carrots, red potatoes, and garlic cloves to the roasting pan.
5. Roast for 15 minutes. Reduce temperature to 375°F, and roast for 1 more hour, basting chicken every 20 minutes.
6. Let chicken rest for 15 minutes before serving.

Curry Chicken Mix

Servings: 2 | Cooking: 25 min

Ingredients
- 2 flatbread
- 7 oz chicken fillet
- 1 tablespoon yogurt
- 1 teaspoon minced garlic
- 1 teaspoon fresh parsley
- ½ teaspoon salt
- ½ teaspoon paprika
- ¼ teaspoon curry powder
- 1 tablespoon tomato sauce

Directions
1. Make the marinade: mix up together yogurt, minced garlic, salt, paprika, and curry powder.
2. Chop the chicken fillet on the medium cubes and put them in the marinade.
3. Mix up the chicken well and leave to marinate for at least 15 minutes.
4. Then put the marinated chicken in the baking tray in one layer and bake it for 25 minutes at 350F. Flip the chicken on another side after 10 minutes of cooking.
5. Then put the cooked chicken on the flatbread and sprinkle with tomato sauce and parsley.

Nutrition: calories 290; fat 10.1; fiber 2.4; carbs 15.9; protein 32.5

Creamy Chicken

Servings: 4 | Cooking: 35 min

Ingredients
- 1-pound chicken breast, skinless, boneless
- 3 oz Mozzarella, sliced
- 1 tomato, sliced
- 1 teaspoon Italian seasoning
- ½ teaspoon salt
- 1 tablespoon sour cream
- 1 teaspoon olive oil

Directions
1. Make the cuts in the chicken breast in the shape of Hasselback.
2. Sprinkle the chicken with Italian seasoning, salt, and sour cream.

3. Massage the chicken breast gently.
4. Fill every chicken breast cut with sliced Mozzarella and sliced tomato.
5. Arrange the chicken breast in the baking dish and sprinkle it with olive oil.
6. Bake the chicken Hasselback for 35 minutes at 355F.

Nutrition: calories 212; fat 8.8; fiber 0.2; carbs 1.6; protein 30.3

Chicken And Celery Quinoa Mix

Servings: 4 | Cooking: 50 min

Ingredients
- 4 chicken things, skinless and boneless
- 1 tablespoon olive oil
- Salt and black pepper to the taste
- 2 celery stalks, chopped
- 2 spring onions, chopped
- 2 cups chicken stock
- ½ cup cilantro, chopped
- ½ cup quinoa
- 1 teaspoon lime zest, grated

Directions
1. Heat up a pot with the oil over medium-high heat, add the chicken and brown for 4 minutes on each side.
2. Add the onion and the celery, stir and sauté everything for 5 minutes more.
3. Add the rest of the ingredients, toss, bring to a simmer and cook over medium-low heat for 35 minutes.
4. Divide everything between plates and serve.

Nutrition: calories 241; fat 12.6; fiber 9.5; carbs 15.6; protein 34.1

Chicken And Nutmeg Butter Sauce

Servings: 4 | Cooking: 30 min

Ingredients
- 4 chicken thighs, skinless, boneless
- 1 teaspoon ground black pepper
- ½ teaspoon salt
- 1 teaspoon paprika
- ¼ cup Cheddar cheese, shredded
- 1 tablespoon cream cheese
- ½ teaspoon garlic powder
- 1 teaspoon fresh dill, chopped
- 1 tablespoon butter
- 1 teaspoon olive oil
- ½ teaspoon ground nutmeg

Directions
1. Grease the baking dish with butter.
2. Then heat up olive oil in the skillet.
3. Meanwhile, rub the chicken thighs with ground nutmeg, garlic powder, paprika, and salt. Add ground black pepper.
4. Roast the chicken thighs in the hot oil over the high heat for 2 minutes from each side.
5. Then transfer the chicken thighs in the prepared baking dish.
6. Mix up together Cheddar cheese, cream cheese, and dill.
7. Top every chicken thigh with cheese mixture and bake for 25 minutes at 365F.

Nutrition: calories 79; fat 7.5; fiber 0.4; carbs 1.2; protein 2.4

Turmeric Chicken And Eggplant Mix

Servings: 4 | Cooking: 30 min

Ingredients
- 2 cups eggplant, cubed
- Salt and black pepper to the taste
- 2 tablespoons olive oil
- 1 cup yellow onion, chopped
- 2 tablespoons garlic, minced
- 2 tablespoons hot paprika
- 1 teaspoon turmeric powder
- 1 and ½ tablespoons oregano, chopped
- 1 cup chicken stock
- 1 pound chicken breast, skinless, boneless and cubed
- 1 cup half and half
- 1 tablespoon lemon juice

Directions
1. Heat up a pan with the oil over medium-high heat, add the chicken and brown for 4 minutes on each side.
2. Add the eggplant, onion and garlic and sauté for 5 minutes more.
3. Add the rest of the ingredients, bring to a simmer and cook over medium heat for 16 minutes.
4. Divide the mix between plates and serve.

Nutrition: calories 392; fat 11.6; fiber 8.3; carbs 21.1; protein 24.2

Honey Chicken

Servings: 5 | Cooking: 25 min

Ingredients
- 5 chicken drumsticks
- 2 oz currant
- ½ teaspoon liquid honey
- 1 teaspoon butter
- 1 teaspoon lime juice
- ½ teaspoon salt
- ¼ cup of water
- ½ teaspoon chili pepper

Directions
1. Mix up together chicken drumsticks with chili pepper and salt.
2. Put butter in the skillet and heat it up.
3. Add chicken drumsticks and cook them for 15 minutes or until they are cooked.
4. Meanwhile, mash currant and mix it up with lime juice, liquid honey, and water.
5. Pour the currant mixture over the drumstick and close the lid.
6. Cook the meal for 5 minutes over the medium heat.

Nutrition: calories 93; fat 3.4; fiber 0.5; carbs 2.2; protein 12.8

Cheddar Chicken Mix

Servings: 4 | Cooking: 20 min

Ingredients
- 4 chicken fillets (4 oz each fillet)
- 1 cup cherry tomatoes
- 1 tablespoon olive oil
- 1 tablespoon fresh basil, chopped
- ½ teaspoon salt
- ½ teaspoon ground black pepper
- 1 teaspoon balsamic vinegar
- 1 teaspoon garlic clove, diced
- 1 oz Cheddar cheese, shredded

Directions
1. Pour olive oil in the skillet and heat it up.
2. Sprinkle the chicken fillets with salt and ground black pepper and put in the hot oil.
3. Roast the chicken for 3 minutes from each side over the medium heat.
4. Then cut the cherry tomatoes on the halves and add in the olive oil.
5. Sprinkle the vegetables with balsamic vinegar, garlic, and basil.
6. Mix up the ingredients well.
7. Sprinkle the chicken with Cheddar cheese and close the lid.
8. Cook the chicken caprese for 10 minutes over the medium heat.

Nutrition: calories 299; fat 17; fiber 1.6; carbs 17.3; protein 21.3

Chicken And Veggie Saute

Servings: 2 | Cooking: 25 min

Ingredients
- 4 oz chicken fillet
- 4 tomatoes, peeled
- 1 bell pepper, chopped
- 1 teaspoon olive oil
- 1 cup of water
- 1 teaspoon salt
- 1 chili pepper, chopped
- ½ teaspoon saffron

Directions
1. Pour water in the pan and bring it to boil.
2. Meanwhile, chop the chicken fillet.
3. Add the chicken fillet in the boiling water and cook it for 10 minutes or until the chicken is tender.
4. After this, put the chopped bell pepper and chili pepper in the skillet.
5. Add olive oil and roast the vegetables for 3 minutes.
6. Add chopped tomatoes and mix up well.
7. Cook the vegetables for 2 minutes more.
8. Then add salt and a ¾ cup of water from chicken.
9. Add chopped chicken fillet and mix up.
10. Cook the saute for 10 minutes over the medium heat.

Nutrition: calories 192; fat 7.2; fiber 3.8; carbs 14.4; protein 19.2

Thyme Chicken And Potatoes

Servings: 4 | Cooking: 50 min

Ingredients
- 1 tablespoon olive oil
- 4 garlic cloves, minced
- A pinch of salt and black pepper
- 2 teaspoons thyme, dried
- 12 small red potatoes, halved

- 2 pounds chicken breast, skinless, boneless and cubed
- 1 cup red onion, sliced
- ¾ cup chicken stock
- 2 tablespoons basil, chopped

Directions
1. In a baking dish greased with the oil, add the potatoes, chicken and the rest of the ingredients, toss a bit, introduce in the oven and bake at 400 degrees F for 50 minutes.
2. Divide between plates and serve.

Nutrition: calories 281; fat 9.2; fiber 10.9; carbs 21.6; protein 13.6

Creamy Chicken And Mushrooms

Servings: 4 | Cooking: 30 min

Ingredients
- 1 red onion, chopped
- 1 tablespoon olive oil
- 2 garlic cloves, minced
- 2 carrots chopped
- Salt and black pepper to the taste
- 1 tablespoon thyme, chopped
- 1 and ½ cups chicken stock
- ½ pound Bella mushrooms, sliced
- 1 cup heavy cream
- 2 chicken breasts, skinless, boneless and cubed
- 2 tablespoons chives, chopped
- 1 tablespoon parsley, chopped

Directions
1. Heat up a Dutch oven with the oil over medium-high heat, add the onion and the garlic and sauté for 5 minutes.
2. Add the chicken and the mushrooms, and sauté for 10 minutes more.
3. Add the rest of the ingredients except the chives and the parsley, bring to a simmer and cook over medium heat for 15 minutes.
4. Add the chives and parsley, divide the mix between plates and serve.

Nutrition: calories 275; fat 11.9; fiber 10.6; carbs 26.7; protein 23.7

Basil Turkey And Zucchinis

Servings: 4 | Cooking: 1 Hour

Ingredients
- 2 tablespoons avocado oil
- 1 pound turkey breast, skinless, boneless and sliced
- Salt and black pepper to the taste
- 3 garlic cloves, minced
- 2 zucchinis, sliced
- 1 cup chicken stock
- ¼ cup heavy cream
- 2 tablespoons basil, chopped

Directions
1. Heat up a pot with the oil over medium-high heat, add the turkey and brown for 5 minutes on each side.
2. Add the garlic and cook everything for 1 minute.
3. Add the rest of the ingredients except the basil, toss gently, bring to a simmer and cook over medium-low heat for 50 minutes.
4. Add the basil, toss, divide the mix between plates and serve.

Nutrition: calories 262; fat 9.8; fiber 12.2; carbs 25.8; protein 14.6

Herbed Almond Turkey

Servings: 4 | Cooking: 40 min

Ingredients
- 1 big turkey breast, skinless, boneless and cubed
- 1 tablespoon olive oil
- ½ cup chicken stock
- 1 tablespoon basil, chopped
- 1 tablespoon rosemary, chopped
- 1 tablespoon oregano, chopped
- 1 tablespoon parsley, chopped
- 3 garlic cloves, minced
- ½ cup almonds, toasted and chopped
- 3 cups tomatoes, chopped

Directions
1. Heat up a pan with the oil over medium-high heat, add the turkey and the garlic and brown for 5 minutes.
2. Add the stock and the rest of the ingredients, bring to a simmer over medium heat and cook for 35 minutes.
3. Divide the mix between plates and serve.

Nutrition: calories 297; fat 11.2; fiber 9.2; carbs 19.4; protein 23.6

Lime Chicken Thighs And Pomegranate Sauce

Servings: 2 | Cooking: 10 min

Ingredients
- 1 tablespoon pomegranate molasses
- 8 oz chicken thighs (4 oz each chicken thigh)
- ½ teaspoon paprika
- 1 teaspoon cornstarch
- ½ teaspoon chili flakes
- ½ teaspoon ground black pepper
- 1 teaspoon olive oil
- ½ teaspoon lime juice

Directions
1. In the shallow bowl mix up together ground black pepper, chili flakes, paprika, and cornstarch.
2. Rub the chicken thighs with spice mixture.
3. Heat up olive oil in the skillet.
4. Add chicken thighs and roast them for 4 minutes from each side over the medium heat.
5. When the chicken thighs are light brown, sprinkle them with pomegranate molasses and roast for 1 minute from each side.

Nutrition: calories 353; fat 21; fiber 0.4; carbs 9.3; protein 30.2

Mediterranean Meatloaf

Servings: 1/8 Loaf | Cooking: 45 min

Ingredients
- 2 lb. ground chicken
- 1/3 cup plain breadcrumbs
- 1 1/2 tsp. salt
- 1 tsp. garlic powder
- 1 tsp. ground black pepper
- 1 tsp. paprika
- 1/2 tsp. dried oregano
- 1/2 tsp. dried thyme
- 2 TB. fresh basil, chopped
- 2 TB. fresh Italian parsley, chopped
- 1 large egg
- 1 large carrot, shredded
- 1 cup fresh or frozen green peas
- 1/2 cup sun-dried tomatoes, chopped
- 1 cup ketchup

Directions
1. Preheat the oven to 400°F. Lightly coat all sides of a 9×5-inch loaf pan with olive oil spray.
2. In a large bowl, combine chicken, breadcrumbs, salt, garlic powder, black pepper, paprika, oregano, thyme, basil, Italian parsley, egg, carrot, green peas, and sun-dried tomatoes.
3. Transfer chicken mixture to the prepared pan, and even out top. Cover the pan with a piece of aluminum foil, and bake for 40 minutes.
4. After 40 minutes have passed, pour ketchup over top of loaf and spread out evenly. Bake for 5 more minutes.
5. Remove meatloaf from the oven, and let rest for 10 minutes before slicing and serving warm.

Lemon Chicken

Servings: 4 | Cooking: 20 min

Ingredients
- 1-pound chicken breast, skinless, boneless
- 3 tablespoons lemon juice
- 1 tablespoon olive oil
- 1 teaspoon ground black pepper

Directions
1. Cut the chicken breast on 4 pieces.
2. Sprinkle every chicken piece with olive oil, lemon juice, and ground black pepper.
3. Then place them in the skillet.
4. Roast the chicken for 20 minutes over the medium heat.
5. Flip the chicken pieces every 5 minutes.

Nutrition: calories 163; fat 6.5; fiber 0.2; carbs 0.6; protein 24.2

Chicken And Mushroom Mix

Servings: 2 | Cooking: 20 min

Ingredients
- 9 oz chicken fillet, cubed
- 1/3 cup cream
- ¼ cup mushrooms, chopped
- 1 teaspoon butter
- ½ onion, diced
- ½ teaspoon ground black pepper
- ½ teaspoon salt
- 1 teaspoon hot pepper
- 1 teaspoon sunflower oil

Directions
1. Sprinkle the chicken cubes with hot pepper and mix up.

2. Pour sunflower oil in the skillet and roast chicken cubes for 5 minutes over the medium heat. Stir them from time to time.
3. Toss butter in the separated skillet and melt it.
4. Add mushrooms and sprinkle them with salt and ground black pepper.
5. Add onion.
6. Cook the vegetables for 10 minutes over the low heat. Stir them with the help of spatula every 3 minutes.
7. Then add cream and bring to boil.
8. Add roasted chicken cubes and mix up well.
9. Close the lid and simmer the meal for 5 minutes.

Nutrition: calories 213; fat 10.7; fiber 0.5; carbs 3; protein 25.2

Chicken And Ginger Cucumbers Mix

Servings: 4 | Cooking: 20 min

Ingredients
- 4 chicken breasts, boneless, skinless and cubed
- 2 cucumbers, cubed
- Salt and black pepper to the taste
- 1 tablespoon ginger, grated
- 1 tablespoon garlic, minced
- 2 tablespoons balsamic vinegar
- 3 tablespoons olive oil
- ¼ teaspoon chili paste
- ½ cup chicken stock
- ½ tablespoon lime juice
- 1 tablespoon chives, chopped

Directions
1. Heat up a pan with the oil over medium-high heat, add the chicken and brown for 3 minutes on each side.
2. Add the cucumbers, salt, pepper and the rest of the ingredients except the chives, bring to a simmer and cook over medium heat for 15 minutes.
3. Divide the mix between plates and serve with the chives sprinkled on top.

Nutrition: calories 288; fat 9.5; fiber 12.1; carbs 25.6; protein 28.6

Dill Chicken Stew

Servings: 2 | Cooking: 25 min
Ingredients
- 1 ½ cup water
- 6 oz chicken fillet
- 1 chili pepper, chopped
- 1 onion, diced
- 1 teaspoon butter
- ½ teaspoon salt
- ½ teaspoon paprika
- 1 tablespoon fresh dill, chopped

Directions
1. Pour water in the saucepan.
2. Add chicken fillet and salt. Boil it for 15 minutes over the medium heat.
3. Then remove the chicken fillet from water and shred it with the help of the fork.
4. Return it back in the hot water.
5. Melt butter in the skillet and add diced onion. Roast it until light brown and transfer in the shredded chicken.
6. Add paprika, dill, chili pepper, and mix up.
7. Close the lid and simmer Posole for 5 minutes.
8. Ladle it in the serving bowls.

Nutrition: calories 207; fat 8.4; fiber 1.7; carbs 6.5; protein 25.7

Chicken Stuffed Zucchini

Servings: 2 | Cooking: 30 min

Ingredients
- 1 zucchini
- ½ cup ground chicken
- ½ teaspoon chipotle pepper
- ½ teaspoon tomato sauce
- 1 oz Swiss cheese, shredded
- ½ teaspoon salt
- 4 tablespoons water

Directions
1. Trim the zucchini and cut it on 2 halves.
2. Remove the zucchini pulp.
3. In the mixing bowl mix up together ground chicken, chipotle pepper, tomato sauce, and salt.
4. Fill the zucchini with chicken mixture and top with Swiss cheese.
5. Place the zucchini boats in the tray. Add water.
6. Bake the boats for 30 minutes at 355F.

Nutrition: calories 137; fat 6.7; fiber 1.1; carbs 4.2; protein 15.2

Creamy Coriander Chicken

Servings: 4 | Cooking: 55 min

Ingredients
- 2 chicken breasts, boneless, skinless and halved

- 2 tablespoons avocado oil
- ½ teaspoon hot paprika
- 1 cup chicken stock
- 1 tablespoon almonds, chopped
- 2 spring onions, chopped
- 2 garlic cloves, minced
- ¼ cup heavy cream
- A handful coriander, chopped
- Salt and black pepper to the taste

Directions
1. Grease a roasting pan with the oil, add the chicken, paprika and the rest of the ingredients except the coriander and the heavy cream, toss, introduce in the oven and bake at 360 degrees F for 40 minutes.
2. Add the cream and the coriander, toss, bake for 15 minutes more, divide between plates and serve.

Nutrition: calories 225; fat 8.9; fiber 10.2; carbs 20.8; protein 17.5

Chicken And Tomato Pan

Servings: 4 | Cooking: 30 min

Ingredients
- 12 oz chicken fillet
- 4 kalamata olives, chopped
- 4 tomatoes, chopped
- 1 yellow onion, diced
- 1 tablespoon olive oil
- ½ cup of water

Directions
1. Pour olive oil in the saucepan.
2. Add diced yellow onion and cook it for 5 minutes. Stir it from time to time.
3. After this, add olives and chopped tomatoes. Mix up well and cook vegetables for 5 minutes more.
4. Meanwhile, chop the chicken fillet.
5. Add the chicken fillet in the tomato mixture and mix up.
6. Close the lid.
7. Simmer the chicken for 20 minutes over the medium heat.

Nutrition: calories 230; fat 10.6; fiber 2.2; carbs 7.6; protein 26

Smoked And Hot Turkey Mix

Servings: 4 | Cooking: 40 min

Ingredients
- 1 red onion, sliced
- 1 big turkey breast, skinless, boneless and roughly cubed
- 1 tablespoon smoked paprika
- 2 chili peppers, chopped
- Salt and black pepper to the taste
- 2 tablespoons olive oil
- ½ cup chicken stock
- 1 tablespoon parsley, chopped
- 1 tablespoon cilantro, chopped

Directions
1. Grease a roasting pan with the oil, add the turkey, onion, paprika and the rest of the ingredients, toss, introduce in the oven and bake at 425 degrees F for 40 minutes.
2. Divide the mix between plates and serve right away.

Nutrition: calories 310; fat 18.4; fiber 10.4; carbs 22.3; protein 33.4

Chicken With Artichokes

Servings: 3 | Cooking: 30 min

Ingredients
- 1 can artichoke hearts, chopped
- 12 oz chicken fillets (3 oz each fillet)
- 1 teaspoon avocado oil
- ½ teaspoon ground thyme
- ½ teaspoon white pepper
- 1/3 cup water
- 1/3 cup shallot, roughly chopped
- 1 lemon, sliced

Directions
1. Mix up together chicken fillets, artichoke hearts, avocado oil, ground thyme, white pepper, and shallot.
2. Line the baking tray with baking paper and place the chicken fillet mixture in it.
3. Then add sliced lemon and water.
4. Bake the meal for 30 minutes at 375F. Stir the ingredients during cooking to avoid burning.

Nutrition: calories 263; fat 8.8; fiber 3.7; carbs 10.9; protein 35.3

Brown Rice, Chicken And Scallions

Servings: 4 | Cooking: 30 min

Ingredients
- 1 and ½ cups brown rice
- 3 cups chicken stock
- 2 tablespoon balsamic vinegar
- 1 pound chicken breast, boneless, skinless and cubed
- 6 scallions, chopped
- Salt and black pepper to the taste
- 1 tablespoon sweet paprika
- 2 tablespoons avocado oil

Directions
1. Heat up a pan with the oil over medium-high heat, add the chicken and brown for 5 minutes.
2. Add the scallions and sauté for 5 minutes more.
3. Add the rice and the rest of the ingredients, bring to a simmer and cook over medium heat for 20 minutes.
4. Stir the mix, divide everything between plates and serve.

Nutrition: calories 300; fat 9.2; fiber 11.8; carbs 18.6; protein 23.8

Greek Chicken Bites

Servings: 6 | Cooking: 20 min

Ingredients
- 1-pound chicken fillet
- 1 tablespoon Greek seasoning
- 1 teaspoon sesame oil
- ½ teaspoon salt
- 1 teaspoon balsamic vinegar

Directions
1. Cut the chicken fingers on small tenders (fingers) and sprinkle them with Greek seasoning, salt, and balsamic vinegar. Mix up well with the help of the fingertips.
2. Then sprinkle chicken with sesame oil and shake gently.
3. Line the baking tray with parchment.
4. Place the marinated chicken fingers in the tray in one layer.
5. Bake the chicken fingers for 20 minutes at 355F. Flip them on another side after 10 minutes of cooking.

Nutrition: calories 154; fat 6.4; fiber 0; carbs 0.8; protein 22

Chicken Kebabs

Servings: 4 | Cooking: 20 min

Ingredients
- 2 chicken breasts, skinless, boneless and cubed
- 1 red bell pepper, cut into squares
- 1 red onion, roughly cut into squares
- 2 teaspoons sweet paprika
- 1 teaspoon nutmeg, ground
- 1 teaspoon Italian seasoning
- ¼ teaspoon smoked paprika
- A pinch of salt and black pepper
- ¼ teaspoon cardamom, ground
- Juice of 1 lemon
- 3 garlic cloves, minced
- ½ cup olive oil

Directions
1. In a bowl, combine the chicken with the onion, the bell pepper and the other ingredients, toss well, cover the bowl and keep in the fridge for 30 minutes.
2. Assemble skewers with chicken, peppers and the onions, place them on your preheated grill and cook over medium heat for 8 minutes on each side.
3. Divide the kebabs between plates and serve with a side salad.

Nutrition: calories 262; fat 14; fiber 2; carbs 14; protein 20

Chicken, Corn And Peppers

Servings: 4 | Cooking: 1 Hour

Ingredients
- 2 pounds chicken breast, skinless, boneless and cubed
- 2 tablespoons olive oil
- 2 garlic cloves, minced
- 1 red onion, chopped
- 2 red bell peppers, chopped
- ¼ teaspoon cumin, ground
- 2 cups corn
- ½ cup chicken stock
- 1 teaspoon chili powder
- ¼ cup cilantro, chopped

Directions
1. Heat up a pot with the oil over medium-high heat, add the chicken and brown for 4 minutes on each side.
2. Add the onion and the garlic and sauté for 5 minutes more.

3. Add the rest of the ingredients, stir, bring to a simmer over medium heat and cook for 45 minutes.
4. Divide into bowls and serve.

Nutrition: calories 332; fat 16.1; fiber 8.4; carbs 25.4; protein 17.4

Spicy Cumin Chicken

Servings: 4 | Cooking: 25 min

Ingredients
- 2 teaspoons chili powder
- 2 and ½ tablespoons olive oil
- Salt and black pepper to the taste
- 1 and ½ teaspoons garlic powder
- 1 tablespoon smoked paprika
- ½ cup chicken stock
- 1 pound chicken breasts, skinless, boneless and halved
- 2 teaspoons sherry vinegar
- 2 teaspoons hot sauce
- 2 teaspoons cumin, ground
- ½ cup black olives, pitted and sliced

Directions
1. Heat up a pan with the oil over medium-high heat, add the chicken and brown for 3 minutes on each side.
2. Add the chili powder, salt, pepper, garlic powder and paprika, toss and cook for 4 minutes more.
3. Add the rest of the ingredients, toss, bring to a simmer and cook over medium heat for 15 minutes more.
4. Divide the mix between plates and serve.

Nutrition: calories 230; fat 18.4; fiber 9.4; carbs 15.3; protein 13.4

Chives Chicken And Radishes

Servings: 4 | Cooking: 30 min

Ingredients
- 2 chicken breasts, skinless, boneless and cubed
- Salt and black pepper to the taste
- 1 tablespoon olive oil
- 1 cup chicken stock
- ½ cup tomato sauce
- ½ pound red radishes, cubed
- 2 tablespoon chives, chopped

Directions
1. Heat up a Dutch oven with the oil over medium-high heat, add the chicken and brown for 4 minutes on each side.
2. Add the rest of the ingredients except the chives, bring to a simmer and cook over medium heat for 20 minutes.
3. Divide the mix between plates, sprinkle the chives on top and serve.

Nutrition: calories 277; fat 15; fiber 9.3; carbs 20.9; protein 33.2

Yogurt Chicken And Red Onion Mix

Servings: 4 | Cooking: 30 min

Ingredients
- 2 pounds chicken breast, skinless, boneless and sliced
- 3 tablespoons olive oil
- ¼ cup Greek yogurt
- 2 garlic cloves, minced
- ½ teaspoon onion powder
- A pinch of salt and black pepper
- 4 red onions, sliced

Directions
1. In a roasting pan, combine the chicken with the oil, the yogurt and the other ingredients, introduce in the oven at 375 degrees F and bake for 30 minutes.
2. Divide chicken mix between plates and serve hot.

Nutrition: calories 278; fat 15; fiber 9.2; carbs 15.1; protein 23.3

Basil Chicken With Olives

Servings: 5 | Cooking: 40 min

Ingredients
- 1.5-pound chicken breast, skinless, boneless
- 3 Kalamata olives, chopped
- 1 teaspoon minced garlic
- 1 teaspoon salt
- 1 teaspoon ground black pepper
- 2 tablespoons sunflower oil
- 1 tablespoon fresh basil, chopped
- ½ teaspoon chili flakes
- 1 tablespoon lemon juice
- ½ teaspoon honey
- ¼ cup of water

Directions
1. Combine together Kalamata olives, minced garlic, salt, ground black pepper, sunflower oil, basil, chili flakes, lemon juice, and honey.
2. Whisk the mixture until homogenous.
3. Chop the chicken breast roughly and arrange it in the baking dish.
4. Pour olives mixture over the chicken.
5. Then mix up it with the help of the fingertips.
6. Add water and cover the baking dish with foil.
7. Pierce the foil with the help of the fork or knife to give the "air" for meat during cooking.
8. Bake the chicken for 40 minutes at 360F.

Nutrition: calories 213; fat 9.3; fiber 0.2; carbs 1.3; protein 29

Chicken Skewers (shish Tawook)

Servings: 1 Skewer | Cooking: 8 min

Ingredients
- 1 1/2 lb. boneless, skinless chicken breasts
- 2 TB. minced garlic
- 3 TB. fresh lemon juice
- 3 TB. extra-virgin olive oil
- 2 TB. Greek yogurt
- 2 TB. tomato paste
- 1 TB. paprika
- 1/2 tsp. cayenne
- 1 tsp. salt
- 1/2 tsp. ground black pepper

Directions
1. Preheat a grill to medium heat.
2. Cut chicken breast into 1-inch cubes and place in a large bowl.
3. Add garlic, lemon juice, extra-virgin olive oil, Greek yogurt, tomato paste, paprika, cayenne, salt, and black pepper, and mix to combine.
4. Skewer chicken, dividing equally among 5 skewers. Place chicken on the grill, and cook for 8 minutes, turning over every 2 minutes to grill all sides.
5. Serve warm with hummus and pita bread.

Oregano Chicken And Zucchini Pan

Servings: 4 | Cooking: 30 min

Ingredients
- 2 cups tomatoes, peeled and crushed
- 1 and ½ pounds chicken breast, boneless, skinless and cubed
- 2 tablespoons olive oil
- Salt and black pepper to the taste
- 1 small yellow onion, sliced
- 2 garlic cloves, minced
- 2 zucchinis, sliced
- 2 tablespoons oregano, chopped
- 1 cup chicken stock

Directions
1. Heat up a pan with the oil over medium-high heat, add the chicken and brown for 3 minute son each side.
2. Add the onion and the garlic and sauté for 4 minutes more.
3. Add the rest of the ingredients except the oregano, bring to a simmer and cook over medium heat and cook for 20 minutes.
4. Divide the mix between plates, sprinkle the oregano on top and serve.

Nutrition: calories 228; fat 9.5; fiber 9.1; carbs 15.6; protein 18.6

Stuffed Chicken

Servings: 2 | Cooking: 35 min

Ingredients
- 10 oz chicken breast, skinless, boneless
- 2 tablespoons fresh cilantro, chopped
- 1 tomato, sliced
- 1 teaspoon fresh parsley, chopped
- 1 teaspoon sour cream
- ½ teaspoon salt
- ½ teaspoon sage
- 1 oz Mozzarella, sliced
- 1 tablespoon pesto sauce

Directions
1. Make the lengthwise cut in the chicken breast and fill it with fresh parsley, cilantro, sliced Mozzarella, and sliced tomatoes. Secure the chicken breast with toothpicks.
2. After this, sprinkle the chicken with sage, salt, sour cream, and pesto sauce.
3. Wrap the stuffed chicken breast in the foil and bake in the preheated to the 365F oven for 35 minutes.

Nutrition: calories 246; fat 9.8; fiber 0.6; carbs 2.5; protein 35.2

Chicken And Avocado Bowl

Servings: 3 | Cooking: 15 min

Ingredients
- 3 chicken drumsticks
- 1 avocado, sliced
- ½ cup cherry tomatoes
- 2 bell peppers
- 1 teaspoon Italian herbs
- 1 teaspoon olive oil
- 1 tablespoon lemon juice
- 1 teaspoon sesame oil
- ½ teaspoon sesame seeds

Directions
1. Sprinkle the chicken drumsticks with lemon juice, Italian herbs, and olive oil and place them in the skillet.
2. Roast the chicken drumsticks for 15 minutes. Flip them every 5 minutes.
3. Meanwhile, cut the cherry tomatoes on the halves.
4. Chop the bell peppers roughly.
5. Place the vegetables in 3 serving plates.
6. Add avocado and sprinkle the ingredients with sesame seeds and sesame oil.
7. Add cooked roasted drumsticks.

Nutrition: calories 276; fat 19.3; fiber 6; carbs 13.2; protein 15.1

Chicken And Grapes Salad

Servings: 4 | Cooking: 0 min

Ingredients
- 7 oz chicken breast, skinless, boneless, cooked
- ½ cup red grapes
- 1 oz celery stalk, chopped
- 1 red onion, sliced
- ½ cup Greek yogurt
- ½ teaspoon honey
- 1 tablespoon fresh parsley, chopped
- 1 cucumber, chopped

Directions
1. Chop the chicken breast and place it in the salad bowl.
2. Add red grapes, celery stalk, sliced red onion, parsley, and cucumber.
3. Mix up the salad mixture.
4. Then mix up together Greek yogurt and honey.
5. Pour Greek yogurt mixture over the salad and stir well.

Nutrition: calories 116; fat 1.9; fiber 1.2; carbs 10.9; protein 14

Lime Turkey And Avocado Mix

Servings: 2 | Cooking: 1 Hour And 10 min

Ingredients
- 2 tablespoons olive oil
- 1 turkey breast, boneless, skinless and halved
- 2 ounces cherry tomatoes, halved
- A handful coriander, chopped
- Juice of 1 lime
- Zest of 1 lime, grated
- Salt and black pepper to the taste
- 2 spring onions, chopped
- 2 avocadoes, pitted, peeled and cubed

Directions
1. In a roasting pan, combine the turkey with the oil and the rest of the ingredients, introduce in the oven and bake at 370 degrees F for 1 hour and 10 minutes.
2. Divide between plates and serve.

Nutrition: calories 301; fat 8.9; fiber 10.2; carbs 19.8; protein 13.5

Coriander Chicken Drumsticks

Servings: 4 | Cooking: 35 min

Ingredients
- 8 chicken drumsticks
- 1 lemon
- 1 teaspoon minced garlic
- 1 teaspoon ground coriander
- 1/3 cup onion, chopped
- ½ teaspoon ground turmeric
- 1 teaspoon paprika
- 1 teaspoon salt
- 1 tablespoon olive oil
- 1 teaspoon butter
- 1/3 cup water

Directions
1. Peel the lemon and chop the lemon pulp. Place it in the saucepan.
2. Add minced garlic, ground coriander, onion, turmeric, paprika, salt, olive oil, and butter.
3. Then add water and bring the mixture to boil. Mix it up.
4. Add chicken drumsticks and close the lid.
5. Simmer the chicken for 30 minutes over the medium-low heat.

Nutrition: calories 206; fat 9.9; fiber 0.9; carbs 3; protein 25.7

Turkey And Asparagus Mix

Servings: 4 | Cooking: 30 min

Ingredients
- 1 bunch asparagus, trimmed and halved
- 1 big turkey breast, skinless, boneless and cut into strips
- 1 teaspoon basil, dried
- 2 tablespoons olive oil
- A pinch of salt and black pepper
- ½ cup tomato sauce
- 1 tablespoon chives, chopped

Directions
1. Heat up a pan with the oil over medium-high heat, add the turkey and brown for 4 minutes.
2. Add the asparagus and the rest of the ingredients except the chives, bring to a simmer and cook over medium heat for 25 minutes.
3. Add the chives, divide the mix between plates and serve.

Nutrition: calories 337; fat 21.2; fiber 10.2; carbs 21.4; protein 17.6

Braised Chicken

Servings: 1 Drumstick | Cooking: 52 min

Ingredients
- 6 chicken drumsticks, skin on
- 3 TB. extra-virgin olive oil
- 2 cups crimini mushrooms, cleaned
- 1 large yellow onion, chopped
- 12 cloves garlic
- 11/2 tsp. salt
- 1 tsp. ground black pepper
- 2 cups water
- 2 TB. tomato paste
- 1/3 cup tomato sauce
- 1 TB. brown sugar, packed
- 1/2 tsp. cayenne

Directions
1. In a large, 3-quart pot over medium heat, brown chicken drumsticks for 10 minutes, rotating every 3 minutes. Remove chicken from the pot, and set aside.
2. In the pot, combine extra-virgin olive oil, crimini mushrooms, yellow onion, garlic, and salt. Cook for 7 minutes.
3. Add black pepper, water, tomato paste, tomato sauce, brown sugar, and cayenne, and simmer for 5 minutes.
4. Return chicken to the pot, reduce heat to low, cover, and simmer for 30 minutes.
5. Serve each drumstick with sauce and some vegetables.

Pesto Chicken Mix

Servings: 4 | Cooking: 40 min

Ingredients
- 4 chicken breast halves, skinless and boneless
- 3 tomatoes, cubed
- 1 cup mozzarella, shredded
- ½ cup basil pesto
- A pinch of salt and black pepper
- Cooking: spray

Directions
1. Grease a baking dish lined with parchment paper with the cooking spray.
2. In a bowl, mix the chicken with salt, pepper and the pesto and rub well.
3. Place the chicken on the baking sheet, top with tomatoes and shredded mozzarella and bake at 400 degrees F for 40 minutes.
4. Divide the mix between plates and serve with a side salad.

Nutrition: calories 341; fat 20; fiber 1; carbs 4; protein 32

Chicken And Salsa Enchiladas

Servings: 5 | Cooking: 15 min

Ingredients
- 5 corn tortillas
- 10 oz chicken breast, boiled, shredded
- 1 teaspoon chipotle pepper
- 3 tablespoons green salsa
- ½ teaspoon minced garlic
- ½ cup cream
- ¼ cup chicken stock
- 1 cup Mozzarella, shredded
- 1 teaspoon butter, softened

Directions
1. Mix up together shredded chicken breast, chipotle pepper, green salsa, and minced garlic.
2. Then put the shredded chicken mixture in the center of every corn tortilla and roll them.
3. Spread the baking dish with softened butter from inside and arrange the rolled corn tortillas.
4. Then pour chicken stock and cream over the tortillas.

5. Top them with shredded Mozzarella.
6. Bake the enchiladas for 15 minutes at 365F.

Nutrition: calories 159; fat 5.3; fiber 1.6; carbs 12.3; protein 15.3

Paprika Chicken And Pineapple Mix

Servings: 4 | Cooking: 15 min

Ingredients
- 2 cups pineapple, peeled and cubed
- 2 tablespoons olive oil
- 1 tablespoon smoked paprika
- 2 pounds chicken breasts, skinless, boneless and cubed
- A pinch of salt and black pepper
- 1 tablespoon chives, chopped

Directions
1. Heat up a pan with the oil over medium-high heat, add the chicken, salt and pepper and brown for 4 minutes on each side.
2. Add the rest of the ingredients, toss, cook for 7 minutes more, divide everything between plates and serve with a side salad.

Nutrition: calories 264; fat 13.2; fiber 8.3; carbs 25.1; protein 15.4

Chicken And Apples Mix

Servings: 4 | Cooking: 40 min

Ingredients
- ½ cup chicken stock
- 1 red onion, sliced
- ½ cup tomato sauce
- 2 green apples, cored and chopped
- 1 pound breast, skinless, boneless and cubed
- 1 teaspoon thyme, chopped
- 1 and ½ tablespoons olive oil
- 1 tablespoon chives, chopped

Directions
1. In a roasting pan, combine the chicken with the tomato sauce, apples and the rest of the ingredients except the chives, introduce the pan in the oven and bake at 425 degrees F for 40 minutes.
2. Divide the mix between plates, sprinkle the chives on top and serve.

Nutrition: calories 292; fat 16.1; fiber 9.4; carbs 15.4; protein 16.4

Oregano Turkey And Peppers

Servings: 4 | Cooking: 1 Hour

Ingredients
- 2 red bell peppers, cut into strips
- 2 green bell peppers, cut into strips
- 1 red onion, chopped
- 4 garlic cloves, minced
- ½ cup black olives, pitted and sliced
- 2 cups chicken stock
- 1 big turkey breast, skinless, boneless and cut into strips
- 1 tablespoon oregano, chopped
- ½ cup cilantro, chopped

Directions
1. In a baking pan, combine the peppers with the turkey and the rest of the ingredients, toss, introduce in the oven at 400 degrees F and roast for 1 hour.
2. Divide everything between plates and serve.

Nutrition: calories 229; fat 8.9; fiber 8.2; carbs 17.8; protein 33.6

Tomato Chicken And Lentils

Servings: 8 | Cooking: 1 Hour

Ingredients
- 2 tablespoons olive oil
- 2 celery stalks, chopped
- 1 red onion, chopped
- 2 tablespoons tomato paste
- 2 garlic cloves, chopped
- ½ cup chicken stock
- 2 cups French lentils
- 1 pound chicken thighs, boneless and skinless
- Salt and black pepper to the taste
- 1 tablespoon cilantro, chopped

Directions
1. Heat up a Dutch oven with the oil over medium-high heat, add the onion and the garlic and sauté for 2 minutes.
2. Add the chicken and brown for 3 minutes on each side.
3. Add the rest of the ingredients except the cilantro, bring to a simmer and cook over medium-low heat for 45 minutes.
4. Add the cilantro, stir, divide the mix into bowls and serve.

Nutrition: calories 249; fat 9.7; fiber 11.9; carbs 25.3; protein 24.3

Chicken and Olives Tapenade

Servings: 4 | Cooking: 25 min

Ingredients
- 2 chicken breasts, boneless, skinless and halved
- 1 cup black olives, pitted
- ½ cup olive oil
- Salt and black pepper to the taste
- ½ cup mixed parsley, chopped
- ½ cup rosemary, chopped
- Salt and black pepper to the taste
- 4 garlic cloves, minced
- Juice of ½ lime

Directions
1. In a blender, combine the olives with half of the oil and the rest of the ingredients except the chicken and pulse well.
2. Heat up a pan with the rest of the oil over medium-high heat, add the chicken and brown for 4 minutes on each side.
3. Add the olives mix, and cook for 20 minutes more tossing often.

Nutrition: calories 291; fat 12.9; fiber 8.5; carbs 15.8; protein 34.2

Turkey, Leeks And Carrots

Servings: 4 | Cooking: 1 Hour

Ingredients
- 1 big turkey breast, skinless, boneless and cubed
- 2 tablespoons avocado oil
- Salt and black pepper to the taste
- 1 tablespoon sweet paprika
- ½ cup chicken stock
- 1 leek, sliced
- 1 carrot, sliced
- 1 yellow onion, chopped
- 1 tablespoon lemon juice
- 1 teaspoon cumin, ground
- 1 tablespoon basil, chopped

Directions
1. Heat up a pan with the oil over medium-high heat, add the turkey and brown for 4 minutes on each side.
2. Add the leeks, carrot and the onion and sauté everything for 5 minutes more.
3. Add the rest of the ingredients, bring to a simmer and cook over medium heat for 40 minutes.
4. Divide the mix between plates and serve.

Nutrition: calories 249; fat 10.7; fiber 11.9; carbs 22.3; protein 17.3

Grilled Chicken On The Bone

Servings: 1 Drumstick And 1 Thigh | Cooking: 40 min

Ingredients
- 4 TB. minced garlic
- 1/2 cup fresh lemon juice
- 1/2 cup extra-virgin olive oil
- 1 TB. dried oregano
- 2 tsp. salt
- 1 tsp. ground black pepper
- 1 tsp. cayenne
- 1 tsp. paprika
- 4 chicken drumsticks
- 4 chicken thighs

Directions
1. In a small bowl, whisk together garlic, lemon juice, extra-virgin olive oil, oregano, salt, black pepper, cayenne, and paprika.
2. Place chicken drumsticks and chicken thighs in a large bowl, pour 1/2 of dressing over chicken, mix to coat evenly, and set in the refrigerator to marinate for 1 hour.
3. Preheat the grill to medium-high heat.
4. Place chicken evenly on the grill, and cook for 5 minutes per side.
5. Reduce heat to medium-low, cover the grill, and cook chicken for 15 minutes per side or until juices run clear and internal temperature of chicken reads 175°F.
6. Remove chicken from the grill, and let rest for 5 minutes before serving warm.

Saffron Chicken Thighs And Green Beans

Servings: 4 | Cooking: 25 min

Ingredients
- 2 pounds chicken thighs, boneless and skinless
- 2 teaspoons saffron powder
- 1 pound green beans, trimmed and halved
- ½ cup Greek yogurt
- Salt and black pepper to the taste
- 1 tablespoon lime juice

- 1 tablespoon dill, chopped

Directions
1. In a roasting pan, combine the chicken with the saffron, green beans and the rest of the ingredients, toss a bit, introduce in the oven and bake at 400 degrees F for 25 minutes.
2. Divide everything between plates and serve.

Nutrition: calories 274; fat 12.3; fiber 5.3; carbs 20.4; protein 14.3

Sage And Nutmeg Chicken

Servings: 6 | Cooking: 20 min

Ingredients
- 2-pound chicken breast, skinless, boneless
- 2 tablespoons lemon juice
- 1 teaspoon sage
- ½ teaspoon ground nutmeg
- ½ teaspoon dried oregano
- 1 teaspoon paprika
- 1 teaspoon onion powder
- 2 tablespoons olive oil
- 1 teaspoon chili flakes
- 1 teaspoon salt
- 1 teaspoon apple cider vinegar

Directions
1. Make the marinade: whisk together apple cider vinegar, salt, chili flakes, olive oil, onion powder, paprika, dried oregano, ground nutmeg, sage, and lemon juice.
2. Then rub the chicken with marinade carefully and leave for 25 minutes to marinate.
3. Meanwhile, preheat grill to 385F.
4. Place the marinated chicken breast in the grill and cook it for 10 minutes from each side.
5. Cut the cooked chicken on the servings.

Nutrition: calories 218; fat 8.6; fiber 0.3; carbs 0.9; protein 32.2

Herbed Chicken

Servings: 4 | Cooking: 40 min

Ingredients
- 2 chicken breasts, skinless, boneless and sliced
- 2 red onions, chopped
- 2 tablespoons olive oil
- 2 garlic cloves, minced
- ½ cup chicken stock
- 1 teaspoon oregano, dried
- 1 teaspoon basil, dried
- 1 teaspoon rosemary, dried
- 1 cup canned tomatoes, chopped
- Salt and black pepper to the taste

Directions
1. Heat up a pot with the oil over medium-high heat, add the chicken and brown for 4 minutes on each side.
2. Add the garlic and the onions and sauté for 5 minutes more.
3. Add the rest of the ingredients, bring to a simmer and cook over medium heat for 25 minutes.
4. Divide everything between plates and serve.

Nutrition: calories 251; fat 11.6; fiber 15.5; carbs 15.6; protein 9.1

Duck And Blackberries

Servings: 4 | Cooking: 25 min

Ingredients
- 4 duck breasts, boneless and skin scored
- 2 tablespoons balsamic vinegar
- Salt and black pepper to the taste
- 1 cup chicken stock
- 4 ounces blackberries
- ¼ cup chicken stock
- 2 tablespoons avocado oil

Directions
1. Heat up a pan with the avocado oil over medium-high heat, add duck breasts, skin side down and cook for 5 minutes.
2. Flip the duck, add the rest of the ingredients, bring to a simmer and cook over medium heat for 20 minutes.
3. Divide everything between plates and serve.

Nutrition: calories 239; fat 10.5; fiber 10.2; carbs 21.1; protein 33.3

Chicken And Onion Mix

Servings: 4 | Cooking: 30 min

Ingredients
- 4 chicken steaks (4 oz each steak)
- ½ cup crushed tomatoes
- ¼ cup fresh cilantro
- 1 garlic clove, diced
- ½ cup of water
- 1 onion, diced
- 1 teaspoon olive oil

- 3 oz Parmesan, grated
- 3 tablespoon Panko breadcrumbs
- 2 eggs, beaten
- 1 teaspoon ground black pepper

Directions
1. Pour olive oil in the saucepan.
2. Add garlic and onion. Roast the vegetables for 3 minutes.
3. Then add fresh cilantro, crushed tomatoes, and water.
4. Simmer the mixture for 5 minutes.
5. Meanwhile, mix up together ground black pepper and eggs.
6. Dip the chicken steaks in the egg mixture.
7. Then coat them in Panko breadcrumbs and again in the egg mixture.
8. Coat the chicken steaks in grated Parmesan.
9. Place the prepared chicken steaks in the crushed tomato mixture.
10. Close the lid and cook chicken parm for 20 minutes. Flip the chicken steaks after 10 minutes of cooking.
11. Serve the chicken parm with crushed tomatoes sauce.

Nutrition: calories 372; fat 21.2; fiber 2.5; carbs 12.3; protein 32.5

Cinnamon Duck Mix

Servings: 4 | Cooking: 20 min

Ingredients
- 4 duck breasts, boneless and skin scored
- Salt and black pepper to the taste
- 1 teaspoon cinnamon powder
- ½ cup chicken stock
- 3 tablespoons chives, chopped
- 2 tablespoons parsley, chopped
- 1 tablespoon olive oil
- 3 tablespoons balsamic vinegar
- 2 red onions, chopped

Directions
1. Heat up a pan with the oil over medium-high heat, add the duck skin side down and cook for 5 minutes.
2. Add the cinnamon and the rest of the ingredients except the chives and cook for 5 minutes more.
3. Flip the duck breasts again, bring the whole mix to a simmer and cook over medium heat for 10 minutes.
4. Add the chives, divide everything between plates and serve.

Nutrition: calories 310; fat 13.5; fiber 9.2; carbs 16.7; protein 15.2

Lemony Turkey And Pine Nuts

Servings: 4 | Cooking: 30 min

Ingredients
- 2 turkey breasts, boneless, skinless and halved
- A pinch of salt and black pepper
- 2 tablespoons avocado oil
- Juice of 2 lemons
- 1 tablespoon rosemary, chopped
- 3 garlic cloves, minced
- ¼ cup pine nuts, chopped
- 1 cup chicken stock

Directions
1. Heat up a pan with the oil over medium-high heat, add the garlic and the turkey and brown for 4 minutes on each side.
2. Add the rest of the ingredients, bring to a simmer and cook over medium heat for 20 minutes.
3. Divide the mix between plates and serve with a side salad.

Nutrition: calories 293; fat 12.4; fiber 9.3; carbs 17.8; protein 24.5

Spicy Mustard Chicken

Preparation: 32 min | Cooking: 36 min | Servings: 4

Ingredients
- 4 chicken breasts
- 2 garlic cloves, crushed
- 1/3 cup chicken broth
- 3 tbsp. Dijon mustard
- tsp chili powder

Directions
1. In a small bowl, mix the mustard, chicken broth, garlic and chili. Marinate the chicken for 30 min.
2. Bake in a prepared to 375 F oven for 35 min.

Nutrition: 302 calories; 18g fat; 49g protein

Walnut and Oregano Crusted Chicken

Preparation: 36 min | Cooking: 13 min | Servings: 4

Ingredients
- 4 skinless, boneless chicken breasts
- 10-12 fresh oregano leaves

- 1/2 cup walnuts, chopped
- 2 garlic cloves, chopped
- 2 eggs, beaten

Directions
1. Blend the garlic, oregano and walnuts in a food processor until a rough crumb is formed. Place this mixture on a plate.
2. Whisk eggs in a deep bowl. Soak each chicken breast in the beaten egg then roll it in the walnut mixture. Place coated chicken on a baking tray and bake at 375 F for 13 min each side.

Nutrition: 304 calories; 54g fat; 14g protein

Chicken and Mushrooms

Preparation: 20 min | Cooking: 7 min | Servings: 4

Ingredients
- 4 chicken breasts, diced
- 2 lbs. mushrooms, chopped
- onion, chopped
- 4 tbsp. extra virgin olive oil
- salt and black, pepper to taste

Directions
1. Heat olive oil in a deep-frying pan over medium-high heat. Brown chicken, stirring, for 2 min each side, or until golden.
2. Add the chopped onion, mushrooms, salt and black pepper, and stir to combine. Adjust heat, cover and simmer for 30 min.
3. Uncover and simmer for 5 more min.

Nutrition: 290 calories; 49g fat; 9g protein

Blue Cheese and Mushroom Chicken

Preparation: 25 min | Cooking: 18 min | Servings: 4

Ingredients
- 4 chicken breast halves
- cup crumbled blue cheese
- 1 cup sour cream
- salt and black pepper, to taste
- 1/2 cup parsley, finely cut

Directions
1. Prep the oven to 350 degrees F. Grease a casserole with nonstick spray. Place all ingredients into it, turn chicken to coat.
2. Bake for 22 min. Sprinkle with parsley and serve.

Nutrition: 287 calories; 46g fat; 10g protein

Chicken and Onion Casserole

Preparation: 16 min | Cooking: 47 min | Servings: 4

Ingredients
- 4 chicken breasts
- 4-5 large onions, sliced
- 2 leeks, cut
- 4 tbsp. extra virgin olive oil
- 1 tsp thyme

Directions
1. Cook olive oil in a large, deep frying pan over medium-high heat. Brown chicken, turning, for 2-3 min each side or until golden. Set aside in a casserole dish.
2. Cut the onions and leeks and add them on and around the chicken, add in olives, thyme, salt and black pepper to taste. Cover it using aluminum foil and bake at 375 F for 35 min, or until the chicken is cooked through. Open then situate back to the oven for 6 min.

Nutrition: 309 calories; 59g fat; 18g protein

Chicken And Mediterranean Tabbouleh

Servings: 2 | Cooking: 30 min

Ingredients
- 6 ounces chicken breast halves, skinless, boneless, broiled or grilled, then sliced
- 4 large leaves romaine and/or butter head (Bibb or Boston) lettuce
- 3/4 cup water
- 3 tablespoons lemon juice
- 2 tablespoons olive oil
- 2 tablespoons green onions, thinly sliced
- 1/8teaspoon ground black pepper
- 1/4 teaspoon salt
- 1/4 cup bulgur
- 1/2 cup tomatoes (1 medium), chopped
- 1/2 cup seeded cucumber, finely chopped
- 1/2 cup Italian parsley, finely chopped
- 1 tablespoon fresh mint, snipped (or 1 teaspoon dried mint, crushed)

Directions
1. In a large sized bowl, combine the bulgur and the water; let stand for 30 minutes. After 30 minutes, drain in the sink through a fine sieve; pressing out the excess water from the bulgur using a large spoon. Return the bulgur into the bowl. Stir in the

cucumber, tomatoes, green onions, parsley, and the mint.
2. Prepare the dressing; put the olive oil, lemon juice, salt, and pepper into a screw-top jar. Cover securely and shake well until well mixed. Pour the dressing over the bulgur mixture; lightly toss to coat the bulgur mixture with the dressing. Cover the bowl and refrigerate to chill for at least 4 hours up to 24 hours, occasionally stirring.
3. When ready to serve, bring the bulgur mixture to room temperature. Divide the romaine and/or butterhead lettuce leaves between 2 shallow bowls, top with the broiled or grilled chicken, and then top with the bulgur mixture.

Nutrition: 294 cal.,13 g total fat (2 g sat. fat,2 g poly. fat, 8 g mono. fat), 72 mg chol., 276 mg sodium, 16 g total carbs., 5 g fiber, 3 g sugar, and 30 g protein.

Chicken Green Bean Soup

Servings: 8 | Cooking: 45 min

Ingredients
- 3 tablespoons olive oil
- 2 chicken breasts, cubed
- 1 shallot, chopped
- 1 garlic clove, chopped
- 1 red bell pepper, cored and diced
- 1 celery stalk, diced
- 2 carrots, diced
- 1 pound green beans, sliced
- 3 cups vegetable stock
- 4 cups water
- 1 bay leaf
- 1 thyme sprig
- 1 can diced tomatoes
- Salt and pepper to taste

Directions
1. Heat the oil in a soup pot and stir in the chicken. Cook for 5 minutes then add the shallot, garlic, bell pepper, celery and carrots.
2. Cook for 5 more minutes then stir in the green beans, stock, water, bay leaf, thyme sprig and tomatoes.
3. Add salt and pepper and cook for 25 minutes.
4. Serve the soup warm and fresh.

Nutrition: Calories:149 Fat:8.1g Protein:11.9g Carbohydrates:8.2g

Chicken Soup

Servings: 2 Cups | Cooking: 1 Hour 10 min

Ingredients
- 1 (3-lb.) whole chicken
- 3 bay leaves
- 5 whole allspice
- 1 (2-in.) cinnamon stick
- 1/2 medium yellow onion, sliced
- 1 1/2 tsp. salt
- 10 cups water
- 5 medium carrots, chopped
- 3 medium stalks celery, chopped
- 5 TB. extra-virgin olive oil
- 1/2 medium yellow onion, chopped
- 1 cup vermicelli noodles
- 1 large potato, peeled and diced
- 1/2 cup fresh parsley, chopped

Directions
1. In a large pot over high heat, combine chicken, bay leaves, allspice, cinnamon stick, sliced yellow onion, 1 teaspoon salt, and water. Bring to a boil, reduce heat to medium-low, and simmer for 40 minutes, skimming any foam that rises to the top.
2. Remove chicken from the pot, and set aside to cool enough to handle. Pick chicken apart, removing skin and bones, and cut into bite-size pieces.
3. Strain broth, discard solids, and return broth and boneless chicken pieces to the pot over medium-low heat.
4. Add carrots and celery, and cook for 10 minutes.
5. In a small saucepan over medium heat, heat 3 tablespoons extra-virgin olive oil. Add chopped yellow onion, and sauté for 5 minutes. Add to the pot.
6. In the same small saucepan over medium heat, heat remaining 2 tablespoons extra-virgin olive oil. Add vermicelli noodles, and cook, stirring to brown evenly, for 3 minutes.
7. Add toasted vermicelli noodles and diced potato to the pot, and cook for 10 minutes.
8. Add parsley, remove from heat, and serve.

Chapter 5: Fish and Seafood Recipes

Cod And Mustard Sauce

Servings: 4 | Cooking: 45 min

Ingredients
- 1-pound cod fillet
- 1 carrot, peeled
- 1 bell pepper, chopped
- 1 white onion, chopped
- 1 eggplant, peeled, chopped
- 2 tablespoons butter
- 1 tablespoon olive oil
- 1 teaspoon coriander seeds
- 1 teaspoon salt
- 1 teaspoon dried dill
- 1 teaspoon honey
- 1 tablespoon Mustard

Directions
1. Chop the cod fillet roughly.
2. Line the baking tray with baking paper and arrange the fish in it.
3. After this, mix up together mustard, honey, dried dill, salt, coriander seeds, olive oil, and butter.
4. Chop the carrot roughly.
5. Put all vegetables in the baking tray and sprinkle with honey mixture.
6. Preheat the oven to 365F.
7. Bake the sheet-pan fish for 45 minutes.
8. When all the vegetables and fish are soft, the meal is cooked.

Nutrition: calories 257; fat 11.6; fiber 6; carbs 15.9; protein 25.1

Garlic Scallops And Peas Mix

Servings: 6 | Cooking: 20 min

Ingredients
- 12 ounces scallops
- 2 tablespoons olive oil
- 4 garlic cloves, minced
- A pinch of salt and black pepper
- ½ cup chicken stock
- 1 cup snow peas, sliced
- ½ tablespoon balsamic vinegar
- 1 cup scallions, sliced
- 1 tablespoon basil, chopped

Directions
1. Heat up a pan with half of the oil over medium-high heat, add the scallops, cook for 5 minutes on each side and transfer to a bowl.
2. Heat up the pan again with the rest of the oil over medium heat, add the scallions and the garlic and sauté for 2 minutes.
3. Add the rest of the ingredients, stir, bring to a simmer and cook for 5 minutes more.
4. Add the scallops to the pan, cook everything for 3 minutes, divide into bowls and serve.

Nutrition: calories 296; fat 11.8; fiber 9.8; carbs 26.5; protein 20.5

Shrimp And Beans Salad

Servings: 4 | Cooking: 4 min

Ingredients
- 1 pound shrimp, peeled and deveined
- 30 ounces canned cannellini beans, drained and rinsed
- 2 tablespoons olive oil
- 1 cup cherry tomatoes, halved
- 1 teaspoon lemon zest, grated
- ½ cup red onion, chopped
- 4 handfuls baby arugula
- A pinch of salt and black pepper

For the dressing:
- 3 tablespoons red wine vinegar
- 2 garlic cloves, minced
- ½ cup olive oil

Directions
1. Heat up a pan with 2 tablespoons oil over medium-high heat, add the shrimp and cook for 2 minutes on each side.
2. In a salad bowl, combine the shrimp with the beans and the rest of the ingredients except the ones for the dressing and toss.
3. In a separate bowl, combine the vinegar with ½ cup oil and the garlic and whisk well.
4. Pour over the salad, toss and serve right away.

Nutrition: calories 207; fat 12.3; fiber 6.6; carbs 15.4; protein 8.7

Lemoney Prawns

Servings: 2 | Cooking: 3 min

Ingredients
- 1/2 lb prawns
- 1/2 cup fish stock
- 1 tbsp fresh lemon juice
- 1 tbsp lemon zest, grated
- 1 tbsp olive oil

- 1 tbsp garlic, minced
- Pepper
- Salt

Directions
1. Add all ingredients into the inner pot of instant pot and stir well.
2. Seal pot with lid and cook on high for 3 minutes.
3. Once done, release pressure using quick release. Remove lid.
4. Drain prawns and serve.

Nutrition: Calories 215 Fat 9.5 g Carbohydrates 3.9 g Sugar 0.4 g Protein 27.6 g Cholesterol 239 mg

Pesto And Lemon Halibut

Servings: 4 | Cooking: 10 min

Ingredients
- 1 tbsp fresh lemon juice
- 1 tbsp lemon rind, grated
- 2 garlic cloves, peeled
- 2 tbsp olive oil
- ¼ cup Parmesan Cheese, freshly grated
- 2/3 cups firmly packed basil leaves
- 1/8 tsp freshly ground black pepper
- ¼ tsp salt, divided
- 4 pcs 6-oz halibut fillets

Directions
1. Preheat grill to medium fire and grease grate with cooking spray.
2. Season fillets with pepper and 1/8 tsp salt. Place on grill and cook until halibut is flaky around 4 minutes per side.
3. Meanwhile, make your lemon pesto by combining lemon juice, lemon rind, garlic, olive oil, Parmesan cheese, basil leaves and remaining salt in a blender. Pulse mixture until finely minced but not pureed.
4. Once fish is done cooking, transfer to a serving platter, pour over the lemon pesto sauce, serve and enjoy.

Nutrition: Calories: 277.4; Fat: 13g; Protein: 38.7g; Carbs: 1.4g

Stuffed Branzino

Servings: 7 | Cooking: 40 min

Ingredients
- 6 oz fennel bulb, trimmed
- 1 teaspoon ground coriander
- ½ teaspoon ground black pepper
- 1 tablespoon lemon juice
- 1 teaspoon salt
- 1 teaspoon dried oregano
- 1 teaspoon dried cilantro
- 1 tablespoon butter, unsalted
- 1.5-pound whole branzino, trimmed, peeled
- 1 tablespoon sunflower oil

Directions
1. Slice fennel bulb.
2. Rub the branzino with ground coriander, black pepper, salt, oregano, and cilantro.
3. Then sprinkle it with lemon juice and sunflower oil.
4. After this, fill the branzino with butter and sliced fennel and wrap the fish in the foil.
5. Bake the fish for 40 minutes at 365F.
6. Then discard the foil from the fish and cut it on the servings.

Nutrition: calories 245; fat 8.4; fiber 0.9; carbs 2.1; protein 39.2

Tomato Olive Fish Fillets

Servings: 4 | Cooking: 8 min

Ingredients
- 2 lbs halibut fish fillets
- 2 oregano sprigs
- 2 rosemary sprigs
- 2 tbsp fresh lime juice
- 1 cup olives, pitted
- 28 oz can tomatoes, diced
- 1 tbsp garlic, minced
- 1 onion, chopped
- 2 tbsp olive oil

Directions
1. Add oil into the inner pot of instant pot and set the pot on sauté mode.
2. Add onion and sauté for 3 minutes.
3. Add garlic and sauté for a minute.
4. Add lime juice, olives, herb sprigs, and tomatoes and stir well.
5. Seal pot with lid and cook on high for 3 minutes.
6. Once done, release pressure using quick release. Remove lid.
7. Add fish fillets and seal pot again with lid and cook on high for 2 minutes.
8. Once done, release pressure using quick release. Remove lid.
9. Serve and enjoy.

Nutrition: Calories 333 Fat 19.1 g Carbohydrates 31.8 g Sugar 8.4 g Protein 13.4 g Cholesterol 5 mg

Steamed Mussels Thai Style

Servings: 4 | Cooking: 15 min

Ingredients
- ¼ cup minced shallots
- ½ tsp Madras curry
- 1 cup dry white wine
- 1 small bay leaf
- 1 tbsp chopped fresh basil
- 1 tbsp chopped fresh cilantro
- 1 tbsp chopped fresh mint
- 2 lbs. mussel, cleaned and debearded
- 2 tbsp butter
- 4 medium garlic cloves, minced

Directions
1. In a large heavy bottomed pot, on medium high fire add to pot the curry powder, bay leaf, wine plus the minced garlic and shallots. Bring to a boil and simmer for 3 minutes.
2. Add the cleaned mussels, stir, cover, and cook for 3 minutes.
3. Stir mussels again, cover, and cook for another 2 or 3 minutes. Cooking: is done when majority of shells have opened.
4. With a slotted spoon, transfer cooked mussels in a large bowl. Discard any unopened mussels.
5. Continue heating pot with sauce. Add butter and the chopped herbs.
6. Season with pepper and salt to taste.
7. Once good, pour over mussels, serve and enjoy.

Nutrition: Calories: 407.2; Protein: 43.4g; Fat: 21.2g; Carbs: 10.8g

Oregano Citrus Salmon

Servings: 2 | Cooking: 15 min

Ingredients
- 2 salmon fillets (5 oz each fish fillet)
- ½ teaspoon garlic powder
- ¾ teaspoon chili flakes
- ¾ teaspoon ground coriander
- ½ teaspoon salt
- 1 tablespoon butter
- ½ teaspoon dried oregano
- 1 orange, peeled

Directions
1. In the shallow bowl make the spice mix from garlic powder, chili flakes, ground coriander, salt, and dried oregano.
2. Then coat the salmon fillets in the spice mix.
3. Slice the orange and place it in the skillet.
4. Add butter and roast the sliced orange until the butter is melted.
5. Then remove the sliced orange from the skillet.
6. Add salmon fillets and roast them for 4 minutes from each side over the medium heat.
7. After this, top the salmon with roasted sliced orange and close the lid.
8. Cook the fish for 5 minutes more over the low heat.

Nutrition: calories 285; fat 14.7; fiber 2.5; carbs 11.6; protein 28.6

Nutmeg Sea Bass

Servings: 4 | Cooking: 10 min

Ingredients
- 1 teaspoon fresh ginger, minced
- 10 oz seabass fillet (4 fillets)
- 1 tablespoon butter
- 1 teaspoon minced garlic
- ¼ teaspoon ground nutmeg
- ½ teaspoon salt

Directions
1. Toss butter in the skillet and melt it.
2. Add minced garlic, ground nutmeg, salt, and fresh ginger.
3. Roast the mixture for 1 minute.
4. Then add seabass fillet.
5. Fry the fish for 3 minutes from each side.

Nutrition: calories 205; fat 13.5; fiber 0.8; carbs 0.6; protein 19.7

Shrimp Kebabs

Servings: 2 | Cooking: 5 min

Ingredients
- 4 King prawns, peeled
- 1 tablespoon lemon juice
- ¾ teaspoon ground coriander
- ½ teaspoon salt
- 1 tablespoon tomato sauce
- 1 tablespoon olive oil

Directions
1. Skew the shrimps on the skewers and sprinkle them with lemon juice, ground coriander, salt, and tomato sauce.
2. Then drizzle the shrimps with olive oil.
3. Preheat grill to 385F.
4. Grill the shrimp kebabs for 2 minutes from each side.

Nutrition: calories 106; fat 7.5; fiber 0.4; carbs 0.6; protein 9.1

Easy Broiled Lobster Tails

Servings: 2 | Cooking: 10 min

Ingredients
- 1 6-oz frozen lobster tails
- 1 tbsp olive oil
- 1 tsp lemon pepper seasoning

Directions
1. Preheat oven broiler.
2. With kitchen scissors, cut thawed lobster tails in half lengthwise.
3. Brush with oil the exposed lobster meat. Season with lemon pepper.
4. Place lobster tails in baking sheet with exposed meat facing up.
5. Place on top broiler rack and broil for 10 minutes until lobster meat is lightly browned on the sides and center meat is opaque.
6. Serve and enjoy.

Nutrition: Calories: 175.6; Protein: 3g; Fat: 10g; Carbs: 18.4g

Cajun Garlic Shrimp Noodle Bowl

Servings: 2 | Cooking: 15 min

Ingredients
- ½ teaspoon salt
- 1 onion, sliced
- 1 red pepper, sliced
- 1 tablespoon butter
- 1 teaspoon garlic granules
- 1 teaspoon onion powder
- 1 teaspoon paprika
- 2 large zucchinis, cut into noodle strips
- 20 jumbo shrimps, shells removed and deveined
- 3 cloves garlic, minced
- 3 tablespoon ghee
- A dash of cayenne pepper
- A dash of red pepper flakes

Directions
1. Prepare the Cajun seasoning by mixing the onion powder, garlic granules, pepper flakes, cayenne pepper, paprika and salt. Toss in the shrimp to coat in the seasoning.
2. In a skillet, heat the ghee and sauté the garlic. Add in the red pepper and onions and continue sautéing for 4 minutes.
3. Add the Cajun shrimp and cook until opaque. Set aside.
4. In another pan, heat the butter and sauté the zucchini noodles for three minutes.
5. Assemble by the placing the Cajun shrimps on top of the zucchini noodles.

Nutrition: Calories: 712; Fat: 30.0g; Protein: 97.8g; Carbs: 20.2g

Red Peppers & Pineapple Topped Mahi-mahi

Servings: 4 | Cooking: 30 min

Ingredients
- ¼ tsp black pepper
- ¼ tsp salt
- 1 cup whole wheat couscous
- 1 red bell pepper, diced
- 2 1/3 cups low sodium chicken broth
- 2 cups chopped fresh pineapple
- 2 tbsp. chopped fresh chives
- 2 tsp. olive oil
- 4 pieces of skinless, boneless mahi mahi (dolphin fish) fillets (around 4-oz each)

Directions
On high fire, add 1 1/3 cups broth to a small saucepan and heat until boiling. Once boiling, add couscous. Turn off fire, cover and set aside to allow liquid to be fully absorbed around 5 minutes.
1. On medium high fire, place a large nonstick saucepan and heat oil.
2. Season fish on both sides with pepper and salt. Add mahi mahi to hot pan and pan fry until golden around one minute each side. Once cooked, transfer to plate.
3. On same pan, sauté bell pepper and pineapples until soft, around 2 minutes on medium high fire.
4. Add couscous to pan along with chives, and remaining broth.
5. On top of the mixture in pan, place fish. With foil, cover pan and continue cooking until fish is

steaming and tender underneath the foil, around 3-5 minutes.

Nutrition: Calories per serving: 302; Protein: 43.1g; Fat: 4.8g; Carbs: 22.0g

Dill Halibut

Servings: 3 | Cooking: 10 min

Ingredients
- 13 oz halibut fillet
- 1/3 cup cream
- ¼ cup dill, chopped
- ½ teaspoon garlic powder
- ¼ teaspoon turmeric
- ¼ teaspoon ground paprika
- 1 teaspoon salt
- 1 teaspoon olive oil

Directions
1. Chop the fish fillet on the big cubes and sprinkle them with garlic powder, turmeric, ground paprika, and salt.
2. Pour olive oil in the skillet and preheat it well.
3. Then place fish in the hot oil and roast it for 2 minutes from each side over the medium heat.
4. Add cream and stir gently with the help of the spatula.
5. Bring the mixture to boil and add dill.
6. Close the lid and cook fish on the medium heat for 5 minutes. Till the fish and creamy sauce are cooked.
7. Serve the halibut cubes with creamy sauce.

Nutrition: calories 170; fat 5.9; fiber 0.7; carbs 3.6; protein 25.1

Kale, Beets And Cod Mix

Servings: 4 | Cooking: 20 min

Ingredients
- 2 tablespoons apple cider vinegar
- ½ cup chicken stock
- 1 red onion, sliced
- 4 golden beets, trimmed, peeled and cubed
- 2 tablespoons olive oil
- Salt and black pepper to the taste
- 4 cups kale, torn
- 2 tablespoons walnuts, chopped
- 1 pound cod fillets, boneless, skinless and cubed

Directions
1. Heat up a pan with the oil over medium-high heat, add the onion and the beets and cook for 3-4 minutes.
2. Add the rest of the ingredients except the fish and the walnuts, stir, bring to a simmer and cook for 5 minutes more.
3. Add the fish, cook for 10 minutes, divide between plates and serve.

Nutrition: calories 285; fat 7.6; fiber 6.5; carbs 16.7; protein 12.5

Shrimp Scampi

Servings: 6 | Cooking: 8 min

Ingredients
- 1 lb whole wheat penne pasta
- 1 lb frozen shrimp
- 2 tbsp garlic, minced
- 1/4 tsp cayenne
- 1/2 tbsp Italian seasoning
- 1/4 cup olive oil
- 3 1/2 cups fish stock
- Pepper
- Salt

Directions
1. Add all ingredients into the inner pot of instant pot and stir well.
2. Seal pot with lid and cook on high for 6 minutes.
3. Once done, release pressure using quick release. Remove lid.
4. Stir well and serve.

Nutrition: Calories 435 Fat 12.6 g Carbohydrates 54.9 g Sugar 0.1 g Protein 30.6 g Cholesterol 116 mg

Orange Rosemary Seared Salmon

Servings: 4 | Cooking: 10 min

Ingredients
- ½ cup chicken stock
- 1 cup fresh orange juice
- 1 tablespoon coconut oil
- 1 tablespoon tapioca starch
- 2 garlic cloves, minced
- 2 tablespoon fresh lemon juice
- 2 teaspoon fresh rosemary, minced
- 2 teaspoon orange zest
- 4 salmon fillets, skins removed

- Salt and pepper to taste

Directions
1. Season the salmon fillet on both sides.
2. In a skillet, heat coconut oil over medium high heat. Cook the salmon fillets for 5 minutes on each side. Set aside.
3. In a mixing bowl, combine the orange juice, chicken stock, lemon juice and orange zest.
4. In the skillet, sauté the garlic and rosemary for 2 minutes and pour the orange juice mixture. Bring to a boil. Lower the heat to medium low and simmer. Season with salt and pepper to taste.
5. Pour the sauce all over the salmon fillet then serve.

Nutrition: Calories: 493; Fat: 17.9g; Protein: 66.7g; Carbs: 12.8g

Salmon And Mango Mix

Servings: 2 | Cooking: 25 min

Ingredients
- 2 salmon fillets, skinless and boneless
- Salt and pepper to the taste
- 2 tablespoons olive oil
- 2 garlic cloves, minced
- 2 mangos, peeled and cubed
- 1 red chili, chopped
- 1 small piece ginger, grated
- Juice of 1 lime
- 1 tablespoon cilantro, chopped

Directions
1. In a roasting pan, combine the salmon with the oil, garlic and the rest of the ingredients except the cilantro, toss, introduce in the oven at 350 degrees F and bake for 25 minutes.
2. Divide everything between plates and serve with the cilantro sprinkled on top.

Nutrition: calories 251; fat 15.9; fiber 5.9; carbs 26.4; protein 12.4

Delicious Shrimp Alfredo

Servings: 4 | Cooking: 3 min

Ingredients
- 12 shrimp, remove shells
- 1 tbsp garlic, minced
- 1/4 cup parmesan cheese
- 2 cups whole wheat rotini noodles
- 1 cup fish broth
- 15 oz alfredo sauce
- 1 onion, chopped
- Salt

Directions
1. Add all ingredients except parmesan cheese into the instant pot and stir well.
2. Seal pot with lid and cook on high for 3 minutes.
3. Once done, release pressure using quick release. Remove lid.
4. Stir in cheese and serve.

Nutrition: Calories 669 Fat 23.1 g Carbohydrates 76 g Sugar 2.4 g Protein 37.8 g Cholesterol 190 mg

Cod And Mushrooms Mix

Servings: 4 | Cooking: 25 min

Ingredients
- 2 cod fillets, boneless
- 4 tablespoons olive oil
- 4 ounces mushrooms, sliced
- Sea salt and black pepper to the taste
- 12 cherry tomatoes, halved
- 8 ounces lettuce leaves, torn
- 1 avocado, pitted, peeled and cubed
- 1 red chili pepper, chopped
- 1 tablespoon cilantro, chopped
- 2 tablespoons balsamic vinegar
- 1 ounce feta cheese, crumbled

Directions
1. Put the fish in a roasting pan, brush it with 2 tablespoons oil, sprinkle salt and pepper all over and broil under medium-high heat for 15 minutes. Meanwhile, heat up a pan with the rest of the oil over medium heat, add the mushrooms, stir and sauté for 5 minutes.
2. Add the rest of the ingredients, toss, cook for 5 minutes more and divide between plates.
3. Top with the fish and serve right away.

Nutrition: calories 257; fat 10; fiber 3.1; carbs 24.3; protein 19.4

Baked Shrimp Mix

Servings: 4 | Cooking: 32 min

Ingredients
- 4 gold potatoes, peeled and sliced
- 2 fennel bulbs, trimmed and cut into wedges
- 2 shallots, chopped
- 2 garlic cloves, minced

- 3 tablespoons olive oil
- ½ cup kalamata olives, pitted and halved
- 2 pounds shrimp, peeled and deveined
- 1 teaspoon lemon zest, grated
- 2 teaspoons oregano, dried
- 4 ounces feta cheese, crumbled
- 2 tablespoons parsley, chopped

Directions
1. In a roasting pan, combine the potatoes with 2 tablespoons oil, garlic and the rest of the ingredients except the shrimp, toss, introduce in the oven and bake at 450 degrees F for 25 minutes.
2. Add the shrimp, toss, bake for 7 minutes more, divide between plates and serve.

Nutrition: calories 341; fat 19; fiber 9; carbs 34; protein 10

Lemon And Dates Barramundi

Servings: 2 | Cooking: 12 min

Ingredients
- 2 barramundi fillets, boneless
- 1 shallot, sliced
- 4 lemon slices
- Juice of ½ lemon
- Zest of 1 lemon, grated
- 2 tablespoons olive oil
- 6 ounces baby spinach
- ¼ cup almonds, chopped
- 4 dates, pitted and chopped
- ¼ cup parsley, chopped
- Salt and black pepper to the taste

Directions
1. Season the fish with salt and pepper and arrange on 2 parchment paper pieces.
2. Top the fish with the lemon slices, drizzle the lemon juice, and then top with the other ingredients except the oil.
3. Drizzle 1 tablespoon oil over each fish mix, wrap the parchment paper around the fish shaping to packets and arrange them on a baking sheet.
4. Bake at 400 degrees F for 12 minutes, cool the mix a bit, unfold, divide everything between plates and serve.

Nutrition: calories 232; fat 16.5; fiber 11.1; carbs 24.8; protein 6.5

Cheesy Crab And Lime Spread

Servings: 8 | Cooking: 25 min

Ingredients
- 1 pound crab meat, flaked
- 4 ounces cream cheese, soft
- 1 tablespoon chives, chopped
- 1 teaspoon lime juice
- 1 teaspoon lime zest, grated

Directions
1. In a baking dish greased with cooking spray, combine the crab with the rest of the ingredients and toss.
2. Introduce in the oven at 350 degrees F, bake for 25 minutes, divide into bowls and serve.

Nutrition: calories 284; fat 14.6; fiber 5.8; carbs 16.5; protein 15.4

Honey Lobster

Servings: 2 | Cooking: 10 min

Ingredients
- 2 lobster tails
- 2 teaspoons butter, melted
- 1 teaspoon honey
- ¼ teaspoon ground paprika
- 1 teaspoon lemon juice
- ¼ teaspoon dried dill

Directions
1. Cut the top of the lobster tail shell to the tip of the tail with the help of the scissors. It will look like "lobster meat in a blanket".
2. Mix up together melted butter, honey, ground paprika, lemon juice, and dried dill.
3. Brush the lobster tails with butter mixture carefully from the top and down.
4. Preheat the oven to 365F.
5. Line the baking tray with parchment and arrange the lobster tails in it.
6. Bake the lobster tails for 10 minutes.

Nutrition: calories 91; fat 3.9; fiber 0.1 carbs 3.1; protein 0.1

Fried Salmon

Servings: 2 | Cooking: 8 min

Ingredients
- 5 oz salmon fillet
- ¼ teaspoon salt

- ½ teaspoon ground black pepper
- 1 tablespoon sunflower oil
- ¼ teaspoon lime juice

Directions
1. Cut the salmon fillet on 2 lengthwise pieces.
2. Sprinkle every fish piece with salt, ground black pepper, and lime juice.
3. Pour sunflower oil in the skillet and preheat it until shimmering.
4. Then place fish fillets in the hot oil and cook them for 3 minutes from each side.

Nutrition: calories 157; fat 11.4; fiber 0.1; carbs 0.3; protein 13.8

Smoked Salmon And Veggies Mix

Servings: 4 | Cooking: 20 min

Ingredients
- 3 red onions, cut into wedges
- ¾ cup green olives, pitted and halved
- 3 red bell peppers, roughly chopped
- ½ teaspoon smoked paprika
- Salt and black pepper to the taste
- 3 tablespoons olive oil
- 4 salmon fillets, skinless and boneless
- 2 tablespoons chives, chopped

Directions
1. In a roasting pan, combine the salmon with the onions and the rest of the ingredients, introduce in the oven and bake at 390 degrees F for 20 minutes.
2. Divide the mix between plates and serve.

Nutrition: calories 301; fat 5.9; fiber 11.9; carbs 26.4; protein 22.4

Berries And Grilled Calamari

Servings: 4 | Cooking: 5 min

Ingredients
- ¼ cup dried cranberries
- ¼ cup extra virgin olive oil
- ¼ cup olive oil
- ¼ cup sliced almonds
- ½ lemon, juiced
- ¾ cup blueberries
- 1 ½ pounds calamari tube, cleaned
- 1 granny smith apple, sliced thinly
- 1 tablespoon fresh lemon juice
- 2 tablespoons apple cider vinegar
- 6 cups fresh spinach
- Freshly grated pepper to taste
- Sea salt to taste

Directions
1. In a small bowl, make the vinaigrette by mixing well the tablespoon of lemon juice, apple cider vinegar, and extra virgin olive oil. Season with pepper and salt to taste. Set aside.
2. Turn on the grill to medium fire and let the grates heat up for a minute or two.
3. In a large bowl, add olive oil and the calamari tube. Season calamari generously with pepper and salt.
4. Place seasoned and oiled calamari onto heated grate and grill until cooked or opaque. This is around two minutes per side.
5. As you wait for the calamari to cook, you can combine almonds, cranberries, blueberries, spinach, and the thinly sliced apple in a large salad bowl. Toss to mix.
6. Remove cooked calamari from grill and transfer on a chopping board. Cut into ¼-inch thick rings and throw into the salad bowl.
7. Drizzle with vinaigrette and toss well to coat salad.
8. Serve and enjoy!

Nutrition: Calories: 567; Fat: 24.5g; Protein: 54.8g; Carbs: 30.6g

Salmon And Zucchini Rolls

Servings: 8 | Cooking: 0 min

Ingredients
- 8 slices smoked salmon, boneless
- 2 zucchinis, sliced lengthwise in 8 pieces
- 1 cup ricotta cheese, soft
- 2 teaspoons lemon zest, grated
- 1 tablespoon dill, chopped
- 1 small red onion, sliced
- Salt and pepper to the taste

Directions
1. In a bowl, mix the ricotta cheese with the rest of the ingredients except the salmon and the zucchini and whisk well.
2. Arrange the zucchini slices on a working surface, and divide the salmon on top.
3. Spread the cheese mix all over, roll and secure with toothpicks and serve right away.

Nutrition: calories 297; fat 24.3; fiber 11.6; carbs 15.4; protein 11.6

Scallions And Salmon Tartar

Servings: 4 | Cooking: 0 min

Ingredients
- 4 tablespoons scallions, chopped
- 2 teaspoons lemon juice
- 1 tablespoon chives, minced
- 1 tablespoon olive oil
- 1 pound salmon, skinless, boneless and minced
- Salt and black pepper to the taste
- 1 tablespoon parsley, chopped

Directions
1. In a bowl, combine the scallions with the salmon and the rest of the ingredients, stir well, divide into small molds between plates and serve.

Nutrition: calories 224; fat 14.5; fiber 5.2; carbs 12.7; protein 5.3

Flavors Cioppino

Servings: 6 | Cooking: 5 min

Ingredients
- 1 lb codfish, cut into chunks
- 1 1/2 lbs shrimp
- 28 oz can tomatoes, diced
- 1 cup dry white wine
- 1 bay leaf
- 1 tsp cayenne
- 1 tsp oregano
- 1 shallot, chopped
- 1 tsp garlic, minced
- 1 tbsp olive oil
- 1/2 tsp salt

Directions
1. Add oil into the inner pot of instant pot and set the pot on sauté mode.
2. Add shallot and garlic and sauté for 2 minutes.
3. Add wine, bay leaf, cayenne, oregano, and salt and cook for 3 minutes.
4. Add remaining ingredients and stir well.
5. Seal pot with a lid and select manual and cook on low for 0 minutes.
6. Once done, release pressure using quick release. Remove lid.
7. Serve and enjoy.

Nutrition: Calories 281 Fat 5 g Carbohydrates 10.5 g Sugar 4.9 g Protein 40.7 g Cholesterol 266 mg

Warm Caper Tapenade On Cod

Servings: 4 | Cooking: 30 min

Ingredients
- ¼ cup chopped cured olives
- ¼ tsp freshly ground pepper
- 1 ½ tsp chopped fresh oregano
- 1 cup halved cherry tomatoes
- 1 lb. cod fillet
- 1 tbsp capers, rinsed and chopped
- 1 tbsp minced shallot
- 1 tsp balsamic vinegar
- 3 tsp extra virgin olive oil, divided

Directions
1. Grease baking sheet with cooking spray and preheat oven to 450oF.
2. Place cod on prepared baking sheet. Rub with 2 tsp oil and season with pepper.
3. Roast in oven for 15 to 20 minutes or until cod is flaky.
4. While waiting for cod to cook, on medium fire, place a small fry pan and heat 1 tsp oil.
5. Sauté shallots for a minute.
6. Add tomatoes and cook for two minutes or until soft.
7. Add capers and olives. Sauté for another minute.
8. Add vinegar and oregano. Turn off fire and stir to mix well.
9. Evenly divide cod into 4 servings and place on a plate.
10. To serve, top cod with Caper-Olive-Tomato Tapenade and enjoy.

Nutrition: Calories: 107; Fat: 2.9g; Protein: 17.6g; Carbs: 2.0g

Spicy Tomato Crab Mix

Servings: 4 | Cooking: 12 min

Ingredients
- 1 lb crab meat
- 1 tsp paprika
- 1 cup grape tomatoes, cut into half
- 2 tbsp green onion, chopped
- 1 tbsp olive oil
- Pepper
- Salt

Directions
1. Add oil into the inner pot of instant pot and set the pot on sauté mode.
2. Add paprika and onion and sauté for 2 minutes.
3. Add the rest of the ingredients and stir well.
4. Seal pot with lid and cook on high for 10 minutes.
5. Once done, release pressure using quick release. Remove lid.
6. Serve and enjoy.

Nutrition: Calories 142 Fat 5.7 g Carbohydrates 4.3 g Sugar 1.3 g Protein 14.7 g Cholesterol 61 mg

Salmon Bake

Servings: 6 | Cooking: 25 min

Ingredients
- 1 teaspoon baking powder
- ½ cup skim milk
- 1 ½ cup wheat flour, whole grain
- ½ teaspoon salt
- 1 egg, beaten
- 8 oz salmon, canned
- 2 oz Cheddar cheese, shredded
- 1 teaspoon olive oil
- 1 teaspoon butter
- ½ teaspoon paprika
- ½ teaspoon ground black pepper
- 1 tablespoon sour cream

Directions
1. Make the pie dough: pour skim milk in the saucepan and reheat it until it is warm but not hot.
2. Then add baking powder, flour, salt, and egg. Knead the non-sticky dough. Add more flour if needed.
3. Make the bun from the dough and cover it with a towel. Let it rest for at least 10 minutes in a warm place.
4. Meanwhile, make the filling for the pie: chop the salmon and combine it with cheese, paprika, sour cream, and ground black pepper. Stir well.
5. Cut the dough on the two pieces.
6. Roll up one piece of dough and arrange it in the non-sticky round springform.
7. Put the filling over the dough.
8. Roll up the second part of the dough and cover the filing.
9. Secure the edges of the pie with the help of the fork or fingertip.
10. Bake the pie for 25 minutes at 360F.
11. When the pie is cooked, chill it to the room temperature and cut on 6 servings.

Nutrition: calories 238; fat 8.4; fiber 1; carbs 25.7; protein 14.6

Baked Trout And Fennel

Servings: 4 | Cooking: 22 min

Ingredients
- 1 fennel bulb, sliced
- 2 tablespoons olive oil
- 1 yellow onion, sliced
- 3 teaspoons Italian seasoning
- 4 rainbow trout fillets, boneless
- ¼ cup panko breadcrumbs
- ½ cup kalamata olives, pitted and halved
- Juice of 1 lemon

Directions
1. Spread the fennel the onion and the rest of the ingredients except the trout and the breadcrumbs on a baking sheet lined with parchment paper, toss them and cook at 400 degrees F for 10 minutes.
2. Add the fish dredged in breadcrumbs and seasoned with salt and pepper and cook it at 400 degrees F for 6 minutes on each side.
3. Divide the mix between plates and serve.

Nutrition: calories 306; fat 8.9; fiber 11.1; carbs 23.8; protein 14.5

Salmon And Corn Salad

Servings: 4 | Cooking: 0 min

Ingredients
- ½ cup pecans, chopped
- 2 cups baby arugula
- 1 cup corn
- ¼ pound smoked salmon, skinless, boneless and cut into small chunks
- 2 tablespoons olive oil
- 2 tablespoon lemon juice
- Sea salt and black pepper to the taste

Directions
1. In a salad bowl, combine the salmon with the corn and the rest of the ingredients, toss and serve right away.

Nutrition: calories 284; fat 18.4; fiber 5.4; carbs 22.6; protein 17.4

Minty Sardines Salad

Servings: 4 | Cooking: 0 min

Ingredients
- 4 ounces canned sardines in olive oil, skinless, boneless and flaked
- 2 teaspoons avocado oil
- 2 tablespoons mint, chopped
- A pinch of salt and black pepper
- 1 avocado, peeled, pitted and cubed
- 1 cucumber, cubed
- 2 tomatoes, cubed
- 2 spring onions, chopped

Directions
1. In a bowl, combine the sardines with the oil and the rest of the ingredients, toss, divide into small cups and keep in the fridge for 10 minutes before serving.

Nutrition: calories 261; fat 7.6; fiber 2.2; carbs 22.8; protein 12.5

Smoked Salmon And Watercress Salad

Servings: 4 | Cooking: 0 min

Ingredients
- 2 bunches watercress
- 1 pound smoked salmon, skinless, boneless and flaked
- 2 teaspoons mustard
- ¼ cup lemon juice
- ½ cup Greek yogurt
- Salt and black pepper to the taste
- 1 big cucumber, sliced
- 2 tablespoons chives, chopped

Directions
1. In a salad bowl, combine the salmon with the watercress and the rest of the ingredients toss and serve right away.

Nutrition: calories 244; fat 16.7; fiber 4.5; carbs 22.5; protein 15.6

Easy Salmon Stew

Servings: 6 | Cooking: 8 min

Ingredients
- 2 lbs salmon fillet, cubed
- 1 onion, chopped
- 2 cups fish broth
- 1 tbsp olive oil
- Pepper
- salt

Directions
1. Add oil into the inner pot of instant pot and set the pot on sauté mode.
2. Add onion and sauté for 2 minutes.
3. Add remaining ingredients and stir well.
4. Seal pot with lid and cook on high for 6 minutes.
5. Once done, release pressure using quick release. Remove lid.
6. Stir and serve.

Nutrition: Calories 243 Fat 12.6 g Carbohydrates 0.8 g Sugar 0.3 g Protein 31 g Cholesterol 78 mg

Oregano Swordfish Mix

Servings: 4 | Cooking: 20 min

Ingredients
- 4 swordfish fillets (oz each fillet)
- 4 sprig fresh rosemary
- 4 teaspoons capers
- ½ teaspoon dried oregano
- 1 tablespoon olive oil
- ½ teaspoon salt
- 1 teaspoon butter
- 1 tablespoon lemon juice
- ¼ teaspoon lemon zest, grated

Directions
1. Toss butter in the skillet and bring it to boil.
2. Add rosemary sprigs, lemon zest, and dried oregano.
3. Boil the ingredients for 20 seconds.
4. Then add swordfish fillets.
5. Roast the fish for 2 minutes from each side over the high heat.
6. Then reduce the heat to medium.
7. Sprinkle the fish with olive oil, salt, lemon juice, and capers.
8. Close the lid and cook the swordfish for 15 minutes over the low heat.

Nutrition: calories 206; fat 10; fiber 0.3; carbs 0.5; protein 27.1

Cheddar Tuna Bake

Servings: 4 | Cooking: 35 min

Ingredients
- ½ cup Cheddar cheese, shredded
- 2 tomatoes, chopped
- 7 oz tuna filet, chopped
- 1 teaspoon ground coriander
- ½ teaspoon salt
- 1 teaspoon olive oil
- ½ teaspoon dried oregano

Directions
1. Brush the casserole mold with olive oil.
2. Mix up together chopped tuna fillet with dried oregano and ground coriander.
3. Place the fish in the mold and flatten well to get the layer.
4. Then add chopped tomatoes and shredded cheese.
5. Cover the casserole with foil and secure the edges.
6. Bake the meal for 35 minutes at 355F.

Nutrition: calories 260; fat 21.5; fiber 0.8; carbs 2.7; protein 14.6

Tarragon Trout And Beets

Servings: 4 | Cooking: 35 min

Ingredients
- 1 pound medium beets, peeled and cubed
- 3 tablespoons olive oil
- 4 trout fillets, boneless
- Salt and black pepper to the taste
- 1 tablespoon chives, chopped
- 1 tablespoon tarragon, chopped
- 3 tablespoon spring onions, chopped
- 2 tablespoons lemon juice
- ½ cup chicken stock

Directions
1. Spread the beets on a baking sheet lined with parchment paper, add salt, pepper and 1 tablespoon oil, toss and bake at 450 degrees F for 20 minutes.
2. Heat up a pan with the rest of the oil over medium-high heat, add the trout and the remaining ingredients, and cook for 4 minutes on each side.
3. Add the baked beets, cook the mix for 5 minutes more, divide everything between plates and serve.

Nutrition: calories 232; fat 5.5; fiber 7.5; carbs 20.9; protein 16.8

Cod And Brussels Sprouts

Servings: 4 | Cooking: 20 min

Ingredients
- 1 teaspoon garlic powder
- 1 teaspoon smoked paprika
- 2 tablespoons olive oil
- 2 pounds Brussels sprouts, trimmed and halved
- 4 cod fillets, boneless
- ½ cup tomato sauce
- 1 teaspoon Italian seasoning
- 1 tablespoon chives, chopped

Directions
1. In a roasting pan, combine the sprouts with the garlic powder and the other ingredients except the cod and toss.
2. Put the cod on top, cover the pan with tin foil and bake at 450 degrees F for 20 minutes.
3. Divide the mix between plates and serve.

Nutrition: calories 188; fat 12.8; fiber 9.2; carbs 22.2; protein 16.8

Salmon Tortillas

Servings: 2 | Cooking: 10 min

Ingredients
- 2 corn tortillas
- 8 oz wild salmon fillet
- 1 teaspoon balsamic vinegar
- ¾ teaspoon cayenne pepper
- ¾ teaspoon salt
- 1 teaspoon Italian herbs
- 1 teaspoon olive oil
- ¼ cup green olives, pitted
- 1 tablespoon fresh cilantro, chopped

Directions
1. Sprinkle salmon fillet with balsamic vinegar, cayenne pepper, salt, Italian herbs, and olive oil.
2. Massage the salmon fillet well with the help of the fingertips.
3. Then preheat skillet well and place salmon fillet inside.
4. Roast the fish for 10 minutes totally.
5. Meanwhile, slice green olives and mix them up with fresh cilantro.
6. Chill the cooked salmon gently and chop it.
7. Arrange the fish on the corn tortillas and sprinkle with cilantro mixture.
8. Fold up the tortillas in the shape of tacos.

Nutrition: calories 233; fat 9.6; fiber 2.9; carbs 14.1; protein 20.6

Tasty Tuna Scaloppine

Servings: 4 | Cooking: 10 min

Ingredients
- ¼ cup chopped almonds
- ¼ cup fresh tangerine juice
- ½ tsp fennel seeds
- ½ tsp ground black pepper, divided
- ½ tsp salt
- 1 tbsp extra virgin olive oil
- 2 tbsp chopped fresh mint
- 2 tbsp chopped red onion
- 4 6-oz sushi-grade Yellowfin tuna steaks, each split in half horizontally
- Cooking: spray

Directions
1. In a small bowl mix fennel seeds, olive oil, mint, onion, tangerine juice, almonds, ¼ tsp pepper and ¼ tsp salt. Combine thoroughly.
2. Season fish with remaining salt and pepper.
3. On medium high fire, place a large nonstick pan and grease with cooking spray. Pan fry fish in two batches cooking each side for a minute.
4. Fish is best served with a side of salad greens or a half cup of cooked brown rice.

Nutrition: Calories per serving: 405; Protein: 27.5g; Fat: 11.9g; Carbs: 27.5

Tuna And Tomato Salad

Servings: 6 | Cooking: 10 min

Ingredients
- ½ cup white beans, canned, drained
- 4 oz tuna fillet
- 1 teaspoon fresh basil, chopped
- 1 scallion, chopped
- ½ cup cherry tomatoes, halved
- 4 Kalamata olives
- ¼ teaspoon ground black pepper
- ½ red onion, peeled, sliced
- 1 tablespoon sesame oil
- ½ tablespoon lemon juice
- ¼ tablespoon Dijon Mustard
- ½ teaspoon butter
- ½ teaspoon salt

Directions
1. Rub the tuna fillet with ground black pepper and sprinkle with lemon juice.
2. Place butter in the skillet and melt it.
3. Add tuna and cook it for 8 minutes (for 4 minutes from each side) over the medium heat.
4. After this, chill the cooked tuna well and chop.
5. In the salad bowl, combine together white beans, chopped basil, scallion, halved cherry tomatoes, sliced red onion, and salt.
6. Slice Kalamata olives and add in the salad bowl.
7. Churn together Dijon mustard and sesame oil. The salad dressing is cooked.
8. Shake the salad well and sprinkle with oil dressing.
9. Mix up the cooked salad directly before serving.

Nutrition: calories 150; fat 5.1; fiber 3.2; carbs 12.1; protein 15

Coriander Shrimps

Servings: 6 | Cooking: 5 min

Ingredients
- 1 hot chili pepper
- ¼ cup fresh coriander leaves
- ½ teaspoon ground cumin
- 2 garlic cloves, peeled
- ½ teaspoon salt
- 1 tablespoon lemon juice
- 2 tablespoons olive oil
- 2-pounds shrimps, peeled

Directions
1. Place in the blender: hot chili pepper, fresh coriander leaves, ground cumin, garlic cloves, salt, lemon juice, and olive oil. Blend the spices until you get the smooth texture of the mixture.
2. After this, place peeled shrimps in the big bowl.
3. Pour the blended spice mass over the shrimps. Mix up well.
4. Then preheat skillet well.
5. Place the shrimps and all spicy mixture in the skillet.
6. Roast the seafood for 5 minutes over the medium heat. Stir the shrimps with the help of the wooden spatula from time to time.
7. Then remove the shrimps from the heat and let them rest for 10 minutes before serving.

Nutrition: calories 223; fat 7.3; fiber 0.1; carbs 2.8; protein 34.6

Leftover Salmon Salad Power Bowls

Servings: 1 | Cooking: 10 min

Ingredients
- ½ cup raspberries
- ½ cup zucchini, sliced
- 1 lemon, juice squeezed
- 1 tablespoon balsamic glaze
- 2 sprigs of thyme, chopped
- 2 tablespoon olive oil
- 4 cups seasonal greens
- 4 ounces leftover grilled salmon
- Salt and pepper to taste

Directions
1. Heat oil in a skillet over medium flame and sauté the zucchini. Season with salt and pepper to taste.
2. In a mixing bowl, mix all ingredients together.
3. Toss to combine everything.
4. Sprinkle with nut cheese.

Nutrition: Calories: 450.3; Fat: 35.5 g; Protein: 23.4g; Carbs: 9.3 g

Roasted Pollock Fillet With Bacon And Leeks

Servings: 2 | Cooking: 30 min

Ingredients
- ¼ cup olive oil
- ½ cup white wine
- 1 ½ lbs. Pollock fillets
- 1 sprig fresh thyme
- 1 tbsp chopped fresh thyme
- 2 tbsp. olive oil
- 4 leeks, sliced

Directions
1. Grease a 9x13 baking dish and preheat oven to 400oF.
2. In baking pan add olive oil and leeks. Toss to combine.
3. Pop into the oven and roast for 10 minutes.
4. Remove from oven; add white wine and 1 tbsp chopped thyme. Return to oven and roast for another 10 minutes.
5. Remove pan from oven and add fish on top. With a spoon, spoon olive oil mixture onto fish until coated fully. Return to oven and roast for another ten minutes.
6. Remove from oven, garnish with a sprig of thyme and serve.

Nutrition: Calories: 442; Carbs: 13.6 g; Protein: 42.9 g; Fat: 24 g

Lemon Rainbow Trout

Servings: 2 | Cooking: 15 min

Ingredients
- 2 rainbow trout
- Juice of 1 lemon
- 3 tablespoons olive oil
- 4 garlic cloves, minced
- A pinch of salt and black pepper

Directions
1. Line a baking sheet with parchment paper, add the fish and the rest of the ingredients and rub.
2. Bake at 400 degrees F for 15 minutes, divide between plates and serve with a side salad.

Nutrition: calories 521; fat 29; fiber 5; carbs 14; protein 52

Salmon With Pesto

Servings: 1 Fillet | Cooking: 10 min

Ingredients
- 2 cups fresh basil
- 2 cloves garlic
- 4 TB. fresh lemon juice
- 1 tsp. salt
- 1 tsp. ground black pepper
- 3 TB. grated Parmesan cheese
- 3 TB. toasted pine nuts
- 1/4 cup plus 2 TB. extra-virgin olive oil
- 2 (6-oz.) salmon fillets
- 1/2 medium lemon

Directions
1. In a food processor fitted with a chopping blade, pulse basil, garlic, 2 tablespoons lemon juice, 1/2 teaspoon salt, and 1/2 teaspoon black pepper 15 times.
2. Add Parmesan cheese, pine nuts, and 1/4 cup extra-virgin olive oil, and pulse 15 more times. Set aside.
3. Set salmon fillets on a plate. Drizzle both sides with remaining 2 tablespoons lemon juice, and season with remaining 1/2 teaspoon salt and remaining 1/2 teaspoon black pepper.
4. In a large, nonstick skillet over medium heat, heat remaining 2 tablespoons extra-virgin olive oil. Add salmon, and cook for 5 minutes per side.

5. Place salmon on a serving plate, spoon 2 tablespoons pesto over each piece, and serve warm.

Baked Sea Bass

Servings: 4 | Cooking: 12 min

Ingredients
- 4 sea bass fillets, boneless
- Sal and black pepper to the taste
- 2 cups potato chips, crushed
- 1 tablespoon mayonnaise

Directions
1. Season the fish fillets with salt and pepper, brush with the mayonnaise and dredge each in the potato chips.
2. Arrange the fillets on a baking sheet lined with parchment paper and bake at 400 degrees F for 12 minutes.
3. Divide the fish between plates and serve with a side salad.

Nutrition: calories 228; fat 8.6; fiber 0.6; carbs 9.3; protein 25

Italian Tuna Pasta

Servings: 6 | Cooking: 5 min

Ingredients
- 15 oz whole wheat pasta
- 2 tbsp capers
- 3 oz tuna
- 2 cups can tomatoes, crushed
- 2 anchovies
- 1 tsp garlic, minced
- 1 tbsp olive oil
- Salt

Directions
1. Add oil into the inner pot of instant pot and set the pot on sauté mode.
2. Add anchovies and garlic and sauté for 1 minute.
3. Add remaining ingredients and stir well. Pour enough water into the pot to cover the pasta.
4. Seal pot with a lid and select manual and cook on low for 4 minutes.
5. Once done, release pressure using quick release. Remove lid.
6. Stir and serve.

Nutrition: Calories 339 Fat 6 g Carbohydrates 56.5 g Sugar 5.2 g Protein 15.2 g Cholesterol 10 mg

Mustard Cod

Servings: 2 | Cooking: 20 min

Ingredients
- 1 tablespoon Dijon mustard
- 2 teaspoons sunflower oil
- 1 white onion, diced
- 1/3 teaspoon minced garlic
- 2 tomatoes, chopped
- ¾ cup black olives, chopped
- 1 teaspoon capers, drained
- 1 tablespoon fresh parsley
- 10 oz cod fillets (5 oz each fish fillet)

Directions
1. Preheat sunflower oil in the skillet over the medium heat.
2. Then place the fish fillets in the hot oil and roast them for 2 minutes from each side.
3. Transfer the fish in the plate.
4. After this, add diced onion in the skillet.
5. Then add minced garlic, tomatoes, and capers. Mix up well and close the lid.
6. Cook the vegetables for 5 minutes over the medium heat.
7. Then ad roasted cod fillets and stir puttanesca well.
8. Close the lid and cook the meal for 10 minutes over the medium-low heat.
9. Transfer the cooked cod in the serving plates and top with the cooked vegetables.

Nutrition: calories 285; fat 12.2; fiber 4.7; carbs 13.9; protein 32.6

Ginger Scallion Sauce Over Seared Ahi

Servings: 4 | Cooking: 6 min

Ingredients
- 1 bunch scallions, bottoms removed, finely chopped
- 1 tbsp rice wine vinegar
- 1 tbsp. Bragg's liquid amino
- 16-oz ahi tuna steaks
- 2 tbsp. fresh ginger, peeled and grated
- 3 tbsp. coconut oil, melted
- Pepper and salt to taste

Directions
1. In a small bowl mix together vinegar, 2 tbsp. oil, soy sauce, ginger and scallions. Put aside.
2. On medium fire, place a large saucepan and heat remaining oil. Once oil is hot and starts to smoke,

sear tuna until deeply browned or for two minutes per side.
3. Place seared tuna on a serving platter and let it stand for 5 minutes before slicing into 1-inch thick strips.
4. Drizzle ginger-scallion mixture over seared tuna, serve and enjoy.

Nutrition: Calories: 247; Protein: 29g; Fat: 1g; Carbs: 8g

Creamy Scallops

Servings: 4 | Cooking: 7 min

Ingredients
- ½ cup heavy cream
- 1 teaspoon fresh rosemary
- ½ teaspoon dried cumin
- ½ teaspoon garlic, diced
- 8 oz bay scallops
- 1 teaspoon olive oil
- ½ teaspoon salt
- ¼ teaspoon chili flakes

Directions
1. Preheat olive oil in the skillet until hot.
2. Then sprinkle scallops with salt, chili flakes, and dried cumin and place in the hot oil.
3. Add fresh rosemary and diced garlic.
4. Roast the scallops for 2 minutes from each side.
5. After this, add heavy cream and bring the mixture to boil. Boil it for 1 minute.

Nutrition: calories 114; fat 7.3; fiber 0.2; carbs 2.2; protein 9.9

Fish And Rice (sayadieh)

Servings: 1 Cup | Cooking: 1½hours

Ingredients
- 1 lb. whitefish fillets (cod, tilapia, or haddock)
- 2 tsp. salt
- 2 tsp. ground black pepper
- 1/4 cup plus 2 TB. extra-virgin olive oil
- 2 large yellow onions, sliced
- 5 cups water
- 1 tsp. turmeric
- 1 tsp. ground coriander
- 1/2 tsp. ground cumin
- 1/4 tsp. ground cinnamon
- 2 cups basmati rice
- 1/2 cup sliced almonds

Directions
1. Season both sides of whitefish with 1 teaspoon salt and 1 teaspoon black pepper.
2. In a skillet over medium heat, heat 1/4 cup extra-virgin olive oil. Add fish, and cook for 3 minutes per side. Remove fish from the pan.
3. Add yellow onions to the skillet, reduce heat to medium-low, and cook for 15 minutes or until golden brown and caramelized.
4. In a 3-quart pot over medium heat, add 1/2 of cooked onions, water, turmeric, coriander, cumin, cinnamon, remaining 1 teaspoon salt, and remaining 1 teaspoon black pepper. Simmer for 20 minutes.
5. Add basmati rice, cover, and cook for 30 minutes.
6. Cut fish into 1/2-inch pieces, fluff rice, and gently fold fish into rice. Cover and cook for 10 more minutes.
7. Remove from heat, and let sit for 10 minutes before serving.
8. Meanwhile, in a small saucepan over low heat, heat remaining 2 tablespoons extra-virgin olive oil. Add almonds, and toast for 3 minutes.
9. Spoon fish and rice onto a serving plate, top with remaining onions and toasted almonds, and serve.

Creamy Bacon-fish Chowder

Servings: 8 | Cooking: 30 min

Ingredients
- 1 1/2 lbs. cod
- 1 1/2 tsp dried thyme
- 1 large onion, chopped
- 1 medium carrot, coarsely chopped
- 1 tbsp butter, cut into small pieces
- 1 tsp salt, divided
- 3 1/2 cups baking potato, peeled and cubed
- 3 slices uncooked bacon
- 3/4 tsp freshly ground black pepper, divided
- 4 1/2 cups water
- 4 bay leaves
- 4 cups 2% reduced-fat milk

Directions
1. In a large skillet, add the water and bay leaves and let it simmer. Add the fish. Cover and let it simmer some more until the flesh flakes easily with fork. Remove the fish from the skillet and cut into large pieces. Set aside the cooking liquid.
2. Place Dutch oven in medium heat and cook the bacon until crisp. Remove the bacon and reserve

the bacon drippings. Crush the bacon and set aside.
3. Stir potato, onion and carrot in the pan with the bacon drippings, cook over medium heat for 10 minutes. Add the cooking liquid, bay leaves, 1/2 tsp salt, 1/4 tsp pepper and thyme, let it boil. Lower the heat and let simmer for 10 minutes. Add the milk and butter, simmer until the potatoes becomes tender, but do not boil. Add the fish, 1/2 tsp salt, 1/2 tsp pepper. Remove the bay leaves.
4. Serve sprinkled with the crushed bacon.

Nutrition: Calories per serving: 400; Carbs: 34.5g; Protein: 20.8g; Fat: 19.7g

Healthy Poached Trout

Servings: 2 | Cooking: 10 min

Ingredients
- 1 8-oz boneless, skin on trout fillet
- 2 cups chicken broth or water
- 2 leeks, halved
- 6-8 slices lemon
- salt and pepper to taste

Directions
1. On medium fire, place a large nonstick skillet and arrange leeks and lemons on pan in a layer. Cover with soup stock or water and bring to a simmer.
2. Meanwhile, season trout on both sides with pepper and salt. Place trout on simmering pan of water. Cover and cook until trout is flaky, around 8 minutes.
3. In a serving platter, spoon leek and lemons on bottom of plate, top with trout and spoon sauce into plate. Serve and enjoy.

Nutrition: Calories per serving: 360.2; Protein: 13.8g; Fat: 7.5g; Carbs: 51.5g

Creamy Curry Salmon

Servings: 2 | Cooking: 20 min

Ingredients
- 2 salmon fillets, boneless and cubed
- 1 tablespoon olive oil
- 1 tablespoon basil, chopped
- Sea salt and black pepper to the taste
- 1 cup Greek yogurt
- 2 teaspoons curry powder
- 1 garlic clove, minced
- ½ teaspoon mint, chopped

Directions
1. Heat up a pan with the oil over medium-high heat, add the salmon and cook for 3 minutes.
2. Add the rest of the ingredients, toss, cook for 15 minutes more, divide between plates and serve.

Nutrition: calories 284; fat 14.1; fiber 8.5; carbs 26.7; protein 31.4

Cod And Cabbage

Servings: 4 | Cooking: 15 min

Ingredients
- 3 cups green cabbage, shredded
- 1 sweet onion, sliced
- A pinch of salt and black pepper
- ½ cup feta cheese, crumbled
- 4 teaspoons olive oil
- 4 cod fillets, boneless
- ¼ cup green olives, pitted and chopped

Directions
1. Grease a roasting pan with the oil, add the fish, the cabbage and the rest of the ingredients, introduce in the pan and cook at 450 degrees F for 15 minutes.
2. Divide the mix between plates and serve.

Nutrition: calories 270; fat 10; fiber 3; carbs 12; protein 31

Pecan Salmon Fillets

Servings: 6 | Cooking: 15 min

Ingredients
- 3 tablespoons olive oil
- 3 tablespoons mustard
- 5 teaspoons honey
- 1 cup pecans, chopped
- 6 salmon fillets, boneless
- 1 tablespoon lemon juice
- 3 teaspoons parsley, chopped
- Salt and pepper to the taste

Directions
1. In a bowl, mix the oil with the mustard and honey and whisk well.
2. Put the pecans and the parsley in another bowl.
3. Season the salmon fillets with salt and pepper, arrange them on a baking sheet lined with parchment paper, brush with the honey and mustard mix and top with the pecans mix.

4. Introduce in the oven at 400 degrees F, bake for 15 minutes, divide between plates, drizzle the lemon juice on top and serve.

Nutrition: calories 282; fat 15.5; fiber 8.5; carbs 20.9; protein 16.8

Shrimp And Mushrooms Mix

Servings: 4 | Cooking: 12 min

Ingredients
- 1 pound shrimp, peeled and deveined
- 2 green onions, sliced
- ½ pound white mushrooms, sliced
- 2 tablespoons balsamic vinegar
- 2 tablespoons sesame seeds, toasted
- 2 teaspoons ginger, minced
- 2 teaspoons garlic, minced
- 3 tablespoons olive oil
- 2 tablespoons dill, chopped

Directions
1. Heat up a pan with the oil over medium-high heat, add the green onions and the garlic and sauté for 2 minutes.
2. Add the rest of the ingredients except the shrimp and cook for 6 minutes more.
3. Add the shrimp, cook for 4 minutes, divide everything between plates and serve.

Nutrition: calories 245; fat 8.5; fiber 45.8; carbs 11.8; protein 17.7

Leeks And Calamari Mix

Servings: 6 | Cooking: 15 min

Ingredients
- 2 tablespoon avocado oil
- 2 leeks, chopped
- 1 red onion, chopped
- Salt and black to the taste
- 1 pound calamari rings
- 1 tablespoon parsley, chopped
- 1 tablespoon chives, chopped
- 2 tablespoons tomato paste

Directions
1. Heat up a pan with the avocado oil over medium heat, add the leeks and the onion, stir and sauté for 5 minutes.
2. Add the rest of the ingredients, toss, simmer over medium heat for 10 minutes, divide into bowls and serve.

Nutrition: calories 238; fat 9; fiber 5.6; carbs 14.4; protein 8.4

Cod With Lentils

Servings: 4 | Cooking: 30 min

Ingredients
- 1 red pepper, chopped
- 1 yellow onion, diced
- 1 teaspoon ground black pepper
- 1 teaspoon butter
- 1 jalapeno pepper, chopped
- ½ cup lentils
- 3 cups chicken stock
- 1 teaspoon salt
- 1 tablespoon tomato paste
- 1 teaspoon chili pepper
- 3 tablespoons fresh cilantro, chopped
- 8 oz cod, chopped

Directions
1. Place butter, red pepper, onion, and ground black pepper in the saucepan.
2. Roast the vegetables for 5 minutes over the medium heat.
3. Then add chopped jalapeno pepper, lentils, and chili pepper.
4. Mix up the mixture well and add chicken stock and tomato paste.
5. Stir until homogenous. Add cod.
6. Close the lid and cook chili for 20 minutes over the medium heat.

Nutrition: calories 187; fat 2.3; fiber 8.8; carbs 21.3; protein 20.6

Honey Garlic Shrimp

Servings: 4 | Cooking: 5 min

Ingredients
- 1 lb shrimp, peeled and deveined
- 1/4 cup honey
- 1 tbsp garlic, minced
- 1 tbsp ginger, minced
- 1 tbsp olive oil
- 1/4 cup fish stock
- Pepper
- Salt

Directions
1. Add shrimp into the large bowl. Add remaining ingredients over shrimp and toss well.
2. Transfer shrimp into the instant pot and stir well.
3. Seal pot with lid and cook on high for 5 minutes.
4. Once done, release pressure using quick release. Remove lid.
5. Serve and enjoy.

Nutrition: Calories 240 Fat 5.6 g Carbohydrates 20.9 g Sugar 17.5 g Protein 26.5 g Cholesterol 239 mg

Pepper Salmon Skewers

Servings: 5 | Cooking: 15 min

Ingredients
- 1.5-pound salmon fillet
- ½ cup Plain yogurt
- 1 teaspoon paprika
- 1 teaspoon turmeric
- 1 teaspoon red pepper
- 1 teaspoon salt
- 1 teaspoon dried cilantro
- 1 teaspoon sunflower oil
- ½ teaspoon ground nutmeg

Directions
1. For the marinade: mix up together Plain yogurt, paprika, turmeric red pepper, salt, and ground nutmeg.
2. Chop the salmon fillet roughly and put it in the yogurt mixture.
3. Mix up well and marinate for 25 minutes.
4. Then skew the fish on the skewers.
5. Sprinkle the skewers with sunflower oil and place in the tray.
6. Bake the salmon skewers for 15 minutes at 375F.

Nutrition: calories 217; fat 9.9; fiber 0.6; carbs 4.2; protein 28.1

Marinated Tuna Steak

Preparation time: 6 min | Cooking time: 18 min | Servings: 4

Ingredients
- Olive oil (2 tbsp.)
- Orange juice (.25 cup)
- Soy sauce (.25 cup)
- Lemon juice (1 tbsp.)
- Fresh parsley (2 tbsp.)
- Garlic clove (1)
- Ground black pepper (.5 tsp.)
- Fresh oregano (.5 tsp.)
- Tuna steaks (4 - 4 oz. Steaks)

Directions
1. Mince the garlic and chop the oregano and parsley.
2. In a glass container, mix the pepper, oregano, garlic, parsley, lemon juice, soy sauce, olive oil, and orange juice.
3. Warm the grill using the high heat setting. Grease the grate with oil.
4. Add to tuna steaks and cook for five to six min. Turn and baste with the marinated sauce.
5. Cook another five min or until it's the way you like it. Discard the remaining marinade.

Nutrition: Calories: 200; Protein: 27.4g; Fat: 7.9g

Garlic and Shrimp Pasta

Preparation: 4 min | Cooking: 16 min | Servings: 4

Ingredients
- 6 ounces whole wheat spaghetti
- 12 ounces raw shrimp, peeled and deveined, cut into 1-inch pieces
- 1 bunch asparagus, trimmed
- 1 large bell pepper, thinly sliced
- 1 cup fresh peas
- 3 garlic cloves, chopped
- 1 and ¼ teaspoons kosher salt
- ½ and ½ cups non-fat plain yogurt
- 3 tablespoon lemon juice
- 1 tablespoon extra-virgin olive oil
- ½ teaspoon fresh ground black pepper
- ¼ cup pine nuts, toasted

Directions
1. Take a large sized pot and bring water to a boil
2. Add your spaghetti and cook them for about min less than the directed package instruction
3. Add shrimp, bell pepper, asparagus and cook for about 2- 4 min until the shrimp are tender
4. Drain the pasta and the contents well
5. Take a large bowl and mash garlic until a paste form
6. Whisk in yogurt, parsley, oil, pepper and lemon juice into the garlic paste
7. Add pasta mix and toss well
8. Serve by sprinkling some pine nuts!

Nutrition: Calories: 406; Fat: 22g; Protein: 26g

Paprika Butter Shrimps

Preparation: 6 min | Cooking: 31 min | Servings: 2

Ingredients
- ¼ tablespoon smoked paprika
- 1/8 cup sour cream
- ½ pound tiger shrimps
- 1/8 cup butter
- Salt and black pepper, to taste

Directions
1. Prep the oven to 390F and grease a baking dish.
2. Mix together all the ingredients in a large bowl and transfer into the baking dish.
3. Situate in the oven and bake for about 15 min.
4. Place paprika shrimp in a dish and set aside to cool for meal prepping. Divide it in 2 containers and cover the lid. Refrigerate for 1-2 days and reheat in microwave before serving.

Nutrition: Calories: 330; Protein: 32.6g; Fat: 21.5g

Nicoise-inspired Salad with Sardines

Preparation: 9 min | Cooking: 16 min | Servings: 4

Ingredients
- 4 eggs
- 12 ounces baby red potatoes (about 12 potatoes)
- 6 ounces green beans, halved
- 4 cups baby spinach leaves or mixed greens
- 1 bunch radishes, quartered (about 1 1/3 cups)
- 1 cup cherry tomatoes
- 20 Kalamata or Nicoise olives (about 1/3 cup)
- 3 (3.75-ounce) cans skinless, boneless sardines packed in olive oil, drained
- 8 tablespoons Dijon Red Wine Vinaigrette

Directions
1. Situate the eggs in a saucepan and cover with water. Bring the water to a boil. Once the water starts to boil, close then turn the heat off. Set a timer for min.
2. Once the timer goes off, strain the hot water and run cold water over the eggs to cool. Peel the eggs when cool and cut in half.
3. Poke each potato a few times using fork. Place them on a microwave-safe plate and microwave on high for 4 to 5 min, until the potatoes are tender. Let cool and cut in half.
4. Place green beans on a microwave-safe plate and microwave on high for 1½ to 2 min, until the beans are crisp-tender. Cool.
5. Place 1 egg, ½ cup of green beans, 6 potato halves, 1 cup of spinach, 1/3 cup of radishes, ¼ cup of tomatoes, olives, and 3 sardines in each of 4 containers. Pour 2 tablespoons of vinaigrette into each of 4 sauce containers.

Nutrition: Calories: 450; Fat: 32g; Protein: 21g

Mediterranean Avocado Salmon Salad

Preparation: 6 min | Cooking: 10 min | Servings: 4

Ingredients
- 1 lb. skinless salmon fillets

Marinade/Dressing:
- 3 tbsp. olive oil
- 2 tbsp. lemon juice fresh, squeezed
- 1 tbsp. red wine vinegar, optional
- 1 tbsp. fresh chopped parsley
- 2 tsp garlic minced
- 1 tsp dried oregano
- 1 tsp salt
- Cracked pepper, to taste

Salad:
- 4 cups Romaine (or Cos) lettuce leaves
- 1 large cucumber
- 2 Roma tomatoes
- 1 red onion
- 1 avocado
- 1/2 cup feta cheese
- 1/3 cup pitted Kalamata olives

Directions
1. Scourge the olive oil, lemon juice, red wine vinegar, chopped parsley, garlic minced, oregano, salt and pepper
2. Fill out half of the marinade into a large, shallow dish, refrigerate the remaining marinade to use as the dressing
3. Coat the salmon in the rest of the marinade
4. Place a skillet pan or grill over medium-high, add 1 tbsp oil and sear salmon on both sides until crispy and cooked through
5. Allow the salmon to cool
6. Distribute the salmon among the containers, store in the fridge for 2-3 days
7. To Serve: Prep the salad by putting the romaine lettuce, cucumber, roma tomatoes, red onion, avocado, feta cheese, and olives in a bowl. Reheat the salmon in the microwave for 30seconds to 1 minute or until heated through.
8. Slice the salmon and arrange over salad. Drizzle the salad with the remaining untouched dressing, serve with lemon wedges.

Nutrition: Calories:411; Fat: 27g; Protein: 28g

Moroccan Fish

Preparation: 9 min | Cooking: 76 min | Servings: 12

Ingredients
- Garbanzo beans (15 oz. Can)
- Red bell peppers (2)
- Large carrot (1)
- Vegetable oil (1 tbsp.)
- Onion (1)
- Garlic (1 clove)
- Tomatoes (3 chopped/14.5 oz can)
- Olives (4 chopped)
- Chopped fresh parsley (.25 cup)
- Ground cumin (.25 cup)
- Paprika (3 tbsp.)
- Chicken bouillon granules (2 tbsp.)
- Cayenne pepper (1 tsp.)
- Salt (to your liking)
- Tilapia fillets (5 lb.)

Directions
1. Drain and rinse the beans. Thinly slice the carrot and onion. Mince the garlic and chop the olives. Throw away the seeds from the peppers and slice them into strips.
2. Warm the oil in a frying pan using the medium temperature setting. Toss in the onion and garlic. Simmer them for approximately five min.
3. Fold in the bell peppers, beans, tomatoes, carrots, and olives.
4. Continue sautéing them for about five additional min.
5. Sprinkle the veggies with the cumin, parsley, salt, chicken bouillon, paprika, and cayenne.
6. Stir thoroughly and place the fish on top of the veggies.
7. Pour in water to cover the veggies.
8. Lower the heat setting and cover the pan to slowly cook until the fish is flaky (about 40 min.

Nutrition: Calories: 268; Protein: 42g; Fat: 5g

Broiled Chili Calamari

Preparation: 9 min | Cooking: 8 min | Servings: 4

Ingredients
- 2 tablespoons extra virgin olive oil
- 1 teaspoon chili powder
- ½ teaspoon ground cumin
- Zest of 1 lime
- Juice of 1 lime
- Dash of sea salt
- 1 and ½ pounds squid, cleaned and split open, with tentacles cut into ½ inch rounds
- 2 tablespoons cilantro, chopped
- 2 tablespoons red bell pepper, minced

Directions
1. Take a medium bowl and stir in olive oil, chili powder, cumin, lime zest, sea salt, lime juice and pepper
2. Add squid and let it marinade and stir to coat, coat and let it refrigerate for 1 h
3. Pre-heat your oven to broil
4. Arrange squid on a baking sheet, broil for 8 min turn once until tender
5. Garnish the broiled calamari with cilantro and red bell pepper
6. Serve and enjoy!

Nutrition: Calories: 159; Fat: 13g; Protein: 3g

Salmon with Corn Pepper Salsa

Preparation: 9 min | Cooking: 12 min | Servings: 2

Ingredients
- 1 garlic clove, grated
- ½ teaspoon mild chili powder
- ½ teaspoon ground coriander
- ¼ teaspoon ground cumin
- 2 limes – 1, zest and juice; 1 cut into wedges
- 2 teaspoons rapeseed oil
- 2 wild salmon fillets
- 1 ear of corn on the cob
- 1 red onion, finely chopped
- 1 avocado, cored, peeled, and finely chopped
- 1 red pepper, deseeded and finely chopped
- 1 red chili, halved and deseeded
- ½ a pack of finely chopped coriander

Directions
1. Boil the corn in water for about 6-8 min until tender.
2. Drain and cut off the kernels.
3. In a bowl, combine garlic, spices, 1 tablespoon of lime juice, and oil; mix well to prepare spice rub.
4. Coat the salmon with the rub.
5. Add the zest to the corn and give it a gentle stir.
6. Heat a frying pan over medium heat.
7. Cook salmon for 4 min on both sides.
8. Serve the cooked salmon with salsa and lime wedges.
9. Enjoy!

Nutrition: Calories: 949; Fat: 57.4g; Protein: 76.8g

Seafood Paella

Preparation: 9 min | Cooking: 41 min | Servings: 4

Ingredients
- 4 small lobster tails (6-12 oz. each)
- 3 tbsp. Extra Virgin Olive Oil
- 1 large yellow onion
- 2 cups Spanish rice
- 4 garlic cloves
- 2 large pinches of Spanish saffron threads
- 1 tsp. Sweet Spanish paprika
- 1 tsp. cayenne pepper
- 1/2 tsp. Aleppo pepper flakes
- 2 large Roma tomatoes
- 6 oz. French green beans
- 1 lb. prawns or large shrimp
- 1/4 cup chopped fresh parsley

Directions
1. Using big pot, add 3 cups of water and bring it to a rolling boil
2. Add in the lobster tails and allow boil briefly, about 1-min or until pink, remove from heat
3. Using tongs situate the lobster tails to a plate and Do not discard the lobster cooking water
4. Allow the lobster is cool, then remove the shell and cut into large chunks.
5. Using a deep pan or skillet over medium-high heat, add 3 tbsp olive oil
6. Add the chopped onions, sauté the onions for 2 min and then add the rice, and cook for 3 more min, stirring regularly
7. Then add in the lobster cooking water and the chopped garlic and, stir in the saffron and its soaking liquid, cayenne pepper, Aleppo pepper, paprika, and salt
8. Gently stir in the chopped tomatoes and green beans, bring to a boil and allow it to slightly reduce, then cover and cook over low heat for 20 min
9. Once done, uncover and spread the shrimp over the rice, push it into the rice slightly, add in a little water, if needed
10. Close and cook for 18 min
11. Then add in the cooked lobster chunks
12. Once the lobster is warmed through, remove from heat allow the dish to cool completely
13. Distribute among the containers, store for 2 days
14. To Serve: Reheat in the microwave for 1-2 min or until heated through. Garnish with parsley and enjoy!

Nutrition: Calories: 536; Fat: 26g; Protein: 50g

Mediterranean Pearl Couscous

Preparation: 4 min | Cooking: 10 min | Servings: 6

Ingredients
For the Lemon Dill Vinaigrette:
- 1 large lemon, juice of
- 1/3 cup Extra virgin olive oil
- 1 tsp dill weed
- 1 tsp garlic powder
- Salt and pepper

For the Israeli Couscous:
- 2 cups Pearl Couscous, Israeli Couscous
- Extra virgin olive oil
- 2 cups grape tomatoes, halved
- 1/3 cup finely chopped red onions
- 1/2 English cucumber
- 15 oz. can chickpeas
- 14 oz. can good quality artichoke hearts
- 1/2 cup Kalamata olives
- 15–20 fresh basil leaves
- 3 oz. fresh baby mozzarella or feta cheese

Directions
1. Make the lemon-dill vinaigrette, scourge lemon juice, olive oil, dill weed, garlic powder, salt and pepper then keep aside
2. In a medium-sized heavy pot, heat two tbsp. of olive oil
3. Sauté the couscous in the olive oil briefly until golden brown, then add cups of boiling water (or follow the instructed on the package), and cook according to package.
4. Once done, drain in a colander, set aside in a bowl and allow to cool
5. In a large mixing bowl, combine the extra virgin olive oil, grape tomatoes, red onions, cucumber, chickpeas, artichoke hearts, and Kalamata olives
6. Then add in the couscous and the basil, mix together gently
7. Now, give the lemon-dill vinaigrette a quick whisk and add to the couscous salad, mix to combine
8. Taste and adjust salt, if needed
9. Distribute among the containers, store for 2-3 days
10. To Serve: Add in the mozzarella cheese, garnish with more fresh basil and enjoy!

Nutrition: Calories: 393; Fat: 13g; Protein: 13g

Potato and Tuna Salad

Preparation: 18 min | Cooking: 0 min | Servings: 4

Ingredients
- 1-pound baby potatoes, scrubbed, boiled
- 1 cup tuna chunks, drained
- 1 cup cherry tomatoes, halved
- 1 cup medium onion, thinly sliced
- 8 pitted black olives
- 2 medium hard-boiled eggs, sliced
- 1 head Romaine lettuce
- Honey lemon mustard dressing
- ¼ cup olive oil
- 2 tablespoons lemon juice
- 1 tablespoon Dijon mustard
- 1 teaspoon dill weed, chopped
- Salt as needed
- Pepper as needed

Directions
1. Take a small glass bowl and mix in your olive oil, honey, lemon juice, Dijon mustard and dill
2. Season the mix with pepper and salt
3. Add in the tuna, baby potatoes, cherry tomatoes, red onion, green beans, black olives and toss everything nicely
4. Arrange your lettuce leaves on a beautiful serving dish to make the base of your salad
5. Top them up with your salad mixture and place the egg slices
6. Drizzle it with the previously prepared Salad Dressing
7. Serve

Nutrition: Calories: 406; Fat: 22g; Protein: 26g

Tuna with Vegetable Mix

Preparation: 8 min | Cooking: 16 min | Servings: 4

Ingredients
- ¼ cup extra-virgin olive oil, divided
- 1 tablespoon rice vinegar
- 1 teaspoon kosher salt, divided
- ¾ teaspoon Dijon mustard
- ¾ teaspoon honey
- 4 ounces baby gold beets, thinly sliced
- 4 ounces fennel bulb, trimmed and thinly sliced
- 4 ounces baby turnips, thinly sliced
- 6 ounces Granny Smith apple, very thinly sliced
- 2 teaspoons sesame seeds, toasted
- 6 ounces tuna steaks
- ½ teaspoon black pepper
- 1 tablespoon fennel fronds, torn

Directions
1. Scourge 2 tablespoons of oil, ½ a teaspoon of salt, honey, vinegar, and mustard.
2. Give the mixture a nice mix.
3. Add fennel, beets, apple, and turnips; mix and toss until everything is evenly coated.
4. Sprinkle with sesame seeds and toss well.
5. Using cast-iron skillet, heat 2 tablespoons of oil over high heat.
6. Carefully season the tuna with ½ a teaspoon of salt and pepper
7. Situate the tuna in the skillet and cook for 4 min, giving 1½ min per side.
8. Remove the tuna and slice it up.
9. Place in containers with the vegetable mix.
10. Serve with the fennel mix, and enjoy!

Nutrition: Calories: 443; Fat: 17.1g; Protein: 16.5g

Tuna Bowl with Kale

Preparation: 4 min | Cooking: 18 min | Servings: 6

Ingredients
- 3 tablespoons extra virgin olive oil
- 1 ½ teaspoons minced garlic
- ¼ cup of capers
- 2 teaspoons sugar
- 15 ounce can of drained and rinsed great northern beans
- 1-pound chopped kale with the center ribs removed
- ½ teaspoon ground black pepper
- 1 cup chopped onion
- 2 ½ ounces of drained sliced olives
- ¼ teaspoon sea salt
- ¼ teaspoon crushed red pepper
- 6 ounces of tuna in olive oil, do not drain

Directions
1. Place a large pot, like a stockpot, on your stove and turn the burner to high heat.
2. Fill the pot about 3-quarters of the way full with water and let it come to a boil.
3. Cook the kale for 2 min.
4. Drain the kale and set it aside.
5. Set the heat to medium and place the empty pot back on the burner.
6. Add the oil and onion. Sauté for 3 to 4 min.
7. Combine the garlic into the oil mixture and sauté for another minute.
8. Add the capers, olives, and red pepper.
9. Cook the ingredients for another minute while stirring.
10. Pour in the sugar and stir while you toss in the kale. Mix all the ingredients thoroughly and ensure the kale is thoroughly coated.

11. Cover the pot and set the timer for 8 min.
12. Put off the heat and stir in the tuna, pepper, beans, salt, and any other herbs that will make this one of the best Mediterranean dishes you've ever made.

Nutrition: Calories: 265, Fats: 12g; Protein: 16g

Greek Baked Cod

Preparation: 9 min | Cooking: 13 min | Servings: 4

Ingredients
- 1 ½ lb. Cod fillet pieces (4–6 pieces)
- 5 garlic cloves, peeled and minced
- 1/4 cup chopped fresh parsley leaves

Lemon Juice Mixture:
- 5 tbsp. fresh lemon juice
- 5 tbsp. extra virgin olive oil
- 2 tbsp. melted vegan butter

For Coating:
- 1/3 cup all-purpose flour
- 1 tsp ground coriander
- 3/4 tsp sweet Spanish paprika
- 3/4 tsp ground cumin
- 3/4 tsp salt
- 1/2 tsp black pepper

Directions
1. Preheat oven to 400F
2. Scourge lemon juice, olive oil, and melted butter, set aside
3. In another shallow bowl, mix all-purpose flour, spices, salt and pepper, set next to the lemon bowl to create a station
4. Pat the fish fillet dry, then dip the fish in the lemon juice mixture then dip it in the flour mixture, brush off extra flour
5. In a cast iron skillet over medium-high heat, add 2 tbsp olive oil
6. Once heated, add in the fish and sear on each side for color, but do not thoroughly cook, remove from heat
7. With the remaining lemon juice mixture, add the minced garlic and mix
8. Drizzle all over the fish fillets
9. Bake for 10 min, for until the it begins to flake easily with a fork
10. Allow the dish to cool completely
11. Distribute among the containers, store for 2-3 days
12. To Serve: Reheat in the microwave for 1-2 min or until heated through. Sprinkle chopped parsley. Enjoy!

Nutrition: Calories: 321; Fat: 18g; Protein: 23g

Pistachio Sole Fish

Preparation: 4 min | Cooking: 11 min | Servings: 4

Ingredients
- 4 (5 ounces boneless sole fillets
- Salt and pepper as needed
- ½ cup pistachios, finely chopped
- Zest of 1 lemon
- Juice of 1 lemon
- 1 teaspoon extra virgin olive oil

Directions
1. Pre-heat your oven to 350 degrees Fahrenheit
2. Prep a baking sheet using parchment paper then keep side
3. Pat fish dry with kitchen towels and lightly season with salt and pepper
4. Take a small bowl and stir in pistachios and lemon zest
5. Place sol on the prepped sheet and press 2 tablespoons of pistachio mixture on top of each fillet
6. Rub fish with lemon juice and olive oil
7. Bake for 10 min until the top is golden and fish flakes with a fork
8. Serve and enjoy!
9. Meal Prep/Storage Options: Store in airtight containers in your fridge for 1-2 days.

Nutrition: Calories: 166; Fat: 6g; Protein: 26g

Baked Tilapia

Preparation: 9 min | Cooking: 16 min | Servings: 4

Ingredients
- 1 lb. tilapia fillets (about 8 fillets)
- 1 tsp olive oil
- 1 tbsp. vegan butter
- 2 shallots finely chopped
- 3 garlic cloves minced
- 1 1/2 tsp ground cumin
- 1 1/2 tsp paprika
- 1/4 cup capers
- 1/4 cup fresh dill finely chopped
- Juice from 1 lemon
- Salt & Pepper to taste

Directions
1. Preheat oven to 375F

2. Prep a rimmed baking sheet using parchment paper or foil
3. Lightly mist with cooking spray, arrange the fish fillets evenly on baking sheet
4. Mix the cumin, paprika, salt and pepper
5. Rub the fish fillets with the spice mixture
6. Scourge the melted butter, lemon juice, shallots, olive oil, and garlic, and brush evenly over fish fillets
7. Top with the capers
8. Bake for 13 min
9. Pull out from oven and allow the dish to cool completely
10. Distribute among the containers, store for 2-3 days
11. To Serve: Reheat in the microwave for 1-2 min or until heated through. Top with fresh dill. Serve!

Nutrition: Calories: 410; Fat: 5g; Protein: 21g

Mediterranean Salmon

Preparation: 9 min | Cooking: 16 min | Servings: 4

Ingredients
- ½ cup of olive oil
- ¼ cup balsamic vinegar
- 4 garlic cloves, pressed
- 4 pieces salmon fillets
- 1 tablespoon fresh cilantro, chopped
- 1 tablespoon fresh basil, chopped
- 1½ teaspoons garlic salt

Directions
1. Combine olive oil and balsamic vinegar.
2. Add salmon fillets to a shallow baking dish.
3. Rub the garlic onto the fillets.
4. Pour vinegar and oil all over, making sure to turn them once to coat them.
5. Season with cilantro, garlic salt, and basil.
6. Keep aside and marinate for 13 min.
7. Preheat the broiler to your oven.
8. Place the baking dish with the salmon about 6 inches from the heat source.
9. Broil for 15 min until both sides are evenly browned and can be flaked with a fork.
10. Make sure to keep brushing with sauce from the pan.
11. Enjoy!

Nutrition: Calories: 459; Fat: 36.2g; Protein: 34.8g

A Great Mediterranean Snapper

Preparation: 11 min | Cooking: 19 min | Servings: 2

Ingredients
- 2 tablespoons extra virgin olive oil
- 1 medium onion, chopped
- 2 garlic cloves, minced
- 1 teaspoon oregano
- 1 can (14 ounces tomatoes, diced with juice
- ½ cup black olives, sliced
- 4 red snapper fillets (each 4 ounces
- Salt and pepper as needed
- Garnish
- ¼ cup feta cheese, crumbled
- ¼ cup parsley, minced

Directions
1. Pre-heat your oven to a temperature of 425-degree Fahrenheit
2. Take a 13x9 inch baking dish and grease it up with non-stick cooking spray
3. Take a large sized skillet and place it over medium heat
4. Add oil and heat it up
5. Add onion, oregano and garlic
6. Sauté for 2 min
7. Add diced tomatoes with juice alongside black olives
8. Bring the mix to a boil
9. Remove the heat
10. Place the fish on the prepped baking dish
11. Season both sides with salt and pepper
12. Spoon the tomato mix over the fish
13. Bake for 10 min
14. Remove the oven and sprinkle a bit of parsley and feta
15. Enjoy!

Nutrition: Calories: 269; Fat: 13g; Protein: 27g

Mediterranean Snapper

Preparation: 9 min | Cooking: 13 min | Servings: 4

Ingredients
- non-stick cooking spray
- 2 tablespoons extra virgin olive oil
- 1 medium onion, chopped
- 2 garlic cloves, minced
- 1 teaspoon oregano
- 1 14-ounce can dice tomatoes
- ½ cup black olives, sliced
- 4 4-ounce red snapper fillets
- Salt

- Pepper
- ¼ cup crumbled feta cheese
- ¼ cup fresh parsley, minced

Directions
1. Preheat oven to 425 degrees Fahrenheit.
2. Brush a 13x9 baking dish with non-stick cooking spray.
3. Cook oil in a large skillet over medium heat.
4. Sauté onion, oregano, garlic for 2 min.
5. Add can of tomatoes and olives, and bring mixture to a boil; remove from heat.
6. Season both sides of fillets with salt and pepper and place in the baking dish.
7. Ladle the tomato mixture evenly over the fish.
8. Bake for 11 min.
9. Pull out from oven and sprinkle with parsley and feta.
10. Enjoy!

Nutrition: Calories: 257; Fat: 9g; Protein: 31.3 g

Heartthrob Mediterranean Tilapia

Preparation: 8 min | Cooking: 16 min | Servings: 4

Ingredients
- 3 tbsp. Sun-dried tomatoes, packed in oil
- 1 tbsp. capers
- 2 tilapia fillets
- 1 tbsp. oil from sun-dried tomatoes
- 1 tbsp. lemon juice
- 2 tbsp. Kalamata olives, chopped and pitted

Directions
1. Pre-heat your oven to 372-degree Fahrenheit.
2. Take a small sized bowl and add sun-dried tomatoes, olives, capers and stir well
3. Keep the mixture on the side
4. Take a baking sheet and transfer the tilapia fillets and arrange them side by side
5. Drizzle olive oil all over them
6. Drizzle lemon juice
7. Bake in your oven for 10-15 min
8. After 10 min, check the fish for a "Flaky" texture
9. Once appropriately cooked, top the fish with tomato mix and serve!

Nutrition: Calories: 183; Fat: 8g; Protein: 18.3g

Spiced Swordfish

Preparation: 10 min | Cooking: 15 min | Servings: 4

Ingredients
- 4 (7 ounces each) swordfish steaks
- 1/2 teaspoon ground black pepper
- 12 cloves of garlic, peeled
- 3/4 teaspoon salt
- 1 1/2 teaspoon ground cumin
- 1 teaspoon paprika
- 1 teaspoon coriander
- 3 tablespoons lemon juice
- 1/3 cup olive oil

Directions
1. Take a blender or food processor, open the lid and add all the ingredients except for swordfish.
2. Close the lid and blend to make a smooth mixture.
3. Pat dry fish steaks.
4. Coat evenly with the prepared spice mixture.
5. Add them over an aluminum foil, cover and refrigerator for 1 h.
6. Preheat a griddle pan over high heat, pour oil and heat it.
7. Add fish steaks.
8. Stir-cook for 5-6 min per side until cooked through and evenly browned.
9. Serve warm.

Anchovy Pasta Mania

Preparation: 10 min | Cooking: 20 min | Servings: 4

Ingredients
- 4 anchovy fillets, packed in olive oil
- ½ pound broccoli, cut into 1-inch florets
- 2 cloves garlic, sliced
- 1-pound whole-wheat penne
- 2 tablespoons olive oil
- ¼ cup Parmesan cheese, grated
- Salt and black pepper, to taste
- Red pepper flakes, to taste

Directions
1. Cook pasta as directed over pack. Drain and set aside.
2. Take a medium saucepan or skillet, add oil.
3. Heat over medium heat.
4. Add anchovies, broccoli, and garlic, and stir-cook until veggies turn tender for 4-5 min.
5. Take off heat and mix in the pasta.
6. Serve warm with Parmesan cheese, red pepper flakes, salt, and black pepper sprinkled on top.

Tuna Nutty Salad

Preparation: 10 min | Cooking: 0 min | Servings: 4

Ingredients
- 1 tablespoon tarragon
- 1 stalk celery
- 1 medium shallot
- 3 tablespoons chives
- 1 (5-oz.) can tuna (covered in olive oil)
- 1 tsp. Dijon mustard
- 2-3 tbsp. mayonnaise
- 1/4 tsp. salt
- 1/8 tsp. pepper
- 1/4 cup pine nuts

Directions
1. Incorporate tuna, shallot, chives, tarragon, and celery.
2. Scourge mayonnaise, mustard, salt, and black pepper.
3. Pour in mayonnaise mixture to salad bowl.
4. Toss well to combine.
5. Add pine nuts and toss again.
6. Serve fresh.

Creamy Shrimp Soup

Preparation: 10 min | Cooking: 35 min | Servings: 6

Ingredients
- 1-pound medium shrimp
- 1 leek, both whites and light green parts, sliced
- 1 medium fennel bulb, chopped
- 2 tablespoons olive oil
- 3 stalks celery, chopped
- 1 clove garlic, minced
- Sea salt and ground pepper to taste
- 4 cups vegetable or chicken broth
- 1 tablespoon fennel seeds
- 2 tablespoons light cream
- Juice of 1 lemon

Directions
1. Take a medium-large cooking pot or Dutch oven, heat oil over medium heat.
2. Add celery, leek, and fennel and stir-cook for about 15 min, until vegetables are softened and browned.
3. Add garlic and season with black pepper and sea salt to taste.
4. Add fennel seed and stir.
5. Pour broth and bring to a boil.
6. Over low heat, simmer mixture for about 20 min, stir in between.
7. Add shrimp and cook until just pink for 3 min.
8. Mix in cream and lemon juice.
9. Serve warm.

Spiced Salmon with Vegetable Quinoa

Preparation: 30 min | Cooking: 10 min | Servings: 4

Ingredients
- 1 cup uncooked quinoa
- 1 teaspoon of salt, divided in half
- ¾ cup cucumbers, seeds removed, diced
- 1 cup of cherry tomatoes, halved
- ¼ cup red onion, minced
- 4 fresh basil leaves, cut in thin slices
- Zest from one lemon
- ¼ teaspoon black pepper
- 1 teaspoon cumin
- ½ teaspoon paprika
- 4 (5-oz.) salmon fillets
- 8 lemon wedges
- ¼ cup fresh parsley, chopped

Directions
1. To a medium-sized saucepan, add the quinoa, 2 cups of water, and ½ teaspoons of the salt. Heat these until the water is boiling, then lower the temperature until it is simmering. Cover the pan and let it cook 20 min or as long as the quinoa package instructs.
2. Turn off the burner under the quinoa and allow it to sit, covered, for at least another 5 min before serving.
3. Right before serving, add the onion, tomatoes, cucumbers, basil leaves, and lemon zest to the quinoa and stir gently. In the meantime (while the quinoa cooks), prepare the salmon.
4. Turn on the oven broiler to high and make sure a rack is in the lower part of the oven. To a small bowl, add the following components: black pepper, ½ teaspoon of the salt, cumin, and paprika. Stir them together.
5. Place foil over the top of a glass or aluminum baking sheet, then spray it with nonstick cooking spray. Place salmon fillets on the foil. Rub the spice mixture over each fillet (about ½ teaspoons of the spice mixture per fillet).
6. Add the lemon wedges to the pan edges near the salmon. Cook the salmon under the broiler for 8-10 min. Your goal is for the salmon to flake apart easily with a fork. Sprinkle the salmon with the parsley, and then serve it with the lemon wedges and vegetable parsley.
7. Serve.

Nutrition: 385 Calories, 12.5g Fat, 35.5g Protein

Baked Cod with Vegetables

Preparation: 15 min | Cooking: 25 min | Servings: 2

Ingredients
- 1 pound (454 g) thick cod fillet, cut into 4 even portions
- ¼ teaspoon onion powder (optional)
- ¼ teaspoon paprika
- 3 tablespoons extra-virgin olive oil
- 4 medium scallions
- ½ cup fresh chopped basil, divided
- 3 tablespoons minced garlic (optional)
- 2 teaspoons salt
- 2 teaspoons freshly ground black pepper
- ¼ teaspoon dry marjoram (optional)
- 6 sun-dried tomato slices
- ½ cup dry white wine
- ½ cup crumbled feta cheese
- 1 (15-ounce / 425-g) can oil-packed artichoke hearts, drained
- 1 lemon, sliced
- 1 cup pitted kalamata olives
- 1 teaspoon capers (optional)
- 4 small red potatoes, quartered

Directions
1. Set oven to 375°F (190°C).
2. Season the fish with paprika and onion powder (if desired).
3. Preheat an ovenproof skillet over medium heat and sear the top side of the cod for about 1 minute until golden. Set aside.
4. Cook the olive oil in the same skillet over medium heat. Add the scallions, ¼ cup of basil, garlic (if desired), salt, pepper, marjoram (if desired), tomato slices, and white wine and stir to combine. Boil then removes from heat.
5. Evenly spread the sauce on the bottom of skillet. Place the cod on top of the tomato basil sauce and scatter with feta cheese. Place the artichokes in the skillet and top with the lemon slices.
6. Scatter with the olives, capers (if desired), and the remaining ¼ cup of basil. Pullout from the heat and transfer to the preheated oven. Bake for 15 to 20 min
7. Meanwhile, place the quartered potatoes on a baking sheet or wrapped in aluminum foil. Bake in the oven for 15 min.
8. Cool for 5 min before serving.

Nutrition: 1168 calories; 60g fat; 64g protein

Grilled Lemon Pesto Salmon

Preparation: 5 min | Cooking: 10 min | Servings: 2

Ingredients
- 10 ounces (283 g) salmon fillet
- 2 tablespoons prepared pesto sauce
- 1 large fresh lemon, sliced
- Cooking spray

Directions
1. Preheat the grill to medium-high heat. Spray the grill grates with cooking spray.
2. Season the salmon well. Spread the pesto sauce on top.
3. Make a bed of fresh lemon slices about the same size as the salmon fillet on the hot grill, and place the salmon on top of the lemon slices.
4. Put any additional lemon slices on top of the salmon.
5. Grill the salmon for 10 min.
6. Serve hot.

Nutrition: 316 calories; 21g fat; 29g protein

Dill Chutney Salmon

Preparation: 5 min | Cooking: 3 min | Servings: 2

Ingredients
Chutney:
- ¼ cup fresh dill
- ¼ cup extra virgin olive oil
- Juice from ½ lemon
- Sea salt, to taste

Fish:
- 2 cups water
- 2 salmon fillets
- Juice from ½ lemon
- ¼ teaspoon paprika
- Salt and freshly ground pepper to taste

Directions
1. Pulse all the chutney ingredients in a food processor until creamy. Set aside.
2. Add the water and steamer basket to the Instant Pot®.
3. Place salmon fillets, skin-side down, on the steamer basket. Drizzle the lemon juice over salmon and sprinkle with the paprika.
4. Click the Manual mode and set the cooking time for 3 min at High Pressure.
5. Once cooking is complete, make a quick pressure release Carefully open the lid.
6. Season the fillets with pepper and salt to taste.

7. Serve topped with the dill chutney.

Nutrition: 636 calories; 41g fat; 65g protein

Steamed Trout with Lemon Herb Crust

Preparation: 10 min | Cooking: 15 min | Servings: 2

Ingredients
- 3 tbsp. olive oil
- 3 garlic cloves
- 2 tbsp. fresh lemon juice
- 1 tbsp. fresh mint
- 1 tbsp. fresh parsley
- ¼ tsp. dried ground thyme
- 1 tsp. sea salt
- 1 lb. (454 g) fresh trout
- 2 cups fish stock

Directions
1. Scourge olive oil, garlic, lemon juice, mint, parsley, thyme, and salt. Rub the marinade onto the fish.
2. Situate a trivet in the Instant Pot®.
3. Fill in the fish stock and position the fish on the trivet.
4. Click the Steam mode and set the cooking time for 15 min at High Pressure.
5. Once cooking is complete, make a quick pressure release.
6. Carefully open the lid.
7. Serve warm.

Nutrition: 477 calories; 30g fat; 52g protein

Lemony Trout with Caramelized Shallots

Preparation: 10 min | Cooking: 20 min | Servings: 2

Ingredients
Shallots:
- 1 teaspoon almond butter
- 2 shallots, thinly sliced
- Dash salt

Trout:
- 1 tablespoon almond butter
- 2 (4-ounce / 113-g) trout fillets
- 3 tablespoons capers
- ¼ cup freshly squeezed lemon juice
- ¼ teaspoon salt
- Dash freshly ground black pepper
- 1 lemon, thinly sliced

Directions
For Shallots:
1. Situate skillet over medium heat, cook the butter, shallots, and salt for 20 min, stirring every 5 min.

For Trout:
1. Using big skillet over medium heat, cook 1 teaspoon of almond butter.
2. Add the trout fillets and cook each side for 3 min, or until flaky. Transfer to a plate and set aside.
3. In the skillet used for the trout, stir in the capers, lemon juice, salt, and pepper, then bring to a simmer. Whisk in the remaining 1 tablespoon of almond butter. Spoon the sauce over the fish.
4. Garnish the fish with the lemon slices and caramelized shallots before serving.
5. Serve.

Nutrition: 344 calories; 18g fat; 21g protein

Hazelnut Crusted Sea Bass

Preparation: 10 min | Cooking: 15 min | Servings: 2

Ingredients
- 2 tablespoons almond butter
- 2 sea bass fillets
- 1/3 cup roasted hazelnuts
- A pinch of cayenne pepper

Directions
1. Ready oven to 425°F (220°C). Line a baking dish with waxed paper.
2. Brush the almond butter over the fillets.
3. Pulse the hazelnuts and cayenne in a food processor.
4. Coat the sea bass with the hazelnut mixture, then transfer to the baking dish.
5. Bake in the prepared oven for 17 min.
6. Cool for 5 min before serving.
7. Serve.

Nutrition: 468 calories; 31g fat; 40g protein

Swordfish Souvlaki

Preparation: 25 min | Cooking: 10 min | Servings: 4

Ingredients
- ½ cup freshly squeezed lemon juice
- ½ cup extra-virgin olive oil
- 1 teaspoon kosher salt
- 1 teaspoon freshly ground black pepper
- 1 teaspoon dried Greek oregano
- 2 pounds swordfish steaks
- 8 ounces cherry tomatoes
- 1 red onion, quartered

Directions
1. Scourge lemon juice, olive oil, salt, pepper, and oregano.
2. Add the fish and marinate in the refrigerator for 10 to 15 min.
3. Heat a grill to medium-high heat.
4. Skewer the swordfish, tomatoes, and red onion, alternating 1 to 2 pieces of fish for each tomato and onion quarter.
5. Grill the kebabs for 10 min.
6. Alternatively, broil the skewers carefully for 3 to 5 min per side, checking frequently.
7. Serve with a squeeze of lemon and Avocado Skordalia /Avocado Garlic Spread.

Nutrition: 493 Calories, 34g Fat, 42g Protein

Stuffed Monkfish

Preparation: 20 min | Cooking: 8 min | Servings: 4

Ingredients
- 4 (6-ounce) fresh white fish fillets
- 6 tablespoons extra-virgin olive oil, divided
- ½ teaspoon sea salt
- ½ teaspoon freshly ground black pepper
- ¼ cup feta cheese
- ¼ cup minced green olives
- ¼ cup minced orange pulp
- 1 tablespoon orange zest
- ½ teaspoon dried dill
- ¼ cup chopped fresh Greek basil

Directions
1. Blend fish with 2 tablespoons of olive oil, salt, and pepper
2. In another bowl, mix together the feta, olives, and orange pulp.
3. Spoon the mixture onto the fish fillets and spread it to coat them.
4. Roll the fillets, inserting 2 toothpicks through to the other side to hold them together.
5. In heavy-bottomed skillet over medium-high heat, heat the remaining olive oil for about 15 seconds.
6. Add the rolled fillets and cook for 6 to 8 min, depending on their thickness, rolling onto each side as they cook.
7. Top each piece with the orange zest, dill, and basil, equally divided.
8. Serve.

Nutrition: 365 Calories, 25g Fat, 29g Protein

Octopus with Figs and Peaches

Preparation: 15 min | Cooking: 10 min | Servings: 4

Ingredients
- 1-pound octopus tentacles
- ¼ cup extra-virgin olive oil
- 1 teaspoon sea salt
- 1 teaspoon black pepper
- 1 teaspoon granulated garlic
- ½ teaspoon dried Greek oregano
- 1 cup fig balsamic vinegar
- 6 fresh figs, halved
- 2 large peaches, quartered
- ¼ cup chopped fresh parsley

Directions
1. In a large bowl, thoroughly mix the octopus, olive oil, salt, pepper, garlic, and oregano to coat well. Marinate in the refrigerator for 2 hs. Bring to room temperature before cooking.
2. In an 8- to 10-inch heavy-bottomed deep skillet over medium-high heat, bring the fig balsamic vinegar to a boil. Reduce the heat to a rolling simmer.
3. Stir with the flat side of a metal spatula so any thickened vinegar is mixed into the liquid instead of sticking to the pan.
4. After about 4 min, when the vinegar is foamy on top, add the octopus and stir quickly, cooking for only 2 to 3 min.
5. Add the figs and peaches to the vinegar remaining in the skillet.
6. Cook for about 1 minute, stirring them into the caramelized vinegar just until coated and soft.
7. Transfer to the serving bowl and gently stir to combine.
8. Top with the parsley.

Nutrition: 304 Calories, 14g Fat, 21g Protein

Steamed Mussels with White Wine and Fennel

Preparation: 20 min | Cooking: 30 min | Servings: 4

Ingredients
- ¼ cup extra-virgin olive oil
- 1 onion, chopped
- 1 teaspoon sea salt
- 4 garlic cloves, minced
- 1 teaspoon red pepper flakes
- 1 fennel bulb
- 1 cup dry white wine
- 4 pounds mussels
- Juice of 2 lemons

Directions
1. Position 8-quart pot over medium-high heat, heat the olive oil.
2. Add the onion and salt. Cook for 5 min, until translucent.
3. Add garlic and red pepper flakes. Cook for 1 minute.
4. Stir in the chopped fennel. Cook for 3 min.
5. Stir in the wine and simmer for about 7 min.
6. Carefully pour the mussels into the pot. Reduce the heat to medium, give everything a good stir, cover the pot, and cook for 5 to 7 min.
7. Remove the opened mussels and divide them among 4 bowls. Re-cover the pot and cook any unopened mussels for 3 min more.
8. Divide any additional opened mussels among the bowls. Discard any unopened mussels. Evenly distribute the broth into the bowls.
9. Garnish with the fennel leaves.

Nutrition: 578 Calories, 23g Fat, 55g Protein

Skillet Braised Cod with Asparagus and Potatoes

Preparation: 20 min | Cooking: 20 min | Servings: 4

Ingredients
- 4 skinless cod fillets
- 1-pound asparagus
- 12 oz. halved small purple potatoes
- Finely grated zest of ½ lemon
- Juice of ½ lemon
- ½ cup white wine
- ¼ cup torn fresh basil leaves
- 1 ½ tbsp. olive oil
- 1 tbsp. capers
- 3 cloves sliced garlic

Directions
1. Take a large and tall pan on the sides and heat the oil over medium-high.
2. Season the cod abundantly with salt and pepper and put in the pan, with the hot oil, for 1 min.
3. Carefully flip for 1 more min and after transferring the cod to a plate and set aside.
4. Add the lemon zest, capers and garlic to the pan and mix to coat with the remaining oil in the pan and cook about 1 minute. Fill in the wine and deglaze the pan.
5. Add lemon juice, potatoes, ½ tsp salt, ¼ tsp pepper and 2 cups of water and boil, decrease heat and simmer for 11 min.
6. Mix the asparagus and cook for 2 min.
7. Bring back the cod filets and any juices accumulated in the pan and cook until the asparagus are tender, for about 3 min.
8. Divide the cod fillets into shallow bowls and add the potatoes and asparagus and mix the basil in the broth left in the pan and pour over the cod.

Nutrition: 461 Calories: 40g Protein:

Mediterranean Tuna Noodle Casserole

Preparation: 15 min | Cooking: 40 min | Servings: 5

Ingredients
- 10 oz. dried egg noodles
- 9 oz. halved frozen artichoke hearts
- 6 oz. drained olive oil packed tuna
- 4 sliced scallions
- 1-pound sliced ¼ inch thick small red potatoes
- 2 cup milk
- ¾ cup finely grated Parmesan cheese
- ¾ cup drained capers
- ½ cup finely chopped flat-leaf parsley
- ½ cup sliced black olives
- ¼ cup flour
- 4 tbsp. unsalted butter
- 2 tsp Kosher salt, divided

Directions
1. Place a grill in the middle of the oven and heat to 400 °F (200 °C).
2. Lightly coat a 2-quart baking tray with oil and set aside.
3. Using big pan of salt water to a boil. Add the noodles and cook for 2 min less than recommended in the package directions.
4. Strain noodles and season immediately with olive oil so that they don't pile up and set aside.

5. Pour the pan with water again and boil. Put the potato slices and cook for 4 min. Drain well, then bring them back to the pan.
6. Cook butter in a small saucepan over medium heat, while the noodles and potatoes are cooking. When it melts and expands, add the flour and cook for about 5 min mixing constantly, until the sauce thickens slightly, about 5 min. Add 1 tsp salt and pepper to taste.
7. Add the egg noodles to the potato pan, then pour the sauce over it. Add and mix the remaining 1 tsp of salt, capers, olive oil, tuna, artichoke hearts, shallots, parsley and ½ cup of Parmesan. Season well.
8. Transfer to the baking tray and distribute it in a uniform layer. Season with the remaining ¼ cup of Parmesan and bake uncovered, about 25 min.

Nutrition: 457 Calories: 37g Protein: 21g Fat

Acquapazza Snapper

Preparation: 10 min | Cooking: 35 min | Servings: 4

Ingredients
- 1 ½ pounds cut into 4 pieces red snapper fillets
- 1 ½ coarsely chopped ripe tomatoes
- 3 cups water
- 2 tbsp. olive oil
- 1 tbsp. chopped thyme leaves
- 1 tbsp. chopped oregano leaves
- ¼ tsp red pepper flakes
- 3 cloves minced garlic

Directions
1. Cook oil in a casserole large enough to hold all 4 pieces of snapper fillets in a single layer over medium heat.
2. Cook garlic and red pepper flakes and add the water, tomatoes, thyme, oregano and simmer. Cover, reduce over medium-low heat and simmer for 15 min.
3. Open it then continue to simmer for 12 min, pressing occasionally on the tomatoes. Taste and season with salt as needed.
4. Put the snapper fillets in the casserole with the skin facing down, if there is skin. Sprinkle with salt, and cook for 9 min.
5. Place the snapper fillets on 4 large, shallow bowls and put the broth around it.
6. Serve immediately.

Nutrition: 501 Calories: 52g Protein: 26g Fat

Grilled Fish with Lemons

Preparation: 8 min | Cooking: 20 min | Servings: 4

Ingredients
- 3-4 Lemons
- 1 Tablespoon Olive Oil
- Sea Salt & Black Pepper to Taste
- 4 Catfish Fillets, 4 Ounces Each
- Nonstick Cooking Spray

Directions
1. Pat your fillets dry using a paper towel and let them come to room temperature. This may take 10 min.
2. Rub the cooking grate of your grill with nonstick cooking spray while it's cold. Once it's coated preheat it to 400 °F (200 °C), cut one lemon in half, setting it to the side and slice your remaining half of the lemon into ¼ inch slices.
3. Get out a bowl and squeeze a tablespoon of juice from your reserved half. Add your oil to the bowl, mixing well.
4. Brush your fish down with the oil and lemon mixture.
5. Situate the lemon slices on the grill and then put our fillets on top. Grill with your lid closed.
6. Turn the fish halfway through if they're more than a half an inch thick.

Nutrition: 147 Calories, 22g Protein, 1g Fat

Seafood Corn Chowder

Preparation: 10 min | Cooking: 12 min | Servings: 4

Ingredients
- 1 tablespoon butter
- 1 cup onion
- 1/3 cup celery
- ½ cup green bell pepper
- ½ cup red bell pepper
- 1 tablespoon white flour
- 14 ounces chicken broth
- 2 cups cream
- 6 ounces evaporated milk
- 10 ounces surimi imitation crab chunks
- 2 cups frozen corn kernels
- ½ teaspoon black pepper
- ½ teaspoon paprika

Directions
1. Place a suitably-sized saucepan over medium heat and add butter to melt.

2. Toss in onion, green and red peppers, and celery, then sauté for 5 min.
3. Stir in flour and whisk well for 2 min.
4. Pour in chicken broth and stir until it boils.
5. Add evaporated milk, corn, surimi crab, paprika, black pepper, and creamer.
6. Cook for 5 min. Serves warm.

Nutrition: 175 calories; 8g protein 7g fat;

Creamy Bell Pepper Soup With Cod Fillets

Servings: 6 | Cooking: 1 Hour

Ingredients
- 2 tablespoons olive oil
- 1 shallot, chopped
- 2 garlic cloves, chopped
- 1 jar roasted red bell peppers, sliced
- 2 cups chicken stock
- 2 cups water
- 1 bay leaf
- 1 thyme sprig
- 1 rosemary sprig
- Salt and pepper to taste
- 4 cod fillets, cubed

Directions
1. Heat the oil in a soup pot and stir in the shallot and garlic. Cook for 2 minutes then add the bell peppers, stock, water and herbs, as well as salt and pepper to taste.
2. Cook for 15 minutes then remove the herbs and puree the soup with an immersion blender.
3. Add the cod fillets and place the soup back on heat.
4. Cook for another 5 minutes.
5. Serve the soup warm and fresh.

Nutrition: Calories:48 Fat:5.0g Protein:0.4g Carbohydrates:1.3g

Cod Potato Soup

Servings: 8 | Cooking: 1 Hour

Ingredients
- 2 tablespoons olive oil
- 2 shallots, chopped
- 1 celery stalk, sliced
- 1 carrot, sliced
- 1 red bell pepper, cored and diced
- 2 garlic cloves, chopped
- 1 ½ pounds potatoes, peeled and cubed
- 1 cup diced tomatoes
- 1 bay leaf
- 1 thyme sprig
- ½ teaspoon dried marjoram
- 2 cups chicken stock
- 6 cups water
- Salt and pepper to taste
- 4 cod fillets, cubed
- 2 tablespoons lemon juice

Directions
1. Heat the oil in a soup pot and stir in the shallots, celery, carrot, bell pepper and garlic.
2. Cook for 5 minutes then stir in the potatoes, tomatoes, bay leaf, thyme, marjoram, stock and water.
3. Season with salt and pepper and cook on low heat for 20 minutes.
4. Add the cod fillets and lemon juice and continue cooking for 5 additional minutes.
5. Serve the soup warm and fresh.

Nutrition: Calories:108 Fat:3.9g Protein:2.2g Carbohydrates:17.1g

White Wine Fish Soup

Servings: 8 | Cooking: 50 min

Ingredients
- 3 tablespoons olive oil
- 2 shallots, chopped
- 2 garlic cloves, chopped
- 1 celery stalk, sliced
- 2 red bell peppers, cored and sliced
- 2 carrots, sliced
- 2 tomatoes, sliced
- 1 cup diced tomatoes
- ½ cup tomato juice
- 2 cups chicken stock
- 2 cups water
- 1 cup dry white wine
- 2 cod fillets, cubed
- 2 flounder fillets, cubed
- 1 pound fresh mussels, cleaned and rinsed
- 1 bay leaf
- 1 thyme sprig
- Salt and pepper to taste

Directions
1. Heat the oil in a soup pot and stir in the shallots, garlic, celery, bell peppers and carrots.
2. Cook for 10 minutes then add the tomatoes and tomato juice, as well as stock, water and wine.
3. Cook for 15 minutes then add the cod, flounder and fresh mussels, as well as the bay leaf and thyme.
4. Adjust the taste with salt and pepper and cook for another 5 minutes.
5. Serve the soup warm and fresh.

Nutrition: Calories:190 Fat:7.4g Protein:15.8g Carbohydrates:10.0g

Chapter 6: Salads & Side Dishes

Balsamic Mushrooms

Servings: 4-6 | Cooking: 7 min

Ingredients
- 1 pound white mushroom, halved (or quartered if they are very large)
- 1 teaspoon salt
- 1/4 cup olive oil
- 1/4 teaspoon red pepper flakes
- 3 tablespoons balsamic vinegar
- Pepper, to taste

Directions
1. In a medium-sized skillet, heat the oil over medium high-heat. Add the mushrooms; cook for about 5 minutes or until golden.
2. Stir in the vinegar, red pepper flakes, and the salt, then season with pepper; cook for 1 minute more. Transfer into a serving bowl.
3. Notes: Serve this dish with your favorite steak. You can also add this to spinach salad to give it a different spin.

Nutrition: 155.3 cal., 13.9 g fat (1.9 g sat. fat), 0 mg chol., 590.1 mg sodium, 5.8 g total carb., 1.2 g fiber, 4.1 g sugar, and 3.6 g protein.

Greek Potato And Corn Salad

Servings: 2 | Cooking: 20 min

Ingredients
- 2 medium potatoes, peeled and cubed
- 2 shallots, chopped
- 1 tablespoon olive oil
- 2 cups corn
- 1 tablespoon dill, chopped
- 1 tablespoon balsamic vinegar
- Salt and black pepper to the taste

Directions
1. Put the potatoes in a pot, add water to cover, bring to a simmer over medium heat, cook for 20 minutes, drain and transfer to a bowl.
2. Add the shallots and the other ingredients, toss and serve cold.

Nutrition: calories 198; fat 5.3; fiber 6.5; carbs 11.6; protein 4.5

Mint Avocado Chilled Soup

Servings: 2 | Cooking: 15 min

Ingredients
- 2 romaine lettuce leaves
- 1 Tablespoon lime juice
- 1 medium ripe avocado
- 1 cup coconut milk, chilled
- 20 fresh mint leaves
- Salt to taste

Directions
1. Put all the ingredients in a blender and blend until smooth.
2. Refrigerate for about 10 minutes and serve chilled.

Nutrition: Calories: 432 Carbs: 16.1g Fats: 42.2g Proteins: 5.2g Sodium: 33mg Sugar: 4.5g

Amazingly Fresh Carrot Salad

Servings: 4 | Cooking: 0 min

Ingredients
- ¼ tsp chipotle powder
- 1 bunch scallions, sliced
- 1 cup cherry tomatoes, halved
- 1 large avocado, diced
- 1 tbsp chili powder
- 1 tbsp lemon juice
- 2 tbsp olive oil
- 3 tbsp lime juice
- 4 cups carrots, spiralized
- salt to taste

Directions
1. In a salad bowl, mix and arrange avocado, cherry tomatoes, scallions and spiralized carrots. Set aside.
2. In a small bowl, whisk salt, chipotle powder, chili powder, olive oil, lemon juice and lime juice thoroughly.
3. Pour dressing over noodle salad. Toss to coat well.
4. Serve and enjoy at room temperature.

Nutrition: Calories: 243.6; Fat: 14.8g; Protein: 3g; Carbs: 24.6g

Feta And Almond Pasta

Servings: 4 | Cooking: 25 min

Ingredients
- 5 oz whole grain macaroni
- 4 oz Feta cheese, crumbled

- 2 eggs, beaten
- ½ teaspoon chili pepper
- 1 teaspoon almond butter
- 1 cup water, for cooking

Directions
1. Mix up together water and macaroni and boil according to the directions of the manufacturer.
2. Then drain water.
3. Add almond butter, chili pepper, and Feta cheese. Mix up well.
4. Transfer the mixture in the casserole mold and flatten well.
5. Pour beaten eggs over the macaroni and bake for 10 minutes at 355F.

Nutrition: calories 262; fat 11.4; fiber 4.2; carbs 27.2; protein 13.9

Italian-style Butter Beans

Servings: 4 | Cooking: 15 min

Ingredients
- 1 can (400 g) chopped tomato
- 1 tablespoon olive oil
- 2 cans (400 g) butter beans, rinsed, drained
- 2 teaspoons sugar
- 4 garlic cloves, crushed
- Small bunch basil, chopped

Directions
1. In a medium-sized saucepan, heat the olive oil. Add the garlic; cook for 1 minute. Add the tomatoes, sugar, and a bit of seasoning.
2. Add the beans and a splash of water. Cover and let simmer for 5 minutes. Stir in the basil; serve.

Nutrition: 140 cal, 4 g fat (1 g sat. fat), 20 g carbs, 6 g sugars, 6 g fiber, 8 g protein, and 1.41 g sodium.

Leeks Salad

Servings: 4 | Cooking: 0 min

Ingredients
- 1 tablespoon olive oil
- 4 leeks, sliced
- 3 garlic cloves, grated
- A pinch of sea salt and white pepper
- ½ teaspoon apple cider vinegar
- A drizzle of olive oil
- 1 tablespoon dill, chopped

Directions
1. In a salad bowl, combine the leeks with the garlic and the rest of the ingredients, toss and serve cold.

Nutrition: calories 71; fat 2.1; fiber 1.1; carbs 1.3; protein 2.4

Broccoli And Mushroom Salad

Servings: 4 | Cooking: 0 min

Ingredients
- ½ pound white mushrooms, sliced
- 1 broccoli head, florets separated and steamed
- 1 garlic clove, minced
- 1 tablespoon balsamic vinegar
- 1 yellow onion, chopped
- 1 tablespoon olive oil
- A pinch of sea salt and black pepper
- A pinch of red pepper flakes

Directions
1. In a bowl, mix the broccoli with the mushrooms and the other ingredients, toss and serve cold.

Nutrition: calories 183; fat 6.5; fiber 4.2; carbs 8.5; protein 4

Tomato Greek Salad

Servings: 4 | Cooking: 15 min

Ingredients
- 1 pound tomatoes, cubed
- 1 cucumber, sliced
- ½ cup black olives
- ¼ cup sun-dried tomatoes, chopped
- 1 red onion, sliced
- ¼ cup parsley, chopped
- Salt and pepper to taste
- 1 tablespoon balsamic vinegar
- 2 tablespoons extra virgin olive oil

Directions
1. Combine the tomatoes, cucumber, black olives, sun-dried tomatoes, onion and parsley in a bowl.
2. Add salt and pepper to taste then stir in the vinegar and olive oil.
3. Mix well and serve the salad fresh.

Nutrition: Calories: 126 Fat: 9.2g Protein: 2.1g Carbohydrates: 11.5g

Saffron Zucchini Mix

Servings: 4 | Cooking: 10 min

Ingredients
- 2 zucchinis, sliced
- A pinch of sea salt and black pepper
- 1 tablespoon white vinegar
- 1 tablespoon olive oil
- 1 teaspoon saffron powder

Directions
1. Heat up a pan with the oil over medium heat, add the zucchinis and sauté for 8 minutes.
2. Add the rest of the ingredients, toss, cook for 2 minutes more, divide between plates and serve.

Nutrition: calories 150; fat 5.2; fiber 4.3; carbs 5; protein 4

Thai Salad With Cilantro Lime Dressing

Servings: 2 | Cooking: 20 min

Ingredients
- ¼ cup cashews
- ¼ cup fresh mint leaves
- ¼ cup fresh Thai basil leaves
- ¼ teaspoon fish sauce
- ½ cup green papaya, julienned
- ½ teaspoon honey
- 1 head green leaf lettuce, chopped
- 1 loose handful fresh cilantro
- 1 tablespoon lime juice
- 1 teaspoon coconut aminos
- 3 tablespoon olive oil
- 3 tangerines, peeled and segmented

Directions
1. Prepare the lime cilantro dressing by mixing honey, fresh cilantro, fish sauce, coconut aminos, lime juice and oil in a mixing bowl. Mix then set aside.
2. Prepare the salad by mixing the remaining six ingredients. Toss everything to distribute the ingredients.
3. Toss the salad dressing into the vegetables.
4. Serve chilled.

Nutrition: Calories: 649.8; Fat: 57.4 g; Protein: 7.5 g; Carbs: 25.8 g;

Green Mediterranean Salad

Servings: 4 | Cooking: 15 min

Ingredients
- 2 cups arugula leaves
- 2 cups baby spinach
- 2 cucumbers, sliced
- 2 celery stalks, sliced
- ½ cup chopped parsley
- ¼ cup chopped cilantro
- 1 lemon, juiced
- 1 tablespoon balsamic vinegar
- Salt and pepper to taste

Directions
1. Combine the arugula and spinach with the rest of the ingredients in a salad bowl.
2. Add salt and pepper to taste and season well with salt and pepper.
3. Serve the salad fresh.

Nutrition: Calories: 38 Fat: 0.4g Protein: 2.1g Carbohydrates: 8.5g

Sautéed Zucchini And Mushrooms

Servings: 1 Cup | Cooking: 12 min

Ingredients
- 3 TB. extra-virgin olive oil
- 1 large white onion, chopped
- 2 cups crimini mushrooms, rinsed and chopped
- 1 tsp. salt
- 1 TB. minced garlic
- 2 medium zucchini, chopped
- 2 TB. fresh thyme
- 1/2 tsp. ground black pepper

Directions
1. In a large skillet over medium heat, heat extra-virgin olive oil. Add white onion, crimini mushrooms, and salt, and toss. Cook for 5 minutes.
2. Stir in garlic, and cook for another 2 minutes.
3. Add zucchini, thyme, and black pepper, and stir to combine. Cook for 5 minutes.
4. Serve warm.

Salad Greens With Pear And Persimmon

Servings: 2 | Cooking: 0 min

Ingredients
- ½ cup chopped pecans, toasted
- 1 ripe persimmon, sliced
- 1 ripe red pear, sliced
- 1 shallot, minced
- 1 tsp minced garlic
- 1 tsp whole grain mustard
- 2 tbsp fresh lemon juice
- 3 tbsp extra virgin olive oil
- 6 cups baby spinach

Directions
1. In a big mixing bowl, mix garlic, olive oil, lemon juice and mustard.
2. Once thoroughly mixed, add remaining ingredients.
3. Toss to coat.
4. Equally divide into two bowls, serve and enjoy.

Nutrition: Calories per serving: 429.1; Protein: 6.2g; Carbs: 39.2g; Fat: 27.5g

Easy Eggplant Salad

Servings: 4 | Cooking: 30 min

Ingredients
- Salt and pepper - to taste
- Eggplant - 2, sliced
- Smoked paprika - 1 tsp.
- Extra virgin olive oil - 2 tbsp.
- Garlic cloves - 2, minced
- Mixed greens - 2 cups
- Sherry vinegar - 2 tbsp.

Directions
1. Mix together garlic, paprika and oil in a small bowl.
2. Place eggplant on a plate and sprinkle with salt and pepper to suit your taste. Next, brush oil mixture onto the eggplant.
3. Cook eggplant on a medium heated grill pan until brown on both sides. Once cooked, put eggplant into a salad bowl.
4. Top with greens and vinegar and greens, serve and eat.

Wheatberry And Walnuts Salad

Servings: 2 | Cooking: 50 min

Ingredients
- ¼ cup of wheat berries
- 1 cup of water
- 1 teaspoon salt
- 2 tablespoons walnuts, chopped
- 1 tablespoon chives, chopped
- ¼ cup fresh parsley, chopped
- 2 oz pomegranate seeds
- 1 tablespoon canola oil
- 1 teaspoon chili flakes

Directions
1. Place wheat berries and water in the pan.
2. Add salt and simmer the ingredients for 50 minutes over the medium heat.
3. Meanwhile, mix up together walnuts, chives, parsley, pomegranate seeds, and chili flakes.
4. When the wheatberry is cooked, transfer it in the walnut mixture.
5. Add canola oil and mix up the salad well.

Nutrition: calories 160; fat 11.8; fiber 1.2; carbs 12; protein 3.4

Lemony Butter Beans With Parsley

Servings: 4 | Cooking: 20 min

Ingredients
- 1 garlic clove, crushed
- 1 large bunch parsley, chopped (or 2 small bunches)
- 1 large onion, sliced
- 1 tablespoon olive oil
- 2 cans (400 g or 14 ounces) butter beans, rinsed, drained
- Zest and juice 1 lemon

Directions
1. In a pan, heat the olive oil. Add the onion; cook for about 10 to 15 minutes or until soft
2. Add the garlic; cook for 1 minute. Stir in the beans, cooking until heated through. Add the lemon juice and zest. Stir in the parsley; serve.

Nutrition: 134 cal, 4 g fat (0 g sat. fat), 19 g carbs, 4 g sugars, 6 g fiber, 8 g protein, and 1.29 g sodium.

Spring Soup Recipe With Poached Egg

Servings: 2 | Cooking: 20 min

Ingredients
- 2 eggs
- 2 tablespoons butter
- 4 cups chicken broth
- 1 head of romaine lettuce, chopped

- Salt, to taste

Directions
1. Boil the chicken broth and lower heat.
2. Poach the eggs in the broth for about 5 minutes and remove the eggs.
3. Place each egg into a bowl and add chopped romaine lettuce into the broth.
4. Cook for about 10 minutes and ladle the broth with the lettuce into the bowls.

Nutrition: Calories: 264 Carbs: 7g Fats: 18.9g Proteins: 16.1g Sodium: 1679mg Sugar: 3.4g

Eggplant Ragoût With Chickpeas, Tomatoes, And Peppers

Servings: 4-6 | Cooking: 45 min

Ingredients
- 5 plum tomatoes; peel, quarter in a lengthwise direction, seed
- 1 can (15-ounces) chickpeas (preferably organic), rinsed, drained
- 1 1/2 pounds eggplant, use plump round ones
- 1 1/4 cups water
- 1 large bell pepper, yellow or red, cored, seeded, cut to 1-inch pieces
- 1 large red onion, cut into 1/2-inch dices
- 1 teaspoon salt, plus more to taste
- 1 teaspoons ground cumin
- 1/4 cup fresh flat-leaf parsley, coarsely chopped
- 2 plump cloves garlic, sliced to thin pieces
- 2 tablespoons olive oil; plus more for brushing the eggplant
- 2 tablespoons tomato paste
- 2 teaspoons paprika
- Black pepper, freshly ground, to taste
- Generous pinch cayenne

Directions
1. Preheat the broiler. In crosswise direction, cut the eggplant to 3/4-inch rounds; brush each side with the olive oil and broil for 2 minutes each side, or until both sides are light gold. Cool; cut to 1-inch pieces.
2. Over medium-high heat, heat 2 tablespoons olive oil in a medium-sized Dutch oven.
3. Add the onion and the bell pepper and sauté for about 12 to 15 minutes or until the onions are slightly browned. About 1-2 minutes before the onion browning is finished, add garlic, cumin, paprika, and the cayenne. Stir in the tomato paste; cook for 1 minutes, stirring.
4. Stir in the 1/4 cup water; boil. With wooden spoon, scrape the juices that stuck on the pan bottom.
5. Add the eggplant, tomatoes, chickpeas, remaining water, and salt; bring to boil. Simmer covered for about 25 minutes or until the veggies are tender, stirring one or 2 times. Stir the parsley in the pot, adjust seasoning, and serve.

Nutrition: 220 cal., 8 g fat (1 g sat. fat, 1 g poly fat, 5 g mono fat), 0 mg chol., 550 mg sodium, 32 g carbs., 8 g fiber, and 6 g protein.

Crispy Watermelon Salad

Servings: 4 | Cooking: 20 min

Ingredients
- 2 flat breads, sliced
- 10 oz. watermelon, cubed
- 4 oz. feta cheese, cubed
- 1 cucumber, sliced
- 2 tablespoons extra virgin olive oil
- 2 tablespoons mixed seeds

Directions
1. Combine flat bread, watermelon, cheese, cucumber, oil and seeds in a salad bowl and mix gently.
2. Serve the salad fresh.

Nutrition: Calories: 167 Fat: 13.2g Protein: 4.9g Carbohydrates: 9.2g

Red Wine Dressed Arugula Salad

Servings: 2 | Cooking: 12 min

Ingredients
- ¼ cup red onion, sliced thinly
- 1 ½ tbsp fresh lemon juice
- 1 ½ tbsp olive oil
- 1 tbsp extra-virgin olive oil
- 1 tbsp red-wine vinegar
- 2 center cut salmon fillets (6-oz each)
- 2/3 cup cherry tomatoes, halved
- 3 cups baby arugula leaves
- Pepper and salt to taste

Directions
1. In a shallow bowl, mix pepper, salt, 1 ½ tbsp olive oil and lemon juice. Toss in salmon fillets and rub with the marinade. Allow to marinate for at least 15 minutes.
2. Grease a baking sheet and preheat oven to 350oF.

3. Bake marinated salmon fillet for 10 to 12 minutes or until flaky with skin side touching the baking sheet.
4. Meanwhile, in a salad bowl mix onion, tomatoes and arugula.
5. Season with pepper and salt. Drizzle with vinegar and oil. Toss to combine and serve right away with baked salmon on the side.

Nutrition: Calories per serving: 400; Protein: 36.6g; Carbs: 5.8g; Fat: 25.6g

Artichoke Farro Salad

Servings: 6 | Cooking: 30 min

Ingredients
- 1 cup faro
- 2 cups vegetable stock
- 6 artichoke hearts, chopped
- ½ cup chopped parsley
- 2 tablespoons chopped cilantro
- 2 garlic cloves, chopped
- 2 tablespoons extra virgin olive oil
- Salt and pepper to taste
- 4 oz. feta cheese, crumbled

Directions
1. Combine the faro and stock in a saucepan and cook on low heat until all the liquid has been absorbed.
2. When done, transfer the faro in a salad bowl then stir in the rest of the ingredients.
3. Adjust the taste with salt and pepper and mix well.
4. Serve the salad fresh.

Nutrition: Calories:171 Fat:9.0g Protein:8.3g Carbohydrates:18.8g

Balsamic Tomato Mix

Servings: 4 | Cooking: 0 min

Ingredients
- 2 pounds cherry tomatoes, halved
- 2 tablespoons olive oil
- 2 tablespoons balsamic vinegar
- 1 garlic clove, minced
- 1 cup basil, chopped
- 1 tablespoon chives, chopped
- Salt and black pepper to the taste

Directions
1. In a bowl, combine the tomatoes with the garlic, basil and the rest of the ingredients, toss and serve as a side salad.

Nutrition: calories 200; fat 5.6; fiber 4.5; carbs 15.1; protein 4.3

Gigantes Plaki

Servings: 4 | Cooking: 2 Hour

Ingredients
- 1 Spanish onion, finely chopped
- 1 teaspoon dried oregano
- 1 teaspoon sugar
- 2 garlic cloves, finely chopped
- 2 tablespoons flat-leaf parsley, chopped, plus more to serve
- 2 tablespoons tomato purée
- 3 tablespoons extra-virgin olive oil, plus more to serve
- 400 g dried butter beans
- 800 g ripe tomatoes, skinned, roughly chopped
- Pinch ground cinnamon

Directions
1. In water, soak the beans overnight, drain, rinse, and then place in a pan filled with water; bring to a boil. When boiling, reduce the heat to a simmer, cooking for about 50 minutes or until the beans are slightly tender but still not soft. Drain and set aside.
2. Preheat the oven to 180C, gas to 4, or fan to 160C.
3. In a large-sized frying pan, heat the olive oil. Add the onion and the garlic; cook for 10 minutes over medium heat or until soft but not browned.
4. Add the tomato puree, cook for 1 minute more. Add the rest of the ingredients; simmer for about 2 to 3 minutes, season generously, then stir in the beans. Pour the mixture into an oven-safe dish; bake for 1 hour, uncovered, without stirring, or until the beans are tender.

Nutrition: 431 cal, 11 g fat (1 g sat. fat), 66 g carbs, 15 g sugars, 19 g fiber, 22 g protein, and 0.2 g sodium.

Squash And Tomatoes Mix

Servings: 6 | Cooking: 20 min

Ingredients
- 5 medium squash, cubed
- A pinch of salt and black pepper

- 3 tablespoons olive oil
- 1 cup pine nuts, toasted
- ¼ cup goat cheese, crumbled
- 6 tomatoes, cubed
- ½ yellow onion, chopped
- 2 tablespoons cilantro, chopped
- 2 tablespoons lemon juice

Directions
1. Heat up a pan with the oil over medium heat, add the onion and pine nuts and cook for 3 minutes.
2. Add the squash and the rest of the ingredients, cook everything for 15 minutes, divide between plates and serve as a side dish.

Nutrition: calories 200; fat 4.5; fiber 3.4; carbs 6.7; protein 4

Chickpeas, Corn And Black Beans Salad

Servings: 4 | Cooking: 0 min

Ingredients
- 1 and ½ cups canned black beans, drained and rinsed
- ½ teaspoon garlic powder
- 2 teaspoons chili powder
- A pinch of sea salt and black pepper
- 1 and ½ cups canned chickpeas, drained and rinsed
- 1 cup baby spinach
- 1 avocado, pitted, peeled and chopped
- 1 cup corn kernels, chopped
- 2 tablespoons lemon juice
- 1 tablespoon olive oil
- 1 tablespoon apple cider vinegar
- 1 teaspoon chives, chopped

Directions
1. In a salad bowl, combine the black beans with the garlic powder, chili powder and the rest of the ingredients, toss and serve cold.

Nutrition: calories 300; fat 13.4; fiber 4.1; carbs 8.6; protein 13

Eggplant And Bell Pepper Mix

Servings: 4 | Cooking: 45 min

Ingredients
- 2 green bell peppers, cut into strips
- 2 eggplants, sliced
- 2 tablespoons tomato paste
- Salt and black pepper to the taste
- 4 garlic cloves, minced
- ¼ cup olive oil
- 1 tablespoon cilantro, chopped
- 1 tablespoon chives, chopped

Directions
1. In a roasting pan, combine the bell peppers with the eggplants and the rest of the ingredients, introduce in the oven and cook at 380 degrees F for 45 minutes.
2. Divide the mix between plates and serve as a side dish.

Nutrition: calories 207; fat 13.3; fiber 10.5; carbs 23.4; protein 3.8

Broccoli Salad With Caramelized Onions

Servings: 4 | Cooking: 25 min

Ingredients
- Extra virgin olive oil - 3 tbsp.
- Red onions - 2, sliced
- Dried thyme - 1 tsp.
- Balsamic vinegar - 2 tbsp. vinegar
- Broccoli - 1 lb., cut into florets
- Salt and pepper - to taste

Directions
1. Heat extra virgin olive oil in a pan over high heat and add in sliced onions. Cook for approximately 10 minutes or until the onions are caramelized. Stir in vinegar and thyme and then remove from stove.
2. Mix together the broccoli and onion mixture in a bowl, adding salt and pepper if desired. Serve and eat salad as soon as possible.

Easy Butternut Squash Soup

Servings: 4 | Cooking: 1 Hour 45 min

Ingredients
- 1 small onion, chopped
- 4 cups chicken broth
- 1 butternut squash
- 3 tablespoons coconut oil
- Salt, to taste
- Nutmeg and pepper, to taste

Directions
1. Put oil and onions in a large pot and add onions.

2. Sauté for about 3 minutes and add chicken broth and butternut squash.
3. Simmer for about 1 hour on medium heat and transfer into an immersion blender.
4. Pulse until smooth and season with salt, pepper and nutmeg.
5. Return to the pot and cook for about 30 minutes.
6. Dish out and serve hot.

Nutrition: Calories: 149 Carbs: 6.6g Fats: 11.6g Proteins: 5.4g Sodium: 765mg Sugar: 2.2g

Mediterranean Veggie Bowl

Preparation: 10 min | Cooking: 20 min | Servings: 4

Ingredients
- 1 cup quinoa, rinsed
- 1½ teaspoons salt, divided
- 2 cups cherry tomatoes, cut in half
- 1 large bell pepper, cucumber
- 1 cup Kalamata olives

Directions
1. Using medium pot over medium heat, boil 2 cups of water. Add the bulgur (or quinoa) and 1 teaspoon of salt. Close and cook for 18 min.
2. To arrange the veggies in your 4 bowls, visually divide each bowl into 5 sections. Place the cooked bulgur in one section. Follow with the tomatoes, bell pepper, cucumbers, and olives.
3. Scourge ½ cup of lemon juice, olive oil, remaining ½ teaspoon salt, and black pepper.
4. Evenly spoon the dressing over the 4 bowls.
5. Serve.

Nutrition: 772 Calories: 6g Protein: 41g Carbohydrates

Grilled Veggie and Hummus Wrap

Preparation: 15 min | Cooking: 10 min | Servings: 6

Ingredients
- 1 large eggplant
- 1 large onion
- ½ cup extra-virgin olive oil
- 6 lavash wraps or large pita bread
- 1 cup Creamy Traditional Hummus

Directions
1. Preheat a grill, large grill pan, or lightly oiled large skillet on medium heat.
2. Slice the eggplant and onion into circles. Rub the vegetables with olive oil and sprinkle with salt.
3. Cook the vegetables on both sides, about 3 to 4 min each side.
4. To make the wrap, lay the lavash or pita flat. Scoop 3 tablespoons of hummus on the wrap.
5. Evenly divide the vegetables among the wraps, layering them along one side of the wrap. Gently fold over the side of the wrap with the vegetables, tucking them in and making a tight wrap.
6. Lay the wrap seam side-down and cut in half or thirds.
7. You can also wrap each sandwich with plastic wrap to help it hold its shape and eat it later.

Nutrition: 362 Calories: 15g Protein: 28g Carbohydrates

Spanish Green Beans

Preparation: 10 min | Cooking: 20 min | Servings: 4

Ingredients
- 1 large onion, chopped
- 4 cloves garlic, finely chopped
- 1-pound green beans, fresh or frozen, trimmed
- 1 (15-ounce) can diced tomatoes

Directions
1. In a huge pot over medium heat, cook olive oil, onion, and garlic; cook for 1 minute.
2. Cut the green beans into 2-inch pieces.
3. Add the green beans and 1 teaspoon of salt to the pot and toss everything together; cook for 3 min.
4. Add the diced tomatoes, remaining ½ teaspoon of salt, and black pepper to the pot; continue to cook for another 12 min, stirring occasionally.
5. Serve warm.

Nutrition: 200 Calories: 4g Protein: 18g Carbohydrates

Roasted Cauliflower and Tomatoes

Preparation: 5 min | Cooking: 25 min | Servings: 4

Ingredients
- 4 cups cauliflower, cut into 1-inch pieces
- 6 tablespoons extra-virgin olive oil, divided
- 4 cups cherry tomatoes
- ½ teaspoon freshly ground black pepper
- ½ cup grated Parmesan cheese

Directions
1. Preheat the oven to 425°F.

2. Add the cauliflower, 3 tablespoons of olive oil, and ½ teaspoon of salt to a large bowl and toss to evenly coat. Fill onto a baking sheet and arrange the cauliflower out in an even layer.
3. In another large bowl, add the tomatoes, remaining 3 tablespoons of olive oil, and ½ teaspoon of salt, and toss to coat evenly. Pour onto a different baking sheet.
4. Put the sheet of cauliflower and the sheet of tomatoes in the oven to roast for 17 to 20 min until the cauliflower is lightly browned and tomatoes are plump.
5. Using a spatula, spoon the cauliflower into a serving dish, and top with tomatoes, black pepper, and Parmesan cheese. Serve warm.

Nutrition: 294 Calories: 9g Protein: 13g Carbohydrates

Rustic Cauliflower and Carrot Hash

Preparation: 10 min | Cooking: 10 min | Servings: 4

Ingredients
- 1 large onion, chopped
- 1 tablespoon garlic, minced
- 2 cups carrots, diced
- 4 cups cauliflower pieces, washed
- ½ teaspoon ground cumin

Directions
1. Using big skillet over medium heat, cook 3 tbsps. of olive oil, onion, garlic, and carrots for 3 min.
2. Cut the cauliflower into 1-inch or bite-size pieces. Add the cauliflower, salt, and cumin to the skillet and toss to combine with the carrots and onions.
3. Cover and cook for 3 min.
4. Throw the vegetables and continue to cook uncovered for an additional 3 to 4 min.
5. Serve warm.

Nutrition: 159 Calories: 3g Protein: 15g Carbohydrates

Roasted Acorn Squash

Preparation: 10 min | Cooking: 35 min | Servings: 6

Ingredients
- 2 acorn squash, medium to large
- 2 tablespoons extra-virgin olive oil
- 5 tablespoons unsalted butter
- ¼ cup chopped sage leaves
- 2 tablespoons fresh thyme leaves

Directions
1. Preheat the oven to 400°F.
2. Cut the acorn squash in half lengthwise. Scoop out the seeds and cut it horizontally into ¾-inch-thick slices.
3. In a large bowl, drizzle the squash with the olive oil, sprinkle with salt, and toss together to coat.
4. Lay the acorn squash flat on a baking sheet.
5. Situate the baking sheet in the oven and bake the squash for 20 min. Flip squash over with a spatula and bake for another 15 min.
6. Cook the butter in a medium saucepan over medium heat.
7. Sprinkle the sage and thyme to the melted butter and let them cook for 30 seconds.
8. Transfer the cooked squash slices to a plate. Spoon the butter/herb mixture over the squash. Season with salt and black pepper. Serve warm.

Nutrition: 188 Calories: 1g Protein: 16g Carbohydrates

Sweet Veggie-Stuffed Peppers

Preparation: 20 min | Cooking: 30 min | Servings: 6

Ingredients
- 6 large bell peppers, different colors
- 3 cloves garlic, minced
- 1 carrot, chopped
- 1 (16-ounce) can garbanzo beans
- 3 cups cooked rice

Directions
1. Preheat the oven to 350°F.
2. Make sure to choose peppers that can stand upright. Cut off the pepper cap and remove the seeds, reserving the cap for later. Stand the peppers in a baking dish.
3. In a skillet over medium heat, cook up olive oil, 1 onion, garlic, and carrots for 3 min.
4. Stir in the garbanzo beans. Cook for another 3 min.
5. Take out the pan from the heat and spoon the cooked ingredients to a large bowl.
6. Add the rice, salt, and pepper; toss to combine.
7. Stuff each pepper to the top and then put the pepper caps back on.
8. Wrap the baking dish using aluminum foil and bake for 25 min.
9. Pull out the foil and bake for 6 min.
10. Serve warm.

Nutrition: 301 Calories: 8g Protein: 50g Carbohydrate

Garlicky Sautéed Zucchini with Mint

Preparation: 5 min | Cooking: 10 min | Servings: 4

Ingredients
- 3 large green zucchinis
- 3 tablespoons extra-virgin olive oil
- 1 large onion, chopped
- 3 cloves garlic, minced
- 1 teaspoon dried mint

Directions
1. Cut the zucchini into ½-inch cubes.
2. Using huge skillet, place over medium heat, cook the olive oil, onions, and garlic for 3 min, stirring constantly.
3. Add the zucchini and salt to the skillet and toss to combine with the onions and garlic, cooking for 5 min.
4. Add the mint to the skillet, tossing to combine. Cook for another 2 min. Serve warm.

Nutrition: 147 Calories: 4g Protein: 12g Carbohydrates

Stewed Okra

Preparation: 5 min | Cooking: 25 min | Servings: 4

Ingredients
- 4 cloves garlic, finely chopped
- 1 pound fresh or frozen okra, cleaned
- 1 (15-ounce) can plain tomato sauce
- 2 cups water
- ½ cup fresh cilantro, finely chopped

Directions
1. In a big pot at medium heat, stir and cook ¼ cup of olive oil, 1 onion, garlic, and salt for 1 minute.
2. Stir in the okra and cook for 3 min.
3. Add the tomato sauce, water, cilantro, and black pepper; stir, cover, and let cook for 15 min, stirring occasionally.
4. Serve warm.

Nutrition: 201 Calories: 4g Protein: 18g Carbohydrates

Moussaka

Preparation: 55 min | Cooking: 40 min | Servings: 6

Ingredients
- 2 large eggplants, onions
- 10 cloves garlic, sliced
- 2 (15-ounce) cans diced tomatoes
- 1 (16-ounce) can garbanzo beans
- 1 teaspoon dried oregano

Directions
1. Slice the eggplant horizontally into ¼-inch-thick round disks. Sprinkle the eggplant slices with 1 teaspoon of salt and place in a colander for 31min.
2. Preheat the oven to 450°F. Pat the slices of eggplant dry with a paper towel and spray each side with an olive oil spray or lightly brush each side with olive oil.
3. Spread eggplant in a layer on a baking sheet. Bake for 10 min.
4. With a spatula, turn it over and bake for 12 min.
5. Using big skillet add the olive oil, onions, garlic, and remaining 1 teaspoon of salt. Cook for 3 min. Add the tomatoes, garbanzo beans, oregano, and black pepper. Simmer for 11 min.
6. Using a deep casserole dish, begin to layer, starting with eggplant, then the sauce. Repeat until all ingredients have been used. Bake in the oven for 20 min.
7. Remove from the oven and serve warm.

Nutrition: 262 Calories: 8g Protein: 35g Carbohydrates

Vegetable-Stuffed Grape Leaves

Preparation: 50 min | Cooking: 45 min | Servings: 7

Ingredients
- 2 cups white rice, rinsed
- 2 large tomatoes, finely diced
- 1 (16-ounce) jar grape leaves
- 1 cup lemon juice
- 4 to 6 cups water

Directions
1. Incorporate rice, tomatoes, 1 onion, 1 green onion, 1 cup of parsley, 3 garlic cloves, salt, and black pepper.
2. Drain and rinse the grape leaves.
3. Prepare a large pot by placing a layer of grape leaves on the bottom. Lay each leaf flat and trim off any stems.
4. Place 2 tablespoons of the rice mixture at the base of each leaf. Fold over the sides, then roll as tight as possible. Situate the rolled grape leaves in the pot, lining up each rolled grape leaf. Continue to layer in the rolled grape leaves.
5. Gently pour the lemon juice and olive oil over the grape leaves, and add enough water to just cover the grape leaves by 1 inch.

6. Lay a heavy plate that is smaller than the opening of the pot upside down over the grape leaves. Cover the pot and cook the leaves over medium-low heat for 45 min. Let stand for 20 min before serving.
7. Serve warm or cold.

Nutrition: 532 Calories: 12g Protein: 80g Carbohydrates

Grilled Eggplant Rolls

Preparation: 30 min | Cooking: 10 min | Servings: 5

Ingredients
- 2 large eggplants
- 4 ounces goat cheese
- 1 cup ricotta
- ¼ cup fresh basil, finely chopped

Directions
1. Slice the tops of the eggplants off and cut the eggplants lengthwise into ¼-inch-thick slices. Sprinkle the slices with the salt and place the eggplant in a colander for 15 to 20 min.
2. In a large bowl, combine the goat cheese, ricotta, basil, and pepper.
3. Preheat a grill, grill pan, or lightly oiled skillet on medium heat. Pat the eggplant slices dry using paper towel and lightly spray with olive oil spray. Place the eggplant on the grill, grill pan or skillet and cook for 3 min on each side.
4. Take out the eggplant from the heat and let cool for 5 min.
5. To roll, lay one eggplant slice flat, place a tablespoon of the cheese mixture at the base of the slice, and roll up. Serve immediately or chill until serving.

Nutrition: 255 Calories: 15g Protein: 19g Carbohydrates

Crispy Zucchini Fritters

Preparation: 15 min | Cooking: 20 min | Servings: 6

Ingredients
- 2 large green zucchinis
- 1 cup flour
- 1 large egg, beaten
- ½ cup water
- 1 teaspoon baking powder

Directions
1. Grate the zucchini into a large bowl.
2. Add the 2 tbsp. of parsley, 3 garlic cloves, salt, flour, egg, water, and baking powder to the bowl and stir to combine.
3. In a large pot or fryer over medium heat, heat oil to 365°F.
4. Drop the fritter batter into 3 cups of vegetable oil. Turn the fritters over using a slotted spoon and fry until they are golden brown, about 2 to 3 min.
5. Strain fritters from the oil and place on a plate lined with paper towels.
6. Serve warm with Creamy Tzatziki or Creamy Traditional Hummus as a dip.

Nutrition: 446 Calories: 5g Protein: 19g Carbohydrates

Green Beans and Potatoes in Olive Oil

Preparation: 12 min | Cooking: 17 min | Servings: 4

Ingredients
- 15 oz. tomatoes (diced)
- 2 potatoes
- 1 lb. green beans (fresh)
- 1 bunch dill, parsley, zucchini
- 1 tbsp. dried oregano

Directions
1. Turn on the sauté function on your instant pot.
2. Pour tomatoes, a cup of water and olive oil. Stir in the rest of the ingredients and stir through.
3. Close the instant pot and click the valve to seal. Set time for fifteen min.
4. When the time has elapsed release pressure. Remove the Fasolakia from the instant pot. Serve and enjoy.

Nutrition: 510 Calories: 20g Protein: 28g Carbohydrates

Cheesy Spinach Pies

Preparation: 20 min | Cooking: 40 min | Servings: 5

Ingredients
- 2 tablespoons extra-virgin olive oil
- 3 (1-pound) bags of baby spinach, washed
- 1 cup feta cheese
- 1 large egg, beaten
- Puff pastry sheets

Directions
1. Preheat the oven to 375°F.
2. Using big skillet over medium heat, cook the olive oil, 1 onion, and 2 garlic cloves for 3 min.

3. Add the spinach to the skillet one bag at a time, letting it wilt in between each bag. Toss using tongs. Cook for 4 min. Once cooked, strain any extra liquid from the pan.
4. Mix feta cheese, egg, and cooked spinach.
5. Lay the puff pastry flat on a counter. Cut the pastry into 3-inch squares.
6. Place a tablespoon of the spinach mixture in the center of a puff-pastry square. Turn over one corner of the square to the diagonal corner, forming a triangle. Crimp the edges of the pie by pressing down with the tines of a fork to seal them together. Repeat until all squares are filled.
7. Situate the pies on a parchment-lined baking sheet and bake for 25 to 30 min or until golden brown. Serve warm or at room temperature.

Nutrition: 503 Calories: 16g Protein: 38g Carbohydrates

Instant Pot Black Eyed Peas

Preparation: 6 min | Cooking: 25 min | Servings: 4

Ingredients
- 2 cups black-eyed peas (dried)
- 1 cup parsley, dill
- 2 slices oranges
- 2 tbsp. tomato paste
- 4 green onions
- 2 carrots, bay leaves

Directions
1. Clean the dill thoroughly with water removing stones.
2. Add all the ingredients in the instant pot and stir well to combine.
3. Lid the instant pot and set the vent to sealing.
4. Set time for twenty-five min. When the time has elapsed release pressure naturally.
5. Serve and enjoy the black-eyed peas.

Nutrition: 506 Calories: 14g Protein: 33g Carbohydrates

Nutritious Vegan Cabbage

Preparation: 35 min | Cooking: 15 min | Servings: 6

Ingredients
- 3 cups green cabbage
- 1 can tomatoes, onion
- Cups vegetable broth
- 3 stalks celery, carrots
- 2 tbsp. vinegar, sage

Directions
1. Mix 1 tbsp. of lemon juice. 2 garlic cloves and the rest of ingredients in the instant pot and. Lid and set time for fifteen min on high pressure.
2. Release pressure naturally then remove the lid. Remove the soup from the instant pot.
3. Serve and enjoy.

Nutrition: 67 Calories: 0.4g Fat 3.8g Fiber

Instant Pot Horta and Potatoes

Preparation: 12 min | Cooking: 17 min | Servings: 4

Ingredients
- 2 heads of washed and chopped greens (spinach, Dandelion, kale, mustard green, Swiss chard)
- 6 potatoes (washed and cut in pieces)
- 1 cup virgin olive oil
- 1 lemon juice (reserve slices for serving)
- 10 garlic cloves (chopped)

Directions
1. Position all the ingredients in the instant pot and lid setting the vent to sealing.
2. Set time for fifteen min. When time is done release pressure.
3. Let the potatoes rest for some time. Serve and enjoy with lemon slices.

Nutrition: 499 Calories: 18g Protein: 41g Carbohydrates

Instant Pot Artichokes with Mediterranean Aioli

Preparation: 7 min | Cooking: 10 min | Servings: 3

Ingredients
- 3 medium artichokes (stems cut off)
- 1 cup vegetable broth
- Mediterranean aioli

Directions
1. Place wire trivet in place in the instant pot then place the artichokes on the wire.
2. Pour vegetable broth over artichokes.
3. Lid the instant pot and put steam mode on. Set time for 10 min. When the time has elapsed allow pressure to release.
4. Remove the artichokes from the instant pot and reserve the remaining broth, about a quarter cup.
5. Half the artichokes and place them on serving bowls. Drizzle broth.

6. Serve with aioli and enjoy.

Nutrition: 30 Calories: 0.1g Fat 3.5g Fiber

Instant Pot Jackfruit Curry

Preparation: 1 h | Cooking: 16 min | Servings: 2

Ingredients
- 1 tbsp. oil
- Cumin seeds, Mustard seeds
- 2 tomatoes (purred)
- 20 oz. can green jackfruit (drained and rinsed)
- 1 tbsp. coriander powder, turmeric.

Directions
1. Turn the instant pot to sauté mode. Add cumin seeds, mustard, ten nigella seeds and allow them to sizzle.
2. Add 2 red chilies and 2 bay leaves and allow cooking for a few seconds.
3. Add chopped 1 onion, 5 garlic cloves, ginger and salt, and pepper to taste. Stir cook for five min.
4. Add other ingredients and a cup of water then lid the instant pot. Set time for seven min on high pressure.
5. When the time has elapsed release pressure naturally, shred the jackfruit and serve.

Nutrition: 369 Calories: 3g Fat 6g Fiber

Instant Pot Collard Greens with Tomatoes

Preparation: 18 min | Cooking: 8 min | Servings: 4

Ingredients
- 1 white onion (diced)
- 3tbsp olive oil
- 3 garlic cloves (minced)
- Cup tomatoes (sun-dried and chopped)
- 1 bunch collard greens (roughly cut and hard stems removed)

Directions
1. Turn on the sauté function on your instant pot.
2. Add onions and olive oil to the instant pot and let cook for three min or lightly browned.
3. Mix in the rest of ingredients simultaneously while stirring.
4. Add salt and pepper to taste and a cup of water. Turn off the sauté function and set to manual. Set time for five min at high pressure.
5. When the time has elapsed, release pressure naturally.

6. Open the lid and drizzle a half lemon juice.
7. Serve and enjoy.

Nutrition: 498 Calories: 19g Protein: 32g Carbohydrates

Instant Pot Millet Pilaf

Preparation: 23 min | Cooking: 11 min | Servings: 4

Ingredients
- 1 cup millet
- Cup apricot and shelled pistachios (roughly chopped)
- 1 lemon juice and zest
- 1 tbsp. olive oil
- Cup parsley (fresh)

Directions
1. Pour one and three-quarter cup of water in your instant pot. Place the millet and lid the instant pot.
2. Adjust time for 10 min on high pressure. When the time has elapsed, release pressure naturally.
3. Remove the lid and add all other ingredients. Stir while adjusting the seasonings.
4. Serve and enjoy

Nutrition: 308 Calories: 11g Fat 6g Fiber

Barley & Mushroom Soup

Preparation: 7 min | Cooking: 27 min | Servings: 6

Ingredients
- ¼ cup red wine
- 2 tablespoons olive oil
- 1 cup carrots, chopped
- 1 cup onion, chopped
- ½ cups mushrooms, chopped
- 2 cups vegetable broth, low sodium
- 1 cup pearled barley, uncooked
- 2 tablespoons tomato paste
- 1 bay leaf
- 6 tablespoons parmesan cheese, grated
- 4 sprigs thyme, fresh

Directions
1. Get out a stockpot and place it over medium heat. Heat your oil and add in your carrots and onion. Cook for five min and frequently stir during this time.
2. Turn your heat up to medium-high before throwing in your mushrooms. Cook for another three min. Make sure to stir frequently.

3. Add in your barley, tomato paste, thyme, wine, broth, and bay leaf. Stir and cover. Bring to boil, and stir a few more times. Reduce to medium-low heat. Cover, and cook for another twelve to fifteen min.
4. Remove your bay leaf and serve topped with cheese.

Nutrition: Calories: 491; Fat: 12g; Protein: 19g

Instant Pot Stuffed Sweet Potatoes

Preparation: 13 min | Cooking: 22 min | Servings: 2

Ingredients
- 2 sweet potatoes (washed thoroughly)
- cup chickpeas, onions
- 2 spring onions
- 1 avocado
- cooked couscous

Directions
1. Pour a cup and half of water in your instant pot then place steam rack in place.
2. Place the sweet potatoes on the rack. Set the valve to sealing and time for seventeen min under high pressure.
3. Meanwhile, roast the chickpeas on your pan with olive oil.
4. Add salt and pepper to taste then paprika. Stir until chickpeas are coated evenly.
5. Cook for a minute then put off the heat.
6. When the instant pot time elapses, release pressure naturally for five min. Let the sweet potatoes cool then remove them from the instant pot.
7. Cut the sweet potatoes lengthwise and use a fork to mash the inside creating a space for toppings.
8. Add the pre-prepared toppings then serve with feta cheese lemon wedges.

Nutrition: 776 Calories; 26g Fat; 23g Protein;

Instant Pot Couscous and Vegetable Medley

Preparation: 9 min | Cooking: 17 min | Servings: 3

Ingredients
- Onion (chopped)
- 1 red bell pepper (chopped)
- cup couscous Israeli, carrot
- Garam masala, cilantro, lemon juice,
- 2 bays leave

Directions
- Put on sauté function on your instant pot then add olive oil.
- Add bay leaves followed by chopped onions the sauté for two min.
- Add pepper and carrots then continue to sauté for one more minute.
- Stir in couscous, Garam masala, salt to taste and a cup and three-quarter of water.
- Switch the sauté function to manual and set for two min. When the time has elapsed naturally release pressure for ten min.
- Fluff the couscous then mix in lemon juice and garnish with cilantro.
- Remove from instant pot and serve when hot

Nutrition: 460 Calories: 5g Fat 13g Protein

Chickpea Pasta Salad

Preparation: 8 min | Cooking: 17 min | Servings: 6

Ingredients
- 2 tablespoons olive oil
- 16 ounces rotelle pasta
- ½ cup cured olives, chopped
- 2 tablespoons oregano, fresh & minced
- 2 tablespoons parsley, fresh & chopped
- 1 bunch green onions, chopped
- ¼ cup red wine vinegar
- 15 ounces canned garbanzo beans, drained & rinsed
- ½ cup parmesan cheese, grated
- sea salt & black pepper to taste

Directions
1. Bring water to boil and cook your pasta al dente per package instructions. Drain it and rinse it using cold water.
2. Get out a skillet and heat your olive oil over medium heat. Add in your scallions, chickpeas, parsley, oregano, and olives. Set the heat to low then cook for twenty min more. Allow this mixture to cool.
3. Toss your chickpea mixture with your pasta and add in your grated cheese, salt, pepper, and vinegar. Chill before serving.

Nutrition: Calories: 445; Fat: 9g; Protein: 13g

Bean Lettuce Wraps

Preparation: 9 min | Cooking: 7 min | Servings: 4

Ingredients
- 15 ounces cannellini beans, canned, drained & rinsed sea salt & black pepper to taste
- ¾ cup tomatoes, fresh & chopped
- ½ cup red onion, diced
- 1 tbsp. olive oil
- ¼ cup parsley, fresh & chopped fine
- 8 romaine lettuce leaves
- ½ cup hummus

Directions
1. Get out a skillet and place it over medium heat. Heat your oil. Once your oil is hot, adding in your onion, and cook for three min. Stir occasionally.
2. Stir in your tomatoes and season with salt and pepper. Cook for another three min. Add in your beans and heat all the way through. Stir it, so it doesn't burn. Remove it from heat, and then mix in your parsley.
3. Spread a tablespoon of hummus on each lettuce leaf and then top with your bean mixture. Fold, and then wrap before serving.

Nutrition: Calories: 405; Fat: 6g; Protein: 10g

Easy Lentil & Rice Bowl

Preparation: 6 min | Cooking: 29 min | Servings: 4

Ingredients
- ¼ cup parsley, curly leaf, fresh & chopped
- 1 ½ tablespoons olive oil
- sea salt & black pepper to taste
- 1 clove garlic, minced
- 1 tablespoon lemon juice, fresh
- 1 (6-oz.) can onion, drained
- ½ cup celery, diced
- ½ cup carrots, diced
- ½ cup instant brown rice, uncooked
- ½ cup green lentils, uncooked
- ¼ vegetable broth, low sodium

Directions
1. Put a saucepan over high heat, and then bring your lentils to a boil with the broth. Cover once it begins to boil, and then lower the heat to medium-low. Cook for eight min.
2. Set the heat to medium, and add in your rice. Stir well, and cover. Cook for fifteen more min. The liquid should be absorbed.
3. Allow it to set off the heat and cover for one minute before stirring.
4. Mix your celery, olives, onion, carrot, and parsley in a bowl while your rice and lentils are cooking.

5. Get out a bowl and whisk your oil, lemon juice, salt, pepper, and garlic together. Set this to the side.
6. When your rice and lentils are cooked, add them to a serving bowl and top with the dressing. Serve immediately.

Nutrition: Calories: 391; Fat: 8g; Protein: 12g

Chickpea Pita Patties

Preparation: 12 min | Cooking: 21 min | Servings: 4

Ingredients
- egg, large
- teaspoons oregano
- ½ cup panko bread crumbs, whole wheat sea salt & black pepper to taste
- 1 tablespoon olive oil
- 1 cucumber, halved lengthwise 6 ounces Greek yogurt, 2%
- clove garlic, minced
- pita bread, whole wheat & halved
- 1 tomato, cut into 4 thick slices
- ½ cup hummus
- 15 ounces chickpeas, drained & rinsed

Directions
1. Get out a large bowl, mash your chickpeas with a potato masher, and then add in your bread crumbs, eggs, hummus, oregano, and pepper. Stir well. Form four patties, and then press them flat on a plate. They should be ¾ inch thick.
2. Get out a skillet, placing it over medium-high heat. Heat the oil until hot, which should take three min. Cook the patties for five min per side.
3. While your patties are cooking, shred half of your cucumber with a grader, and then stir your shredded cucumber, garlic, and yogurt together to make a tzatziki sauce. Slice the remaining cucumber into slices that are a quarter of an inch thick before placing them to the side.
4. Toast your pita bread, and then assemble your sandwich with each one having a tomato slice, a few slices of cucumber, chickpea patty, and drizzle each one with your sauce to serve.

Nutrition: Calories: 387; Fat: 7g; Protein: 11g

Mushrooms with Soy Sauce Glaze

Preparation: 11 min | Cooking: 28 min | Servings: 2

Ingredients
- 2 tablespoons butter
- 1 (8 oz.) package sliced white mushrooms
- 2 cloves garlic, minced
- 2 teaspoons soy sauce
- ground black pepper to taste

Directions
1. Undo the butter in a skillet; add the mushrooms; cook and stir until the mushrooms are soft and released about 5 min.
2. Stir in the garlic; keep cooking and stir for 1 minute. Pour the soy sauce; cook the mushrooms in the soy sauce until the liquid has evaporated, about 4 min.

Nutrition: Calories: 455; Fat: 11g; Protein: 18g

California Grilled Vegetable Sandwich

Preparation: 6 min | Cooking: 17 min | Servings: 4

Ingredients
- 1/4 cup mayonnaise
- 3 garlic cloves, minced
- 1 tablespoon lemon juice
- 1/8 cup olive oil
- 1 cup sliced red peppers
- 1 small zucchini, sliced
- 1 red onion, sliced
- 1 small yellow pumpkin, sliced
- 2 pieces of focaccia bread (4 x 6 inch), split horizontally
- 1/2 cup of crumbled feta cheese

Directions
1. Combine the mayonnaise, chopped garlic, and lemon juice in a bowl. Chill in the fridge.
2. Preheat the grill on high heat.
3. Brush the vegetables with olive oil on each side. Brush the grill with oil. Place the pepper and zucchini closest to the grill center and add the onions and squash pieces. Bake for about 3 min, turn around and cook for another 3 min. Peppers can take a little longer. Remove from the grill and set aside.
4. Spread a little mayonnaise mixture on the sliced sides of the bread and sprinkle with feta cheese. Place the cheese on the grill and cover with the lid for 2 to 3 min.
5. Get away from the grill and brush with the vegetables. Enjoy open face grilled sandwiches.

Nutrition: Calories: 461; Fat: 12g; Protein: 21g

Delicious Sweet Potato Casserole

Preparation: 11 min | Cooking: 26 min | Servings: 12

Ingredients
- 4 cups sweet potatoes, diced
- 1/2 cup white sugar
- 2 beaten eggs
- 1/2 teaspoon of salt
- 4 tablespoons of soft butter
- 1/2 cup milk
- 1/2 teaspoon vanilla extract
- 1/2 cup packed brown sugar
- 1/3 cup all-purpose flour
- 3 tablespoons butter
- 1/2 cup soft chopped pecans

Directions
1. Preheat the oven to 165 degrees (325° F). Put the sweet potatoes in a medium-sized pan with water to cover. Cook over medium heat until soft; drain and crush.
2. Combine sweet potatoes, white sugar, eggs, salt, butter, milk, and vanilla extract in a large bowl. Mix until smooth. Transfer to a baking dish.
3. Put sugar and flour in a bowl. Cut the butter until the mixture is coarse. Stir in the pecans. Now sprinkle the mixture over the sweet potato mixture.
4. Bake in the prepared oven for 31 min or until light brown.

Nutrition: Calories: 445; Fat: 9g; Protein: 13g

Light and Fluffy Spinach Quiche

Preparation: 9 min | Cooking: 21 min | Servings: 6

Ingredients
- 1/2 cup light mayonnaise
- 1/2 cup milk
- 4 lightly beaten eggs
- 8 oz. grated cheddar cheese
- 1 packet of chopped spinach frozen, thawed, and drained
- 1/4 cup chopped onion
- 1 (9-inch) uncooked pie crust

Directions
1. Put the oven to 200 degrees. Cover a baking sheet with aluminum foil.
2. In a large bowl, mix mayonnaise and milk until smooth. Stir in the eggs. Arrange the spinach, cheese, and onion in the pie and form several layers. Pour in the egg mixture.

3. Place the quiche on the prepared baking sheet. Cover the quiche with aluminum foil.
4. Bake for 45 min in the oven. Open and bake for 12 min.

Nutrition: Calories: 465; Fat: 13g; Protein: 21g

Spicy Bean Salsa

Preparation: 9 min | Cooking: 7 min | Servings: 12

Ingredients

- 1 (15 oz.) can black beans
- 1 can of whole-grain corn
- 1/2 cup chopped onion
- 1/2 cup chopped green pepper
- 1 can diced jalapeño pepper
- 1 can of tomato cubes, drained
- 1 cup of Italian dressing
- 1/2 teaspoon of garlic salt

Directions

1. Mix black-eyed peas, black beans, corn, onion, green pepper, jalapeño peppers, and tomatoes. Season with Italian dressing and salt with garlic; mix well. Put in the fridge overnight to mix the flavors.

Nutrition: Calories: 421; Fat: 7g; Protein: 19g

Hot Artichoke and Spinach Dip

Preparation: 12 min | Cooking: 22 min | Servings: 12

Ingredients

- 1/4 cup mayonnaise
- 1 (8-oz) package cream cheese, softened
- 1/4 cup grated Parmesan cheese
- 1/4 cup grated Romano cheese
- 1 clove garlic, peeled and minced
- 1/2 teaspoon dried basil
- 1/4 teaspoon garlic
- salt and pepper to taste
- 1 (14-oz) artichoke hearts, drained
- 1/2 cup frozen spinach
- 1/4 cup shredded mozzarella cheese

Directions

1. Prep oven to 350 F. Lightly grease a small baking dish.
2. Scourge cream cheese, mayonnaise, Parmesan cheese, Romano cheese, garlic, basil, garlic salt, salt, and pepper. Gently stir in artichoke hearts and spinach.
3. Transfer the mixture to the baking dish. Top with mozzarella cheese. Bake in the prepared oven for 25 min., until bubbly and lightly browned.

Nutrition: Calories: 475; Fat: 14g; Protein: 26g

Harvest Salad

Preparation: 14 min | Cooking: 9 min | Servings: 6

Ingredients

- 1/2 cup chopped nuts
- 1 bunch of spinach, rinsed and torn into bite-sized pieces
- 1/2 cup dried cranberries
- 1/2 cup of crumbled blue cheese
- 2 tomatoes, minced
- 1 avocado - peeled, seeded, and diced
- 1/2 red onion, thinly sliced
- 2 tablespoons red raspberry jam (with seeds)
- 2 tablespoons red wine vinegar
- 1/3 cup walnut oil
- freshly ground black pepper
- salt

Directions

1. Preheat the oven to 200 degrees. Put the nuts on a baking sheet. Grill in the oven for 7 min.
2. Combine spinach, walnuts, cranberries, blue cheese, tomatoes, avocado, and red onion in a large bowl.
3. Mix jam, vinegar, walnut oil, pepper, and salt in a small bowl. Pour the salad dressing just before serving and mix well.

Nutrition: Calories: 411; Fat: 8g; Protein: 16g

Sweet Potato Casserole Dessert

Preparation: 9 min | Cooking: 26 min | Servings: 18

Ingredients

- 4 1/2 cups of cooked sweet potatoes
- 1/2 cup melted butter
- 1/3 cup milk
- 1 cup white sugar
- 1/2 teaspoon vanilla extract
- 2 eggs, beaten
- 1 cup light brown sugar
- 1/2 cup all-purpose flour
- 1/3 cup butter
- 1 cup chopped pecans

Directions

1. Preheat the oven to 175 degrees (350° F).

2. Combine mashed potatoes, 1/2 cup butter, milk, sugar, vanilla extract, and eggs in a large bowl. Arrange the sweet potato mixture in the prepared baking dish.

3. Combine brown sugar and flour in a small bowl. Add 1/3 cup butter until the mixture is crumbly, and add the pecans. Sprinkle the pecan mixture over the sweet potatoes.

4. Bake in the prepared oven for 25 min or until golden brown.

Nutrition: Calories: 435; Fat: 12g; Protein: 19g

Cranberry Sauce

Preparation: 6 min | Cooking: 17 min | Servings: 11

Ingredients

- 12 ounces cranberries
- 1 cup white sugar
- 1 cup of orange juice

Directions

1. Using saucepan, dissolve the sugar in the orange juice.

2. Stir in the cranberries and cook until the cranberries begin to appear (about 10 min). Pull out from heat and put the sauce in a bowl. The cranberry sauce becomes thicker as it cools.

Nutrition: Calories: 497; Fat: 16g; Protein: 26g

Vegetarian Meatloaf

Preparation: 19 min | Cooking: 31 min | Servings: 8

Ingredients

- 1 bottle of barbecue sauce
- 1 package of vegetarian burgers (12 oz.)
- 1 green pepper, minced
- 1/3 cup chopped onion
- 1 clove garlic
- 1/2 cup breadcrumbs
- 3 tablespoons Parmesan cheese
- 1 beaten egg
- 1/4 teaspoon dried thyme
- 1/4 c. dried basil
- 1/4 teaspoon
- Salt and pepper to taste

Directions

1. Preheat the oven to 165 degrees (325° F). Grease a 5 x 9-inch light bread pan.

2. Blend half of the barbecue sauce with the vegetarian burgers, green pepper, onion, garlic, breadcrumbs, parmesan cheese, and egg. Season with thyme, basil, parsley, salt, and pepper put in the bread pan.

3. Bake for 45 min in the prepared oven. Pour the rest of the barbecue sauce onto the bread and continue to cook for 15 min.

Nutrition: Calories: 449; Fat: 14g; Protein: 23g

Eggs Over Kale Hash

Servings: 4 | Cooking: 20 min

Ingredients

- 4 large eggs
- 1 bunch chopped kale

- Dash of ground nutmeg
- 2 sweet potatoes, cubed
- 1 14.5-ounce can of chicken broth

Directions

1. In a large non-stick skillet, bring the chicken broth to a simmer. Add the sweet potatoes and season slightly with salt and pepper. Add a dash of nutmeg to improve the flavor.

2. Cook until the sweet potatoes become soft, around 10 minutes. Add kale and season with salt and pepper. Continue cooking for four minutes or until kale has wilted. Set aside.

3. Using the same skillet, heat 1 tablespoon of olive oil over medium high heat.

4. Cook the eggs sunny side up until the whites become opaque and the yolks have set. Top the kale hash with the eggs. Serve immediately.

Nutrition: Calories per serving: 158; Protein: 9.8g; Carbs 18.5g; Fat: 5.6g

Baba Ganoush

Servings: 2 Tablespoons | Cooking: 50 min

Ingredients

- 2 large eggplants
- 4 TB. extra-virgin olive oil
- 1 large white onion, chopped
- 1 TB. minced garlic
- 3 TB. fresh lemon juice
- 1 tsp. salt
- 1/2 tsp. ground black pepper
- 1/2 medium red bell pepper, ribs and seeds removed, and finely diced
- 1/2 medium green bell pepper, ribs and seeds removed, and finely diced
- 3 TB. fresh parsley, finely chopped
- 1/2 tsp. cayenne
- 3 medium radishes, finely diced
- 3 whole green onions, finely chopped

Directions

1. Preheat a grill top or a grill to medium-low heat.

2. Place eggplants on the grill, and roast on all sides for 40 minutes, turning every 5 minutes. Immediately place eggplants on a plate, cover with plastic wrap, let cool for 15 minutes.

3. Remove eggplant stems, and peel off as much skin as possible. (It's okay if it doesn't all come off.)

4. In a food processor fitted with a chopping blade, pulse eggplant 7 times. Transfer eggplant to a medium bowl.

5. In a medium saucepan over low heat, heat 2 tablespoons extra-virgin olive oil. Add white onion, and sauté, stirring occasionally, for 10 minutes. Add onions to eggplant.

6. Add garlic, lemon juice, salt, black pepper, red bell pepper, green bell pepper, and parsley to eggplant, and stir well.

7. Spread baba ganoush on a serving plate, and drizzle remaining 2 tablespoons extra-virgin olive oil over top. Sprinkle with cayenne, radishes, and green onions.

8. Serve cold or at room temperature.

Leek And Potato Soup

Servings: 8 | Cooking: 1 Hour

Ingredients

- 3 tablespoons olive oil
- 3 leeks, sliced
- 4 garlic cloves, chopped
- 6 potatoes, peeled and cubed
- 2 cups vegetable stock
- 2 cups water
- 1 thyme sprig
- 1 rosemary sprig
- Salt and pepper to taste

Directions

1. Heat the oil in a soup pot and stir in the leeks. Cook for 15 minutes until slightly caramelized.

2. Add the garlic and cook for 2 more minutes.

3. Add the rest of the ingredients and season with salt and pepper.

4. Cook on low heat for 20 minutes then remove the herb sprigs and puree the soup with an immersion blender.

5. Serve the soup fresh.

Nutrition: Calories:179 Fat:5.5g Protein:3.4g Carbohydrates:30.6g

Mast-o Khiar (Aka Persian Yogurt And Cucumbers)

Servings: 8 | Cooking: 10 min

Ingredients

- 4 cup yogurt, plain Greek
- 2 teaspoon mint, dried
- 2 teaspoon dill, dried
- 1/4 teaspoon black pepper, ground
- 1/2 teaspoon salt
- 1 1/2 cup Persian cucumbers, diced

Directions

1. Combine all the ingredients in a medium-sized bowl.

Nutrition: 62 cal., 4 g total fat (0.8 g sat. fat), 0 mg chol., 1 mg sodium, 81 mg pot., 7.2 g total carbs., 1.3 g fiber, 5.5 g sugar, 0.8 g protein, 0% vitamin A, 0% vitamin C, 1% calcium, and 3% iron.

Homemade Greek Yogurt

Servings: ½ Cup | Cooking: 20 min

Ingredients

- 1 gal. whole milk
- 2 cups plain Greek yogurt

Directions

1. In a large pot over medium-low heat, bring whole milk to a simmer until a froth starts to form on the surface. If you have a thermometer, bring the milk to 185°F.

2. Remove from heat, and let milk cool to lukewarm, or 110°F.

3. Pour all but about 2 cups milk into a large plastic container.

4. Pour remaining 2 cups milk into a smaller bowl. Add Greek yogurt, and stir until well combined.

5. Slowly pour milk and yogurt mixture into the large bowl of milk, and stir well.

6. Cover the bowl with a lid, and set aside where it won't be disturbed. Cover it with a towel, and let it sit overnight.

7. The next morning, gently transfer the bowl to the refrigerator. Chill for at least 1 day.

8. The next day, gently pour off clear liquid that's formed on top of yogurt, leaving just a little liquid remaining.

9. Serve, or store in the refrigerator for up to 2 weeks.

Curried Chicken, Chickpeas And Raita Salad

Servings: 8 | Cooking: 15 min

Ingredients

- 1 cup red grapes, halved
- 3-4 cups rotisserie chicken, meat coarsely shredded
- 2 tbsp cilantro
- 1 cup plain yogurt
- 2 medium tomatoes, chopped
- 1 tsp ground cumin
- 1 tbsp curry powder
- 2 tbsp olive oil
- 1 tbsp minced peeled ginger
- 1 tbsp minced garlic
- 1 medium onion, chopped
- ¼ tsp cayenne
- ½ tsp turmeric
- 1 tsp ground cumin
- 1 19-oz can chickpeas, rinsed, drained and patted dry

- 1 tbsp olive oil
- ½ cup sliced and toasted almonds
- 2 tbsp chopped mint
- 2 cups cucumber, peeled, cored and chopped
- 1 cup plain yogurt

Directions

1. To make the chicken salad, on medium low fire, place a medium nonstick saucepan and heat oil.

2. Sauté ginger, garlic and onion for 5 minutes or until softened while stirring occasionally.

3. Add 1 ½ tsp salt, cumin and curry. Sauté for two minutes.

4. Increase fire to medium high and add tomatoes. Stirring frequently, cook for 5 minutes.

5. Pour sauce into a bowl, mix in chicken, cilantro and yogurt. Stir to combine and let it stand to cool to room temperature.

6. To make the chickpeas, on a nonstick fry pan, heat oil for 3 minutes.

7. Add chickpeas and cook for a minute while stirring frequently.

8. Add ¼ tsp salt, cayenne, turmeric and cumin. Stir to mix well and cook for two minutes or until sauce is dried.

9. Transfer to a bowl and let it cool to room temperature.

10. To make the raita, mix ½ tsp salt, mint, cucumber and yogurt. Stir thoroughly to combine and dissolve salt.

11. To assemble, in four 16-oz lidded jars or bowls layer the following: curried chicken, raita, chickpeas and garnish with almonds.

12. You can make this recipe one day ahead and refrigerate for 6 hours before serving.

Nutrition: Calories per serving: 381; Protein: 36.1g; Carbs: 27.4g; Fat: 15.5g

Bulgur Tomato Pilaf

Servings: 1 Cup | Cooking: 27 min

Ingredients

- 1 lb. ground beef
- 3 TB. extra-virgin olive oil
- 1 large yellow onion, finely chopped
- 2 medium tomatoes, diced
- 11/2 tsp. salt
- 1 tsp. ground black pepper
- 2 cups plain tomato sauce
- 2 cups water
- 2 cups bulgur wheat, grind #2

Directions

1. In a large, 3-quart pot over medium heat, brown beef for 5 minutes, breaking up chunks with a wooden spoon.

2. Add extra-virgin olive oil and yellow onion, and cook for 5 minutes.

3. Stir in tomatoes, salt, and black pepper, and cook for 5 minutes.

4. Add tomato sauce and water, and simmer for 10 minutes.

5. Add bulgur wheat, and cook for 2 minutes. Remove from heat, cover, and let sit for 5 minutes. Uncover, fluff bulgur with a fork, cover, and let sit for 5 more minutes.

6. Serve warm.

Garbanzo And Kidney Bean Salad

Servings: 4 | Cooking: 0 min

Ingredients

- 1 (15 ounce) can kidney beans, drained
- 1 (15.5 ounce) can garbanzo beans, drained
- 1 lemon, zested and juiced
- 1 medium tomato, chopped
- 1 teaspoon capers, rinsed and drained
- 1/2 cup chopped fresh parsley
- 1/2 teaspoon salt, or to taste
- 1/4 cup chopped red onion
- 3 tablespoons extra virgin olive oil

Directions

1. In a salad bowl, whisk well lemon juice, olive oil and salt until dissolved.

2. Stir in garbanzo, kidney beans, tomato, red onion, parsley, and capers. Toss well to coat.

3. Allow flavors to mix for 30 minutes by setting in the fridge.

4. Mix again before serving.

Nutrition: Calories per serving: 329; Protein: 12.1g; Carbs: 46.6g; Fat: 12.0g

Rice & Currant Salad Mediterranean Style

Servings: 4 | Cooking: 50 min

Ingredients

- 1 cup basmati rice
- salt
- 2 1/2 Tablespoons lemon juice
- 1 teaspoon grated orange zest
- 2 Tablespoons fresh orange juice
- 1/4 cup olive oil
- 1/2 teaspoon cinnamon
- Salt and pepper to taste
- 4 chopped green onions
- 1/2 cup dried currants
- 3/4 cup shelled pistachios or almonds
- 1/4 cup chopped fresh parsley

Directions

1. Place a nonstick pot on medium high fire and add rice. Toast rice until opaque and starts to smell, around 10 minutes.

2. Add 4 quarts of boiling water to pot and 2 tsp salt. Boil until tender, around 8 minutes uncovered.

3. Drain the rice and spread out on a lined cookie sheet to cool completely.

4. In a large salad bowl, whisk well the oil, juices and spices. Add salt and pepper to taste.

5. Add half of the green onions, half of parsley, currants, and nuts.

6. Toss with the cooled rice and let stand for at least 20 minutes.

7. If needed adjust seasoning with pepper and salt.

8. Garnish with remaining parsley and green onions.

Nutrition: Calories per serving: 450; Carbs: 50.0g; Protein: 9.0g; Fat: 24.0g

Orange, Dates And Asparagus On Quinoa Salad

Servings: 8 | Cooking: 25 min

Ingredients

- ¼ cup chopped pecans, toasted
- ½ cup white onion, finely chopped
- ½ jalapeno pepper, diced
- ½ lb. asparagus, sliced into 2-inch lengths, steamed and chilled
- ½ tsp salt
- 1 cup fresh orange sections
- 1 cup uncooked quinoa
- 1 tsp olive oil
- 2 cups water
- 2 tbsp minced red onion
- 5 dates, pitted and chopped
- ¼ tsp freshly ground black pepper
- ¼ tsp salt
- 1 garlic clove, minced
- 1 tbsp extra virgin olive oil
- 2 tbsp chopped fresh mint
- 2 tbsp fresh lemon juice
- Mint sprigs – optional

Directions

1. On medium high fire, place a large nonstick pan and heat 1 tsp oil.

2. Add white onion and sauté for two minutes.

3. Add quinoa and for 5 minutes sauté it.

4. Add salt and water. Bring to a boil, once boiling, slow fire to a simmer and cook for 15 minutes while covered.

5. Turn off fire and leave for 15 minutes, to let quinoa absorb the remaining water.

6. Transfer quinoa to a large salad bowl. Add jalapeno pepper, asparagus, dates, red onion, pecans and oranges. Toss to combine.

7. Make the dressing by mixing garlic, pepper, salt, olive oil and lemon juice in a small bowl.

8. Pour dressing into quinoa salad along with chopped mint, mix well.

9. If desired, garnish with mint sprigs before serving.

Nutrition: Calories: 265.2; Carbs: 28.3g; Protein: 14.6g; Fat: 10.4g

Stuffed Tomatoes With Green Chili

Servings: 6 | Cooking: 55 min

Ingredients

- 4 oz Colby-Jack shredded cheese
- ¼ cup water
- 1 cup uncooked quinoa
- 6 large ripe tomatoes
- ¼ tsp freshly ground black pepper
- ¾ tsp ground cumin
- 1 tsp salt, divided
- 1 tbsp fresh lime juice
- 1 tbsp olive oil
- 1 tbsp chopped fresh oregano
- 1 cup chopped onion
- 2 cups fresh corn kernels
- 2 poblano chilies

Directions

1. Preheat broiler to high.

2. Slice lengthwise the chilies and press on a baking sheet lined with foil. Broil for 8 minutes. Remove from oven and let cool for 10 minutes. Peel the chilies and chop coarsely and place in medium sized bowl.

3. Place onion and corn in baking sheet and broil for ten minutes. Stir two times while broiling. Remove from oven and mix in with chopped chilies.

4. Add black pepper, cumin, ¼ tsp salt, lime juice, oil and oregano. Mix well.

5. Cut off the tops of tomatoes and set aside. Leave the tomato shell intact as you scoop out the tomato pulp.

6. Drain tomato pulp as you press down with a spoon. Reserve 1 ¼ cups of tomato pulp liquid and discard the rest. Invert the tomato shells on a wire rack for 30 mins and then wipe the insides dry with a paper towel.

7. Season with ½ tsp salt the tomato pulp.

8. On a sieve over a bowl, place quinoa. Add water until it covers quinoa. Rub quinoa grains for 30 seconds together with hands; rinse and drain. Repeat this procedure two times and drain well at the end.

9. In medium saucepan bring to a boil remaining salt, ¼ cup water, quinoa and tomato liquid.

10. Once boiling, reduce heat and simmer for 15 minutes or until liquid is fully absorbed. Remove from heat and fluff quinoa with fork. Transfer and mix well the quinoa with the corn mixture.

11. Spoon ¾ cup of the quinoa-corn mixture into the tomato shells, top with cheese and cover with the tomato top. Bake in a preheated 350ºF oven for 15 minutes and then broil high for another 1.5 minutes.

Nutrition: Calories per serving: 276; Carbs: 46.3g; Protein: 13.4g; Fat: 4.1g

Red Wine Risotto

Servings: 8 | Cooking: 25 min

Ingredients

- Pepper to taste
- 1 cup finely shredded Parmigian-Reggiano cheese, divided
- 2 tsp tomato paste
- 1 ¾ cups dry red wine
- ¼ tsp salt

- 1 ½ cups Italian 'risotto' rice
- 2 cloves garlic, minced
- 1 medium onion, freshly chopped
- 2 tbsp extra-virgin olive oil
- 4 ½ cups reduced sodium beef broth

Directions

1. On medium high fire, bring to a simmer broth in a medium fry pan. Lower fire so broth is steaming but not simmering.

2. On medium low heat, place a Dutch oven and heat oil.

3. Sauté onions for 5 minutes. Add garlic and cook for 2 minutes.

4. Add rice, mix well, and season with salt.

5. Into rice, add a generous splash of wine and ½ cup of broth.

6. Lower fire to a gentle simmer, cook until liquid is fully absorbed while stirring rice every once in a while.

7. Add another splash of wine and ½ cup of broth. Stirring once in a while.

8. Add tomato paste and stir to mix well.

9. Continue cooking and adding wine and broth until broth is used up.

10. Once done cooking, turn off fire and stir in pepper and ¾ cup cheese.

11. To serve, sprinkle with remaining cheese and enjoy.

Nutrition: Calories: 231; Carbs: 33.9g; Protein: 7.9g; Fat: 5.7g

Chicken Pasta Parmesan

Servings: 1 | Cooking: 20 min

Ingredients

- ¼ cup prepared marinara sauce
- ½ cup cooked whole wheat spaghetti
- 1 oz reduced fat mozzarella cheese, grated
- 1 tbsp olive oil
- 2 tbsp seasoned dry breadcrumbs
- 4 oz skinless chicken breast

Directions

1. On medium high fire, place an ovenproof skillet and heat oil.

2. Pan fry chicken for 3 to 5 minutes per side or until cooked through.

3. Pour marinara sauce, stir and continue cooking for 3 minutes.

4. Turn off fire, add mozzarella and breadcrumbs on top.

5. Pop into a preheated broiler on high and broil for 10 minutes or until breadcrumbs are browned and mozzarella is melted.

6. Remove from broiler, serve and enjoy.

Nutrition: Calories: 529; Carbs: 34.4g; Protein: 38g; Fat: 26.6g

Tasty Lasagna Rolls

Servings: 6 | Cooking: 20 min

Ingredients

- ¼ tsp crushed red pepper
- ¼ tsp salt
- ½ cup shredded mozzarella cheese
- ½ cups parmesan cheese, shredded
- 1 14-oz package tofu, cubed
- 1 25-oz can of low-sodium marinara sauce
- 1 tbsp extra virgin olive oil
- 12 whole wheat lasagna noodles
- 2 tbsp Kalamata olives, chopped
- 3 cloves minced garlic
- 3 cups spinach, chopped

Directions

1. Put enough water on a large pot and cook the lasagna noodles according to package instructions. Drain, rinse and set aside until ready to use.

2. In a large skillet, sauté garlic over medium heat for 20 seconds. Add the tofu and spinach and cook until the spinach wilts. Transfer this mixture in a

bowl and add parmesan olives, salt, red pepper and 2/3 cup of the marinara sauce.

3. In a pan, spread a cup of marinara sauce on the bottom. To make the rolls, place noodle on a surface and spread ¼ cup of the tofu filling. Roll up and place it on the pan with the marinara sauce. Do this procedure until all lasagna noodles are rolled.

4. Place the pan over high heat and bring to a simmer. Reduce the heat to medium and let it cook for three more minutes. Sprinkle mozzarella cheese and let the cheese melt for two minutes. Serve hot.

Nutrition: Calories: 304; Carbs: 39.2g; Protein: 23g; Fat: 19.2g

Raisins, Nuts And Beef On Hashweh Rice

Servings: 8 | Cooking: 50 min

Ingredients

- ½ cup dark raisins, soaked in 2 cups water for an hour
- 1/3 cup slivered almonds, toasted and soaked in 2 cups water overnight
- 1/3 cup pine nuts, toasted and soaked in 2 cups water overnight
- ½ cup fresh parsley leaves, roughly chopped
- Pepper and salt to taste
- ¾ tsp ground cinnamon, divided
- ¾ tsp cloves, divided
- 1 tsp garlic powder
- 1 ¾ tsp allspice, divided
- 1 lb. lean ground beef or lean ground lamb
- 1 small red onion, finely chopped
- Olive oil
- 1 ½ cups medium grain rice

Directions

1. For 15 to 20 minutes, soak rice in cold water. You will know that soaking is enough when you can snap a grain of rice easily between your thumb and index finger. Once soaking is done, drain rice well.

2. Meanwhile, drain pine nuts, almonds and raisins for at least a minute and transfer to one bowl. Set aside.

3. On a heavy cooking pot on medium high fire, heat 1 tbsp olive oil.

4. Once oil is hot, add red onions. Sauté for a minute before adding ground meat and sauté for another minute.

5. Season ground meat with pepper, salt, ½ tsp ground cinnamon, ½ tsp ground cloves, 1 tsp garlic powder, and 1 ¼ tsp allspice.

6. Sauté ground meat for 10 minutes or until browned and cooked fully. Drain fat.

7. In same pot with cooked ground meat, add rice on top of meat.

8. Season with a bit of pepper and salt. Add remaining cinnamon, ground cloves, and allspice. Do not mix.

9. Add 1 tbsp olive oil and 2 ½ cups of water. Bring to a boil and once boiling, lower fire to a simmer. Cook while covered until liquid is fully absorbed, around 20 to 25 minutes.

10. Turn of fire.

11. To serve, place a large serving platter that fully covers the mouth of the pot. Place platter upside down on mouth of pot, and invert pot. The inside of the pot should now rest on the platter with the rice on bottom of plate and ground meat on top of it.

12. Garnish the top of the meat with raisins, almonds, pine nuts, and parsley.

13. Serve and enjoy.

Nutrition: Calories per serving: 357; Carbs: 39.0g; Protein: 16.7g; Fat: 15.9g

Yangchow Chinese Style Fried Rice

Servings: 4 | Cooking: 20 min

Ingredients

- 4 cups cold cooked rice
- 1/2 cup peas
- 1 medium yellow onion, diced
- 5 tbsp olive oil

- 4 oz frozen medium shrimp, thawed, shelled, deveined and chopped finely
- 6 oz roast pork
- 3 large eggs
- Salt and freshly ground black pepper
- 1/2 tsp cornstarch

Directions

1. Combine the salt and ground black pepper and 1/2 tsp cornstarch, coat the shrimp with it. Chop the roasted pork. Beat the eggs and set aside.

2. Stir-fry the shrimp in a wok on high fire with 1 tbsp heated oil until pink, around 3 minutes. Set the shrimp aside and stir fry the roasted pork briefly. Remove both from the pan.

3. In the same pan, stir-fry the onion until soft, Stir the peas and cook until bright green. Remove both from pan.

4. Add 2 tbsp oil in the same pan, add the cooked rice. Stir and separate the individual grains. Add the beaten eggs, toss the rice. Add the roasted pork, shrimp, vegetables and onion. Toss everything together. Season with salt and pepper to taste.

Nutrition: Calories per serving: 556; Carbs: 60.2g; Protein: 20.2g; Fat: 25.2g

Cinnamon Quinoa Bars

Servings: 4 | Cooking: 30 min

Ingredients

- 2 ½ cups cooked quinoa
- 4 large eggs
- 1/3 cup unsweetened almond milk
- 1/3 cup pure maple syrup
- Seeds from ½ whole vanilla bean pod or 1 tbsp vanilla extract
- 1 ½ tbsp cinnamon
- 1/4 tsp salt

Directions

1. Preheat oven to 375oF.

2. Combine all ingredients into large bowl and mix well.

3. In an 8 x 8 Baking pan, cover with parchment paper.

4. Pour batter evenly into baking dish.

5. Bake for 25-30 minutes or until it has set. It should not wiggle when you lightly shake the pan because the eggs are fully cooked.

6. Remove as quickly as possible from pan and parchment paper onto cooling rack.

7. Cut into 4 pieces.

8. Enjoy on its own, with a small spread of almond or nut butter or wait until it cools to enjoy the next morning.

Nutrition: Calories per serving: 285; Carbs: 46.2g; Protein: 8.5g; Fat: 7.4g

Cucumber Olive Rice

Servings: 8 | Cooking: 10 min

Ingredients

- 2 cups rice, rinsed
- 1/2 cup olives, pitted
- 1 cup cucumber, chopped
- 1 tbsp red wine vinegar
- 1 tsp lemon zest, grated
- 1 tbsp fresh lemon juice
- 2 tbsp olive oil
- 2 cups vegetable broth
- 1/2 tsp dried oregano
- 1 red bell pepper, chopped
- 1/2 cup onion, chopped
- 1 tbsp olive oil
- Pepper
- Salt

Directions

1. Add oil into the inner pot of instant pot and set the pot on sauté mode.

2. Add onion and sauté for 3 minutes.

3. Add bell pepper and oregano and sauté for 1 minute.
4. Add rice and broth and stir well.
5. Seal pot with lid and cook on high for 6 minutes.
6. Once done, allow to release pressure naturally for 10 minutes then release remaining using quick release. Remove lid.
7. Add remaining ingredients and stir everything well to mix.
8. Serve immediately and enjoy it.

Nutrition: Calories 229 Fat 5.1 g Carbohydrates 40.2 g Sugar 1.6 g Protein 4.9 g Cholesterol 0 mg

Chicken And White Bean

Servings: 8 | Cooking: 70 min

Ingredients

- 2 tbsp fresh cilantro, chopped
- 2 cups grated Monterey Jack cheese
- 3 cups water
- 1/8 tsp cayenne pepper
- 2 tsp pure chile powder
- 2 tsp ground cumin
- 1 4-oz can chopped green chiles
- 1 cup corn kernels
- 2 15-oz cans shite beans, drained and rinsed
- 2 garlic cloves
- 1 medium onion, diced
- 2 tbsp extra virgin olive oil
- 1 lb. chicken breasts, boneless and skinless

Directions

1. Slice chicken breasts into ½-inch cubes and with pepper and salt, season it.
2. On high fire, place a large nonstick fry pan and heat oil.
3. Sauté chicken pieces for three to four minutes or until lightly browned.
4. Reduce fire to medium and add garlic and onion.
5. Cook for 5 to 6 minutes or until onions are translucent.
6. Add water, spices, chilies, corn and beans. Bring to a boil.
7. Once boiling, slow fire to a simmer and continue simmering for an hour, uncovered.
8. To serve, garnish with a sprinkling of cilantro and a tablespoon of cheese.

Nutrition: Calories per serving: 433; Protein: 30.6g; Carbs: 29.5g; Fat: 21.8g

Chorizo-kidney Beans Quinoa Pilaf

Servings: 4 | Cooking: 35 min

Ingredients

- ¼ pound dried Spanish chorizo diced (about 2/3 cup)
- ¼ teaspoon red pepper flakes
- ¼ teaspoon smoked paprika
- ½ teaspoon cumin
- ½ teaspoon sea salt
- 1 3/4 cups water
- 1 cup quinoa
- 1 large clove garlic minced
- 1 small red bell pepper finely diced
- 1 small red onion finely diced
- 1 tablespoon tomato paste
- 1 15-ounce can kidney beans rinsed and drained

Directions

1. Place a nonstick pot on medium high fire and heat for 2 minutes. Add chorizo and sauté for 5 minutes until lightly browned.
2. Stir in peppers and onion. Sauté for 5 minutes.
3. Add tomato paste, red pepper flakes, salt, paprika, cumin, and garlic. Sauté for 2 minutes.
4. Stir in quinoa and mix well. Sauté for 2 minutes.
5. Add water and beans. Mix well. Cover and simmer for 20 minutes or until liquid is fully absorbed.

6. Turn off fire and fluff quinoa. Let it sit for 5 minutes more while uncovered.

7. Serve and enjoy.

Nutrition: Calories per serving: 260; Protein: 9.6g; Carbs: 40.9g; Fat: 6.8g

Belly-filling Cajun Rice & Chicken

Servings: 6 | Cooking: 20 min

Ingredients

- 1 tablespoon oil
- 1 onion, diced
- 3 cloves of garlic, minced
- 1-pound chicken breasts, sliced
- 1 tablespoon Cajun seasoning
- 1 tablespoon tomato paste
- 2 cups chicken broth
- 1 ½ cups white rice, rinsed
- 1 bell pepper, chopped

Directions

1. Press the Sauté on the Instant Pot and pour the oil.

2. Sauté the onion and garlic until fragrant.

3. Stir in the chicken breasts and season with Cajun seasoning.

4. Continue cooking for 3 minutes.

5. Add the tomato paste and chicken broth. Dissolve the tomato paste before adding the rice and bell pepper.

6. Close the lid and press the rice button.

7. Once done cooking, do a natural release for 10 minutes.

8. Then, do a quick release.

9. Once cooled, evenly divide into serving size, keep in your preferred container, and refrigerate until ready to eat.

Nutrition: Calories per serving: 337; Carbohydrates: 44.3g; Protein: 26.1g; Fat: 5.0g

Quinoa & Black Bean Stuffed Sweet Potatoes

Servings: 8 | Cooking: 60 min

Ingredients

- 4 sweet potatoes
- ½ onion, diced
- 1 garlic glove, crushed and diced
- ½ large bell pepper diced (about 2/3 cups)
- Handful of diced cilantro
- ½ cup cooked quinoa
- ½ cup black beans
- 1 tbsp olive oil
- 1 tbsp chili powder
- ½ tbsp cumin
- ½ tbsp paprika
- ½ tbsp oregano
- 2 tbsp lime juice
- 2 tbsp honey
- Sprinkle salt
- 1 cup shredded cheddar cheese
- Chopped spring onions, for garnish (optional)

Directions

1. Preheat oven to 400oF.

2. Wash and scrub outside of potatoes. Poke with fork a few times and then place on parchment paper on cookie sheet. Bake for 40-45 minutes or until it is cooked.

3. While potatoes are baking, sauté onions, garlic, olive oil and spices in a pan on the stove until onions are translucent and soft.

4. In the last 10 minutes while the potatoes are cooking, in a large bowl combine the onion mixture with the beans, quinoa, honey, lime juice, cilantro and ½ cup cheese. Mix well.

5. When potatoes are cooked, remove from oven and let cool slightly. When cool to touch, cut in half (hot dog style) and scoop out most of the insides. Leave a thin ring of potato so that it will hold its shape. You

can save the sweet potato guts for another recipe, such as my veggie burgers (recipe posted below).

6. Fill with bean and quinoa mixture. Top with remaining cheddar cheese.

7. (If making this a freezer meal, stop here. Individually wrap potato skins in plastic wrap and place on flat surface to freeze. Once frozen, place all potatoes in large zip lock container or Tupperware.)

8. Return to oven for an additional 10 minutes or until cheese is melted.

Nutrition: Calories per serving: 243; Carbs: 37.6g; Protein: 8.5g; Fat: 7.3g

Feta, Eggplant And Sausage Penne

Servings: 6 | Cooking: 30 min

Ingredients

- ¼ cup chopped fresh parsley
- ½ cup crumbled feta cheese
- 6 cups hot cooked penne
- 1 14.5oz can diced tomatoes
- ¼ tsp ground black pepper
- 1 tsp dried oregano
- 2 tbsp tomato paste
- 4 garlic cloves, minced
- ½ lb. bulk pork breakfast sausage
- 4 ½ cups cubed peeled eggplant

Directions

1. On medium high fire, place a nonstick, big fry pan and cook for seven minutes garlic, sausage and eggplant or until eggplants are soft and sausage are lightly browned.

2. Stir in diced tomatoes, black pepper, oregano and tomato paste. Cover and simmer for five minutes while occasionally stirring.

3. Remove pan from fire, stir in pasta and mix well.

4. Transfer to a serving dish, garnish with parsley and cheese before serving.

Nutrition: Calories: 376; Carbs: 50.8g; Protein: 17.8g; Fat: 11.6g

Bell Peppers 'n Tomato-chickpea Rice

Servings: 4 | Cooking: 35 min

Ingredients

- 2 tablespoons olive oil
- 1/2 chopped red bell pepper
- 1/2 chopped green bell pepper
- 1/2 chopped yellow pepper
- 1/2 chopped red pepper
- 1 medium onion, chopped
- 1 clove garlic, minced
- 2 cups cooked jasmine rice
- 1 teaspoon tomato paste
- 1 cup chickpeas
- salt to taste
- 1/2 teaspoon paprika
- 1 small tomato, chopped
- Parsley for garnish

Directions

1. In a large mixing bowl, whisk well olive oil, garlic, tomato paste, and paprika. Season with salt generously.

2. Mix in rice and toss well to coat in the dressing.

3. Add remaining ingredients and toss well to mix.

4. Let salad rest to allow flavors to mix for 15 minutes.

5. Toss one more time and adjust salt to taste if needed.

6. Garnish with parsley and serve.

Nutrition: Calories per serving: 490; Carbs: 93.0g; Protein: 10.0g; Fat: 8.0g

Lipsmacking Chicken Tetrazzini

Servings: 8 | Cooking: 3 Hours

Ingredients

- Toasted French bread slices
- ¾ cup thinly sliced green onion

- 2/3 cup grated parmesan cheese
- 10 oz dried spaghetti or linguine, cooked and drained
- ¼ tsp ground nutmeg
- ¼ tsp ground black pepper
- 2 tbsp dry sherry
- ¼ cup chicken broth or water
- 1 16oz jar of Alfredo pasta sauce
- 2 4.5oz jars of sliced mushrooms, drained
- lbs. skinless chicken breasts cut into ½ inch slices

Directions

1. In a slow cooker, mix mushrooms and chicken.

2. In a bowl, mix well nutmeg, pepper, sherry, broth and alfredo sauce before pouring over chicken and mushrooms.

3. Set on high heat, cover and cook for two to three hours.

4. Once chicken is cooked, pour over pasta, garnish with green onion and serve with French bread on the side.

Nutrition: Calories: 505; Carbs: 24.7g; Protein: 35.1g; Fat: 30.2g

Spaghetti In Lemon Avocado White Sauce

Servings: 6 | Cooking: 30 min

Ingredients

- Freshly ground black pepper
- Zest and juice of 1 lemon
- 1 avocado, pitted and peeled
- 1-pound spaghetti
- Salt
- 1 tbsp Olive oil
- 8 oz small shrimp, shelled and deveined
- ¼ cup dry white wine
- 1 large onion, finely sliced

Directions

1. Let a big pot of water boil. Once boiling add the spaghetti or pasta and cook following manufacturer's instructions until al dente. Drain and set aside.

2. In a large fry pan, over medium fire sauté wine and onions for ten minutes or until onions are translucent and soft.

3. Add the shrimps into the fry pan and increase fire to high while constantly sautéing until shrimps are cooked around five minutes. Turn the fire off. Season with salt and add the oil right away. Then quickly toss in the cooked pasta, mix well.

4. In a blender, until smooth, puree the lemon juice and avocado. Pour into the fry pan of pasta, combine well. Garnish with pepper and lemon zest then serve.

Nutrition: Calories: 206; Carbs: 26.3g; Protein: 10.2g; Fat: 8.0g

Simple Penne Anti-pasto

Servings: 4 | Cooking: 15 min

Ingredients

- ¼ cup pine nuts, toasted
- ½ cup grated Parmigiano-Reggiano cheese, divided
- 8oz penne pasta, cooked and drained
- 1 6oz jar drained, sliced, marinated and quartered artichoke hearts
- 1 7 oz jar drained and chopped sun-dried tomato halves packed in oil
- 3 oz chopped prosciutto
- 1/3 cup pesto
- ½ cup pitted and chopped Kalamata olives
- 1 medium red bell pepper

Directions

1. Slice bell pepper, discard membranes, seeds and stem. On a foiled lined baking sheet, place bell pepper halves, press down by hand and broil in oven for eight minutes. Remove from oven, put in a sealed bag for 5 minutes before peeling and chopping.

2. Place chopped bell pepper in a bowl and mix in artichokes, tomatoes, prosciutto, pesto and olives.

3. Toss in ¼ cup cheese and pasta. Transfer to a serving dish and garnish with ¼ cup cheese and pine nuts. Serve and enjoy!

Nutrition: Calories: 606; Carbs: 70.3g; Protein: 27.2g; Fat: 27.6g

Kidney Beans And Beet Salad

Servings: 4 | Cooking: 15 min

Ingredients

- 1 14.5-ounce can kidney beans, drained and rinsed
- 1 tablespoon pomegranate syrup or juice
- 2 tablespoons olive oil
- 4 beets, scrubbed and stems removed
- 4 green onions, chopped
- Juice of 1 lemon
- Salt and pepper to taste

Directions

1. Bring a pot of water to boil and add beets. Simmer for 10 minutes or until tender. Drain beets and place in ice bath for 5 minutes.
2. Peel bets and slice in halves.
3. Toss to mix the pomegranate syrup, olive oil, lemon juice, green onions, and kidney beans in a salad bowl.
4. Stir in beets. Season with pepper and salt to taste.
5. Serve and enjoy.

Nutrition: Calories per serving: 175; Protein: 6.0g; Carbs: 22.0g; Fat: 7.0g

Filling Macaroni Soup

Servings: 6 | Cooking: 45 min

Ingredients

- 1 cup of minced beef or chicken or a combination of both
- 1 cup carrots, diced
- 1 cup milk
- ½ medium onion, sliced thinly
- 3 garlic cloves, minced
- Salt and pepper to taste
- 2 cups broth (chicken, vegetable or beef)
- ½ tbsp olive oil
- 1 cup uncooked whole wheat pasta like macaroni, shells, even angel hair broken to pieces
- 1 cup water

Directions

1. In a heavy bottomed pot on medium high fire heat oil.
2. Add garlic and sauté for a minute or two until fragrant but not browned.
3. Add onions and sauté for 3 minutes or until soft and translucent.
4. Add a cup of minced meat. You can also use whatever leftover frozen meat you have.
5. Sauté the meat well until cooked around 8 minutes. While sautéing, season meat with pepper and salt.
6. Add water and broth and bring to a boil.
7. Once boiling, add pasta. I use any leftover pasta that I have in the pantry. If all you have left is spaghetti, lasagna, angel hair or fettuccine, just break them into pieces—around 1-inch in length before adding to the pot.
8. Slow fire to a simmer and cook while covered until pasta is soft.
9. Halfway through cooking the pasta, around 8 minutes I add the carrots.
10. Once the pasta is soft, turn off fire and add milk.
11. Mix well and season to taste again if needed.
12. Serve and enjoy.

Nutrition: Calories: 125; Carbs: 11.4g; Protein: 10.1g; Fat: 4.3g

Squash And Eggplant Casserole

Servings: 2 | Cooking: 45 min

Ingredients

- ½ cup dry white wine

- 1 eggplant, halved and cut to 1-inch slices
- 1 large onion, cut into wedges
- 1 red bell pepper, seeded and cut to julienned strips
- 1 small butternut squash, cut into 1-inch slices
- 1 tbsp olive oil
- 12 baby corn
- 2 cups low sodium vegetable broth
- Salt and pepper to taste
- ¼ cup parmesan cheese, grated
- 1 cup instant polenta
- 2 tbsp fresh oregano, chopped
- 1 garlic clove, chopped
- 2 tbsp slivered almonds
- 5 tbsp parsley, chopped
- Grated zest of 1 lemon

Directions

1. Preheat the oven to 350 degrees Fahrenheit.

2. In a casserole, heat the oil and add the onion wedges and baby corn. Sauté over medium high heat for five minutes. Stir occasionally to prevent the onions and baby corn from sticking at the bottom of the pan.

3. Add the butternut squash to the casserole and toss the vegetables. Add the eggplants and the red pepper.

4. Cover the vegetables and cook over low to medium heat.

5. Cook for about ten minutes before adding the wine. Let the wine sizzle before stirring in the broth. Bring to a boil and cook in the oven for 30 minutes.

6. While the casserole is cooking inside the oven, make the topping by spreading the slivered almonds on a baking tray and toasting under the grill until they are lightly browned.

7. Place the toasted almonds in a small bowl and mix the remaining ingredients for the toppings.

8. Prepare the polenta. In a large saucepan, bring 3 cups of water to boil over high heat.

9. Add the polenta and continue whisking until it absorbs all the water.

10. Reduce the heat to medium until the polenta is thick. Add the parmesan cheese and oregano.

11. Serve the polenta on plates and add the casserole on top. Sprinkle the toppings on top.

Nutrition: Calories: 579.3; Carbs: 79.2g; Protein: 22.2g; Fat: 19.3g

Blue Cheese And Grains Salad

Servings: 4 | Cooking: 40 min

Ingredients

- ¼ cup thinly sliced scallions
- ½ cup millet, rinsed
- ½ cup quinoa, rinsed
- 1 ½ tsp olive oil
- 1 Bartlett pear, cored and diced
- 1/8 tsp ground black pepper
- 2 cloves garlic, minced
- 2 oz blue cheese
- 2 tbsp fresh lemon juice
- 2 tsp dried rosemary
- 4 4-oz boneless, skinless chicken breasts
- 6 oz baby spinach
- olive oil cooking spray
- ¼ cup fresh raspberries
- 1 tbsp pure maple syrup
- 1 tsp fresh thyme leaf
- 2 tbsp grainy mustard
- 6 tbsp balsamic vinegar

Directions

1. Bring millet, quinoa, and 2 ¼ cups water on a small saucepan to a boil. Once boiling, slow fire to a simmer and stir once. Cover and cook until water is fully absorbed and grains are soft around 15 minutes. Turn off fire, fluff grains with a fork and set aside to cool a bit.

2. Arrange one oven rack to highest position and preheat broiler. Line a baking sheet with foil, and grease with cooking spray.

3. Whisk well pepper, oil, rosemary, lemon juice and garlic. Rub onto chicken.

4. Place chicken on prepared pan, pop into the broiler and broil until juices run clear and no longer pin inside around 12 minutes.

5. Meanwhile, make the dressing by combining all ingredients in a blender. Blend until smooth.

6. Remove chicken from oven, cool slightly before cutting into strips, against the grain.

7. To assemble, place grains in a large salad bowl. Add in dressing and spinach, toss to mix well.

8. Add scallions and pear, mix gently and evenly divide into four plates. Top each salad with cheese and chicken.

9. Serve and enjoy.

Nutrition: Calories: 530.4; Carbs: 77g; Protein: 21.4g; Fat: 15.2g

Creamy Artichoke Lasagna

Servings: 8 | Cooking: 70 min

Ingredients

- 1 cup shredded mozzarella cheese
- 2 cups light cream
- ¼ cup all-purpose flour
- 1 cup vegetable broth
- ¾ tsp salt
- 1 egg
- 1 cup snipped fresh basil
- 1 cup finely shredded Parmesan cheese
- 1 15-oz carton ricotta cheese
- 4 cloves garlic, minced
- ½ cup pine nuts
- 3 tbsp olive oil
- 9 dried lasagna noodles, cooked, rinsed in cold water and drained
- 15 fresh baby artichokes
- ¼ cup lemon juice
- 3 cups water

Directions

1. Prepare in a medium bowl lemon juice and water. Put aside. Slice off artichoke base and remove yellowed outer leaves and cut into quarters. Immediately soak sliced artichokes in prepared liquid and drain after a minute.

2. Over medium fire, place a big saucepan with 2 tbsp oil and fry half of garlic, pine nuts and artichokes. Stir frequently and cook until artichokes are soft around ten minutes. Turn off fire and transfer mixture to a big bowl and quickly stir in salt, egg, ½ cup of basil, ½ cup of parmesan cheese and ricotta cheese. Mix thoroughly.

3. In a small bowl mix flour and broth. In same pan, add 1 tbsp oil and fry remaining garlic for half a minute. Add light cream and flour mixture. Stir constantly and cook until thickened. Remove from fire and stir in ½ cup of basil.

4. In a separate bowl mix ½ cup parmesan and mozzarella cheese.

5. Assemble the lasagna by layering the following in a greased rectangular glass dish: lasagna, 1/3 of artichoke mixture, 1/3 of sauce, sprinkle with the dried cheeses and repeat layering procedure until all ingredients are used up.

6. For forty minutes, bake lasagna in a pre-heated oven of 350oF. Remove lasagna from oven and before serving, let it stand for fifteen minutes.

Nutrition: Calories: 425; Carbs: 41.4g; Protein: 21.3g; Fat: 19.8g

Brown Rice Pilaf With Butternut Squash

Servings: 8 | Cooking: 50 min

Ingredients

- Pepper to taste
- A pinch of cinnamon
- 1 tsp salt
- 2 tbsp chopped fresh oregano
- ½ cup chopped fennel fronds

- ½ cup white wine
- 1 ¾ cups water + 2 tbsp, divided
- 1 cup instant or parboiled brown rice
- 1 tbsp tomato paste
- 1 garlic clove, minced
- 1 large onion, finely chopped
- 3 tbsp extra virgin olive oil
- 2 lbs. butternut squash, peeled, halved and seeded

Directions

1. In a large hole grater, grate squash.
2. On medium low fire, place a large nonstick skillet and heat oil for 2 minutes.
3. Add garlic and onions. Sauté for 8 minutes or until lightly colored and soft.
4. Add 2 tbsp water and tomato paste. Stir well to combine and cook for 3 minutes.
5. Add rice, mix well to coat in mixture and cook for 5 minutes while stirring frequently.
6. If needed, add squash in batches until it has wilted so that you can cover pan.
7. Add remaining water and increase fire to medium high.
8. Add wine, cover and boil. Once boiling, lower fire to a simmer and cook for 20 to 25 minutes or until liquid is fully absorbed.
9. Stir in pepper, cinnamon, salt, oregano, and fennel fronds.
10. Turn off fire, cover and let it stand for 5 minutes before serving.

Nutrition: Calories: 147; Carbs: 22.1g; Protein: 2.3g; Fat: 5.5g

Cranberry And Roasted Squash Delight

Servings: 8 | Cooking: 60 min

Ingredients

- ¼ cup chopped walnuts
- ¼ tsp thyme
- ½ tbsp chopped Italian parsley
- 1 cup diced onion
- 1 cup fresh cranberries
- 1 small orange, peeled and segmented
- 2 tsp canola oil, divided
- 4 cups cooked wild rice
- 4 cups diced winter squash, peeled and cut into ½-inch cubes
- Pepper to taste

Directions

1. Grease roasting pan with cooking spray and preheat oven to 400oF.
2. In prepped roasting pan place squash cubes, add a teaspoon of oil and toss to coat. Place in oven and roast until lightly browned, around 40 minutes.
3. On medium high fire, place a nonstick fry pan and heat remaining oil. Once hot, add onions and sauté until lightly browned and tender, around 5 minutes.
4. Add cranberries and continue stir frying for a minute.
5. Add remaining ingredients into pan and cook until heated through around four to five minutes.
6. Best served warm.

Nutrition: Calories: 166.2; Protein: 4.8g; Carbs: 29.1g; Fat: 3.4g

Mexican Quinoa Bake

Servings: 4 | Cooking: 40 min

Ingredients

- 3 cups sweet potato, peeled, diced very small (about 1 large sweet potato)
- 2 cups cooked quinoa
- 1 cup shredded sharp cheddar cheese
- 2 Tbs chili powder
- T Tbs paprika
- 1 1/4 cup salsa of your choice
- 1 red bell pepper, diced
- 1 large carrot, diced

- 3 Tbs canned green chiles
- 1 small onion, diced
- 3 garlic cloves, minced
- 2 cups cooked black beans

Directions

1. Preheat oven to 400OF.
2. Dice, chop, measure and prep all ingredients.
3. Combine all ingredients in one big bowl and toss ingredients well.
4. Spray a 9 X 13-inch pan with cooking spray and pour all ingredients in.
5. Bake for 35-40 minutes or until sweet potato pieces are slightly mushy, cheese is melted and items are heated all the way through.
6. Let sit for about 5 minutes, scoop into bowls and enjoy!

Nutrition: Calories per serving: 414; Carbs: 56.6g; Protein: 22.0g; Fat: 13.0g

Spanish Rice Casserole With Cheesy Beef

Servings: 2 | Cooking: 32 min

Ingredients

- 2 tablespoons chopped green bell pepper
- 1/4 teaspoon Worcestershire sauce
- 1/4 teaspoon ground cumin
- 1/4 cup shredded Cheddar cheese
- 1/4 cup finely chopped onion
- 1/4 cup chile sauce
- 1/3 cup uncooked long grain rice
- 1/2-pound lean ground beef
- 1/2 teaspoon salt
- 1/2 teaspoon brown sugar
- 1/2 pinch ground black pepper
- 1/2 cup water
- 1/2 (14.5 ounce) can canned tomatoes
- 1 tablespoon chopped fresh cilantro

Directions

1. Place a nonstick saucepan on medium fire and brown beef for 10 minutes while crumbling beef. Discard fat.
2. Stir in pepper, Worcestershire sauce, cumin, brown sugar, salt, chile sauce, rice, water, tomatoes, green bell pepper, and onion. Mix well and cook for 10 minutes until blended and a bit tender.
3. Transfer to an ovenproof casserole and press down firmly. Sprinkle cheese on top and cook for 7 minutes at 400OF preheated oven. Broil for 3 minutes until top is lightly browned.
4. Serve and enjoy with chopped cilantro.

Nutrition: Calories per serving: 460; Carbohydrates: 35.8g; Protein: 37.8g; Fat: 17.9g

Kidney Bean And Parsley-lemon Salad

Servings: 6 | Cooking: 0 min

Ingredients

- ¼ cup lemon juice (about 1 ½ lemons)
- ¼ cup olive oil
- ¾ cup chopped fresh parsley
- ¾ teaspoon salt
- 1 can (15 ounces) chickpeas, rinsed and drained, or 1 ½ cups cooked chickpeas
- 1 medium cucumber, peeled, seeded and diced
- 1 small red onion, diced
- 2 cans (15 ounces each) red kidney beans, rinsed and drained, or 3 cups cooked kidney beans
- 2 stalks celery, sliced in half or thirds lengthwise and chopped
- 2 tablespoons chopped fresh dill or mint
- 3 cloves garlic, pressed or minced
- Small pinch red pepper flakes

Directions

1. Whisk well in a small bowl the pepper flakes, salt, garlic, and lemon juice until emulsified.

2. In a serving bowl, combine the prepared kidney beans, chickpeas, onion, celery, cucumber, parsley and dill (or mint).

3. Drizzle salad with the dressing and toss well to coat.

4. Serve and enjoy.

Nutrition: Calories per serving: 228; Protein: 8.5g; Carbs: 26.2g; Fat: 11.0g

Italian White Bean Soup

Servings: 4 | Cooking: 50 min

Ingredients

- 1 (14 ounce) can chicken broth
- 1 bunch fresh spinach, rinsed and thinly sliced
- 1 clove garlic, minced
- 1 stalk celery, chopped
- 1 tablespoon lemon juice
- 1 tablespoon vegetable oil
- 1 onion, chopped
- 1/4 teaspoon ground black pepper
- 1/8 teaspoon dried thyme
- 2 (16 ounce) cans white kidney beans, rinsed and drained
- 2 cups water

Directions

1. Place a pot on medium high fire and heat pot for a minute. Add oil and heat for another minute.

2. Stir in celery and onion. Sauté for 7 minutes.

3. Stir in garlic and cook for another minute.

4. Add water, thyme, pepper, chicken broth, and beans. Cover and simmer for 15 minutes.

5. Remove 2 cups of the bean and celery mixture with a slotted spoon and set aside.

6. With an immersion blender, puree remaining soup in pot until smooth and creamy.

7. Return the 2 cups of bean mixture. Stir in spinach and lemon juice. Cook for 2 minutes until heated through and spinach is wilted.

8. Serve and enjoy.

Nutrition: Calories per serving: 245; Protein: 12.0g; Carbs: 38.1g; Fat: 4.9g

Citrus Quinoa & Chickpea Salad

Servings: 4 | Cooking: 0 min

Ingredients

- 2 cups cooked quinoa
- 1 can chickpeas, drained & rinsed
- 1 ripe avocado, diced
- 1 red bell pepper, diced
- 1/2 red onion, diced
- 1/4 cup lime juice
- 1/2 tbsp garlic powder
- 1/2 tbsp paprika
- 1/4-1/2 cup chopped cilantro
- 1 tbsp chopped jalapenos
- Sea salt to taste

Directions

1. Add all ingredients in a large bowl and mix well.

2. Enjoy right away or refrigerate for later.

Nutrition: Calories per serving: 300; Carbs: 43.5g; Protein: 10.3g; Fat: 10.9g

Chickpea Salad Moroccan Style

Servings: 6 | Cooking: 0 min

Ingredients

- 1/3 cup crumbled low-fat feta cheese
- ¼ cup fresh mint, chopped
- ¼ cup fresh cilantro, chopped
- 1 red bell pepper, diced
- 2 plum tomatoes, diced
- 3 green onions, sliced thinly
- 1 large carrot, peeled and julienned

- 3 cups BPA free canned chickpeas or garbanzo beans
- Pinch of cayenne pepper
- ¼ tsp salt
- ¼ tsp pepper
- 2 tsp ground cumin
- 3 tbsp fresh lemon juice
- 3 tbsp olive oil

Directions

1. Make the dressing by whisking cayenne, black pepper, salt, cumin, lemon juice and oil in a small bowl and set aside.

2. Mix together feta, mint, cilantro, red pepper, tomatoes, onions, carrots and chickpeas in a large salad bowl.

3. Pour dressing over salad and toss to coat well.

4. Serve and enjoy.

Nutrition: Calories per serving: 300; Protein: 13.2g; Carbs: 35.4g; Fat: 12.8g

Garlicky Peas And Clams On Veggie Spiral

Servings: 4 | Cooking: 15 min

Ingredients

- 2 tbsp chopped fresh basil
- ½ cup pre-shredded Parmesan cheese
- 1 cup frozen green peas
- ¼ tsp crushed red pepper
- ¼ cup dry white wine
- 1 cup organic vegetable broth
- 3 cans chopped clams, clams and juice separated
- 1 ½ tsp bottled minced garlic
- 2 tbsp olive oil
- 6 cups zucchini, spiral

Directions

1. Bring a pot of water to a rolling boil and blanch zucchini for 4 minutes on high fire. Drain and let stand for a couple of minutes to continue cooking.

2. On medium high fire, add a large nonstick saucepan and heat oil. Add and sauté for a minute the garlic. Pour in wine, broth and clam juice.

3. Once liquid is boiling, low fire to a simmer and add pepper. Continue cooking and stirring for 5 minutes.

4. Add peas and clams, cook until heated through or around two minutes.

5. Toss in zucchini, mix well. Cook until heated through.

6. Add basil and cheese, toss to mix well then remove from fire.

7. Transfer equally to four serving bowls and enjoy.

Nutrition: Calories: 210; Carbs: 24.0g; Protein: 8.5g; Fat: 9.2g

Leek, Bacon And Pea Risotto

Servings: 4 | Cooking: 60 min

Ingredients

- Salt and pepper to taste
- 2 tbsp fresh lemon juice
- ½ cup grated parmesan cheese
- ¾ cup frozen peas
- 1 cup dry white wine
- 2 ½ cups Arborio rice
- 4 slices bacon (cut into strips)
- 12 cups low sodium chicken broth
- 2 leeks cut lengthwise

Directions

1. In a saucepan, bring the broth to a simmer over medium flame.

2. On another skillet, cook bacon and stir continuously to avoid the bacon from burning. Cook more for five minutes and add the leeks and cook for two more minutes.

3. Increase the heat to medium high and add the rice until the grains become translucent.

4. Add the wine and stir until it evaporates.

5. Add 1 cup of broth to the mixture and reduce the heat to medium low. Stir constantly for two minutes.

6. Gradually add the remaining broth until the rice becomes al dente and it becomes creamy.

7. Add the peas and the rest of the broth.

8. Remove the skillet or turn off the heat and add the Parmesan cheese.

9. Cover the skillet and let the cheese melt. Season the risotto with lemon juice, salt and pepper.

10. Serve the risotto with more parmesan cheese.

Nutrition: Calories: 742; Carbs: 57.6g; Protein: 38.67g; Fat: 39.6g

Chickpea Fried Eggplant Salad

Servings: 4 | Cooking: 10 min

Ingredients

- 1 cup chopped dill
- 1 cup chopped parsley
- 1 cup cooked or canned chickpeas, drained
- 1 large eggplant, thinly sliced (no more than 1/4 inch in thickness)
- 1 small red onion, sliced in 1/2 moons
- 1/2 English cucumber, diced
- 3 Roma tomatoes, diced
- 3 tbsp Za'atar spice, divided
- oil for frying, preferably extra virgin olive oil
- Salt
- 1 large lime, juice of
- 1/3 cup extra virgin olive oil
- 1–2 garlic cloves, minced
- Salt & Pepper to taste

Directions

1. On a baking sheet, spread out sliced eggplant and season with salt generously. Let it sit for 30 minutes. Then pat dry with paper towel.

2. Place a small pot on medium high fire and fill halfway with oil. Heat oil for 5 minutes. Fry eggplant in batches until golden brown, around 3 minutes per side. Place cooked eggplants on a paper towel lined plate.

3. Once eggplants have cooled, assemble the eggplant on a serving dish. Sprinkle with 1 tbsp of Za'atar.

4. Mix dill, parsley, red onions, chickpeas, cucumbers, and tomatoes in a large salad bowl. Sprinkle remaining Za'atar and gently toss to mix.

5. Whisk well the vinaigrette ingredients in a small bowl. Drizzle 2 tbsp of the dressing over the fried eggplant. Add remaining dressing over the chickpea salad and mix.

6. Add the chickpea salad to the serving dish with the fried eggplant.

7. Serve and enjoy.

Nutrition: Calories per serving: 642; Protein: 16.6g; Carbs: 25.9g; Fat: 44.0g

Turkey And Quinoa Stuffed Peppers

Servings: 6 | Cooking: 55 min

Ingredients

- 3 large red bell peppers
- 2 tsp chopped fresh rosemary
- 2 tbsp chopped fresh parsley
- 3 tbsp chopped pecans, toasted
- ¼ cup extra virgin olive oil
- ½ cup chicken stock
- ½ lb. fully cooked smoked turkey sausage, diced
- ½ tsp salt
- 2 cups water
- 1 cup uncooked quinoa

Directions

1. On high fire, place a large saucepan and add salt, water and quinoa. Bring to a boil.

2. Once boiling, reduce fire to a simmer, cover and cook until all water is absorbed around 15 minutes.

3. Uncover quinoa, turn off fire and let it stand for another 5 minutes.

4. Add rosemary, parsley, pecans, olive oil, chicken stock and turkey sausage into pan of quinoa. Mix well.

5. Slice peppers lengthwise in half and discard membranes and seeds. In another boiling pot of water, add peppers, boil for 5 minutes, drain and discard water.

6. Grease a 13 x 9 baking dish and preheat oven to 350oF.

7. Place boiled bell pepper onto prepared baking dish, evenly fill with the quinoa mixture and pop into oven.

8. Bake for 15 minutes.

Nutrition: Calories: 255.6; Carbs: 21.6g; Protein: 14.4g; Fat: 12.4g

Brussels Sprouts 'n White Bean Medley

Servings: 4 | Cooking: 15 min

Ingredients

- 1 tsp salt
- 2 tbsp olive oil
- 3 cans white beans, drained and rinsed
- 3 medium onions, peeled and sliced
- 3tbsp lemon juice
- 4 ½ cups Brussels sprouts, cleaned and sliced in half
- 6 garlic cloves, smashed, peeled, and minced
- Pepper to taste

Directions

1. Place a saucepan on medium high fire and heat for 2 minutes.

2. Add oil and heat for a minute.

3. Sauté garlic and onions for 3 minutes.

4. Stir in Brussels Sprouts and sauté for 5 minutes.

5. Stir in white beans and sauté for 5 minutes.

6. Season with pepper and salt.

Nutrition: Calories per serving: 371; Protein: 21.4g; Carbs: 57.8g; Fat: 8.1g

Pastitsio An Italian Dish

Servings: 8 | Cooking: 30 min

Ingredients

- 2 tbsp chopped fresh flat leaf parsley
- ¾ cup shredded mozzarella cheese
- 1 3oz package of fat free cream cheese
- ½ cup 1/3 less fat cream cheese
- 1 can 14.5-oz of diced tomatoes, drained
- 2 cups fat free milk
- 1 tbsp all-purpose flour
- ¾ tsp kosher salt
- 5 garlic cloves, minced
- 1 ½ cups chopped onion
- 1 tbsp olive oil
- 1 lb. ground sirloin
- Cooking: spray
- 8 oz penne, cooked and drained

Directions

1. On medium high fire, place a big nonstick saucepan and for five minutes sauté beef. Keep on stirring to break up the pieces of ground meat. Once cooked, remove from pan and drain fat.

2. Using same pan, heat oil and fry onions until soft around four minutes while occasionally stirring.

3. Add garlic and continue cooking for another minute while constantly stirring.

4. Stir in beef and flour, cook for another minute. Mix constantly.

5. Add the fat free cream cheese, less fat cream cheese, tomatoes and milk. Cook until mixture is smooth and heated. Toss in pasta and mix well.

6. Transfer pasta into a greased rectangular glass dish and top with mozzarella. Cook in a preheated broiler for four minutes. Remove from broiler and garnish with parsley before serving.

Nutrition: Calories: 263; Carbs: 17.8g; Protein: 24.1g; Fat: 10.6g

Rice And Chickpea Stew

Servings: 6 | Cooking: 60 min

Ingredients

- ½ cup chopped fresh cilantro
- ¼ tsp freshly ground pepper
- ¼ tsp salt
- 2/3 cup brown basmati rice
- 3 cups peeled and diced sweet potato
- 2 15-oz cans chickpeas, rinsed
- 4 cups reduced-sodium chicken broth
- 1 cup orange juice
- 2 tsp ground coriander
- 2 tsp ground cumin
- 3 medium onions, halved and thinly sliced
- 1 tbsp extra virgin olive oil

Directions

1. On medium fire, place a large nonstick fry pan and heat oil.
2. Sauté onions for 8 minutes or until soft and translucent.
3. Add coriander and cumin, sauté for half a minute.
4. Add broth and orange juice.
5. Add salt, rice, sweet potato, and chickpeas.
6. Bring to a boil, once boiling lower fire to a simmer, cover and cook.
7. Stir occasionally, cook for 45 minutes or until potatoes and rice are tender.
8. Season with pepper.
9. Stew will be thick, if you want a less thick soup, just add water and adjust salt and pepper to taste.
10. To serve, garnish with cilantro.

Nutrition: Calories per serving: 332; Protein: 13.01g; Carbs: 55.5g; Fat: 7.5g

Mediterranean Diet Pasta With Mussels

Servings: 4 | Cooking: 20 min

Ingredients

- 1 tbsp finely grated lemon zest
- ¼ cup chopped fresh parsley
- Freshly ground pepper to taste
- ¼ tsp salt
- Big pinch of crushed red pepper
- ¾ cup dry white wine
- 2 lbs. mussels, cleaned
- Big pinch of saffron threads soaked in 2 tbsp of water
- 1 can of 15 oz crushed tomatoes with basil
- 2 large cloves garlic, chopped
- ¼ cup extra virgin olive oil
- 8 oz whole wheat linguine or spaghetti

Directions

1. Cook your pasta following the package label, drain and set aside while covering it to keep it warm.
2. On medium heat, place a large pan and heat oil. Sauté for two to three minutes the garlic and add the saffron plus liquid and the crushed tomatoes. Let it simmer for five minutes.
3. On high heat and in a different pot, boil the wine and mussels for four to six minutes or until it opens. Then transfer the mussels into a clean bowl while disposing of the unopened ones.
4. Then, with a sieve strain the mussel soup into the tomato sauce, add the red pepper and continue for a minute to simmer the sauce. Lastly, season with pepper and salt.
5. Then transfer half of the sauce into the pasta bowl and toss to mix. Then ladle the pasta into 4 medium sized serving bowls, top with mussels, remaining sauce, lemon zest and parsley in that order before serving.

Nutrition: Calories: 402; Carbs: 26.0g; Protein: 35.0g; Fat: 17.5g

Sun-dried Tomatoes And Chickpeas

Servings: 6 | Cooking: 22 min

Ingredients

- 1 red bell pepper
- 1/2 cup parsley, chopped
- 1/4 cup red wine vinegar
- 2 14.5-ounce cans chickpeas, drained and rinsed
- 2 cloves garlic, chopped
- 2 cups water
- 2 tablespoons extra-virgin olive oil
- 4 sun-dried tomatoes
- Salt to taste

Directions

1. Lengthwise, slice bell pepper in half. Place on baking sheet with skin side up. Broil on top rack for 5 minutes until skin is blistered.
2. In a brown paper bag, place the charred bell pepper halves. Fold bag and leave in there for 10 minutes. Remove pepper and peel off skin. Slice into thin strips.
3. Meanwhile, microwave 2 cups of water to boiling. Add the sun-dried tomatoes and leave in to reconstitute for 10 minutes. Drain and slice into thin strips.
4. Whisk well olive oil, garlic, and red wine vinegar.
5. Mix in parsley, sun-dried tomato, bell pepper, and chickpeas.
6. Season with salt to taste and serve.

Nutrition: Calories per serving: 195; Protein: 8.0g; Carbs: 26.0g; Fat: 7.0g

Puttanesca Style Bucatini

Servings: 4 | Cooking: 40 min

Ingredients

- 1 tbsp capers, rinsed
- 1 tsp coarsely chopped fresh oregano
- 1 tsp finely chopped garlic
- 1/8 tsp salt
- 12-oz bucatini pasta
- 2 cups coarsely chopped canned no-salt-added whole peeled tomatoes with their juice
- 3 tbsp extra virgin olive oil, divided
- 4 anchovy fillets, chopped
- 8 black Kalamata olives, pitted and sliced into slivers

Directions

1. Cook bucatini pasta according to package directions. Drain, keep warm, and set aside.
2. On medium fire, place a large nonstick saucepan and heat 2 tbsp oil.
3. Sauté anchovies until it starts to disintegrate.
4. Add garlic and sauté for 15 seconds.
5. Add tomatoes, sauté for 15 to 20 minutes or until no longer watery. Season with 1/8 tsp salt.
6. Add oregano, capers, and olives.
7. Add pasta, sautéing until heated through.
8. To serve, drizzle pasta with remaining olive oil and enjoy.

Nutrition: Calories: 207.4; Carbs: 31g; Protein: 5.1g; Fat: 7g

Garlic Avocado-pesto And Zucchini Pasta

Servings: 2 | Cooking: 0 min

Ingredients

- salt and pepper to taste
- 1 tbsp pine nuts
- 1 tbsp cashew nuts
- 1 lemon juice
- 4 cloves garlic, minced
- 1 small ripe avocado
- 2 cups zucchini, spiral
- 2 tbsp olive oil
- 2 tbsp grated Pecorino Cheese
- ½ cup packed fresh basil leaves

Directions

1. In a food processor grind pine nuts and cashew nuts to a fine powder.
2. Add basil leaves, cheese, olive oil, ripe avocado, garlic, lemon juice, salt and pepper to taste and process until you have a smooth mixture.
3. Arrange zucchini pasta on two plates and top evenly with the Avocado pesto mixture.
4. Serve and enjoy.

Nutrition: Calories: 353; Carbs: 17.0g; Protein: 5.5g; Fat: 31.9g

Mushroom Chickpea Marsala

Servings: 4 | Cooking: 20 min

Ingredients

- 2 tbsp olive oil
- 8 oz. baby portobello mushrooms, sliced
- 2 garlic cloves, minced
- 1 cup dry Marsala wine
- 2 tbsp lemon juice, or to taste
- 1 tsp rubbed sage
- 1/2 tsp black pepper
- 1/4 tsp salt
- 2 tbsp chopped fresh parsley
- 1-14 oz. can or 1 3/4 cups cooked chickpeas, rinsed and drained

Directions

1. On medium fire, place a large saucepan and heat oil.
2. Add mushrooms, cover and cook for 5 minutes.
3. Stir in garlic and cook for 2 minutes.
4. Add wine, lemon juice, sage, salt and pepper. Deglaze pot.
5. Simmer for 10 minutes while covered.
6. Add chickpeas and mix well. Cook for 3 minutes.
7. Remove pot from fire and stir in parsley.
8. Serve and enjoy.

Nutrition: Calories per serving: 159; Protein: 6.1g; Carbs: 16.8g; Fat: 8.5g

Creamy Alfredo Fettuccine

Servings: 4 | Cooking: 25 min

Ingredients

- Grated parmesan cheese
- ½ cup freshly grated parmesan cheese
- 1/8 tsp freshly ground black pepper
- ½ tsp salt
- 1 cup whipping cream
- 2 tbsp butter
- 8 oz dried fettuccine, cooked and drained

Directions

1. On medium high fire, place a big fry pan and heat butter.
2. Add pepper, salt and cream and gently boil for three to five minutes.
3. Once thickened, turn off fire and quickly stir in ½ cup of parmesan cheese. Toss in pasta, mix well.
4. Top with another batch of parmesan cheese and serve.

Nutrition: Calories: 202; Carbs: 21.1g; Protein: 7.9g; Fat: 10.2g

Chickpea-crouton Kale Caesar Salad

Servings: 4 | Cooking: 35 min

Ingredients

- 1 large bunch Tuscan kale, stem removed & thinly sliced
- ½ cup toasted pepitas
- 1 cup chickpeas, rinsed and drained
- 1 tbsp Dijon mustard
- 1 tbsp Nutritional yeast
- 2 tbsp olive oil
- salt and pepper, to taste
- ½ cup silken tofu

- 2 tablespoons olive oil
- 1 lemon, zested and juiced
- 1 clove garlic
- 2 teaspoons capers, drained
- 2 tablespoons Nutritional yeast
- 1 teaspoon Dijon mustard
- salt and pepper, to taste

Directions

1. Heat oven to 350oF. Toss the chickpeas in the garlic, Dijon, Nutritional yeast, olive oil, and salt and pepper. Roast for 30-35 minutes, until browned and crispy.

2. In a blender, add all dressing ingredients. Puree until smooth and creamy.

3. In a large salad bowl, toss the kale with dressing to taste, massaging lightly to tenderize the kale.

4. Top with the chickpea croutons, pepitas, and enjoy!

Nutrition: Calories per serving: 327; Protein: 11.9g; Carbs: 20.3g; Fat: 23.8g

Lemon Asparagus Risotto

Servings: 5 | Cooking: 6 min

Ingredients

- 1 tablespoons olive oil
- 1 shallot, chopped
- 1 clove of garlic, minced
- 1 ½ cup Arborio rice
- 1/3 cup white wine
- 3 cups vegetable broth
- 1 teaspoon lemon zest
- 2 teaspoon thyme leaves
- Salt and pepper to taste
- 1 bunch asparagus spears, trimmed
- 1 tablespoons butter
- 2 tablespoons parmesan cheese, grated

Directions

1. Heat olive oil in a pot for 2 minutes.
2. Sauté the shallot and garlic until fragrant, around 2 minutes.
3. Add the Arborio rice and stir for 2 minutes before adding the white wine.
4. Pour in the vegetable broth. Season with salt and pepper to taste.
5. Stir in the lemon zest and thyme leaves.
6. Cover and cook on medium fire for 15 minutes.
7. Stir in the asparagus spears and allow to simmer for 3 minutes.
8. Add the butter and sprinkle with parmesan cheese.
9. Turn off fire and let it sit covered for 10 minutes.

Nutrition: Calories per serving: 179; Carbohydrates: 21.4g; Protein:5.7g; Fat: 12.9g

Seafood Paella With Couscous

Servings: 4 | Cooking: 15 min

Ingredients

- ½ cup whole wheat couscous
- 4 oz small shrimp, peeled and deveined
- 4 oz bay scallops, tough muscle removed
- ¼ cup vegetable broth
- 1 cup freshly diced tomatoes and juice
- Pinch of crumbled saffron threads
- ¼ tsp freshly ground pepper
- ¼ tsp salt
- ½ tsp fennel seed
- ½ tsp dried thyme
- 1 clove garlic, minced
- 1 medium onion, chopped
- 2 tsp extra virgin olive oil

Directions

1. Put on medium fire a large saucepan and add oil. Stir in the onion and sauté for three minutes before

adding: saffron, pepper, salt, fennel seed, thyme, and garlic. Continue to sauté for another minute.

2. Then add the broth and tomatoes and let boil. Once boiling, reduce the fire, cover and continue to cook for another 2 minutes.

3. Add the scallops and increase fire to medium and stir occasionally and cook for two minutes. Add the shrimp and wait for two minutes more before adding the couscous. Then remove from fire, cover and set aside for five minutes before carefully mixing.

Nutrition: Calories: 117; Carbs: 11.7g; Protein: 11.5g; Fat: 3.1g

Amazingly Good Parsley Tabbouleh

Servings: 4 | Cooking: 15 min

Ingredients

- ¼ cup chopped fresh mint
- ¼ cup lemon juice
- ¼ tsp salt
- ½ cup bulgur
- ½ tsp minced garlic
- 1 cup water
- 1 small cucumber, peeled, seeded and diced
- 2 cups finely chopped flat-leaf parsley
- 2 tbsp extra virgin olive oil
- 2 tomatoes, diced
- 4 scallions, thinly sliced
- Pepper to taste

Directions

1. Cook bulgur according to package instructions. Drain and set aside to cool for at least 15 minutes.

2. In a small bowl, mix pepper, salt, garlic, oil, and lemon juice.

3. Transfer bulgur into a large salad bowl and mix in scallions, cucumber, tomatoes, mint, and parsley.

4. Pour in dressing and toss well to coat.

5. Place bowl in ref until chilled before serving.

Nutrition: Calories: 134.8; Carbs: 13g; Protein: 7.2g; Fat: 6g

Greek Farro Salad

Servings: 4 | Cooking: 15 min

Ingredients

- ½ teaspoon fine-grain sea salt
- 1 cup farro, rinsed
- 1 tablespoon olive oil
- 2 garlic cloves, pressed or minced
- ½ small red onion, chopped and then rinsed under water to mellow the flavor
- 1 avocado, sliced into strips
- 1 cucumber, sliced into thin rounds
- 15 pitted Kalamata olives, sliced into rounds
- 1-pint cherry tomatoes, sliced into rounds
- 2 cups cooked chickpeas (or one 14-ounce can, rinsed and drained)
- 5 ounces mixed greens
- Lemon wedges
- ⅛ teaspoon salt
- 1 ¼ cups plain Greek yogurt
- 1 ½ tablespoon lightly packed fresh dill, roughly chopped
- 1 ½ tablespoon lightly packed fresh mint, torn into pieces
- 1 tablespoon lemon juice (about ½ lemon)
- 1 tablespoon olive oil

Directions

1. In a blender, blend and puree all herbed yogurt ingredients and set aside.

2. Then cook the farro by placing in a pot filled halfway with water. Bring to a boil, reduce fire to a simmer and cook for 15 minutes or until farro is tender. Drain well. Mix in salt, garlic, and olive oil and fluff to coat.

3. Evenly divide the cooled farro into 4 bowls. Evenly divide the salad ingredients on the 4 farro bowl. Top with ¼ of the yogurt dressing.

4. Serve and enjoy.

Nutrition: Calories per serving: 428; Protein: 17.7g; Carbs: 47.6g; Fat: 24.5g

Exotic Chickpea Tagine

Servings: 4 | Cooking: 45 min

Ingredients

- 4 tsp sliced toasted almonds
- 1 cup whole wheat couscous, cooked according to manufacturer's instructions
- Freshly squeezed juice of ½ lemon, plus additional to taste
- 1 19-oz can chickpeas, drained and rinsed
- ½ cup water
- ¼ cup packed dried apricots, sliced
- 1 medium zucchini, quartered and cut into ½-inch chunks
- 4 plum tomatoes, cored and chopped
- ¼ tsp turmeric
- 1 whole cinnamon stick
- 1 tsp ground cumin
- 2 tsp honey, plus additional to taste
- ½ tsp harissa paste plus additional to taste
- 3 quarter-sized pieces of peeled fresh ginger
- 2 garlic cloves, roughly chopped
- 2 small carrots, sliced lengthwise, then cut into ½-inch thick slices
- 1 ½ cups cubed, peeled butternut squash
- ½ tsp salt plus additional to taste
- 1 red onion, quartered and thickly sliced
- 1 ½ tbsp extra virgin olive oil

Directions

1. On medium low fire, place a heavy and large pot. Heat oil and sauté onions and salt until onions are soft and translucent.

2. Add carrots and sauté for another 5 minutes. Add ginger, garlic and butternut squash. Sauté for 5 minutes and lower fire to medium.

3. Add turmeric, cinnamon stick, cumin, honey and harissa. Sauté for a minute or until fragrant. Stir in apricots, zucchini and tomatoes. Add water and bring to a boil. Once boiling, lower fire to a simmer, cover and cook for 20 minutes or until vegetables are tender.

4. Stir in lemon juice and chickpeas. Increase fire to medium and continue cooking dish uncovered for 5 to 10 minutes or until sauce has thickened.

5. Season dish to taste. Adjust seasoning like lemon, honey and harissa if needed.

6. Serve tagine over couscous and garnished with sliced almonds.

Nutrition: Calories per serving: 345; Protein: 13.2g; Carbs: 54.1g; Fat: 10.0g

Zucchini And Brown Rice

Servings: 1 Cup | Cooking: 50 min

Ingredients

- 2 TB. extra-virgin olive oil
- 2 large zucchini, diced
- 1 (16-oz.) can artichoke hearts, rinsed and drained
- 1 TB. fresh dill
- 1 tsp. ground black pepper
- 1 tsp. salt
- 4 cups chicken or vegetable broth
- 2 cups basmati brown rice

Directions

1. In a large, 3-quart pot over medium heat, heat extra-virgin olive oil. Add zucchini, and cook for 3 minutes.

2. Add artichoke hearts, and cook for 2 minutes.

3. Add dill, black pepper, salt, and chicken broth, and bring to a simmer. Stir in basmati brown rice, cover, reduce heat to low, and cook for 40 minutes.

4. Remove from heat, uncover, fluff with a fork, cover, and let sit for another 15 minutes. Serve with Greek yogurt.

Perfect Herb Rice

Servings: 4 | Cooking: 4 min

Ingredients

- 1 cup brown rice, rinsed
- 1 tbsp olive oil
- 1 1/2 cups water
- 1/2 cup fresh mix herbs, chopped
- 1 tsp salt

Directions

1. Add all ingredients into the inner pot of instant pot and stir well.
2. Seal pot with lid and cook on high for 4 minutes.
3. Once done, allow to release pressure naturally for 10 minutes then release remaining using quick release. Remove lid.
4. Stir well and serve.

Nutrition: Calories 264 Fat 9.9 g Carbohydrates 36.7 g Sugar 0.4 g Protein 7.3 g Cholesterol 0 mg

Baked Parmesan And Eggplant Pasta

Servings: 8 | Cooking: 50 min

Ingredients

- ½ tsp dried basil
- ½ cup grated Parmesan cheese, divided
- 8-oz mozzarella cheese, shredded and divided
- 6 cups spaghetti sauce
- 2 cups Italian seasoned breadcrumbs
- ½ lb. ground beef
- 6 cups eggplant, spiralized
- 1 tbsp olive oil

Directions

1. Grease a 9x13 baking dish and preheat oven to 350oF.
2. On medium high fire, place a nonstick large saucepan and heat oil. Sauté ground beef until cooked around 8 minutes. Pour in spaghetti sauce and cook until heated through.
3. Scoop out two cups of spaghetti meat sauce and set aside.
4. Add eggplant spirals in saucepan and mix well.
5. Scoop out half of eggplant spaghetti into baking dish, top with half of mozzarella cheese and cover with breadcrumbs. Top again with the remaining spaghetti, mozzarella and Parmesan cheese.
6. Pop into oven and bake until tops are golden brown around 35 minutes.
7. Remove from oven and evenly slice into 8 pieces.
8. Serve and enjoy while warm.

Nutrition: Calories: 297; Carbs: 26.6g; Protein: 22.9g; Fat: 11.1g

Greek Couscous Salad And Herbed Lamb Chops

Servings: 4 | Cooking: 30 min

Ingredients

- ¼ tsp salt
- ½ cup crumbled feta
- ½ cup whole wheat couscous
- 1 cup water
- 1 medium cucumber, peeled and chopped
- 1 tbsp finely chopped fresh parsley
- 1 tbsp minced garlic
- 2 ½ lbs. lamb loin chops, trimmed of fat
- 2 medium tomatoes, chopped
- 2 tbsp finely chopped fresh dill
- 2 tsp extra virgin olive oil
- 3 tbsp lemon juice

Directions

1. On medium saucepan, add water and bring to a boil.
2. Ibn a small bowl, mix salt, parsley, and garlic. Rub onto lamb chops.
3. On medium high fire, place a large nonstick saucepan and heat oil.

4. Pan fry lamb chops for 5 minutes per side or to desired doneness. Once done, turn off fire and keep warm.

5. On saucepan of boiling water, add couscous. Once boiling, lower fire to a simmer, cover and cook for two minutes.

6. After two minutes, turn off fire, cover and let it stand for 5 minutes.

7. Fluff couscous with a fork and place into a medium bowl.

8. Add dill, lemon juice, feta, cucumber, and tomatoes in bowl of couscous and toss well to combine.

9. Serve lamb chops with a side of couscous and enjoy.

Nutrition: Calories: 524.1; Carbs: 12.3g; Protein: 61.8g; Fat: 25.3g

Fresh Herbs And Clams Linguine

Servings: 4 | Cooking: 10 min

Ingredients

- ½ tsp freshly ground black pepper
- ¾ tsp salt
- 2 tbsp butter
- lbs. littleneck clams
- ½ cup white wine
- 4 garlic cloves, sliced
- ¼ tsp crushed red pepper
- 2 cups vertically sliced red onion
- 2 tbsp olive oil
- 2 tsp grated lemon zest
- 1 tbsp chopped fresh oregano
- 1/3 cup parsley leaves
- 8-oz linguine, cooked and drained

Directions

1. Chop finely lemon rind, oregano and parsley. Set aside.

2. On medium high fire, place a nonstick fry pan with olive oil and fry for four minutes garlic, red pepper and onion.

3. Add clams and wine and cook until shells have opened, around five minutes. Throw any unopened clam.

4. Transfer mixture into a large serving bowl. Add pepper, salt, butter and pasta. Toss to mix well. Serve with parsley garnish.

Nutrition: Calories: 507; Carbs: 53.9g; Protein: 34.2g; Fat: 16.8g

Garbanzo And Lentil Soup

Servings: 8 | Cooking: 90 min

Ingredients

- 1 14.5-oz can petite diced tomatoes, undrained
- 2 15-oz cans Garbanzo beans, rinsed and drained
- 1 cup lentils
- 6 cups vegetable broth
- ¼ tsp ground cayenne pepper
- ½ tsp ground cumin
- 1 tsp turmeric
- 1 tsp garam masala
- 1 tsp minced garlic
- 2 tsp grated fresh ginger
- 1 cup diced carrots
- 1 cup chopped celery
- 2 onions, chopped

Directions

1. On medium high fire, place a heavy bottomed large pot and grease with cooking spray.

2. Add onions and sauté until tender, around three to four minutes.

3. Add celery and carrots. Cook for another five minutes.

4. Add cayenne pepper, cumin, turmeric, ginger, garam masala and garlic, cook for half a minute.

5. Add diced tomatoes, garbanzo beans, lentils and vegetable broth. Bring to a boil.

6. Once boiling, slow fire to a simmer and cook while covered for 90 minutes. Occasionally stir soup.

7. If you want a thicker and creamier soup, you can puree ½ of the pot's content and mix in.

8. Once lentils are soft, turn off fire and serve.

Nutrition: Calories per serving: 196; Protein: 10.1g; Carbs: 33.3g; Fat: 3.6g

Pasta And Tuna Salad

Servings: 4 | Cooking: 12 min

Ingredients

- ¼ cup mayonnaise
- ¼ cup sliced carrots
- ½ cup chopped zucchini
- 2 cups whole wheat macaroni, uncooked
- 1/3 cup diced onion
- 2 5-oz cans low-sodium tuna, water pack

Directions

1. In a pot of boiling water, cook macaroni according to manufacturer's instructions.

2. Drain macaroni, run under cold tap water until cool and set aside.

3. Drain and discard tuna liquid.

4. Place tuna in a salad bowl.

5. Add zucchini, carrots, drained macaroni and onion. Toss to mix.

6. Add mayonnaise and mix well.

7. Serve and enjoy.

Nutrition: Calories: 168.2; Carbs: 24.6g; Protein: 5.3g; Fat: 5.4g

Quinoa Buffalo Bites

Servings: 4 | Cooking: 15 min

Ingredients

- 2 cups cooked quinoa
- 1 cup shredded mozzarella
- 1/2 cup buffalo sauce
- 1/4 cup +1 Tbsp flour
- 1 egg
- 1/4 cup chopped cilantro
- 1 small onion, diced

Directions

1. Preheat oven to 350oF.

2. Mix all ingredients in large bowl.

3. Press mixture into greased mini muffin tins.

4. Bake for approximately 15 minutes or until bites are golden.

5. Enjoy on its own or with blue cheese or ranch dip.

Nutrition: Calories per serving: 212; Carbs: 30.6g; Protein: 15.9g; Fat: 3.0g

Feta On Tomato-black Bean

Servings: 8 | Cooking: 0 min

Ingredients

- 1/2 red onion, sliced
- 1/4 cup crumbled feta cheese
- 1/4 cup fresh dill, chopped
- 2 14.5-ounce cans black beans, drained and rinsed
- 2 tablespoons extra-virgin olive oil
- 4 Roma or plum tomatoes, diced
- Juice of 1 lemon
- Salt to taste

Directions

1. Except for feta, mix well all ingredients in a salad bowl.

2. Sprinkle with feta.

3. Serve and enjoy.

Nutrition: Calories per serving: 121; Protein: 6.0g; Carbs: 15.0g; Fat: 5.0g

Nutty And Fruity Amaranth Porridge

Servings: 2 | Cooking: 30 min

Ingredients

- ¼ cup pumpkin seeds
- ½ cup blueberries
- 1 medium pear, chopped
- 1 tbsp raw honey
- 1 tsp cinnamon
- 2 cups filtered water
- 2/3 cups whole-grain amaranth

Directions

1. In a nonstick pan with cover, boil water and amaranth. Slow fire to a simmer and continue cooking until liquid is absorbed completely, around 25-30 minutes.
2. Turn off fire.
3. Mix in cinnamon, honey and pumpkin seeds. Mix well.
4. Pour equally into two bowls.
5. Garnish with pear and blueberries.
6. Serve and enjoy.

Nutrition: Calories: 393.4; Carbs: 68.5g; Protein: 10.5g; Fat: 8.6g

Black Beans And Quinoa

Servings: 6 | Cooking: 30 min

Ingredients

- ½ cup chopped cilantro
- 2 15-oz cans black beans, rinsed and drained
- 1 cup frozen corn kernels
- Pepper and salt to taste
- ¼ tsp cayenne pepper
- 1 tsp ground cumin
- 1 ½ cups vegetable broth
- ¾ cup quinoa
- 3 cloves garlic, chopped
- 1 onion, chopped
- 1 tsp vegetable oil

Directions

1. On medium fire, place a saucepan and heat oil.
2. Add garlic and onions. Sauté for 5 minutes or until onions are soft.
3. Add quinoa. Pour vegetable broth and bring to a boil while increasing fire.
4. As you wait for broth to boil, season quinoa mixture with pepper, salt, cayenne pepper, and cumin.
5. Once boiling, reduce fire to a simmer, cover and simmer around 20 minutes or until liquid is fully absorbed.
6. Once liquid is fully absorbed, stir in black beans and frozen corn. Continue cooking until heated through, around 5 minutes.
7. To serve, add cilantro, toss well to mix, and enjoy.

Nutrition: Calories per serving: 262; Carbs: 47.1g; Protein: 13.0g; Fat: 2.9g

Veggie Pasta With Shrimp, Basil And Lemon

Servings: 4 | Cooking: 5 min

Ingredients

- 2 cups baby spinach
- ½ tsp salt
- 2 tbsp fresh lemon juice
- 2 tbsp extra virgin olive oil
- 3 tbsp drained capers
- ¼ cup chopped fresh basil
- 1 lb. peeled and deveined large shrimp
- 4 cups zucchini, spirals

Directions

1. Bring a pot of water to a rolling boil and blanch zucchini and shrimp for 3 minutes or until desired softness is achieved. Remove from fire, drain and let stand for a minute while draining.

2. Meanwhile, in a large salad bowl, mix salt, lemon juice, olive oil, capers and basil.

3. Toss in zucchini and shrimps. Toss to mix well.

4. Evenly divide into 4 serving plates, top with ¼ cup of spinach, serve and enjoy.

Nutrition: Calories: 51; Carbs: 4.4g; Protein: 1.8g; Fat: 3.4g

Kasha With Onions And Mushrooms

Servings: 4 | Cooking: 40 min

Ingredients

- ½ tsp pepper
- ½ tsp rubbed sage
- ¾ cup carrot juice
- 1 cup water
- 1 cup whole grain kasha
- 1 tbsp olive oil
- 12oz shiitake mushrooms
- 2 large onions, thinly sliced
- 2 tsp sugar
- Salt to taste

Directions

1. In a large skillet, heat oil over medium high heat and add onions and sugar. Cook until the onions are brown.

2. Add the sage, mushrooms and pepper stir constantly until the mushrooms are tender. Set aside.

3. In the same skillet, place kasha and cook over medium heat. Stir constantly until lightly toasted.

4. Combine carrot juice, water and salt in a saucepan and bring to a boil over medium heat.

5. Add kasha and cook until tender.

6. Fluff with fork and transfer the contents to the skillet with the onion and sugar mixture.

7. Toss until well combined.

8. Serve and enjoy.

Nutrition: Calories: 254.5; Carbs: 46.8 g; Protein: 6.7g; Fat: 4.5g

Chickpea Alfredo Sauce

Servings: 4 | Cooking: 0 min

Ingredients

- ¼ teaspoon ground nutmeg
- ¼ teaspoon sea salt or to taste
- 1 clove garlic minced
- 2 cups chickpeas, rinsed and drained
- 1 tablespoon white miso paste
- 1-½ cups water
- 2 tablespoons lemon juice
- 3 tablespoons Nutritional yeast

Directions

1. Add all ingredients in a blender.

2. Puree until smooth and creamy.

Nutrition: Calories per serving: 123; Protein: 6.2g; Carbs: 20.2g; Fat: 2.4g

Lime-cilantro Rice Chipotle Style

Servings: 10 | Cooking: 17 min

Ingredients

- 1 can vegetable broth
- ¾ cup water
- 2 tablespoons canola oil
- 3 tablespoons juice of lime juice
- 2 cups long grain white rice, rinsed
- Zest of 1 lime
- ½ cup cilantro, chopped
- ½ teaspoon salt

Directions

1. Place everything in the pot and give a good stir.

2. Give a good stir and close the lid.

3. Seal off the vent.

4. Press the Rice button and adjust the cooking time to 17 minutes.

5. Do natural pressure release.

6. Fluff the rice before serving.

7. Once cooled, evenly divide into serving size, keep in your preferred container, and refrigerate until ready to eat.

Nutrition: Calories per serving: 166; Carbohydrates: 31.2g; Protein:2.7 g; Fat: 3.1g

Lentils And Rice (mujaddara With Rice)

Servings: 1 Cup | Cooking: 1 Hour 10 min

Ingredients

- 1/4 cup extra-virgin olive oil
- 1 large yellow onion, finely chopped
- 2 tsp. salt
- 2 cups green or brown lentils, picked over and rinsed
- 6 cups water
- 1 cup long-grain rice or brown rice
- 1 TB. cumin

Directions

1. In a large, 3-quart pot over medium-low heat, heat extra-virgin olive oil. Add yellow onion and 1 teaspoon salt, and cook, stirring intermittently, for 10 minutes.

2. Add green lentils and water, and cook, stirring intermittently, for 20 minutes.

3. Stir in long-grain rice, remaining 1 teaspoon salt, and cumin. Cover and cook, stirring intermittently, for 40 minutes.

4. Serve warm or at room temperature with tzatziki sauce or a Mediterranean salad.

Gorgonzola And Chicken Pasta

Servings: 8 | Cooking: 40 min

Ingredients

- 12 oz pastas, cooked and drained
- ¼ cup snipped fresh Italian parsley
- 2/3 cup Parmesan cheese
- 1 cup crumbled Gorgonzola cheese
- 2 cups whipping cream
- 8 oz stemmed fresh cremini or shiitake mushrooms
- 3 tbsp olive oil
- ½ tsp ground pepper
- ½ tsp salt
- 1 ½ lbs. skinless chicken breast, cut into ½-inch slices

Directions

1. Season chicken breasts with ¼ tsp pepper and ¼ tsp salt.

2. On medium high fire, place a nonstick pan with 1 tbsp oil and stir fry half of the chicken until cooked and lightly browned, around 5 minutes per side. Transfer chicken to a clean dish and repeat procedure to remaining batch of uncooked chicken.

3. In same pan, add a tablespoon of oil and stir fry mushroom until liquid is evaporated and mushrooms are soft, around eight minutes. Stir occasionally.

4. Add chicken back to the mushrooms along with cream and simmer for three minutes. Then add the remaining pepper and salt, parmesan cheese and ½ cup of Gorgonzola cheese. Cook until mixture is uniform. Turn off fire.

5. Add pasta into the mixture, tossing to combine. Transfer to serving dish and garnish with remaining Gorgonzola cheese and serve.

Nutrition: Calories: 358; Carbs: 23.1g; Protein: 27.7g; Fat: 17.1g

Pasta Shells Stuffed With Feta

Servings: 10 | Cooking: 40 min

Ingredients

- Cooking spray
- 20 jumbo pasta shells, cooked and drained
- 2 garlic cloves, minced

- 5 oz frozen chopped spinach, thawed, drained and squeezed dry
- 1 9oz package frozen artichoke hearts, thawed and chopped
- ¼ tsp freshly ground black pepper
- ½ cup fat free cream cheese softened
- 1 cup crumbled feta cheese
- 1 cup shredded provolone cheese, divided
- 1 8oz can no salt added tomato sauce
- 1 28oz can fire roasted crushed tomatoes with added puree
- ¼ cup chopped pepperoncini peppers
- 1 tsp dried oregano

Directions

1. On medium fire, place a medium fry pan and for 12 minutes cook tomato sauce, crushed tomatoes, peppers and oregano. Put aside.

2. In a medium bowl, mix garlic, spinach, artichoke, black pepper, cream cheese, feta cheese and ½ cup provolone. Evenly stuff these to the cooked pasta shells.

3. Grease a rectangular glass dish and arrange all the pasta shells within. Cover with tomato mixture and top with provolone.

4. Bake for 25 minutes in a preheated 3750F oven.

Nutrition: Calories: 284; Carbs: 38.5g; Protein: 15.9g; Fat: 8.3g

Kefta Styled Beef Patties With Cucumber Salad

Servings: 4 | Cooking: 10 min

Ingredients

- 2 pcs of 6-inch pita, quartered
- ½ tsp freshly ground black pepper
- 1 tbsp fresh lemon juice
- ½ cup plain Greek yogurt; fat free
- 2 cups thinly sliced English cucumber
- ½ tsp ground cinnamon
- ½ tsp salt
- 1 tsp ground cumin
- 2 tsp ground coriander
- 1 tbsp peeled and chopped ginger
- ¼ cup cilantro, fresh
- ¼ cup plus 2 tbsp fresh parsley, chopped and divided
- 1 lb. ground sirloin

Directions

1. On medium high fire, preheat a grill pan coated with cooking spray.

2. In a medium bowl, mix together cinnamon, salt, cumin, coriander, ginger, cilantro, parsley and beef. Then divide the mixture equally into four parts and shaping each portion into a patty ½ inch thick.

3. Then place patties on pan cooking each side for three minutes or until desired doneness is achieved.

4. In a separate bowl, toss together vinegar and cucumber.

5. In a small bowl, whisk together pepper, juice, 2 tbsp parsley and yogurt.

6. Serve each patty on a plate with ½ cup cucumber mixture and 2 tbsp of the yogurt sauce.

Nutrition: Calories per serving: 313; Carbs: 11.7g; Protein: 33.9g; Fat: 14.1g

Italian Mac & Cheese

Servings: 4 | Cooking: 6 min

Ingredients

- 1 lb whole grain pasta
- 2 tsp Italian seasoning
- 1 1/2 tsp garlic powder
- 1 1/2 tsp onion powder
- 1 cup sour cream
- 4 cups of water
- 4 oz parmesan cheese, shredded
- 12 oz ricotta cheese
- Pepper

- Salt

Directions

1. Add all ingredients except ricotta cheese into the inner pot of instant pot and stir well.
2. Seal pot with lid and cook on high for 6 minutes.
3. Once done, allow to release pressure naturally for 5 minutes then release remaining using quick release. Remove lid.
4. Add ricotta cheese and stir well and serve.

Nutrition: Calories 388 Fat 25.8 g Carbohydrates 18.1 g Sugar 4 g Protein 22.8 g Cholesterol 74 mg

Saffron Green Bean-quinoa Soup

Servings: 6 | Cooking: 20 min

Ingredients

- 2 tablespoons extra virgin olive oil
- 1 large leek, white and light green parts only, halved, washed, and sliced
- 2 cloves garlic, minced
- 8 ounces fresh green beans, trimmed and chopped into 1" pieces
- 2 large pinches saffron, or one capsule
- 15 ounces chickpeas and liquid (do not rinse!)
- 1 large tomato, seeded and chopped into 1" pieces
- salt and freshly ground pepper, to taste
- freshly chopped basil, for serving
- 1 large carrot, chopped into 1/2" pieces
- 1 large celery stalk, chopped into 1/2" pieces
- 1 large zucchini, chopped into 1/2" pieces
- 1/2 cup quinoa, rinsed
- 4-5 cups vegetable stock

Directions

1. Place a large pot on medium fire and heat olive oil for 2 minutes.
2. Stir in celery and carrots. Cook for 6 minutes or until soft.
3. Mix in garlic and leek. Sauté for 3 minutes.
4. Add the zucchini and green beans, and sauté 1 minute more.
5. Pour in broth and saffron. Bring to a boil. Stir in chickpeas and quinoa. Cook until quinoa is soft, around 11 minutes while covered.
6. Stir in the diced tomato and salt and pepper, to taste, and remove from heat.
7. Serve the soup with the freshly chopped basil and enjoy!

Nutrition: Calories per serving: 196; Protein: 7.9g; Carbs: 26.6g; Fat: 7.5g

Black Bean Hummus

Servings: 8 | Cooking: 0 min

Ingredients

- 10 Greek olives
- ¼ tsp paprika
- ¼ tsp cayenne pepper
- ½ tsp salt
- ¾ tsp ground cumin
- 1 ½ tbsp tahini
- 2 tbsp lemon juice
- 1 15-oz can black beans, drain and reserve liquid
- 1 clove garlic

Directions

1. In food processor, mince garlic.
1. Add cayenne pepper, salt, cumin, tahini, lemon juice, 2 tbsp reserved black beans liquid, and black beans.
2. Process until smooth and creamy. Scrape the side of processor as needed and continue pureeing.
3. To serve, garnish with Greek olives and paprika.
4. Best eaten as a dip for pita bread or chips.

Nutrition: Calories per serving: 205; Protein: 12.1g; Carbs: 34.4g; Fat: 2.9g

White Bean And Tuna Salad

Servings: 4 | Cooking: 8 min

Ingredients

- 1 (12 ounce) can solid white albacore tuna, drained
- 1 (16 ounce) can Great Northern beans, drained and rinsed
- 1 (2.25 ounce) can sliced black olives, drained
- 1 teaspoon dried oregano
- 1/2 teaspoon finely grated lemon zest
- 1/4 medium red onion, thinly sliced
- 3 tablespoons lemon juice
- 3/4-pound green beans, trimmed and snapped in half
- 4 large hard-cooked eggs, peeled and quartered
- 6 tablespoons extra-virgin olive oil
- Salt and ground black pepper, to taste

Directions

1. Place a saucepan on medium high fire. Add a cup of water and the green beans. Cover and cook for 8 minutes. Drain immediately once tender.
2. In a salad bowl, whisk well oregano, olive oil, lemon juice, and lemon zest. Season generously with pepper and salt and mix until salt is dissolved.
3. Stir in drained green beans, tuna, beans, olives, and red onion. Mix thoroughly to coat.
4. Adjust seasoning to taste.
5. Spread eggs on top.
6. Serve and enjoy.

Nutrition: Calories per serving: 551; Protein: 36.3g; Carbs: 33.4g; Fat: 30.3g

Beans And Spinach Mediterranean Salad

Servings: 4 | Cooking: 30 min

Ingredients

- 1 can (14 ounces) water-packed artichoke hearts, rinsed, drained and quartered
- 1 can (14-1/2 ounces) no-salt-added diced tomatoes, undrained
- 1 can (15 ounces) cannellini beans, rinsed and drained
- 1 small onion, chopped
- 1 tablespoon olive oil
- 1/4 teaspoon pepper
- 1/4 teaspoon salt
- 1/8 teaspoon crushed red pepper flakes
- 2 garlic cloves, minced
- 2 tablespoons Worcestershire sauce
- 6 ounces fresh baby spinach (about 8 cups)
- Additional olive oil, optional

Directions

1. Place a saucepan on medium high fire and heat for a minute.
2. Add oil and heat for 2 minutes. Stir in onion and sauté for 4 minutes. Add garlic and sauté for another minute.
3. Stir in seasonings, Worcestershire sauce, and tomatoes. Cook for 5 minutes while stirring continuously until sauce is reduced.
4. Stir in spinach, artichoke hearts, and beans. Sauté for 3 minutes until spinach is wilted and other ingredients are heated through.
5. Serve and enjoy.

Nutrition: Calories per serving: 187; Protein: 8.0g; Carbs: 30.0g; Fat: 4.0g

Grilled Veggie And Pasta With Marinara Sauce

Servings: 4 | Cooking: 30 min

Ingredients

- 8 oz whole wheat spaghetti
- 1 sweet onion, sliced into ¼-inch wide rounds
- 1 zucchini, sliced lengthwise
- 1 yellow summer squash, sliced lengthwise
- 2 red peppers, sliced into chunks
- 1/8 tsp freshly ground black pepper
- ½ tsp dried oregano

- 1 tsp sugar
- 1 tbsp chopped fresh basil or 1 tsp dried basil
- 2 tbsp chopped onion
- ½ tsp minced garlic
- salt
- 10 large fresh tomatoes, peeled and diced
- 2 tbsp extra virgin olive oil, divided

Directions

1. Make the marinara sauce by heating on medium high fire a tablespoon of oil in a large fry pan.
2. Sauté black pepper, oregano, sugar, basil, onions, garlic, salt and tomatoes. Once simmering, lower fire and allow to simmer for 30 minutes or until sauce has thickened.
3. Meanwhile, preheat broiler and grease baking pan with cooking spray.
4. Add sweet onion, zucchini, squash and red peppers in baking pan and brush with oil. Broil for 5 to 8 minutes or until vegetables are tender. Remove from oven and transfer veggies into a bowl.
5. Bring a large pot of water to a boil. Once boiling, add pasta and cook following manufacturer's instructions. Once al dente, drain and divide equally into 4 plates.
6. To serve, equally divide marinara sauce on to pasta, top with grilled veggies and enjoy.

Nutrition: Calories: Carbs: 41.9g; Protein: 8.3g; Fat: 6.2g

Chicken And Sweet Potato Stir Fry

Servings: 6 | Cooking: min

Ingredients

- ¼ tsp salt
- ½ cups quinoa, rinsed and drained
- 1 clove garlic, minced
- 1 cup frozen peas
- 1 cup water
- 1 jalapeno chili pepper, chopped
- 1 medium onion, chopped
- 1 medium-sized red bell pepper, chopped
- 1 tsp cumin, ground
- 1/8 tsp black pepper
- 12oz boneless chicken
- 1med sweet potatoes, cubed
- 3 tbsp fresh cilantro, chopped
- 4 tsp canola oil

Directions

1. Bring to a boil water and quinoa over medium heat. Simmer until the quinoa has absorbed the water.
2. In a small saucepan, put the sweet potatoes and enough water to cover the potatoes. Bring to a boil. Drain the potatoes and discard the water.
3. In a skillet, add the chicken and cook until brown. Transfer to a bowl.
4. Using the same skillet, heat 2 tablespoon of oil and sauté the onions and jalapeno pepper for one minute.
5. Add the bell pepper, cumin and garlic. Cook for three minutes until the vegetables have softened.
6. Add the peas and chicken. Cook for two minutes before adding the sweet potato and quinoa.
7. Stir cilantro and add salt and pepper to taste.
8. Serve and enjoy.

Nutrition: Calories: 187.6; Carbs: 18g; Protein: 16.3g; Fat: 5.6g

Shrimp Paella Made With Quinoa

Servings: 7 | Cooking: 40 min

Ingredients

- 1 lb. large shrimp, peeled, deveined and thawed
- 1 tsp seafood seasoning
- 1 cup frozen green peas
- 1 red bell pepper, cored, seeded & membrane removed, sliced into ½" strips
- ½ cup sliced sun-dried tomatoes, packed in olive oil
- Salt to taste

- ½ tsp black pepper
- ½ tsp Spanish paprika
- ½ tsp saffron threads (optional turmeric)
- 1 bay leaf
- ¼ tsp crushed red pepper flakes
- 3 cups chicken broth; fat free, low sodium
- 1 ½ cups dry quinoa, rinse well
- 1 tbsp olive oil
- 2 cloves garlic, minced
- 1 yellow onion, diced

Directions

1. Season shrimps with seafood seasoning and a pinch of salt. Toss to mix well and refrigerate until ready to use.

2. Prepare and wash quinoa. Set aside.

3. On medium low fire, place a large nonstick skillet and heat oil. Add onions and for 5 minutes sauté until soft and tender.

4. Add paprika, saffron (or turmeric), bay leaves, red pepper flakes, chicken broth and quinoa. Season with salt and pepper.

5. Cover skillet and bring to a boil. Once boiling, lower fire to a simmer and cook until all liquid is absorbed, around ten minutes.

6. Add shrimp, peas and sun-dried tomatoes. For 5 minutes, cover and cook.

7. Once done, turn off fire and for ten minutes allow paella to set while still covered.

8. To serve, remove bay leaf and enjoy with a squeeze of lemon if desired.

Nutrition: Calories: 324.4; Protein: 22g; Carbs: 33g; Fat: 11.6g

Fasolakia – Potatoes & Green Beans In Olive Oil

Servings: 4 | Cooking: 25 min

Ingredients

- 1 1/2 onion, sliced thin
- 1 bunch of dill, chopped
- 1 cup water
- 1 large zucchini, quartered
- 1 lb. green beans frozen
- 1 tsp dried oregano
- 1/2 bunch parsley, chopped
- 1/2 cup extra virgin olive oil
- 15 oz can diced tomatoes
- 2 potatoes, quartered
- salt and pepper, to taste

Directions

1. Place a pot on medium high fire and heat pot for 2 minutes.

2. Add oil and heat for 3 minutes.

3. Stir in onions and sauté for 2 minutes. Stir in dill, oregano, and potatoes. Cook for 3 minutes. Season with pepper and salt.

4. Add dice tomatoes and water. Cover and simmer for 10 minutes.

5. Stir in zucchini and green beans. Cook for 5 minutes.

6. Adjust seasoning to taste, turn off fire, and stir in parsley.

7. Serve and enjoy.

Nutrition: Calories per serving: 384; Protein: 5.9g; Carbs: 30.6g; Fat: 27.9g

Pesto Pasta And Shrimps

Servings: 4 | Cooking: 15 min

Ingredients

- ¼ cup pesto, divided
- ¼ cup shaved Parmesan Cheese
- 1 ¼ lbs. large shrimp, peeled and deveined
- 1 cup halved grape tomatoes
- 4-oz angel hair pasta, cooked, rinsed and drained

Directions

1. On medium high fire, place a nonstick large fry pan and grease with cooking spray.

2. Add tomatoes, pesto and shrimp. Cook for 15 minutes or until shrimps are opaque, while covered.

3. Stir in cooked pasta and cook until heated through.

4. Transfer to a serving plate and garnish with Parmesan cheese.

Nutrition: Calories: 319; Carbs: 23.6g; Protein: 31.4g; Fat: 11g

Seafood And Veggie Pasta

Servings: 4 | Cooking: 20 min

Ingredients

- ¼ tsp pepper
- ¼ tsp salt
- 1 lb raw shelled shrimp
- 1 lemon, cut into wedges
- 1 tbsp butter
- 1 tbsp olive oil
- 2 5-oz cans chopped clams, drained (reserve 2 tbsp clam juice)
- 2 tbsp dry white wine
- 4 cloves garlic, minced
- 4 cups zucchini, spiraled (use a veggie spiralizer)
- 4 tbsp Parmesan Cheese
- Chopped fresh parsley to garnish

Directions

1. Ready the zucchini and spiralize with a veggie spiralizer. Arrange 1 cup of zucchini noodle per bowl. Total of 4 bowls.

2. On medium fire, place a large nonstick saucepan and heat oil and butter.

3. For a minute, sauté garlic. Add shrimp and cook for 3 minutes until opaque or cooked.

4. Add white wine, reserved clam juice and clams. Bring to a simmer and continue simmering for 2 minutes or until half of liquid has evaporated. Stir constantly.

5. Season with pepper and salt. And if needed add more to taste.

6. Remove from fire and evenly distribute seafood sauce to 4 bowls.

7. Top with a tablespoonful of Parmesan cheese per bowl, serve and enjoy.

Nutrition: Calories: 324.9; Carbs: 12g; Protein: 43.8g; Fat: 11.3g

Cilantro-dijon Vinaigrette On Kidney Bean Salad

Servings: 4 | Cooking: 0 min

Ingredients

- 1 15-oz. can kidney beans, drained and rinsed
- 1/2 English cucumbers, chopped
- 1 Medium-sized heirloom tomato, chopped
- 1 bunch fresh cilantro, stems removed, chopped (about 1 1/4 cup)
- 1 red onion, chopped (about 1 cup)
- 1 large lime or lemon, juice of
- 3 tbsp Private Reserve or Early Harvest Greek extra virgin olive oil
- 1 tsp Dijon mustard
- ½ tsp fresh garlic paste, or finely chopped garlic
- 1 tsp sumac
- Salt and pepper, to taste

Directions

1. In a small bowl, whisk well all vinaigrette ingredients.

2. In a salad bowl, combine cilantro chopped veggies, and kidney beans.

3. Add vinaigrette to salad and toss well to mix.

4. For 30 minutes allow for flavors to mix and set in the fridge.

5. Mix and adjust seasoning if needed before serving.

Nutrition: Calories per serving: 154; Protein: 5.5g; Carbs: 18.3g; Fat: 7.4g

Tasty Mushroom Bolognese

Servings: 6 | Cooking: 65 min

Ingredients

- ¼ cup chopped fresh parsley
- 1.5 oz Parmigiano-Reggiano cheese, grated
- 1 tbsp kosher salt
- 10-oz whole wheat spaghetti, cooked and drained
- ¼ cup milk
- 1 14-oz can whole peeled tomatoes
- ½ cup white wine
- 2 tbsp tomato paste
- 1 tbsp minced garlic
- 8 cups finely chopped cremini mushrooms
- ½ lb. ground pork
- ½ tsp freshly ground black pepper, divided
- ¾ tsp kosher salt, divided
- 2 ½ cups chopped onion
- 1 tbsp olive oil
- 1 cup boiling water
- ½-oz dried porcini mushrooms

Directions

1. Let porcini stand in a boiling bowl of water for twenty minutes, drain (reserve liquid), rinse and chop. Set aside.
2. On medium high fire, place a Dutch oven with olive oil and cook for ten minutes cook pork, ¼ tsp pepper, ¼ tsp salt and onions. Constantly mix to break ground pork pieces.
3. Stir in ¼ tsp pepper, ¼ tsp salt, garlic and cremini mushrooms. Continue cooking until liquid has evaporated, around fifteen minutes.
4. Stirring constantly, add porcini and sauté for a minute.
5. Stir in wine, porcini liquid, tomatoes and tomato paste. Let it simmer for forty minutes. Stir occasionally. Pour milk and cook for another two minutes before removing from fire.
6. Stir in pasta and transfer to a serving dish. Garnish with parsley and cheese before serving.

Nutrition: Calories: 358; Carbs: 32.8g; Protein: 21.1g; Fat: 15.4g

Delicious Chicken Pasta

Servings: 4 | Cooking: 17 min

Ingredients

- 3 chicken breasts, skinless, boneless, cut into pieces
- 9 oz whole-grain pasta
- 1/2 cup olives, sliced
- 1/2 cup sun-dried tomatoes
- 1 tbsp roasted red peppers, chopped
- 14 oz can tomatoes, diced
- 2 cups marinara sauce
- 1 cup chicken broth
- Pepper
- Salt

Directions

1. Add all ingredients except whole-grain pasta into the instant pot and stir well.
2. Seal pot with lid and cook on high for 12 minutes.
3. Once done, allow to release pressure naturally. Remove lid.
4. Add pasta and stir well. Seal pot again and select manual and set timer for 5 minutes.
5. Once done, allow to release pressure naturally for 5 minutes then release remaining using quick release. Remove lid.
6. Stir well and serve.

Nutrition: Calories 615 Fat 15.4 g Carbohydrates 71 g Sugar 17.6 g Protein 48 g Cholesterol 100 mg

Garlicky Lemon-parsley Hummus

Servings: 8 | Cooking: 0 min

Ingredients

- ¼ cup tahini
- ¼ teaspoon fine grain sea salt

- ⅓ cup fresh lemon juice
- ¾ cup chopped parsley
- 1 tablespoon olive oil, plus more for drizzling
- 1 ½ cans (15 ounces each) chickpeas, rinsed and drained
- 5 cloves garlic, peeled and roughly chopped
- Dash freshly ground black pepper

Directions

1. Place all ingredients in a blender and puree until smooth and creamy.
2. Transfer to a bowl and adjust seasoning if needed.
3. If dip dries up, just add more olive oil and mix well.
4. Serve and enjoy with carrot sticks.

Nutrition: Calories per serving: 131; Protein: 4.9g; Carbs: 13.8g; Fat: 7.0g

Black Eyed Peas Stew

Servings: 4 | Cooking: 20 min

Ingredients

- ½ cup extra virgin olive oil, divided
- 1 cup fresh dill, stems removed, chopped
- 1 cup fresh parsley, stems removed, chopped
- 1 cup water
- 2 bay leaves
- 2 carrots, peeled and sliced
- 2 cups black eyed beans, drained and rinsed
- 2 slices orange with peel and flesh
- 2 Tablespoons tomato paste
- 4 green onions, thinly sliced
- Salt and pepper, to taste

Directions

1. Place a pot on medium high fire and heat. Add ¼ cup oil and heat for 3 minutes.
2. Stir in bay leaves and tomato paste. Sauté for 2 minutes.
3. Stir in carrots and a up of water. Cover and simmer for 5 minutes.
4. Stir in dill, parsley, beans, and orange. Cover and cook for 3 minutes or until heated through.
5. Season with pepper and salt to taste.
6. Stir in remaining oil and green onions cook for 2 minutes.
7. Serve and enjoy.

Nutrition: Calories per serving: 376; Protein: 8.8g; Carbs: 25.6g; Fat: 27.8g

Breakfast Salad From Grains And Fruits

Servings: 6 | Cooking: 20 min

Ingredients

- ¼ tsp salt
- ¾ cup bulgur
- ¾ cup quick cooking brown rice
- 1 8-oz low fat vanilla yogurt
- 1 cup raisins
- 1 Granny Smith apple
- 1 orange
- 1 Red delicious apple
- 3 cups water

Directions

1. On high fire, place a large pot and bring water to a boil.
2. Add bulgur and rice. Lower fire to a simmer and cook for ten minutes while covered.
3. Turn off fire, set aside for 2 minutes while covered.
4. In baking sheet, transfer and evenly spread grains to cool.
5. Meanwhile, peel oranges and cut into sections. Chop and core apples.
6. Once grains are cool, transfer to a large serving bowl along with fruits.
7. Add yogurt and mix well to coat.

8. Serve and enjoy.

Nutrition: Calories: 48.6; Carbs: 23.9g; Protein: 3.7g; Fat: 1.1g

Pasta Primavera Without Cream

Servings: 6 | Cooking: 30 min

Ingredients

- ½ cup grated Romano cheese
- 3 tbsp balsamic vinegar
- 1/3 cup chopped fresh parsley
- 1/3 cup chopped fresh basil
- 2 tsp lemon zest
- 2 cloves garlic, sliced thinly
- ¼ large yellow onion, sliced thinly
- 1 tbsp butter
- 1 tbsp Italian seasoning
- ¼ tsp coarsely ground black pepper
- ¼ tsp salt
- ¼ cup olive oil, divided
- 5 spears asparagus, trimmed and cut into 1-inch pieces
- 1 cup fresh green beans, trimmed and cut into 1-inch pieces
- ½ pint grape tomatoes
- ½ red bell pepper, julienned
- 1 carrot, julienned
- 1 zucchini, chopped
- 1 package 12-oz penne pasta

Directions

1. Cook pasta according to manufacturer's instructions, drain and rinse in running cold water.
2. Line baking sheet with aluminum foil and preheat oven to 450oF.
3. Mix thoroughly together in a bowl Italian seasoning, lemon juice, pepper, salt, 2 tbsp olive oil, asparagus, green beans, tomatoes, red bell pepper, carrot, zucchini and squash.
4. Arrange veggies in baking sheet and bake until tender for 15 minutes. Remove from oven.
5. In a large skillet, heat butter and stir fry garlic and onion until soft.
6. Add balsamic vinegar, parsley, basil, lemon zest and pasta. Continue cooking until heated through while gently tossing around the pasta.
7. Remove from fire and transfer to a large serving bowl and mix in the roasted veggies.
8. Serve and enjoy.

Nutrition: Calories: 406; Carbs: 54.4g; Protein: 15.4g; Fat: 13.6g

Spicy Sweet Red Hummus

Servings: 8 | Cooking: 0 min

Ingredients

- 1 (15 ounce) can garbanzo beans, drained
- 1 (4 ounce) jar roasted red peppers
- 1 1/2 tablespoons tahini
- 1 clove garlic, minced
- 1 tablespoon chopped fresh parsley
- 1/2 teaspoon cayenne pepper
- 1/2 teaspoon ground cumin
- 1/4 teaspoon salt
- 3 tablespoons lemon juice

Directions

1. In a blender, add all ingredients and process until smooth and creamy.
2. Adjust seasoning to taste if needed.
3. Can be stored in an airtight container for up to 5 days.

Nutrition: Calories per serving: 64; Protein: 2.5g; Carbs: 9.6g; Fat: 2.2g

Veggies And Sun-dried Tomato Alfredo

Servings: 4 | Cooking: 30 min

Ingredients
- 2 tsp finely shredded lemon peel
- ½ cup finely shredded Parmesan cheese
- 1 ¼ cups milk
- 2 tbsp all-purpose flour
- 8 fresh mushrooms, sliced
- 1 ½ cups fresh broccoli florets
- 4 oz fresh trimmed and quartered Brussels sprouts
- 4 oz trimmed fresh asparagus spears
- 1 tbsp olive oil
- 4 tbsp butter
- ½ cup chopped dried tomatoes
- 8 oz dried fettuccine

Directions

1. In a boiling pot of water, add fettuccine and cook following manufacturer's instructions. Two minutes before the pasta is cooked, add the dried tomatoes. Drain pasta and tomatoes and return to pot to keep warm. Set aside.

2. On medium high fire, in a big fry pan with 1 tbsp butter, fry mushrooms, broccoli, Brussels sprouts and asparagus. Cook for eight minutes while covered, transfer to a plate and put aside.

3. Using same fry pan, add remaining butter and flour. Stirring vigorously, cook for a minute or until thickened. Add Parmesan cheese, milk and mix until cheese is melted around five minutes.

4. Toss in the pasta and mix. Transfer to serving dish. Garnish with Parmesan cheese and lemon peel before serving.

Nutrition: Calories: 439; Carbs: 52.0g; Protein: 16.3g; Fat: 19.5g

Aioli Sauce

Servings: 4 | Cooking: 4 min

Ingredients
- 1 cup olive oil
- 1 lemon, juice
- 1 whole egg
- 1/2 teaspoon mustard, good prepared
- 1/2 teaspoon salt
- 2 large garlic cloves (or 3 medium)
- White pepper, to taste

Directions

1. Except for the oil, put the rest of the ingredients into a food processor with the steel blade attached; process for 2 minutes at HIGH.

2. With the motor still running, pour the olive oil in the pierced food pusher. Pour in small parts if it is too small to contain all the oil at once.

3. Let the oil drip in; process 2 minutes more. Open the processor and transfer the aioli into a serving bowl.

Nutrition: 454 cal., 51.7 g total fat (7.6 g sat. fat), 41 mg chol., 308 mg sodium, 33 mg pot., 0.9 g total carbs., 0 g fiber, 0 g sugar, 1.6 g protein, 1% vitamin A, 6% vitamin C, 1% calcium, and 2% iron.

Italian Meatball Soup

Servings: 8 | Cooking: 1 Hour

Ingredients
- 4 cups chicken stock
- 4 cups water
- 1 shallot, chopped
- 2 red bell peppers, cored and diced
- 1 carrot, diced
- 1 celery stalk, diced
- 2 tomatoes, diced
- 1 cup tomato juice
- ½ teaspoon dried oregano
- 1 teaspoon dried basil
- 1 pound ground chicken
- 2 tablespoons white rice
- 1 lemon, juiced
- Salt and pepper to taste
- 2 tablespoons chopped parsley

Directions

1. Combine the stock, water, shallot, bell peppers, carrot, celery, tomatoes, tomato juice, oregano and basil in a soup pot.

2. Add salt and pepper to taste and cook for 10 minutes.

3. Make the meatballs by mixing the chicken with rice and parsley.

4. Form small meatballs and drop them in the hot soup.

5. Continue cooking for another 15 minutes then add the lemon juice.

6. Serve the soup right away.

Nutrition: Calories:150 Fat:4.7g Protein:18.0g Carbohydrates:8.8g

Dill And Tomato Frittata

Servings: 6 | Cooking: 35 min

Ingredients

- pepper and salt to taste
- 1 tsp red pepper flakes
- 2 garlic cloves, minced
- ½ cup crumbled goat cheese – optional
- 2 tbsp fresh chives, chopped
- 2 tbsp fresh dill, chopped
- 4 tomatoes, diced
- 8 eggs, whisked
- 1 tsp coconut oil

Directions

1. Grease a 9-inch round baking pan and preheat oven to 3250F.

2. In a large bowl, mix well all ingredients and pour into prepped pan.

3. Pop into the oven and bake until middle is cooked through around 30-35 minutes.

4. Remove from oven and garnish with more chives and dill.

Eggs With Dill, Pepper, And Salmon

Servings: 6 | Cooking: 15 min

Ingredients

- pepper and salt to taste
- 1 tsp red pepper flakes
- 2 garlic cloves, minced
- ½ cup crumbled goat cheese
- 2 tbsp fresh chives, chopped
- 2 tbsp fresh dill, chopped
- 4 tomatoes, diced
- 8 eggs, whisked
- 1 tsp coconut oil

Directions

1. In a big bowl whisk the eggs. Mix in pepper, salt, red pepper flakes, garlic, dill and salmon.

2. On low fire, place a nonstick fry pan and lightly grease with oil.

3. Pour egg mixture and whisk around until cooked through to make scrambled eggs.

4. Serve and enjoy topped with goat cheese.

Nutrition: Calories per serving: 141; Protein: 10.3g; Carbs: 6.7g; Fat: 8.5g

Kale And Red Pepper Frittata

Servings: 4 | Cooking: 23 min

Ingredients

- Salt and pepper to taste
- ½ cup almond milk
- 8 large eggs
- 2 cups kale, rinsed and chopped
- 3 slices of crispy bacon, chopped
- 1/3 cup onion, chopped
- ½ cup red pepper, chopped
- 1 tablespoon coconut oil

Directions

1. Preheat the oven to 350F.

2. In a medium bowl, combine the eggs and almond milk. Season with salt and pepper. Set aside.

3. In a skillet, heat the coconut oil over medium flame and sauté the onions and red pepper for three minutes or until the onion is translucent. Add in the kale and cook for 5 minutes more.

4. Add the eggs into the mixture along with the bacon and cook for four minutes or until the edges start to set.

5. Continue cooking the frittata in the oven for 15 minutes.

Nutrition: Calories per serving: 242; Protein: 16.5g; Carbs: 7.0g; Fat: 16.45g

Tahini Sauce

Servings: 4 | Cooking: 15 min

Ingredients

- 1 cup tahini sesame seed paste, made from light colored seeds
- 1/4 cup freshly squeezed lemon juice, or more to taste
- 1/4 teaspoon salt, or more to taste
- 3 cloves raw garlic (or 5 cloves roasted garlic)
- 3/4 cup lukewarm water, or more for consistency
- 2 teaspoon fresh parsley, minced, optional

Directions

1. Put the tahini paste, lemon juice, lukewarm water, and salt in the food processor; process, scraping the sides periodically until the mixture is ivory-colored and creamy.

2. If using a blender, break the thick parts of the mixture every 30 seconds using a long-handles spoon; this will prevent the blender blades from clogging.

3. Process or blend until the sauce turns into a smooth, rich paste.

4. If the mixture is too thick, slowly add water until the texture is according to your desired consistency.

5. If using tahini as a topping for meat dish or hummus, make the sauce creamy and thick.

6. If using as a condiment for falafel or fits, make it more liquid.

7. Taste the sauce often during processing or blending. If desired, add more salt or lemon juice.

8. Pour the sauce into a bowl once it's blended according to your needed consistency and desired flavor. If desired, stir parley until well mixed or just sprinkle the top with parsley leaves to garnish.

Nutrition: 364 cal., 32.4 g total fat (4.6 g sat. fat), 0 mg chol., 221 mg sodium, 279 mg pot., 13.8 g total carbs., 5.7 g fiber, 0.6 g sugar, 10.5 g protein, 2% vitamin A, 13% vitamin C, 26% calcium, and 30% iron.

Mediterranean Wild Mushroom Pie

Servings: 6-8 | Cooking: 20 min

Ingredients

- 250 grams wild mushrooms, sliced or halved
- 200 grams squash, sliced into small pieces (or pumpkin)
- 2 tablespoons vegetable oil
- 2 tablespoons sundried tomato paste
- 2 small courgettes or zucchini, cut into thin slices
- 15 grams fresh parsley, chopped
- 100 ml cream, dairy-free (I used Oatly)
- 1 large onion, cut in half and slice finely
- 1 large clove garlic, crushed
- 1 block (500 grams) vegan short-crust pastry
- Salt and pepper

Directions

1. Roll out the vegan short-crust pastry and line into a 10-inch baking tray with loose-bottom. Trim off any excess pastry and then blind bake the pastry (see notes) for at 200C for about 15 minutes. Before filling the tart, remove the baking paper carefully.

2. Add vegetable oil into a frying pan. Add the onion and sauté for about 3 to 4 minutes. Put the garlic and the squash; cook for couple of minutes or until squash starts to soften. If necessary, add some water. Add the mushrooms, courgettes, and parsley. Carefully stir and season with salt and generously season with pepper.

3. Mix the tomato paste with the cream. Stir the mixture into the pan.

4. Adjust seasoning according to taste and then transfer into the prepared pastry shell; bake for 20 minutes or until the blind baked pastry is golden browned.

Nutrition: 225 cal.,7 g total fat (1.7 g sat. fat), 2 mg chol., 796 mg sodium, 425 mg pot., 35.7 g total carbs., 2.5 g fiber, 7.4 g sugar, 6.4 g protein, 7% vitamin A, 25% vitamin C, 3% calcium, and 17% iron

Simple And Easy Hummus

Servings: 4-5 | Cooking: 5 min

Ingredients

- 1 can (15 ounce) chickpeas, drained and then rinsed
- 2 garlic cloves
- 3 tablespoons tahini
- 3 tablespoons olive oil
- 2 tablespoons lemon juice
- 1/2 teaspoon salt

Directions

1. Put all the ingredients in a food processor or a blender; process or blend until the texture is pasty.

Nutrition: 548 cal., 23 g total fat (3.1 g sat. fat), 0 mg chol., 331 mg sodium, 992 mg pot., 67.5 g total carbs., 19.6 g fiber, 11.6 g sugar, 22.6 g protein, 2% vitamin A, 14% vitamin C, 16% calcium, and 43% iron.

Grilled Mediterranean Vegetables

Servings: 8 | Cooking: 25 min

Ingredients

- 6 zucchini and/or yellow squash sliced into 1/4-inch thick (about 2 1/2 pounds total),
- 2 cups couscous
- 2 bunches scallions, trimmed
- 1/2 cup olive oil
- 1 quart cherry tomatoes (preferably on the vine)
- 1 large eggplant, sliced into 1/4-inch thick (about 1 pound)
- Kosher salt and black pepper
- Spiced Chili Oil or store-bought harissa (North African chili sauce, found in the international aisle)

Directions

1. Cook the couscous according to the directions on the package.

2. Meanwhile, preheat the grill to medium.

3. In a large-sized bowl, toss the squash, zucchini, tomatoes, eggplant, and scallions, with 1 teaspoon of salt, 1/2 teaspoon of pepper, and the olive oil.

4. Working in batches, grill the veggies, covered, occasionally turning, until tender. The squash and the eggplant will be done after about 4-6 minutes. The scallions and the tomatoes will be done after about 1-2 minutes.

5. Serve with the couscous and drizzle with the spiced chili oil.

Nutrition: 347 cal.,15 g total fat (2 g sat. fat), 0 mg chol., 269mg sodium, 49 g total carbs., 7 g fiber, 10 g protein, 72 mg calcium, and 2 mg iron.

Greek Salad And Mediterranean Vinaigrette

Servings: 2-4 | Cooking: 15 min

Ingredients

- 4 Persian cucumbers, sliced into rounds (or 1 English cucumber)
- 4 campari tomatoes, cut into wedges
- 2 tablespoons Vinaigrette
- 2 ounces feta cheese, crumbled
- 1/8 cup Kalamata olives
- 1/4 small red onion, thinly sliced
- 1 tablespoon capers

Directions

1. Except for the vinaigrette, put all of the ingredients into a large-sized salad bowl. Drizzle with the vinaigrette; toss to evenly coat. Serve.

Nutrition: 148 cal.,8.1 g total fat (3.1 g sat. fat), 13 mg chol., 271 mg sodium, 751 mg pot., 17.3 g total carbs.,

3.3 g fiber, 9.2 g sugar, 5.2 g protein, 28% vitamin A, 43% vitamin C, 14% calcium, and 8% iron

Cream Of Asparagus Soup

Servings: 6 | Cooking: 35 min

Ingredients

- 2 tablespoons olive oil
- 1 shallot, chopped
- 2 garlic cloves, chopped
- 2 bunches asparagus, trimmed and chopped
- 2 cups chicken stock
- 1 cup water
- 1 teaspoon lemon juice
- Salt and pepper to taste
- ½ cup heavy cream

Directions

1. Heat the oil in a soup pot and stir in the shallot and garlic. Cook for 2 minutes then add the asparagus, stock, water and lemon juice.

2. Adjust the taste with salt and pepper and cook for 10 minutes.

3. When done, remove from heat and add the cream.

4. Puree the soup with an immersion blender.

5. Serve the soup warm.

Nutrition: Calories:90 Fat:8.6g Protein:1.5g Carbohydrates:2.9g

Mediterranean-style Spread

Servings: 14 | Cooking: 5 min

Ingredients

- 1 container (4 ounces) crumbled feta cheese
- 1 package (8 ounces) cream cheese, softened
- 1/4 cup sour cream
- 2 teaspoons dried dill weed
- 2 teaspoons garlic powder

Directions

1. Mix all the ingredients until well blended; cover and chill in the fridge for 30 minutes before serving.

Nutrition: 88 cal., 8.2 g total fat (5.3 g sat. fat), 27 mg chol., 141 mg sodium, 39 mg pot., 1.3 g total carbs., 0 g fiber, 0 g sugar, 2.6 g protein, 6% vitamin A, 0% vitamin C, 6% calcium, and 2% iron.

Spicy Tortilla Soup

Servings: 10 | Cooking: 1 Hour

Ingredients

- 3 tablespoons olive oil
- 1 sweet onion, chopped
- 2 garlic cloves, chopped
- ½ teaspoon cumin powder
- ½ teaspoon chili powder
- 1 celery stalk, sliced
- 2 carrots, grated
- 1 can diced tomatoes
- 2 tablespoons tomato paste
- 1 can kidney beans, drained
- 1 cup canned sweet corn, drained
- 4 cups vegetable stock
- 4 cups water
- Salt and pepper to taste
- 1 avocado, peeled and sliced
- ¼ cup chopped parsley
- 1 lime, juiced

Directions

1. Heat the oil in a soup pot and stir in the onion, garlic, cumin powder, chili powder, celery and carrots.

2. Cook for 5 minutes then add the rest of the ingredients, except the parsley, avocado and lime juice.

3. Continue cooking the soup for 20-25 minutes then add the parsley and avocado slices, as well as lime juice.

4. Serve the soup fresh.

Nutrition: Calories:174 Fat:8.6g Protein:5.8g Carbohydrates:21.1g

Muhammara Spread

Servings: 2 Tablespoons | Cooking: 30 min

Ingredients

- 2 large red bell peppers
- 1 1/2 cups walnuts
- 1/4 cup plain breadcrumbs
- 1 TB. crushed red pepper flakes
- 3 cloves garlic
- 3 TB. lemon juice
- 3 TB. pomegranate molasses
- 1 TB. paprika
- 1 tsp. cumin
- 1 tsp. salt
- 1/2 tsp. ground black pepper
- 2 TB. extra-virgin olive oil

Directions

1. Preheat a grill top or a grill to medium heat.

2. Place red bell peppers on the grill, and cook on all sides for about 20 minutes or until charred. Immediately place peppers on a plate, cover with plastic wrap, let cool for 10 minutes.

3. Preheat the oven to 450°F.

4. When peppers are cool enough to handle, peel off skin. (It's okay if it doesn't all come off.) Remove stalks and seeds.

5. Spread walnuts evenly on a baking sheet, and bake for 7 minutes or until they're lightly toasted. Be sure not to burn them.

6. In a food processor fitted with a chopping blade, blend roasted red bell peppers, toasted walnuts, breadcrumbs, crushed red pepper flakes, garlic, lemon juice, pomegranate molasses, paprika, cumin, salt, black pepper, and extra-virgin olive oil for 2 minutes or until well combined, intermittently scraping down the sides of the food processor bowl with a rubber spatula.

7. Serve cold or at room temperature.

Mixed Greens And Ricotta Frittata

Servings: 8 | Cooking: 35 min

Ingredients

- 1 tbsp pine nuts
- 1 clove garlic, chopped
- 1/4 cup fresh mint leaves
- 3/4 cup fresh parsley leaves
- 1 cup fresh basil leaves
- 8-oz part-skim ricotta
- 1 tbsp red-wine vinegar
- 1/2 + 1/8 tsp freshly ground black pepper, divided
- 1/2 tsp salt, divided
- 10 large eggs
- 1 lb chopped mixed greens
- Pinch of red pepper flakes
- 1 medium red onion, finely diced
- 1/3 cup + 2 tbsp olive oil, divided

Directions

1. Preheat oven to 350°F.

2. On medium high fire, place a nonstick skillet and heat 1 tbsp oil. Sauté onions until soft and translucent, around 4 minutes. Add half of greens and pepper flakes and sauté until tender and crisp, around 5 minutes.

3. Remove cooked greens and place in colander. Add remaining uncooked greens in skillet and sauté until tender and crisp, when done add to colander.

4. Allow cooked veggies to cool enough to handle, then squeeze dry and place in a bowl.

5. Whisk well 1/4 tsp pepper, 1/4 tsp salt, Parmesan and eggs in a large bowl.

6. In bowl of cooked vegetables, add 1/8 tsp pepper, ricotta and vinegar. Mix thoroughly. Then pour into bowl of eggs and mix well.

7. On medium fire, place same skillet used previously and heat 1 tbsp oil. Pour egg mixture and cook for 8 minutes or until sides are set. Turn off fire,

place skillet inside oven and bake for 15 minutes or until middle of frittata is set.

8. Meanwhile, make the pesto by processing pine nuts, garlic, mint, parsley and basil in a food processor until coarsely chopped. Add 1/3 cup oil and continue processing. Season with remaining pepper and salt. Process once again until thoroughly mixed.

9. To serve, slice the frittata in 8 equal wedges and serve with a dollop of pesto.

Nutrition: Calories per serving: 280; Protein: 14g; Carbs: 8g; Fat: 21.3g

Baked Mediterranean Halibut

Servings: 2 | Cooking: 12 min

Ingredients

- 100 grams (3 1/2 ounces) watercress
- 142 ml double cream
- 2 pieces (175 grams or 6 ounce each) halibut steaks
- 2 tablespoons lemon juice
- 2 tablespoons extra-virgin olive oil
- 25 g (1 ounce) parmesan cheese, grated
- 25 grams (1 ounce) olives, pitted, chopped
- 25 grams (1 ounce) sundried tomatoes, chopped
- Basil leaves, to garnish
- Salt and black pepper, to season

Directions

1. Preheat the oven to 190C or fan to 170C or gas to 6.

2. Lightly grease a small-sized oven-safe dish.

3. Season both sides of the halibut steaks with salt and pepper. Place the seasoned halibut steaks into the prepared dish.

4. Pour the cream over the fish and dot each halibut steak with the sundried tomatoes and the olive. Sprinkle with the parmesan cheese. Cook in the oven for about12 to 15 mnutes or until the fish flakes when you gently press them and the cheese is golden.

5. Mix the olive oil and the lemon juice; season with salt and pepper. Add the watercress; toss to coat.

6. Place the halibut steaks into serving plates, divide the watercress mixture between each serving, and if desired, garnish with the basil leaves.

Nutrition: 7231 cal.,187.9 g total fat (39.9 g sat. fat), 2085 mg chol., 3930 mg sodium, 801 mg pot., 23.8 g total carbs., 13 g fiber, 8.9 g sugar, 7.7 g protein, 3% vitamin A, 30% vitamin C, 17% calcium, and 21% iron

Mediterranean Baba Ghanoush

Servings: 4 | Cooking: 25 min

Ingredients

- 1 bulb garlic
- 1 red bell pepper, halved and seeded
- 1 tbsp chopped fresh basil
- 1 tbsp olive oil
- 1 tsp black pepper
- 2 eggplants, sliced lengthwise
- 2 rounds of flatbread or pita
- Juice of 1 lemon

Directions

1. Grease grill grate with cooking spray and preheat grill to medium high.

2. Slice tops of garlic bulb and wrap in foil. Place in the cooler portion of the grill and roast for at least 20 minutes.

3. Place bell pepper and eggplant slices on the hottest part of grill.

4. Grill for at least two to three minutes each side.

5. Once bulbs are done, peel off skins of roasted garlic and place peeled garlic into food processor.

6. Add olive oil, pepper, basil, lemon juice, grilled red bell pepper and grilled eggplant.

7. Puree until smooth and transfer into a bowl.

8. Grill bread at least 30 seconds per side to warm.

9. Serve bread with the pureed dip and enjoy.

Nutrition: Calories: 213.6; Carbs: 36.3g; Protein: 6.3g; Fat: 4.8g

Mushroom, Spinach And Turmeric Frittata

Servings: 6 | Cooking: 35 min

Ingredients

- ½ tsp pepper
- ½ tsp salt
- 1 tsp turmeric
- 5-oz firm tofu
- 4 large eggs
- 6 large egg whites
- ¼ cup water
- 1 lb fresh spinach
- 6 cloves freshly chopped garlic
- 1 large onion, chopped
- 1 lb button mushrooms, sliced

Directions

1. Grease a 10-inch nonstick and oven proof skillet and preheat oven to 350oF.

2. Place skillet on medium high fire and add mushrooms. Cook until golden brown.

3. Add onions, cook for 3 minutes or until onions are tender.

4. Add garlic, sauté for 30 seconds.

5. Add water and spinach, cook while covered until spinach is wilted, around 2 minutes.

6. Remove lid and continue cooking until water is fully evaporated.

7. In a blender, puree pepper, salt, turmeric, tofu, eggs and egg whites until smooth. Pour into skillet once liquid is fully evaporated.

8. Pop skillet into oven and bake until the center is set around 25-30 minutes.

9. Remove skillet from oven and let it stand for ten minutes before inverting and transferring to a serving plate.

10. Cut into 6 equal wedges, serve and enjoy.

Nutrition: Calories per serving: 166; Protein: 15.9g; Carbs: 12.2g; Fat: 6.0g

White Bean Kale Soup

Servings: 8 | Cooking: 1 Hour

Ingredients

- 2 tablespoons olive oil
- 1 shallot, chopped
- 2 garlic cloves, chopped
- 1 red pepper, chopped
- 1 celery stalk, diced
- 2 carrots, diced
- 1 can white beans, drained
- 2 tablespoons lemon juice
- 1 can diced tomatoes
- 2 cups vegetable stock
- 6 cups water
- Salt and pepper to taste
- 1 bunch kale, shredded

Directions

1. Heat the oil in a soup pot and stir in the shallot, garlic, red pepper, celery and carrots. Cook for 2 minutes until softened.

2. Add the rest of the ingredients and season with salt and pepper.

3. Cook on low heat for 30 minutes.

4. Serve the soup warm or chilled.

Nutrition: Calories:136 Fat:3.8g Protein:6.8g Carbohydrates:19.8g

Hearty Brown Lentil Soup

Servings: 2 Cups | Cooking: 1 Hour 20 min

Ingredients

- 2 cups brown lentils, picked over and rinsed
- 14 cups water
- 2 tsp. salt
- 1/4 cup long-grain rice
- 1/2 lb. lean ground beef
- 1 tsp. ground black pepper

- 3 TB. extra-virgin olive oil
- 1 medium yellow onion, chopped
- 1 TB. cumin
- 1/2 cup fresh parsley, chopped
- 2 medium potatoes, peeled and medium diced

Directions

1. In a large pot over medium-low heat, combine brown lentils, water, and 1 teaspoon salt. Bring to a simmer, and cook, stirring occasionally, for 1 hour.

2. Remove the pot from heat. Using a handheld immersion blender or in a food processor fitted with a chopping blade, blend lentils for 1 or 2 minutes or until smooth. If desired, strain soup to remove any pulp from lentil skins.

3. Set the pot over low heat, add long-grain rice, and cook, stirring occasionally to stop rice from clumping, for 10 minutes.

4. In a small bowl, combine ground beef, 1/2 teaspoon salt, and 1/2 teaspoon black pepper. Form mixture into about 20 to 30 (1/2-inch) meatballs.

5. In a small skillet over medium heat, cook meatballs for 6 minutes, turning over every 2 minutes until browned on all sides. Add cooked meatballs to soup.

6. In the small skillet, heat extra-virgin olive oil. Add yellow onion, and sauté for 5 minutes. Add onion to soup.

7. Add remaining 1/2 teaspoon salt, remaining 1/2 teaspoon black pepper, cumin, parsley, and potatoes to soup, and stir to combine. Cook for 5 minutes.

8. Remove from heat, and serve.

Cheesy Vegetable Soup

Servings: 8 | Cooking: 1 Hour

Ingredients

- 2 tablespoons olive oil
- 2 garlic cloves, chopped
- 2 shallots, chopped
- 2 carrots, diced
- 1 celery stalk, chopped
- 2 red bell peppers, cored and diced
- 1 zucchini, cubed
- 1 red pepper, sliced
- 1 cup diced tomatoes
- 2 cups vegetable stock
- 6 cups water
- ½ teaspoon dried basil
- ½ teaspoon dried oregano
- Salt and pepper to taste
- 4 oz. grated Cheddar cheese

Directions

1. Heat the oil in a soup pot and stir in the garlic, shallots, carrots and celery.

2. Cook for 5 minutes then add the bell pepper, zucchini, red pepper, tomatoes, stock and water.

3. Season with salt and pepper, as well as basil and oregano and cook for 20 minutes on low heat.

4. When done, pour into serving bowls and top with cheese.

5. Serve the soup warm and fresh.

Nutrition: Calories:120 Fat:8.5g Protein:4.8g Carbohydrates:7.1g

Tomato-bacon Quiche

Servings: 6 | Cooking: 47 min

Ingredients

- 2 small medium sized tomatoes, sliced
- ¼ tsp black pepper
- ¼ tsp salt
- ¼ tsp ground mustard
- ½ cup fresh spinach, chopped
- 2/4 cups cauliflower, ground into rice
- 5 slices nitrate free bacon, cooked and chopped
- 3 tbsp unsweetened plain almond milk
- ½ cup organic white eggs
- 5 eggs, beaten
- 1/8 tsp sea salt

- 1 tbsp butter
- 1 tsp flax meal
- 1 ½ tbsp coconut flour
- 1 egg, beaten
- 2 small to medium sized organic zucchini, grated

Directions

1. Grease a pie dish and preheat oven to 400oF.
2. Grate zucchini, drain and squeeze dry.
3. In a bowl, add dry zucchini and remaining crust ingredients and mix well.
4. Place in bottom of pie plate and press down as if making a pie crust. Pop in the oven and bake for 9 minutes.
5. Meanwhile in a large mixing bowl, whisk well black pepper, salt, mustard, almond milk, egg whites, and egg.
6. Add bacon, spinach, and cauliflower rice. Mix well. Pour into baked zucchini crust, top with tomato slices.
7. Pop back in the oven and bake for 28 minutes. If at 20 minutes baking time top is browning too much, cover with parchment paper for remainder of cooking time.
8. Once done cooking, remove from oven, let it stand for at least ten minutes.
9. Slice into equal triangles, serve and enjoy.

Nutrition: Calories per serving: 154; Protein: 11.6g; Carbs: 3.4g; Fat: 10.3g

Spicy Silan Aka Date Syrup

Servings: 10 | Cooking: 5 min

Ingredients

- 1 cup silan (date honey)
- 1 teaspoon hot Spanish paprika
- 1 teaspoon parsley flakes
- 1 teaspoon salt
- 1/2 teaspoon black pepper
- 1 tablespoon garlic powder

Directions

1. Simply mix the date honey with 1-2 teaspoons of the grilling sauce.

Nutrition: 107 cal., 0 g total fat (0 g sat. fat), 0 mg chol., 234 mg sodium, 34 mg pot., 28.7 g total carbs., 0 g fiber, 28.1 g sugar, 0.3 g protein, 2% vitamin A, 1% vitamin C, 0% calcium, and 1% iron.

Fried Caprese Pistachio Bites

Servings: 10 | Cooking: 1 min

Ingredients

- 20 pieces bocconcini cheese
- 2 tablespoons of protein packed nut free hemp basil pesto (or store bought)
- 2 Tablespoons of Balsamic Vinegar
- 1/3 cup pistachios, crushed
- 1/3 cup panko breadcrumbs (or gluten free breadcrumbs, rice cereal)
- 1/2 of an egg
- 1/2 cup of all-purpose flour (for gluten free use rice flour)
- 1 pint of grape tomatoes
- Baby mini mushrooms, optional
- Fresh minced basil for sprinkling
- 2 pinches salt, divided

Directions

1. Line a tray with wax paper or parchment paper. Put the bocconcini in the tray and cover with a plastic wrap; freeze for at least 6 hours or overnight or until the cheeses are completely hard.
2. Put the flour in a bowl.
3. In another bowl, add the pesto, egg, vinegar, and a pinch of salt.
4. In another bowl, mix the pistachio with the breadcrumbs.
5. Preheat an electric fryer or fill a small pot with oil half full until the heat is 375F.
6. Dredge each bocconcini cheese in the flour, shaking off any excess. Drop into the basil pesto mix, rolling it well to coat.

7. Finally, roll in the bowl with pistachio, making sure the entire surface is covered with the coating well. Put the coated balls on a plate mined with wax paper.

8. Repeat the process with the rest of the cheese balls and the coatings. If you want some fried mushrooms, follow the process to coat them.

9. Fry the coated bocconcini and, if adding, the mushrooms for about 1 minute and, if needed, 30 seconds more, depending the temperature of your oil or how crowded the pot is. Drain each on paper towels and sprinkle with a pinch of salt.

Nutrition: 105 cal., 7.3 g total fat (3.1 g sat. fat), 22 mg chol., 182.7 mg sodium, 3.9 g total carbs., 0.5 g fiber, 0.9 g sugar, 6.1 g protein, 6% vitamin A, 4% vitamin C, 13% calcium, and 3% iron.

Dill, Havarti & Asparagus Frittata

Servings: 4 | Cooking: 20 min

Ingredients

- 1 tsp dried dill weed or 2 tsp minced fresh dill
- 4-oz Havarti cheese cut into small cubes
- 6 eggs, beaten well
- Pepper and salt to taste
- 1 stalk green onions sliced for garnish
- 3 tsp. olive oil
- 2/3 cup diced cherry tomatoes
- 6-8 oz fresh asparagus, ends trimmed and cut into 1 ½-inch lengths

Directions

1. On medium-high the fire, place a large cast-iron pan and add oil. Once oil is hot, stir-fry asparagus for 4 minutes.

2. Add dill weed and tomatoes. Cook for two minutes.

3. Meanwhile, season eggs with pepper and salt. Beat well.

4. Pour eggs over the tomatoes.

5. Evenly spread cheese on top.

6. Preheat broiler.

7. Lower the fire to low, cover pan, and let it cook for 10 minutes until the cheese on top has melted.

8. Turn off the fire and transfer pan in the oven and broil for 2 minutes or until tops are browned.

9. Remove from the oven, sprinkle sliced green onions, serve, and enjoy.

Nutrition: Calories per serving: 244; Protein: 16.0g; Carbs: 3.7g; Fat: 18.3g

Pistachio Oil Drizzled Robiola, And Pickled Fig Crostini

Servings: 12 | Cooking: 15 min

Ingredients

- 6 dried figs
- 2 tablespoons sugar
- 2 tablespoons pistachios, toasted and shelled
- 12 slices ciabatta bread
- 1/4 cup extra-virgin olive oil
- 1/2 cup red wine vinegar
- 1/4 cup water
- Robiola cheese, at room temperature

Directions

1. In a saucepan, combine the sugar, red wine vinegar, dried figs, and water; bring the mixture to a simmer. When simmering, remove from the heat; let sit for about 30 minutes or until the figs are soft. When the figs are soft, cut the figs into halves in a lengthwise manner. Alternatively, you can use 6 pieces fresh figs halve d lengthwise.

2. Crush the pistachios into fine pieces and then combine with the olive oil.

3. Grill the slices of ciabatta bread.

4. Spread the cheese over the warm toasted bread slices. Top with each with a fig half and then drizzle with the pistachio oil.

Nutrition: 132.8 cal., 5.8 g total fat (1 g sat. fat), 120.7 mg sodium, , 1.2 mg chol., 18.44 g total carbs., 1 g fiber, 4.7 g sugar, and 2.8 g protein.

Mediterranean Lentil Sloppy Joes

Preparation: 6 min | Cooking: 16 min | Servings: 4

Ingredients

- 1 tablespoon extra-virgin olive oil
- 1 cup chopped onion (about ½ medium onions)
- 1 cup chopped bell pepper, any color (about 1 medium bell pepper)
- 2 garlic cloves, minced (about 1 teaspoon)
- 1 (15-ounce) can lentils, drained and rinsed
- 1 (14.5-ounce) can low-sodium or no-salt-added diced tomatoes
- 1 teaspoon ground cumin
- 1 teaspoon dried thyme
- ¼ teaspoon kosher or sea salt
- 4 whole-wheat pita breads, split open
- 1½ cups chopped seedless cucumber (1 medium cucumber)
- 1 cup chopped romaine lettuce

Directions

1. Using medium saucepan over medium-high heat, heat the oil. Add the onion and bell pepper and cook for 4 min, stirring frequently. Cook the garlic 1 minute.

2. Add the lentils, tomatoes (with their liquid), cumin, thyme, and salt. Cook at medium heat for 10 min.

3. Stuff the lentil mixture inside each pita. Lay the cucumbers and lettuce on top of the lentil mixture and serve.

Nutrition: Calories: 334; Fat: 5g; Protein: 16g

Zucchini-Eggplant Gratin

Preparation: 11 min | Cooking: 20 min | Servings: 6

Ingredients

- 1 large eggplant, finely chopped (about 5 cups)
- 2 large zucchini, finely chopped (about 3¾ cups)
- ¼ teaspoons freshly ground black pepper
- ¼ teaspoon kosher or sea salt
- 3 tablespoons extra-virgin olive oil, divided
- 1 tablespoon all-purpose flour
- ¾ cup 2% milk
- 1/3 cup plus 2 tablespoons Parmesan cheese
- 1 cup chopped tomato (about 1 large tomato)
- 1 cup diced or shredded fresh mozzarella (about 4 ounces)
- ¼ cup fresh basil leaves

Directions

1. Preheat the oven to 425°F.

2. Mix the eggplant, zucchini, pepper, and salt.

3. Using big skillet over medium-high heat, heat 1 tablespoon of oil. Add half the veggie mixture to the skillet. Stir a few times, then close and cook for 5 min, stirring occasionally. Pour the cooked veggies into a baking dish. Situate the skillet back on the heat, add 1 tablespoon of oil, and repeat with the remaining veggies. Add the veggies to the baking dish.

4. While the vegetables are cooking, heat the milk in the microwave for 1 minute. Set aside.

5. Place a medium saucepan over medium heat. Add the remaining tablespoon of oil and flour, and whisk together for about 1 minute, until well blended.

6. Slowly pour the warm milk into the oil mixture, whisking the entire time. Continue to whisk frequently until the mixture thickens a bit. Stir in 1/3 cup of Parmesan cheese, and whisk until melted. Pour the cheese sauce over the vegetables in the baking dish and mix well.

7. Gently mix in the tomatoes and mozzarella cheese. Roast in the oven for 10 min, or until the gratin is almost set and not runny. Garnish with the fresh basil leaves and the remaining 2 tablespoons of Parmesan cheese before serving.

Nutrition: Calories: 207; Fat: 14g; Protein: 11g

Tuscan Bread Dipper

Preparation: 6 min | Cooking: 0 min | Servings: 8

Ingredients

- ¼ cup balsamic vinegar
- ¼ cup extra virgin olive oil

- ¼ teaspoon salt
- ½ tbsp. fresh basil, minced
- ½ teaspoon pepper
- 1 ½ teaspoon Italian seasoning
- 2 cloves garlic minced
- 8 pieces Food for Life Brown Rice English Muffins

Directions

1. In a small bowl mix well all ingredients except for bread. Allow herbs to steep in olive oil-balsamic vinegar mixture for at least 30 min.

2. To serve, toast bread, cut each muffin in half and serve with balsamic vinegar dip.

Nutrition: Calories: 168.5; Protein: 5.2g; Fat: 4.1g

Sandwich with Spinach and Tuna Salad

Preparation: 9 min | Cooking: 0 min | Servings: 4

Ingredients

- 1 cup fresh baby spinach
- 8 slices 100% whole wheat sandwich bread
- ¼ tsp freshly ground black pepper
- ½ tsp salt free seasoning blend
- Juice of one lemon
- 2 tbsp. olive oil
- ½ tsp dill weed
- 2 ribs celery, diced

Directions

1. In a medium bowl, mix well dill weed, celery, onion, cucumber and tuna. Add lemon juice and olive oil and mix thoroughly. Season with pepper and salt-free seasoning blend.

2. To assemble sandwich, you can toast bread slices, on top of one bread slice layer ½ cup tuna salad, top with ¼ cup spinach and cover with another slice of bread. Repeat procedure to remaining ingredients, serve and enjoy.

Nutrition: Calories: 272.5; Protein: 10.4g; Fat: 9.7g

Chapter 7: Dessert Recipes

Soothing Red Smoothie

Servings: 2 | Cooking: 3 min

Ingredients

- 4 plums, pitted
- ¼ cup raspberry
- ¼ cup blueberry
- 1 tablespoon lemon juice
- 1 tablespoon linseed oil

Directions

1. Place all Ingredients in a blender.
2. Blend until smooth.
3. Pour in a glass container and allow to chill in the fridge for at least 30 minutes.

Nutrition: Calories per serving: 201; Carbs: 36.4g; Protein: 0.8g; Fat: 7.1g

Minty Orange Greek Yogurt

Servings: 1 | Cooking: 5 min

Ingredients

- 6 tablespoons Greek yogurt; fat-free
- 4 fresh mint leaves, thinly sliced
- 1 large orange, peeled, quartered, and then sliced crosswise
- 1 1/2 teaspoons honey

Directions

1. Stir together the honey and the yogurt.
2. Place the orange slices into a dessert glass. Spoon the honeyed yogurt over the orange slices in the glass and scatter the mint on top of the yogurt.

Nutrition: 171 cal., 34 g total carbs, 5 g fiber, and 11 g protein.

Yogurt Mousse With Sour Cherry Sauce

Servings: 6 | Cooking: 1 Hour

Ingredients

- 1 ½ cups Greek yogurt
- 1 teaspoon vanilla extract
- 4 tablespoons honey
- 1 ½ cups heavy cream, whipped
- 2 cups sour cherries
- ¼ cup white sugar
- 1 cinnamon stick

Directions

1. Combine the yogurt with vanilla and honey in a bowl.
2. Fold in the whipped cream then spoon the mousse into serving glasses and refrigerate.
3. For the sauce, combine the cherries, sugar and cinnamon in a saucepan. Allow to rest for 10 minutes then cook on low heat for 10 minutes.
4. Cool the sauce down then spoon it over the mousse.
5. Serve it right away.

Nutrition: Calories:245 Fat:12.1g Protein:5.8g Carbohydrates:29.7g

Fruit Salad With Orange Blossom Water

Servings: 8 | Cooking: 3 min

Ingredients

- 4 oranges, peeled and cut into bite-sized pieces
- 8 dried figs, quartered
- 2 Medjool dates, pitted then chopped
- ½ cup pomegranate seeds
- 2 tablespoons honey
- 2 tablespoons orange blossom water
- 2 bananas, peeled and sliced
- ¼ cup pistachio nuts, shelled and chopped

Directions

1. In a large mixing bowl, toss in all the ingredients except for the pistachio nuts.
2. Let the fruits rest in the fridge for at least 8 hours before serving.
3. Garnish with chopped pistachios before serving.

Nutrition: Calories per serving: 185; Carbs: 43g; Protein: 3g; Fat: 2g

Vanilla Apple Pie

Servings: 8 | Cooking: 50 min

Ingredients

- 3 apples, sliced
- ½ teaspoon ground cinnamon
- 1 teaspoon vanilla extract
- 1 tablespoon Erythritol
- 7 oz yeast roll dough
- 1 egg, beaten

Directions

1. Roll up the dough and cut it on 2 parts.
2. Line the springform pan with baking paper.
3. Place the first dough part in the springform pan.
4. Then arrange the apples over the dough and sprinkle it with Erythritol, vanilla extract, and ground cinnamon.
5. Then cover the apples with remaining dough and secure the edges of the pie with the help of the fork.
6. Make the small cuts in the surface of the pie.
7. Brush the pie with beaten egg and bake it for 50 minutes at 375F.
8. Cool the cooked pie well and then remove from the springform pan.
9. Cut it on the servings.

Nutrition: calories 139; fat 3.6; fiber 3.1; carbs 26.1; protein 2.8

Spinach Pancake Cake

Servings: 6 | Cooking: 15 min

Ingredients

- 1 cup heavy cream
- ¼ cup Erythritol
- 1 cup fresh spinach, chopped
- ½ cup skim milk
- 1 teaspoon vanilla extract
- 1 cup all-purpose flour
- ½ cup of rice flour
- 1 teaspoon baking powder
- 1 teaspoon olive oil
- 1 egg, beaten
- ¼ teaspoon ground clove
- 1 teaspoon butter

Directions

1. Blend the spinach until you get puree mixture.
2. After this, add skim milk, vanilla extract, all-purpose flour, and rice flour.
3. Add baking powder, egg, and ground clove.
4. Blend the ingredients until you get a smooth and thick batter.
5. Then add olive oil and pulse the batter for 30 seconds more.
6. Heat up butter in the skillet.
7. Ladle 1 ladle of the crepe batter in the skillet and flatten it in the shape of crepe.
8. Cook it for 1.5 minutes from one side and them flip into another side and cook for 20 seconds more.
9. Place the cooked crepe in the plate.
10. Repeat the same steps will all crepe batter.
11. Make the cake filling: whip the heavy cream with Erythritol.
12. Spread every crepe with sweet whipped cream.
13. Store the cake in the fridge for up to 2 days.

Nutrition: calories 228; fat 10; fiber 1; carbs 38.8; protein 5.1

Blueberry Frozen Yogurt

Servings: 6 | Cooking: 30 min

Ingredients

- 1-pint blueberries, fresh
- 2/3 cup honey

- 1 small lemon, juiced and zested
- 2 cups yogurt, chilled

Directions

1. In a saucepan, combine the blueberries, honey, lemon juice, and zest.
2. Heat over medium heat and allow to simmer for 15 minutes while stirring constantly.
3. Once the liquid has reduced, transfer the fruits in a bowl and allow to cool in the fridge for another 15 minutes.
4. Once chilled, mix together with the chilled yogurt.

Nutrition: Calories per serving: 233; Carbs:52.2 g; Protein:3.5 g; Fat: 2.9g

Apple Pear Compote

Servings: 6 | Cooking: 45 min

Ingredients

- 4 apples, cored and cubed
- 2 pears, cored and cubed
- 1 cinnamon stick
- 1 star anise
- 2 whole cloves
- 1 orange peel
- 4 cups water
- 2 tablespoons lemon juice

Directions

1. Combine all the ingredients in a saucepan.
2. Place over low heat and cook for 25 minutes.
3. Serve the compote chilled.

Nutrition: Calories:110 Fat:0.5g Protein:0.8g Carbohydrates:28.6g

Cream Cheese Cake

Servings: 2 | Cooking: 60 min

Ingredients

- 2 teaspoons cream cheese
- 1 cup Erythritol
- 2 egg whites
- ½ teaspoon lemon juice
- ½ teaspoon vanilla extract
- 2 strawberries, sliced

Directions

1. Whisk the egg whites until you get soft peaks.
2. Keep whisking and gradually add Erythritol and lemon juice.
3. Whisk the egg whites till you get strong peak mass.
4. After this, mix up together cream cheese and vanilla extract.
5. Line the baking tray with baking paper.
6. With the help of the spoon make egg white nests in the tray.
7. Bake the egg white nests for 60 minutes at 205F.
8. When the "nests' are cooked, fill them with vanilla cream cheese and top with sliced strawberries.

Nutrition: calories 36; fat 1.3; fiber 0.3; carbs 121.4; protein 3.9

Nutmeg Lemon Pudding

Servings: 6 | Cooking: 20 min

Ingredients

- 2 tablespoons lemon marmalade
- 4 eggs, whisked
- 2 tablespoons stevia
- 3 cups almond milk
- 4 allspice berries, crushed
- ¼ teaspoon nutmeg, grated

Directions

1. In a bowl, mix the lemon marmalade with the eggs and the other ingredients and whisk well.
2. Divide the mix into ramekins, introduce in the oven and bake at 350 degrees F for 20 minutes.
3. Serve cold.

Nutrition: calories 220; fat 6.6; fiber 3.4; carbs 12.4; protein 3.4

Yogurt Panna Cotta With Fresh Berries

Servings: 6 | Cooking: 1 Hour

Ingredients

- 2 cups Greek yogurt
- 1 cup milk
- 1 cup heavy cream
- 2 teaspoons gelatin powder
- 4 tablespoons cold water
- 4 tablespoons honey
- 1 teaspoon vanilla extract
- 1 teaspoon lemon zest
- 1 pinch salt
- 2 cups mixed berries for serving

Directions

1. Combine the milk and cream in a saucepan and heat them up.

2. Bloom the gelatin in cold water for 10 minutes.

3. Remove the milk off heat and stir in the gelatin until dissolved.

4. Add the vanilla, lemon zest and salt and allow to cool down.

5. Stir in the yogurt then pour the mixture into serving glasses.

6. When set, top with fresh berries and serve.

Nutrition: Calories:219 Fat:9.7g Protein:10.8g Carbohydrates:22.6g

Flourless Chocolate Cake

Servings: 8 | Cooking: 1 Hour

Ingredients

- 8 oz. dark chocolate, chopped
- 4 oz. butter, cubed
- 6 eggs, separated
- 1 teaspoon vanilla extract
- 1 pinch salt
- 4 tablespoons white sugar
- Berries for serving

Directions

1. Combine the chocolate and butter in a heatproof bowl and melt them together until smooth.

2. When smooth, remove off heat and place aside.

3. Separate the eggs.

4. Mix the egg yolks with the chocolate mixture.

5. Whip the egg whites with a pinch of salt until puffed up. Add the sugar and mix for a few more minutes until glossy and stiff.

6. Fold the meringue into the chocolate mixture then pour the batter in a 9-inch round cake pan lined with baking paper.

7. Bake in the preheated oven at 350F for 25 minutes.

8. Serve the cake chilled.

Nutrition: Calories:324 Fat:23.2g Protein:6.4g Carbohydrates:23.2g

Strawberry And Avocado Medley

Servings: 4 | Cooking: 5 min

Ingredients

- 2 cups strawberry, halved
- 1 avocado, pitted and sliced
- 2 tablespoons slivered almonds

Directions

1. Place all Ingredients in a mixing bowl.

2. Toss to combine.

3. Allow to chill in the fridge before serving.

Nutrition: Calories per serving: 107; Carbs: 9.9g; Protein: 1.6g; Fat: 7.8g

Creamy Mint Strawberry Mix

Servings: 6 | Cooking: 30 min

Ingredients

- Cooking: spray
- ¼ cup stevia
- 1 and ½ cup almond flour
- 1 teaspoon baking powder
- 1 cup almond milk
- 1 egg, whisked
- 2 cups strawberries, sliced
- 1 tablespoon mint, chopped
- 1 teaspoon lime zest, grated
- ½ cup whipping cream

Directions

1. In a bowl, combine the almond with the strawberries, mint and the other ingredients except the cooking spray and whisk well.

2. Grease 6 ramekins with the cooking spray, pour the strawberry mix inside, introduce in the oven and bake at 350 degrees F for 30 minutes.

3. Cool down and serve.

Nutrition: calories 200; fat 6.3; fiber 2; carbs 6.5; protein 8

Watermelon Ice Cream

Servings: 2 | Cooking: 5 min

Ingredients

- 8 oz watermelon
- 1 tablespoon gelatin powder

Directions

1. Make the juice from the watermelon with the help of the fruit juicer.

2. Combine together 5 tablespoons of watermelon juice and 1 tablespoon of gelatin powder. Stir it and leave for 5 minutes.

3. Then preheat the watermelon juice until warm, add gelatin mixture and heat it up over the medium heat until gelatin is dissolved.

4. Then remove the liquid from the heat and pout it in the silicone molds.

5. Freeze the jelly for 30 minutes in the freezer or for 4 hours in the fridge.

Nutrition: calories 46; fat 0.2; fiber 0.4; carbs 8.5; protein 3.7

Creamy Pie

Servings: 6 | Cooking: 30 min

Ingredients

- ¼ cup lemon juice
- 1 cup cream
- 4 egg yolks
- 4 tablespoons Erythritol
- 1 tablespoon cornstarch
- 1 teaspoon vanilla extract
- 3 tablespoons butter
- 6 oz wheat flour, whole grain

Directions

1. Mix up together wheat flour and butter and knead the soft dough.

2. Put the dough in the round cake mold and flatten it in the shape of pie crust.

3. Bake it for 15 minutes at 365F.

4. Meanwhile, make the lemon filling: Mix up together cream, egg yolks, and lemon juice. When the liquid is smooth, start to heat it up over the medium heat. Stir it constantly.

5. When the liquid is hot, add vanilla extract, cornstarch, and Erythritol. Whisk well until smooth.

6. Brin the lemon filling to boil and remove it from the heat.

7. Cool it to the room temperature.

8. Cook the pie crust to the room temperature.

9. Pour the lemon filling over the pie crust, flatten it well and leave to cool in the fridge for 25 minutes.

Nutrition: calories 225; fat 11.4; fiber 0.8; carbs 34.8; protein 5.2

Hazelnut Pudding

Servings: 8 | Cooking: 40 min

Ingredients

- 2 and ¼ cups almond flour
- 3 tablespoons hazelnuts, chopped
- 5 eggs, whisked
- 1 cup stevia
- 1 and 1/3 cups Greek yogurt
- 1 teaspoon baking powder
- 1 teaspoon vanilla extract

Directions

1. In a bowl, combine the flour with the hazelnuts and the other ingredients, whisk well, and pour into a cake pan lined with parchment paper,

2. Introduce in the oven at 350 degrees F, bake for 30 minutes, cool down, slice and serve.

Nutrition: calories 178; fat 8.4; fiber 8.2; carbs 11.5; protein 1.4

Mediterranean Cheesecakes

Servings: 1 Cheesecake | Cooking: 20 min

Ingredients

- 4 cups shredded phyllo (kataifi dough)
- 1/2 cup butter, melted
- 12 oz. cream cheese
- 1 cup Greek yogurt
- 3/4 cup confectioners' sugar
- 1 TB. vanilla extract
- 2 TB. orange blossom water
- 1 TB. orange zest
- 2 large eggs
- 1 cup coconut flakes

Directions

1. Preheat the oven to 450°F.

2. In a large bowl, and using your hands, combine shredded phyllo and melted butter, working the two together and breaking up phyllo shreds as you work.

3. Using a 12-cup muffin tin, add 1/3 cup shredded phyllo mixture to each tin, and press down to form crust on the bottom of the cup. Bake crusts for 8 minutes, remove from the oven, and set aside.

4. In a large bowl, and using an electric mixer on low speed, blend cream cheese and Greek yogurt for 1 minute.

5. Add confectioners' sugar, vanilla extract, orange blossom water, and orange zest, and blend 1 minute.

6. Add eggs, and blend for about 30 seconds or just until eggs are incorporated.

7. Lightly coat the sides of each muffin tin with cooking spray.

8. Pour about 1/3 cup cream cheese mixture over crust in each tin. Do not overflow.

9. Bake for 12 minutes.

10. Spread shredded coconut on a baking sheet, and place in the oven with cheesecakes to toast for 4 or 5 minutes or until golden brown. Remove from the oven, and set aside.

11. Remove cheesecakes from the oven, and cool for 1 hour on the countertop.

12. Place the tin in the refrigerator, and cool for 1 more hour.

13. To serve, dip a sharp knife in warm water and then run it along the sides of cheesecakes to loosen from the tin. Gently remove cheesecakes and place on a serving plate.

14. Sprinkle with toasted coconut flakes, and serve.

Melon Cucumber Smoothie

Servings: 2 | Cooking: 5 min

Ingredients

- ½ cucumber
- 2 slices of melon
- 2 tablespoons lemon juice
- 1 pear, peeled and sliced
- 3 fresh mint leaves
- ½ cup almond milk

Directions

1. Place all Ingredients in a blender.

2. Blend until smooth.

3. Pour in a glass container and allow to chill in the fridge for at least 30 minutes.

Nutrition: Calories per serving: 253; Carbs: 59.3g; Protein: 5.7g; Fat: 2.1g

Mediterranean Style Fruit Medley

Servings: 7 | Cooking: 5 min

Ingredients

- 4 fuyu persimmons, sliced into wedges
- 1 ½ cups grapes, halved
- 8 mint leaves, chopped
- 1 tablespoon lemon juice
- 1 tablespoon honey
- ½ cups almond, toasted and chopped

Directions

1. Combine all Ingredients in a bowl.
2. Toss then chill before serving.

Nutrition: Calories per serving:159; Carbs: 32g; Protein: 3g; Fat: 4g

White Wine Grapefruit Poached Peaches

Servings: 6 | Cooking: 40 min

Ingredients

- 4 peaches
- 2 cups white wine
- 1 grapefruit, peeled and juiced
- ¼ cup white sugar
- 1 cinnamon stick
- 1 star anise
- 1 cardamom pod
- 1 cup Greek yogurt for serving

Directions

1. Combine the wine, grapefruit, sugar and spices in a saucepan.
2. Bring to a boil then place the peaches in the hot syrup.
3. Lower the heat and cover with a lid. Cook for 15 minutes then allow to cool down.
4. Carefully peel the peaches and place them in a small serving bowl.
5. Top with yogurt and serve right away.

Nutrition: Calories:157 Fat:0.9g Protein:4.2g Carbohydrates:20.4g

Cinnamon Stuffed Peaches

Servings: 4 | Cooking: 5 min

Ingredients

- 4 peaches, pitted, halved
- 2 tablespoons ricotta cheese
- 2 tablespoons of liquid honey
- ¾ cup of water
- ½ teaspoon vanilla extract
- ¾ teaspoon ground cinnamon
- 1 tablespoon almonds, sliced
- ¾ teaspoon saffron

Directions

1. Pour water in the saucepan and bring to boil.
2. Add vanilla extract, saffron, ground cinnamon, and liquid honey.
3. Cook the liquid until the honey is melted.
4. Then remove it from the heat.
5. Put the halved peaches in the hot honey liquid.
6. Meanwhile, make the filling: mix up together ricotta cheese, vanilla extract, and sliced almonds.
7. Remove the peaches from honey liquid and arrange in the plate.
8. Fill 4 peach halves with ricotta filling and cover them with remaining peach halves.
9. Sprinkle the cooked dessert with liquid honey mixture gently.

Nutrition: calories 113; fat 1.8; fiber 2.8; carbs 23.9; protein 2.7

Eggless Farina Cake (namoura)

Servings: 1 Piece | Cooking: 40 min

Ingredients

- 2 cups farina
- 1/2 cup semolina
- 1/2 cup all-purpose flour
- 1 TB. baking powder
- 1 tsp. active dry yeast
- 1/2 cup sugar
- 1/2 cup plain Greek yogurt
- 1 cup whole milk
- 3/4 cup butter, melted
- 1/4 cup water
- 2 TB. tahini paste
- 15 almonds
- 2 cups Simple Syrup

Directions

1. In a large bowl, combine farina, semolina, all-purpose flour, baking powder, yeast, sugar, Greek yogurt, whole milk, butter, and water. Set aside for 15 minutes.

2. Preheat the oven to 375°F.

3. Spread tahini paste evenly in the bottom of a 9×13-inch baking pan, and pour in cake batter. Arrange almonds on top of batter, about where each slice will be. Bake for 45 minutes or until golden brown.

4. Remove cake from the oven, and using a toothpick, poke holes throughout cake for Simple Syrup to seep into. Pour syrup over cake, and let cake sit for 1 hour to absorb syrup.

5. Cool cake completely before cutting and serving.

Banana And Berries Trifle

Servings: 10 | Cooking: 5 min

Ingredients

- 8 oz biscuits, chopped
- ¼ cup strawberries, chopped
- 1 banana, chopped
- 1 peach, chopped
- ½ mango, chopped
- 1 cup grapes, chopped
- 1 tablespoon liquid honey
- 1 cup of orange juice
- ½ cup Plain yogurt
- ¼ cup cream cheese
- 1 teaspoon coconut flakes

Directions

1. Bring the orange juice to boil and remove it from the heat.

2. Add liquid honey and stir until it is dissolved.

3. Cool the liquid to the room temperature.

4. Add chopped banana, peach, mango, grapes, and strawberries. Shake the fruits gently and leave to soak the orange juice for 15 minutes.

5. Meanwhile, with the help of the hand mixer mix up together Plain yogurt and cream cheese.

6. Then separate the chopped biscuits, yogurt mixture, and fruits on 4 parts.

7. Place the first part of biscuits in the big serving glass in one layer.

8. Spread it with yogurt mixture and add fruits.

9. Repeat the same steps till you use all ingredients.

10. Top the trifle with coconut flakes.

Nutrition: calories 164; fat 6.2; fiber 1.3; carbs 24.8; protein 3.2

Mixed Berry Sorbet

Servings: 8 | Cooking: 2 ½ Hours

Ingredients

- 2 cups water
- ½ cup white sugar

- 2 cups mixed berries
- 1 tablespoon lemon juice
- 2 tablespoons honey
- 1 teaspoon lemon zest
- 1 mint sprig

Directions

1. Combine the water, sugar, berries, lemon juice, honey and lemon zest in a saucepan.
2. Bring to a boil and cook on low heat for 5 minutes.
3. Add the mint sprig and remove off heat. Allow to infuse for 10 minutes then remove the mint.
4. Pour the syrup into a blender and puree until smooth and creamy.
5. Pour the smooth syrup into an airtight container and freeze for at least 2 hours.
6. Serve the sorbet chilled.

Nutrition: Calories:84 Fat:0.1g Protein:0.4g Carbohydrates:21.3g

Almonds And Oats Pudding

Servings: 4 | Cooking: 15 min

Ingredients

- 1 tablespoon lemon juice
- Zest of 1 lime
- 1 and ½ cups almond milk
- 1 teaspoon almond extract
- ½ cup oats
- 2 tablespoons stevia
- ½ cup silver almonds, chopped

Directions

1. In a pan, combine the almond milk with the lime zest and the other ingredients, whisk, bring to a simmer and cook over medium heat for 15 minutes.
2. Divide the mix into bowls and serve cold.

Nutrition: calories 174; fat 12.1; fiber 3.2; carbs 3.9; protein 4.8

Chocolate Rice

Servings: 4 | Cooking: 20 min

Ingredients

- 1 cup of rice
- 1 tbsp cocoa powder
- 2 tbsp maple syrup
- 2 cups almond milk

Directions

1. Add all ingredients into the inner pot of instant pot and stir well.
2. Seal pot with lid and cook on high for 20 minutes.
3. Once done, allow to release pressure naturally for 10 minutes then release remaining using quick release. Remove lid.
4. Stir and serve.

Nutrition: Calories 474 Fat 29.1 g Carbohydrates 51.1 g Sugar 10 g Protein 6.3 g Cholesterol 0 mg

Lemon And Semolina Cookies

Servings: 6 | Cooking: 20 min

Ingredients

- ½ teaspoon lemon zest, grated
- 4 tablespoons Erythritol
- 4 tablespoons semolina
- 2 tablespoons olive oil
- 8 tablespoons wheat flour, whole grain
- 1 teaspoon vanilla extract
- ½ teaspoon ground clove
- 3 tablespoons coconut oil
- ¼ teaspoon baking powder
- ¼ cup of water

Directions

1. Make the dough: in the mixing bowl combine together lemon zest, semolina, olive oil, wheat flour, vanilla extract, ground clove, coconut oil, and baking powder.
2. Knead the soft dough.

3. Make the small cookies in the shape of walnuts and press them gently with the help of the fork.

4. Line the baking tray with the baking paper.

5. Place the cookies in the tray and bake them for 20 minutes at 375F.

6. Meanwhile, bring the water to boil.

7. Add Erythritol and simmer the liquid for 2 minutes over the medium heat. Cool it.

8. Pour the cooled sweet water over the hot baked cookies and leave them for 10 minutes.

9. When the cookies soak all liquid, transfer them in the serving plates.

Nutrition: calories 165; fat 11.7; fiber 0.6; carbs 23.7; protein 2

Strawberry Sorbet

Servings: 2 | Cooking: 20 min

Ingredients

- 1 cup strawberries, chopped
- 1 tablespoon of liquid honey
- 2 tablespoons water
- 1 tablespoon lemon juice

Directions

1. Preheat the water and liquid honey until you get homogenous liquid.

2. Blend the strawberries until smooth and combine them with honey liquid and lemon juice.

3. Transfer the strawberry mixture in the ice cream maker and churn it for 20 minutes or until the sorbet is thick.

4. Scoop the cooked sorbet in the ice cream cups.

Nutrition: calories 57; fat 0.3; fiber 1.5; carbs 14.3; protein 0.6

Halva (halawa)

Servings: ¼ Cup | Cooking: 10 min

Ingredients

- 1 1/2 cups honey
- 1 1/2 cups tahini paste
- 1 cup pistachios, coarsely chopped

Directions

1. Pour honey into a saucepan, set over low heat, and bring to 240°F.

2. In another saucepan over low heat, bring tahini paste to 120°F.

3. In a bowl, whisk together heated honey and tahini paste until smooth. Fold in pistachios.

4. Line a loaf pan with parchment paper and spray with cooking spray. Pour tahini mixture into the loaf pan, and refrigerate for 2 days to set.

5. Cut halva into bite-size pieces, and serve.

Semolina Cake

Servings: 6 | Cooking: 30 min

Ingredients

- ½ cup wheat flour, whole grain
- ½ cup semolina
- 1 teaspoon baking powder
- ½ cup Plain yogurt
- 1 teaspoon vanilla extract
- 4 tablespoons Erythritol
- 1 teaspoon lemon rind
- 2 tablespoons olive oil
- 1 tablespoon almond flakes
- 4 teaspoons liquid honey
- ½ cup of orange juice

Directions

1. Mix up together wheat flour, semolina, baking powder, Plain yogurt, vanilla extract, Erythritol, and olive oil.

2. Then add lemon rind and mix up the ingredients until smooth.

3. Transfer the mixture in the non-sticky cake mold, sprinkle with almond flakes, and bake for 30 minutes at 365F.

4. Meanwhile, bring the orange juice to boil.

5. Add liquid honey and stir until dissolved.

6. When the cake is cooked, pour the hot orange juice mixture over it and let it rest for at least 10 minutes.

7. Cut the cake into the servings.

Nutrition: calories 179; fat 6.1; fiber 1.1; carbs 36.3; protein 4.5

Shredded Phyllo And Sweet Cheese Pie (knafe)

Servings: 1/8 Pie | Cooking: 30 min

Ingredients

- 1 lb. pkg. shredded phyllo (kataifi dough)
- 1 cup butter, melted
- 1/2 cup whole milk
- 2 TB. semolina flour
- 1 lb. ricotta cheese
- 2 cups mozzarella cheese, shredded
- 2 TB. sugar
- 1 cup Simple Syrup

Directions

1. 1 cup Simple Syrup

2. In a food processor fitted with a chopping blade, pulse shredded phyllo and butter 10 times. Transfer mixture to a bowl.

3. In a small saucepan over low heat, warm whole milk.

4. Stir in semolina flour, and cook for 1 minute.

5. Rinse the food processor, and to it, add ricotta cheese, mozzarella cheese, sugar, and semolina mixture. Blend for 1 minute.

6. Preheat the oven to 375°F.

7. In a 9-inch-round baking dish, add 1/2 of shredded phyllo mixture, and press down to compress. Add cheese mixture, and spread out evenly. Add rest of shredded phyllo mixture, spread evenly, and gently press down. Bake for 40 minutes or until golden brown.

8. Let pie rest for 10 minutes before serving with Simple Syrup drizzled over top.

Lemon Pear Compote

Servings: 6 | Cooking: 15 min

Ingredients

- 3 cups pears, cored and cut into chunks
- 1 tsp vanilla
- 1 tsp liquid stevia
- 1 tbsp lemon zest, grated
- 2 tbsp lemon juice

Directions

1. Add all ingredients into the inner pot of instant pot and stir well.

2. Seal pot with lid and cook on high for 15 minutes.

3. Once done, allow to release pressure naturally for 10 minutes then release remaining using quick release. Remove lid.

4. Stir and serve.

Nutrition: Calories 50 Fat 0.2 g Carbohydrates 12.7 g Sugar 8.1 g Protein 0.4 g Cholesterol 0 mg

Banana Kale Smoothie

Servings: 3 | Cooking: 5 min

Ingredients

- 2 cups kale leaves
- 1 cup almond milk
- ½ cup crushed ice
- 1 banana, peeled
- 1 apple, peeled and cored
- A dash of cinnamon

Directions

1. Place all Ingredients in a blender.

2. Blend until smooth.

3. Pour in a glass container and allow to chill in the fridge for at least 30 minutes.

Nutrition: Calories per serving: 165; Carbs: 32.1g; Protein: 2.3g; Fat: 4.2g

Cinnamon Pear Jam

Servings: 12 | Cooking: 4 min

Ingredients

- 8 pears, cored and cut into quarters
- 1 tsp cinnamon
- 1/4 cup apple juice
- 2 apples, peeled, cored and diced

Directions

1. Add all ingredients into the inner pot of instant pot and stir well.
2. Seal pot with lid and cook on high for 4 minutes.
3. Once done, allow to release pressure naturally. Remove lid.
4. Blend pear apple mixture using an immersion blender until smooth.
5. Serve and enjoy.

Nutrition: Calories 103 Fat 0.3 g Carbohydrates 27.1 g Sugar 18 g Protein 0.6 g Cholesterol 0 mg

Apple And Walnut Salad

Servings: 6 | Cooking: 5 min

Ingredients

- Juice from ½ orange
- Zest from ½ orange, grated
- 2 tablespoons honey
- 1 tablespoon olive oil
- 4 medium Gala apples, cubed
- 8 dried apricots, chopped
- ¼ cup walnuts, toasted and chopped

Directions

1. In a small bowl, whisk together the orange juice, zest, honey, and olive oil. Set aside.
2. In a larger bowl, toss the apples, apricots, and walnuts.
3. Drizzle with the vinaigrette and toss to coat all Ingredients.
4. Serve chilled.

Nutrition: Calories per serving: 178; Carbs: 30g; Protein: 1g; Fat: 6g

Phyllo Custard Pockets (shaabiyat)

Servings: 1 Pocket | Cooking: 10 min

Ingredients

- 8 phyllo sheets
- 1/2 cup butter, melted
- 21/4 cups Ashta Custard (recipe later in this chapter)
- 1 cup Simple Syrup (recipe later in this chapter)
- 1/2 cup pistachios, ground

Directions

1. Preheat the oven to 450°F.
2. Lay out a sheet of phyllo dough, brush with butter, and layer another sheet of phyllo dough on top. Cut sheets into 3 equal-size columns, each about 3 or 4 inches wide.
3. Place 3 tablespoons Ashta Custard at one end of each column, and fold the bottom-right corner up and over custard. Pull up bottom-left corner, and repeat folding each corner up to the opposite corner, forming a triangle as you fold.
4. Place triangle pockets on a baking sheet, brush with butter, and bake for 10 minutes or until golden brown.
5. Serve warm or cold, drizzled with Simple Syrup and sprinkled with pistachios.

Chocolate Baklava

Servings: 4 | Cooking: 35 min

Ingredients

- 24 sheets (14 x 9-inch) frozen whole-wheat phyllo (filo) dough, thawed
- 1/8 teaspoon salt
- 1/3 cup toasted walnuts, chopped coarsely

- 1/3 cup almonds, blanched toasted, chopped coarsely
- 1/2 teaspoon ground cinnamon
- 1/2 cup water
- 1/2 cup hazelnuts, toasted, chopped coarsely
- 1/2 cup pistachios, roasted, chopped coarsely
- 3/4 cup honey
- 1/2 cup of butter, melted
- 1 cup chocolate-hazelnut spread (I used Nutella)
- 1 piece (3-inch) cinnamon stick
- Cooking: spray

Directions

1. Into medium-sized saucepan, combine the water, honey, and the cinnamon stick; stir until the honey is dissolved. Increase the heat/flame to medium; continue cooking for about 10 minutes without stirring. A candy thermometer should read 230F. Remove the saucepan from the heat and then keep warm. Remove and discard the cinnamon stick.

2. Preheat the oven to 350F.

3. Put the chocolate-hazelnut spread into microwavable bowl; microwave the spread for about 30 seconds on HIGH or until the spread is melted.

4. In a bowl, combine the hazelnuts, pistachios, almonds, walnuts, ground cinnamon, and the salt.

5. Lightly grease with the cooking spray a 9x13-inch ceramic or glass baking dish.

6. Put 1 sheet lengthwise into the bottom of the prepared baking dish, extending the ends of the sheet over the edges of the dish. Lightly brush the sheet with the butter. Repeat the process with 5 sheets phyllo and a light brush of butter. Drizzle 1/3 cup of the melted chocolate-hazelnut spread over the buttered phyllo sheets. Sprinkle about 1/3 of the nut mixture (1/2 cup) over the spread.

7. Repeat the process, layering phyllo sheet, brush of butter, spread, and with nut mixture. For the last, nut mixture top layer, top with 6 phyllo sheets, pressing each phyllo gently into the dish and brushing each sheet with butter.

8. Slice the layers into 24 portions by making 3 cuts lengthwise and then 5 cuts crosswise with a sharp knife; bake for about 35 minutes at 350F or until the phyllo sheets are golden.

9. Remove the dish from the oven, drizzle the honey sauce over the baklava. Pace the dish on a wire rack and let cool. Cover and store the baklavas at normal room temperature if not serving right away.

Nutrition: 238 Cal, 13.4 g total fat (4.3 g sat. fat, 5.6 g mono fat, 2 g poly fat), 4 g protein, 27.8 g total carbs., 1.6 g fiber, 10 mg chol., 1.3 mg iron, 148 mg sodium, and 29 mg calcium.

Apricot Rosemary Muffins

Servings: 12 | Cooking: 1 Hour

Ingredients

- 2 eggs
- 1/3 cup white sugar
- 1 teaspoon vanilla extract
- 1 cup buttermilk
- ¼ cup olive oil
- 1 ½ cups all-purpose flour
- ¼ teaspoon salt
- 1 teaspoon baking powder
- ¼ teaspoon baking soda
- 4 apricots, pitted and diced
- 1 teaspoon dried rosemary

Directions

1. Combine the eggs, sugar and vanilla in a bowl and mix until double in volume.

2. Stir in the oil and buttermilk and mix well.

3. Fold in the flour, salt, baking powder and baking soda then add the apricots and rosemary and mix gently.

4. Spoon the batter in a muffin tin lined with muffin papers and bake in the preheated oven at 350F for 20-25 minutes or until the muffins pass the toothpick test.

5. Serve the muffins chilled.

Nutrition: Calories:140 Fat:5.4g Protein:3.4g Carbohydrates:20.1g

Blueberry Yogurt Mousse

Servings: 4 | Cooking: 0 min

Ingredients

- 2 cups Greek yogurt
- ¼ cup stevia
- ¾ cup heavy cream
- 2 cups blueberries

Directions

1. In a blender, combine the yogurt with the other ingredients, pulse well, divide into cups and keep in the fridge for 30 minutes before serving.

Nutrition: calories 141; fat 4.7; fiber 4.7; carbs 8.3; protein 0.8

Pistachio Cheesecake

Servings: 6 | Cooking: 10 min

Ingredients

- ½ cup pistachio, chopped
- 4 teaspoons butter, softened
- 4 teaspoon Erythritol
- 2 cups cream cheese
- ½ cup cream, whipped

Directions

1. Mix up together pistachios, butter, and Erythritol.

2. Put the mixture in the baking mold and bake for 10 minutes at 355F.

3. Meanwhile, whisk together cream cheese and whipped cream.

4. When the pistachio mixture is baked, chill it well.

5. After this, transfer the pistachio mixture in the round cake mold and flatten in one layer.

6. Then put the cream cheese mixture over the pistachio mixture, flatten the surface until smooth.

7. Cool the cheesecake in the fridge for 1 hour before serving.

Nutrition: calories 332; fat 33; fiber 0.5; carbs 7.4; protein 7

Almond Citrus Muffins

Servings: 6 | Cooking: 30 min

Ingredients

- 2 eggs, beaten
- 1 ½ cup whole wheat flour
- ½ cup almond meal
- 1 teaspoon vanilla extract
- 1 tablespoon butter, softened
- 1 teaspoon orange zest, grated
- 1 tablespoon orange juice
- ¾ cup Erythritol
- 1 oz orange pulp
- 1 teaspoon baking powder
- ½ teaspoon lime zest, grated
- Cooking: spray

Directions

1. Combine together almond meal, eggs, whole wheat flour, vanilla extract, butter, orange zest, orange juice, and orange pulp.

2. Add lime zest and baking powder.

3. Then add Erythritol.

4. With the help of the hand mixer mix up the ingredients.

5. When the mixture is soft and smooth, it is done.

6. Spray the muffin molds with cooking spray from inside and preheat the oven to 365F.

7. Fill ½ part of every muffin mold with muffin batter and transfer them in the oven.

8. Cook the muffins for 30 minutes.

9. Then check if the muffins are cooked by piercing them with a toothpick (if it is dry, the muffins are cooked; if it is not dry, bake the muffins for 5-7 minutes more.)

Nutrition: calories 204; fat 7.7; fiber 1.9; carbs 57.1; protein 6.8

Custard-filled Pancakes (atayef)

Servings: 1 Pancake | Cooking: 15 min

Ingredients

- 1 cup all-purpose flour
- 1/2 cup whole-wheat flour
- 1 cup whole milk
- 1/2 cup water
- 1 tsp. active dry yeast
- 1 tsp. baking powder
- 1/2 tsp. salt
- 2 TB. sugar
- 2 cups Ashta Custard
- 1/2 cup ground pistachios
- 1 cup Simple Syrup

Directions

1. In a large bowl, whisk together all-purpose flour, whole-wheat flour, whole milk, water, yeast, baking powder, salt, and sugar. Set aside for 30 minutes.

2. Preheat a nonstick griddle over low heat.

3. Spoon 3 tablespoons batter onto the griddle, and cook pancake for about 30 seconds or until bubbles form along entire top of pancake. Do not flip over pancake. You're only browning the bottom.

4. Transfer pancake to a plate, and let cool while cooking remaining pancakes. Do not overlap the pancakes while letting them cool.

5. Form pancake into a pocket by folding pancake into a half-moon, and pinch together the edges, but only halfway up.

6. Spoon Ashta Custard into a piping bag or a zipper-lock plastic bag, snip off the corner, and squeeze about 2 tablespoons custard into each pancake pocket. Sprinkle custard with pistachios.

7. Serve pancakes chilled with Simple Syrup drizzled on top.

Mediterranean Bread Pudding (aish El Saraya)

Servings: 1/9 Of Pudding | Cooking: 20 min

Ingredients

- 8 slices white bread, crust removed
- 1 cup sugar
- 1/2 cup water
- 1 TB. fresh lemon juice
- 2 cups Simple Syrup (recipe later in this chapter)
- 4 cups Ashta Custard (recipe later in this chapter)
- 1/2 cup coconut flakes, toasted
- 1/2 cup pistachios, ground
- 1 strawberry, sliced

Directions

1. Preheat the oven to 450°F.

2. Place slices of bread on a baking sheet, and toast for 10 minutes or until bread is golden brown and dry.

3. In a small saucepan over medium-low heat, combine sugar, water, and lemon juice. Simmer for 5 to 7 minutes or until sugar reaches a dark golden brown color.

4. Carefully pour hot dark brown syrup into an 8×8-inch baking dish, shifting the dish from side to side to spread syrup around bottom of dish.

5. Place 4 slices of bread on top of brown syrup. Pour 1 cup of Simple Syrup over bread, spread 2 cups Ashta Custard over bread, and add another layer of 4 slices of bread. Pour remaining 1 cup Simple Syrup over bread, and spread remaining 2 cups Ashta Custard over top bread layer.

6. Cover the dish with plastic wrap, and refrigerate for 4 hours.

7. Decorate top of dish with toasted coconut, pistachios, and strawberry slices, and serve.

Cinnamon Apple Rice Pudding

Servings: 8 | Cooking: 15 min

Ingredients

- 1 cup of rice
- 1 tsp vanilla
- 1/4 apple, peeled and chopped
- 1/2 cup water
- 1 1/2 cup almond milk
- 1 tsp cinnamon

- 1 cinnamon stick

Directions

1. Add all ingredients into the instant pot and stir well.
2. Seal pot with lid and cook on high for 15 minutes.
3. Once done, release pressure using quick release. Remove lid.
4. Stir and serve.

Nutrition: Calories 206 Fat 11.5 g Carbohydrates 23.7 g Sugar 2.7 g Protein 3 g Cholesterol 0 mg

Pomegranate Granita With Lychee

Servings: 7 | Cooking: 5 min

Ingredients

- 500 millimeters pomegranate juice, organic and sugar-free
- 1 cup water
- ½ cup lychee syrup
- 2 tablespoons lemon juice
- 4 mint leaves
- 1 cup fresh lychees, pitted and sliced

Directions

1. Place all Ingredients in a large pitcher.
2. Place inside the fridge to cool before serving.

Nutrition: Calories per serving: 96; Carbs: 23.8g; Protein: 0.4g; Fat: 0.4g

Lime Grapes And Apples

Servings: 2 | Cooking: 25 min

Ingredients

- ½ cup red grapes
- 2 apples
- 1 teaspoon lime juice
- 1 teaspoon Erythritol
- 3 tablespoons water

Directions

1. Line the baking tray with baking paper.
2. Then cut the apples on the halves and remove the seeds with the help of the scooper.
3. Cut the apple halves on 2 parts more.
4. Arrange all fruits in the tray in one layer, drizzle with water, and bake for 20 minutes at 375F.
5. Flip the fruits on another side after 10 minutes of cooking.
6. Then remove them from the oven and sprinkle with lime juice and Erythritol.
7. Return the fruits back in the oven and bake for 5 minutes more.
8. Serve the cooked dessert hot or warm.

Nutrition: calories 142; fat 0.4; fiber 5.7; carbs 40.1; protein 0.9

Mediterranean Baked Apples

Servings: 4 | Cooking: 25 min

Ingredients

- 1.5 pounds apples, peeled and sliced
- Juice from ½ lemon
- A dash of cinnamon

Directions

1. Preheat the oven to 250F.
2. Line a baking sheet with parchment paper then set aside.
3. In a medium bowl, apples with lemon juice and cinnamon.
4. Place the apples on the parchment paper-lined baking sheet.
5. Bake for 25 minutes until crisp.

Nutrition: Calories per serving: 90; Carbs: 23.9g; Protein: 0.5g; Fat: 0.3g

Poached Cherries

Servings: 5 | Cooking: 10 min

Ingredients

- 1 pound fresh and sweet cherries, rinsed, pitted
- 3 strips (1x3 inches each) orange zest,
- 3 strips (1x3 inches each) lemon zest,
- 2/3 cup sugar
- 15 peppercorns
- 1/4 vanilla bean, split but not scraped
- 1 3/4 cups water

Directions

1. In a saucepan, mix the water, citrus zest, sugar, peppercorns, and vanilla bean; bring to a boil, stirring until the sugar is dissolved.
2. Add the cherries; simmer for about 10 minutes until the cherries are soft, but not falling apart.
3. Skim any foam from the surface and let the poached cherries cool.
4. Refrigerate with the poaching liquid. Before serving, strain the cherries.

Nutrition: 170 cal., 1 g total fat (0 g sat. fat, 0 g mono fat, 0.5 g poly fat), 0 mg chol., 0 mg sodium, 42 g total carbs., and 2 g fiber.

Watermelon Salad

Servings: 6 | Cooking: 0 min

Ingredients

- 14 oz watermelon
- 1 oz dark chocolate
- 3 tablespoons coconut cream
- 1 teaspoon Erythritol
- 2 kiwi, chopped
- 1 oz Feta cheese, crumbled

Directions

1. Peel the watermelon and remove the seeds from it.
2. Chop the fruit and place in the salad bowl.
3. Add chopped kiwi and crumbled Feta. Stir the salad well.
4. Then mix up together coconut cream and Erythritol.
5. Pour the cream mixture over the salad.
6. Then shave the chocolate over the salad with the help of the potato peeler.
7. The salad should be served immediately.

Nutrition: calories 90; fat 4.4; fiber 1.4; carbs 12.9; protein 1.9

Easy Fruit Compote

Servings: 2 | Cooking: 15 min

Ingredients

- 1-pound fresh fruits of your choice
- 2 tablespoons maple syrup
- A dash of salt

Directions

1. Slice the fruits thinly and place them in a saucepan.
2. Add the honey and salt.
3. Heat the saucepan over medium low heat and allow the fruits to simmer for 15 minutes or until the liquid has reduced.
4. Make sure that you stir constantly to prevent the fruits from sticking at the bottom of your pan and eventually burning.
5. Transfer in a lidded jar.
6. Allow to cool.
7. Serve with slices of whole wheat bread or vegan ice cream.

Nutrition: Calories per serving:218; Carbs: 56.8g; Protein: 0.9g; Fat: 0.2g

Minty Tart

Servings: 6 | Cooking: 30 min

Ingredients

- 1 cup tart cherries, pitted
- 1 cup wheat flour, whole grain
- 1/3 cup butter, softened

- ½ teaspoon baking powder
- 1 tablespoon Erythritol
- ¼ teaspoon dried mint
- ¾ teaspoon salt

Directions

1. Mix up together wheat flour and cutter.
2. Add baking powder and salt. Knead the soft dough.
3. Then place the dough in the freezer for 10 minutes.
4. When the dough is solid, remove it from the freezer and grate with the help of the grater. Place ¼ part of the grated dough in the freezer.
5. Sprinkle the springform pan with remaining dough and place tart cherries on it.
6. Sprinkle the berries with Erythritol and dried mint and cover with ¼ part of dough from the freezer.
7. Bake the cake for 30 minutes at 365F. The cooked tart will have a golden brown surface.

Nutrition: calories 177; fat 10.4; fiber 0.9; carbs 21; protein 2.4

Papaya Cream

Servings: 2 | Cooking: 0 min

Ingredients

- 1 cup papaya, peeled and chopped
- 1 cup heavy cream
- 1 tablespoon stevia
- ½ teaspoon vanilla extract

Directions

1. In a blender, combine the cream with the papaya and the other ingredients, pulse well, divide into cups and serve cold.

Nutrition: calories 182; fat 3.1; fiber 2.3; carbs 3.5; protein 2

Orange-sesame Almond Tuiles

Servings: 20 | Cooking: 45 min

Ingredients

- 3/4 cup unblanched or blanched sliced almonds
- 3 tablespoons orange juice, freshly squeezed
- 3 tablespoons (about 1 1/2 ounce) unsalted or salted butter
- 2 tablespoons white sesame seeds
- 10 tablespoons granulated sugar
- 1/8 cup whole-wheat flour
- 1/8 cup all-purpose flour
- 1 tablespoon toasted sesame oil
- 1 1/2 teaspoons black sesame seeds
- Grated zest of 1 orange, preferably organic

Directions

1. In a small-sized saucepan, warm the butter, sesame oil, orange zest, orange juice, and sugar over low heat until the mixture is smooth. Remove from the heat, Stir the flour, almonds and the sesame seeds; let the batter rest for 1 hour at normal room temperature.
2. Preheat the oven to 375F. Line 2 pieces baking sheet with parchment paper.
3. Set a rolling pin on a folded dishtowel. Ready a wire rack.
4. Measuring by level tablespoons, drop batter into the prepared baking sheets, placing only 4 on each sheet and spacing them apart evenly.
5. With dampened fingers, slightly flatten the batter. Place one baking sheet in the oven, bake the tuiles for about 8 to 9 minutes, rotating the baking sheet halfway through baking, until the cookies are evenly browned. Let the cookies cool slightly for 1 minute.
6. With a metal spatula, lift each cookie of the baking sheet and then drape them over the rolling pin. Let them cool in the rolling pin and then transfer to a wire rack. Repeat the process with the remaining batter. Serve the tuiles a few hours after baking.

Nutrition: 78 cal., 4.7 g total fat (1.4 g sat. fat), 5 mg chol., 13 mg sodium, 39 mg pto., 8.6 g total carbs., 0.7 g fiber, 6.4 g sugar, and 1.1 g protein.

Strawberry Ice Cream

Servings: 6 | Cooking: 1 ¼ Hours

Ingredients

- 1 pound strawberries, hulled
- 1 cup Greek yogurt
- 1 cup heavy cream
- 3 tablespoons honey
- 1 teaspoon lime zest

Directions

1. Combine all the ingredients in a blender and pulse until well mixed and smooth.

2. Pour the mixture into your ice cream machine and churn for 1 hour or according to your machine's instructions.

3. Serve the ice cream right away.

Nutrition: Calories:150 Fat:8.3g Protein:4.3g Carbohydrates:16.4g

Creamy Strawberries

Servings: 4 | Cooking: 5 min

Ingredients

- 6 tablespoons almond butter
- 1 tablespoon Erythritol
- 1 cup milk
- 1 teaspoon vanilla extract
- 1 cup strawberries, sliced

Directions

1. Pour milk in the saucepan.

2. Add Erythritol, vanilla extract, and almond butter.

3. With the help of the hand mixer mix up the liquid until smooth and bring it to boil.

4. Then remove the mixture from the heat and let it cool.

5. The cooled mixture will be thick.

6. Put the strawberries in the serving glasses and top with the thick almond butter dip.

Nutrition: calories 192; fat 14.9; fiber 3.1; carbs 10.4; protein 7.3

Almond Rice Dessert

Servings: 4 | Cooking: 20 min

Ingredients

- 1 cup white rice
- 2 cups almond milk
- 1 cup almonds, chopped
- ½ cup stevia
- 1 tablespoon cinnamon powder
- ½ cup pomegranate seeds

Directions

1. In a pot, mix the rice with the milk and stevia, bring to a simmer and cook for 20 minutes, stirring often.

2. Add the rest of the ingredients, stir, divide into bowls and serve.

Nutrition: calories 234; fat 9.5; fiber 3.4; carbs 12.4; protein 6.5

Greek Yogurt Pie

Servings: 8 | Cooking: 1 Hour

Ingredients

- 1 package phyllo dough sheets
- 4 cups plain yogurt
- 4 eggs
- ½ cup white sugar
- 1 teaspoon vanilla extract
- 1 teaspoon lemon zest
- 1 teaspoon orange zest

Directions

1. Mix the yogurt, eggs, sugar, vanilla and citrus zest in a bowl.

2. Layer 2 phyllo sheets in a deep dish baking pan then pour a few tablespoons of yogurt mixture over the dough.

3. Continue layering the phyllo dough and yogurt in the pan.

4. Bake in the preheated oven at 350F for 40 minutes.

5. Allow the pie to cool down before serving.

Nutrition: Calories:175 Fat:3.8g Protein:9.9g Carbohydrates:22.7g

Five Berry Mint Orange Infusion

Servings: 12 | Cooking: 10 min

Ingredients

- ½ cup water
- 3 orange pekoe tea bags
- 3 sprigs of mint
- 1 cup fresh strawberries
- 1 cup fresh golden raspberries
- 1 cup fresh raspberries
- 1 cup blackberries
- 1 cup fresh blueberries
- 1 cup pitted fresh cherries
- 1 bottle Sauvignon Blanc
- ½ cup pomegranate juice, natural
- 1 teaspoon vanilla

Directions

1. In a saucepan, bring water to a boil over medium heat. Add the tea bags, mint and stir. Let it stand for 10 minutes.

2. In a large bowl, combine the rest of the ingredients.

3. Put in the fridge to chill for at least 3 hours.

Nutrition: Calories per serving: 140; Carbs: 32.1g; Protein: 1.2g; Fat: 1.5g

Cocoa Yogurt Mix

Servings: 2 | Cooking: 0 min

Ingredients

- 1 tablespoon cocoa powder
- ¼ cup strawberries, chopped
- ¾ cup Greek yogurt
- 5 drops vanilla stevia

Directions

1. In a bowl, mix the yogurt with the cocoa, strawberries and the stevia and whisk well.

2. Divide the mix into bowls and serve.

Nutrition: calories 200; fat 8; fiber 3.4; carbs 7.6; protein 4.3

Frozen Strawberry Greek Yogurt

Servings: 16 | Cooking: 15 min

Ingredients

- 3 cups Greek yogurt, plain, low-fat (2%)
- 2 teaspoons vanilla
- 1/8 teaspoon salt
- 1/4 cup freshly squeezed lemon juice
- 1 cup sugar
- 1 cup strawberries, sliced

Directions

1. In a medium-sized bowl, except for the strawberries, combine the rest of the ingredients; whisking until the mixture is smooth.

2. Transfer the yogurt into a 1 1/2 or 2-quart ice cream make and freeze according to the manufacturer's direction, adding the strawberry slices for the last minute. Transfer into an airtight container and freeze for about 2-4 hours. Before serving, let stand for 15 minutes at room temperature.

Nutrition: 86 cal., 1 g total fat (1 g sat. fat), 3 mg chol., 16g carbs., 0 g fiber, 15 g sugar, and 4 g protein.

Almond Peaches Mix

Servings: 4 | Cooking: 10 min

Ingredients

- 1/3 cup almonds, toasted

- 1/3 cup pistachios, toasted
- 1 teaspoon mint, chopped
- ½ cup coconut water
- 1 teaspoon lemon zest, grated
- 4 peaches, halved
- 2 tablespoons stevia

Directions

1. In a pan, combine the peaches with the stevia and the rest of the ingredients, simmer over medium heat for 10 minutes, divide into bowls and serve cold.

Nutrition: calories 135; fat 4.1; fiber 3.8; carbs 4.1; protein 2.3

Raisin Pecan Baked Apples

Servings: 6 | Cooking: 4 min

Ingredients

- 6 apples, cored and cut into wedges
- 1 cup red wine
- 1/4 cup pecans, chopped
- 1/4 cup raisins
- 1/4 tsp nutmeg
- 1 tsp cinnamon
- 1/3 cup honey

Directions

1. Add all ingredients into the instant pot and stir well.
2. Seal pot with lid and cook on high for 4 minutes.
3. Once done, allow to release pressure naturally for 10 minutes then release remaining using quick release. Remove lid.
4. Stir well and serve.

Nutrition: Calories 229 Fat 0.9 g Carbohydrates 52.6 g Sugar 42.6 g Protein 1 g Cholesterol 0 mg

Walnuts Cake

Servings: 4 | Cooking: 40 min

Ingredients

- ½ pound walnuts, minced
- Zest of 1 orange, grated
- 1 and ¼ cups stevia
- eggs, whisked
- 1 teaspoon almond extract
- 1 and ½ cup almond flour
- 1 teaspoon baking soda

Directions

1. In a bowl, combine the walnuts with the orange zest and the other ingredients, whisk well and pour into a cake pan lined with parchment paper.
2. Introduce in the oven at 350 degrees F, bake for 40 minutes, cool down, slice and serve.

Nutrition: calories 205; fat 14.1; fiber 7.8; carbs 9.1; protein 3.4

Spiced Cookies

Servings: 6 | Cooking: 30 min

Ingredients

- 1 egg, beaten
- 1 teaspoon vanilla extract
- ½ teaspoon ground cinnamon
- 1 teaspoon ground turmeric
- 1 tablespoon butter, softened
- 1 cup wheat flour
- 1 teaspoon baking powder
- 4 tablespoons pumpkin puree
- 1 tablespoon Erythritol

Directions

1. Put all ingredients in the mixing bowl and knead the soft and non-sticky dough.
2. After this, line the baking tray with baking paper.
3. Make 6 balls from the dough and press them gently with the help of the spoon.
4. Arrange the dough balls in the tray.
5. Bake the cookies for 30 minutes at 355F.

6. Chill the cooked cookies well and store them in the glass jar.

Nutrition: calories 111; fat 2.9; fiber 1.1; carbs 20.2; protein 3.2

Scrumptious Cake With Cinnamon

Servings: 8 | Cooking: 40 min

Ingredients

- 1 lemon
- 4 eggs
- 1 tsp cinnamon
- ¼ lb. sugar
- ½ lb. ground almonds

Directions

1. Preheat oven to 350oF. Then grease a cake pan and set aside.

2. On high speed, beat for three minutes the sugar and eggs or until the volume is doubled.

3. Then with a spatula, gently fold in the lemon zest, cinnamon and almond flour until well mixed.

4. Then pour batter on prepared pan and bake for forty minutes or until golden brown.

5. Let cool before serving.

Nutrition: Calorie per Servings: 253; Carbs: 21.1g; Protein: 8.8g; Fats: 16.3g

Yogurt Cake

Servings: 1 Piece | Cooking: 55 min

Ingredients

- 1 cup plain Greek yogurt
- 1 cup sugar
- 2 large eggs
- 1 TB. vanilla extract
- 4 TB. fresh lemon juice
- 1 TB. lemon zest
- 1/2 cup vegetable or light olive oil
- 13/4 cups all-purpose flour
- 2 tsp. baking powder
- 1/2 tsp. salt
- 1 cup confectioners' sugar

Directions

1. Preheat the oven to 350°F. Lightly coat a 9-inch-round cake pan with cooking spray, and dust the pan using about 2 tablespoons all-purpose flour.

2. In a large bowl, using an electric mixer on medium speed, blend Greek yogurt, sugar, eggs, vanilla extract, 2 tablespoons lemon juice, lemon zest, and vegetable oil for about 2 minutes.

3. Add all-purpose flour, baking powder, and salt, and blend for 2 more minutes.

4. Pour batter into the prepared cake pan, and bake for 55 minutes or until a toothpick inserted in center of cake comes out clean. Cool cake completely.

5. In a small bowl, whisk together confectioners' sugar and remaining 2 tablespoons lemon juice to make glaze.

6. When cake is cool, pour glaze over top, cut, and serve.

Chunky Apple Sauce

Servings: 16 | Cooking: 12 min

Ingredients

- 4 apples, peeled, cored and diced
- 1 tsp vanilla
- 4 pears, diced
- 2 tbsp cinnamon
- 1/4 cup maple syrup
- 3/4 cup water

Directions

1. Add all ingredients into the instant pot and stir well.

2. Seal pot with lid and cook on high for 12 minutes.

3. Once done, allow to release pressure naturally for 10 minutes then release remaining using quick release. Remove lid.

4. Serve and enjoy.

Nutrition: Calories 75 Fat 0.2 g Carbohydrates 19.7 g Sugar 13.9 g Protein 0.4 g Cholesterol 0 mg

Olive Oil Cake

Servings: 1 Piece | Cooking: 45 min

Ingredients

- 2 large eggs
- 3/4 cup sugar
- 1/2 cup light olive oil
- 1 cup plain Greek yogurt
- 3 TB. fresh orange juice
- 2 TB. orange zest
- 1 3/4 cups all-purpose flour
- 1/2 tsp. salt
- 2 tsp. baking powder
- 1/2 tsp. baking soda
- 3/4 cup dried cranberries
- 2 TB. confectioners' sugar

Directions

1. Preheat the oven to 350°F. Lightly coat a 9-inch-round cake pan or Bundt pan with cooking spray, and dust with about 2 tablespoons all-purpose flour.
2. In a large bowl, and using an electric mixer on medium speed, blend eggs and sugar for 2 minutes.
3. Blend in light olive oil, Greek yogurt, orange juice, and orange zest for 2 more minutes.
4. Add all-purpose flour, salt, baking powder, and baking soda and blend for 1 more minute.
5. Using a spatula or wooden spoon, fold cranberries into batter.
6. Pour batter into the prepared pan, and bake for 45 minutes or until a toothpick inserted in center of cake comes out clean.
7. Cool cake completely.
8. Dust top of cake with confectioners' sugar, cut, and serve.

Grapes Stew

Servings: 4 | Cooking: 10 min

Ingredients

- 2/3 cup stevia
- 1 tablespoon olive oil
- 1/3 cup coconut water
- 1 teaspoon vanilla extract
- 1 teaspoon lemon zest, grated
- 2 cup red grapes, halved

Directions

1. Heat up a pan with the water over medium heat, add the oil, stevia and the rest of the ingredients, toss, simmer for 10 minutes, divide into cups and serve.

Nutrition: calories 122; fat 3.7; fiber 1.2; carbs 2.3; protein 0.4

Lemon Cranberry Sauce

Servings: 8 | Cooking: 14 min

Ingredients

- 10 oz fresh cranberries
- 3/4 cup Swerve
- 1/4 cup water
- 1 tsp lemon zest
- 1 tsp vanilla extract

Directions

1. Add cranberries and water into the instant pot.
2. Seal pot with lid and cook on high for 1 minute.
3. Once done, allow to release pressure naturally for 10 minutes then release remaining using quick release. Remove lid.
4. Set pot on sauté mode.
5. Add remaining ingredients and cook for 2-3 minutes.
6. Pour in container and store in fridge.

Nutrition: Calories 21 Fat 0 g Carbohydrates 25.8 g Sugar 23.9 g Protein 0 g Cholesterol 0 mg

Delectable Mango Smoothie

Servings: 2 | Cooking: 5 min

Ingredients

- 2 cups diced mango
- 1 carrot, peeled and sliced roughly
- 1 orange, peeled and segmented
- Fresh mint leaves

Directions

1. Place the mango, carrot, and oranges in a blender.
2. Pulse until smooth.
3. Pour in a glass container and allow to chill before serving.
4. Garnish with mint leaves on top.

Nutrition: Calories per serving: 134; Carbs: 33.6g; Protein: 2g; Fat: 0.7g; Sugar

Blackberries And Pomegranate Parfait

Servings: 4 | Cooking: 20 min

Ingredients

- 1 cup Plain yogurt
- 1 tablespoon coconut flakes
- 1 tablespoon liquid honey
- 4 teaspoons peanuts, chopped
- 1 cup blackberries
- 1 tablespoon pomegranate seeds

Directions

1. Mix up together plain yogurt and coconut flakes.
2. Put the mixture in the freezer.
3. Meanwhile, combine together liquid honey and blackberries.
4. Place ½ part of blackberry mixture in the serving glasses.
5. Then add ¼ part of the cooled yogurt mixture.
6. Sprinkle the yogurt mixture with all peanuts and cover with ½ part of remaining yogurt mixture.
7. Then add remaining blackberries and top the dessert with yogurt.
8. Garnish the parfait with pomegranate seeds and cool in the fridge for 20 minutes.

Nutrition: calories 115; fat 3.1; fiber 3; carbs 13; protein 5.1

Yellow Cake With Jam Topping

Servings: 1 Piece | Cooking: 20 min

Ingredients

- 5 large eggs
- 11/4 cups sugar
- 1 TB. vanilla extract
- 2 cups all-purpose flour
- 2 tsp. baking powder
- 1/2 tsp. salt
- 1/2 cup whole milk
- 1/2 cup butter, melted
- 2 cups apricot or peach jam
- 1/4 cup sweetened condensed milk
- 2 TB. hot water

Directions

1. Preheat the oven to 350°F. Lightly coat a 9×13-inch cake pan with cooking spray, and dust with about 2 tablespoons all-purpose flour.
2. In a large bowl, and using an electric mixer on medium speed, beat eggs for 3 minutes.
3. Add sugar and vanilla extract, and beat for 2 more minutes.
4. Add all-purpose flour, baking powder, salt, whole milk, and melted butter, and blend for 1 minute.
5. Pour batter into the prepared pan, and bake for 20 minutes or until a toothpick inserted in center of cake comes out clean.
6. Cool cake completely.
7. In a small bowl, whisk together apricot jam, sweetened condensed milk, and hot water.
8. Pour jam icing over cake, letting it run over the edges, cut, and serve.

Raspberry Tart

Servings: 6 | Cooking: 20 min

Ingredients

- 3 tablespoons butter, softened
- 1 cup wheat flour, whole wheat
- 1 teaspoon baking powder
- 1 egg, beaten
- 4 tablespoons pistachio paste
- 2 tablespoons raspberry jam

Directions

1. Knead the dough: combine together softened butter, flour, baking powder, and egg. You should get the non-sticky and very soft dough.
2. Put the dough in the springform pan and flatten it with the help of the fingertips until you get pie crust.
3. Bake it for 10 minutes at 365F.
4. After this, spread the pie crust with raspberry jam and then with pistachio paste.
5. Bake the tart at 365F for another 10 minutes.
6. Cool the cooked tart and cut on the servings.

Nutrition: calories 311; fat 11; fiber 1.3; carbs 24.7; protein 4.5

Coconut Risotto Pudding

Servings: 6 | Cooking: 20 min

Ingredients

- 3/4 cup rice
- 1/2 cup shredded coconut
- 1 tsp lemon juice
- 1/2 tsp vanilla
- oz can coconut milk
- 1/4 cup maple syrup
- 1 1/2 cups water

Directions

1. Add all ingredients into the instant pot and stir well.
2. Seal pot with lid and cook on high for 20 minutes.
3. Once done, allow to release pressure naturally for 10 minutes then release remaining using quick release. Remove lid.
4. Blend pudding mixture using an immersion blender until smooth.
5. Serve and enjoy.

Nutrition: Calories 205 Fat 8.6 g Carbohydrates 29.1 g Sugar 9 g Protein 2.6 g Cholesterol 0 mg

Mango And Honey Cream

Servings: 6 | Cooking: 30 min

Ingredients

- 2 cups coconut cream, chipped
- 6 teaspoons honey
- 2 mango, chopped

Directions

1. Blend together honey and mango.
2. When the mixture is smooth, combine it with whipped cream and stir carefully.
3. Put the mango-cream mixture in the serving glasses and refrigerate for 30 minutes.

Nutrition: calories 272; fat 19.5; fiber 3.6; carbs 27; protein 2.8

Raw Truffles

Servings: 6 | Cooking: 30 min

Ingredients

- ½ pound dates, pitted
- ½ cup water, hot
- 2 tablespoons raw honey
- ½ teaspoon vanilla extract
- 2 tablespoons cocoa powder
- 1 cup shredded coconut
- 1 tablespoon chia seeds
- 1 oz. candied orange, diced
- Extra cocoa powder for coating

Directions

1. Combine the hot water, dates, honey and vanilla in a food processor and pulse until well mixed.
2. Add the rest of the ingredients and mix well.
3. Form small balls and roll them through cocoa powder.
4. Serve right away.

Nutrition: Calories:196 Fat:4.8g Protein:1.7g Carbohydrates:41.3g

Baked Peaches

Servings: 4 | Cooking: 30 min

Ingredients

- 4 teaspoons stevia
- 4 peaches, halved and pitted
- 1 teaspoon vanilla extract
- 3 tablespoons honey

Directions

1. Arrange the peaches on a baking sheet lined with parchment paper, add the stevia, honey and vanilla and bake at 350 degrees F for 30 minutes.
2. Divide them between plates and serve.

Nutrition: calories 176; fat 4.5; fiber 7.6; carbs 11.5; protein 5

Greek Yogurt Muesli Parfaits

Servings: 4 | Cooking: 10 min

Ingredients

- 4 cups Greek yogurt
- 1 cup whole wheat muesli
- 2 cups fresh berries of your choice

Directions

1. Layer the four glasses with Greek yogurt at the bottom, muesli on top, and berries.
2. Repeat the layers until the glass is full.
3. Place in the fridge for at least 2 hours to chill.

Nutrition: Calories per serving: 280; Carbs: 36g; Protein:23 g; Fat: 4g

Lemon Cream

Servings: 6 | Cooking: 10 min

Ingredients

- 2 eggs, whisked
- 1 and ¼ cup stevia
- 10 tablespoons avocado oil
- 1 cup heavy cream
- Juice of 2 lemons
- Zest of 2 lemons, grated

Directions

1. In a pan, combine the cream with the lemon juice and the other ingredients, whisk well, cook for 10 minutes, divide into cups and keep in the fridge for 1 hour before serving.

Nutrition: calories 200; fat 8.5; fiber 4.5; carbs 8.6; protein 4.5

Sweet Tropical Medley Smoothie

Servings: 4 | Cooking: 5 min

Ingredients

- 1 banana, peeled
- 1 sliced mango
- 1 cup fresh pineapple
- ½ cup coconut water

Directions

2. Place all Ingredients in a blender.
3. Blend until smooth.
4. Pour in a glass container and allow to chill in the fridge for at least 30 minutes.

Nutrition: Calories per serving:73 ; Carbs: 18.6g; Protein: 0.8g; Fat: 0.5g.

Mediterranean Fruit Tart

Servings: 1/8 Of Tart | Cooking: 15 min

Ingredients

- 21/4 cups all-purpose flour
- 1/2 tsp. salt
- 2 TB. sugar
- 1 cup cold butter
- 1/2 cup shortening
- 5 TB. ice water
- 2 cups Ashta Custard (recipe earlier in this chapter)
- 10 strawberries, sliced
- 2 kiwi, peeled and sliced
- 1 cup blueberries
- 1 cup peach or apricot jam
- 3 TB. water

Directions

1. In a food processor fitted with a chopping blade, pulse 2 cups all-purpose flour, salt, and sugar 5 times.
2. Add butter and shortening, and blend for 1 minute or until mixture is crumbly. Transfer mixture to a medium bowl.
3. Add ice water to batter, and mix just until combined.
4. Place dough on a piece of plastic wrap, form into a flat disc, and refrigerate for 20 minutes.
5. Preheat the oven to 450°F.
6. Dust your workspace with flour, and using a rolling pin, roll out dough to 1/8 inch thickness. Place rolled-out dough into a 9-inch tart pan, press to mold into pan, and cut off excess dough. Bake for 13 minutes.
7. Let tart cool for 10 minutes.
8. Place tart shell on a serving dish, and fill with Ashta Custard. Arrange strawberry slices, kiwi slices, and blueberries on top of tart.
9. In a small saucepan over medium heat, heat peach jam and water, stirring, for 2 minutes.
10. Using a pastry brush, brush top of fruit and tart with warmed jam.
11. Serve chilled and store in the refrigerator.

Green Tea And Vanilla Cream

Servings: 4 | Cooking: 0 min

Ingredients

- 14 ounces almond milk, hot
- 2 tablespoons green tea powder
- 14 ounces heavy cream
- 3 tablespoons stevia
- 1 teaspoon vanilla extract
- 1 teaspoon gelatin powder

Directions

1. In a bowl, combine the almond milk with the green tea powder and the rest of the ingredients, whisk well, cool down, divide into cups and keep in the fridge for 2 hours before serving.

Nutrition: calories 120; fat 3; fiber 3; carbs 7; protein 4

Semolina Pie

Servings: 6 | Cooking: 1 Hour

Ingredients

- ½ cup milk
- 3 tablespoons semolina
- ½ cup butter, softened
- 8 Phyllo sheets
- 2 eggs, beaten
- 3 tablespoons Erythritol
- 1 teaspoon lemon rind
- 1 tablespoon lemon juice
- 1 teaspoon vanilla extract
- 2 tablespoons liquid honey
- 1 teaspoon ground cinnamon
- ¼ cup of water

Directions

1. Melt ½ part of all butter.
2. Then brush the casserole glass mold with the butter and place 1 Phyllo sheet inside.

3. Brush the Phyllo sheet with butter and cover it with second Phyllo sheet.

4. Make the dessert filling: heat up milk, and add semolina.

5. Stir it carefully.

6. After this, add remaining softened butter, Erythritol, and vanilla extract.

7. Bring the mixture to boil and simmer it for 2 minutes.

8. Remove it from the heat and cool to the room temperature.

9. Then add beaten eggs and mix up well.

10. Pour the semolina mixture in the mold over the Phyllo sheets, flatten it if needed.

11. Then cover the semolina mixture with remaining Phyllo sheets and brush with remaining melted butter.

12. Cut the dessert on the bars.

13. Bake galaktoboureko for 1 hour at 365F.

14. Then make the syrup: bring to boil lemon juice, honey, and water and remove the liquid from the heat.

15. Pour the syrup over the hot dessert and let it chill well.

Nutrition: calories 304; fat 18; fiber 1.1; carbs 39.4; protein 6.1

Vanilla Apple Compote

Servings: 6 | Cooking: 15 min

Ingredients

- 3 cups apples, cored and cubed
- 1 tsp vanilla
- 3/4 cup coconut sugar
- 1 cup of water
- 2 tbsp fresh lime juice

Directions

1. Add all ingredients into the inner pot of instant pot and stir well.

2. Seal pot with lid and cook on high for 15 minutes.

3. Once done, allow to release pressure naturally for 10 minutes then release remaining using quick release. Remove lid.

4. Stir and serve.

Nutrition: Calories 76 Fat 0.2 g Carbohydrates 19.1 g Sugar 11.9 g Protein 0.5 g Cholesterol 0 mg

Cold Lemon Squares

Servings: 4 | Cooking: 0 min

Ingredients

- 1 cup avocado oil+ a drizzle
- 2 bananas, peeled and chopped
- 1 tablespoon honey
- ¼ cup lemon juice
- A pinch of lemon zest, grated

Directions

1. In your food processor, mix the bananas with the rest of the ingredients, pulse well and spread on the bottom of a pan greased with a drizzle of oil.

2. Introduce in the fridge for 30 minutes, slice into squares and serve.

Nutrition: calories 136; fat 11.2; fiber 0.2; carbs 7; protein 1.1

Minty Coconut Cream

Servings: 2 | Cooking: 0 min

Ingredients

- 1 banana, peeled
- 2 cups coconut flesh, shredded
- 3 tablespoons mint, chopped
- 1 and ½ cups coconut water
- 2 tablespoons stevia
- ½ avocado, pitted and peeled

Directions

1. In a blender, combine the coconut with the banana and the rest of the ingredients, pulse well, divide into cups and serve cold.

Nutrition: calories 193; fat 5.4; fiber 3.4; carbs 7.6; protein 3

Cherry Cream

Servings: 4 | Cooking: 0 min

Ingredients

- 2 cups cherries, pitted and chopped
- 1 cup almond milk
- ½ cup whipping cream
- 3 eggs, whisked
- 1/3 cup stevia
- 1 teaspoon lemon juice
- ½ teaspoon vanilla extract

Directions

1. In your food processor, combine the cherries with the milk and the rest of the ingredients, pulse well, divide into cups and keep in the fridge for 2 hours before serving.

Nutrition: calories 200; fat 4.5; fiber 3.3; carbs 5.6; protein 3.4

Warm Peach Compote

Servings: 4 | Cooking: 1 Minute

Ingredients

- 4 peaches, peeled and chopped
- 1 tbsp water
- 1/2 tbsp cornstarch
- 1 tsp vanilla

Directions

1. Add water, vanilla, and peaches into the instant pot.
2. Seal pot with lid and cook on high for 1 minute.
3. Once done, allow to release pressure naturally. Remove lid.
4. In a small bowl, whisk together 1 tablespoon of water and cornstarch and pour into the pot and stir well.
5. Serve and enjoy.

Nutrition: Calories 66 Fat 0.4 g Carbohydrates 15 g Sugar 14.1 g Protein 1.4 g Cholesterol 0 mg

Honey Walnut Bars

Servings: 8 | Cooking: 30 min

Ingredients

- 5 oz puff pastry
- ½ cup of water
- 3 tablespoons of liquid honey
- 1 teaspoon Erythritol
- 1/3 cup butter, softened
- ½ cup walnuts, chopped
- 1 teaspoon olive oil

Directions

1. Roll up the puff pastry and cut it on 6 sheets.
2. Then brush the tray with olive oil and arrange the first puff pastry sheet inside.
3. Grease it with butter gently and sprinkle with walnuts.
4. Repeat the same steps with 4 puff pastry sheets.
5. Then sprinkle the last layer with walnuts and Erythritol and cove with the sixth puff pastry sheet.
6. Cut the baklava on the servings.
7. Bake the baklava for 30 minutes.
8. Meanwhile, bring to boil liquid honey and water.
9. When the baklava is cooked, remove it from the oven.
10. Pour hot honey liquid over baklava and let it cool till the room temperature.

Nutrition: calories 243; fat 19.6; fiber 0.8; carbs 15.9; protein 3.3

Lime Vanilla Fudge

Servings: 6 | Cooking: 0 min

Ingredients

- 1/3 cup cashew butter
- 5 tablespoons lime juice

- ½ teaspoon lime zest, grated
- 1 tablespoons stevia

Directions

1. In a bowl, mix the cashew butter with the other ingredients and whisk well.

2. Line a muffin tray with parchment paper, scoop 1 tablespoon of lime fudge mix in each of the muffin tins and keep in the freezer for 3 hours before serving.

Nutrition: calories 200; fat 4.5; fiber 3.4; carbs 13.5; protein 5

Pear Sauce

Servings: 6 | Cooking: 15 min

Ingredients

- 10 pears, sliced
- 1 cup apple juice
- 1 1/2 tsp cinnamon
- 1/4 tsp nutmeg

Directions

1. Add all ingredients into the instant pot and stir well.

2. Seal pot with lid and cook on high for 15 minutes.

3. Once done, allow to release pressure naturally for 10 minutes then release remaining using quick release. Remove lid.

4. Blend the pear mixture using an immersion blender until smooth.

5. Serve and enjoy.

Nutrition: Calories 222 Fat 0.6 g Carbohydrates 58.2 g Sugar 38 g Protein 1.3 g Cholesterol 0 mg

Honey Cream

Servings: 2 | Cooking: 5 min

Ingredients

- ½ cup cream
- ¼ cup milk
- 2 teaspoons honey
- 1 teaspoon vanilla extract
- 1 tablespoons gelatin
- 2 tablespoons orange juice

Directions

1. Mix up together milk and gelatin and leave it for 5 minutes.

2. Meanwhile, pour cream in the saucepan and bring it to boil.

3. Add honey and vanilla extract.

4. Remove the cream from the heat and stir well until honey is dissolved.

5. After this, add gelatin mixture (milk+gelatin) and mix it up until gelatin is dissolved.

6. After this, place 1 tablespoon of orange juice in every serving glass.

7. Add the cream mixture over the orange juice.

8. Refrigerate the pannacotta for 30-50 minutes in the fridge or until it is solid.

Nutrition: calories 100; fat 4; fiber 0; carbs 11; protein 4.6

Dragon Fruit, Pear, And Spinach Salad

Servings: 4 | Cooking: 3 min

Ingredients

- 5 ounces spinach leaves, torn
- 1 dragon fruit, peeled then cubed
- 2 pears, peeled then cubed
- 10 ounces organic goat cheese
- 1 cup pecan, halves
- 6 ounces blackberries
- 6 ounces raspberries
- 8 tablespoons olive oil
- 8 tablespoons red wine vinegar
- 1 tablespoon poppy seeds

Directions

1. In a mixing bowl, combine all Ingredients except for the poppy seeds.

2. Place inside the fridge and allow to chill before serving.

3. Sprinkle with poppy seeds on top before serving.

Nutrition: Calories per serving:321; Carbs: 27.2g; Protein: 3.3g; Fat: 3.1g

Mediterranean Biscotti

Servings: 3 | Cooking: 1 Hour

Ingredients

- 2 eggs
- 1 cups whole-wheat flour
- 1 cup all-purpose flour
- 3/4 cup parmesan cheese, grated
- 2 teaspoons baking powder
- 2 tablespoons sugar
- 1/4 cup sun-dried tomato, finely chopped
- 1/4 cup Kalamata olive, finely chopped
- 1/3 cup olive oil
- 1/2 teaspoon salt
- 1/2 teaspoon black pepper, cracked
- 1 teaspoon dried oregano (preferably Greek)
- 1 teaspoon dried basil

Directions

1. Into a large-sized bowl, beat the eggs and the sugar together. Pour in the olive; beat until smooth.

2. In another bowl, combine the flours, baking powder, pepper, salt, oregano, and basil. Stir the flour mix into the egg mixture, stirring until blended.

3. Stir in the cheese, tomatoes, and olives; stirring until thoroughly combined.

4. Divide the dough into 2 portions; shape each into 10-inch long logs. Place the logs into a parchment-lined cookie sheet; flatten the log tops slightly.

5. Bake for about 30 minutes in a preheated 375F oven or until the logs are pale golden and not quite firm to the touch.

6. Remove from the oven; let cool on the baking sheet for 3 minutes. Transfer the logs into a cutting board; slice each log into 1/2-inch diagonal slices using a serrated knife.

7. Place the biscotti slices on the baking sheet, return into the 325F oven, and bake for about 20 to 25 minutes until dry and firm. Flip the slices halfway through baking. Remove from the oven, transfer on a wire rack and let cool.

Nutrition: 731.6 Cal, 36.5 g total fat (9 g sat. fat), 146 mg chol., 1238.4 mg sodium, 77.8 g carb., 3.5 g fiber, 10.7 g sugar, and 23.3 g protein.

Kataifi

Servings: 8-10 | Cooking: 30 min

Ingredients

- 1 kilogram almonds, blanched and then chopped
- 1 teaspoon cinnamon
- 1/4 kilogram kataifi phyllo
- 2 eggs
- 4 tablespoons sugar
- 400 g butter
- 1 1/2 kilograms sugar
- 1 lemon rind
- 1 teaspoon lemon juice
- 5 cups water

Directions

1. Preheat the oven to 170C.

2. Put the sugar, eggs, cinnamon, and the almonds in a bowl.

3. With your fingers, open the kataifi pastry gently. Lay it on a piece of marble and wood. Put 1 tablespoon of the almond mixture in one end and then roll the pastry into a log or a cylinder. Make sure you fold the pastry a little tight so the filling is enclosed securely. Repeat the process with the remaining pastry and almond mixture.

4. Melt the butter and put into a baking dish.

5. Brush the kataifi rolls with the melted butter, covering all the sides.

6. Place into baking sheets and bake for about 30 minutes.

7. Meanwhile, prepare the syrup.

8. Except for the lemon juice, cook the rest of the syrup ingredients for about 5-10 minutes. Add the lemon juice and let cook for a few minutes until the syrup is slightly thick.

9. After baking the kataifi, pour the syrup over the still warm rolls.

10. Cover the pastry with a clean towel. Let cool as the kataifi absorbs the syrup.

Nutrition: 1085 cal., 83.3 total fat (24.6 g sat. fat), 119 mg chol., 248 mg sodium, 759 mg pot., 76.6 g total carbs., 12.7 g fiber, 59.1 g sugar, and 22.6 g protein.

Walnuts Kataifi

Servings: 2 | Cooking: 50 min

Ingredients

- 7 oz kataifi dough
- 1/3 cup walnuts, chopped
- ½ teaspoon ground cinnamon
- ¾ teaspoon vanilla extract
- 4 tablespoons butter, melted
- ¼ teaspoon ground clove
- 1/3 cup water
- 3 tablespoons honey

Directions

1. For the filling: mix up together walnuts, ground cinnamon, and vanilla extract. Add ground clove and blend the mixture until smooth.

2. Make the kataifi dough: grease the casserole mold with butter and place ½ part of kataifi dough.

3. Then sprinkle the filling over the kataifi dough.

4. After this, sprinkle the filling with 1 tablespoon of melted butter.

5. Sprinkle the filling with remaining kataifi dough.

6. Make the roll from ½ part of kataifi dough and cut it.

7. Gently arrange the kataifi roll in the tray.

8. Repeat the same steps with remaining dough. In the end, you should get 2 kataifi rolls.

9. Preheat the oven to 355F and place the tray with kataifi rolls inside.

10. Bake the dessert for 50 minutes or until it is crispy.

11. Meanwhile, make the syrup: bring the water to boil.

12. Add honey and heat it up until the honey is dissolved.

13. When the kataifi rolls are cooked, pour the hot syrup over the hot kataifi rolls.

14. Cut every kataifi roll on 2 pieces.

15. Serve the dessert with remaining syrup.

Nutrition: calories 120; fat 1.5; fiber 0; carbs 22; protein 3

Cinnamon Tea

Servings: 1 Cup | Cooking: 32 min

Ingredients

- 6 cups water
- 1 (3-in.) cinnamon stick
- 6 TB. Ahmad Tea, Ceylon tea, or your favorite
- 3 TB. sugar

Directions

1. In a teapot over low heat, bring water and cinnamon stick to a simmer for 30 minutes. Remove cinnamon stick.

2. Stir in Ahmad tea and sugar, and simmer for 2 minutes.

3. Remove from heat, and let sit for 10 minutes.

4. Strain tea into tea cups, and serve warm.

Tiny Orange Cardamom Cookies

Servings: 80 | Cooking: 12 min

Ingredients

- 1/2 cup whole-wheat flour
- 1/2 cup all-purpose flour
- 1 large egg

- 1 tablespoon sesame seeds, toasted, optional (salted roasted pistachios, chopped)
- 1 teaspoon orange zest
- 1 teaspoon vanilla extract
- 1/2 cup butter, softened
- 1/2 cup sugar
- 1/4 teaspoon ground cardamom

Directions

1. Preheat the oven to 375F.

2. In a medium bowl, blend the orange zest and the sugar thoroughly, and then blend in the cardamom.

3. Add the butter and with a mixer, beat until the mixture is fluffy and light. Beat in the egg and the vanilla into the mixture.

4. With the mixer on low speed, mix in the flours into the mixture.

5. Line 3 baking sheets with parchment paper. Using a level teaspoon measure, drop batter of the cookie mixture onto the sheets.

6. Top each cookie with a pinch of sesame seeds or nuts, if desired; bake for 1bout 10-12 minutes or until the cookies are brown at the edges and crisp.

7. When baked, transfer the cookies on a cooling rack and let them cool completely.

Nutrition: 113 Cal, 1.4 g protein, 6.5 g total fat (3.8 g sat. fat) 12 g total carbs., 0.3 g fiber, 46 mg sodium, and 29 mg chol.

Chocolate Ganache

Preparation: 10 min | Cooking: 3 min | Servings: 16

Ingredients

- 9 ounces bittersweet chocolate, chopped
- cup heavy cream
- 1 tablespoon dark rum (optional)

Directions

1. Put the chocolate in a medium bowl. Heat the cream in a small saucepan over medium heat.

2. Bring to a boil. When the cream has reached a boiling point, pour the chopped chocolate over it and beat until smooth. Stir the rum if desired.

3. Allow the ganache to cool slightly before you pour it on a cake. Begin in the middle of the cake and work outside. For a fluffy icing or chocolate filling, let it cool until thick and beat with a whisk until light and fluffy.

Nutrition: 142 calories; 10.8g fat; 1.4g protein

Chocolate Covered Strawberries

Preparation: 15 min | Cooking: 4 min | Servings: 24

Ingredients

- 16 ounces milk chocolate chips
- 2 tablespoons shortening
- 1-pound fresh strawberries with leaves

Directions

1. In a bain-marie, melt chocolate and shortening, occasionally stirring until smooth. Pierce the tops of the strawberries with toothpicks and immerse them in the chocolate mixture.

2. Turn the strawberries and put the toothpick in Styrofoam so that the chocolate cools.

Nutrition: 115 calories; 7.3g fat; 12.7g carbohydrates

Strawberry Angel Food Dessert

Preparation: 15 min | Cooking: 0 minute| Servings: 18

Ingredients

- angel cake (10 inches)
- packages of softened cream cheese
- 1 container (8 oz.) of frozen fluff, thawed
- 1 liter of fresh strawberries, sliced
- 1 jar of strawberry icing

Directions

1. Crumble the cake in a 9 x 13-inch dish.

2. Beat the cream cheese and 1 cup sugar in a medium bowl until the mixture is light and fluffy. Stir in the whipped topping. Crush the cake with your hands, and spread the cream cheese mixture over the cake.

3. Combine the strawberries and the frosting in a bowl until the strawberries are well covered. Spread

over the layer of cream cheese. Cool until ready to serve.

Nutrition: 261 calories; 11g fat; 3.2g protein

Key Lime Pie

Preparation: 8 min | Cooking: 9 min | Servings: 8

Ingredients

- (9-inch) prepared graham cracker crust
- cups of sweetened condensed milk
- 1/2 cup sour cream
- 3/4 cup lime juice
- 1 tablespoon grated lime zest

Directions

1. Preheat the oven to 175 ° C (350 ° F).

2. Combine the condensed milk, sour cream, lime juice, and lime zest in a medium bowl. Mix well and pour into the graham cracker crust.

3. Bake in the preheated oven for 5 to 8 min until small hole bubbles burst on the surface of the cake.

4. Cool the cake well before serving. Decorate with lime slices and whipped cream if desired.

Nutrition: 553 calories; 20.5g fat; 10.9g protein

Ice Cream Sandwich Dessert

Preparation: 20 min | Cooking: 0 minute | Servings: 12

Ingredients

- 22 ice cream sandwiches
- Frozen whipped topping in 16 oz. container, thawed
- 1 jar (12 oz.) Caramel ice cream
- 1 1/2 cups of salted peanuts

Directions

1. Cut a sandwich with ice in two. Place a whole sandwich and a half sandwich on a short side of a 9 x 13-inch baking dish. Repeat this until the bottom is covered; alternate the full sandwich, and the half sandwich.

2. Spread half of the whipped topping. Pour the caramel over it. Sprinkle with half the peanuts. Repeat the layers with the rest of the ice cream sandwiches, whipped cream, and peanuts.

3. Cover and freeze for up to 2 months. Remove from the freezer 20 min before serving. Cut into squares.

Nutrition: 559 calories; 28.8g fat; 10g protein

Bananas Foster

Preparation: 5 min | Cooking: 5 min | Servings: 4

Ingredients

- 2/3 cup dark brown sugar
- 1/2 teaspoons vanilla extract
- 1/2 teaspoon of ground cinnamon
- bananas, peeled and cut lengthwise and broad
- 1/4 cup chopped nuts, butter

Directions

1. Melt the butter in a deep-frying pan over medium heat. Stir in sugar, 3 ½ tbsp. of rum, vanilla, and cinnamon.

2. When the mixture starts to bubble, place the bananas and nuts in the pan. Bake until the bananas are hot, 1 to 2 min. Serve immediately with vanilla ice cream.

Nutrition: 534 calories; 23.8g fat; 4.6g protein

Rhubarb Strawberry Crunch

Preparation: 15 min | Cooking: 45 min | Servings: 18

Ingredients

- 3 tablespoons all-purpose flour
- 3 cups of fresh strawberries, sliced
- 3 cups of rhubarb, cut into cubes
- 1/2 cup flour
- 1 cup butter

Directions

1. Preheat the oven to 190 ° C.

2. Combine 1 cup of white sugar, 3 tablespoons flour, strawberries and rhubarb in a large bowl. Place the mixture in a 9 x 13-inch baking dish.

3. Mix 1 1/2 cups of flour, 1 cup of brown sugar, butter, and oats until a crumbly texture is obtained. You may want to use a blender for this. Crumble the mixture of rhubarb and strawberry.

4. Bake in the preheated oven for 45 min or until crispy and light brown.

Nutrition: 253 calories; 10.8g fat; 2.3g protein

Frosty Strawberry Dessert

Preparation: 5 min | Cooking: 21 min | Servings: 16

Ingredients

- cup flour, white sugar, whipped cream
- 1/2 cup chopped walnuts, butter
- cups of sliced strawberries
- tablespoons lemon juice
- 1/4 cup brown sugar

Directions

1. Preheat the oven to 175 ° C (350 ° F).

2. Mix the flour, brown sugar, nuts, and melted butter in a bowl. Spread on a baking sheet and bake for 20 min in the preheated oven until crispy. Remove from the oven and let cool completely.

3. Beat the egg whites to snow. Keep beating until you get firm spikes while slowly adding sugar. Mix the strawberries in the lemon juice and stir in the egg whites until the mixture turns slightly pink. Stir in the whipped cream until it is absorbed.

4. Crumble the walnut mixture and spread 2/3 evenly over the bottom of a 9-inch by 13-inch dish. Place the strawberry mixture on the crumbs and sprinkle the rest of the crumbs. Place in the freezer for two hs.

5. Take them out of the freezer a few min before serving to facilitate cutting.

Nutrition: 184 calories; 9.2g fat; 2.2g protein

Dessert Pie

Preparation: 16 min | Cooking: 18 min | Servings: 12

Ingredients

- cup all-purpose flour
- 1 package of cream cheese
- 8 oz. whipped cream topping
- 1 (4-oz) package of instant chocolate pudding
- 1/2 cup butter, white sugar

Directions

1. Preheat the oven to 175 ° C (350 ° F).

2. In a large bowl, mix butter, flour and 1/4 cup sugar until the mixture looks like coarse breadcrumbs. Push the mixture into the bottom of a 9 x 13-inch baking dish. Bake in the preheated oven for 15 to 18 min or until lightly browned to allow cooling to room temperature.

3. In a large bowl, beat cream cheese and 1/2 cup sugar until smooth. Stir in half of the whipped topping. Spread the mixture over the cooled crust.

4. Mix the pudding in the same bowl according to the instructions on the package. Spread over the cream cheese mixture.

5. Garnish with the remaining whipped cream. Cool in the fridge.

Nutrition: 376 calories; 23g fat; 3.6g protein

Fruit Dip

Preparation: 5 min | Cooking: 0 minute | Servings: 12

Ingredients

- (8-oz) package cream cheese, softened
- 1 (7-oz) jar marshmallow crème

Directions

1. Use an electric mixer to combine the cream cheese and marshmallow

2. Beat until everything is well mixed.

Nutrition: 118 calories; 6.6g fat; 13.4g carbohydrates

Sugar-Coated Pecans

Preparation: 15 min | Cooking: 1 h | Servings: 12

Ingredients

- egg white
- 1 tablespoon water
- 1-pound pecan halves
- 1 cup white sugar
- 1/2 teaspoon ground cinnamon

Directions

1. Preheat the oven to 120 ° C (250 ° F). Grease a baking tray.

2. In a bowl, whisk the egg whites and water until frothy. Combine the sugar, ¾ tsp. salt, and cinnamon in another bowl.

3. Add the pecans to the egg whites and stir to cover the nuts. Remove the nuts and mix them with the sugar until well covered. Spread the nuts on the prepared baking sheet.

4. Bake for 1 h at 250 ° F (120 ° C). Stir every 15 min.

Nutrition: 328 calories; 27.2g fat; 3.8g protein

Jalapeño Popper Spread

Preparation: 10 min | Cooking: 3 min | Servings: 32

Ingredients

- 2 packets of cream cheese, softened
- cup mayonnaise
- 1 (4-gram) can chopped green peppers, drained
- grams diced jalapeño peppers, canned, drained
- 1 cup grated Parmesan cheese

Directions

1. In a large bowl, mix cream cheese and mayonnaise until smooth. Stir the bell peppers and jalapeño peppers.

2. Pour the mixture into a microwave oven and sprinkle with Parmesan cheese.

3. Microwave on maximum power, about 3 min.

Nutrition: 110 calories; 11.1g fat; 2.1g protein

Brown Sugar Smokies

Preparation: 10 min | Cooking: 4 min | Servings: 12

Ingredients

- 1-pound bacon
- (16 ounces) package little smoky sausages
- 1 cup brown sugar, or to taste

Directions

1. Preheat the oven to 175 ° C (350 ° F).

2. Cut the bacon in three and wrap each strip around a little sausage. Place sausages wrapped on wooden skewers, several to one place the kebabs on a baking sheet and sprinkle generously with brown sugar.

3. Bake until the bacon is crispy, and the brown sugar has melted.

Nutrition: 356 calories; 27.2g fat; 9g protein

Banana & Tortilla Snacks

Preparation: 5 min | Cooking: 0 minute| Servings: 1

Ingredients

- flour tortilla (6 inches)
- tablespoons peanut butter
- 1 tablespoon honey
- 1 banana
- tablespoons raisins

Directions

1. Lay the tortilla flat. Spread peanut butter and honey on the tortilla.

2. Place the banana in the middle and sprinkle the raisins.

3. Wrap and serve.

Nutrition: 520 calories; 19.3g fat; 12.8g protein

Caramel Popcorn

Preparation: 30 min | Cooking: 1 h | Servings: 20

Ingredients

- 2 cups brown sugar
- 1/2 cup of corn syrup
- 1/2 teaspoon baking powder

- teaspoon vanilla extract
- 5 cups of popcorn

Directions

1. Preheat the oven to 95° C (250° F). Put the popcorn in a large bowl.

2. Melt 1 cup of butter in a medium-sized pan over medium heat. Stir in brown sugar, 1 tsp. of salt, and corn syrup. Bring to a boil, constantly stirring — Cook without stirring for 4 min. Then remove from heat and stir in the soda and vanilla.

3. Pour in a thin layer on the popcorn and stir well.

4. Place in two large shallow baking tins and bake in the preheated oven, stirring every 15 min for an h. Remove from the oven and let cool completely before breaking into pieces.

Nutrition: 14g fat; 253 calories; 32.8g carbohydrates

Apple and Berries Ambrosia

Preparation: 15 min | Cooking: 0 min | Serves 4

Ingredients

- 2 cups unsweetened coconut milk, chilled
- 2 tablespoons raw honey
- 1 apple, peeled, cored, and chopped
- 2 cups fresh raspberries
- 2 cups fresh blueberries

Directions

1. Spoon the chilled milk in a large bowl, and then mix in the honey. Stir to mix well.

2. Then mix in the remaining ingredients. Stir to coat the fruits well and serve immediately.

Nutrition: 386 calories; 21.1g fat; 4.2g protein

Chocolate, Almond, and Cherry Clusters

Preparation: 15 min | Cooking: 3 min | Servings: 5

Ingredients

- 1 cup dark chocolate (60% cocoa or higher), chopped
- 1 tablespoon coconut oil
- ½ cup dried cherries
- 1 cup roasted salted almonds

Directions

1. Line a baking sheet with parchment paper.

2. Melt the chocolate and coconut oil in a saucepan for 3 min. Stir constantly.

3. Turn off the heat and mix in the cherries and almonds.

4. Drop the mixture on the baking sheet with a spoon. Place the sheet in the refrigerator and chill for at least 1 h or until firm.

5. Serve chilled.

Nutrition: 197 calories; 13.2g fat; 4.1g protein

Mascarpone and Fig Crostini

Preparation: 8 min | Cooking: 15 min | Servings: 6

Ingredients

- 1 long French baguette
- 4 tbsp. (½ stick) salted butter, melted
- 1 (8 oz.) tub mascarpone cheese
- 1 (12 oz.) jar fig jam or preserves
- 1 tbsp. sugar

Directions

1. Preheat the oven to 350°F.

2. Portion the bread to ¼-inch-thick slices.

3. Arrange the sliced bread on a sheet and rub each slice with the melted butter and small amount of sugar.

4. Next, put the baking sheet into your oven and toast the bread for 5 to 7 min, just until it turns to golden brown.

5. Let the bread cool slightly. Then, spread about a teaspoon or so of the mascarpone cheese on each piece of bread.

6. Lastly, put a teaspoon or so of the jam on top. Serve immediately.

Nutrition: 281 calories; 18g fat; 4g fiber

Chocolate and Avocado Mousse

Preparation: 40 min | Cooking: 5 min | Servings: 5

Ingredients

- 8 ounces (227 g) dark chocolate (60% cocoa or higher), chopped
- ¼ cup unsweetened coconut milk
- 2 tablespoons coconut oil
- 2 ripe avocados, deseeded
- ¼ cup raw honey

Directions

1. Put the chocolate in a saucepan. Pour in the coconut milk and add the coconut oil.
2. Cook for 3 min or until the chocolate and coconut oil melt. Stir constantly.
3. Put the avocado in a food processor, and then drizzle with honey and melted chocolate. Pulse to combine until smooth.
4. Pour the mixture in a serving bowl, then sprinkle with salt. Refrigerate to chill for 30 min and serve.

Nutrition: 654 calories; 46.8g fat; 7.2g protein

Coconut Blueberries with Brown Rice

Preparation: 55 min | Cooking: 10 min | Servings: 4

Ingredients

- 1 cup fresh blueberries
- 2 cups unsweetened coconut milk
- 1 teaspoon ground ginger
- ¼ cup maple syrup
- 2 cups cooked brown rice

Directions

1. Put all the ingredients, except for the brown rice, in a pot. Stir to combine well.
2. Cook over medium-high heat for 7 min or until the blueberries are tender.
3. Pour in the brown rice and cook for 3 more minute or until the rice is soft. Stir constantly.
4. Serve immediately.

Nutrition: 470 calories; 24.8g fat; 6.2g protein

Glazed Pears with Hazelnuts

Preparation: 10 min | Cooking: 20 min | Servings: 4

Ingredients

- 4 pears, peeled, cored, and quartered lengthwise
- 1 cup apple juice
- 1 tablespoon grated fresh ginger
- ½ cup pure maple syrup
- ¼ cup chopped hazelnuts

Directions

1. Put the pears in a pot, then pour in the apple juice. Bring to a boil over medium-high heat, and then reduce the heat to medium-low. Stir constantly.
2. Cover and simmer for an additional 15 min or until the pears are tender.
3. Meanwhile, combine the ginger and maple syrup in a saucepan. Bring to a boil over medium-high heat. Stir frequently. Turn off the heat and transfer the syrup to a small bowl and let sit until ready to use.
4. Transfer the pears in a large serving bowl with a slotted spoon, then top the pears with syrup.
5. Spread the hazelnuts over the pears and serve immediately.

Nutrition: 287 calories; 3.1g fat; 2.2g protein

Lemony Blackberry Granita

Preparation: 10 min | Cooking: 0 min | Servings: 4

Ingredients

- 1 pound (454 g) fresh blackberries
- 1 teaspoon chopped fresh thyme
- ¼ cup freshly squeezed lemon juice
- ½ cup raw honey
- ½ cup water

Directions

1. Put all the ingredients in a food processor, then pulse to purée.
2. Pour the mixture through a sieve into a baking dish. Discard the seeds remain in the sieve.

3. Put the baking dish in the freezer for 2 hs. Remove the dish from the refrigerator and stir to break any frozen parts.

4. Return the dish back to the freezer for an h, then stir to break any frozen parts again.

5. Return the dish to the freezer for 4 hs until the granita is completely frozen.

6. Remove it from the freezer and mash to serve.

Nutrition: 183 calories; 1.1g fat; 2.2g protein

Lemony Tea and Chia Pudding

Preparation: 30 min | Cooking: 0 min | Servings: 4

Ingredients

- 2 teaspoons Matcha green tea powder (optional)
- 2 tablespoons ground chia seeds
- 1 to 2 dates
- 2 cups unsweetened coconut milk
- Zest and juice of 1 lime

Directions

1. Put all the ingredients in a food processor and pulse until creamy and smooth.

2. Pour the mixture in a bowl, then wrap in plastic. Store in the refrigerator for at least 20 min, then serve chilled.

Nutrition: 225 calories; 20.1g fat; 3.2g protein

Mint Banana Chocolate Sorbet

Preparation: 4 h 5 min | Cooking: 0 min | Serves 1

Ingredients

- 1 frozen banana
- 1 tablespoon almond butter
- 2 tablespoons minced fresh mint
- 2 to 3 tablespoons dark chocolate chips (60% cocoa or higher)
- 2 to 3 tablespoons goji (optional)

Directions

1. Put the banana, butter, and mint in a food processor. Pulse to purée until creamy and smooth.

2. Add the chocolate and goji, then pulse for several more times to combine well.

3. Pour the mixture in a bowl or a ramekin, then freeze for at least 4 hs before serving chilled.

Nutrition: 213 calories; 9.8g fat; 3.1g protein

Yogurt Sundae

Preparation: 5 min | Cooking: 0 min | Servings: 1

Ingredients

- ¾ cup plain Greek yogurt
- ¼ cup fresh mixed berries (blueberries, strawberries, blackberries)
- 2 tablespoons walnut pieces
- 1 tablespoon ground flaxseed
- 2 fresh mint leaves, shredded

Directions

1. Pour the yogurt into a tall parfait glass and sprinkle with the mixed berries, walnut pieces, and flaxseed.

2. Garnish with the shredded mint leaves and serve immediately.

Nutrition: 236 calories; 10.8g fat; 21.1g protein

Raspberry Yogurt Basted Cantaloupe

Preparation: 15 min | Cooking: 0 min | Servings: 6

Ingredients

- 2 cups fresh raspberries, mashed
- 1 cup plain coconut yogurt
- ½ teaspoon vanilla extract
- 1 cantaloupe, peeled and sliced
- ½ cup toasted coconut flakes

Directions

1. Combine the mashed raspberries with yogurt and vanilla extract in a small bowl. Stir to mix well.

2. Place the cantaloupe slices on a platter, then top with raspberry mixture and spread with toasted coconut.

3. Serve immediately.

Nutrition: 75 calories; 4.1g fat; 1.2g protein

Simple Apple Compote

Preparation: 15 min | Cooking: 10 min | Servings: 4

Ingredients

- 6 apples, peeled, cored, and chopped
- ¼ cup raw honey
- 1 teaspoon ground cinnamon
- ¼ cup apple juice

Directions

1. Put all the ingredients in a stockpot. Stir to mix well, then cook over medium-high heat for 10 min or until the apples are glazed by honey and lightly saucy. Stir constantly.

2. Serve immediately.

Nutrition: 246 calories; 0.9g fat; 1.2g protein

Simple Peanut Butter and Chocolate Balls

Preparation: 45 min | Cooking: 0 min | Servings: 15

Ingredients

- ¾ cup creamy peanut butter
- ¼ cup unsweetened cocoa powder
- 2 tablespoons softened almond butter
- ½ teaspoon vanilla extract
- 1¾ cups maple sugar

Directions

1. Line a baking sheet with parchment paper.

2. Combine all the ingredients in a bowl. Stir to mix well.

3. Divide the mixture into 15 parts and shape each part into a 1-inch ball.

4. Arrange the balls on the baking sheet and refrigerate for at least 30 min, then serve chilled.

Nutrition: 146 calories; 8.1g fat; 4.2g protein

Simple Spiced Sweet Pecans

Preparation: 4 min | Cooking: 17 min | Servings: 4

Ingredients

- 1 cup pecan halves
- 3 tablespoons almond butter
- 1 teaspoon ground cinnamon
- ½ teaspoon ground nutmeg
- ¼ cup raw honey

Directions

1. Preheat the oven to 350°F (180°C). Line a baking sheet with parchment paper.

2. Combine all the ingredients in a bowl. Stir to mix well, then spread the mixture in the single layer on the baking sheet with a spatula.

3. Bake in the preheated oven for 16 min or until the pecan halves are well browned.

4. Serve immediately.

Nutrition: 324 calories; 29.8g fat; 3.2g protein

Overnight Oats with Raspberries

Preparation: 5 min | Cooking: 0 min | Servings: 2

Ingredients

- 2/3 cup unsweetened almond milk
- ¼ cup raspberries
- 1/3 cup rolled oats
- 1 teaspoon honey
- ¼ teaspoon turmeric

Directions

1. Place the almond milk, raspberries, rolled oats, honey, turmeric, 1/8 tsp. cinnamon, and a pinch of ground cloves in a mason jar. Cover and shake to combine.

2. Transfer to the refrigerator for at least 8 hs, preferably 24 hs.

3. Serve chilled.

Nutrition: 81 calories; 1.9g fat; 2.1g protein

Blackberry-Yogurt Green

Preparation: 5 min | Cooking: 0 min | Serves 2

Ingredients

- 1 cup plain Greek yogurt
- 1 cup baby spinach
- ½ cup frozen blackberries
- ½ cup unsweetened almond milk
- ¼ cup chopped pecans

Directions

1. Process the yogurt, baby spinach, blackberries, almond milk, and ½ tsp. ginger in a food processor until smoothly blended.

2. Divide the mixture into two bowls and serve topped with the chopped pecans.

Nutrition: 201 calories; 14.5g fat; 7.1g protein

Minty Watermelon Salad

Preparation: 10 min | Cooking: 0 minute | Servings: 6

Ingredients

- 1 medium watermelon
- 1 c. fresh blueberries
- 2 tbsp. fresh mint leaves
- 2 tbsp. lemon juice
- 1/3 c. honey

Directions

1. Cut the watermelon into 1-inch cubes. Put them in a bowl.

2. Evenly distribute the blueberries over the watermelon.

3. Next, finely chop the mint leaves and put them into a separate bowl.

4. Add the lemon juice and honey to the mint and whisk together.

5. Drizzle the mint dressing over the watermelon and blueberries. Serve cold.

Nutrition: 296 calories; 23g fat; 3.3g fiber;

Creamy Rice Pudding

Preparation: 11 min | Cooking: 50 min | Servings: 6

Ingredients

- 1¼ c. long-grain rice
- 5 c. whole milk
- 1 c. sugar
- 1 tbsp. rose water or orange blossom water
- 1 tsp. cinnamon

Directions

1. First, rinse the rice under cold water for 30 seconds.

2. Put the rice, milk, and sugar in a large pot. Bring to a gentle boil while continually stirring.

3. Turn the heat down to low and let simmer for 40 to 45 min, stirring every 3 to 4 min so that the rice does not stick to the bottom of the pot.

4. Next, add the rose water at the end and simmer for 5 min.

5. Divide the pudding into 6 bowls. Sprinkle the top with cinnamon. Lastly, cool for at least 1 h before serving. Store in the fridge.

Nutrition: 303 calories; 21g fat; 2g fiber;

Ricotta-Lemon Cheesecake

Preparation: 14 min | Cooking: 1 h | Servings: 8

Ingredients

- 2 (8 oz.) packages full-fat; cream cheese
- 1 (16 oz.) container full-fat; ricotta cheese
- 1½ c. granulated sugar
- 1 tbsp. lemon zest
- 5 eggs

Directions

1. Preheat the oven to 350°F.

2. Next, using a mixer, blend together the cream cheese and ricotta cheese.

3. Blend in the sugar and lemon zest.

4. Blend in the eggs; drop in 1 egg at a time, blend for 10 seconds, and repeat.

5. Line a 9-inch spring form pan with a parchment paper and nonstick spray. Bind the lower part of the pan with foil.

6. Pour the cheesecake batter into the pan.

7. To make a water bath, get a baking or roasting pan larger than the cheesecake pan. Fill the roasting pan about 1/3 of the way up with warm water.

8. Put the cheesecake pan into the water bath.

9. Situate the whole thing in the oven and let the cheesecake bake for 1 h.

10. After baking is complete, remove the cheesecake pan from the water bath and remove the foil. Let the cheesecake cool approximately for 1 h on the countertop. Lastly, put it in the fridge to cool for at least 3 hs before serving.

Nutrition: 311 calories; 20g fat; 6g fiber;

Strawberry Coconut Parfait

Preparation: 7 min | Cooking: 0 min | Servings: 1

Ingredients

- 1 c. plain unsweetened coconut yogurt
- 1 tbsp. raw honey
- ½ tsp. vanilla powder
- 1 c. chopped strawberries
- ½ c. Granola

Directions

1. First, in your small bowl, mix together the coconut yogurt, honey, and vanilla powder until combined.

2. In a large glass, spoon one-third of the yogurt mixture into the bottom, followed by one-third of the strawberries, then one-third of the granola. Repeat the same layers twice more.

3. Serve immediately.

4. If you're making extra parfaits, store the yogurt and the granola separately and put the parfait together right before serving, so the granola will not get soggy.

Nutrition: 281 calories; 16g fat; 1g fiber;

Moroccan Stuffed Dates

Preparation: 16 min | Cooking: 0 minute| Servings: 30

Ingredients

- 1 lb. dates
- 1 cup blanched almonds
- 1/4 cup sugar
- 1 1/2 tbsp. orange flower water
- 1/4 teaspoon cinnamon

Directions

1. Process the almonds, sugar and cinnamon in a food processor. Add 1 tbsp. butter and orange flower water and process until a smooth paste is formed.

2. Roll small pieces of almond paste the same length as a date. Take one date, make a vertical cut and discard the pit.

3. Insert a piece of the almond paste and press the sides of the date firmly around.

4. Repeat with all the remaining dates and almond paste.

Nutrition: 208 calories; 12g fat; 6g protein

Almond Cookies

Preparation: 13 min | Cooking: 10 min | Servings: 30

Ingredients

- 1 cup almonds, blanched, toasted and finely chopped
- 1 cup powdered sugar
- 4 egg whites
- 2 tbsp. flour
- 1/2 tsp vanilla extract

Directions

1. Preheat oven to 320 F. Blend the almonds in a food processor until finely chopped.

2. Beat egg whites and sugar until thick. Add in vanilla extract and a pinch of cinnamon. Gently stir in almonds and flour. Place tablespoonful of mixture on two lined baking trays.

3. Bake for 10 min, or until firm. Turn oven off, leave the door open and leave cookies to cool. Dust with powdered sugar.

Nutrition: 219 calories; 16g fat; 8g protein

Spanish Nougat

Preparation: 17 min | Cooking: 15 min | Servings: 24

Ingredients

- 1 1/2 cup honey
- 3 egg whites
- 1 ¾ cup almonds, roasted and chopped

Directions

1. Pour the honey into a saucepan and bring it to a boil over medium-high heat, then set aside to cool. Beat the egg whites to a thick glossy meringue and fold them into the honey.

2. Bring the mixture back to medium-high heat and let it simmers, constantly stirring, for 15 min. When the color and consistency change to dark caramel, remove from heat, add the almonds and mix trough.

3. Line a 9x13 inch pan with foil and pour the hot mixture on it. Cover with another piece of foil and even out. Let cool completely. Place a wooden board weighted down with some heavy cans on it. Leave like this for 3-4 days, so it hardens and dries out. Slice into 1-inch squares.

Nutrition: 189 calories; 12g fat; 5g protein

Cinnamon Butter Cookies

Preparation: 12 min | Cooking: 15 min | Servings: 24

Ingredients

- 2 cups flour
- 1/2 cup sugar
- 5 tbsp. butter
- 3 eggs
- 1 tbsp. cinnamon

Directions

1. Cream the butter and sugar until light and fluffy. Combine the flour and the cinnamon. Beat eggs into the butter mixture. Gently add in the flour.

2. Turn the dough onto a lightly floured surface and knead just once or twice until smooth.

3. Form a roll and divide it into 24 pieces. Line baking sheets with parchment paper or grease them. Roll each piece of cookie dough into a long thin strip, then make a circle, flatten a little and set it on the prepared baking sheet.

4. Bake cookies, in batches, in a preheated to 350 F oven, for 12 to 15 min. Set aside to cool on a cooling rack.

Nutrition: 199 calories; 13g fat; 4g protein

Pumpkin Baked with Dry Fruit

Preparation: 18 min | Cooking: 15 min | Servings: 6

Ingredients

- lb. pumpkin, cut into medium pieces
- 1 cup dry fruit (apricots, plums, apples, raisins)
- 1/2 cup brown sugar

Directions

1. Soak the dry fruit in some water, drain and discard the water. Cut the pumpkin in medium cubes. At the bottom of a pot arrange a layer of pumpkin pieces, then a layer of dry fruit and then again, some pumpkin.

2. Add a little water. Cover the pot and bring to boil. Simmer until there is no more water left. When almost ready add the sugar. Serve warm or cold.

Nutrition: 200 calories; 14g fat; 7g protein

Best French Meringues

Preparation: 15 min | Cooking: 2 hs | Servings: 36

Ingredients

- 4 egg whites
- 2 1/4 cups powdered sugar

Directions

1. Preheat the oven to 200 F. and line a baking sheet.

2. In a glass bowl, beat egg whites with an electric mixer. Add in sugar a little at a time, while continuing to beat at medium speed. When the egg white mixture becomes stiff and shiny like satin, transfer to a large

pastry bag. Pipe the meringue onto the lined baking sheet with the use of a large star tip.

3. Place the meringues in the oven and leave the oven door slightly ajar. Bake for 2 1/2 hs, or until the meringues are dry, and can easily be removed from the pan.

Nutrition: 210 calories; 16g fat; 9g protein

Cinnamon Palmier

Preparation: 9 min | Cooking: 17 min | Servings: 30

Ingredients

- 1/3 cup granulated sugar
- 2 tsp cinnamon
- 1/2 lb. puff pastry
- 1 egg, beaten (optional)

Directions

1. Stir together the sugar and cinnamon. Roll the pastry dough into a large rectangle. Spread the cinnamon sugar in an even layer over the dough.

2. Starting at the long ends of the rectangle, loosely roll each side inward until they meet in the middle. If needed, brush it with the egg to hold it together.

3. Slice the pastry roll crosswise into 1/4-inch pieces and arrange them on a lined with parchment paper baking sheet. Bake cookies in a preheated to 400 F oven for 12-15 min, until they puff and turn golden brown. Serve warm or at room temperature.

Nutrition: 211 calories; 17g fat; 6g protein

Baked Apples

Preparation: 17 min | Cooking: 10 min | Servings: 4

Ingredients

- 8 medium sized apples
- 1/3 cup walnuts, crushed
- 3/4 cup sugar
- 3 tbsp. raisins, soaked in brandy or dark rum
- 2 oz. butter

Directions

1. Peel and carefully hollow the apples. Prepare stuffing by beating the butter, 3/4 cup of sugar, crushed walnuts, raisins and cinnamon.

2. Stuff the apples with this mixture and place them in an oiled dish. Sprinkle the apples with 1-2 tablespoons of water and bake in a moderate oven. Serve warm with a scoop of vanilla ice cream.

Nutrition: 219 calories; 12g fat; 5g protein

Quick Peach Tarts

Preparation: 14 min | Cooking: 10 min | Servings: 4

Ingredients

- 1 sheet frozen ready-rolled puff pastry
- 1/4 cup light cream cheese spread
- 2 tablespoons sugar
- a pinch of cinnamon
- 4 peaches, peeled, halved, stones removed, sliced

Directions

1. Line a baking tray with baking paper. Cut the pastry into 4 squares and place them on the prepared tray. Using a spoon, mix cream cheese, sugar, vanilla and cinnamon. Spread over pastry squares. Arrange peach slices on top.

2. Bake in a preheated to 350 F oven for 10 min, or until golden.

Nutrition: 205 calories; 13g fat; 4g protein

Bulgarian Rice Pudding

Preparation: 8 min | Cooking: 15 min | Serving 4-5

Ingredients

- 1 cup short-grain white rice
- 6 tbsp. sugar
- 1 1/2 cup whole milk, water
- 1 cinnamon stick
- 1 strip lemon zest

Directions

1. Place the rice in a saucepan, cover with water and cook over low heat for about 15 min.

2. Add milk, sugar, a cinnamon stick and lemon zest and cook over very low heat, stirring frequently, until the mixture is creamy.

3. Do not let it boil. When ready, discard the cinnamon stick and lemon zest.

4. Serve warm or at room temperature.

Nutrition: 187 calories; 10g fat; 3g protein

Caramel Cream

Preparation: 18 min | Cooking: 1 h | Servings: 8

Ingredients

- 1 1/2 cup sugar
- 4 cups cold milk
- 8 eggs
- 2 tsp vanilla powder

Directions

1. Melt 1/4 of the sugar in a non-stick pan over low heat. When the sugar has turned into caramel, pour it into 8 cup-sized ovenproof pots covering only the bottoms.

2. Whisk the eggs with the rest of the sugar and the vanilla, and slowly add the milk. Stir the mixture well and divide between the pots.

3. Place the 8 pots in a larger, deep baking dish. Pour 3-4 cups of water into the dish. Place the baking dish in a preheated to 280 F oven for about an h and bake but do not let the water boil, as the boiling will overcook the cream and make holes in it: if necessary, add cold water to the baking dish.

4. Remove the baking dish from the oven; remove the pots from the dish. Place a shallow serving plate on top, then invert each pot so that the cream unmolds. The caramel will form a topping and sauce.

Nutrition: 213 calories; 16g fat; 8g protein

Yogurt-Strawberries Ice Pops

Preparation: 4 hs| Cooking: 0 minute| Servings: 8-9

Ingredients

- 3 cups yogurt
- 3 tbsp. honey
- 2 cups strawberries, quartered

Directions

1. Strain the yogurt in a clean white dishtowel. Combine the strained yogurt with honey.

2. Blend the strawberries with a blender then gently fold the strawberry puree into the yogurt mixture until just barely combined, with streaks remaining.

3. Divide evenly among the molds, insert the sticks and freeze for 3 to 4 hs until solid.

Nutrition: 216 calories; 16g fat; 8g protein

Fresh Strawberries in Mascarpone and Rose Water

Preparation: 11 min | Cooking: 0 minute| Servings: 4

Ingredients

- 6 oz. strawberries, washed
- 1 cup mascarpone cheese
- 1/2 teaspoon rose water
- 1/2 teaspoon vanilla extract
- 1/4 cup white sugar

Directions

1. In a bowl, combine together the mascarpone cheese, sugar, rose water and vanilla. Divide the strawberries into 4 dessert bowls.

2. Add two dollops of mascarpone mixture on top and serve.

Nutrition: 197 calories; 10g fat; 3g protein

Delicious French Éclairs

Preparation: 23 min | Cooking: 43 min | Servings: 12

Ingredients

- 1/2 cup butter
- 1 cup boiling water
- 1 cup sifted flour
- 4 eggs
- a pinch of salt

Directions

1. In a medium saucepan, combine butter, salt, and boiling water. Bring to the boil, then reduce heat and add a cup of flour all at once, stirring vigorously until mixture forms a ball.

2. Remove from heat and add eggs, one at a time, whisking well to incorporate completely after each addition. Continue beating until the mixture is thick and shiny and breaks from the spoon.

3. Pipe or spoon onto a lined baking sheet then bake for 20 min in a preheated to 450 F oven. Reduce heat to 350 F and bake for 20 min more, or until golden.

4. Set aside to cool and fill with sweetened whipped cream or custard.

Nutrition: 220 calories; 17g fat; 5g protein

Blueberry Yogurt Dessert

Preparation: 18 min | Cooking: 0 minute| Servings: 6

Ingredients

- 1/3 cup blueberry jam
- 1 cup fresh blueberries
- 2 tbsp. powdered sugar
- 1 cup heavy cream
- 2 cups yogurt

Directions

1. Strain the yogurt in a piece of cheesecloth.

2. In a large bowl, beat the cream and powdered sugar until soft peaks form. Add strained yogurt and 1 tsp. of vanilla and beat until medium peaks form and the mixture is creamy and thick.

3. Gently fold half the fresh blueberries and the blueberry jam into cream mixture until just barely combined, with streaks remaining. Divide dessert among 6 glass bowls, top with fresh blueberries and serve.

Nutrition: 208 calories; 12g fat; 6g protein

Banana Yogurt with Walnuts

Servings: 2 | Kcal per serving: 236

Ingredients

- 2 tablespoons toasted and chopped walnuts
- 2 bananas (chunked)
- 225 grams Greek yogurt

Directions

1. Prepare 2 serving glasses.

2. Place yogurt at the bottom of each glass, top with banana, and add another layer of yogurt. Continue the sequence until the glass is full.

3. Sprinkle with walnuts on top, and serve at once.

Manufactured by Amazon.ca
Bolton, ON